NOVELL'S

Guide to Troubleshooting
TCP/IP

D1519118

NOVELL'S

Guide to Troubleshooting
TCP/IP

SILVIA HAGEN AND STEPHANIE LEWIS

Novell Press, San Jose

Novell's Guide to Troubleshooting TCP/IP
Published by
Novell Press
2211 North First Street
San Jose, CA 95131

Copyright © 1999 Novell, Inc. All rights reserved. No part of this book, including interior design, cover design, and icons, may be reproduced or transmitted in any form, by any means (electronic, photocopying, recording, or otherwise) without the prior written permission of the publisher.

ISBN: 0-7645-4562-0

Printed in the United States of America

10 9 8 7 6 5 4 3 2 1

1B/RV/QZ/ZZ/FC

Distributed in the United States by IDG Books Worldwide, Inc.

Distributed by CDG Books Canada Inc. for Canada; by Transworld Publishers Limited in the United Kingdom; by IDG Norge Books for Norway; by IDG Sweden Books for Sweden; by IDG Books Australia Publishing Corporation Pty. Ltd. for Australia and New Zealand; by TransQuest Publishers Pte Ltd. for Singapore, Malaysia, Thailand, Indonesia, and Hong Kong; by Gotop Information Inc. for Taiwan; by ICG Muse, Inc. for Japan; by Intersoft for South Africa; by Eyrolles for France; by International Thomson Publishing for Germany, Austria and Switzerland; by Distribuidora Cuspide for Argentina; by LR International for Brazil; by Galileo Libros for Chile; by Ediciones ZETA S.C.R. Ltda. for Peru; by WS Computer Publishing Corporation, Inc., for the Philippines; by Contemporanea de Ediciones for Venezuela; by Express Computer Distributors for the Caribbean and West Indies; by Micronesia Media Distributor, Inc. for Micronesia; by Chips Computadoras S.A. de C.V. for Mexico; by Editorial Norma de Panama S.A. for Panama; by American Bookshops for Finland.

For general information on IDG Books Worldwide's books in the U.S., please call our Consumer Customer Service department at 800-762-2974. For reseller information, including discounts and premium sales, please call our Reseller Customer Service department at 800-434-3422.

For information on where to purchase IDG Books Worldwide's books outside the U.S., please contact our International Sales department at 317-596-5530 or fax 317-596-5692.

For consumer information on foreign language translations, please contact our Customer Service department at 800-434-3422, fax 317-596-5692, or e-mail rights@idgbooks.com.

For information on licensing foreign or domestic rights, please phone +1-650-655-3109.

For sales inquiries and special prices for bulk quantities, please contact our Sales department at 650-655-3200 or write to IDG Books Worldwide, 919 E. Hillsdale Blvd., Suite 400, Foster City, CA 94404.

For information on using IDG Books Worldwide's books in the classroom or for ordering examination copies, please contact our Educational Sales department at 800-434-2086 or fax 317-596-5499.

For press review copies, author interviews, or other publicity information, please contact our Public Relations department at 650-655-3000 or fax 650-655-3299.

For authorization to photocopy items for corporate, personal, or educational use, please contact Novell, Inc., Copyright Permission, 1555 North Technology Way, Mail Stop ORM-C-311, Orem, UT 84097-2395 or fax 801-228-7077.

For general information on Novell Press books in the U.S., including information on discounts and premiums, contact IDG Books Worldwide at 800-434-3422 or 650-655-3200. For information on where to purchase Novell Press books outside the U.S., contact IDG Books International at 650-655-3021 or fax 650-655-3295.

Library of Congress Cataloging-in-Publication Data

Hagen, Silvia, (date)
   Novell's guide to troubleshooting TCP/IP / Silvia Hagen and Stephanie Lewis.
      p.   cm.
   Includes index.
   ISBN 0-7645-4562-0 (alk. paper)
   1. TCP/IP (Computer network protocol) I. Lewis, Stephanie, 1960– . II. Title.
   TK5105.585.H34 1999   99-33557
   004.6'2—dc21   CIP

John Kilcullen, *CEO, IDG Books Worldwide, Inc.*
Steven Berkowitz, *President, IDG Books Worldwide, Inc.*
Richard Swadley, *Senior Vice President & Publisher, Technology*
The IDG Books Worldwide logo is a registered trademark or trademark under exclusive license to IDG Books Worldwide, Inc. from International Data Group, Inc. in the United States and/or other countries.

Marcy Shanti, *Publisher, Novell Press, Novell, Inc.*

Novell Press and the Novell Press logo are trademarks of Novell, Inc.

Welcome to Novell Press

Novell Press, the world's leading provider of networking books, is the premier source for the most timely and useful information in the networking industry. Novell Press books cover fundamental networking issues as they emerge — from today's Novell and third-party products to the concepts and strategies that will guide the industry's future. The result is a broad spectrum of titles for the benefit of those involved in networking at any level: end user, department administrator, developer, systems manager, or network architect.

Novell Press books are written by experts with the full participation of Novell's technical, managerial, and marketing staff. The books are exhaustively reviewed by Novell's own technicians and are published only on the basis of final released software, never on prereleased versions.

Novell Press at IDG Books Worldwide is an exciting partnership between two companies at the forefront of the knowledge and communications revolution. The Press is implementing an ambitious publishing program to develop new networking titles centered on the current versions of NetWare, GroupWise, BorderManager, ManageWise, and networking integration products.

Novell Press books are translated into several languages and sold throughout the world.

Marcy Shanti
Publisher
Novell Press, Novell, Inc.

Novell Press

Publisher
Marcy Shanti

IDG Books Worldwide

Acquisitions Editor
Jim Sumser

Development Editor
Kurt Stephan

Technical Editors
Neil Cashell
Praveen Joshi

Copy Editors
William McManus
Larisa North

Illustrator
Donna Reynolds

Production
Publication Services

Proofreading and Indexing
Publication Services

About the Authors

Silvia Hagen started her networking career in 1990 as a Novell instructor and has since trained hundreds of system engineers. Today she is a professional consultant and analyst for many mid- and large-size companies throughout Europe. She consults them on large-scale NDS designs, migrations to NetWare 4/5 in multi-platform environments, integration of NT, and optimization of network communications. She is the author of the successful and unique NDS Troubleshooting Workshop, which is taught regularly throughout Europe. Silvia currently holds certifications for Novell's Master CNE and Master CNI, Microsoft's MCP and MCT, and Sniffer University Instructor. She lives and works in Zurich, Switzerland. When she is not sitting in front of a computer, she loves music, reading, swimming, skiing, and driving cute little fast cars like the Z3 roadster. For more information about Silvia, go to www.sunny.ch or send an e-mail to shagen@sunny.ch.

Stephanie Lewis is a professional network analyst, consultant, and speaker who has been working in the networked-computer industry since 1985. She is a Novell Master CNE, Master CNI, and Microsoft MCSE and MCT. Stephanie has been involved in the design, implementation, and troubleshooting of many large-scale, multi-platform, multi-protocol networks. Her broad client base includes city and county governments, police and fire departments, and service and industrial firms. She is also a Certified Protocol Analyst and works with many companies on packet-level education and analysis. Stephanie can be reached at slewis@pncg.com.

This book is dedicated to my wonderful daughter Marina and to everyone who helps to make our world a better place.

— Silvia Hagen

This book is dedicated to my parents, Mike and Karen Lewis. They gave me both the analytical and creative abilities I use every day, and learned what TCP/IP stands for so they could tell their friends that their daughter wrote a book.

— Stephanie Lewis

Foreword

TCP/IP has become the dominant force in today's internetwork communications. It is the key protocol stack used on the Internet, and many private companies who have not deployed an IP-based network are scrambling to integrate it into their corporate structure.

The greatest skillset you can acquire today is the capability to effectively troubleshoot TCP/IP communications. Naturally, the most effective method is through packet-level analysis. It's time to dust off that analyzer software/hardware and start working at the communications level—and this is the perfect opportunity to get started.

Silvia and Stephanie have captured the flavor (and packets) of the IP communications stack and have paired these packets with detailed information and fabulous examples of how IP elements function. As you read this fascinating work, capture your own network packets and compare them to the defined functionality and troubleshooting tips that are packed into this book. You can easily contrast the general TCP/IP communications defined in this book with your network communications.

With *Novell's Guide to Troubleshooting TCP/IP*, you will be able to efficiently troubleshoot and analyze your TCP/IP network. This is a must-read for anyone who plans to run a TCP/IP network.

Use the troubleshooting methods described herein with a variety of analyzer products to become a thoroughly self-sufficient, effective IP network analyst.

Enjoy!

Laura A. Chappell
Senior Protocol Analyst
The Network Analysis Institute
www.netanalysis.org

Preface

The network is down and it's your responsibility to fix it. Now.

And you don't know where to start.

If you've ever been in this situation, you know very well how frustrating it can be to deal with the TCP/IP protocol stack. With so many different protocols performing so many different functions, how can you possibly know where to start? Is it the router? The IP address? The subnet mask? DHCP? SNMP? Or DNS? Novell or UNIX or NT? This book not only tells you where to start, but how to troubleshoot common TCP/IP problems on multiple platforms.

Novell's Guide to Troubleshooting TCP/IP provides comprehensive, easy-to-understand technical coverage of the protocol stack from the packet level view. We use analysis products — and show you how to do the same — to uncover the true communication that occurs in the TCP/IP environment. This book covers each of the protocols in depth, beginning with its function. Each protocol is then dissected, and the fields and field values are detailed for you to understand. A case study using that particular protocol is covered in depth at the end of almost every chapter to help you understand how the analyzer is used in the troubleshooting process.

Next time the network is down, be ready.

Who Should Read This Book?

This book is a must-read for anyone who installs, configures, designs, or troubleshoots TCP/IP networks on any platform. Whether you are just beginning to use network analysis tools, are an experienced network analyst, or somewhere in between, this book is for you. We've provided examples that show just what you should be seeing on the wire, plus real-life case studies to assist in the troubleshooting process.

If you are just beginning, you should start with Chapters 1 and 2, which explain the analysis and troubleshooting methods and tools. You will learn about the physical components of networking, and the frame structures of Ethernet and Token Ring.

Intermediate- to advanced-level readers may wish to begin digging into the real protocols of the TCP/IP suite. We show how IP and TCP really function in Chapters 4 and 10. You will learn to use ICMP as a great troubleshooting tool in

Chapter 6. If routing protocols are your problem, learn the difference between distance vector and link state protocols, and issues specific to each, in Chapters 7 and 8. Not all TCP/IP implementations are the same: you'll see how Novell, Microsoft, and different vendors implement this protocol suite.

No matter the level of your experience, this packet level view of the TCP/IP protocols is the type of communications analysis and troubleshooting training you won't get anywhere else. See what it looks like when things go right, and learn what it looks like when things go wrong. But most of all, have fun. Happy troubleshooting!

How This Book is Organized

Novell's Guide to Troubleshooting TCP/IP is separated into six logically organized parts:

Part I: Analysis Basics

The first part of the book contains the following chapters:

Chapter 1: Overview of TCP/IP Analysis

This chapter shows how the TCP/IP stack is formed and used, and gives a basis for further analysis. Data flow and network design considerations are discussed. The role of network hardware such as hubs, switches, bridges, and routers and their effects on infrastructure are explained.

Chapter 2: Analyzers and Other TCP/IP Troubleshooting Tools

The second chapter gives an overview of the analysis process. Different analysis methods and products are discussed, and a number of vendor-specific tools are used.

Chapter 3: Troubleshooting the LInk for Ethernet and Token Ring Networks

In this chapter, you are introduced to the frame types and communication methods used by these popular topologies. Common Ethernet infrastructure problems and solutions are defined, including runts, collisions, fragments, alignment/CRC problems. Token Ring specific errors are defined, including soft errors and burst errors. Topology rules for cabling are defined.

Part II: Analyzing and Troubleshooting the Internet Layer

The second part of the book consists of the following chapters:

Chapter 4: The Internet Protocol (IP)

This chapter defines the function of the IP protocol, proper IP addressing, and IP packet structure and field values. You'll learn how routing decisions are made by clients and gateways, plus the pros and cons of using the default gateway property of many client TCP/IP software products.

Chapter 5: Address Resolution Protocol/Reverse Address Resolution Protocol (ARP/RARP)

The fifth chapter defines the ARP/RARP protocol function and packet structures. You'll discover how ARP is used to communicate with other hosts on the network.

Chapter 6: Internet Control Message Protocol (ICMP)

This chapter shows how ICMP can be used as a troubleshooting tool. Discussion of the function, packet structures, and message types is also included.

Chapter 7: Routing Information Protocol

Chapter 7 gives a functional description of the RIP1 and RIP2 routing protocols. Possible issues surrounding this protocol are defined and differences between these versions of the routing protocol are discussed, along with packet structure and field values.

Chapter 8: Open Shortest Path First (OSPF)

This chapter discusses the functionality of the OSPF link state protocol. It discusses routing decisions and components of this routing protocol, as well as configuration parameters and packet structures.

Part III: Analyzing and Troubleshooting the Host-to-Host (Transport) Layer

The third part of this book includes the following chapters:

Chapter 9: User Datagram Protocol (UDP)

This chapter gives a functional description of UDP and applications that use UDP for transport. An analysis of a UDP session is covered, along with the UDP packet structure and values.

Chapter 10: Transmission Control Protocol (TCP)

Chapter 10 discusses the most popular transport in the TCP/IP protocol suite — TCP. The function of TCP is discussed, along with the handshake, sliding window, flow control, and other features of this transport protocol. TCP sessions are analyzed, and the TCP packet structure and field values are given.

Part IV: Analyzing and Troubleshooting the Application Layer

The following chapters are included in the fourth part of the book:

Chapter 11: Dynamic Host Configuration Protocol (DHCP) and BOOTP

This chapter covers the use and function of DHCP, analysis of a session, and how addresses are leased. Address renewal and popular DHCP options are discussed, along with the packet structure and field values.

Chapter 12: Domain Name System (DNS)

Chapter 12 discusses the use and function of DNS, legal and illegal DNS names, and lookup types. DNS authorities, root servers, and zones are also covered. A DNS session is analyzed, and packet structures and field values are given.

Chapter 13: Simple Network Management Protocol (SNMP)

This chapter teaches how the SNMP protocol, MIB databases, and Structure of Management Information is used to manage devices on a TCP/IP network. SNMP commands and security issues are discussed. An SNMP session is analyzed, and packet structures are detailed.

Chapter 14: Service Location Protocol (SLP)

In this chapter, the function of this protocol (new to NetWare 5) is explored, and the SLP communication process and packet structure are detailed.

Part V: Vendor Implementation of TCP/IP

The fifth part of the book includes the following chapters:

Chapter 15: Novell TCP/IP Implementation

Chapter 15 details the TCP/IP support available in NetWare products. Discussion focuses on SNMP, DHCP, DNS, and SNMP support. Native IP architecture and implementation is discussed, and a sample communication session is analyzed.

Chapter 16: Microsoft Implementation

This chapter details the TCP/IP support available in Microsoft products. Focus is on the DNS and DHCP support available, along with Microsoft implementations of NetBIOS over TCP/IP and Windows Internet Naming Service. NetBIOS node types are discussed, and a sample configuration is described.

Chapter 17: UNIX TCP/IP Implementation/Configuration

This chapter describes the differences between several UNIX vendor verions of TCP/IP. Discussion focuses on Linux, Sun and HP installations, utilities, and configuration for DNS, DHCP, and ICMP support.

Part VI: Other TCP/IP Communications and Issues

Part VI of the book consists of the following chapters:

Chapter 18: Miscellaneous TCP/IP Communications

This chapter details important TCP/IP protocols including the Network Time Protocol, IGMP, and Cisco's IGRP and EIGRP.

Chapter 19: IP Tunneling

Chapter 19 discusses IP tunneling and types of tunneling products. Virtual private networks and IPv6 tunneling are discussed, and a sample session is analyzed.

Chapter 20: IP Version 6

The final chapter of the book discusses the newest version of the TCP/IP protocol — version 6. Functionality is discussed, along with addressing methods and transition implementation. Packet structures are defined, and the use of dual IP layers is considered.

Appendixes

In addition, *Novell's Guide to Troubleshooting TCP/IP* contains the following valuable reference appendixes for your use:

- ▶ Appendix A: Hex-Decimal-Binary Conversion Chart

- ▶ Appendix B: IP Addressing Rules/RFC 1878

- ▶ Appendix C: UDP/TCP Well-Known Port List

- ▶ Appendix D: RFC Index

- ▶ Appendix E: Analyzer Manufacturer List

- ▶ Appendix F: Ethertype Assignments

- ▶ Appendix G: Ethernet Vendor Addresses

- ▶ Appendix H: Ethernet Multicast Addresses

- ▶ Appendix I: Internet Multicast Addresses

- ▶ Appendix J: IP Option Numbers

- ▶ Appendix K: ICMP Code Types (v4 and v6)

- ▶ Appendix L: TCP Options (Parameters)

- ▶ Appendix M: DNS and DHCP/BOOTP Parameters

- ▶ Appendix N: ARP/RARP Parameters

Contacting the Authors

We hope you have as much fun reading this book as we had writing it. Now that it is complete, we must go back to our primary jobs—troubleshooting TCP/IP. We will share our trace files with you on either of our Web sites. If you wish to contact Silvia Hagen, you may reach her at shagen@sunny.ch. Her Web address is www.sunny.ch. Stephanie Lewis may be reached at slewis@pncg.com or on the Web at www.pncg.com. You may also see one of us speaking publicly or through other articles that we've written. Enjoy, and keep in touch.

Acknowledgments

This book represents a collaborative effort by two authors who live and work on different continents. We wish to thank those responsible for pioneering e-mail and the telephone system. Without those tools, this book would not have been possible.

Seriously, we first want to thank Laura Chappell for talking us into writing this book. (Laura, why didn't you tell us what we were getting ourselves into?) Her encouragement, guidance, and support during this process was invaluable.

We next thank our friends, families, and coworkers for helping us to write a book that weighs more than Stephanie's dog!

From Silvia:

The book would never have been accomplished if my wonderful daughter Marina had not supported me during the whole process with her love, patience, and by cheering me up and cooking meals for me. What helped her was the fact that she was proud to have a mum that writes a book. Thank you, Marina; you are the sunshine of my life.

Many friends and neighbors also contributed in many ways. Marianne Schüpfer kept my office running, and Madlen Voigt made sure my apartment was still a nice place to come home to. Edith Luginbühl took care of my daughter while I was working. Thank you also to my friends Meta Castelberg, Franziska Birchler, Monika Bär, Christine and Hansruedi Schütz, Claudio Zanetti, Stefan Oehen, and Stefan Schätti.

And all my love to Stephanie. I am glad we did this book together. Knowing that you were sitting there on another continent struggling through the same process made it much easier. And when late at night, after writing on the book, all my friends here were asleep and no one was around to talk to, I could call you, and talking to you always cheered me up. Thank you, girlfriend. What's our next project?

Many of my customers have supported this book too: Thomas Allemann and Jürg Wegmüller at Zurich Insurance, Antonio Licuria, Jan Brunschwig and Toni Mosimann at UBS, and Roland Cunz, Lorenz Waller, and Bruno Felix at Bank Sarasin.

From Stephanie:

To all of my wonderful friends and family, I wholeheartedly thank you for supporting me during the writing of this book. Thank you for pretending to understand TCP/IP and giving me perspective. In particular, I wish to thank Alan Frank for making me write when I wanted to play, and Stacy Lewis who made me play when I wanted to write. I couldn't have done it without the two of you.

Thank you to my business partner, Jim Zantow, who kept the office running (and hired more people) while I was writing or speaking or somewhere on the road discussing TCP/IP. I promise I'll come back to work now, if I still have an office. To my assistant, Suzanne Gaulke, thank you for keeping my chapters and my head together during this process. And finally, to Silvia Hagen, who always seemed to call me just as I was giving up — isn't it time for you to get some sleep?

Collectively:

Many people contributed to this book as technical advisors. We wish to thank Stefan Marzohl for his invaluable input to the chapter on OSPF and Bob Vergidis for his contribution to the UNIX chapter. Don Prefontaine at Network Associates gave his input and help on many chapters. Thanks to Keith Parsons at Network Associates for all his input, and Adrian Tschopp and Walter Hofstetter at Network Associates Switzerland, who helped us with Sniffer Pro. Marcus Williamson, Peter Van Lone, and Alan Frank deserve thanks for reviewing chapters and offering a lot of substantial input. (Network Associates, Sniffer, Total Network Visibility, and Net Tools are registered trademarks of Network Associates and its affiliates in the United States and other countries. Network Associates, Inc., 3965 Freedom, Circle Santa Clara, CA 95054; 408-988-3832; fax: 408-970-9727; www.nai.com.)

Novell has been a great help too, especially Frank Berzau, Roger Holm, John McGowan, Robert Kumiega, Matthias Baqué, Todd Rupper, Kirk Kimball, and Petra Rohde. Thanks to Cricket Liu, as well as Roger Grandjean and Henry Lehir from Genesis Communications on DNS issues. Thank you also to Neil Cashell and Praveen Joshi, who checked the technical accuracy of the manusscript.

Cisco Switzerland has been supporting this project; we wish to thank Michael Ganser, Yves Bron, and Stefan Ruoss.

We thank vendors who were open to answering many questions on product-specific issues. Thank you to James Kempf and Michael Witt at Sun, Frank Zimmermann, Michael Wyrsch, Markus Hinnen and Thomas Wacker at Hewlett-Packard, and Ulrich Abderhalden at IBM Switzerland, Paul Lupus at Shomiti, Andy Moon at Packetware, and Nick Wells at Caldera. Thanks also to Hannes

Lubich, Urs Keller, Ingo Hiepler, Anja Spittler (the girl who loves printers so much), Mark Miller, Shawn Rogers, Wolfgang Zweimüller, Roger Lapuh from Bay Networks, Uri Raz, Chuck Bolz, and Richard Renzetti for their assistance.

We thank Jim Sumser at IDG Books, who took a risk to start this project with two first-time authors. We know we did not disappoint you and hope this is not the last book we do together.

We also thank all of the folks at IDG Books Worldwide, especially Kurt Stephan, who accompanied us through the whole process. He has always been very kind, supportive, and understanding. Instead of hassling us and putting even more pressure on us, he was a great help, and cheered us up when we felt like breaking down. Thank you Kurt; we appreciate your support a lot. Special thanks also to Larisa North of IDG Books for her skillful management of the copyediting process.

Finally, we give thanks to all that brought light and inspiration to this piece of work: the power of the mountains in Switzerland, the beauty of the desert flowers in Phoenix, the calming lakes, the night sky, and music we both shared kept our spirits high during the hours at the computer.

Contents at a Glance

Contents

Part III　Troubleshooting and Analyzing the Host-to-Host (Transport) Layer　　373

Part V   Vendor Implementation of TCP/IP   603

Analysis Basics

Overview of TCP/IP Analysis

So, you're ready to learn how to troubleshoot and analyze your TCP/IP network. You've come to the right place! We will help you every step of the way. Welcome to a world of fun and excitement — knowing exactly what is going on at the wire level can be a very liberating experience. Why guess at the problem when you can analyze it?

The term *TCP/IP* stands for *Transmission Control Protocol/Internet Protocol*. The TCP/IP protocol suite consists of many different protocols, each unique in its own respect, so reviewing the entire suite can be a bit overwhelming. The good news is that TCP/IP is a very organized suite of protocols in its network implementation. When you begin to analyze your TCP/IP network, simply take it one step at a time — don't try to do it all at once.

Before you begin to study the analysis process, you need to understand how communication takes place between computers on the network, using the protocol stack.

The Protocol Stack

Similar to a language, a *protocol* is the method by which computers can communicate on a network. A *protocol stack* is simply a group of protocols that work together. A protocol stack may be something other than TCP/IP, such as the group of protocols found in AppleTalk, Novell's IPX/SPX, or IBM's SNA, but for purposes of this book, "protocol stack" refers to TCP/IP.

The need for a protocol stack in a network is similar to the need for a common language when making a telephone call. When you pick up the telephone and dial a number, all the hardware is present to help you make that call — the fiber optic phone line is in the ground and the phone line is working on your end. However, if the other party answers in a language that is foreign to you, how do you communicate with that person? Obviously, communication is easiest if you both speak the same language.

Like the hardware for your telephone, your computer network has cable configured for network communication. And, similar to the need for a common language with which to communicate by telephone, computers need to have the same protocol stack, so that communication can occur across the network hardware, using the same language.

Understanding Layering Concepts

A protocol stack is like a group of people that work together, each having a very specific job description. Each specific area of a protocol stack is called a *layer*. Using a *layered approach* means that during transmission and receipt of a packet of information between computers, each layer touches the packet and passes it on to the next in line, as shown in Figure 1.1.

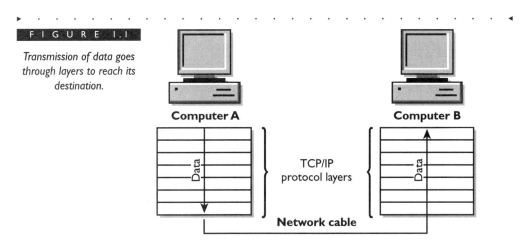

FIGURE 1.1

Transmission of data goes through layers to reach its destination.

The process is sort of like a relay race to the top (or bottom, depending on the data direction) of the stack. At the bottom of the protocol stack in each computer is the physical connection to the network. In Figure 1.1, Computer A has made a request of Computer B. The communication starts when the user types a request on Computer A. When the user presses Enter to execute the request, data begins in the topmost (upper) layers. As the data continues its journey to Computer B, it passes through all the layers in the protocol stack in Computer A. When it reaches the network cable, the signal is transmitted and received by Computer B.

When Computer B receives the data packet, the packet begins its journey back up the protocol stack to Computer B's upper layers. When the packet reaches the topmost layer, Computer B can respond to the request. Notice that both Computers A and B have identical protocol stacks, which is required for them to be able to communicate over the network.

Why Layer?

At first glance, one simple process seemingly should be able to transmit data from one computer to another. After all, how hard can it be to get data from point A to point B? We've been doing it for years! True enough, but remember that the TCP/IP protocol is not just one protocol — it's a suite that contains potentially hundreds of protocols. Each layer represents a unique set of protocols that performs a specific function, such as putting data on the wire or moving data between buildings.

TCP/IP is kind of like a pit crew at the Indianapolis 500, one of the most highly profiled car races in the United States. (Remember, the TCP/IP protocol stack is like a highly trained group of people.) At the Indy 500, when a car makes a pit stop, many people immediately go to work on the car. One person changes the oil, another changes the tires, and yet another fills the gas tank. Everyone has a job to do. Fluids are checked and windows are washed — and the car returns to the track in 30 seconds. One person could never accomplish a task like that as efficiently as that crew.

Similarly, one layer of a protocol stack could never accomplish what an entire stack can accomplish, which is why the protocol stack is layered.

▶ · ◀

Protocol Models

The previous section describes very generally how data is transmitted up and down the protocol stack in the layered approach. Two distinct layered models can be used:

▸ Open Systems Interconnection (OSI) model (seven layers)

▸ Advanced Research Projects Agency (ARPA) TCP/IP model (four layers)

The following sections review in detail each model and its layers.

Open Systems Interconnection Model

When an application is developed, it must follow a specific series of steps to work properly on a computer or network system. Supporting the many operations models that application developers have conceived is nearly impossible, so structured application development is essential. To standardize the way that applications work, the OSI seven-layer communications model (shown in Figure 1.2) was developed, which works independently from vendor-specific requirements. The OSI model was developed jointly by the International Standards Organization (ISO) and the International Telephone and Telegraph Consultative Committee (CCITT).

► . . . . ◄

FIGURE 1.2

OSI 7-Layer Model

The OSI model has seven layers.

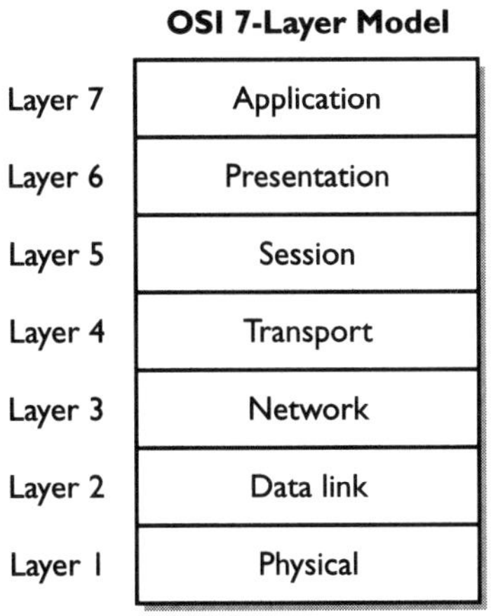

Layer 7	Application
Layer 6	Presentation
Layer 5	Session
Layer 4	Transport
Layer 3	Network
Layer 2	Data link
Layer 1	Physical

By building communications software according to the OSI model, developers know the exact guidelines by which they must develop their software. By using the layered approach, developers don't need to worry about any other function except their design focus, which may be as diverse as e-mail systems and database design. A database designer shouldn't have to worry about the intricate details of e-mail, and vice versa.

Each layer in the model is responsible for a different function. One or more protocols on each layer may perform that layer's function in a somewhat different manner, but the basic function is defined at each layer. The functions of the seven layers of the OSI model are shown in Table 1.1, beginning with the bottom layer and working up.

	LAYER NUMBER	**LAYER NAME**	**FUNCTION DESCRIPTION**
T A B L E 1.1 *OSI 7-Layer Model and the Functionality of Each Layer*	1	Physical	Defines the communication channel (such as Ethernet or Token Ring), formats the binary data appropriately, and transmits the data between computers on the wire. This is the layer between the network card and the wire.
	2	Data-link	Responsible for properly framing data for transmission before putting it out on the wire. Similar to packaging a letter in an envelope before mailing, this layer makes sure that Ethernet data goes onto an Ethernet cable, Token Ring data goes onto a Token Ring cable, and so on.
	3	Network	Has several job functions, including proper addressing, packet routing, and error notification. This layer actually instructs data where to go and how to get there.
	4	Transport	Used by data to reach its destination. After the network layer gives direction to the data, this layer picks up the data and takes it to its destination. This layer is also responsible for some error correction and *flow control* (a method to tell transmitting systems to slow down when sending data).

LAYER NUMBER	LAYER NAME	FUNCTION DESCRIPTION
5	Session	Whereas all the preceding layers format the data, this layer takes the formatted data and creates a logical connection with the remote computer. After the session is established, higher-level processes, such as file transfer, may take place.
6	Presentation	Used to encode/decode, encrypt and decrypt and compress data, if necessary. An example of data that uses this layer is compression for streaming video.
7	Application	The top of the protocol stack; allows users to access specific functions, such as file transfer or e-mail. It is the interface between the computer and the user.

Because the OSI model is a vendor-independent model, different protocols are at work at each layer, depending on the protocol stack. The TCP/IP model, however, is specific to a single suite of protocols. The next section looks at that model and the protocols involved.

Advanced Research Projects Agency TCP/IP Protocol Model

Beginning as a research project in the late 1960s, the Department of Defense Advanced Research Projects Agency (ARPA, later known as DARPA) funded the development of techniques for using reliable packet-switching networks. This original network, called ARPANET, linked only a few key universities and research agencies, and allowed these entities to share expensive computing resources. The success of ARPANET was unexpected, and by the 1980s, hundreds of organizations connected together to form what has now become the Internet. The original ARPANET protocols were replaced by the TCP/IP protocol suite, using a simpler, four-layer communication model.

The protocol model for TCP/IP consists of the four layers shown in Figure 1.3.

FIGURE 1.3

TCP/IP 4-layer model

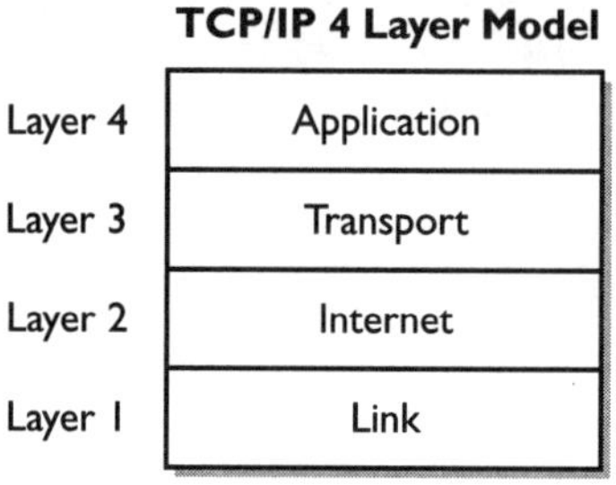

TCP/IP 4 Layer Model

Layer 4	Application
Layer 3	Transport
Layer 2	Internet
Layer 1	Link

As with the OSI model, each layer performs a specific, important function within the network. The four layers and their functions are shown in Table 1.2.

TABLE 1.2

TCP/IP 4-Layer Model and the Functionality of Each Layer

LAYER NUMBER DESCRIPTION	LAYER NAME	FUNCTION
1	Link	Handles the transmission of the data from the network card to the physical medium. Similar to the OSI physical layer.
2	Internet	Responsible for the movement of packets around the network. Tells the packets how to get to the destination.
3	Transport (Host to Host)	Provides data flow between two hosts in either a *reliable* or *unreliable* method, depending on the application request.
4	Application	Provides a user interface to the user input. Examples of application layer processes include e-mail, file transfer, and terminal emulation.

As already mentioned, each layer performs a specific function, although several protocols may be available to perform that function. For example, an application layer "function" is a broad category that defines the process of such things as sending e-mail, Web browsing, or terminal emulation. Each process carried out at this layer is performed by a different protocol, even though the function, an application, is the same. Figure 1.4 shows a detailed view of the specific protocols that may be invoked at each layer.

FIGURE 1.4

TCP/IP protocol suite

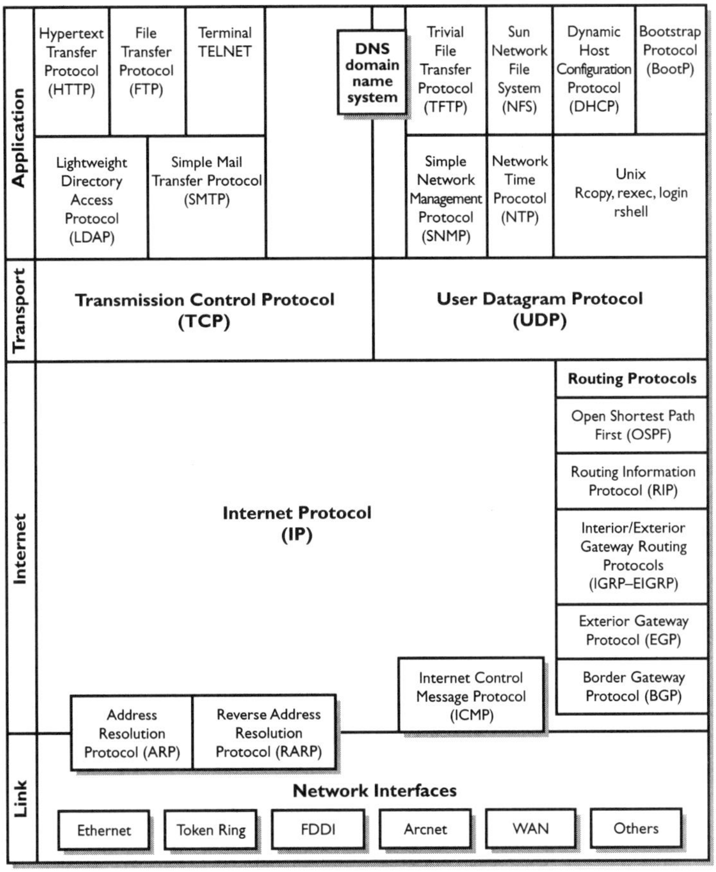

Application

| Hypertext Transfer Protocol (HTTP) | File Transfer Protocol (FTP) | Terminal TELNET | DNS domain name system | Trivial File Transfer Protocol (TFTP) | Sun Network File System (NFS) | Dynamic Host Configuration Protocol (DHCP) | Bootstrap Protocol (BootP) |
| Lightweight Directory Access Protocol (LDAP) | Simple Mail Transfer Protocol (SMTP) | | | Simple Network Management Protocol (SNMP) | Network Time Procotol (NTP) | Unix Rcopy, rexec, login rshell | |

Transport

| Transmission Control Protocol (TCP) | User Datagram Protocol (UDP) |

Internet

Internet Protocol (IP)

Routing Protocols
- Open Shortest Path First (OSPF)
- Routing Information Protocol (RIP)
- Interior/Exterior Gateway Routing Protocols (IGRP–EIGRP)
- Exterior Gateway Protocol (EGP)
- Border Gateway Protocol (BGP)

Internet Control Message Protocol (ICMP)

Address Resolution Protocol (ARP) | Reverse Address Resolution Protocol (RARP)

Link

Network Interfaces

| Ethernet | Token Ring | FDDI | Arcnet | WAN | Others |

As this figure demonstrates, the TCP/IP suite includes many protocols. This book looks at most of these protocols in great depth. For now, though, you need to understand specifically how data is transmitted between computers via the models and the layers.

Comparing the Model Layers

Figure 1.5 shows how the seven-layer OSI model compares to the four-layer TCP/IP model.

FIGURE 1.5

Comparing the OSI model to the TCP/IP model

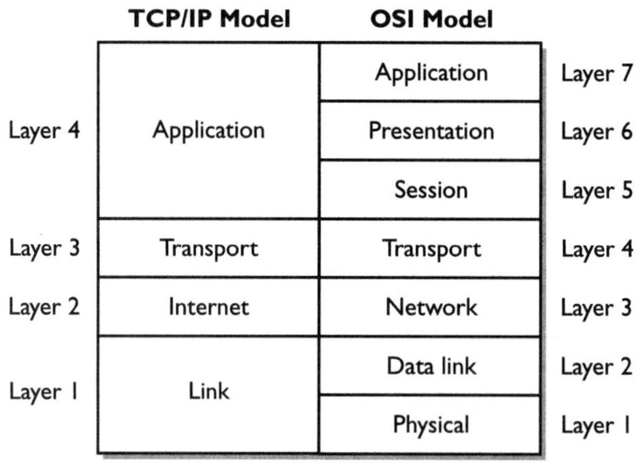

	TCP/IP Model	**OSI Model**	
Layer 4	Application	Application	Layer 7
		Presentation	Layer 6
		Session	Layer 5
Layer 3	Transport	Transport	Layer 4
Layer 2	Internet	Network	Layer 3
Layer 1	Link	Data link	Layer 2
		Physical	Layer 1

The TCP/IP model combines the ISO physical and data-link layers into a single layer, the link layer. The function of the TCP/IP Internet layer is much the same as the ISO network layer. The transport layer in each model performs roughly the same function. An aggregation of the top three ISO layers (session, presentation, and application) functions similarly to the single application layer of the TCP/IP model. The reason for this comparison is that many vendors don't implement a specific four-layer approach to TCP/IP. Therefore, using the ISO model to display the TCP/IP architecture of a specific vendor sometimes is easier than cramming that architecture into four layers.

Data Flow Within the Model

As data moves through the layers, each layer appends its own information, called a *header,* to the original data before it puts the data on the wire. The receiving computer strips the headers, one by one, as the data moves up the stack to its final destination, the user.

The best way to describe this process is through an analogy. Suppose that you're taking a trip to another country. The clothes that you pack for the trip are analogous to the application data. Using the TCP/IP model's layered approach, you take the following steps to get your clothing (data) to the destination country:

1. Pack your clothes in a suitcase (application layer).

2. Drive to the airport (transport layer).

3. Check your luggage at the gate and put a destination tag on it (Internet layer).

4. Get in the plane and fly to the other country (link layer).

You take the same steps in reverse to retrieve your clothing:

4. Arrive at the destination and retrieve your luggage from the baggage claim — hopefully they didn't lose it (link layer).

3. Get directions to the hotel (Internet layer).

2. Drive the car and your luggage to the hotel (transport layer).

1. Open the suitcase and unpack your clothes (application layer).

This process is illustrated further in Figures 1.6 and 1.7.

FIGURE 1.6

Sending data to its destination

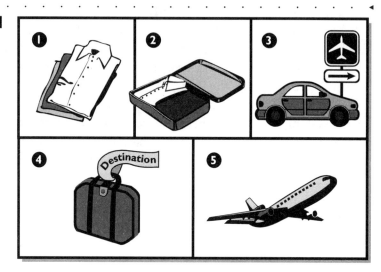

FIGURE 1.7

Unpacking retrieved data

Notice how the process works, moving down the layers when going to the airport and in reverse at arrival time. The same is true for communications between computers. The appending of header information sometimes is referred to as *frame construction*, whereas the stripping of header information sometimes is referred to as *frame reduction*. Figure 1.8 depicts the actual construction and reduction process when two computers are exchanging file information by using File Transfer Protocol (FTP).

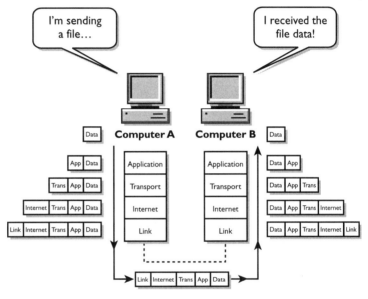

FIGURE 1.8

Multiple headers are appended to the user data

Computer A begins an FTP transmission to Computer B. As the data begins to travel down the stack, several headers are added, starting with the application header. Each subsequent layer looks at the data, plus the appended header, and adds its own header before passing the packet to the next level in the stack. This process ends with the link layer header, before wire transmission takes place. Upon receipt of the data packet, Computer B's protocol stack strips each header to reveal a new header while passing the data up the stack. When all the headers are removed, the original FTP application is able to report the data to the end user, who is viewing the computer screen.

The protocols operating at each layer are allowed to communicate only with the layer directly above or below them. Skipping layers is not allowed.

NOTE

TCP/IP Communication Methods Between Computers

No matter which vendor implementation of TCP/IP is used, a computer configured with the TCP/IP protocol suite follows one of two models for communications. The two types of processes are the following, each of which is discussed in this section:

- Client/server model

- Peer-to-peer model

Client/Server Communications

In the client/server model, one computer is assumed to be making a request (the client) while another computer is servicing the request (the server), as shown in Figure 1.9.

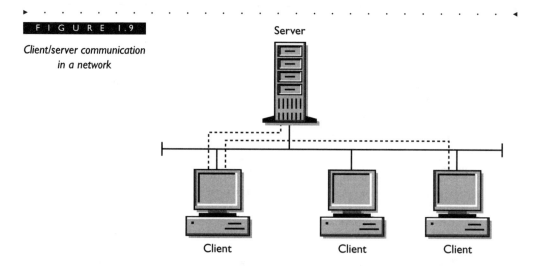

Server

Client   Client   Client

Two types of client/server communication may take place in a TCP/IP environment—*iterative* and *concurrent* server connections.

An iterative server goes through the steps illustrated in Figure 1.10 when communicating with a client. The client makes a request of the server, which is waiting for the request to arrive. On arrival, the server processes the client request and sends the response back to the client. The server then returns to the waiting mode and waits for another request.

FIGURE 1.10

Iterative server communication

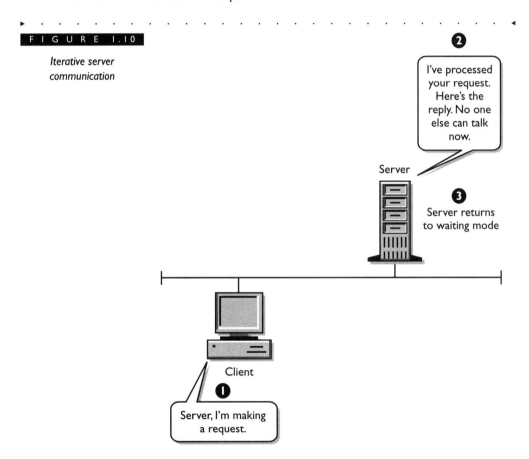

In contrast, a concurrent server works as shown in Figure 1.11. The concurrent server begins by waiting for a request to arrive. When the request arrives, the server starts a new process to handle the request. As other requests come in, the server simply starts more new processes, to handle multiple requests.

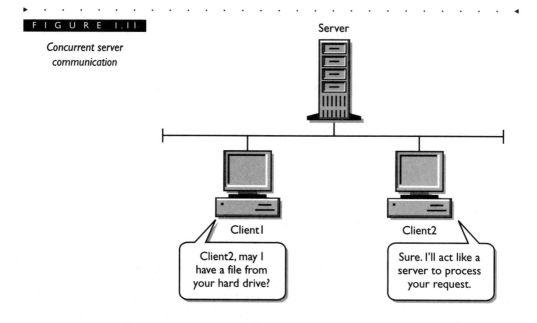

FIGURE 1.11

*Concurrent server
communication*

The following are the two possible protocols that an application may use for transport:

▸ **User Datagram Protocol (UDP):** A *connectionless* transport protocol, which means that no acknowledgement of the packet receipt is required between computers.

▸ **Transmission Control Protocol (TCP):** A *connection-oriented* protocol, which means that it requires acknowledgements for every data transmission.

For more information on UDP and TCP, refer to Chapters 9 and 10, respectively.

X-REF

In the client/server model, the usual rule is that UDP requests are serviced iteratively, whereas TCP requests are serviced concurrently.

Peer-to-Peer TCP/IP Communication

In a TCP/IP environment, a client may also have server components, enabling it to execute *peer-to-peer* communications, as shown in Figure 1.12.

FIGURE 1.12

Peer-to-peer TCP/IP communications enable computers to be both a client and a server.

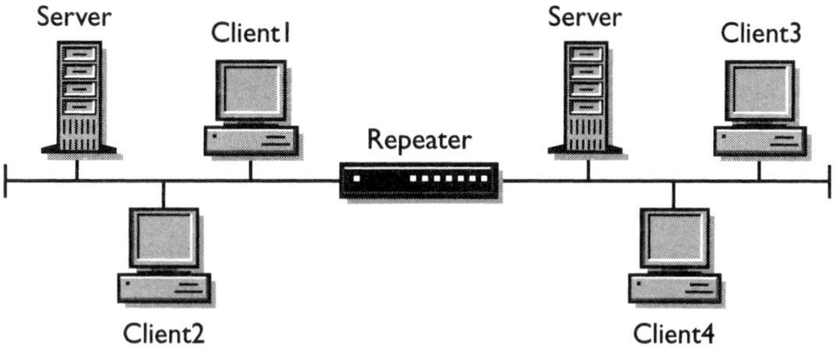

An example of a peer-to-peer operating system is the Microsoft Windows environment. Users in this environment can share files with the server, but files on local hard drives can also be shared directly between the computers without any help from the designated server. Contrast this with a Novell system using DOS-based clients, in which case the clients can communicate with the server, but can't communicate directly with each other without help from the server.

Layering and the Troubleshooting Process

This model and layering talk is the kind of stuff that people love to hate. Lots of people ask why they have to learn this. The truth is, when troubleshooting and analyzing networks, the more that you understand about the functionality of the layers and their associated protocols, the easier it is to understand a problem. Remember, each layer serves a particular function. If that function is working properly, then move on to other layers to troubleshoot. Some of the more common layer-specific problems are listed in Table 1.3.

TABLE 1.3	LAYER	COMMON PROBLEMS
Common Problems in Each OSI Layer	Application	Slow response or processing; file locking; long searches for files or directories; denial of rights or network privileges; looping requests
	Presentation	Data compression; garbled data due to improper formatting
	Session	Dropped connections; computer names can't be found; handshaking and improper negotiation
	Transport	Retransmission of packets; frozen windows; timeouts; overflows
	Network	Slowdown or bottlenecks in routers or switches (due to improper configuration or underpowered hardware)
	Data Link	Alignment; cyclic redundancy check (CRC) errors, usually due to packet damage between start and end points, but may be due to bad cables
	Physical	Collisions (late), beaconing, and other communications errors, such as loss of signal, magnetic interference, radio frequency interference, and improper grounding; cabling problems due to noncompliance with standards

When troubleshooting the network, always troubleshoot the lower layers first, working your way up to the upper layers, and change only one thing at a time.

 Troubleshoot the lower layers first and work your way up.

NOTE

The number of cabling systems that are out of specification is amazing, which causes quite a bit of trouble on the network. Chapter 3 gives specifics on what you should have in your Ethernet or Token Ring network. Don't violate the specification just because someone said you could. The specification exists for a reason.

► · ◄

Internetworking in the TCP/IP Environment

So far, this chapter has discussed how data flows through the network in a single, small environment. This section reviews what happens as the network grows, what the options are for expanding the network, and how expansion affects the layered communication.

Several hardware-based methods are available to use when network expansion is needed. Perhaps you have too many computers on a physical segment and need to break it up, or need to interconnect two local area networks (LANs) into a wide area network (WAN). The following are the four common hardware devices used to connect or extend networks:

- ► Hubs/repeaters

- ► Bridges

- ► Routers

- ► Switches

The following sections review how each of these devices is used in an IP network.

Repeaters and Hubs

As communication signals pass down a cable, they gradually weaken, which is called *attenuation*. Attenuation is normal in a growing network environment, but it isn't suitable for reliable communication between computers. When network cables are too long or out of specification (wrong cable type), the signal strength can become so weak that network communication is almost impossible.

To help combat signal loss, a device called a *repeater* may be added to the network. The repeater can extend a signal over a longer distance, making communication more reliable. A repeater is a common device used in a coaxial-based network system, as shown in Figure 1.13.

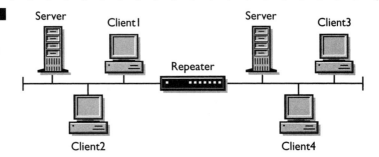

FIGURE 1.13

A coaxial-based network can be extended with the use of a repeater.

In a twisted-pair environment, a special type of repeater, called a *hub,* may be used. In this scenario, the hub has several ports, each attaching to a computer, as shown in Figure 1.14. A hub or repeater is simply a device that amplifies the signals sent to it. Amplified data is then sent out to all the ports on the hub. All devices on the hub or repeater share the same bandwidth.

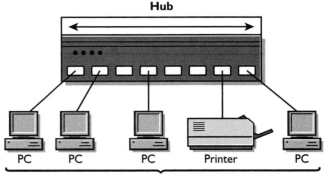

FIGURE 1.14

Twisted-pair networking using a hub

Hubs and repeaters are transparent to the network computers. Adding one of these devices is almost the same as adding more cable to the network — it just makes the network bigger. Hubs may contain modules for management, or may contain more sophisticated processes, as an option.

How Does Data Flow Through a Hub or Repeater?

When you install a hub or repeater on a network, the data flow is exactly the same as it was before — everybody sees everything on the network. Eventually, the network will need to be broken into segments, at which point a different connecting device needs to be used, such as a bridge, router, or switch.

Bridges

A *bridge* is another type of LAN extension device. However, unlike a repeater or hub, a bridge is a more intelligent device, insofar as it doesn't send all data everywhere. Instead, a bridge sends data across the LAN based on the media access control (MAC) address of the network interface card (NIC). Bridges communicate at the data-link layer of the OSI model, near the bottom of the protocol stack, which means that they don't rely on any upper-layer protocols to communicate, as shown in Figure 1.15.

FIGURE 1.15

Bridges operate at the data-link layer

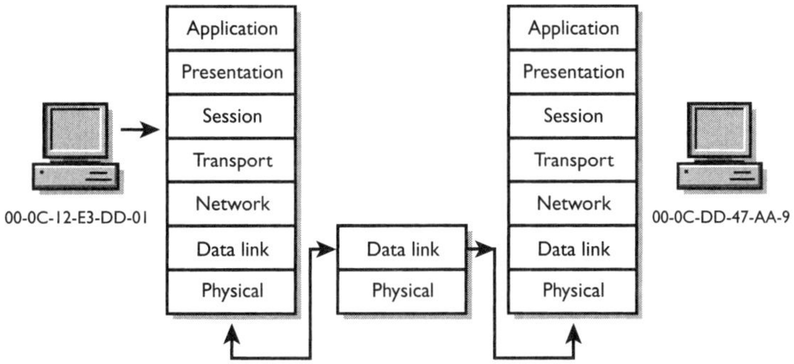

To send data across the network, a bridge needs only the MAC address of the NIC, which makes the bridge a very simple device to install in a network.

Why Use a Bridge?

Several reasons exist for why a bridge may be used within a LAN. First, a bridge is a popular and stable technology. The second, and most common reason, that network managers install bridges is simply to separate traffic. With Ethernet, for example, as a network segment becomes more heavily used, and increasingly more computers connect to the network, collisions and retransmission occurrences skyrocket. This causes network users to complain that the network is too slow, because the computers are fighting for network bandwidth, as shown in Figure 1.16.

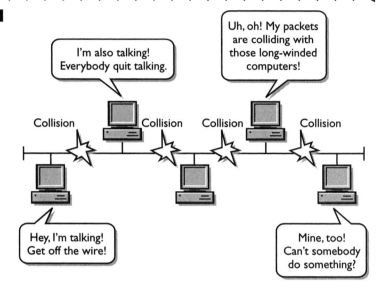

FIGURE 1.16

Too many devices on a network cause bandwidth contention.

By installing a bridge, you can begin to separate computers on one side of the bridge from computers on the other side. Data packets cross the bridge only as needed. An example of a bridge is shown in Figure 1.17.

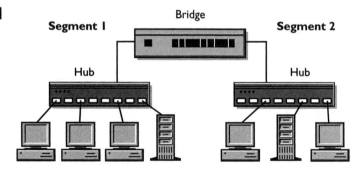

FIGURE 1.17

Using a bridge to separate network traffic

Another reason that bridges are popular is that they can be used across networks using nonrouteable protocols. Two examples of nonrouteable protocols are Digital Equipment Corporation's (DEC) Local Area Transport (LAT) protocol, and Network Basic Input/Output System (NetBIOS), used by Microsoft and IBM systems. Both of these protocols are designed to operate within the boundaries of a single Ethernet segment. So, what happens when the network grows and a new segment is added? Only some of the network users can use resources that rely on these protocols, unless a bridge is installed.

What Are the Types of Bridges?

As bridge technology has improved and grown, several types of bridges have been developed. Three of the most popular types of bridges are the following:

▸ **Transparent bridge:** A *transparent bridge* is a device that is used to connect two or more identical segments. Though these segments may operate at different speeds, they must be the same technology, such as Ethernet, as shown in Figure 1.18. The transparent bridge doesn't modify packets in any way — it makes its forwarding decisions based solely on MAC layer information. In this scenario, the computers on each side of the bridge are unaware of the presence of the device.

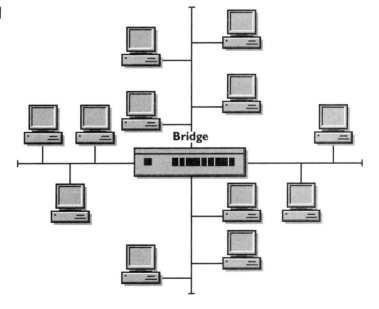

FIGURE 1.18

A transparent bridge connects multiple identical segments.

For more information on MAC layer differences, refer to Chapter 3.

X-REF

▶ **Source route bridge:** Specific to the Token Ring or Fiber Distributed Data Interface (FDDI) transmission medium, this bridge is used to connect two identical Token Ring or FDDI segments, though they may be running at different speeds. The source route bridge is different from the transparent bridge in its use of special *explorer frames*, which are used to discover routes to a specific end station. In source route bridging, each LAN segment and bridge are given an ID number, so that routes through the network can be identified, as shown in Figure 1.19. The source route bridge can modify a frame during the forwarding process. Routing decisions can be set in the Token Ring header, to control how routing takes place for specific packets, allowing packets to take different communication paths in the network.

FIGURE 1.19

A source route bridge uses explorer broadcasts to determine routes.

Ring B

Source route bridge 3

Ring A

Source route bridge 1

Ring D

Server A

Computer A

Source route bridge 2

Ring C

❸ File server receives both broadcasts and determines there are two routes between itself and Computer A

❶ Computer A sends an Explorer broadcast to Rings B and C

❷ Rings B and C both send the Explorer packet to Ring D

▶ **Translation bridge:** Has the toughest job of all bridging technologies: to connect different types of LAN segments and modify or translate forwarded frames before sending them across the bridge, as shown in Figure 1.20.

This is somewhat of a "two-faced" bridge, because it speaks to each LAN segment using its own proper frame header. In Figure 1.20, the translation bridge connecting the Ethernet and the Token Ring segment appears as a transparent bridge to each segment. Therefore, the stations on the Ethernet segment don't know they are communicating with a Token Ring computer, and the same is true for the Token Ring nodes. Meanwhile, the bridge is doing some pretty fancy work.

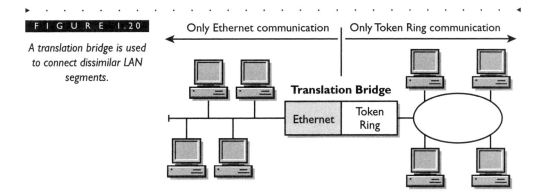

FIGURE 1.20

A translation bridge is used to connect dissimilar LAN segments.

How Do Bridges Work?

To explain how bridges work, this section focuses on how standard transparent bridges operate, using as an example the small, bridged network in Figure 1.21. In this example, a bridge is used to separate the sample network into logical segments. Three users are on each side of the bridge, and the network has just been powered on. No device knows about any other device.

A bridge operates in *promiscuous mode*, which means that the Ethernet traffic on each side of the bridge is received by the bridge. So, basically, the bridge sees everything and is a big snoop. For every packet sent on the network, regardless of the segment, the bridge looks at the source MAC address, trying to learn which computers belong to the different segments connected to the bridge. The bridge stores the entries that it learns about in a *bridge table*, which it uses to forward

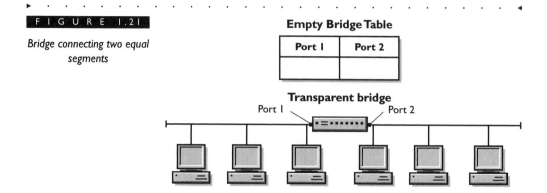

F I G U R E   1.21

Bridge connecting two equal segments

packets intelligently. The process is called the *bridge learning process,* which works like this:

1. Computer A sends a packet addressed to Computer X.

2. The bridge notices that Computer A is on its Port 1 (because it just saw a packet from Computer A) and updates its routing table with Computer A's MAC address.

3. The bridge looks in its routing table for Computer X, but finds no entry, so it doesn't know whether to forward the packet.

4. The bridge performs a process called *flooding,* in which it sends the packet on all ports, looking for Computer X. (The packet is addressed to Computer X, so only that computer will respond. All other computers ignore the packet).

5. Computer X receives the packet and processes it.

These steps are further illustrated in Figure 1.22.

FIGURE 1.22

*Bridge learns MAC
addresses*

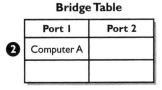

Bridge Table

Port 1	Port 2
❷ Computer A	

❸ Bridge has no table entry for Computer X

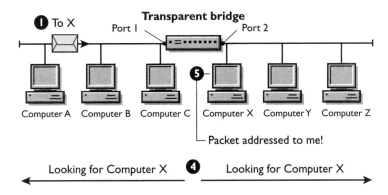

So, what happens when Computer X responds to Computer A? The process works like this:

1. Computer X sends a packet addressed to Computer A.

2. The bridge learns that Computer X is on Port 2 and updates its table with Computer X's MAC address. (Remember, the bridge is promiscuous and looks at everything on the network.)

3. The bridge looks in its table, notices that Computer A is on another segment, and realizes that the packet needs to be forwarded.

4. The bridge forwards the packet to Computer A.

Figure 1.23 illustrates this process.

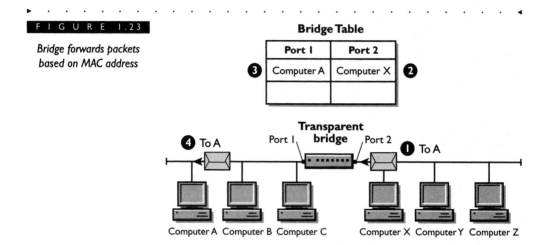

Bridge Table

Bridge forwards packets based on MAC address

This process continues for as many packets as are sent on the wire. The bridge continues learning and fills its table, as shown in Figure 1.24.

Complete bridge table

Port 1	Port 2
00-OC-DD-EI-A7-01 (Computer A)	00-AE-CC-27-39-22 (Computer X)
OC-00-DD-AE-37-02 (Computer B)	OC-OD-CL-01-39-28 (Computer Y)
00-OC-BI-93-65-01 (Computer C)	OC-00-DC-13-27-93 (Computer Z)

After the table is built, the bridge can decide what to do with packets — forward them or leave them on the segment. For example, in Figure 1.24, the MAC addresses for Computers A and B have been entered into the bridge table. According to the bridge table, both computers are on the same segment. When traffic comes from Computer A to Computer B, the bridge knows that this traffic shouldn't be forwarded. However, if Computer A wants to talk to Computer X again, the bridge knows that the packets must be forwarded.

Bridge Traffic Rules

You must be aware of a few "bridge traffic rules" when using bridging technology:

> ► **Rule #1:** If the bridge table is incomplete and an unknown address is received, the bridge must flood all ports (send the packet out to all connected segments).

> ► **Rule #2:** If a broadcast packet is sent, the broadcast must be sent on to other segments.

These rules mean that although bridging technology is simple and easy to set up, it segments only physical cabling, not necessarily traffic patterns on the network. As such, this isn't a good Internet technology. Imagine what would happen if you were looking to communicate with another computer on your corporate network and that broadcast request went around the world. (Well, okay, limitations do exist on how many bridges can be in a network, but you get the idea.)

For this reason, routing technology is heavily used in the TCP/IP environment.

Routers

So far, you have explored how a network can be expanded by using a hub, repeater, or bridge. However, none of these hardware technologies is a good way to connect networks together. Today, some corporate networks span the globe, the Internet, and different types of hardware and software, all working together. This is accomplished through a hardware device called a *router*.

What Is a Router?

For two networks to communicate, they first must be physically connected in some manner. However, just having the physical connection isn't enough; the device connecting them must be smart enough to be able to send (or *route*) packets between networks. Figure 1.25 shows how two networks may be connected with a router.

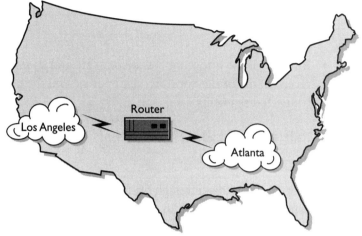

*Two networks connected
with a router*

The router's job is to capture packets from the network in Atlanta and send them to the network in Los Angeles. Likewise, the router must be able to take packets from Los Angeles and send them to Atlanta.

As more networks are connected through routers, the routers' job becomes more complex. Consider the larger internetwork depicted in Figure 1.26, in which the routing principles become much more complex. Router 1 must know that it needs to pass packets through not only to Network 2, but also to Networks 3, 4, and 5. Consider the Internet, and the millions of computers and networks that it connects. Routers have a tough job!

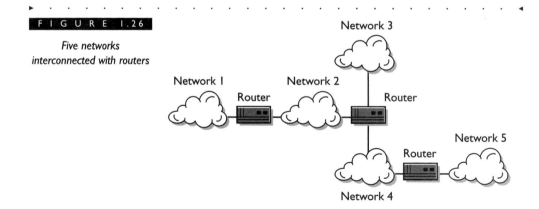

*Five networks
interconnected with routers*

How Do Routers Work?

By now, you might have guessed that a router isn't just a simple device. Often, it's a large machine with enough memory to hold all the information about the networks for which it sends packets. Additionally, a router is an intelligent device that makes decisions to route based on network numbers, not on MAC addresses, like a bridge.

Making the Routing Decision   In a TCP/IP environment, each network has its own address, as does each of the devices. The *network address* describes the actual network, such as 192.168.1.0. The *host address* is assigned to a specific device within a network.

To help you understand this concept better, consider how mail is delivered to your house. Every city, there are streets, such as Main Street or First Street. These street names must be unique throughout the city. The same goes for network numbers—they must be unique. Mail first comes to the post office and is sorted and given to the mail delivery person. When the mailperson delivers mail, he or she first looks at the street to which the mail should be delivered. Let's say that it's on Main Street. The mailperson takes an appropriate route to get to Main street. Once he or she is on Main Street, the mailperson must look for the proper house number. When the proper house number is found, the mail is delivered.

Like street names in a city, network numbers must be unique. The router on the internetwork is responsible for getting the mailperson to the appropriate street within the larger network.

X-REF

For detailed information on IP addressing, refer to Chapter 4.

Routers maintain a *routing information table (RIT)* to keep track of the different routes available, along with MAC addresses for specific computers. A router decides when and how to route a packet that it receives on one of its ports. A router may have several ports (or attached networks), as shown in Figure 1.27.

Router with multiple ports

Network 216.12.45.0
(First Street)

Computer A

Router   Network 145.30.17.0
(Second Street)

Network 207.26.1.0
(Main Street)

Computer X

Network 101.65.32.0
(Third Street)

This figure shows an interconnected network, with each segment having a specific (and unique) network number. Notice that the router is connected to all networks, which means that traffic will flow through that single router to get between networks. Let's take a look at how the data actually travels through the router.

How Does Data Flow Through a Router?   Before an originating computer sends a packet in an IP network, it compares its own source IP address with the destination IP address, to determine whether that packet needs to go through a router. For example, in Figure 1.28, the originating computer makes a decision regarding whether the packet is destined for its own local network or some other network. When it decides that the destination is on some other network, it calls on the router for help.

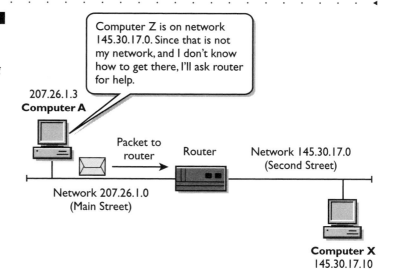

Originating computer compares IP addresses to determine whether routing is needed

The originating computer first looks in its own internal routing table to locate the routing information needed to send the packet to another network. If that information doesn't exist in the originating computer's internal routing table, it sends the packet for processing to the *default router,* which is the router that is configured in the TCP/IP parameters of the originating computer. The default router can then send the packet on the next hop toward its final destination.

By configuring a default router within the computer's TCP/IP parameters, the originating computer no longer has to decide which router it should communicate with if the network has several routers. The originating computer sends a *unicast* directly to the router, a type of transmission between a single sender and a single receiver (such as a computer and a router). Differentiating this method from the promiscuous mode of a bridge is important—when using unicast, the router hardware is already more performance-dedicated, because it doesn't have to look at every packet on the network, as a bridge does.

A router operates in unicast mode. A bridge operates in promiscuous mode.

IMPORTANT

The originating computer now has made a decision to send a packet to the router. The following list explores the path that the packet takes as it travels through the router to the other (remote) network:

1. Router receives the packet.

2. The packet type is checked. If it is an IP packet, the data-link header is stripped.

3. Router looks at the destination IP address.

4. Router searches RIT to find the appropriate route.

5. The router builds a new header for the packet and sends it out a different port.

The following sections look at these steps in a little more detail.

Step 1: Router Receives the Packet   Figure 1.29 shows two networks, Network 1 and Network 2, connected with a router. Computer A wants to communicate with Computer X. Computer A has decided that Computer X isn't on its local network and thus is configured to send the packet to the default router connected to Network 1.

F I G U R E   1.29

Computer A sends packet to the default router

Network 1
207.26.1.0

Router

Network 2
145.30.17.0

Port 1   Port 2
MAC 00-CO-AA-01-23-18   MAC AA-01-BB-79-23-08
IP 207.26.1.1   IP 145.30.17.1

Computer A
MAC-DD-01-CB-35-78-91
IP 207.26.1.10

Computer X
MAC-CC-03-29-A9-37-EF
IP 145.30.17.10

Step 2: The Packet Type Is Checked The router examines the packet to determine the packet type, as shown in Figure 1.30, and determines that the packet is a valid IP packet.

FIGURE 1.30

*Router examines packet for
the valid packet type*

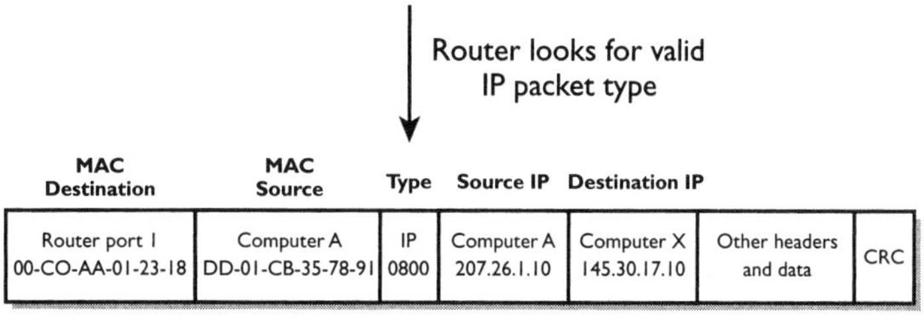

Router looks for valid
IP packet type

MAC Destination	MAC Source	Type	Source IP	Destination IP		
Router port 1 00-CO-AA-01-23-18	Computer A DD-01-CB-35-78-91	IP 0800	Computer A 207.26.1.10	Computer X 145.30.17.10	Other headers and data	CRC

Step 3: Router Looks at the Source and Destination IP Address The router makes sure that it checks the source and destination IP address, as shown in Figure 1.31. Notice that in this packet, Computer A's IP address (207.26.1.10) and Computer X's IP address (145.30.17.10) are listed as the source and destination IP addresses, respectively.

FIGURE 1.31

*Router checks source and
destination IP address*

MAC Destination	MAC Source	Type	Source IP	Destination IP		
Router port 1 00-CO-AA-01-23-18	Computer A DD-01-CB-35-78-91	IP 0800	Computer A 207.26.1.10	Computer X 145.30.17.10	Other headers and data	CRC

Router views source and
destination IP addresses

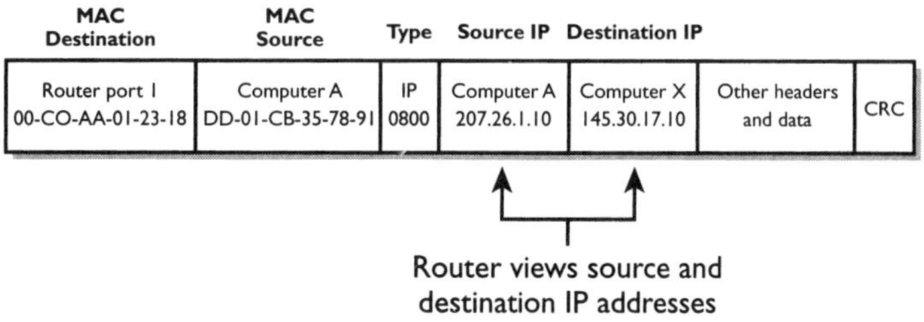

Step 4: Router Searches RIT to Find Appropriate Route to Destination The router searches its RIT for information about how to send a packet from Network 1 (207.26.10.0) to Network 2 (145.30.17.0). It finds an entry in its table, as shown in Figure 1.32.

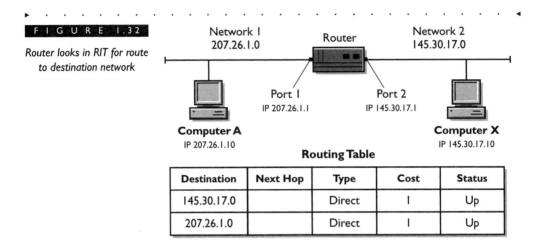

FIGURE 1.32

Router looks in RIT for route to destination network

Network 1
207.26.1.0

Router

Network 2
145.30.17.0

Port 1
IP 207.26.1.1

Port 2
IP 145.30.17.1

Computer A
IP 207.26.1.10

Computer X
IP 145.30.17.10

Routing Table

Destination	Next Hop	Type	Cost	Status
145.30.17.0		Direct	1	Up
207.26.1.0		Direct	1	Up

The router determines that it knows how to communicate with Network 2, because its RIT entry says the router is directly connected to Network 2. It must send a packet out its second port to reach its destination. If the router doesn't know how to communicate to Network 2, it could perform an Address Resolution Protocol (ARP) process to attempt communication with the destination computer. (The ARP process is discussed in later chapters.)

Additionally, another router may exist between the networks. In that case, the router forwards the packet to the *next hop router,* a router that has informed the original router that it can reach the destination network. Using this process, a packet may go through several routers before actually arriving at its destination.

The Routing Information Protocol that routers use to communicate routes is discussed in detail in Chapter 7.

X-REF

Step 5: Router Builds New Header for Packet and Sends It Out a Different Port
Before the router can transmit the packet, it must replace the Ethernet header that it originally stripped. The router places a new header on the packet, using its own MAC address as the source address, and the destination MAC address of Computer X, as shown in Figure 1.33.

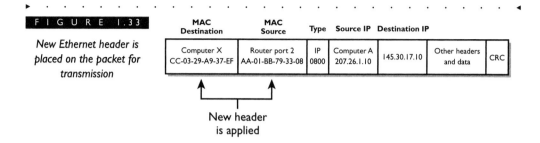

New Ethernet header is placed on the packet for transmission

When the packet is received by the remote computer, the process works in reverse. Namely, the computer responds to the router port from which the information came. The router then strips the header, finds the route back to the originating network, places a new header, and sends the packet out the original port. This process continues until the communication stops between the two end nodes. The packet returning to Computer A through the router is shown in Figure 1.34.

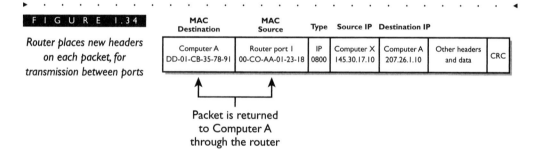

Router places new headers on each packet, for transmission between ports

Routers play a key role in TCP/IP communication — they truly can segment and direct traffic. Later chapters in the book discuss how routers communicate among themselves and how they learn routes.

The advantage of having routers in a large TCP/IP network, such as the Internet, is that they work transparently to the users. Today, a network user sends an e-mail message and it magically appears in the mailbox of the recipient, whether that person is 10 miles or 10,000 miles away. The process of routing involves the network layer of the communication model, instead of the link layer, as with a bridge. Using this layer in the model allows communication to be more highly configured. By contrasting that to the bridge, which uses only the MAC address for packet forwarding, you can see why routers are used more frequently than bridges in today's networking environments.

Switches

A *switch* is another hardware device that can be used to segment network traffic. A switch operates like a bridge, insofar as it uses the MAC address to decide whether to forward a packet. However, a switch may be used to connect to devices and network segments, whereas a bridge can connect only two segments. Figure 1.35 shows a network with a switch that is connected directly to a server, a workstation, and a hub, which branches off to many other computers. This is the type of configuration that you normally see in a switched environment.

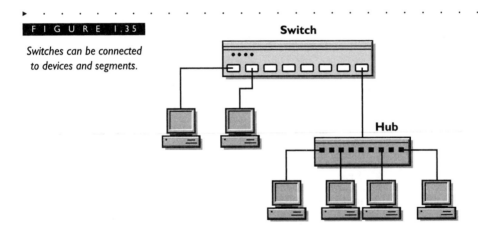

▶ · ◀

F I G U R E 1.35

Switches can be connected to devices and segments.

As mentioned earlier, networks grow. As more computers are placed on a network segment, the probability for packet collisions increases. A switch is used to segment the network logically, while keeping it functioning as a single, nonrouted network. This process is called separating the *collision domain*.

Although a switch operates similarly to how the transparent bridge operates, some very important differences exist:

> ▶ A switch can operate at a much higher speed than a bridge or a hub. Ethernet speeds have reached 100MBps and higher, and switches allow communication to take place at almost wire speeds. Switches can also

accommodate different device speeds within the same switch, such as a 10MBps and 100MBps Ethernet segment.

▸ By logically separating computers and reducing the chance of collisions, switching technology improves overall network performance.

How Do Switches Work?

In a switched environment, devices connected to the switch share the same device bandwidth, as shown in Figure 1.36.

F I G U R E   1.36

Switched devices use the same bandwidth

Shared bandwidth

Switch

Switches have multiple ports and, like a bridge, learn the MAC addresses from the data packets passing through the switches. For each connection request, a circuit between ports is established. The next several figures follow the path that a packet takes when a computer on one port wants to communicate with a computer on another port. On boot up, the switch has no entries in its address table, as shown in Figure 1.37.

F I G U R E   1.37

Switch boots up and has no MAC address entries

Switch Address Table

Port 1	Port 2	Port 3	Port 4

When Computer A sends its request to the switch, the switch updates its MAC address table to reflect Computer A's location (Port 1). It then looks in its address table to find the MAC address of Computer X. However, no current entry to Computer X exists, because the switch just started and has communicated only with Computer A, as shown in Figure 1.38.

FIGURE 1.38

Switch updates its MAC address table with Computer A's MAC address and port location

2 Table is updated

5 Table is updated

Switch Address Table

Port 1	Port 2	Port 3	Port 4	Port 5	Port 6	Port 7	Port 8
Computer A MAC			Computer X MAC				

So what does the switch do? Any guesses? Well, it floods all ports with the packet destined for Computer X. Computer X receives the packet and responds to Computer A. At this point, the switch updates its MAC address table to reflect the location of Computer X (Port 4). Then, it establishes a circuit between Port 1 and Port 4, to allow the computers to communicate freely, as shown in Figure 1.39.

FIGURE 1.39

Switch updates its MAC address table and establishes a communication circuit

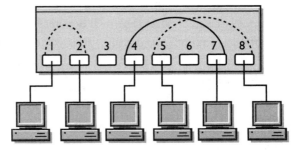

Switch

This process may take place with several computers simultaneously, resulting in many circuits running concurrently within the switch. Figure 1.39 shows several conversations running in the switch.

NOTE

Many people wonder why switching doesn't help network speed in a single-server 10MBps environment. The simple answer is that all circuits go to the same place—the server. For better performance, upgrade the 10MBps link between the server and the switch to a 100MBps link.

Normal traffic on a switch is sent by using circuits. However, when broadcast packets are sent on a switch, the broadcasts go everywhere. When sending data between ports on a switch, the switch device itself may be configured in numerous ways. The four most popular types of switching methods are the following:

▸ *Cut-through:* The fastest configuration to transmit packets between ports. A switch starts to forward a received packet to its destination before receiving the end of the frame. Thus, packets are transmitted very quickly. However, because the end of the frame contains error information in the form of a *cyclic redundancy check (CRC)*, error packets are forwarded just like packets without errors, resulting in unnecessary packet pieces floating around on the wire.

▸ *Store-and-forward:* Switches read an entire packet into the switch and store it in a receive buffer (an alternative to the cut-through method). After the packet integrity is verified, the packet is sent to its destination. This results in a slower switching process, but doesn't put bad packets on the wire unknowingly.

▸ *Adaptive:* A switch starts in cut-through mode but begins to experience excessive errors or bad packets, so it automatically converts itself to store-and-forward mode. Using adaptive mode, the packets are read into the switch, buffered, and inspected, and all the bad packets are discarded. When the number of error packets returns to an acceptable level, the switch returns to cut-though mode. Many switches today incorporate the adaptive switching method.

▶ *Fragment free:* Method of packet forwarding on an Ethernet segment that guarantees transmission after receipt of the first 64 bytes of a packet. Any received packet with a length less than 64 bytes is considered to be a *fragment*, or corrupt packet. This is similar to the cut-through mode of operation, insofar as the packet is sent to the destination before all the data is received.

Remember, a switch is simply an extension of the network. Unlike a router, which connects internetworks, a switch is a device that makes virtual connections between ports to allow communication to occur between two systems on separate ports. Switched systems are not as scaleable as routed systems, due to their bridge-like architecture.

Switching for the Future

This section looks at how switching prospects are evolving for the future.

Layer 2 Switches   So far, this chapter has described *layer 2 switching*, which performs packet forwarding by NIC MAC address. A layer 2 switch performs its function at the physical layer of the OSI model, which means that it's very dependent on understanding the actual physical interconnection hardware (such as Ethernet or Token Ring) that connects the network. A switch was originally designed for workgroups or small to midsize networks, but as networks have grown, new ways of managing switched traffic have been developed.

Virtual LAN (VLAN) Technology   The most common layer 2 switching technology is a *virtual LAN (VLAN),* a group of hosts or network devices that forms a single bridging domain. VLANs are formed to group related users, regardless of the physical connections of their hosts to the network. Users on a VLAN can be as close as the next room or as far away as the next country, but generally are grouped by department or team. For example, sales departments in different buildings may be connected to one VLAN, while the accounting departments may be connected to another VLAN. In general, the idea of a VLAN is to group users so that most of their traffic stays within the VLAN.

One of the greatest advantages of a VLAN is its capability to segment broadcast traffic within the VLAN. In a layer 2 switch environment, when a broadcast packet is sent to the switch, it goes everywhere. Yuck! In a VLAN environment, the broadcasts can be contained within the logical broadcast domain, as shown in Figure 1.40.

FIGURE 1.40

Broadcast traffic with a switch vs. a VLAN

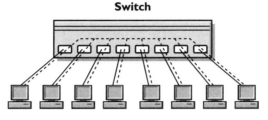

Switch

Broadcast is sent and goes everywhere

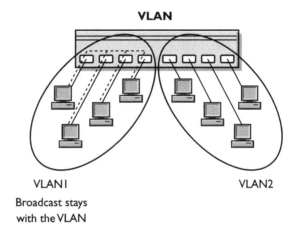

VLAN

VLAN1   VLAN2

Broadcast stays
with the VLAN

VLANs also provide extra security within what otherwise would be a less-secure environment. If a router is included within a VLAN, users outside that VLAN can communicate with users inside the VLAN. However, if a VLAN has no router, no traffic may travel outside the VLAN, which creates a highly secure environment.

Performance is also increased when a VLAN is established, because powerful users may be grouped together to use a dedicated server, for example. Additionally, computers in a VLAN can be programmed to join and leave VLAN groups. A user can be assigned to a VLAN one day and move to another physical location. By using switching technology, recabling may be required to move the user back into the workgroup. However, in a VLAN environment, the user's prior VLAN group information can simply be reprogrammed on the switch.

Layer 3 Switches Layer 3 switching technology has provoked quite a bit of discussion lately. A layer 3 switch is both a switch operating at layer 2 and a router operating at layer 3. Layer 3 switches integrate both routing and switching, for processing at super-fast speeds, thus eliminating the dependence on slow routers resulting from latency and memory configuration. Layer 3 switching attempts to meet the ever-increasing demand for more speed. Additionally, any growing network that still uses layer 2 "bridge-like" technology is bound to run into problems, such as broadcast storms, looping data, and possibly even addressing problems, and can benefit significantly from layer 3 switching.

Many manufacturers have developed technologies based around the layer 3 switching process. Currently, there are several types of layer 3 switches. These are generally referred to as:

▸ Routing switches

▸ Switched routers

▸ Flow or IP switch

In a standard routing situation, when data must be routed, it moves through layer 2 (for the MAC address) and layer 3 (for the IP address) in the protocol stacks of both the sending and receiving stations. Typical communication takes a path like that shown in Figure 1.41.

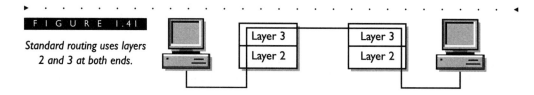

FIGURE 1.41

Standard routing uses layers 2 and 3 at both ends.

Routing switches probably are the simplest layer 3 switch to understand. A routing switch uses standard, nonproprietary routing protocols to move data between the switches. Routing calculations take place in layer 3 only when the routing switch doesn't know the destination of a received packet. When the destination is known, standard switching takes place, as shown in Figure 1.42.

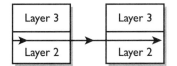

FIGURE 1.42

Routing switches use layer 3 to route and layer 2 to process packets.

Does the switch already know the route? Use layer 2.

Layer 3 → Layer 3

Layer 2 → Layer 2

Does the switch need to find the route? Use layer 3 then layer 2.

Switched routers, also known as *tag-switching routers*, use a slightly different approach to switching. This type of switch uses a special tag-distribution protocol to place a tag on the packet as it moves through the network. Routing and packet processing first takes place at layer 3. When the tag switch receives a packet with a tag, it uses the tag as an index to look up information in its internal *tag information base (TIB)*, which is similar to a routing or bridge table. Each entry in the TIB has an entry for the incoming tag, with one or more subentries. A subentry gives the switch information regarding the routing of the packet, such as an interface number and outgoing MAC information.

When an entry that is equal to the packet tag is found for the incoming tag, the switch goes to work. Looking at the subentries, the switch replaces the tag and the link-level (layer 2) information in the packet. It then sends the packet to the outgoing interface through layer 2, as shown in Figure 1.43.

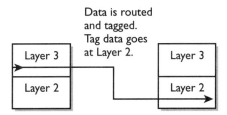

FIGURE 1.43

Switched (tag-switching) routers calculate and process data at layers 2 and 3.

Data is routed and tagged. Tag data goes at Layer 2.

Layer 3 — Layer 3

Layer 2 — Layer 2

By using this method, packet processing at layer 3 is reduced. However, it does require routers to be set up and properly configured with the tag-distribution protocol, for maximum efficiency.

Flow switches, also called *IP switches*, use yet another form of processing to pass packets between routers, although it's similar to a tag switch. In this type of switch, routing (layer 3) is the first function invoked. Both routing and processing of the packet take place until the switch discovers the beginning of a *flow*, a sequence of packets from a source to a destination that gets the same forwarding treatment at a router.

Multiple packets sent to the same destination from the source generally require a router to look at each packet, requiring the router to perform the same function over and over until all the packets are processed. Using a flow switch, the flow is recognized by using a flow protocol. When a flow is detected, the packets are processed at layer 2 until the flow is finished. This type of layer 3 switching is popular in ATM and frame-relay networks, where long-lived flows in traffic occur. The data handling is shown in Figure 1.44.

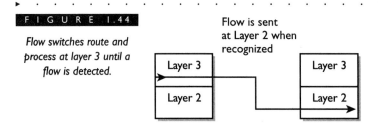

FIGURE 1.44

Flow switches route and process at layer 3 until a flow is detected.

Several fields that are processed by the switch can be used to characterize a flow. The IP source and destination addresses are used, along with the packet's port number. A *port* is used in TCP/IP networking to identify a specific process, such as FTP or Simple Mail Transfer Protocol (SMTP). Ipsilon Networks, Inc., a manufacturer of IP switches, defines two types of flows:

▸ **Host pair flow:** A flow of traffic between two computers, based on IP address.

▸ **Port pair flow:** A flow of traffic between two computers, based on IP address *and* port address. Using port pair flow, for example, the switch may understand not only that Computer A is maintaining a conversation with Computer B, but also that it is performing a file transfer.

Layer 4 Switches   If layer 2 switching is bridging technology and layer 3 switching is routing technology, what type of technology is layer 4 switching? To answer this question, review the layer names. Layer 4 is the *transport layer*, responsible for the coordination of communication between the source and destination computers.

The protocols that function in this layer, UDP and TCP, include port numbers that uniquely identify which application protocols a user is requesting. For example, suppose that a user is making a terminal-emulation request (session request) to a mainframe using a Telnet protocol application. The Telnet port number is 23.

Well-known port numbers are discussed in later chapters.

X-REF

In a layer 4 switch, port information included with each packet forms the basis for routing decisions. The layer 4 switch is capable of making the forwarding decision based not only on the MAC address (as in layer 2) and IP address (as in layer 3), but also on the transport protocol port number. Additionally, new protocols, such as the Resource Reservation Protocol (RSVP), enable a host to request specific qualities of service (sometimes called *service class*) from the network for a particular application or data stream. RSVP isn't a routing protocol, but it does work with existing routing protocols, and it consults with routing tables to find routes. After a route is found, RSVP is used to reserve resources along a data path, resulting in efficient and rapid communication.

One of the greatest advantages of the layer 4 switch process is that it can differentiate between applications when performing routing decisions. For example, traffic for an enterprise application may be assigned forwarding rules that are different from those assigned to traffic coming from the Internet, even if they need to travel over the same network infrastructure.

Another advantage of layer 4 switching is the ability to filter data. This isn't a new concept — it's a *firewall*. Traffic is interrogated at the switch before processing. If a packet arrives at the switch using a port that is filtered, the packet is discarded. This eliminates the need for separate firewall security hardware.

Case Study — What Can Go Wrong

Although many things *can* go wrong within a network environment, one of the biggest problem areas is the misconfiguration of bridges, routers, and switches.

The Problem

In this case study, a customer called with a problem: one of its segments couldn't talk to a server on the other side of a bridge. This is a large network, so Figure 1.45 (the drawing supplied by the customer) shows only the specific part of the network having the trouble.

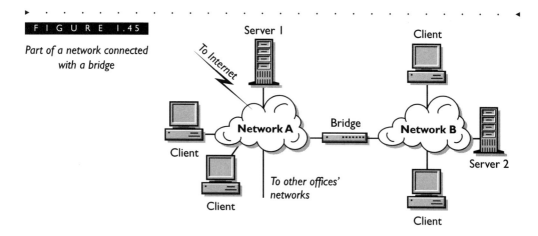

FIGURE 1.45

Part of a network connected with a bridge

Users on Network A could talk to the server on Network A, but every time they attempted to communicate with the server on Network B, the server would display an error message, and no communication was established.

The Analysis

Two Ethernet networks connected by a bridge were having the connection problem. We asked questions regarding what kind of applications they were running, what type of cabling, and so forth. The error message at the server stated that it thought it was seeing bad packets on the network, so that's where we started.

We placed a cable tester on Network A. All cables checked out fine. We placed two analyzers on Network A—a handheld hardware product and a Sniffer. No bad packets, fragments, or other errors were detected.

Network A seemed fine.

After checking Network A, we turned our attention to the device that connected the two systems—a bridge. The customer told us that they had identical Ethernet networks on both sides of the bridge (of course, that was our first question), so the bridge did not seem suspect. Not until we probed a bit deeper into Network B's configuration did we find the problem.

We called Network B's administrator and asked them to check their network card configuration. To our surprise, the network cards were Token Ring! Apparently, the only thing that was the same about these two networks was the physical cable — the rest of the data was formatted for Token Ring on Network B, whereas Ethernet was the choice for Network A. The bridge was a transparent bridge with no translation. Therefore, every time a packet tried to cross the bridge, the bridge had no idea how to convert it from Token Ring to Ethernet, or the other way around.

The Solution

This is a clear case in which the hardware is not right for the job. The solution is to either install a translational bridge or put a router between the networks. The customer chose a router, and everything is working fine.

· ·

Summary

This chapter delivered the very important basics of troubleshooting by defining the model used for data communications in the TCP/IP network. It compared the TCP/IP and OSI models, their differences, and their layers. It also explored how data moves through the layers, and common problems found at each layer. Finally, it discussed hardware for connecting and extending networks, and data flow through different kinds of hardware.

## CHAPTER 2

Analyzers and Other TCP/IP Troubleshooting Tools

Realistically, you can't troubleshoot or analyze a TCP/IP network without appropriate tools. Luckily, almost every TCP/IP operating system implementation includes built-in tools that not only are useful, but usually are required for successful operation of the network. You probably already know how to PING, but do you know how to PING properly?

This chapter discusses some of the built-in tools that are available in the Novell, Windows (95/98 and NT), Linux, and UNIX operating systems. Proper use of the tools, along with options for each command, are discussed.

Of course, to really analyze and troubleshoot the network, you *must* have a protocol analyzer of some kind — and know how to use it! This chapter looks at some popular analyzers that we use to troubleshoot our client's networks, along with some tips and tricks for placing your analyzer on the network for maximum results.

This chapter also introduces some third-party utilities that you may find helpful for use with your TCP/IP network.

▶ · ◀

The Built-In Tools

The great news about the TCP/IP implementation is that quite a few tools are available for troubleshooting — and they're free. The most widely used built-in tools are the following:

▶ **PING:** Checks device status

▶ **Traceroute:** Discovers packet route between two hosts

▶ **NETSTAT:** Provides network statistics

▶ **ARP:** Manipulates device's ARP (Address Resolution Protocol) table

▶ **CONFIG (and variations):** Shows configuration information

▶ **ROUTE:** Manually change routing information

▶ **NBTSTAT:** Used with NetBIOS over TCP/IP implementations

The following sections look at each of these utilities in turn and how they should be used.

Checking Device Status with the PING Utility

Different vendors use the PING utility to check the status of the device. This section reviews how you might use PING for troubleshooting.

What Is PING?

You're probably familiar with the PING command. PING is probably the most useful and most widely used utility associated with the TCP/IP protocols. The purpose of PING is to determine IP-level connectivity between hosts. PING sends request and reply messages, using the Internet Control Message Protocol (ICMP), to test functionality.

ICMP is discussed in depth in Chapter 6.

X-REF

When PING is used, it generates an ICMP Echo Request and message to be sent to the destination host. The destination host replies by using a matching ICMP Echo Reply. If you receive an Echo Reply, you know that the hardware is functioning in the other computer.

Vendor Implementation of PING

PING is usually implemented at the command line. However, several third-party utilities have graphical methods of issuing PING commands. Essentially, though the interface may be different, the function is the same — to verify connectivity. Table 2.1 lists several manufacturers' implementations of the PING command.

TABLE 2.1	IF YOU ARE USING:	THE PING COMMAND IS:
PING Commands by Vendor	Novell NetWare	LOAD PING or LOAD TPING (at the server console)
	Microsoft Windows NT	PING (at the command line)
	Microsoft Windows 95/98	PING (at the command line)
	Linux	ping (at the command line)
	UNIX	ping (at the command line)

The simplest way to issue a PING command is to use the vendor's PING utility along with an IP address of the destination. Figure 2.1 shows the output generated by the PING utility on a Windows workstation:

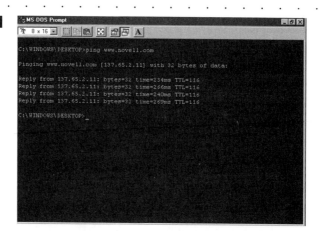

FIGURE 2.1

PING from a Windows workstation

Most PING results are quite similar. Notice the first line, which provides not only the IP address of `www.novell.com`, but also the domain name. Other information included in the PING for each result line is as follows:

▸ **Bytes:** Specifies the number of data bytes included in the Echo Request packet and returned in the Echo Reply.

▸ **Time:** Specifies the elapsed time between the beginning of the request and the receipt of the reply.

▸ **TTL:** Specifies the value of the Time To Live field in the IP header of the Echo Reply packet. This is used so that packets cannot "live" on the network forever.

Novell PING

Novell implements the PING command on the server via two NetWare Loadable Modules: TPING (trivial PING) and PING. The TPING utility is used much like the command-line utility on a UNIX or Windows host. To invoke the TPING utility at the server console, simply go to the server console (or use the RCONSOLE remote utility to display the console) and type:

```
LOAD TPING host [packetsize [retrycount]]
```

as shown in Figure 2.2.

F I G U R E   2.2

TPING at the Novell console

 NetWare 5 does not require the LOAD portion of the command. Simply type TPING at the console prompt.

TIP

You can use the *packetsize* parameter to change the size of the outgoing packet (the default is 64) and the *retry count* to manipulate retries (the default is 5) for a destination that cannot be reached.

The results of the TPING command show a device as either ALIVE or NOT RESPONDING. Figure 2.3 shows the result of a successful TPING.

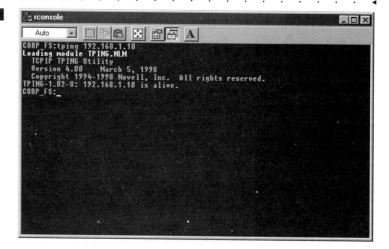

The PING.NLM from Novell also runs on the server console. This utility gives some extra information not usually found in other vendor implementations of PING without using additional command-line parameters. This being the case, this command has very few options. Invoke PING on the fileserver console by typing **LOAD PING** (or just **PING** if you are using NetWare 5). Figure 2.4 shows the first configuration screen.

Notice that only two options are available: the number of seconds to pause between PING commands, and the packet size to send. To begin the PING, simply type the hostname or IP address in the Host Name area.

After the PING command is activated, it continuously transmits Echo Requests across the network. Our advice to you—*don't leave PING.NLM running all the time!* We've actually had to troubleshoot "overloaded" networks because somebody left this utility running. (The IPXPING utility in NetWare, used to verify IPX connectivity, also can make a mess of your IPX-based Novell network if left running.)

Thus, the reason this utility should be used carefully is that it not only runs continuously, but you can actually add additional hosts to PING—sort of like a PING party. You add additional hosts to the PING.NLM by pressing the Insert key. Figure 2.5 shows the PING utility sending requests to several hosts simultaneously.

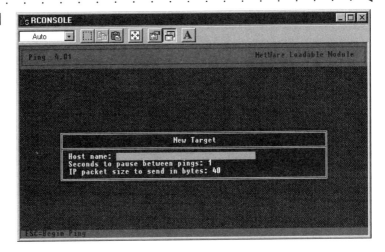

Loading the PING.NLM at the fileserver console

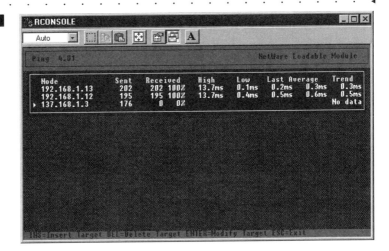

PING.NLM requesting multiple hosts

All joking aside, we really like this utility. The constantly updating table on the fileserver console gives some great information about the following PING statistics:

- **Node:** Specifies the IP address of the destination host

- **Sent:** How many packets were sent

- **Received:** How many packets were received

- **High:** Shows the longest round-trip time of the packets received

- **Low:** Shows the shortest round-trip time of the packets received

- **Last:** Round-trip time of the most recently received display

- **Average:** Specifies the average round-trip time of the replies received

- **Trend:** Shows current trending information for round-trip times. You may also see one of four information messages in this field, as shown in Figure 2.5:

  - **No Data:** Indicates that not enough data is being received to determine status

  - **Down:** Indicates that no replies have been received

  - **Failing:** Indicates that two-thirds of the requests have not received replies

  - **Drop:** Indicates that one-third of the requests have not received replies

Use the PING.NLM to compute round-trip statistics between servers, and even routing inside a single server.

TIP

PING Syntax and Command-Line Arguments

The PING tool, available in all implementations of TCP/IP, has several command-line arguments. The following is the proper command-line operation of PING:

```
PING [-t] [-a] [-n count] [-l length] [-f] [-I ttl] [-v tos]
[-r count] [-s count] [-j computer-list]|[-k computer list]
[-w timeout] destination_list
```

Table 2.2 describes each of the command-line arguments.

T A B L E   2.2

*PING Command-Line
Arguments*

PING ARGUMENT	DESCRIPTION
-t	PINGs repeatedly until interrupted (please don't leave this running on the network!).
-a	Shows the name of the computer assigned to the IP address used in the PING command.
-n *count*	Specifies the number of times to PING the computer.
-l *length*	The number of bytes to send to the destination computer.
-f	Tells routers not to fragment the packet.
-I *ttl*	Modifies the TTL field to the specified value. Defaults vary from 30 hops in UNIX, to 32 in Windows 95, to 64 for Novell, and 128 in Windows NT.
-v *tos*	Sets the Type of Service field to the specified value.
-r *count*	Displays the route taken by the packet between hosts. The value of *count* can be between 1 and 9 routers.
-s *count*	Displays the timestamp for the number of hops specified in the *count* value.
-j *computer_list* or *hosts*	Uses the loose route specified by *computer_list* or *hosts*. Computers must touch every router in the list, but may visit other routers along the way.
-k *computer_list* or *hosts*	Uses the strict route specified by *computer_list* or *hosts*. Computers *must* touch every router in the list in the exact order, and no other router visits are allowed by the packet.
-w *timeout*	Specifies a timeout interval, in milliseconds.
Destination-list	Gives an exact list of computers to PING.

As already mentioned, the simplest way to use PING is to type the command with the host IP address. However, with all the options available, PING becomes a very handy utility.

PING and the Maximum Transmission Unit (MTU)

Data can be transmitted between hosts using a MTU length of 1,500 bytes. The MTU is simply the largest message size that the host can receive without breaking up, or *fragmenting*, the packet. This is pretty standard in networks today.

MTU fragmentation is discussed in detail in Chapter 4.

X-REF

So, how do you know whether the packet is being fragmented? What is the maximum MTU size that your network can accept? PING can help you to determine this by utilizing the -f and the -l options in the PING command. Consider the example in Figure 2.6.

▶ . . . . ◀

F I G U R E 2.6

PING with maximum MTU size

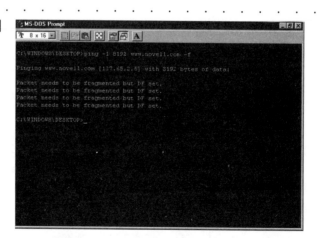

In this scenario, we attempted to PING using a maximum MTU of 8192 and told the system not to fragment the packet. The routers between our local device and the destination device could not process a packet with such a large MTU, so it gave us a PING error message stating that fragmentation was needed but not allowed. We can now use the PING utility with smaller packets to determine the maximum MTU for this particular communication session. It is important to note that, after a packet is fragmented, a device with a larger MTU capability will not increase the MTU for that path. So, after that packet is fragmented and the size is set, the size stays the same throughout that session.

The message shown in Figure 2.6 is one of four messages that may be encountered when using the PING utility.

PING Error Messages

The error messages displayed by PING are significant in troubleshooting the packet routes and communication within the network. Some of the most common PING results (other than a successful PING) are the following:

▸ **Destination Unreachable:** This error generally means that some routing problem exists within the network. Though communication is active, the requesting host received an error message stating that the device or network cannot be found.

▸ **Bad IP Address:** Don't trust this one! This usually means that a DNS name is spelled wrong or that DNS name resolution cannot be performed for some reason. It does not necessarily mean that communication is inactive. Try using the IP address, instead, for better results.

▸ **Packet Needs to Be Fragmented but DF Set:** Indicates that the message MTU size is too large to pass through a network device (such as a router). Also indicates that the Do Not Fragment bit has been set, instructing the device to keep the packet in one piece.

▸ **Request Timed Out:** Indicates that the device either does not exist or is very slow in responding. You will see this quite a bit in a larger network, because data packets tend to get lost in transmission. Figure 2.7 depicts an Internet PING to Novell during a busy time.

In Figure 2.7, two PING requests were made to www.novell.com. Notice that the first set of PING communication replies came back just fine. A short time later, when another PING command was sent, only two of the four replies came back properly. This is normal (especially for the Internet). A good idea in this case would be to use the -w parameter and increase the timeout value.

FIGURE 2.7

PING with request
timing out

If you're curious about the traffic of the Internet and subsequent packet loss around the world, check out
http://www.InternetTrafficReport.com/index.html.

PINGing Properly

Usually, when a person uses the PING utility and gets an error message, such as Request Timed Out, they assume it's the other computer's fault, reboot, and try again. Figure 2.8 shows the steps to using PING properly.

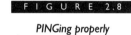

FIGURE 2.8

PINGing properly

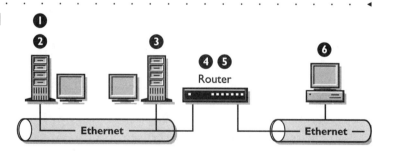

ANALYZERS AND OTHER TCP/IP TROUBLESHOOTING TOOLS

Basically, PINGing properly involves six steps. For the example in Figure 2.8, assume that the workstations on both ends of the routed segments cannot communicate. Follow these steps to determine the problem area:

1. **PING the loopback.** The loopback is a built-in mechanism inside the TCP/IP stack at the device. Simply type **PING LOOPBACK**. When you get PING response packets, you can assume that the TCP/IP capability is loaded in memory, but it does not mean that you have a correct IP configuration or that your hardware is working properly.

2. **PING your own IP address.** If you can PING your own IP address, you can assume that you have verified IP connectivity, although you still may not have a correct configuration. In other words, the hardware is working.

3. **PING an IP address of someone else on your cable segment.** Steps 1 and 2 made sure the hardware was working—this step tell you whether IP is configured properly for your cable segment. If you can communicate with your neighbor, you have IP configuration properly set up.

4. **PING your side of the router.** Every router has at least two interfaces: one that connects to your cable segment and one that connects to another segment. PING the router interface that is connected to your cable segment. (Sometimes, this is called your *default gateway.*)

5. **PING the other side of the router.** If you can PING across the router, you have verified that the LAN or WAN segment on the other side is operational.

6. **PING the destination.** By now, you should be able to PING the destination. If you cannot, then it really is the destination computer's fault.

Some people do this in reverse. It doesn't matter which way you perform the steps, as long as you do it methodically.

Discovering Packet Routes Between Two Hosts by Using Traceroute

The Traceroute utility is a routing utility that initially was used on UNIX systems. Its implementation has been ported to Novell in the form of the IPTRACE.NLM, and to Microsoft in the form of the Tracert command.

Traceroute is used to determine the route that a packet takes from source to destination. This utility will identify all routers and transmission details as a packet passes through an internetwork. Using ICMP TTL messages, the routes are identified by using repeated testing. This process is thoroughly described in Chapter 6.

Though Traceroute could conceivably discover an unlimited amount of systems through which a packet passes, most vendors limit the hop count to 30. This is usually sufficient to cover very large network installations.

Vendor Implementation of Traceroute

Table 2.3 shows vendor implementation of the Traceroute utility and the commands used.

TABLE 2.3	IF YOU ARE USING:	THE TRACE COMMAND IS:
Traceroute Commands	Novell NetWare	LOAD IPTRACE (at the server console)
	Microsoft Windows NT	TRACERT (at the command line)
	Microsoft Windows 95/98	TRACERT (at the command line)
	Linux	traceroute (at the command line)
	UNIX	traceroute (at the command line)

The simplest way to use the Traceroute command is by typing the command and IP address or hostname. Figure 2.9 shows the results of a TRACERT command to www.novell.com.

F I G U R E 2.9

TRACERT command results

Do not trust this utility on a mesh network, such as the Internet. Packets do not take the same route each time, and Traceroute results will vary.

IMPORTANT

Notice in Figure 2.9 that the results list not only the IP address, but also the hostname of the system forwarding the packet. Additionally, the Traceroute output lists three route trip times for each hop in the route, due to the fact that three requests were transmitted for each result line. The result lines with asterisks (*) mean that packets were dropped or lost in transmission.

Novell IPTRACE.NLM

Novell implements the trace utility at the server by using a NetWare Loadable Module (NLM) called IPTRACE.NLM. This utility is called from the console command prompt using the following syntax:

```
LOAD IPTRACE <DESTINATION(DNS Name or IP Address)>
[Hops=maximum hops (default 30)] [Wait=maximum wait time
(default=5 seconds)] [Port=Destination Port (default: 40001,
cannot take a value less than 6000)] [Noresolve]
[NewLog(restart iptrace.log)]
```

The following are the functions of the console command-line parameters:

▸ **Destination:** Specifies either a DNS name or IP address.

▸ **Hops:** Maximum number of hops to be traced. The default is 30.

▸ **Wait:** Specifies the maximum amount of time (in milliseconds) that IPTRACE should wait for replies. The default is five seconds.

▸ **Port:** Specifies the port number on the destination system to which the IPTRACE messages should be sent — the default is 40,001.

▸ **Noresolve:** Tells IPTRACE specifically not to resolve hostnames to IP addresses.

▸ **Newlog:** Begins a new trace log. By default, the log file IPTRACE.LOG is stored in the SYS:\ETC directory. This is a useful historical look at trace results. Figure 2.10 shows the IPTRACE.LOG file on our NetWare 5 server.

FIGURE 2.10

IPTRACE.LOG results

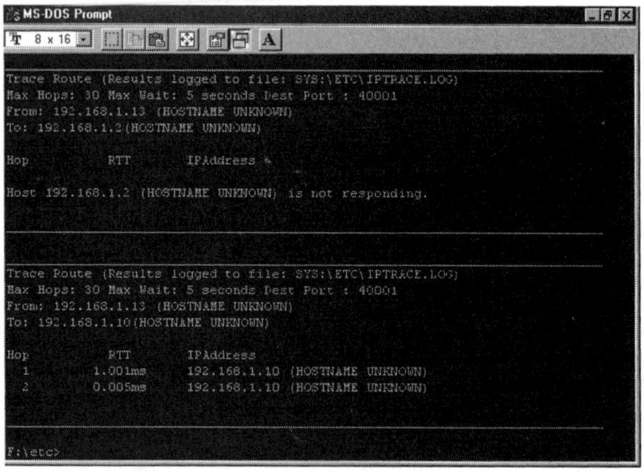

Traceroute Syntax and Command-Line Arguments

Microsoft's TRACERT program and the UNIX implementation of traceroute has the following syntax:

```
TRACERT  (or traceroute for UNIX) [-d] [-h maximum_hops] [-j
computer_list or hosts] [-w timeout] hostname
```

Table 2.4 describes each of the arguments.

TABLE 2.4

*TRACERT Command-Line
Arguments*

TRACERT ARGUMENT	DESCRIPTION
-d	Will not attempt to convert the IP addresses of computers between the local computer and the destination computer.
-h *maximum_hops*	Specifies the maximum number of hops between the local computer and the destination.
-j *computer_list* or *host*	Uses the loose route specified by *computer_list* or *host*. Computers must touch every router in the list, but may visit other routers along the way.
-w *timeout*	Waits the number of milliseconds specified in the *timeout* for each reply.
hostname	The name or IP address of the target host.

Viewing Network Statistics with TCPCON and NETSTAT

Novell's TCPCON.NLM is a utility that performs many functions, including viewing network statistics. Other TCP/IP implementations use the NETSTAT command to display the current TCP/IP network connections and protocol statistics. It is a command-line program that proves very useful in determining network performance issues.

Vendor Implementation of NETSTAT

Table 2.5 shows vendor implementation of NETSTAT and the commands used.

TABLE 2.5	IF YOU ARE USING:	THE STATUS COMMAND IS:
Vendor Implementation of NETSTAT	Novell NetWare	LOAD TCPCON (at the server console)
	Microsoft Windows NT	NETSTAT (at the command line)
	Microsoft Windows 95/98	NETSTAT (at the command line)
	Linux	netstat (at the command line)
	UNIX	netstat (at the command line)

NETSTAT has quite a few command-line options that are very helpful. A NETSTAT command issued at a command prompt with no options specified gives a simple list of the system's current active connections, as shown in Figure 2.11.

FIGURE 2.11

NETSTAT output

For each session, the following information is reported:

- ▸ **Proto:** The transport protocol (TCP or UDP) for that particular session.

- ▸ **Local Address:** The address of the originating workstation; consists of the name or IP address of the workstation, followed by the port number used by the originating host.

▶ **Foreign Address:** The remote address of the session; consists of the name or IP address of the remote host, followed by the port number used by the remote host.

▶ **State:** The state of the TCP connection. A connection can be in one of several states during the session, as described briefly here (further discussion of states is found in Chapter 10):

- **LISTEN:** A host is waiting for a connection request from any remote TCP and port.

- **SYN-SENT:** A connection request has been sent, and the host is waiting for a connection reply.

- **SYN-RECEIVED:** A host has received and sent a connection request, and is waiting for a confirming connection request acknowledgment.

- **ESTABLISHED:** Specifies an open and normal connection.

- **FIN-WAIT-1:** A host is finished and is waiting for a connection termination request from the remote TCP, or an acknowledgment of the connection termination request previously sent.

- **FIN-WAIT-2:** A host is waiting for a connection termination request from the remote host.

- **CLOSE-WAIT:** A host is waiting for a connection termination request from the local user.

- **CLOSING:** A host is waiting for a connection termination request acknowledgment from the remote host.

- **LAST-ACK:** A host has previously sent a termination request and is waiting for an acknowledgment.

- **TIME-WAIT:** The host is waiting for enough time to pass to be sure that the remote received the acknowledgment of its connection termination request.

- **CLOSED:** Represents no connection state at all.

Novell TCPCON

Novell uses an NLM called TCPCON to display and modify many TCP/IP statistics. To use the utility, simply type **LOAD TCPCON** at the fileserver console. A main screen, such as the one displayed in Figure 2.12, appears.

F I G U R E   2.12

TCPCON main screen

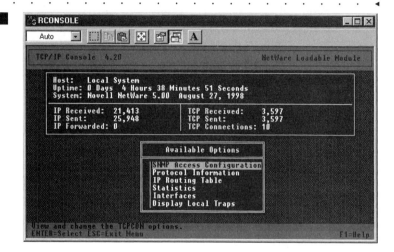

To view the statistics given by the NETSTAT command with no parameters, shown earlier using TCPCON, choose Protocol Information ➪ TCP ➪ TCP Connections ➪ Enter. This displays the statistics table, as shown in Figure 2.13.

F I G U R E   2.13

Protocol Connections Table in TCPCON

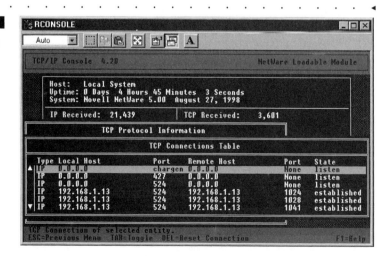

The connections list is a scrollable list that gives the same information as the NETSTAT command.

TIP

Use the Tab key in the TCPCON protocol statistics to toggle port numbers/names and IP hostnames/addresses.

NETSTAT Syntax and Command-Line Arguments

Table 2.6 describes the common functions available in NETSTAT and TCPCON, and the method of viewing for each utility.

TABLE 2.6

NETSTAT and TCPCON
Statistics

FUNCTION DESCRIPTION	NETSTAT ARGUMENT	TCPCON METHOD
Displays all connections plus listening ports	-a	Protocol Information ⇨ TCP ⇨ TCP Connections shows listening ports, by default
Displays Ethernet statistics	-e or -I (Linux)	Interfaces menu option — choose the interface and press Enter
Displays address and port numbers	-n	Protocol Information ⇨ TCP ⇨ TCP Connections Table — Tab to toggle
Displays protocol statistics	-p *protocol* (Microsoft) For Linux: -t — TCP -u — UDP -w — RAW -x — Sockets Note: -s may be used to display a summary for all protocols, including ICMP, TDP, UDP, or IP	Choose Protocol Information ⇨ Protocol and Statistics Choose Statistics ⇨ Protocol
Display routing table	-r	IP Routing Table menu — Enter

As you can probably already see, the NETSTAT or TCPCON information is very useful in troubleshooting the TCP/IP network. Take, for example, the statistics for the network interface card. Simply by performing a NETSTAT -e command (or using the Interfaces table in TCPCON), you can be on top of errors or overloaded interfaces, as shown in Figure 2.14.

You can view Novell fileserver interface statistics with the TCPCON utility, as shown in Figure 2.15.

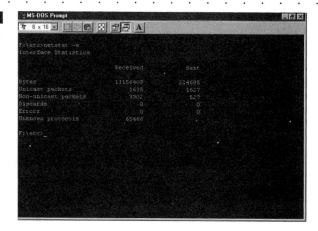

FIGURE 2.14

Results from the NETSTAT -e command

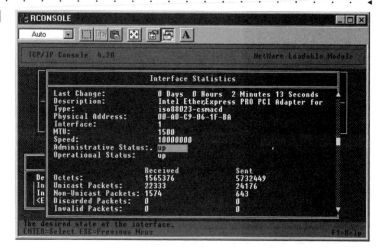

FIGURE 2.15

TCPCON interface statistics

General protocol statistics can be shown by using the NETSTAT –s command (Microsoft and some Linux/UNIX versions only), shown in Figure 2.16.

FIGURE 2.16

*NETSTAT -s command
output*

IP Statistics

Packets received	= 5463
Received header errors	= 280
Received address errors	= 0
Datagrams forwarded	= 0
Unknown protocols received	= 0
Received packets discarded	= 0
Received packets delivered	= 5183
Output requests	= 2141
Routing discards	= 0
Discarded output packets	= 0
Output packet no route	= 0
Reassembly required	= 0
Reassembly successful	= 0
Reassembly failures	= 0
Datagrams successfully fragmented	= 0
Datagrams failing fragmentation	= 4
Fragments created	= 0

ICMP Statistics

	Received	Sent
Messages	107	157
Errors	0	0
Destination unreachable	0	1
Time exceeded	88	0
Parameter problems	0	0
Source quenches	0	0
Redirects	0	0
Echos	0	156
Echo replies	19	0
Timestamps	0	0
Timestamp replies	0	0
Address masks	0	0
Address masks replies	0	0

TCP Statistics

Active opens	= 61
Passive opens	= 0
Failed connection attempts	= 0
Reset connections	= 27
Current connections	= 1
Segments received	= 1038
Segments sent	= 1007
Segments retransmitted	= 15

UDP Statistics

Datagrams received	= 4015
No ports	= 130
Receive errors	= 0
Datagrams sent	= 962

These statistics are particularly helpful in diagnosing error conditions. Notice the error reports for each of the protocols listed in Figure 2.16. Specifically, look at Received Header Errors, Received Address Errors, and so on, which indicate a possible routing problem in the network or a possible hardware failure.

Specific protocol statistics can also be viewed in TCPCON by using the Statistics menu and choosing a specific protocol. Figure 2.17 shows statistics for the IP protocol.

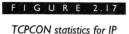

FIGURE 2.17

TCPCON statistics for IP

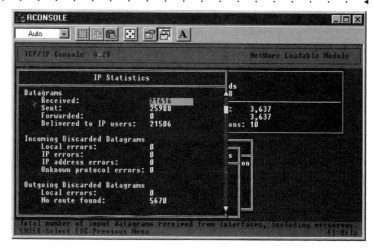

Again, you should look for any local errors or addressing errors. Notice that the No Route Found statistic displays a count of 5670. This number shows how many IP datagrams were discarded due to an unknown route. For this server, it usually means that some significant routing problem exists on the network that should be looked into.

Manipulating the ARP Cache

The Address Resolution Protocol (ARP) provides IP address-to-MAC (media access control—also known as *physical*) address mapping. The ARP command is used to change those address mappings.

In a broadcast network, such as Ethernet or Token Ring, hosts on the network may know the IP address to which they want to communicate. However, routing and communication must take place on the cable, which uses MAC addresses to send data. Therefore, a host requesting communication with another host must first retrieve the MAC address of the host that belongs to the destination IP address. It does this through the ARP process. Resolved ARP entries are then placed into a cache, located in the memory of the device.

ARP is discussed in detail in Chapter 5.

X-REF

Vendor Implementation of ARP

Table 2.7 illustrates vendor implementation of the ARP utility and the commands used.

TABLE 2.7	IF YOU ARE USING:	THE ARP COMMAND IS:
ARP Vendor Implementation	Novell NetWare	LOAD TCPCON (at the server console)
	Microsoft Windows NT	ARP (at the command line)
	Microsoft Windows 95/98	ARP (at the command line)
	Linux	arp (at the command line)
	UNIX	arp (at the command line)

To use the ARP command, at least one command-line argument must be used. The following is the common ARP command syntax:

```
ARP -a [ipaddress]

ARP -d ipaddress

ARP -s ipaddress hwaddress
```

Further ARP command-line arguments are shown in Table 2.8.

T A B L E   2.8

*ARP Syntax and Command-
Line Arguments*

FUNCTION ARGUMENT	DESCRIPTION
-a *ipaddress*	Displays the contents of the ARP cache. The *ipaddress* parameter is optional. If used, it displays only the cache entry for the specified IP address.
-N *if_addr* (Microsoft only)	Causes ARP to display only the cache values associated with the *if_addr* variable. The variable is the interface address and is used when multiple adapters are in the system.
-t *type* (Linux/UNIX)	Used to specify the type of adapter to view ARP information. Some possible values are: ax25, ether, and pronet.
-d *ipaddress*	Deletes an ARP entry from the cache.
-s *ipaddress hwaddress*	Adds a permanent IP-to-MAC address mapping in the ARP cache. The hardware address must be written in hexadecimal format, with each value separated by a colon.

Using TCPCON to View ARP Information

Unlike the systems previously described, Novell uses the TCPCON utility to view and manipulate the ARP cache. Figure 2.18 illustrates the ARP information in TCPCON.

F I G U R E   2.18

*Viewing ARP information
using TCPCON*

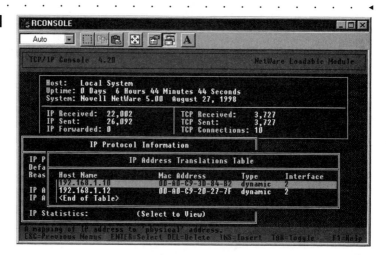

To view ARP information, choose Protocol Information ⇨ IP ⇨ IP Address Translations. The ARP cache will appear. Entries are added by using the Insert key, and are removed by placing the cursor over the entry and pressing the Delete key.

Viewing TCP/IP Configuration Information

Many times, while troubleshooting a TCP/IP network, you will need to know the exact configuration of the host you are working on. Several built-in commands are available that can give you just the information you need.

Table 2.9 shows common vendor configuration commands.

T A B L E 2.9 Configuration Commands	IF YOU ARE USING:	THE CONFIGURATION COMMAND IS:
	Novell NetWare	CONFIG (at the server console)
	Microsoft Windows NT	IPCONFIG (at the command line)
	Microsoft Windows 95/98	WINIPCFG (at the command line)
	Linux	ifconfig (at the command line)
	UNIX	ifconfig (at the command line)

Using the configuration commands gives different output, depending on the operating system. The following sections explore each vendor's implementation of configuration.

Novell CONFIG

The Novell CONFIG command is performed at the fileserver console. It simply displays configuration information and protocol bindings for each adapter in the server, as shown in Figure 2.19.

▶ · ◀

F I G U R E   2 . 1 9

NetWare CONFIG
command

File server name: CORP_FS
IPX internal network number: 34804953
Server Up Time: 6 Hours 57 Minutes 57 seconds

Intel EtherExpress PRO PCI Adapter for spec A3.31
    Version 3.51   April 2, 1998
    Hardware setting: Slot 10007, I/O ports FF80h to FF9Fh,
Memory FFBED000h to FFBEDFFFh,
    Interrupt Bh
    Node address: 00A0C9061FBA
    Frame type: ETHERNET 802.3
    Board name: E100B_1_E83
    LAN protocol: IPX network 490D9DE0

Intel EtherExpress PRO PCI Adapter for spec A3.31
    Version 3.51   April 2, 1998
    Hardware setting: Slot 10007, I/O ports FF80h to FF9Fh,
Memory FFBED000h to FFBEDFFFh,
    Interrupt Bh
    Node address: 00A0C9061FBA
    Frame type: ETHERNET_II
    Board name: E100B_1_EII
    LAN protocol: ARP
    LAN protocol: IP Address 192.168.1.13 Mask
FF.FF.FF.0(255.255.255.0)
               Interfaces 1

Tree Name: DOLLY
Bindery Context(s):
    .corp

CORP_FS:

By using this command at the fileserver console, you can very quickly see which frame types, protocols, and hardware addresses are used on the network. Additionally, basic server information is displayed at a glance.

Windows NT IPCONFIG

Windows NT provides a utility called IPCONFIG that is used to retrieve adapter information from an NT Workstation or NT Server. IPCONFIG can be used alone or with one of three optional command-line arguments. Figure 2.20 shows the standard IPCONFIG output.

FIGURE 2.20

IPCONFIG output

```
Windows NT IP Configuration


Ethernet adapter E100B1:

    IP Address . . . . . . . . . : 192.168.1.10
    Subnet Mask . . . . . . . . : 255.255.255.0
    Default Gateway  . . . . . :
```

Using one of the three optional command-line parameters will produce different results. Table 2.10 gives a description of the IPCONFIG parameters.

TABLE 2.10

IPCONFIG Arguments

IPCONFIG ARGUMENT	DESCRIPTION
/renew *adapter*	Used only when DHCP is active. Causes the IP address lease to be renewed for the adapter specified (such as E100B1 in Figure 2.20).
/release *adapter*	Used only when DHCP is active. Causes an IP address to be released from an adapter.
/all	Causes IPCONFIG to display a more complete listing, including the hardware address, DNS, WINS, NetBIOS, and other characteristics.

An example of the IPCONFIG /ALL output is given in Figure 2.21.

IPCONFIG /all displays detailed configuration information for all adapters in the NT Workstation or Server.

The NT Server Resource Kit includes a GUI-based configuration called WINTIPCFG.

TIP

FIGURE 2.21

IPCONFIG /ALL output

Windows NT IP Configuration

```
Host Name  . . . . . . . . . . . . . . : dpexec2x-nt.domain1
    DNS Servers  . . . . . . . . . . . :
    Node Type . . . . . . . . . . . . . : Broadcast
    NetBIOS Scope ID . . . . . . . . . :
    IP Routing Enabled . . . . . . . . : No
    WINS Proxy Enabled . . . . . . . . : No
    NetBIOS Resolution Uses DNS   . : No


Ethernet adapter E100B1:

    Description  . . . . . . . . . . . . : Intel EtherExpress PRO/100B PCI LAN Adapter
    Physical Address   . . . . . . . . . : 00-A0-C9-3D-84-B2
    DHCP Enabled  . . . . . . . . . . . : No
    IP Address . . . . . . . . . . . . . : 192.168.1.10
    Subnet Mask . . . . . . . . . . . . : 255.255.255.0
    Default Gateway  . . . . . . . . . . :
```

Windows 95/98 WINIPCFG

Windows 95/98 includes a graphical version of the IPCONFIG utility called
WINIPCFG. It is copied to the hard drive during Windows installation, but is not
placed on the menu. To use the WINIPCFG utility, follow these steps.

1. Select Start ⇨ Run.

2. Type **WINIPCFG** in the command box. You will see a screen similar to the
one shown in Figure 2.22.

Notice the drop-down box in this utility, which allows the user to select the
interface. Statistics can be gathered separately for all interfaces in the system,
including dial-up connections.

Linux/UNIX ifconfig

Linux and UNIX systems use the *ifconfig* command not only to view configuration
information, but also to configure systems. The *ifconfig* command follows this syntax:

```
ifconfig interface [address [parameters]]
```

▶ • ◀

FIGURE 2.22	
WINIPCFG output	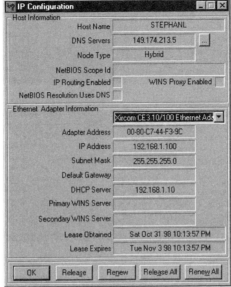

The *interface* argument specifies the interface name, while the *address* designates the IP address of the interface. Common parameters for the *ifconfig* command are shown in Table 2.11.

TABLE 2.11	IFCONFIG ARGUMENT	DESCRIPTION
Common ifconfig Parameters	allmulti	Sets multicast mode. Used in UNIX, but not Linux.
	-allmulti	Turns off multicast mode.
	arp	Turns on ARP capability. Set to On by default.
	-arp	Turns ARP off.
	broadcast	Sets the broadcast address if different than a normal IP broadcast for a class-based IP network.
	down	Disables the interface.
	mtu	Sets the MTU size for the interface. Ethernet default is 1500.

Continued

TABLE 2.11	IFCONFIG ARGUMENT	DESCRIPTION
Common ifconfig Parameters (continued)	netmask	Sets the subnet mask for the interface.
	promisc	Sets an interface to promiscuous mode. (All packets are then received, regardless of the destination.)
	-promisc	Turns off promiscuous mode.
	up	Makes an interface available to the system.

Changing Routing Information with ROUTE

As packets are routed throughout the network, hosts make tables in memory, called *routing tables,* that specify the paths that packets should take to reach a destination. Generally, these routes are learned, but sometimes you need to manipulate the routes that packets take to a destination, for efficiency or proper data flow.

Vendor Implementation of ROUTE

The ROUTE command is included in all vendors' TCP/IP stacks. Table 2.12 shows the proper ROUTE commands for each operating system.

TABLE 2.12	IF YOU ARE USING:	THE ROUTE COMMAND IS:
ROUTE Commands	Novell NetWare	TCPCON (at the server console)
	Microsoft Windows NT	ROUTE (at the command line)
	Microsoft Windows 95/98	ROUTE (at the command line)
	Linux	route (at the command line)
	UNIX	route (at the command line)

Novell TCPCON

To view or change route information in a Novell server environment, simply enter the command **LOAD TCPCON** at the fileserver console. Routing information will be found by choosing the IP Routing Table menu option and pressing Enter. Routing entries are shown in a table format similar to Figure 2.23.

FIGURE 2.23

Viewing routing tables in TCPCON

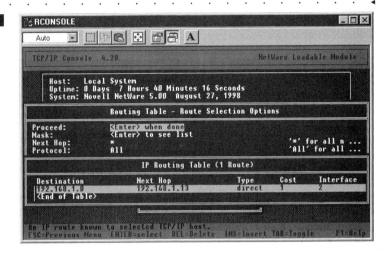

Linux/UNIX

The Linux implementation of the route command is quite simple: either you view the routing table, add entries, or delete entries. The syntax for the route command is

```
route add|del ipaddress
```

Simply use the route command alone to view the routing table.

Microsoft NT and Windows 95/98

The Microsoft implementation of the ROUTE command uses quite a few command-line arguments and parameters. The syntax for the Microsoft ROUTE command uses one of the following four primary commands, followed by arguments:

▸ **PRINT:** Displays the routing table

▸ **ADD:** Adds a new entry to the routing table

▸ **DELETE:** Deletes an entry from the routing table

▸ **CHANGE:** Modifies an entry in the routing table

The following is the syntax for the use of these command:

```
ROUTE [-f] [command [destination] [MASK netmask] [gateway]]
```

Table 2.13 describes the arguments used with this implementation of ROUTE.

T A B L E   2 . 1 3

ROUTE Arguments

ROUTE ARGUMENT	DESCRIPTION
-f	If used without one of the primary commands, the -f argument deletes all entries from the routing table. When used with any of the primary commands, it clears the routing table prior to running the command.
command	Any one of the four primary commands: ADD, PRINT, DELETE, CHANGE.
destination	Specifies the host to which to send the command.
MASK netmask	Specifies a subnet mask value to be associated with this route entry. If not specified, if defaults to 255.255.255.255.
gateway	Specifies a gateway to be used.

An example of routing information is shown in Figure 2.24.

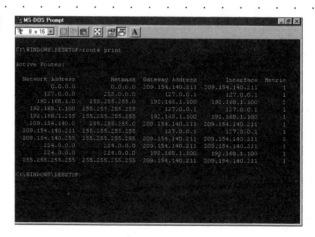

F I G U R E   2 . 2 4

Microsoft results for the ROUTE PRINT command

Viewing NetBIOS Information with NBTSTAT

The NBTSTAT program is a utility that displays TCP/IP statistics and current connections for a system using NetBIOS over TCP/IP. Generally, this is limited to Microsoft Windows installations. In a Windows installation, "friendly" names are used to identify computers. Unlike a simple IP number, this adds a layer of complexity to the network. Now, instead of mapping IP addresses to MAC numbers, you must also map registered names to IP addresses before resolving the MAC address. This can be a broadcast resolution or some other named file procedure.

NetBIOS and its use is discussed in detail in Chapter 16.

X-REF

The NBTSTAT syntax is the following:

```
NBTSTAT [-a RemoteName] [-A IP address] [-c] [-n] [-r] [-R]
[-s] [-S] [interval] ]
```

It is one of the few Windows utilities for which arguments are case-sensitive. Notice the capital A, R, and S commands. Like the ROUTE command, this command requires arguments to direct its output. Table 2.14 shows the command-line arguments available with the NBTSTAT program.

TABLE 2.14

NBTSTAT Command-Line Arguments

NBTSTAT ARGUMENT	DESCRIPTION
-a RemoteName	Lists a remote computer's name table by name.
-A IP address	Lists a remote computer's name table by IP address.
-c	Lists the names in the local cache, including the IP addresses.
-n	Shows the local NetBIOS names.
-r	Lists names resolved either by broadcast or WINS resolution.
-R	Purges and reloads an LMHOSTS file.

Continued

TABLE 2.14

NBTSTAT Command-Line
Arguments (continued)

NBTSTAT ARGUMENT	DESCRIPTION
-s	Shows all client and server sessions. Lists sessions table converting destination IP addresses to hostnames via the hosts file.
-S	Shows all client and server sessions listed by IP address.
RemoteName	The remote host computer name.
IP Address	The dotted decimal notation of the IP address.
Interval	Redisplays some statistics, stopping shortly between displays. Use Ctrl+C to stop the display. If the *interval* is not used, statistics are displayed one time.

In Figure 2.25, a common use for the NBTSTAT command is shown using the -r argument. At least 12 names have been registered using a broadcast on the network. That means the computers all yelled out their names so that anyone running NetBIOS could hear them on this network. Where would we be without friendly names?

FIGURE 2.25

NBTSTAT registration statistics

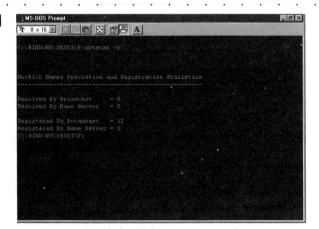

Getting Down to Business — Using an Analyzer

Though the built-in tools are useful in their own way, the best way to learn about the protocols is simply to use a tool that looks at the packets. Get an analyzer and learn to use it properly. No better tool exists for really troubleshooting your network.

When you watch the packets traversing the network cable, you can clearly see where the data is going. This book is filled with useful information that you can use only if you're looking at the packet through the software interface of an analyzer. This section discusses two different types of analysis tools:

- ▶ Network monitoring tools

- ▶ Protocol analyzers

A third category of analysis, discussed later in the chapter, is called *application analysis*, which watches the network for patterns relating to overuse of applications, such as the Internet or a database. This tool uses traffic statistics to discover better ways to use bandwidth (or to find employees that are viewing videos on the Internet during working hours).

Network Monitoring Tools

The very simplest form of a traffic tool is software that tracks the total number of packets sent throughout the network. A network monitor should show statistical information, such as total number of errors, lost packets, discarded packets, and so on. Most vendors ship some sort of monitoring tool with their software. Novell ships TCPCON.NLM, for example, which provides a great deal of packet monitoring. TCPCON.NLM was discussed in the previous section.

Microsoft ships the PerfMon (Performance Monitor) program for Windows NT, which can be configured to show graphical statistics on all aspects of the operating system, including hardware statistics and networking protocol statistics. Figure 2.26 is an example of the statistics shown using PerfMon.

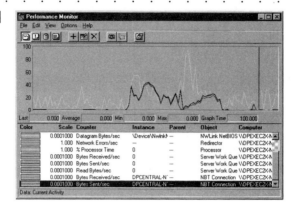

FIGURE 2.26

PerfMon statistics

Though all the network monitoring tools give general statistics and packet breakdown, this is not enough to diagnose routing or flow-control problems that may occur on a TCP/IP network. This is the job of a true protocol analyzer.

Protocol Analyzers

If you don't have an analyzer, you need to get one and learn how to use it. You will be amazed at all the data problems and traffic-flow problems that you may catch on your network with this tool. (We know, your network is running fine, right?)

All sorts of analyzers are available on the market, and the features and benefits offered by one manufacturer over another may vary greatly. Before going into specific vendor analyzers, take a look at the analysis types currently available.

Analyzer Types

It is important to understand the different types of analyzers available today:

▶ Standalone analyzers

▶ Distributed analyzers

▶ Mirror port analyzers

▸ Handheld analyzers

▸ Application analyzers

▸ RMON probes

Standalone Analyzers

A standalone analyzer is simply a tool that is placed on a single network segment to capture traffic. Generally, the least costly of all the analyzers, the standalone analyzer can capture traffic only for the segment where it is located, as shown in Figure 2.27.

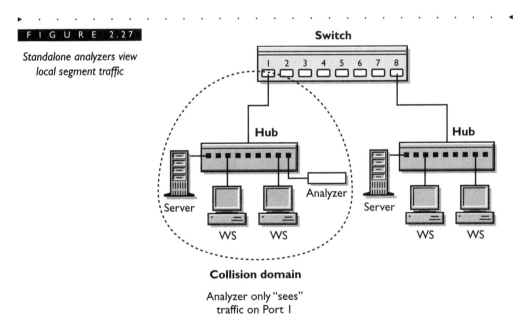

FIGURE 2.27

Standalone analyzers view local segment traffic

This is a good analyzer to use for small to medium-size hubbed networks that don't have a lot of routers, switches, or virtual LANs (VLANs) installed. This is a great way to start analyzing the network, but as the network grows, another solution may be better.

Distributed Analyzers

In a distributed analyzer scenario, a multiple-segment LAN or WAN is managed from a single location. The monitoring device is called a *management console*. With this type of analysis solution, a piece of software called an *agent* is installed on each network segment. The agents then simply collect the data and report to the management console. This means that trending statistics are always available in this type of solution. Additionally, the console can capture network traffic by asking the agents to look at the packets and send those packets back to the console. Captured traffic can then be analyzed by using the console. This type of analysis is very useful in a switched environment, where traffic is logically segmented, as shown in Figure 2.28.

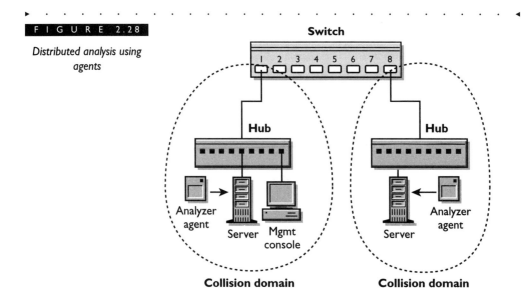

FIGURE 2.28

Distributed analysis using agents

In Figure 2.28, analyzer agents are placed on switch segments 1 and 8. The agents gather information and send it to the management console located on segment 1.

Mirror Port Analyzers

In a switched environment, it is sometimes necessary to capture data directly from the switch by using a mirror port analyzer. This is important for a switch because the design of the switch technology is such that data does not flow through all the ports, like a hub might do. Instead, a switch sets up a virtual connection between two ports during a communication session. Therefore, it is not possible to see all data flowing through a switch. A mirror (sometimes called *monitor port*) analyzer simply attaches to a switch with a specially designated mirror port and allows the network analyst to capture traffic to and from all ports on the switch, as shown in Figure 2.29.

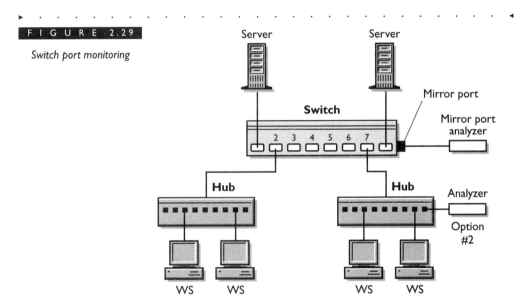

FIGURE 2.29

Switch port monitoring

Of course, not all switches come with a mirror port. For those that do not have a special mirror port and analyzer, you can do a few things to work around a possible "left out" segment. Figure 2.29 shows a monitor port analyzer connecting directly to the switch. However, suppose that you don't have that port. Analyzer Option #2 in Figure 2.29 shows that by placing a hub on the port switch and connecting an analyzer to the hub, you can effectively monitor a segment that may not otherwise be captured.

Handheld Analyzers

A handheld analyzer is very much like a standalone analyzer — except that it is simply a device that plugs into the network. Push a few buttons, and you see your network's statistics. Some handheld analyzers, such as Microtest's COMPAS, give real-time statistics only. Other handheld products, such as Fluke LANMeter, also capture packets and offer a full range of LAN and WAN standalone and distributed analysis products.

Application Analyzers

This newer classification of analysis products actually analyzes application traffic. With Service Level Agreements (SLAs) in effect for so many companies, how can you tell which applications are really contending for network resources? Who is using the Web to watch movies? How does an application that works properly over a LAN function on a WAN? Application analyzers can answer these questions, and others, for you.

RMON Probes

Another method for getting around the switched LAN problem is to use a *probe,* a device that can monitor and report statistics on several LAN segments simultaneously. Using this type of device, a management console or protocol analyzer that supports the RMON standard can be used to query the probe. The probe then sends the statistics to a central location for viewing and manipulation.

The two RMON standards are RMON1 and RMON2. The RMON1 standard, though a huge step forward in remote LAN management, only supported the physical and MAC layers of the protocol stack, which meant limited functionality. With the addition of the RMON2 standard, network layer and application layer traffic can be monitored and reported, giving network managers a much better view of the situation of the LAN.

Network Analyzer Manufacturers

Knowing who makes analyzers is the first step toward choosing an analyzer solution. Analyzers come in all kinds of shapes, sizes, and price ranges, and generally you get what you pay for. We find that a combination of analyzers actually works best for us, and we have some favorites that we discuss in this section that we use in our lab or in the field. We are constantly on the lookout to review analysis solutions, so if you have a product that you would like us to look at, please let us know. Here are the products we use in our everyday life, along with their classifications:

- ▸ Novell

  - • LANalyzer (standalone)

  - • ManageWise (distributed)

- ▸ **Network Associates (formerly Network General Corporation)**

  - • Sniffer Pro (distributed)

  - • Sniffer Basic (standalone)

- ▸ **AG Group**

  - • EtherPeek (standalone)

- ▸ **Triticom**

  - • LANdecoder32 (standalone)

- ▸ **Microsoft**

  - • Network Monitor (standalone)

- ▸ **Handheld Analyzers**

  - • Microtest COMPAS (standalone)

Novell LANalyzer

Three cheers for LANalyzer for Windows! This is the product we use extensively for health-check and standalone analysis. The interface is simple and uses a standard dashboard interface, so all statistics are easily viewed from the main screen, as shown in Figure 2.30.

F I G U R E   2.30

*LANalyzer's Dashboard
gives overall statistics*

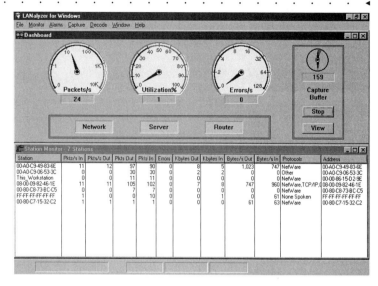

LANalyzer gives you the capability to view IPX, IP, AppleTalk DECnet, and SNA protocols, to name a few.

A LANalyzer update is required if you want to look at the new NetWare 5 protocols. Visit support.novell.com **for that update.**

NOTE

Novell ManageWise

ManageWise is Novell's distributed version of the LANalyzer product. It actually uses LANalyzer agents on the servers throughout the network, and a LANalyzer-style interface for capture analysis.

ManageWise has many features that are not typically part of a strict analysis solution, because its function is complete network management. Those features include desktop management, remote control, virus protection, and network mapping. It also has some great management tools for third-party products, such as routers and hubs, along with other operating systems, such as Windows 95 and Windows NT.

Network Associates Sniffer Pro and Sniffer Basic

Network Associates is probably the most popular analysis manufacturer around today. The Sniffer product is available for both the distributed-analysis solution (Distributed Sniffer) and the standalone arena (Sniffer Basic, formerly NetXRay). Sniffer Pro is a wonderful Windows-based product that gives quite a bit of statistical information from its main screen, as shown in Figure 2.31.

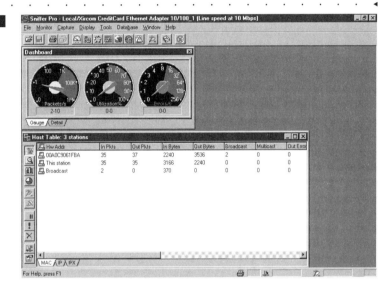

FIGURE 2.31

Sniffer Pro's Dashboard screen

This book was written using Sniffer Pro screen captures, so you will see quite a bit of this product throughout. One of the greatest things about this analyzer is its expert system. It gives layer-by-layer troubleshooting advice, which can be very helpful when sorting through thousands of packets.

Sniffer has add-on modules to support applications such as Oracle, Sybase, and SQL. Additionally, it supports hundreds of protocols, including IP, IPX, AppleTalk, Microsoft, and VINES, to name a few.

For more information on the Sniffer product line, visit www.nai.com.

AG Group EtherPeek

This analyzer started out as a Macintosh-based product, and has now moved to Ethernet and Token Ring topologies, and has products available for Windows. This is an out-of-the-box, ready-to-use product and has enhancements that keep the product on our favorites list. It has plug-ins for expert packet analysis and it supports all the major protocol suites (including IP, AppleTalk, NetWare IPX/SPX, NetBEUI, NetBIOS, DECnet, SMB, OSI TARP, and more). Plus, it can even read and write Sniffer files. The installation is simple and the interface is great for capturing, as shown in Figure 2.32.

F I G U R E   2 . 3 2

EtherPeek's main screen

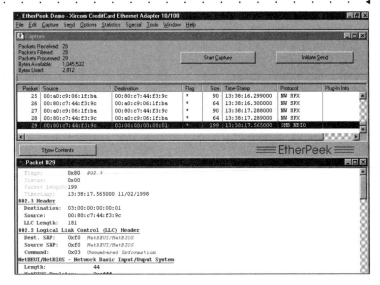

The AG Group also offers training for its product and has a free IP utility toolkit located on its Web site, `www.aggroup.com`.

Triticom LANdecoder32

This is a great analyzer to have in your toolbox if you want to capture through different interfaces, such as a modem connected to the Internet. Triticom's LANdecoder32 will read and write many different types of files, and has a very broad range of protocol decodes, including Microsoft, IP, IPX, IBM, AppleTalk, and many others. The company also has decode packages available for other analyzers, such as LANalyzer.

The LANdecoder32 has an interface similar to the EtherPeek product, with general capture information filling the screen. An expert system is provided to give insight into the problems encountered on the LAN. Figure 2.33 shows the LANdecoder32 product interface.

FIGURE 2.33

LANdecoder32's main screen

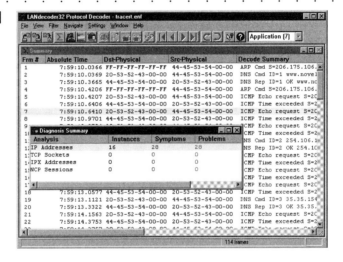

 For more information on this product, visit Triticom's Web site at `www.triticom.com.`

Microsoft NetMon

Microsoft Network Monitor (NetMon) is, so far, the best analyzer that we've found for analyzing Microsoft networks. And why not? Microsoft wrote most of the System Message Block (SMB)-based protocols. The basic version of NetMon comes free with all Windows NT Workstations and Servers. It must be installed separately, because it is not part of the NT installation process. The free version will successfully capture packets going to and from an NT Server, but will *not* capture traffic across the entire network. To capture all traffic, an Systems Management Server (SMS) must be purchased and placed on the server.

The NetMon interface is easy to use and quite intuitive, as shown in Figure 2.34.

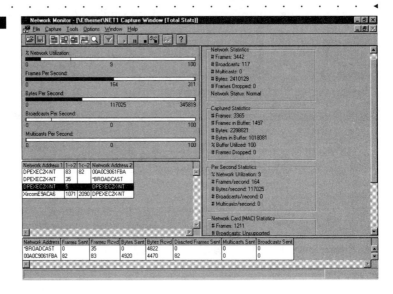

From the main screen, NetMon gives you a dashboard-style feel, only without the dials. Though its strength is in capturing and decoding SMB and other Microsoft protocols, it does a good job with IP, IPX, and AppleTalk, as well.

Microtest COMPAS

Another product in our bag of tricks is the simple-to-use Microtest COMPAS. Designed for 10Mbps networks (hopefully, it will make a 100Mbps version soon), COMPAS delivers real-time IP, IPX, and NT statistics. Because it is handheld, it falls into the standalone category of analyzers. Some of the things COMPAS will do include:

- ▸ IP PING testing

- ▸ Duplicate IP testing

- ▸ NT domain configuration

- ▸ IPX analysis

▸ Health statistics

▸ Broadcast statistics

▸ Network talkers by frame type

 For more information about the Microtest COMPAS, visit the company's Web site at www.microtest.com.

The previous list of tools is just a brief overview of the network-analysis tools available. Because these tools are in our lab, we use them extensively and know them well. Some other available network-analysis tools include those listed in Table 2.15.

TABLE 2.15

Well-Known Network Analyzers

ANALYZER CLASSIFICATION	MANUFACTURER NAME	PRODUCT NAME	WEB ADDRESS
Standalone through distributed	Wandel & Golterman	LinkView and Domino	www.wg.com
Distributed and RMON2	Shomiti	Surveyor	www.shomiti.com
Standalone	Network Instruments	Observer	www.networkinstruments.com
Standalone	Proteon	LANTracer	www.lantracer.com
Standalone	Precision Guesswork	LANWatch32	www.guesswork.com
Distributed	Hewlett-Packard	OpenView	www.hp.com
Application	Technically Elite	MeterWare	www.tecelite.com
Application	Compuware	EcoScope	www.compuware.com
Application	Vital Signs Software	VitalSuite	www.vitalsigns.com
Handheld	Fluke	One Touch and LANMeter	www.fluke.com

▶ · ◀

Analyzer Characteristics

So, now you know about quite a few different products available. How do you know whether a product will meet your needs? How do you know whether an analyzer is really capturing the data that is on the network, and that no data is missing? Before you select an analyzer solution, you must be sure that it has certain characteristics that are required just to analyze the network properly. Everything else is a bonus. Here's what we look for when looking at new analysis tools:

- ▶ Promiscuous mode capability

- ▶ Available decodes

- ▶ Expert system

- ▶ Health statistics

- ▶ Packet filtering (display and capture)

- ▶ Ease of use

- ▶ Media types supported

- ▶ Cost

- ▶ Available training

Promiscuous Mode

To examine all traffic on the network, your network interface card (NIC) must support *promiscuous mode*. This mode, in short, means that the interface can see and capture *all* packets on the network segment, not just the ones specifically addressed to it. Normally, an NIC scans each packet as it travels through the network, and checks the hardware address in the data-link portion of the header as the packet goes by. If the packet is that of the NIC (or the broadcast address), the packet is passed to the NIC for processing. If the packet contains the address of another NIC, then the packet is discarded by the NIC and never processed by the system. This is not a good thing to happen in the machine being used for network analysis.

When talking to your NIC vendor about promiscuous mode, ask about the following areas:

- Broadcast capability (packets that are addressed to all stations)

- Unicast capability (packets addressed to a single station)

- Multicast capability (packets addressed to a group of stations)

- Error packets

Error packets is an especially important area—some cards, though they are called "promiscuous," do not pass errors up the stack to the analysis machine. Imagine your horror if you are analyzing a network with obvious errors that can't be seen by your analyzer! How embarrassing!

 Get promiscuous-mode drivers for your analysis system. All other cards in the network can have nonpromiscuous drivers.

NOTE

Available Decodes

A *decode* is simply the proper breakdown of the packet for viewing inside the analyzer. Some analyzers have more decodes than others, and decodes can often be added to an analyzer. LANalyzer, for example, has a new decode package to work with protocols that are new or changed in NetWare 5. New decodes include: DHCP, BOOTP, SMTP, SLP, RADIUS, and NCP/TCPIP.

The new decodes for LANalyzer for Windows can be found at support.novell.com.

Good decodes are extremely important for anyone who is serious about analyzing LAN communications. (Who would want to try to figure out those hexadecimal characters by hand?)

Expert System

After you capture the traffic, what do you do with it? Where do you start looking? With the help of an expert system, you can quickly go to the problem areas on the network. Sniffer has one of the most widely recognized expert systems around. The expert system makes judgment calls based on the packets captured. The expert can, for example, tell you that a duplicate IP address is on the network, as shown in Figure 2.35.

Now that you know you have a duplicate IP address, you simply double-click the message to show the stations and solve the problem.

Some expert systems take the form of a text manual instead. Novell's LANalyzer, for example, has a tutorial and expert system built in. The tutorial can be read at your leisure, while the expert advises you when an alarm or threshold is triggered within the software.

FIGURE 2.35

Sniffer expert system

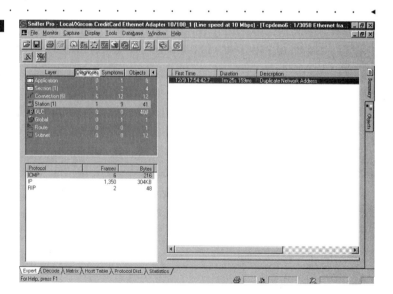

Network Health Information/Station Information

One of the first things that we do when we go into a new network is simply plug in the analyzer and get a feel for the flow on the network. No packet capture yet — we just look to answer some basic questions, such as the following:

▸ Who are the top talkers?

▸ Who are the top receivers?

▸ What devices send the most broadcasts?

▸ What protocols are on the network?

These and other questions can be answered very quickly by looking at the main screen of most analyzers. LANalyzer, for example, gives you all of this information on the first screen, as shown in Figure 2.36.

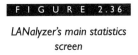

FIGURE 2.36

LANalyzer's main statistics screen

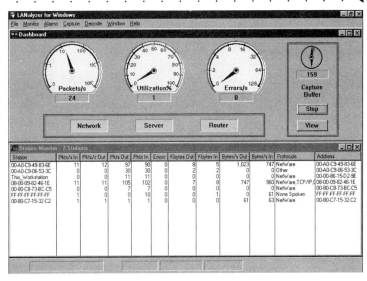

A brief glance at this screen indicates who is broadcasting on the network, and which devices are taking bandwidth. Looking at this screen has helped us in many analysis situations.

A story comes to mind: We were once called in to analyze a large network to find the source of a "network too slow" problem. After plugging in the analyzer, the first thing that we saw was that the top broadcaster on the network was a fax machine! Because the top broadcaster should be a server or some other frequently used device, this seemed strange. After asking some of the employees whether a mass fax was being sent, we were given the reply "We don't use the fax. It's broken." A closer look at the fax device revealed a failing NIC that was continuously broadcasting its presence. After we turned off the fax machine, the network speed went back to normal. Not even one packet capture was needed.

Another good reason to look at the main screen first is to see the type of protocols being used on the network. We go to many places where people say that the only protocol they are using is TCP/IP. A quick look at the network reveals a little IPX, NetBEUI, AppleTalk, and some DECnet thrown in there somewhere. (Just kidding, they're not all like that.) Sometimes, protocols can creep into the network without anyone's knowledge. A quick look at Sniffer's Protocol Distribution screen is helpful, as shown in Figure 2.37. This network has a little bit of everything mixed in.

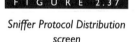

F I G U R E 2.37

Sniffer Protocol Distribution screen

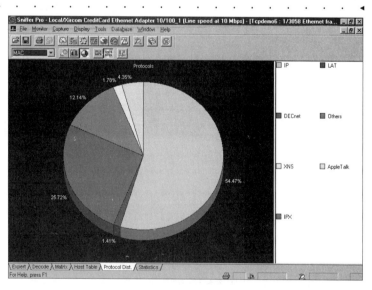

Packet Filtering (Capture and Display)

After you see the overall statistics of the network, using the main analyzer screen, you need to be able to capture traffic that you actually want to see. For example, suppose that you suspect a problem exists between a particular workstation and a server. If you had to capture all traffic on the network, how could you see just the traffic between the two suspect devices? The following are the two ways to filter traffic:

▸ Capture filter

▸ Display filter

A *capture filter* is applied while capturing is taking place. If you knew the addresses of the NICs in the preceding example, you could simply tell the analyzer to capture traffic between those two devices. Figure 2.38 shows an example of a capture filter used with LANalyzer.

A *display filter*, on the other hand, is a post-capture filter. If you have just captured 5,000 packets, you can drill down and filter the display so that you can see just the information that you want. None of the other packets is ever lost — just hidden from view for the time being. A display filter applied after the capture is also very useful. Most analyzers have either a capture or display filter, or both. Sniffer allows filters to be defined and saved for later use, as shown in Figure 2.39.

FIGURE 2.38

LANalyzer's Capture Filter

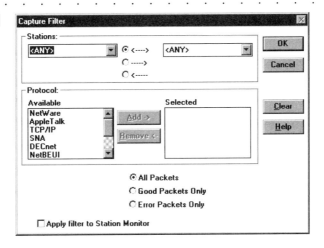

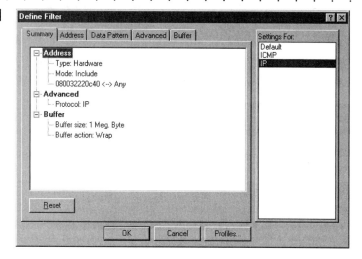

FIGURE 2.39

Sniffer saved filters

Ease of Use

An analyzer is a very personal choice—you must feel comfortable with the interface and how the product functions as a whole. We tend to like Windows-based analyzers, with point-and-click functionality. Many of these types of analyzers have come out recently, enabling people to get involved in network analysis for situations in which they never had been able to before.

Media Types Supported

This is an important factor. You need an analyzer that supports all the topology types in your network, including Ethernet, Token Ring, FDDI, ATM (if you have it), and so on. Buying an Ethernet analyzer won't do you any good if you can't analyze FDDI traffic on your backbone. Most midrange to high-end analyzers have plug-ins that you can add later for more functionality. Ask the vendor about media support before you buy it.

Cost

Analyzers can range from free to thousands of dollars. You must determine your analysis budget before you start looking. We have talked about analyzers in all price ranges in this section, and depending on how much analysis you will do, you may want to start with a lower-end product, such as Sniffer Basic or LANalyzer, and move to Sniffer Pro, Distributed Sniffer, or ManageWise in the future as you learn more about analysis.

Available Training

No matter which analyzer solution you choose, you must learn to use the product. This type of software doesn't come with wizards or flashy things — it's simply there to help you make your network the best it can be. Get training! The manufacturer may give training, or an independent classroom or network analysis institute may be nearby, where you can get training on many different vendor products.

Third-Party Tools

Now that you know about the built-in tools and several analyzers that are available, we'll talk about some of our favorite third-party tools. We use many of these tools on a daily basis — most are free and some are shareware, but they're all great. Our list of favorites includes:

> ► **AG Group IP utilities** (`www.aggroup.com`): Go to this Web site and download these great IP utilities. The Windows interface is easy to use and puts IP statistics in your hands. Figure 2.40 shows the AGGroup's main screen and some of the tools available.

▶ · ◀

FIGURE 2.40

AGGroup IP utilities

▶ **Net3Group Subnet Calculator (`www.net3group.com`):** Another favorite is the Net3Group's Subnet Calculator. With this calculator, subnetting IP addresses is a breeze. Simply enter the parameters, and the calculator computes the network ID, subnet ID, and host ID for you. Figure 2.41 showcases the calculator's Windows interface. Net3Group also makes NetSense, a post-capture utility, and ProConvert, to convert packet types between analyzers.

▶ **NetLab (`members.tripod.com/~adanil`):** Another full-featured freeware IP utility program, similar to the AGGroup utilities. Includes options for Finger, WhoIs, Time, PING (and a no-fragment option), Trace, DNS, Info, and more. Figure 2.42 gives a sample of the main screen, which is very easy to use.

FIGURE 2.41

Net3Group Subnet
Calculator

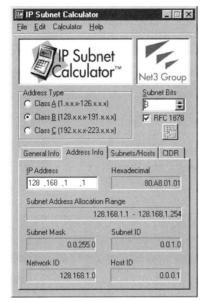

FIGURE 2.42

NetLab main screen

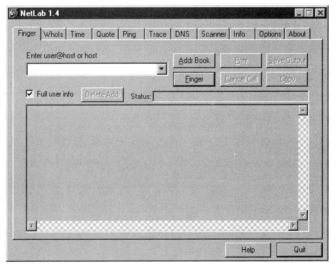

▸ **PING Plotter** (`www.nessoft.com/pingplotter`): PING Plotter is a visual tracing utility. Use PING Plotter to actually "see" where your packets are going, as shown in Figure 2.43.

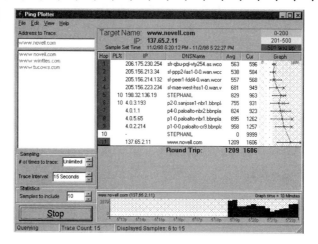

PING Plotter visual trace

▸ **IpSwitch WS_PING ProPack** (`www.ipswitch.com`): The most comprehensive PPING utility group that we use. We especially like the LDAP information and SNMP features, along with the workstation hardware configuration information and throughput statistics, as shown in Figure 2.44. IpSwitch also makes other popular Internet utilities, such as WS_FTP, Imail Server, and FTP Devkit.

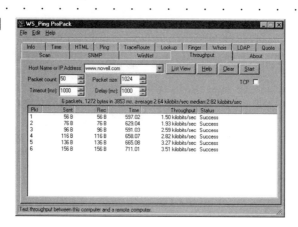

WS_PING ProPack throughput statistics

Summary

This chapter examined the tools that are available to assist you with trouble-shooting and analyzing a TCP/IP network. Built-in TCP/IP tools and vendor implementations were detailed. Guidelines and analyzer characteristics were discussed, and several analysis products were introduced.

Troubleshooting the Link for Ethernet and Token Ring Networks

To connect to a network, a cabling system must be in place to connect every device that needs to communicate, which doesn't mean that only one type of cable may be installed at any single location — in fact, the opposite is true. Several different types of cable may be installed and used in the TCP/IP network, as long as consistency is maintained through routers to the end device. This chapter looks into common LAN cabling types and the Link of the TCP/IP communication model.

Overview of the Link Layer

The *Link* layer is one of the most important areas of the TCP/IP network, because each device must use the Link layer of the DARPA model (corresponding to the OSI model's physical layer) to communicate. Regardless of what kind of device, whether a printer, a file server, or a workstation, each device must be able to communicate at the most basic level on the network — the cable system. Errors at this layer in the model can be propagated throughout the network, causing retransmissions, delays, and service slowdown in the network. Figure 3.1 illustrates how a packet moves between devices at this layer.

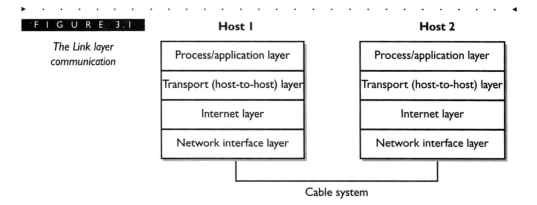

FIGURE 3.1

The Link layer communication

Host I

| Process/application layer |
| Transport (host-to-host) layer |
| Internet layer |
| Network interface layer |

Host 2

| Process/application layer |
| Transport (host-to-host) layer |
| Internet layer |
| Network interface layer |

Cable system

The Link layer is often one of the most overlooked trouble areas in the entire network. Cabling rules are often broken out of necessity or misunderstanding, which causes problematic networks with communication errors. Network analysis at this layer can assist in troubleshooting cable, network interface, or other device errors.

Local Area Network Topology Types

As previously stated, when installing a TCP/IP network, the selection must include a type of cabling to use. The specific cabling type generally is referred to as *topology*. Many types of topology are available for a network such as this, including LAN and WAN topologies. The topology selected for the LAN determines how the data is transmitted across the network, how workstations access that data, and the type of network cards that are used in the devices. This chapter focuses on the two most popular types of LAN topologies:

- Ethernet

- Token Ring

Ethernet Topology and Implementation

Though several topologies are currently in use, the Ethernet system is by far the most popular. The Ethernet topology is supported and maintained by a large variety of vendors, and its specifications are readily available to those who want to manufacture Ethernet devices.

For purposes of this book, "Ethernet" refers to the IEEE Ethernet and 802.3 CSMA/CD network standards.

NOTE

The devices on the Ethernet wiring system use a *Carrier Sense Multiple Access/Collision Detection (CSMA/CD)* method of communication, which means that all stations potentially have access to the wire at the same time. CSMA/CD and its operation are detailed later in this chapter. First, the physical wiring characteristics of the Ethernet network are discussed.

An Ethernet network may operate at either the 10Mbps or 100Mbps speed. Ethernet wiring systems can also be accommodated by several types of physical cable, including coaxial-based cable and unshielded twisted pair (UTP).

Coaxial and UTP cable are only two types used by Ethernet. Other popular implementation methods exist, including fiber-optic cable.

TIP

Although the 100Mbps Ethernet obviously is faster than the 10Mbps types, the CSMA/CD access method and format of the data on the Ethernet wiring system is the same for all speeds, regardless of the operational speed. This creates some interesting "rules" for cabling the Ethernet network. This section explores the popular implementations of 10Mbps and 100Mbps Ethernet LANs.

Coaxial 10Base2 (Thinnet)

10Base2 networks use thin coaxial cable and are limited to a 10Mbps speed. Coaxial cable is flexible and allows direct attachment to an Ethernet device through the use of a special T connector. Coaxial-based Ethernet cable is joined in a daisy chain configuration, in which one computer connects to the next, and the next, and so on. This is a low-cost Ethernet implementation and is used in many smaller networks, although it generally isn't installed in new networks. Figure 3.2 illustrates the components of a 10Base2 or bus network.

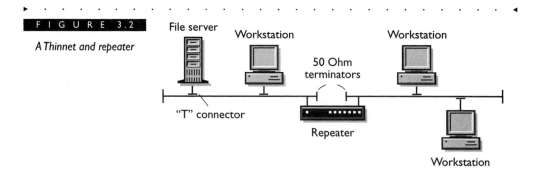

FIGURE 3.2

A Thinnet and repeater

Thinnet Cabling System

Notice the cable lengths and distances in Figure 3.2. Thinnet is based on cable that carries the RG58 A/U 50-ohm rating. It is important in this system that 50-ohm terminating resistors be placed at each end of the Thinnet segment. Standards also note that a single grounding point may (and should) be placed on the Ethernet cable. If more than one grounding point is placed on the cable, signal interruption may occur.

Thinnet networks may be enlarged by using devices called *repeaters,* also shown in Figure 3.2. A repeater simply regenerates a signal from one Thinnet segment to another, effectively increasing the overall length of the network.

General rules for Thinnet are outlined in Table 3.1.

TABLE 3.1	DESCRIPTION	STANDARD
Coaxial Cable Standards	Number of devices per segment	30
	Maximum segments	5 segments/4 repeaters
	Maximum segment length	185 meters/607 feet
	Total network length	925 Meters/3034 feet
	Short cable length between devices	.5 meter/1.6 feet

Though you may be tempted to run a cable segment longer or shorter than the standards require, don't do it! Some vendors make network cards that can send a signal further down the cable than the written standards. Later in this chapter, you'll learn why cable standards exist and why the rules should not be taken lightly.

10BaseT/100BaseTX (UTP)

The 10BaseT and 100BaseTX specifications use UTP cable to maintain communication on the network at either 10Mbps (10BaseT standard) or 100Mbps (100BaseT standard). The *T* in the standards' names specifies *unshielded twisted pair (UTP)* cable, which is something like telephone wire, in which one pair of twisted wire is used to receive data signals, and the other pair is used to transmit data signals. These networks are configured in a star configuration, in which a single segment runs from each workstation to a central location, such as a hub or switch. Figure 3.3 shows how a UTP network is put together.

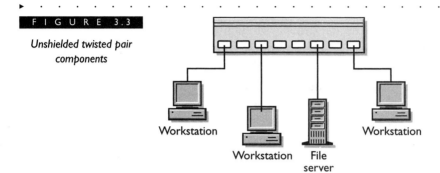

FIGURE 3.3	
Unshielded twisted pair components	Workstation Workstation Workstation File server

The topology and communication method generally is the same for both the 10Mbps and 100Mbps networks, but differences in cable quality do exist. The 10BaseT standard is designed to be used on lower-quality, Category 3 voice-grade cabling, whereas the 100BaseTX standard uses a minimum Category 5 cable to provide a high-quality signal to the desktop. However, distance standards do exist and should be followed. Table 3.2 gives general distance and specifications for a UTP network.

TABLE 3.2	DESCRIPTION	STANDARD
UTP Cable Standards	Number of devices per segment	2 (one device and one hub port)
	Maximum segments	5 segments/4 repeaters between nodes
	Maximum segment length	100 meters/328 feet
	Number of connected hubs	4 maximum
	Shortest patch cable	1 meter/3 feet

Cable Categories

As previously mentioned, a Category 3 cable works for a 10Mbps network. However, many people choose to use higher-quality, Category 5 cable connectors and wire centers, for greater reliability. As networks have grown, the need for higher-speed applications and data transfer rates has created the need for a reliable, high-performance network infrastructure that allows for future growth. Because the original levels, or categories, were defined, the world has been exposed to newer and faster methods of communication. Today's Gigabit Ethernet and ATM standards are seriously pushing the performance limits of existing cables. So, how do you know whether your network will grow into the future? Start with standards, such as Category 5 at a minimum, and make sure your cables meet that minimum.

Category 5

Category 5 is simply a minimum performance requirement. Cables are tested in megahertz (MHz). Cables that meet Category 5 standards are tested only to 100MHz, because no standards exist today for cable over 100MHz. This doesn't mean that you don't need to test over 100MHz — many networking technologies today require this. Additionally, cable testers can verify and test cable to much higher ratings, such as 300MHz. The Category performance standard is defined by three separate electrical properties:

- **Attenuation:** The loss of signal power over distance, which is expressed in decibels (dB). Attenuation increases with frequency and temperature. The more attenuation, the more dB loss that occurs, and ultimately cable problems arise. A low power-loss (dB) rating is desired.

- **Near End Crosstalk (NEXT):** The energy from one pair of wires in a cable creating a disturbance in another pair. An example of this kind of interference is when you can hear a faint conversation of another party when you are on the phone. In this case, signals from the other party's conversation are strong enough to interfere with yours. NEXT is also expressed in dBs, but in this situation, the desired dB rating should be high.

- **Impedance:** The resistance to the flow of current in a circuit. Factors such as installation can impair the cable performance. If installation procedures are not followed precisely, that great Category 5 cable installed in the building may only perform to Category 3 or 4 standards. Environment can also play a big part in cable degradation. Placing a wiring closet in a hot, humid room can affect cable performance, and that new application that runs the office may not work well.

Emerging Standards

Two new standards, Categories 6 and 7, are in the process of being defined. Current indicators show that, while Category 5 supports communication at frequencies up to 100MHz, Category 6 will support up to 200MHz, and Category 7 will support up to 600MHz communication.

An enhanced version of Category 5 (known as Cat 5e) already is available through many cabling and components vendors. Today, a properly designed and installed cabling system that meets the Category 5 standards utilizes high-speed communication technology, such as Gigabit Ethernet.

Cabling is always a consideration when a network grows. Too often, extra cable is pulled to inappropriate distances, and too many nodes are placed on the segment. Though this sometimes is meant as a temporary change to an existing network, it ultimately can alter the data flow of the entire network and cause problems that you wouldn't otherwise see. Having a reputable vendor check your cable to see whether your network is in compliance with Category standards is a good idea.

Ethernet Communication

Different types of cable require different access methods when transmitting. This section explores the methods used by the Ethernet cable system during data transfer.

Ethernet Addressing

Before discussing the Ethernet frame types and fields, you need to understand how the hardware addresses are maintained. Ethernet uses a 6-byte (48-bit) addressing scheme to identify hosts on the network. Every computer attached to an Ethernet network is assigned a unique 6-byte number know as its Ethernet address, also referred to as the *media access control (MAC)* address or *node* address. Ultimately, this address is used to send data to the next appropriate node in the network.

Many utilities are available to help find the MAC address of your workstation or server. Figure 3.4 shows a Windows 95 workstation address.

F I G U R E 3.4

Workstation Ethernet address

Use the WINIPCFG utility from the Windows 95 workstation (or IPCONFIG /ALL on your NT Workstation) to display the computer's MAC address. To use WINIPCFG, click on Start ➪ Run ➪ and type **WINIPCFG** in the command line. This utility shows you not only MAC address information, but also a lot of TCP/IP information.

From the Novell server, a simple CONFIG command displays the Ethernet address of the server, as shown in Figure 3.5.

F I G U R E 3.5

Ethernet address from a Novell file server

```
rconsole                                                        _ □ ×

Auto         ▼  [ ] 📋 📋 🔲 📋 📋  A
        LAN protocol: IPX network 0A0572E4

Intel 82557-Based PCI LAN adapter
        Version 1.47    June 20, 1996
        Hardware setting: Slot 3, I/O ports 0A00h to 0A1Fh, Memory E79FF000h to E79
FFFFFh, Interrupt 9h
        Node address: 00A0C9EE3EDE
        Frame type: ETHERNET_II
        Board name: E100B_1_EII
        LAN protocol: ARP
        LAN protocol: IP  address 208.170.66.131  mask FF.FF.FF.80  interfaces 1

NetWare/IP Server
        Version 3.02c   October 28, 1997
        Hardware setting: I/O Port ABCDh
        Node address: 7E0000AA4283
        Frame type: NWIP
        Board name: NWIP_1
        LAN protocol: IPX network 000000EE

Tree Name: PNCG
Bindery Context(s):
        CORP

NWFS01:_
```

The Ethernet address is a 6-byte address. The first 3 bytes are used by the Ethernet manufacturer to identify the network interface card (NIC) uniquely. This is called the *Organizational Unique Identifier (OUI)*. A partial OUI list is shown in Figure 3.6.

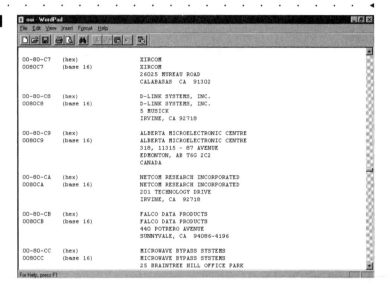

F I G U R E   3 . 6

Partial OUI list sorted by vendor (6-byte) number

Compare the vendor number 0080C7 with the workstation address in Figure 3.4, shown earlier. By using this list, you can see that the NIC was manufactured by Xircom. Pretty great, isn't it?

The complete OUI list can be found in Appendix G or at `www.cavebear.com/CaveBear/Ethernet/vendor.html`.

X-REF

The Ethernet addresses must remain unique throughout the network. Although you can assign your own numbers, this usually isn't recommended. Vendors have stamping machines that maintain unique NIC addresses. Theoretically, no two NICs have the same Ethernet address, although this isn't always the case in practice.

Media Access Method

When working on any Ethernet LAN, you need to understand how communication takes place on the wire. Ethernet uses the CSMA/CD protocol, mentioned earlier, to determine when and how a station may transmit on the wire.

CSMA/CD is simply a method of deciding which and when stations transmit on the wire. The term *Carrier Sense* means that before a station will transmit, it stops and listens to see whether some other station currently has use of the Ethernet wire. If another station is talking, the second station continues to wait until the line is clear.

Multiple Access means that when a station has completed a transmission, it is allowed to access the wire again immediately for another transmission. Other media, such as Token Ring, do not allow this kind of access.

Collision Detection is the ability of the Ethernet hardware to detect colliding packets on the wire. Normal Ethernet operation means that, occasionally, two stations will begin transmitting at the same time (after detecting an open line). The two packets simultaneously on the wire interfere with each other and collide, requiring the stations to retransmit. Collisions and the resulting errors are discussed later in this chapter.

The transmitting and receiving stations on an Ethernet system have very different jobs to perform.

CSMA/CD Transmit Procedure

The CSMA/CD transmit procedure is the same for all Ethernet devices. A transmitting device must perform several steps to get data out on the wire for the receiving device to pick up.

1. **Listen to check whether transmission can occur.** The sending device continually listens and monitors the cable segment to check whether it is idle. The cable must be unused by another device for 9.6 microseconds before the station will attempt to transmit, as shown in Figure 3.7. If another device is using the Ethernet cable, the sending device must wait a specified amount of time before reattempting the transmission. A device normally won't transmit when it knows some other device is using the cable, which would be like pushing someone out of the way while waiting in line for a movie.

2. Transmit the data. After the cable has been idle for 9.6 microseconds, data transmission occurs. The sending device turns on the carrier (alerting other devices to the cable usage) and puts the data on the wire. The transmitting station calculates a special value, called a *cyclic redundancy check (CRC),* and appends it to the end of the data before transmission. The receiving station uses this CRC to calculate the frame integrity.

3. Listen for and detect collisions. As previously stated, stations on the Ethernet segment might begin transmitting data simultaneously. When this happens, the packets eventually collide, and fragments are left on the cable. Therefore, the sending stations listen for this behavior for a short period of time after sending the packet. Different types of collisions can occur. These normal-use collisions, called *early collisions,* are detected and corrected by the sending devices. The next section looks further into the early collision process.

The Early Collision Process

An *early collision* is any collision that occurs before 512 bits (64 bytes) of the frame have been transmitted onto the wire. A collision is detected when the electrical signals of the two devices overlap, creating abnormal voltage on the wire. The following steps outline the collision-and-recovery process. For this scenario, a very simple two-station network is used, but this could apply to any number of devices.

1. Station A transmits. A potential transmitting station detects that the wire has been idle for 9.6 microseconds, as shown in Figure 3.7. After detecting idle time, Station A begins to transmit, starting with the 64-bit preamble.

2. Station B transmits. Before the frame from Station A has had time to travel down the length of the wire, Station B decides to transmit. It detects that the cable has been idle for 9.6 microseconds, so it begins to transmit, as shown in Figure 3.8.

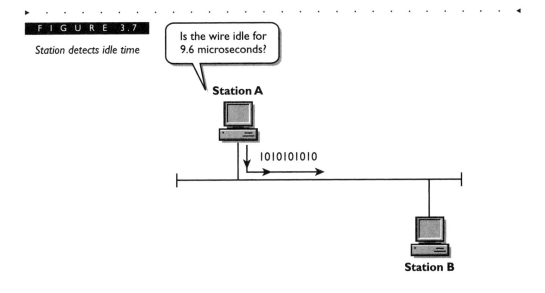

FIGURE 3.7

Station detects idle time

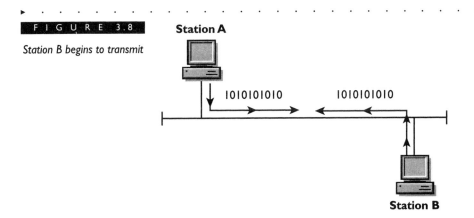

FIGURE 3.8

Station B begins to transmit

3. Collision occurs. Somewhere between Stations A and B on the wire, the packets collide. Abnormal voltage occurs and travels down the wire to both Stations A and B, as shown in Figure 3.9.

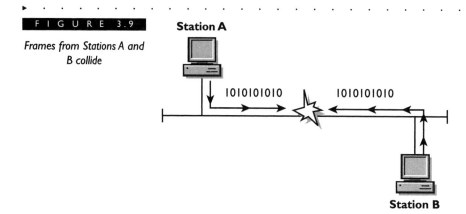

4. **Station B begins jam signal.** The station closest to the point where the collision actually occurred is the first to detect the collision. In this example, assume that Station B hears the collision first. Station B is responsible at this point to notify all stations on the wire that a collision has occurred. This is called a *jam signal*, which consists of a 32-bit transmission that can be any value except for the value of the valid checksum for the previous frame. Usually, a jam consists of all ones, or zeroes and ones. The jam is shown in Figure 3.10.

Station A

32 bit jam

Station B

5. Both Stations A and B perform backoff algorithm and retransmit. If a station were to retransmit immediately on notification of a collision, it could be immediately involved in another collision. To avoid this, stations calculate and prepare for retransmission. This calculation is called the *truncated binary exponential backoff algorithm,* which is described next.

Backoff Algorithm Process

The retransmission process is usually dismissed as a totally random retransmission time, but that's not really true. The algorithm calculation for the backoff process is expressed as follows:

$$slot\ time = (2^n - 1) =$$

The value of n is the number of successive collisions. *Slot time* is the number of random time values that a device may select after a retransmission, to calculate its resend time. A single slot time is equal to 512 bits (or 51.2 microseconds). The device always has an option of immediate resend, or a value of 0. The process is explained next.

Upon First Collision Upon the first collision, stations back off and perform their calculation of slot time (see Figure 3.11):

1. Calculate slot time = $(2^1-1)=1$. This is the first collision, so 1 is placed in the field to replace n.

2. Devices choose an available slot time based on the calculation in Step 1. Zero is always available. After the first collision, the value of the slot time is 1, which leaves only two values available — 0 and 1. Each device must choose a slot time for retransmission. If the devices both choose the same slot time, another collision occurs immediately.

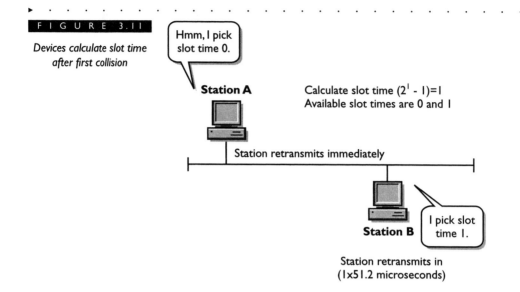

Devices calculate slot time after first collision

After the first collision, a 50% probability exists that another collision between the stations will occur, because the stations have only two time values from which to choose. After ten collisions, a maximum random number, 1023, is reached. Additionally, a 16-attempt limit exists, at which point the device gives up and stops retransmitting.

Upon Second Collision Upon the second collision, the stations back off and perform their calculation of slot time (see Figure 3.12):

1. Calculate slot time = $(2^2-1)=3$. Because it is the second collision, 2 is placed in the field to replace n.

2. After the second collision, the value of the slot time is 3. Stations can now choose 0, 1, 2, or 3 when selecting a time to retransmit, resulting in a lower probability of another collision.

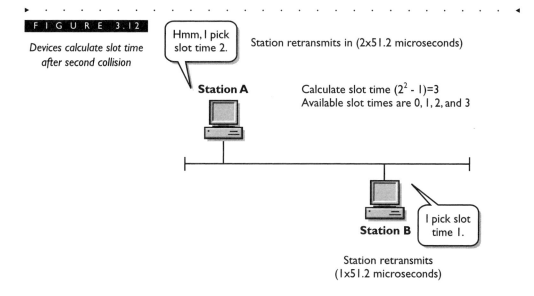

FIGURE 3.12

Devices calculate slot time after second collision

Station B has now performed the backoff algorithm and may be ready to retransmit the interrupted frame, which is commonly referred to as a *runt*. Station A, after detecting the collision, also sends a jam and performs the backoff algorithm. Eventually, the data crosses the wire uninterrupted.

CSMA/CD Receive Procedure

Like the transmitting process on an Ethernet network, a receiving station performs many jobs to process an incoming packet. On an Ethernet network, all devices can "see" all the packets on the wire, regardless of the address of the final destination. After a device receives a packet and determines that the packet has the appropriate length (minimum 64 bytes) and isn't a fragment, the device performs the following steps:

1. **Look at the destination address.** The device checks whether the destination address is addressed to itself, a broadcast, or some other type of address, such as a multicast. A *broadcast* is a message sent to all devices, whereas a *multicast* is a special type of communication that is sent to a group of devices, such as servers, or to a group of users, as with a

streaming video. All stations on the Ethernet network may perform this step to determine whether they should process the packet.

2. **Verify valid CRC.** After the packet is received and its length and valid address are verified, the receiver is responsible for validating the packet's integrity, which is called the *cyclic redundancy check*. The purpose of the CRC is to make sure that a packet went from its source to the destination without changing any of the data inside the packet. This is implemented in the NIC hardware and performed automatically, although software-based CRC implementations do exist.

3. **Process the packet.** After the receiving station receives the packet and verifies its frame length and integrity, the station must go to work. At this point, network interface layer connectivity is guaranteed. The receiving station looks further into the packet to determine what to do next. Even though network interface layer connectivity is proven at this point, other communication errors might still exist, such as a wrong frame type or protocol.

Ethernet Framing

Whenever data is sent across a network, it must be encapsulated in a specific frame format, to guarantee compatibility between devices. Ethernet has four different frame types available. For TCP/IP networks, either one of only two frame types generally is used on a network: Ethernet_II or Ethernet_SNAP, which are described later in this section.

Frame Sizing

Ethernet frames are variable in length, but some standards exist: an Ethernet frame must be no less than 64 bytes and no more than 1518 bytes (including header, data, and CRC).

A NIC driver may generate properly formed packets that are consistently too long or too short. If, for some reason, a frame that is sent contains less than the minimum 64 bytes, pad bytes should be inserted to ensure that the frame meets the proper minimum-length requirements. Conversely, if a packet is over the 1518-byte maximum, but has no errors, it is considered to be an *oversized packet*.

TIP

Consistent over- or undersized packets floating around the network are often caused by an outdated driver. Identify the device generating the packets and get an update from the manufacturer.

Although the network may seem to work properly with these packet sizes, they are considered to be in violation of the Ethernet framing standard. Some devices may tolerate this situation, but others may not. Knowingly violating the framing rules isn't a good idea.

Preamble

All Ethernet frames begin with a *preamble,* which is required so that the communicating stations can synchronize their clocks and agree on how long a unit of time is. The preamble consists of 8 bytes of alternating 1s and 0s, and it always ends in 11, as shown in Figure 3.13.

F I G U R E   3.13

Preamble

Preamble – 8 bytes

Data | 101010101010...1011 ← Preamble always ends with "1011" to indicate beginning of data

IMPORTANT

The jam signal is different from the preamble, because a jam is 32 bits whereas the preamble is 64 bits.

When a station begins to transmit the preamble, a change in voltage occurs on the cable. Another station on that cable "hears" the change in voltage and tries to get an idea of the transmitting station's clock signal. This may take some time, and the receiving station doesn't know how many bits of the preamble it may have missed. Therefore, it waits for the 11, signaling the start of the Ethernet frame, and begins processing from that point forward. The preamble data never enters the NIC's memory, and is considered a normal loss during the synchronization process. Because this data is never in the NIC buffer, it isn't shown in an analyzer, but you can be sure that it's out there on the network.

Ethernet_II

Ethernet_II frame types are the most widely used with TCP/IP communication. The following sections define the Ethernet II frame structure, shown in Figure 3.14.

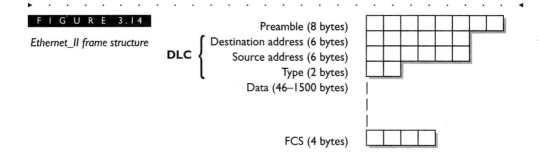

Ethernet_II frame structure

DLC {

Preamble (8 bytes)
Destination address (6 bytes)
Source address (6 bytes)
Type (2 bytes)
Data (46–1500 bytes)

FCS (4 bytes)

Destination Address

The Destination Address field is a 6-byte field that contains the MAC address of the station that is to receive the packet. Remember, the first 3 bytes identify the hardware manufacturer. A destination address of all ones (or FF-FF-FF-FF-FF-FF) denotes a broadcast address.

Source Address

The Source Address field is also a 6-byte field that specifies the sending MAC address. The source address could be a workstation, server, router, or other device. The source address is never a broadcast address (FF-FF-FF-FF-FF-FF).

Ethertype

Immediately following the Source Address field is the Ethertype (or Type) field, which specifies the upper-layer protocol that will be used when processing this frame. Some of the common Ethertypes are listed in Table 3.3, and a full list appears in Appendix F.

TABLE 3.3	ETHERTYPE DESCRIPTION	HEX CODE VALUE
Common Ethertype Code Values	Internet Protocol (IP)	0x0800
	Address Resolution Protocol (ARP)	0x0806
	Reverse Address Resolution Protocol (RARP)	0x8035
	EtherTalk (AppleTalk over Ethernet)	0x809B
	AppleTalk Address Resolution Protocol	0x80F3
	Internet Protocol version 6 (IPv6)	0x86DD

All the Ethernet frames begin with a Destination Address, Source Address, and a 2-byte field used for either length or (in this case) Ethertype. Somehow, the devices need to be able to know when they are seeing an Ethernet_II frame type. A station looks in the 2-byte field to determine whether it should use the Ethernet_II frame type. All Ethernet_II frames have a type-code value higher than 0x05DC (hex) or 1500 decimal. When the receiving station sees a value lower than 0x05DC (hex), it interprets this as one of the other frame types and looks further at other defining fields to discover the appropriate frame type.

TIP

All Ethernet_II frame types have a value higher than 0x05DC (hex) or 1500 decimal.

Data

The Data field is where the upper-layer protocol headers begin. The length of this field is a variable length between 46 and 1500 bytes.

FCS (Frame Check Sequence)

The last 4 bytes of the frame are for the FCS. The FCS field contains the CRC checksum data. This field is designed to provide error checking for the frame, and it is an important part of communications. The FCS ensures that only frames with valid data are processed and used in the network, and that bad frames that don't pass the error check are discarded.

The error check calculation and reversal process works like this:

1. The transmitting station calculates a CRC and places a value in the FCS field before sending the packet.

2. Packet is transmitted and sent to another station.

3. The receiving station performs a CRC calculation on the FCS field and compares the results. If the value is the same as when the packet was sent, the packet is processed.

The CRC error checking is performed by the Ethernet hardware. Figure 3.15 shows an example of an Ethernet_II frame.

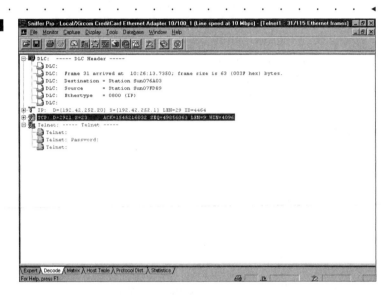

Notice the Ethertype field (0800) that designates IP as the upper-layer protocol. The IP (Internet) layer then passes the packet to TCP, which is handed off to a Telnet application. (Could that user be ready to enter a login password?)

Ethernet_SNAP

The Ethernet_SNAP (Sub Network Access Protocol) frame type is also available for use on the TCP/IP network. This frame type was derived from older types, to create an area for the Ethertype codes for TCP/IP (called the SNAP information). Otherwise, it is identical to an Ethernet_802.2 frame type. This following list describes the fields in an Ethernet_SNAP frame, illustrated in Figure 3.16:

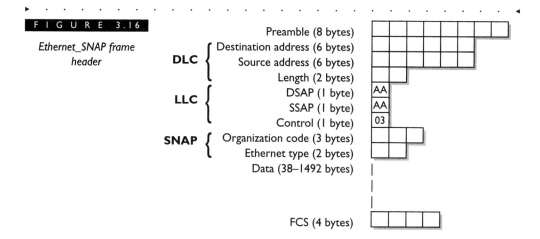

FIGURE 3.16

Ethernet_SNAP frame header

- **Destination Address:** A 6-byte field that contains the MAC address of the station that is to receive the packet. Remember, the first 3 bytes identify the hardware manufacturer. A destination address of all ones (or FF-FF-FF-FF-FF-FF) denotes a broadcast address.

- **Source Address:** A 6-byte field that specifies the sending MAC address. The source address could be a workstation, server, router, or other device. The source address is never a broadcast address (FF-FF-FF-FF-FF-FF).

- **Length:** Contains the amount of data in the frame, not including the preamble or the 4-byte CRC. Remember, an Ethernet frame can be no shorter than 64 bytes and no longer than 158 bytes in total length.

- **Destination Service Access Point (DSAP):** Simply a pointer to a particular memory buffer in the receiving station. The DSAP field is prefilled with 0xAA (hex) to denote the SNAP frame type.

- **Source Service Access Point (SSAP):** Like the DSAP area, the SSAP field is filled with 0xAA (hex) to denote the SNAP frame type.

- **Control Byte:** A single byte in the Ethernet_SNAP frame, it contains a value of 0x03, or an unnumbered format. The unnumbered format denotes that a connectionless service, such as IP, will be used.

▶ **Organization Code (SNAP header):** Constitutes the first 3 bytes of the SNAP header portion of the frame. This generally is filled with the first 3 bytes of the source hardware address, such as a vendor code. It can also be set to zero.

▶ **Ethertype (SNAP header):** Follows immediately after the Source Address field. Just like the Ethernet_II frame, this field (also called Type) specifies the upper-layer protocol that is used when processing this frame. Some of the common Ethertypes were previously listed in Table 3.3, and a full list appears in Appendix F.

▶ **Data:** Where the upper-layer protocol headers begin. The length of this field is a variable length between 38 and 1492 bytes. Notice that this is a different data length than what is available in the Ethernet_II frame type. The reason for this is the additional overhead taken by the Logical Link Control (LLC) and the SNAP header information.

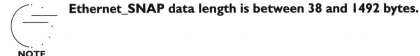

Ethernet_SNAP data length is between 38 and 1492 bytes.

NOTE

Remember, the overall length of an Ethernet frame can't exceed 1518 bytes. It makes sense that if we add more information to the header portion, we must reduce the length of some other field. The only field where this can be done is the Data field. Eight bytes have been added to the header, consisting of the following fields, thus reducing the data portion by 8 bytes overall:

- DSAP   1 byte
- SSAP   1 byte
- Control   1 byte
- Organization   3 bytes
- Ethertype   2 bytes

▸ **FCS:** The last 4 bytes of the frame, as with the Ethernet_II frame. The FCS field contains checksum data called the CRC. This field is designed to provide error checking for the frame and is important part of communications. The FCS ensures that only frames with valid data are processed and used in the network, and that bad frames that don't pass the error check are discarded.

Figure 3.17 shows an example of an Ethernet_SNAP frame.

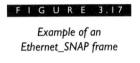

F I G U R E   3 . 1 7

Example of an Ethernet_SNAP frame

NOTE

Novell supports both the Ethernet_II and Ethernet_SNAP frame types and allows both types to run concurrently. Microsoft supports only a single concurrent frame type and uses Ethernet_II by default.

To support the Ethernet_SNAP frame type on an MS TCP/IP stack, the Registry must be manually changed to force the transmission of Ethernet_SNAP. One interesting note, however, is Windows NT's behavior in versions 3.5, 3.51, and 4.0, when TCP/IP is configured to use SNAP. If a SNAP-encapsulated ARP request gets a response with an Ethernet_II format ARP reply, or if an Ethernet_II ARP request is received, TCP/IP automatically switches to using Ethernet_II frames on that link. To configure Microsoft NT TCP/IP to use Ethernet_SNAP frames, use the Regedit command to make the following changes to the Registry:

I. Under the HKEY_LOCAL_MACHINE subtree, go to \SYSTEM\CurrentControlSet\Services\Tcpip\Parameters and click Edit ➪ New ➪ DWORD value to add a new subkey.

2. Name the key by using the following parameters:

- Value: ArpUseEtherSNAP

- Data Type: REG_DWORD — Boolean

- Data Range: 0 or 1 (False or True)

- Default: 0 (False)

3. Change the value from 0 to 1 to enable Ethernet_SNAP.

Configuring the Ethernet_SNAP frame type on a Microsoft NT Server is documented in Microsoft Article ID Q140913 on its support Web site.

TIP

Fast Ethernet

Virtually anyone who has used a network has at some point wished for more network bandwidth. Providing for faster applications, voice, multimedia, and response necessitates a faster infrastructure, such as Fast (100Mbps) Ethernet.

Introduction to Fast Ethernet

If you understand how standard (10Mbps) Ethernet is configured, then you already understand quite a bit about how Fast Ethernet works. Fast Ethernet uses the same cabling and CSMA/CD access method as 10BaseT.

Coaxial-based networks are not Fast Ethernet-compliant — they are limited to a 10Mbps transfer speed.

WARNING

On the most basic level, Fast Ethernet is simply regular Ethernet, but ten times faster. Whenever possible, the same rules and design characteristics of 10BaseT apply to Fast Ethernet.

Differences Between 10Mbps and 100Mbps

Because the access method for these two Ethernet systems is essentially the same, the differences boil down to hardware — cabling and hubs/switches. In the 10Mbps systems of the past, lower-grade cable was used for communication. This worked fine for these lower-bandwidth systems, but it isn't sufficient for a Fast Ethernet environment. Fast Ethernet (100Mbps) requires a Category 5 standard *at a minimum* to ensure proper data transmission.

The second largest difference between 10Mbps and 100Mbps is how the hubs are implemented. A 10Mbps system has the capability to link or cascade together up to four hubs in a single system. A Fast Ethernet environment is limited to a single hub, which makes designing a large network somewhat difficult.

The reason for the single-hub limitation is to create a proper collision domain within the network system. A *collision domain* is a single CSMA/CD network in which a collision occurs if two computers attached to the system transmit simultaneously. For example, a collision domain in the 10BaseT network shown in Figure 3.18 is the entire end-to-end network.

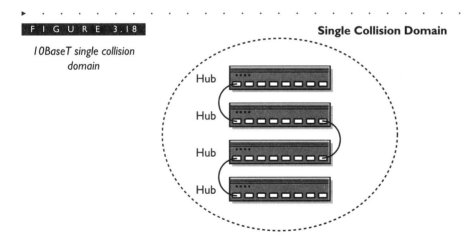

FIGURE 3.18

10BaseT single collision domain

Single Collision Domain

In this situation, collisions can (and do) occur frequently. To decrease the chance of frequent collisions occurring, the collision domain may be split into smaller collision domains. This frequently is done by using a bridge or switch device, as illustrated in Figure 3.19.

F I G U R E   3.19

10BaseT or 100BaseT with multiple collision domains

The reason that the collision domain must be smaller in a 100Mbps system is simple — on the Ethernet segment, ten times as many 100Mbps bits can take up the space previously occupied by a single 10Mbps collision domain.

Integrating 100Mbps and 10Mbps Ethernet

This section assumes that the cabling on the existing 10Mbps Ethernet network has already been upgraded to use 100Mbps, so that the performance benefit of the new standard will be realized. Here are some general guidelines to follow when mixing the technologies, each of which is explained in the sections that follow:

1. Break it up

2. Eliminate bottlenecks

3. Work from major devices to minor ones

Step 1: Break It Up   Chances are, the Ethernet network that you use today has grown from a relatively small system to an (almost) unmanageable beast. The first step is to define which areas are high-traffic areas. Look to the segments where routing takes place, or high-utilization server areas. How do you know which segments have the highest utilization? Simply plug in your analyzer — it will tell you the average bandwidth utilization.

IMPORTANT

> *Bandwidth utilization* **refers to network utilization (traffic on the cable), not the processor utilization of server-class computers.**

Break the network into smaller collision domains, as previously discussed. Switches are the popular choice for breaking the network into smaller, manageable collision domains. Implementing a 10/100 switch is useful when preparing to go to an all-100Mbps network.

Step Two: Eliminate Bottlenecks   In some instances, a switch will break up collision domains but not necessarily improve bandwidth. Remember, the NIC in the computer *must* support the faster standard. Figure 3.20 shows what happens when a 10/100 switch is installed in preparation for a 100Mbps network installation.

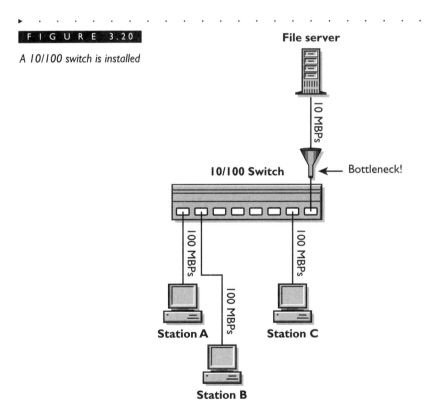

FIGURE 3.20

A 10/100 switch is installed

Bottlenecks such as slow servers and routers, once identified, should be upgraded to use 100Mbps Ethernet cards. Most manufacturers sell 10/100 switching cards that can determine the speed automatically and detect the duplex mode automatically.

WARNING

Automatic speed and duplex detection does not automatically guarantee better performance.

Factors affecting the auto-negotiation process are discussed later in this chapter.

Step 3: Work from Major Devices to Minor Ones After you install the new network cards in the major components of the system, (in other words, routers and servers), the rest of the network can begin its upgrade process. The following are the two ways that can implement 100Mbps technology at the workstations:

▸ Equip the workstations with 10/100 dual speed cards

▸ Upgrade to 100Mbps cards only

Using the 10/100 cards is probably a better idea in the long run, because the reconfiguration of the computer workstation is minimal. With the 100Mbps cards, a new driver and configuration setup must be performed at each computer, requiring a potentially significant cost in labor.

Auto-Negotiation

As previously mentioned, auto-negotiation is an optional part of the Ethernet standard. Auto-negotiation enables devices to exchange information about their abilities over a segment. Two features provided by auto-negotiation are the following:

▸ Automatic speed matching (either 10Mbps or 100Mbps)

▸ Full duplex or half duplex operation

Speed and Fast Link Pulses The automatic speed matching feature is designed to give the device the best possible speed of operation over a link. Auto-negotiation works using a concept called *Fast Link Pulse (FLP)*, a modified version of the 10BaseT standard, which verifies link integrity. Usually, FLP signals are verified at startup, but they may also be manually configured through the device setup.

The FLP signals will coexist with a 10BaseT Normal Link Pulse (NLP) signal, so a device that requires a slower link can communicate, even if it attempts communication with a device sending FLP signals. FLP signals occur during idle times on the network and should not interfere with normal traffic.

Full and Half Duplex Links   In addition to providing speed synchronization between devices, auto-negotiation can also be used to determine the duplex mode of the connected devices. Ethernet communicates in one of two modes:

- **Half duplex:** The normal Ethernet standard. Half duplex states that one type of communication (either transmit or receive) is occurring on the cable at any one time. In other words, a device cannot receive and send simultaneously.

- **Full duplex:** A performance enhancement designed to allow devices at each end of the full duplex link to send and receive data simultaneously over the link. The theory is that, because only two devices are on a link (one at the workstation and one at the switch port), a single channel of communication exists at all times between them. Therefore, data should be sent and received simultaneously.

NOTE

The full duplex standard is an emerging standard. Because no written standard exists, different vendor implementations of this part of the auto-negotiation may vary widely.

If you have equipment from several different vendors, it is a good idea to turn the duplex negotiation off. Don't assume that full duplex implementation from one vendor will work correctly with another vendor's equipment. Leaving full duplex capability turned on with multivendor networks can cause performance degradation across the entire network.

Common Ethernet Network Problems

Many network problems occur for one of two reasons:

- The cabling rules weren't followed correctly

> ▸ A network card or device, such as router, hub, or switch, has
> malfunctioned

This section explores some of the common issues and problems associated with
an Ethernet network.

Propagation Delay/Cable Segment Too Long

As previously stated, the minimum frame size in an Ethernet network is 64
bytes (512 bits). You've also read that the Ethernet maximum cable for 10BaseT is
100 meters, and for 10Base2 networks is 185 meters. A much more obscure fact
is that these two specifications actually are directly related.

Propagation delay is the length of time that a signal takes to transmit from one
place to another. A direct correlation exists between the amount of data sent in a
frame and the amount of time that it takes to communicate that data on the wire.
This is a carefully calculated amount, which results in the cable-length
specifications adhered to by manufacturers (discussed earlier in this chapter).

So, what happens when the cable segment is too long? Nodes beginning to
transmit at one end of the cable are not aware that other nodes may also be
transmitting. This results in a condition called a *late collision,* which isn't normal
on an Ethernet network, and is usually caused by a violation of the cabling
specifications. The next section explores different collision types.

Late Collisions

Normal (or early) collisions were described previously in the chapter. A *late
collision* is any collision that occurs after 64 bytes (512 bits) are transmitted. Late
collisions may occur when cabling specs are violated. The following steps outline
the late collision process. This scenario uses the same two-station network example
that was described in the early collision process, although, again, this scenario
could be any number of devices.

1. **Station A transmits.** A potential transmitting station will detect that the
   wire has been idle for 9.6 microseconds. Station A begins to transmit,
   starting with the 64-bit preamble. Station A finishes the preamble and
   transmits the beginning 32 bytes (256 bits) of the frame, as shown in

Figure 3.21. If the cable were in spec and Station B attempted to transmit at this time, an early (normal) collision would occur. But, the cable system isn't in spec, so Station A continues to transmit bits and finishes sending the first 64 bytes (512 bit) of the frame. At this point, Station A stops listening for collisions.

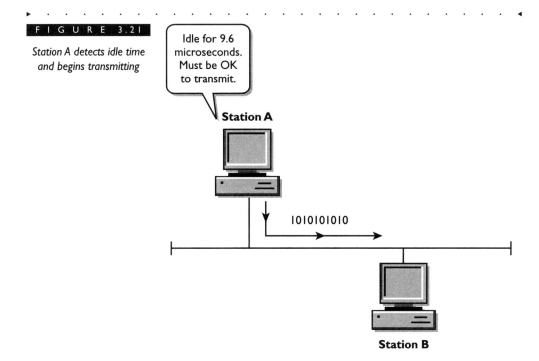

FIGURE 3.21

Station A detects idle time and begins transmitting

Idle for 9.6 microseconds. Must be OK to transmit.

Station A

1010101010

Station B

2. **Station B transmits.** Before the frame from Station A has had time to travel down the length of the wire, Station B decides to transmit. It detects that the cable has been idle for 9.6 microseconds, so it begins to transmit, just before the electrical signal from Station A would have reached Station B, as shown in Figure 3.22.

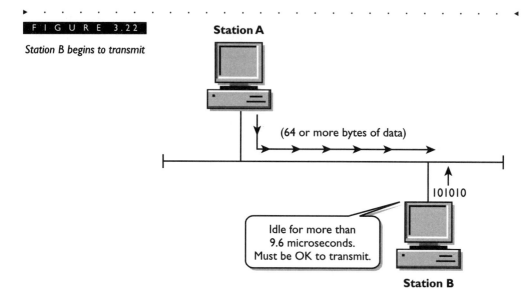

FIGURE 3.22

Station B begins to transmit

Station A

(64 or more bytes of data)

101010

Idle for more than
9.6 microseconds.
Must be OK to transmit.

Station B

3. **Collision occurs.** Very close to Station B, the packets collide. Abnormal
   voltage occurs and travels down the wire to both Stations A and B, as
   shown in Figure 3.23.

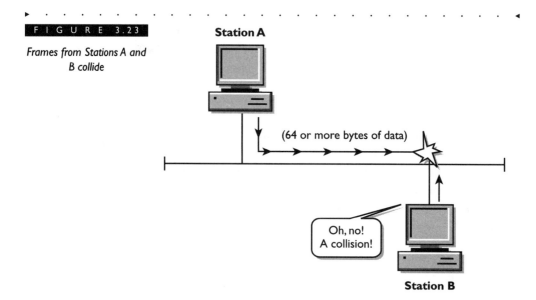

FIGURE 3.23

*Frames from Stations A and
B collide*

Station A

(64 or more bytes of data)

Oh, no!
A collision!

Station B

4. Station B begins jam signal. Station B is very close to the collision and sends a jam signal, which consists of the same 32-bit transmission used in an early collision. Station B then begins the normal backoff algorithm, to determine when to retransmit, as shown in Figure 3.24.

FIGURE 3.24

Station B transmits a jam and backoff

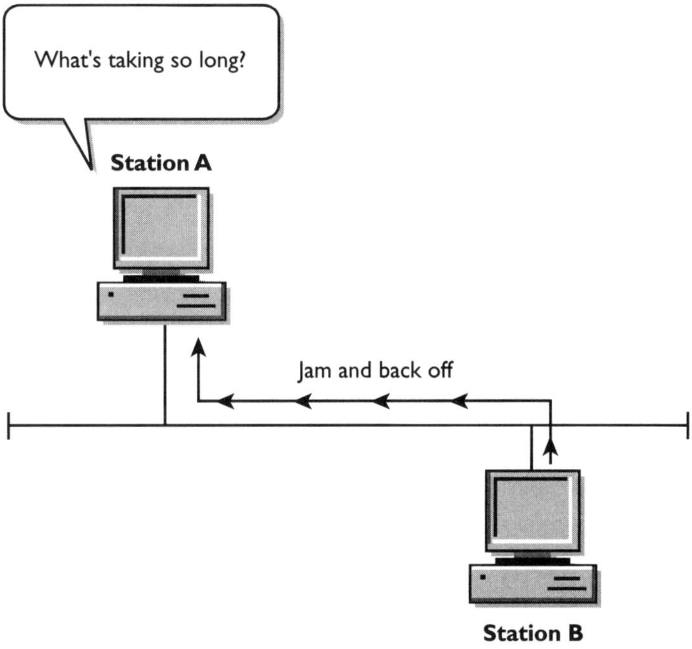

What's taking so long?

Station A

Jam and back off

Station B

Herein lies the problem. Station B is aware of the collision and performs the proper steps to remedy the situation. However, by the time the jam and collision information reaches Station A, it is no longer listening, because it stopped listening when 64 bytes were successfully transmitted. Station A has no idea that a collision has just occurred.

After the network card misses a collision event, the upper layers are responsible for recovery and retransmission. In this case, recovery time increases drastically. Statistics show that a network interface usually can recover from a collision and retransmit in about 2 to 3 milliseconds. When the upper protocol layers are responsible for recovery and retransmission, it can take up to 100 times longer.

CRC/Alignment Errors

If a frame is damaged during transmission, it fails the CRC performed by the receiving station. These errors aren't normal and usually are caused by the various cabling problems described throughout this chapter. Unlike a late collision, which occurs after 64 bytes are transmitted, the frame generally is less than 64 bytes with a bad CRC. Although they can be generated by a lengthy segment, CRC errors typically are related to another type of cable problem. Table 3.4 describes some of these common cable problems.

TABLE 3.4

Common Causes of CRC Errors

POSSIBLE CRC CAUSE	PROBLEM DESCRIPTION
Improper termination	Signals reach the end of the cable and reflect back on the wire
Improper grounding	Data flow corrupted by noise
Faulty network card	Network cards don't listen to activity properly; they should be replaced
Failing hub or switch device	Ports that fail can disrupt the network data flow by sending intermittent bad data on the wire
Interference (noise)	Electromagnetic interference caused by running cables too close to fluorescent lights or high voltage cabinets, motors, or other high-power devices
Kinked or failing cable	Cable that has been bent improperly

Token Ring Topology

Token Ring is the term normally used to refer the IEEE 802.5 specification. Token Ring devices are connected in a series, resulting in a ring that is closed. This topology uses a deterministic access approach for communication, which is much different than the Ethernet CSMA/CD method. Token Ring is less forgiving than Ethernet when it is out of spec, so you need to follow the rules of Token Ring installation carefully. IBM, Madge, and other vendors publish specifications that vary depending on the cable type being used. Many cable types are available with

Token Ring, ranging from STP, to UTP, to fiber. Notice that Token Ring can use STP cable, whereas Ethernet cannot.

Token Ring networks are built in a *star wired ring* topology. The physical network resembles a star (hub and spoke), wherein all cables come to and from a central location, but the electrical signals on the network are actually closed, as in a ring. Figure 3.25 illustrates the Token Ring basic topology.

FIGURE 3.25

Basic Token Ring topology

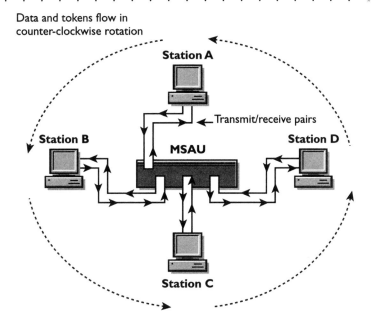

Data and tokens flow in counter-clockwise rotation

Station A

◄ Transmit/receive pairs

Station B

MSAU

Station D

Station C

The network is physically wired, with all the nodes connected to a device called a *multistation access unit (MAU)*. In a twisted-pair cable installation, (a common standard, consisting of a single cable with two pairs), one pair serves as the inbound, or receiving, portion of the ring, and the other pair serves as the outbound, or transmit, wire pair. In this implementation, all Token Ring stations are connected to the MAUs, which are then wired together using patch cables to form one large ring.

Token Ring Implementation

Several different methods are used to install and maintain a Token Ring network. This section discusses some of the common cable types, speeds, and network access algorithms for Token Ring.

4Mbps

The first Token Ring networks were 4Mbps implementations of Token Ring. All data and tokens are sent at the strict 4Mbps rate. This normally isn't installed for new Token Ring networks, but is still used in many legacy networks around the world.

16Mbps

This has the same function and configuration as the 4Mbps ring, but operates at 16Mbps. The two data rates cannot be mixed on the same network.

16Mbps with Early Token Release

In the Token Ring system, only one token can be on the ring at a time. In larger networks, this is inefficient, due to the wait time before a station can transmit. *Early Token Release* technology enables a station to transmit a new, free token while another token is already in use on the ring. This enables the ring to have multiple, simultaneous data transmissions on the ring.

High-Speed Token Ring

Many current Token Ring network users are feeling the crunch of a bandwidth-limited network. The network itself is too costly and works too well to tear apart, but when topologies such as Ethernet and Gigabit Ethernet offer speeds that are more than ten times the capacity of Token Ring, it's hard to settle for 16Mbps.

However, a High-Speed Token Ring standard is on the way. It is expected to run at 100Mbps on copper wire, and a Gigabit Token Ring specification is already under way. The new specification is backward-compatible with current Token Ring standards, which is just one of the benefits of the new spec.

Cabling Types

Several different types of cable can be used in the Token Ring network. Three of the most popular are the following:

- Shielded twisted pair

- ▸ Unshielded twisted pair

- ▸ Fiber optic

Shielded Twisted Pair (STP) Most cables of this type belong to a family of cables called the *IBM Cabling System*. Type 1 is the most commonly used STP cable. Table 3.5 shows some of the common cable types in the IBM family.

TABLE 3.5

Common IBM Cable Types

CABLE TYPE	DESCRIPTION
Type 1	Shielded data-grade cable with two solid-wire twisted pairs. Available in both indoor and outdoor versions.
Type 2	An indoor cable with four solid-wire twisted pairs of 24 AWG (American Wire Gauge) wire. Contains four voice-grade wires along with four data-grade wires.
Type 3	Unused existing telephone wire or EIA (Electronic Industries Association) Category 3 wire (4Mbps operation). Better wire is needed for 16Mbps operation.
Type 4	Not defined.
Type 5	100/140–micron fiber cable used for fiber-optic repeater links.
Type 6	Often used for patch cables. Can be used for MAU-to-MAU connections or from a wall outlet.

Because this type of cable is shielded, rings can be larger than the typical UTP ring. In theory, rings using STP can have up to 250 nodes attached to one ring. STP is costlier than UTP and is less flexible, making it more difficult to work with.

Unshielded Twisted Pair (UTP) UTP probably is the most common type of cable currently used in networking. This cable is small, flexible, easy to work with, readily available, and inexpensive. UTP rings can, in theory, have up to 72 nodes attached to one ring. This is less than the STP installation, mostly due to the fact that the cables are unshielded, and thus signal loss may be greater. Networks using UTP can often be enlarged by using a repeating device, to repeat the signals sent throughout the network.

Fiber Optic Fiber optic is usually used in a Token Ring network to extend the size of the ring that interconnects the MAUs beyond normal limitations.

Media Access Method

Unlike Ethernet, which uses a collision-detection access method, Token Ring uses a *deterministic* method when transmitting data across a network cable. This section discusses how data is sent and received on a network that is using Token Ring.

Token Passing Technology and Process

Token Ring is unique in that, although it is wired in a star configuration, electrical pulses travel through the system as if it were a completely closed ring. Each station in a Token Ring network has a separate transmitter and receiver port. The transmitter port on one station is connected to the receiver port on the next station. The *upstream neighbor* is used to refer to the transmitting station, which transmits over the ring to the *downstream neighbor*, as illustrated in Figure 3.26.

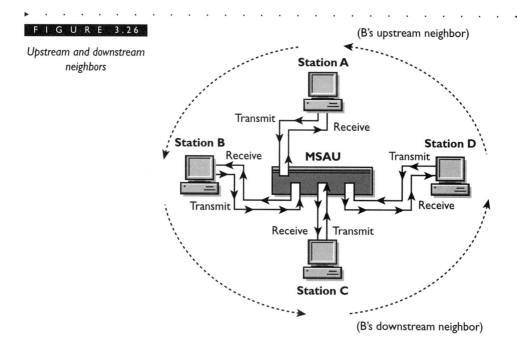

FIGURE 3.26

Upstream and downstream neighbors

(B's upstream neighbor)

(B's downstream neighbor)

Each downstream neighbor receives bits on the cable attached to its nearest upstream neighbor station. It then turns around and repeats the bits to the next station. Remember the game of "telephone" when you were a kid? One person has a secret, they tell it to the next, and the next, and the next, until finally it comes back to you. That's how Token Ring works.

The true process of transmitting and receiving on a Token Ring has a few more steps and rules to follow. Token Ring is *deterministic* in its approach to network communication, meaning that, in due time, each station gets a chance to transmit and receive data. This is unlike an Ethernet system, in which collisions occur when two devices communicate simultaneously. The token simply passes around the ring from station to station until a device captures it and uses it to send data. The data transmission follows these steps:

1. **Station captures a token.** When the adapter receives information to send, it must capture a free token on the ring before it can send the information. The station hardware monitors the ring for a free token. Only one station at a time can use the token. When a free token passes to the station from the upstream neighbor, the station waiting to transmit grabs the token and begins to make it into a format that can transmit data on the wire. That is, it must put frame information on the token, and data into the frame.

2. **Data is transmitted.** After the token is captured, the device that captured it may transmit data until it is finished, or until the token-holding timer expires (8.9 milliseconds). It is important to know that the frames are repeated and checked for errors *at each station between the sender and receiver*. If an error is found, the station sets a bit in the frame, announcing to the other stations that an error was detected. This tells the other stations not to report the error again. When the frame reaches the destination, the frame is copied into the receiving station's adapter buffer for processing. The receiving station changes two more bits in the frame, the Address Recognized Indicator (ARI) and the Frame Copied (FC) bits, and passes the frame to the next neighbor and on again throughout the ring.

3. **Frame stripped from the ring.** The original sending station should never repeat its own frames. By not repeating its own frames, it is said to have "stripped the frame" from the wire. The original sending station also looks

to see which bits are set. First, it looks to see whether the receiving station set the ARI bit (if it was connected to the ring and functioning). Then, it checks whether the frame was copied. If these bits are not set or some combination is not set, the frame is considered to have an error. Errors could occur any time in the transmission process.

4. **New free token transmit.** After the data is transmitted and stripped from the ring by the original sending station, that adapter is responsible for transmitting a free token. This allows other devices on the network to communicate.

Token Ring can also be configured for prioritized token passing. In this case, a device not only follows the steps previously outlined, but can also be configured to take priority over other stations in the ring. Therefore, a station with a higher priority can capture the token before a station with a lower priority.

WARNING

In prioritized token passing, a station can take priority over another station, and therefore capture the token "out of turn."

The Prioritized Token Passing rules also state that if a station has priority, it must lower its priority to its original value the next time that it sees a free token. This ensures that every device on the network gets a chance to communicate.

Active and Standby Monitor

Every station on the Token Ring network is either an Active Monitor (AM) or a Standby Monitor (SM). The AM is chosen in a process called *monitor contention*. One AM must be on the ring at all times. The AM is responsible for making sure that token passing is available, because without that, no communication occurs on the ring. Table 3.6 describes the functions of the AM.

As stated in the table, an *Active Monitor Present (AMP)* frame is generated every seven seconds on a properly functioning Token Ring network. Figure 3.27 illustrates a trace taken with a good Active Monitor.

TROUBLESHOOTING THE LINK FOR ETHERNET AND TOKEN RING NETWORKS

T A B L E   3.6

Active Monitor Responsibilities

ACTIVE MONITOR FUNCTION	DESCRIPTION
Provide master clocking	Creates the mandatory master clock signal on the wire. All stations synchronize to this clock, so no need exists for extensive synchronization before data can be transmitted, as is necessary with Ethernet.
Initiate ring polling	Sends an Active Monitor Present frame every seven seconds.
Provide 24-bit latency buffer	Buffers data on the ring so that a token may not be stripped from the ring before all of the bits have been sent.
Monitor ring polling	Notification for all devices of the nearest upstream neighbor. Polling occurs every seven seconds.
Ensure proper token operation	Watches for corrupted and lost frames, or a prioritization problem. Active Monitor may purge and restart the ring to initiate a new token.

F I G U R E   3.27

Active Monitor Present frames

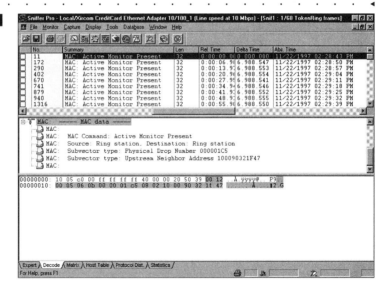

Every other station on the ring is configured as a Standby Monitor, which is required on the ring, and its function is built into the adapter hardware. The job

of the Standby Monitor is basically to monitor the Active Monitor. The SM initiates monitor contention (or election) if any one of the following situations occurs:

- A token has not been passed for more than 2.6 seconds

- No AMP frame has appeared for 15 seconds

- The AM clock is significantly different from the SM clock

Monitor Contention

When the Active Monitor isn't properly performing its duties, the Standby Monitors can initiate *monitor contention,* an election process that excludes the AM — the assumption being that a problem exists with the AM, which caused the contention in the first place.

For a station to participate in the monitor contention process, it must be designated as a "participant."

TIP

Not all stations contend to be the Active Monitor. Those that do participate are either:

- The first station that notices the absence of the AM

- Designated specifically as a participant when the driver was loaded

When monitor contention occurs, the following steps take place:

1. **Monitor contention is initiated.** A station on the ring notices that the AM has disappeared. This is triggered by an absence of the polling on the network, errors coming from the AM, or the complete absence of the AM device. The station that notices is generally the nearest downstream neighbor of the AM station.

2. **Station transmits Claim Token.** The ring station that noticed the absence of the AM enters Claim Token Transmit mode and begins to transmit a special MAC frame called a *Claim Token MAC frame,* without regard for the token process. Figure 3.28 shows a Claim Token MAC frame.

FIGURE 3.28

Claim Token MAC frame

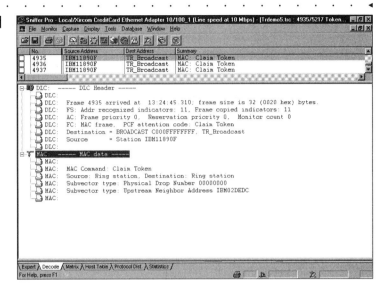

3. **Contention process begins.** The station that started the monitor contention process continues the Claim Token process until either:

   ▸ Another station with a higher adapter address sends a Claim Token. If this happens, the station that initiated the request goes into Repeat mode and sends the Claim Token around the ring.

   ▸ The station receives three of its own Claim Token frames. When this happens, as shown in Figure 3.28, the station "wins" the monitor contention process and becomes the new Active Monitor.

4. **New station becomes Active Monitor.** After the new station becomes AM, it first sets up all the AM functions in its chipset, which include clocking, polling, and 24-bit latency. Next, the new AM executes a ring purge. Then, it restarts the ring-polling process and transmits a free token. The new AM is up and running. Figure 3.29 illustrates the new AM setup process.

F I G U R E 3.29

A new Active Monitor is chosen.

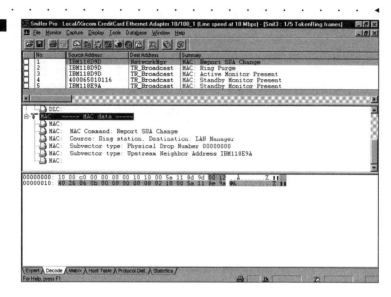

Notice that the new AM immediately purges the ring, to start with a new free token.

The Ring-Polling Process

Mentioned earlier is the ring-polling process that occurs every seven seconds. It is initiated by the AM and serves a very important purpose — to allow every station on the ring to learn about its nearest active upstream neighbor (NAUN). When a station knows its NAUN, it can inform the rest of the ring when the neighbor can't be found. This is valuable in isolating a fault in the Token Ring network. The following steps illustrate the ring polling process:

1. A neighbor-notification timer in the AM expires, which begins the ring-polling process. Station A (the AM) sends out an AMP frame as a broadcast (see Figure 3.30). Station A sets to 0 the ARI and FC bits, which are used by all the devices to determine the NAUN.

2. Station B receives the frame and sees that the ARI and FC bits are set to 0. Station B recognizes that Station A must be its NAUN. It records Station A's address and sets the ARI and FC bits to 1. It then repeats the frame, around the ring, as shown in Figure 3.31.

▼ . . . . ◆ . . . .

FIGURE 3.30

Active Monitor starts ring polling

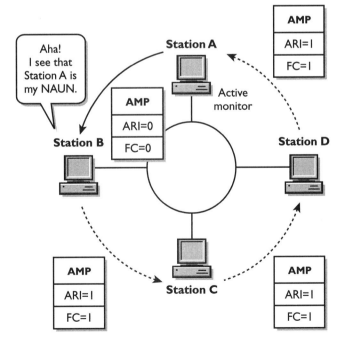

Station A

Active Monitor Poll (AMP)

ARI=0

FC=0

Active monitor

Station B

Station D

Station C

▶ . . . . ◀

FIGURE 3.31

Station B repeats the frame

AMP

ARI=1

FC=1

Aha! I see that Station A is my NAUN.

Station A

Active monitor

AMP

ARI=0

FC=0

Station B

Station D

AMP

ARI=1

FC=1

Station C

AMP

ARI=1

FC=1

. . . . .

3. All other stations on the ring see that the ARI and FC bits are set to 1, so they know they aren't the nearest station to the sending device. They repeat the frame until it returns to Station A, who strips the frame from the wire. Station B waits 20 milliseconds and then sends out a SMP frame, shown in Figure 3.32, to announce its SM presence.

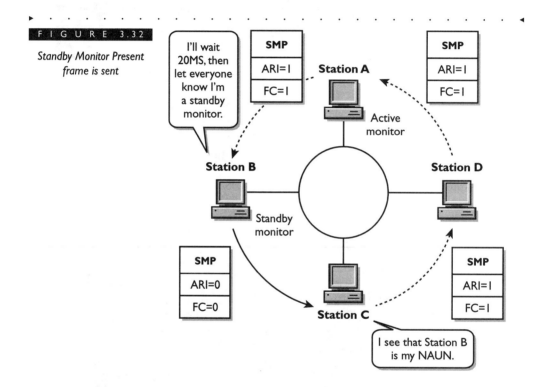

FIGURE 3.32

Standby Monitor Present frame is sent

4. Station C receives the SMP frame and the process occurs again for Stations C and D, until all SM stations are identified.

When an analyzer is used to capture the AM and SM traffic, the screen looks like that shown in Figure 3.33.

Ring polling

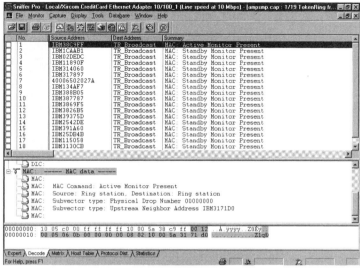

Ring Purge

The ring-purge process is initiated by an AM, to restart the ring operation to a known state. If a station receives a Ring Purge command, it immediately stops whatever it's doing, resets its timers, and enters *Bit Repeat mode*. The AM continues to send the Ring Purge frames until it receives its own frame back. At that time, the AM stops sending Ring Purge frames and issues a new token.

A single Ring Purge frame is usually sent in response to a monitor contention operation or the generation of a new token by the AM. Additionally, a single Ring Purge frame may happen as stations enter and leave the ring. Multiple Ring Purge frames viewed in your analyzer could indicate a ring problem or an analyzer placement issue. For example, if the analyzer is placed downstream from the AM and upstream from the actual problem, the analyzer will pick up many Ring Purge frames before the ring recovers.

Beaconing

When a fault occurs in the Token Ring network, the process of isolating the problem is referred to as *beaconing*. This is an attempt by the stations on the ring to report (and hopefully recover from) a hardware failure. When beaconing occurs, all stations on the ring are notified that the Token protocol has been suspended.

The Beacon frames are sent every 20 milliseconds, without the need for a free token. A Beacon frame contains the address of the station's NAUN, which provides clues as to where the actual ring fault may lie in the network.

Frame Structures

Token Ring uses different types of frames to perform different functions on the network. A Token Ring network generally consists of these frame classifications:

- Token frames

- LLC frames

- MAC frames

The following sections explore the functions and abilities of each type.

Token Frames

A Token frame is a very important part of the Token Ring network. A Token frame has only three fields, as shown in Figure 3.34 and listed next. The token itself takes only 3 bytes. The token is part of every Token Ring frame and is common to all Token Ring frames.

F I G U R E   3.34

Token Frame format

Start delimiter (SDEL) (1 byte)
Access control byte (1 byte)
Ending delimiter (EDEL)

- **Start Delimiter:** Designates the start of the frame. This field doesn't appear in an analyzer.

- **End Delimiter:** Designates the end of the frame. This field doesn't appear in an analyzer.

- **Access Control Byte:** Performs different functions at the bit level — the type of data (token or frame), the priority of the token or frame, priority reservation, and monitor counts.

LLC (Data) Frames

In a Token Ring network, data is carried by frames that include the LLC header (the same header discussed in the Ethernet section of this chapter). The format of the Data frames can be encapsulated in one of two ways:

▸ Token

▸ Token_SNAP

The format of a Token Ring frame is illustrated in Figure 3.35.

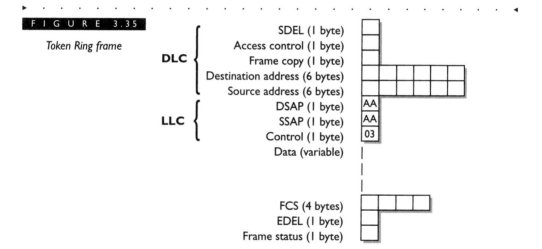

FIGURE 3.35

Token Ring frame

DLC {
SDEL (1 byte)
Access control (1 byte)
Frame copy (1 byte)
Destination address (6 bytes)
Source address (6 bytes)

LLC {
DSAP (1 byte)   AA
SSAP (1 byte)   AA
Control (1 byte)   03

Data (variable)

FCS (4 bytes)
EDEL (1 byte)
Frame status (1 byte)

The Token_SNAP frame includes all of the preceding data, plus a SNAP header after the LLC (DSAP, SSAP, and Control) information. All the Address, LLC, and SNAP fields common to Token Ring are also common to Ethernet (see the LLC and SNAP field descriptions earlier in this chapter).

The Data field in the Token or Token_SNAP frame may include routing or upper-layer protocol information. The Data field is variable in length, and upper limits of packet size can be determined and changed by adapter drivers. However, the common data packet size for Token Ring is a total of 4202 bytes.

The Frame Status field contains the Address Recognized Indicator and Frame Copied Indicator information discussed earlier. Figure 3.36 shows a valid Token Data frame captured in an analyzer.

FIGURE 3.36

Token frame

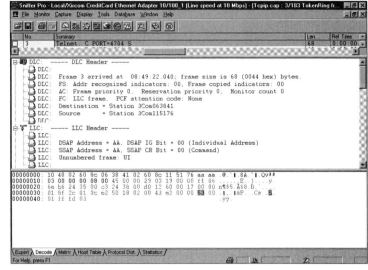

Notice the AA values of the for the DSAP and SSAP fields in the LLC header. This designates that this packet is a TCP/IP packet — the same as Ethernet, even though the data link information is different. Figure 3.37 depicts a Token_SNAP frame.

FIGURE 3.37

Token_SNAP frame

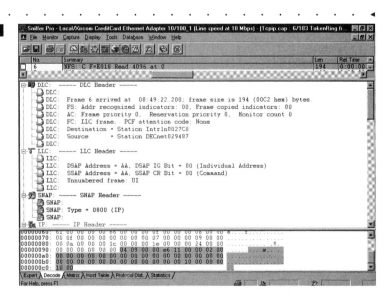

Once again, in this frame, the value of the SNAP information, Type (0080), designates that an IP header is coming next. This, too, is the same as Ethernet.

Management Frames (MAC)

Token Ring management, or MAC, frames are a wonderful part of the Token protocol. Instead of carrying user data, MAC frames carry only Token Ring management or error information. MAC frames are specific to a single ring cable — they cannot cross a bridge or a router of any kind. The frame format is exactly the same as the LLC frames previously described, except that MAC information resides in the sixth field instead of LLC information. Figure 3.38 illustrates a Ring Purge MAC frame.

FIGURE 3.38

Ring Purge MAC frame

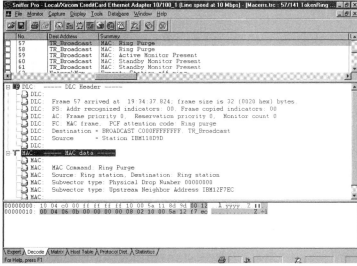

Notice how the MAC information comes directly after the data link portion of the packet. MAC command information is displayed in the analyzer by using Major Vector ID information. Table 3.7 illustrates the Major Vector IDs available.

	MAJOR VECTOR DESCRIPTION	MAJOR VECTOR ID (IN HEX)
T A B L E 3.7	Response	00h
Token Ring Major Vector Codes	Beacon	02h
	Claim Token	03h
	Ring Purge	04h
	Active Monitor Present (AMP)	05h
	Standby Monitor Present (SMP)	06h
	Duplicate Address Test	07h
	Lobe Media Test	08h
	Transmit Forward	09h
	Remove Ring Station	0Bh
	Change Parameters	0Ch
	Initialize Ring Station	0Dh
	Request Station Address	0Eh
	Request Station State	0Fh
	Request Station Attachment	10h
	Request Initialization	20h
	Report Station Address	22h
	Report Station State	23h
	Report Station Attachment	24h
	Report New Active Monitor	25h
	Report NAUN Change	26h
	Report Ring Poll Failure	27h
	Report Active Monitor Error	28h
	Report Soft Error	29h
	Report Transmit Forward	2Ah

Now that you know some of the management frames available in the Token Ring network, take a look at some common errors that may occur with this topology.

Common Token Ring Network Problems

Token Ring network errors can commonly be categorized into two distinct areas: *hard errors* and *soft errors*. This section explores some of these errors.

Hard Errors

A *hard error* generally is something that the ring can't fix by itself. This includes cable breaks, failing adapters, switch ports, hubs, MAUs, patch cables, and generally all the hardware components involved in the network.

Probably the most common type of hard error is a signal loss error, which usually is caused by cable that doesn't meet specifications. (Remember the late collisions in Ethernet?) This problem can also be created by noise on the line, and kinked or broken cable, which may cause a short. When a hard error occurs, the AM makes an attempt to fix the problem by purging the ring. Figure 3.39 illustrates the first step the AM takes in a potentially catastrophic situation.

FIGURE 3.39

Continuous ring purge

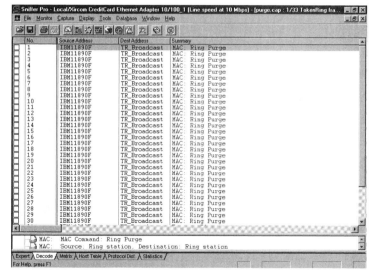

The next step for this ring is the monitor contention phase, and then beaconing. Beaconing is the ultimate hard error and will require human intervention. Get out those cabling tools.

Soft Errors

Soft errors are more common in a Token Ring network (assuming that the cable plant is well designed and implemented). When a soft error occurs, the station waits for two seconds to see whether other errors may be on the ring. After two seconds, the soft error report is sent to the Ring Error Monitor, which is a device on the ring that is designed to record or take action on an error. Table 3.8 describes some of the more common soft errors, as defined by the IEEE committee, and gives some ideas of where to begin troubleshooting when you see these errors in the analyzer.

T A B L E   3 . 8

Token Ring Soft Error Description

ERROR TYPE	DESCRIPTION	WHERE TO LOOK FOR AN ERROR PROBLEM
Abort Delimiter	Station detected an invalid ending delimiter, a Claim Token, or Beacon frame and aborted its transmission.	An adapter can usually recover from this error. If it can't, it removes itself from the ring. Replace it.
A/C Error	Caused by an adapter that doesn't set the ARI bit.	Faulty adapter. Replace the card.
Burst Errors	Cable has had no activity for at least 5 half-bit times (also known as *burst-five*).	Usually due to noise on the line from background interference or faulty hardware.
Frame Copied Error	An adapter recognized a MAC frame addressed to a specific address, and the ARI or FC bits are already set to 1.	Indicates a duplicate MAC address, though stations on the ring test for this, and it should never happen.
Frequency Error	AM clock and ring clock differ greatly in their timing.	AM clock may be faulty or cable may be out of spec.
Internal Error	Caused when a station has a recoverable internal error.	Adapter is in marginal operating condition. Replace the network card.
Line Error	Usually indicates corruption in the Data frame.	A single source indicates faulty hardware, and multiple sources indicates cabling problems.
Lost Frames	The number of times a station has transmitted and not received the entire frame in return.	Usually due to noise.
Receiver Congestion	Caused by an adapter recognizing a frame addressed to it, but lacking available buffer area to copy the frame.	Usually hardware related — older boards have smaller buffers.

▶ • ◀

Case Study — What Can Go Wrong

Now that you've reviewed how data moves around the physical cable, take a look at a real-life cabling problem.

The Problem

A customer calls with complaints about network performance. Stations are freezing up, getting error messages, and taking a long time to communicate with the server. The cable installation is new and the customer has recently changed from a hub to a switch environment. The general layout of the network and some key stations are show in Figure 3.40.

▶ • ◀

FIGURE 3.40

Network layout

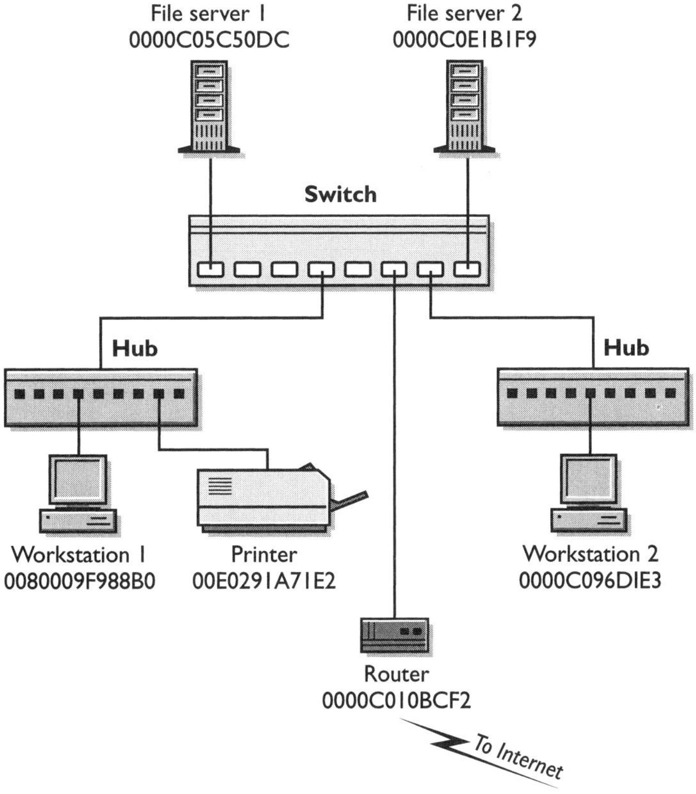

File server 1
0000C05C50DC

File server 2
0000C0E1B1F9

Switch

Hub

Hub

Workstation 1
0080009F988B0

Printer
00E0291A71E2

Workstation 2
0000C096D1E3

Router
0000C010BCF2

To Internet

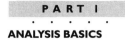
The Analysis

The customer sends a LANalyzer trace that it took from its network on a day when the problems seemed to be at their worst. Figure 3.41 shows the trace. Several things stand out in this trace, which should be analyzed in the following order:

FIGURE 3.41

Customer trace

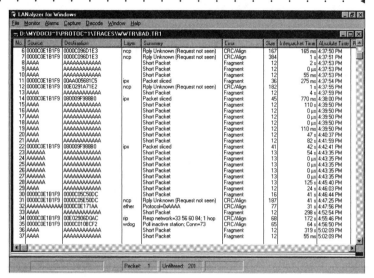

I. Look at the Error column. It shows nothing but CRC/Alignment errors and fragments for every frame. Obviously, a cable plant problem is present. We need to look further to figure this one out.

2. Look at the MAC addresses in the Source Address and Destination Address fields to discover some of the nodes involved in this problem. Look to see whether they are in the same collision domain. After a quick review of the key station diagram in Figure 3.40, we discover that the MAC addresses involved in this problem are *not* in the same collision domain. For example, address 080009F988B0 is a workstation located off a hub, and 0000C096D1E3 is a workstation located on another hub connected to a completely different switch port.

3. So, now we determine what is common to both Workstation 1 and Workstation 2 (two devices in different collision domains). The answer presents three possibilities: the switch, Fileserver 1, and Fileserver 2.

4. A closer look at the Source Address field in this trace reveals that for each full address decode, station 0000C0E1B1F9 (FS2) is shown.

5. At this point, a definite pattern becomes clear — each time station 0000C0E1B1F9 (FS2) transmits, its transmission is followed by several fragments. Could this network card be faulty?

6. The client replaces the network card and send another trace, shown in Figure 3.42.

FIGURE 3.42

Client's second trace

LANalyzer for Windows
File Monitor Alarms Capture Decode Window Help
D:\MYDOCU~1\PROTOC~1\TRACES\WWTR\TOANY3.TR1

No.	Source	Destination	Layer	Summary	Error	Size	Interpacket Time	Absolute Time	Relative Time
1	0000C0E1B1F9	00AA005681C5	ipx	Packet sliced	Fragment	37	0 µs	1:44:56 PM	0 µs
2	0000C0E1B1F9	00E0290EE2AF	ncp	Rply Unknown (	CRC/Align	103	2 s	1:44:57 PM	2 s
3	0000C0E1B1F9	00E0290EE2AF	ncp	Rply Unknown (	CRC/Align	306	7 s	1:45:04 PM	9 s
4	0000C0E1B1F9	00E0291A71E2	ipx	Packet sliced	Fragment	28	7 s	1:45:12 PM	16 s
5	0000C0E1B1F9	00E0290EE2AF	ncp	Rply Unknown (	CRC/Align	263	1 s	1:45:13 PM	17 s
6	0000C0E1B1F9	00E0291A71E2	ncp	Burst Packet;	CRC/Align	832	1 s	1:45:14 PM	18 s
7	0000C0E1B1F9	00E0290EE2AF	ncp	Rply Unknown (	CRC/Align	117	1 s	1:45:15 PM	20 s
8	0000C0E1B1F9	00E0290EE2AF	ncp	Rply Unknown (	CRC/Align	283	4 s	1:45:20 PM	24 s
9	0000C0E1B1F9	00E0290EE2AF	ipx	Packet sliced	Fragment	25	2 s	1:45:21 PM	26 s
10	0000C0E1B1F9	00E0290EE2AF	ipx	Packet sliced	Fragment	47	385 ms	1:45:22 PM	26 s
11	0000C0E1B1F9	00E0290EE2AF	ncp	Rply Unknown (	CRC/Align	173	1 s	1:45:23 PM	27 s
12	0000C0E1B1F9	00E0291A6FED	ncp	Rply Unknown (	CRC/Align	465	1 s	1:45:24 PM	28 s
13	0000C0E1B1F9	00E0291A6FED	ncp	Rply Unknown (	CRC/Align	236	990 ms	1:45:25 PM	29 s
14	0000C0E1B1F9	00E0290EE2AF	ncp	Rply Unknown (	CRC/Align	284	2 s	1:45:27 PM	32 s
15	0000C0E1B1F9	00E0290EE2AF	ncp	Rply Unknown (	CRC/Align	372	3 s	1:45:30 PM	35 s
16	0000C0E1B1F9	00E0290EE2AF	ncp	Rply Unknown (	CRC/Align	308	6 s	1:45:37 PM	41 s
17	0000C0E1B1F9	00E0290EE2AF	ncp	Rply Unknown (	CRC/Align	479	2 s	1:45:39 PM	43 s
18	0000C0E1B1F9	080009F988B0	ipx	Packet sliced	Fragment	35	7 s	1:45:46 PM	50 s
19	0000C0E1B1F9	080009F988B0	ipx	Packet sliced	Fragment	50	6 s	1:45:52 PM	56 s
20	0000C0E1B1F9	00E0290EE2AF	ncp	Rply Unknown (	CRC/Align	358	2 s	1:45:54 PM	58 s
21	0000C0E1B1F9	00E0290EE2AF	ncp	Rply Unknown (	CRC/Align	387	12 s	1:46:06 PM	70 s
22	0000C0E1B1F9	00E0290EE2AF	ncp	Rply Unknown (	CRC/Align	525	6 s	1:46:11 PM	76 s
23	0000C0E1B1F9	00E0290EE2AF	ncp	Rply Unknown (	CRC/Align	266	1 s	1:46:12 PM	77 s
24	0000C0E1B1F9	00E0290EE2AF	ncp	Rply Unknown (	CRC/Align	263	3 s	1:46:15 PM	79 s
25	0000C0E1B1F9	00E0290EE2AF	ncp	Rply Unknown (	CRC/Align	563	11 s	1:46:26 PM	91 s
26	0000C0E1B1F9	00E0290EE2AF	ncp	Rply Unknown (	CRC/Align	113	1 s	1:46:28 PM	92 s
27	0000C0E1B1F9	00E0290EE2AF	ncp	Rply Unknown (	CRC/Align	466	1 s	1:46:29 PM	93 s
28	0000C0E1B1F9	00E0290EE2AF	ncp	Rply Unknown (	CRC/Align	145	9 s	1:46:37 PM	102 s
29	0000C0E1B1F9	00E0290EE2AF	ipx	Packet sliced	Fragment	36	3 s	1:46:41 PM	105 s
30	0000C0E1B1F9	0060B043EA8C	ipx	Packet sliced	Fragment	35	4 s	1:46:45 PM	109 s
31	0000C0E1B1F9	0060B043EA8C	ipx	Packet sliced	Fragment	37	170 s	1:49:35 PM	279 s
32	0000C0E1B1F9	00E0290EE2AF	ncp	Rply Unknown (	CRC/Align	282	8 s	1:49:43 PM	287 s
33	0000C0E1B1F9	00AA00163F84	ncp	Rply Unknown (	CRC/Align	68	35 s	1:50:18 PM	322 s
34	0000C0E1B1F9	00E0290EE2AF	ncp	Rply Unknown (	CRC/Align	65	1 s	1:50:20 PM	324 s

Packet: 1   Unfiltered: 102

7. This time, we see most of the fragments disappear, but still an abnormal amount of CRC/Alignment errors, as depicted in the Error column of the trace. Studying the Source Address field, we see that every bad packet source is FS2. As you learned in this chapter, CRC errors are usually cabling problems. Twisted-pair cabling has only two nodes per section (the

switch/hub port and the device). Quite a few stations are involved in this trace. Does it seem logical that FS2 or every other device must be bad?

8. A cable tester is used to verify the cable that FS2 is using. The cable is tested from the switch to the wallplate. Everything is fine, and the cable to the wallplate is well within spec. The only other cable to test is the patch cable that goes from the wall to FS2. This cable fails the test!

The Solution

After failing the patch cable test, a technician is dispatched and replaces the cable that runs from 00C0E1B1F9 (FS2) to the wall. The customer takes a new trace, and all errors are gone.

► · ◄

Summary

This chapter explored the common problems associated with different network topologies. Ethernet and Token Ring structure, cable requirements, and specifications were discussed. Additionally, the media access methods and differences in communication between Ethernet and Token Ring were examined, and common problems were defined.

Analyzing and Troubleshooting the Internet Layer

The Internet Protocol (IP)

The Internet Protocol (IP) is the workhorse of the TCP/IP protocol suite. No matter what upper-layer protocol or application wants to send data, that data will be transported as an IP datagram.

This chapter explains how IP works. It discusses packet structure, addressing rules, subnetting, and the routing process. It also reviews the fragmentation process in detail. After you learn how things should work, you'll be presented some sample traces and shown how to identify IP-related problems.

At the end of the chapter, a troubleshooting decision tree is provided that helps you to ask the right questions when you encounter communication problems.

X-REF

> **This chapter covers IP version 4. For information on IP version 6 (also called IPng), refer to Chapter 20.**

Overview of IP Functionality

IP is a connectionless protocol, primarily responsible for addressing and routing packets between hosts and networks by using the shortest path. It is defined in RFC 791.

Connectionless means that a session is not established before exchanging data. Each packet is treated independently. A sequence of packets sent from one host to another may travel over different paths.

IP is unreliable. Delivery is not guaranteed. It always makes a *best effort* attempt to deliver a packet. Along the way, a packet may be lost, delivered out of sequence, duplicated, or delayed. Reliability is the responsibility of a higher-layer protocol or of the application. For example, if the router's buffer is full, it discards incoming packets by setting the Time To Live (TTL) field to zero. No retransmission or recovery option exists. The only reaction is an ICMP Source Quench message to the sender. No acknowledgment is given when data is received.

X-REF

> **Refer to Chapter 6 to learn about ICMP (Internet Control Message Protocol).**

IP always looks the same, regardless of what the underlying physical structure is (Token Ring, Ethernet, ATM).

Recall that every piece of TCP or UDP data that is sent over a network goes through the IP layer at both end hosts and at every intermediate router.

NOTE

IP Header Structure

Figure 4.1 shows the format of the IP header. The following paragraphs discuss every field in detail. The default size of an IP header is 20 bytes, unless options are defined. Options can be specified at the end of the header. Check the last field in the detailed header description.

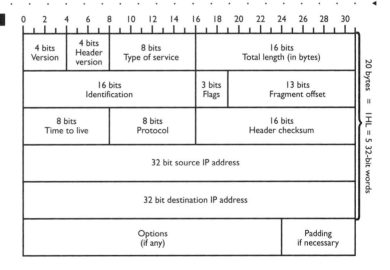

F I G U R E 4.1

Fields in the IP header

The 4 bytes in the 32-bit value are transmitted in the following order: bits 0 – 7; bits 8 – 15; bits 16 – 23; and then bits 24 – 31. This is called *big endian byte ordering* and is required for all binary integers in the TCP/IP headers as they travel through the network. Other formats exist, such as little endian format. Machines that store binary integers in other formats must convert the header values into the network byte order before transmitting the data.

Version

This field has 4 bits and contains the version of IP. The current version is 4.

Header Length

This field has 4 bits and specifies the length of the Internet header. The number in this field denotes the number of 32-bit words in the header, including any options. The default size of an IP header without options is 20 bytes. Therefore, the default value for this field is 5. The header can be extended only in 4-byte increments.

Because this is a 4-bit field, the header length is limited to 60 bytes (15 × 4 bytes).

Type Of Service (TOS)

This 8-bit field specifies reliability, precedence, delay, and throughput parameters for the datagram. It is rarely implemented these days, but may be used in the future. An upper-layer protocol at the sender would have to specify the importance of the datagram. Check RFC 1700 and RFC 2474 for more information. Figure 4.2 shows the details for the TOS fields.

Total Length

This is a 16-bit field that specifies the length of the entire datagram, in bytes (IP header and IP payload). By using this field and the Header Length field, you can determine where the data portion of the IP datagram starts and what its length is. Because this is a 16-bit field, the maximum size of an IP datagram is 65,535 bytes.

This field is required in the IP header, because some data links (such as Ethernet) pad small frames to be a minimum length. The minimum Ethernet frame size is 46 bytes (data size excluding header). An IP datagram can be smaller. If the Total Length field wasn't provided, IP wouldn't know how much of a 46-byte Ethernet frame was really an IP datagram.

F I G U R E 4.2

The details of the TOS field

0	1	2	3	4	5	6	7
Precedence			D	T	R	C	res.

Precedence usually set to 000 which means "Routine"	Bit 3 Delay 0=Normal delay 1=Low delay
	Bit 4 Throughput 0=Normal throughput 1=High throughput
	Bit 5 Reliability 0=Normal reliability 1=High reliability
	Bit 6 Cost
	Bit 7 Reserved

Other settings:

111	Network control
110	Internetwork control
101	CRITIC/ECP
100	Flash override
011	Flash
010	Immediate
001	Priority
000	Routine

Identification

This is a 16-bit field that is used to identify a datagram uniquely. If an IP datagram is too big for the underlying physical structure, IP can fragment the datagram into smaller packets. The Identification number usually increments by one, or some consistent value. All packets belonging to one datagram have the same original identification, which is used to reassemble the fragments at the receiving host. (Fragmentation is explained in detail later in this chapter, during which discussion this field is referenced.)

RFC 791 says that this field should be chosen by the upper layer that is using IP to send the datagram. Therefore, two consecutive datagrams, one sent by TCP and one sent by UDP, can have the same Identification field. The reassembly algorithm can handle this.

Use the Identification field when setting a filter in your analyzer, to capture all the fragments that belong to the same datagram.

TIP

Flags

The Flags field has 3 bits and is used for fragmentation and reassembly of datagrams. It is explained in great detail later in this chapter. The settings are the following:

Bit 0   Reserved, must be zero

Bit 1   0=May Fragment, 1=Don't Fragment

Bit 2   0=Last Fragment, 1=More Fragments

Fragment Offset

This 13-bit field indicates the position of the fragment's data relative to the beginning of the data in the original datagram. This field is used to put the packet back together at the receiving host. The fragment offset is 0×0 if a datagram is unfragmented or if it is the first fragment.

Time To Live (TTL)

This 8-bit field sets an upper limit to the number of routers through which a datagram can pass. The time is measured in units of seconds. Thus, the maximum time to live is 255 seconds (4.25 minutes). The TTL field limits the lifetime of the datagram. It is initialized by the sending host and is decremented by one by every router that handles the datagram. The router also decrements the field by one for every second that the packet stays in its buffer. Some routers permit you to decrement by a value greater than one. The counter is decremented the moment the packet enters the router. When this field reaches 0, the datagram is discarded and the sender is notified with an ICMP message (Time exceeded).

This field can be configured to reduce loop conditions. If, for example, the maximum hop count is 10 in your network, it can be set to 10 initially. The initial value of the TTL field depends on the TCP/IP stack that you are using. Some default values for this field are as follows:

UNIX   30

Windows 95, NT 3.51   32

Windows NT 4.0   128

This field is used by the traceroute utility to determine the route that a packet takes through a network.

Refer to Chapter 6 for details on ICMP and to learn how ping and traceroute work.

X-REF

Protocol

This 8-bit field identifies the Upper Layer Protocol (ULP), which should receive the data portion of the datagram:

1	ICMP
6	TCP
17	UDP
88	IGRP
89	OSPF

For a detailed explanation of all the protocol codes, check the Assigned Numbers document, RFC 1700.

Header Checksum

This field has 16 bits. The header checksum is calculated over the IP header only. TCP, UDP, ICMP, and IGMP (Internet Group Management Protocol) all have their own checksum in their headers to cover their header and data.

When a host discovers a checksum error, it discards the datagram without notifying the sender. Because every router modifies the IP header (TTL), the IP header checksum is recalculated at each hop in its journey from source to destination. If the router corrupts data in the packet before calculating a new checksum, this corruption goes undetected if another checksum doesn't exist on a higher layer.

Source IP Address

This field has 32 bits and contains the address of the sending host. The Source IP Address field remains the same, no matter how many routers the datagram has to cross on its way to the destination. It contains the hexadecimal representation of the more familiar dotted decimal IP address.

Destination IP Address

This field has 32 bits and contains the address of the receiving host or group of hosts. As with the Source IP Address field, this field never changes, no matter what path the datagram takes through the network. It contains the hexadecimal representation of the more familiar dotted decimal IP address.

Options

This is the first field beyond the default header size of 20 bytes. In the detail window in Figure 4.3, the analyzer shows *no options* after the destination IP address. This field has a variable length and the maximum is 40 bytes. The IP header can be extended only in 4-byte increments. If the options are smaller, the field is padded with zeros, up to 4 bytes. These options are rarely used and are not always supported.

The options currently defined are the following:

‣ Security and handling restrictions (RFC 1108)

‣ Record route (see ping options)

‣ Timestamp (see ping options)

‣ Loose source routing (specify a list of IP addresses that must be traversed by the datagram)

‣ Strict source routing (only the addresses in the list can be traversed)

Figure 4.3 shows how the IP header looks in a protocol decode.

Look at the highlighted first 4 bits of the header, which indicate that the IP Version is 4 and the header has the default Length of 20 bytes. The 20 bytes would be expressed by 5 (five 32-bit words). The lower portion of the screen shows the hexadecimal decode of that field. The field that is highlighted in the upper-right part is also highlighted in the hexadecimal window. The value is 45 for the first byte. So, if you don't trust your analyzer's decode, you can look at the hexadecimal window to figure out how the information looks and whether your analyzer properly translates it.

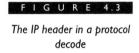

FIGURE 4.3

The IP header in a protocol decode

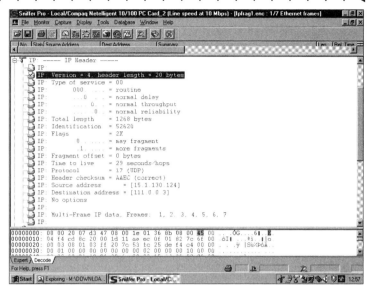

The next fields in the detail window are the *TOS bits interpreted*, the *Total Length* field, and the *Identification number*. The *Flags* field indicates that more fragments belonging to that transfer will follow. The value of 0 in the *Fragment Offset* field indicates that this is the first packet. Every following packet will have a different offset. By using that field, the IP layer at the receiving host will be able to pass the packets up in the correct order.

The next two fields are the TTL and Protocol fields. The value for UDP is 17. You don't have to remember all of those codes, because the analyzer performs a translation for you.

The next fields are the *Header Checksum*, *Source and Destination Addresses*, and *Options* fields.

IP Addressing Basic Rules

A unique IP address is required for all hosts and network components that communicate using TCP/IP. This chapter describes the addressing rules for IPv4.

IPv6 addressing rules are discussed in Chapter 20.

X-REF

Network ID and Host ID

The IP address identifies a host's location on the network, the same way that a street address identifies a house on a street. An IP address must be globally unique and have a uniform format.

Each IP address has two parts: the network ID and the host ID. All systems on the same segment must have the same network ID, which must be unique to the internetwork. The host ID identifies a workstation, a router, a server, or other TCP/IP host within a segment. The host ID must be unique to the network ID.

Each IP address is 32-bits long and is composed of four 8-bit fields, also called *octets*. Octets are separated by periods. The octet represents a decimal number in the range 0 to 255. This is called *dotted decimal notation*. Figure 4.4 illustrates the relation between the host ID and network ID.

FIGURE 4.4

The relation between host ID and network ID

Host

Host address   1 45 . 1 . 0 . 20

Network ID   Host ID

Host ID must be unique within network 145.1

Network ID must be unique to the internetwork

Network 145.1.0.0

The discussion thus far on IP addressing is about how things were defined in 1981 in RFC 791. The significance of an IPv4 32-bit address has changed substantially due to the exponential growth of the Internet. The rule that an Internet address has to be globally unique is not exactly true anymore. The widespread use of NAT (Network Address Translation), for instance, has changed IP addressing rules.

NOTE

The basic concepts are explained here as a starting point. If you want to delve into this topic a little more, read RFC 2101, which is a memo on current IPv4 address behavior.

Back to the basics. Each bit in an octet has an assigned decimal value. The low-order bit has a decimal value of 1. The high-order bit has a decimal value of 128. Therefore, if all bits are set to 1, the highest possible decimal value is 255.

Table 4.1 explains how to convert binary numbers to decimal numbers.

TABLE 4.1	BINARY CODE	BIT VALUES	DECIMAL VALUE
Binary-to-Decimal Conversion Table	0000 0000	0	0
	0000 0001	1	1
	0000 0011	2+1	3
	0000 0111	4+2+1	7
	0000 1111	8+4+2+1	15
	0001 1111	16+8+4+2+1	31
	0011 1111	32+16+8+4+2+1	63
	0111 1111	64+32+16+8+4+2+1	127
	1111 1111	128+64+32+16+8+4+2+1	255

TIP

Appendix A contains a binary-decimal-hex conversion chart. You can also use the Calculator in the Windows 95/NT Accessories group. Enable scientific mode to do the conversion.

The fact that the Internet address contains the network information has some drawbacks:

▶ If a host moves from one network to another, its address must change.

▶ If a network outgrows the number of possible hosts, the whole addressing scheme must be changed.

▶ Multihomed hosts (hosts with more than one network interface) can be reached by different addresses. The destination address used defines which interface will receive the datagram.

> ▸ If one of the network interfaces fails on a multihomed host, an application using that IP address as destination address cannot reach the host, although it is up and running.

Address Classes

The Internet community has defined five IP address classes to accommodate networks of different sizes.

The address class tells us which bits are used for the network ID and for the host ID. It also defines the maximum possible number of networks and the maximum number of hosts per network. Figure 4.5 gives an overview of the address classes.

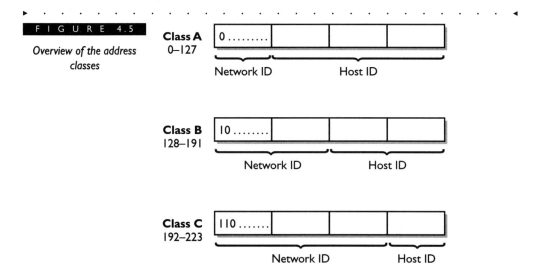

Class A
0–127

Network ID   Host ID

Class B
128–191

Network ID   Host ID

Class C
192–223

Network ID   Host ID

To explain the network ID and host ID concept, the figure shows only Classes A to C. Classes D and E are a little different, as you'll learn in the following descriptions of the address classes:

> ▸ **Class A addresses:** Designed for very large networks with many hosts. They are identified by bit 0 = 0. The range is 1.0.0.0 to 127.255.255.255. Bits 1 through 7 identify the network ID, and the remaining 24 bits represent the host ID. With a 7-bit network ID only 128 Class A network addresses are available. Of these, 0 and 127 are reserved. This allows for

126 Class A networks with each having approximately 16 million hosts. All the Class A addresses are assigned, as shown in Figure 4.6.

FIGURE 4.6

Format of a Class A address

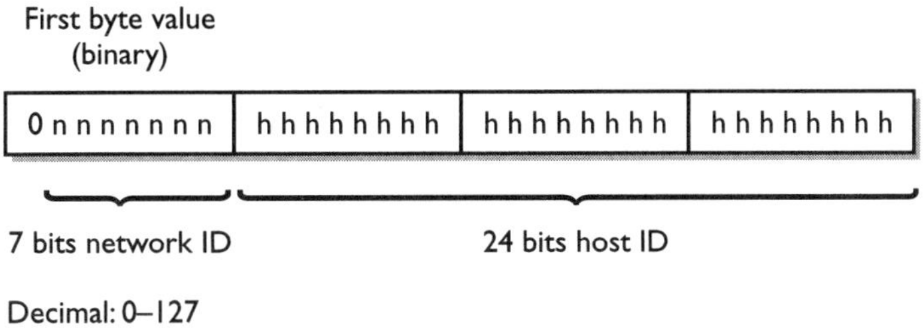

First byte value (binary)

| 0 n n n n n n n | h h h h h h h h | h h h h h h h h | h h h h h h h h |

7 bits network ID   24 bits host ID

Decimal: 0–127

▶ **Class B addresses:** Assigned to medium- to large-sized networks (see Figure 4.7). They are identified by bits 0 and 1 having a value of 10 (binary). The range is 128.0.0.0 to 191.255.255.255. Bits 2 through 15 identify the network ID, and the remaining 16 bits represent the host ID. This allows for 16,384 networks, of which 2 are reserved (all 0 and all 1), and approximately 65,000 hosts per network.

FIGURE 4.7

Format of a Class B address

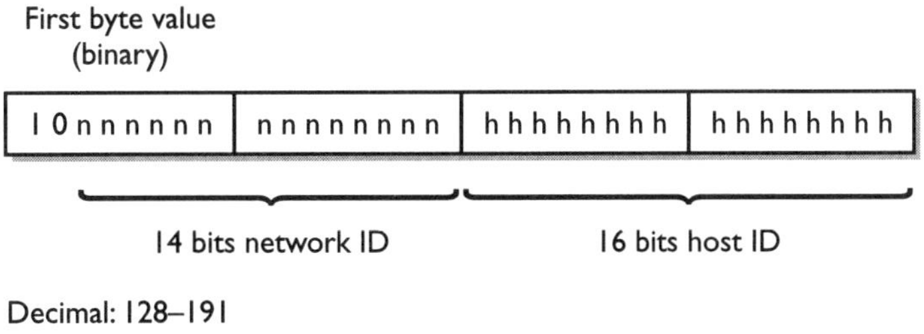

First byte value (binary)

| 1 0 n n n n n n | n n n n n n n n | h h h h h h h h | h h h h h h h h |

14 bits network ID   16 bits host ID

Decimal: 128–191

▶ **Class C addresses:** Used for small LANs (see Figure 4.8). They are identified by bits 0 to 2 having a value of 110 (binary). The range is 192.0.0.0 to 223.255.255.255. Bits 3 through 23 identify the network ID, and the remaining 8 bits represent the host ID. This allows for approximately 2 million networks and 256 hosts per network. (0 and 255 can't be used as host IDs, so the number is 254 hosts per network.)

FIGURE 4.8

Format of a Class C address

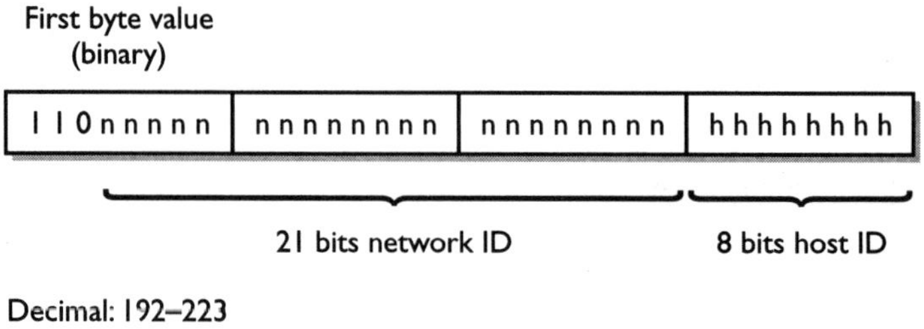

First byte value (binary)

| I I 0 n n n n n | n n n n n n n n | n n n n n n n n | h h h h h h h h |

21 bits network ID   8 bits host ID

Decimal: 192–223

▶ **Class D addresses:** Used for multicast group usage (see Figure 4.9). They are identified by bits 0 to 3 having a value of 1110 (binary). The range is 224.0.0.0 to 239.255.255.255. The remaining 28 bits designate the specific group in which the host participates. No network or host bits are in the multicast group operations. Packets are passed to a selected subset of hosts on a network. Only hosts registered for the multicast address accept the packet. ICMP Router Discovery, OSPF (Open Shortest Path First) and SLP (Service Location) are examples of protocols that use multicast packets.

FIGURE 4.9

Format of a Class D address

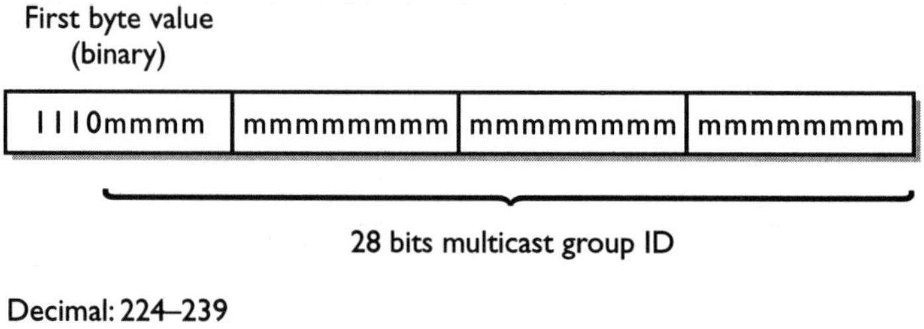

First byte value (binary)

| I I I 0 m m m m | m m m m m m m m | m m m m m m m m | m m m m m m m m |

28 bits multicast group ID

Decimal: 224–239

▶ **Class E addresses:** An experimental class, not available for general use and reserved for future use. Bits 0 to 4 are set to 11110 (binary). The range is 240.0.0.0 to 247.255.255.255. The format of a Class E address is shown in Figure 4.10.

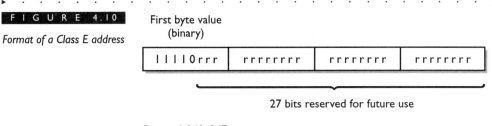

FIGURE 4.10

Format of a Class E address

First byte value (binary)

| 1 1 1 1 0 r r r | r r r r r r r r | r r r r r r r r | r r r r r r r r |

27 bits reserved for future use

Decimal: 240–247

Addressing Guidelines

This is a summary of the most important guidelines, as described in RFC 1700, the Assigned Numbers document.

▸ Network ID can't be 127. This ID is reserved for loopback functions. When this address is used as a destination, no traffic is sent across the network. It should never appear on the network or in a routing table. Essentially, it is used to test the TCP/IP protocol stack internally.

▸ Network ID and host ID can't be 255 (all bits set to 1). 255 is the broadcast address. (But, see the accompanying note for the exception.)

▸ Network ID and host ID can't be 0 (all bits set to 0).

▸ Host ID must be unique to the network.

NOTE

UNIX implementations based on UNIX BSD 4.2 and earlier use 0 as the broadcast address. This was before the broadcast address was defined as 255 in the RFC. Those broadcasts are ignored by other hosts. Also, the BSD 4.2 hosts ignore broadcasts to 255.

The Internet Assigned Numbers Authority (IANA) has reserved the following three blocks of the IP address space for private networks. Check RFC 1918 for details.

▸ 10.0.0.0 through 10.255.255.255

▸ 172.16.0.0 through 172.31.255.255

▸ 192.168.0.0 through 192.168.255.255

The first block is a single Class A network number. The second block is a set of 16 contiguous Class B network numbers. The third block is a set of 256 contiguous Class C network numbers.

An enterprise that decides to use IP addresses out of this private space can do so without any coordination with IANA or an Internet registry. The address space can thus be used by many enterprises. Addresses within this private address space are unique only within the enterprise. Routers should not route these addresses. (See the accompanying note.)

If two companies using the same private address space want to merge their networks, at least one of them has to change its addressing scheme.

NOTE

Routers in networks not using private address space, especially those of Internet service providers, are expected to be configured to reject (filter out) routing information about private networks. If such a router receives such information, the rejection shall not be treated as a routing protocol error (RFC 1918).

Subnetting

Figure 4.4, earlier in the chapter, showed the relation between network ID and host ID. To interpret an IP address exactly, you need to know which part of the address designates the network and which part designates the host, which is the role of the *subnet mask*. It masks a portion of the IP address to distinguish the network ID from the host ID. IP uses the mask to determine whether a host is located on the local network or on a remote network.

Subnet Masks

A *default* subnet mask based on the address class is used on networks that are not divided into subnets (sometimes referred to as a *natural mask*). All TCP/IP hosts require not only a unique address but also a subnet mask, even on a single-segment network.

Table 4.2 shows the subnet masks for the default subnets.

T A B L E   4.2

Bits Used for the Subnet Mask

ADDRESS CLASS	BITS USED FOR SUBNET MASK	DOTTED DECIMAL NOTATION
Class A	11111111 00000000 00000000 00000000	255.0.0.0
Class B	11111111 11111111 00000000 00000000	255.255.0.0
Class C	11111111 11111111 11111111 00000000	255.255.255.0

All bits in the subnet mask that are set to 1 indicate that this bit is used for the network portion of the address. All bits that are part of the host ID are set to 0 in the subnet mask. The following is an example for a Class C address:

IP address   192.137.250.200

Subnet mask 255.255.255.0

If you check the binary representation of the preceding subnet mask, you find that all bits are set to 1 in the first three octets. This indicates that the first three octets are the network ID of this address. So, you know that the following is true:

Network ID   192.137.250.z

Host ID   w.x.y.200

You may want to divide your network into multiple subnets. This can be done by taking bits away from the host ID and using them for the network ID.

The following is an example for a Class C address. Suppose that you need 6 subnets and you know that none of the subnets will have more than 30 hosts. Table 4.4 (which appears later in this chapter) shows that using 3 additional bits for the subnet mask supports 6 subnets and 30 hosts per subnet. The following is a detailed explanation for the preceding example Class C IP address:

IP address   192.137.250.200

Binary   **1100 0000.1000 1001.1111 1010.110**0 1000

Class C mask   1111 1111.1111 1111.1111 1111.0000 0000   255.255.255.0

Subnet mask   **1111 1111.1111 1111.1111 1111.1110** 0000   255.255.255.224

The subnet mask specifies that the first 27 bits of the IP address define the network ID. The subnet mask takes 3 bits away from the default host ID part for a Class C address and uses them for the network ID portion of the address. To clarify this, the bits appear in bold that belong to the network portion according to the subnet mask in the binary representation of the IP address. You now know that the network ID is 192.127.250.192 and the host ID is w.x.y.8.

With 3 bits for the subnet mask, you have eight possibilities for setting the network ID. Table 4.3 shows all available options.

T A B L E 4.3	BINARY	DECIMAL	BIT VALUES
The 8 Subnets with 3 Subnet Mask Bits	000x xxxx	0	0+0+0
	001x xxxx	32	0+0+32
	010x xxxx	64	0+64+0
	011x xxxx	96	0+64+32
	100x xxxx	128	128+0+0
	101x xxxx	160	128+0+32
	110x xxxx	192	128+64+0
	111x xxxx	224	128+64+32

The use of all binary zeros or all binary ones in the subnet and node parts of the address should be avoided, according to RFCs 791 and 950. The current standards-based practice allows all zeros and all ones for the subnet (RFC 1878). We currently don't recommend that you use it. It works only if all of your routers support this configuration. According to the safe old rule, subnet 0 and subnet 224 are not possible. You can have 6 subnets with 3 bits in the mask with the numbers 32, 64, 96, 127, 160, and 192.

Formulas for Calculating Subnets and Hosts

The formula for calculating the number of possible subnets is 2^x, where x is the number of masked bits taken from the host ID part of the address and used for the subnet mask. Note that this formula includes using all zeros and all ones for the subnet. This can be done according to RFC 1878. Newer implementations allow you to configure this. Be careful when using this method, because it works only if all routers in the network support this configuration. Test it thoroughly before using it.

The formula for calculating the number of possible hosts is 2^x-2, where x is the number of the remaining unmasked bits that can be used for the host part of the address. Remember that all zeros and all ones for the host ID aren't allowed. That rule is included in the preceding formula.

Table 4.4 lists the number of possible subnets and nodes per subnet, depending on how many bits are used for the subnet mask. The number-of-nodes calculation is based on the assumption that this is a subnetted Class C address.

TABLE 4.4

Subnet Mask Table

NO. OF SUBNET BITS	BINARY	DECIMAL	NO. OF POSSIBLE SUBNETS	NO. OF NODES PER SUBNET
1	1000 0000	128	0	126
2	1100 0000	192	2	62
3	1110 0000	224	6	30
4	1111 0000	240	14	14
5	1111 1000	248	30	6
6	1111 1100	252	62	2
7	1111 1110	254	126	0
8	1111 1111	255	254	0

Note in this table that a subnet mask with only 1 bit isn't possible. If you apply the old rule that the subnet address shouldn't consist of all zeros or all ones, it leaves no subnets for that example. (For consistency, this line is shown in the binary representation.)

Also, if you take 7 or 8 bits from a Class C address, it leaves no hosts. So, you can't use this subnet mask. (Again, for consistency, these lines in Table 4.4 are shown in the binary representation.)

RFC 1878, "Variable Length Subnet Table For IPv4," is a nice source of information for subnetting. It gives you a list of all possible subnets for Class A, B, and C networks. It provides network IDs, host ranges, and IP broadcast addresses. It considers subnet with all zeros and all ones as valid.

A subnet mask calculator is also available on the Web. You can find it at http://www.telusplanet.net/public/sparkman/netcalc.htm. **Another cool utility is the IP Subnet Calculator by the Net3 Group, which you can find at** http://www.net3group.com. **The Net3 Group has a lot of interesting things on its page, including ProConvert, a tool that you can use to convert trace files from one analyzer format to another.**

The Importance of Configuring the Subnet Mask

Every host in a TCP/IP network needs to be configured with the following information:

▸ An IP address

▸ The subnet mask

▸ The address of a default gateway that is in the same network

Many problems arise because subnet masks haven't been defined properly. In Figure 4.11, Host A wants to communicate with Host B. Host A compares Host B's address with its own subnet mask and finds that B isn't on the same network. Now, Host A addresses the frame to the MAC address of the router's interface and puts B's IP address in the IP header of the datagram.

▶ . . . . ◀

F I G U R E   4.11

Host A

The subnet mask being used to determine whether a host is on the local or on a remote network

IP address   132.10.1.55
Subnet mask 255.255.255.0

Subnet 132.10.1.0

Port 1

Port 2

Router

Subnet 132.10.2.0

IP address   132.10.2.7
Subnet mask 255.255.255.0

Host B

If the subnet mask was configured to be 255.255.0.0, Host A would have determined that Host B is on the same network and thus would have tried to send the datagram to the MAC address of Host B, by ARPing for B's MAC address. ARP (Address Resolution Protocol) broadcasts don't cross routers and, therefore, Host A would be unable to determine B's MAC address.

The same thing happens at the router: Upon receiving the packet from Host A, the router strips off the MAC header, examines the IP destination address, compares it against its subnet mask, and determines that the destination network is 132.10.2.0. Next, the router checks its port 2 ARP table and tries to find the MAC address for Host B. If the entry isn't in the router's ARP table, it sends an ARP request. (ARP is discussed in Chapter 5.)

TIP

For troubleshooting with your analyzer: If you work in a subnetted environment, make sure that you have properly configured your analyzer with the subnet masks that you use. Otherwise, it will use the default Class A, B, and C network masks or whatever the analyzer manufacturer deemed appropriate.

. . . . .

Unicast, Multicast, and Broadcast

The bulk of today's network traffic is *unicast,* which means that a separate copy of the data is sent to every host that needs it. When data is *broadcast*, a single copy of the data is sent to all hosts on the network. If data needs to be sent to only some of the hosts in a network, both methods waste bandwidth. Unicast wastes bandwidth by sending a separate copy to every host. Broadcast wastes bandwidth by sending the data to all the hosts on the network, whether they want it or not. Broadcasting also slows the performance of the hosts. Each host has to process the broadcast packet, regardless of whether it is of interest. *Multicasting* takes the strengths of both approaches and avoids their weaknesses. It sends a single copy of the data to all the hosts that need it.

Broadcasting and multicasting always use UDP, because they send messages to multiple recipients. TCP is connection-oriented and implies a connection between two hosts.

Refer to Chapter 9 for information on UDP; refer to Chapter 10 for information on TCP.

X-REF

To understand broadcasting and multicasting, you need to understand the filtering that takes place on each host each time that a frame passes by on the cable. The network interface card (NIC) sees every frame on the cable and makes a decision regarding whether to receive the frame and deliver it to the device driver. Usually, the NIC receives only those frames that have the destination address of either the interface's hardware address or the broadcast address. A *promiscuous mode card* would receive a copy of every frame.

This difference explains why you need a card and a driver that support promiscuous mode for capturing packets with a network analyzer. Only promiscuous mode cards and drivers capture all the packets on the wire.

NOTE

The NIC receives the frame. If the MAC checksum is correct, the NIC passes the frame to the device driver, which checks whether the frame specifies a protocol that is supported (IP, ARP). Additional multicast filtering may be performed if a multicast group is used in the destination address. If the frame type specifies an IP datagram, it is passed up to IP. IP performs filtering based on the source and destination address and passes the datagram to the next layer (TCP or UDP).

Each time that UDP or TCP receives a datagram from IP, it performs filtering based on the port number. If the destination port number currently isn't used, the datagram is discarded and an ICMP Port Unreachable message is sent out (see Figure 4.12).

FIGURE 4.12

Filtering process at the different layers when a host sees a frame on the cable

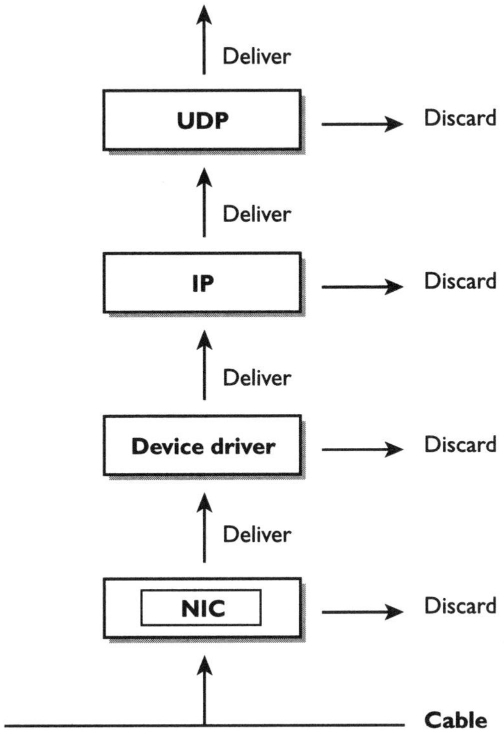

This figure shows the unnecessary processing load that broadcasts can put on hosts. Consider an application that uses UDP broadcast. Only 10 out of 30 hosts in a subnet use the application. All of the 20 hosts that don't use the application have to process the datagram up to the UDP layer before they can discard it.

Broadcasts

Different forms of broadcasts include the following types.

Limited Broadcast

The address is 255.255.255.255 and can be used as the destination address of an IP datagram during the host configuration process, when the host doesn't know its IP address or subnet mask. A Limited Broadcast frame is never forwarded by any router, it appears only on the local cable.

Directed Broadcast

The directed broadcast address has all host ID bits set to 1. A router must forward a Directed Broadcast by default, but should also have an option to disable this. The format of a Directed Broadcast for a Class B address looks like this:

n.n.255.255   (n for network ID)

Subnet Broadcast

The subnet broadcast address has the host ID set to all 1s, but has a specific subnet ID. It can be determined only if the destination's subnet mask is known. The following are three examples:

ADDRESS	SUBNET MASK	BROADCAST?
131.1.2.255	255.255.255.0	This is a broadcast
131.1.3.255	255.255.240.0	This is NOT a broadcast
131.1.15.255	255.255.240.0	This is a broadcast

In the first example, with the subnet mask of 255.255.255.0, all the host ID bits (the last byte) are set to 1 in the binary representation of 131.1.2.255. Therefore, this is a broadcast.

In the second example, with the subnet mask set to 255.255.240.0, the leftmost 4 bits of the third byte are used for the mask. If you look at the binary representation of 131.1.3.255, you'll find that the first 2 bits of the host ID part are set to 0. Thus, this is *not* a broadcast.

In the third example, the address 131.1.15.255 is used with the mask 255.255.240.0. Again, the mask indicates that the network portion of the address uses 4 bits of the third byte, leaving 4 bits plus the last byte for the host ID. If you look at the binary representation of 131.1.15.255, you'll find that all the host ID bits are set to 1. Therefore, this is a broadcast.

All-Subnets Broadcast
In this case, not only the host ID but also the subnet ID are set to all 1s. This broadcast will not only go out to a specific subnet, it will be broadcast onto all subnets. For example:

ADDRESS	SUBNET MASK	BROADCAST TYPE
131.1.255.255	255.255.255.0	All-subnets broadcast
131.1.255.255	255.255.0.0	Directed broadcast

If you are unfamiliar with subnet masks, refer to the earlier section on subnetting.

Multicasting
Multicasting is a *push* model. Compare this to the way that your radio works. A sending station uses a certain frequency. If you want to listen to that radio station, you tune your radio to receive that frequency. A similar thing happens with multicasting. If you are interested in receiving certain multicast frames, you configure your NIC to listen to a certain multicast address. The sender of the data doesn't care who is tuned in to receive that information.

A multicast group address is the combination of the high-order bits of 1110 and the multicast group ID. The set of hosts listening to a particular IP multicast address is called a *host group*.

Multicasting is used by OSPF, for instance, to send Hello messages or Link State messages. It is also used with SLP. Have a look at the trace file in Figure 4.13. You can see two frames issued by OSPF router 192.28.101.130. The Hello Message goes to multicast address 224.0.0.5 and the Link State Update goes to multicast address 224.0.0.6. Only hosts that are registered in those multicast groups will process the frame.

F I G U R E 4.13

Multicast frames in a trace file

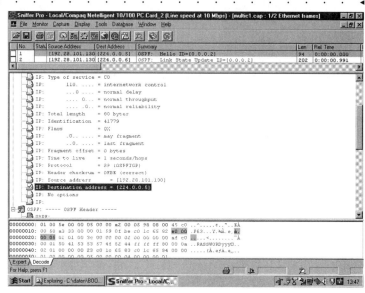

The following are some rules that apply to multicasting:

▸ The host group can span multiple networks if routers support multicasting.

▸ Membership in a host group is dynamic — hosts join and leave the group at will.

▸ There is no restriction on the number of hosts that can join the group.

▸ One host can be a member of multiple groups.

▸ To send a message to a multicast group, the sending host doesn't have to be a member of the multicast group.

IP multicast addresses can be used only as destination addresses. The range is 224.0.0.0 through 239.255.255.255.

NOTE

Some multicast group addresses are assigned as well-known addresses by IANA. They are called *permanent host groups*. These well-known multicast addresses are listed in RFC 1700. Multicasting is defined in RFC 1112. Here are some examples of multicast addresses:

224.0.0.0	Base address (reserved)
224.0.0.1	All hosts on this subnet
224.0.0.2	All routers on this subnet
224.0.0.5	OSPF Hello Message
224.0.0.6	OSPF Link State Update
224.0.0.9	RIP 2 routers
224.0.0.10	IGRP routers

Converting Multicast Group Addresses to Ethernet Addresses

The RFCs define how to map IP multicast addresses to Ethernet multicast addresses: IANA owns an Ethernet address block, which is 00:00:5e (hex). The first byte of an Ethernet multicast address must be 01.

To map an IP multicast address to an Ethernet multicast address, take the low-order 23 bits of the IP multicast address and place them into the low-order 23 bits of the special Ethernet multicast address 01.00.5E.00.00.00. For example:

IP multicast 224.0.0.2 maps to Ethernet multicast 01.00.5E.00.00.02

The upper 5 bits of the multicast group ID are ignored. Therefore, this mapping is not unique. 32 different multicast group IDs map to each Ethernet address. The device driver over the IP module must perform filtering of multicast frames; otherwise, the host will have to receive all multicast frames.

Multicasting on a single network is simple. The process is as follows:

1. The sender specifies a multicast IP address as the destination address.

2. The device driver converts this to a multicast Ethernet address and sends it.

3. The device driver of the receiving host must enable reception of the multicast frame (called *joining a multicast group*).

If a multicast group spans more than one network, the router needs a protocol to determine whether any hosts on a specific physical network belong to the particular multicast group. This protocol is called *IGMP (Internet Group Management Protocol),* which is covered in Chapter 18.

FDDI networks use the same mapping between the Class D address and the 48-bit FDDI address. Token Ring networks normally use a different mapping, due to limitations in most Token Ring controllers.

X-REF

Multicasting will be used increasingly more in the future. IGMP plays an important role for multicast functionality in routed environments. Refer to Chapter 18 to learn about IGMP. Chapter 8 covers OSPF and Chapter 14 covers SLP, two protocols that use multicasting.

Supernetting and CIDR (Classless Interdomain Routing)

Subnetting takes bits away from the host ID portion of the address and uses them for the network portion. With supernetting, you do the opposite. *Supernetting* borrows bits from the network ID and masks them as part of the host ID, for more efficient routing. Here's an example:

- No Class B address is available

- A range of 8 Class C addresses can be allocated

- Each Class C network can allocate 254 hosts, making a total of 2,032 hosts possible

- The network ID is 220.22.168.0 to 220.22.175.0

Without supernetting, the routing table would look like the one in Table 4.5.

T A B L E 4.5	NETWORK ID	SUBNET MASK
Routing Table Without Supernetting	220.22.168.0	255.255.255.0
	220.22.169.0	255.255.255.0
	220.22.170.0	255.255.255.0
	220.22.171.0	255.255.255.0
	220.22.172.0	255.255.255.0
	220.22.173.0	255.255.255.0
	220.22.174.0	255.255.255.0
	220.22.175.0	255.255.255.0

The binary representation of the eight networks looks like this:

167	1010 1000
168	1010 1001
169	1010 1010
170	1010 1011
171	1010 1100
172	1010 1101
173	1010 1110
174	1010 1111

The first 5 bits of the octets are identical; they differ only in the last 3 bits. Therefore, by setting the subnet mask to 255.255.248.0, the routing table has only one entry for all 8 networks. The Binary representation of 248 is **1111 1**000, masking the first 5 bits for the subnet ID. This is why we choose 255.255.248.0 as the subnet mask for these subnets.

Table 4.6 shows the same routing table with supernetting.

T A B L E 4.6	NETWORK ID	SUBNET MASK
The same Routing Table with Supernetting	220.22.168.0	255.255.248.0

The basic concept of CIDR is to consolidate several Class C network addresses into one logical network. This is possible only if the addresses share the same high-order bits. The subnet mask is shortened to take bits away from the network portion of the address and add them to the host portion. CIDR is described in RFC 1518/1519.

The routing protocols being used must be able to carry the 32-bit mask in addition to the 32-bit address. OSPF and RIP 2 are both capable of doing this. RIP 1 does not support subnet mask information. Routing decisions are now based on masking operations of the entire 32-bit address. Whether the address is Class A, B, or C makes no difference.

With CIDR, you can enable route summarization, which makes your routing tables smaller and the performance better. No class distinctions exist any more, and the routing is based on the 32-bit IP address plus a 32-bit mask.

IP on the Router

A *router* is a forwarding device that examines the IP protocol header. It has at least two logical interfaces. It removes the link layer header (also called the MAC header) with which it received the message, modifies the IP header by decrementing the TTL, and then replaces the link layer header for retransmission. A host that acts as a dedicated router may only have the protocols up to the IP layer implemented. No need exists for TCP or UDP on a dedicated router.

NOTE

Originally, the term "gateway" was used to refer to dedicated hosts that route packets. Today, the term "router" is used; "gateway" now refers to an application program that connects two services, such as an "e-mail gateway." Depending on what documentation you are reading, these terms may be used either way.

The Routing Process

When a packet is received at a router, the MAC header is stripped off, the IP address of the next hop is determined, and a new MAC header is applied, with the routers MAC address in the DLC Source field and the next hop's MAC address in the DLC Destination field. Remember, the IP header addressing information never changes. Figure 4.14 illustrates the difference in the MAC header and the information in the IP header of a frame going through a router.

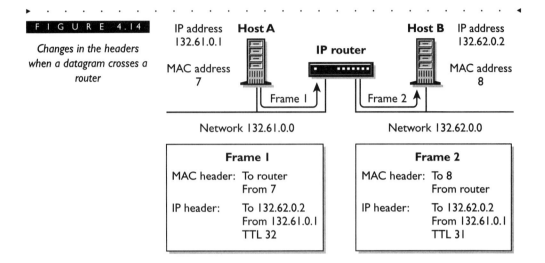

FIGURE 4.14

Changes in the headers when a datagram crosses a router

When the packet comes into the router, here is what happens:

1. The MAC layer checks whether the packet is good (error checking).

2. Is the packet addressed to me or is it a broadcast? If no, discard it; if yes, go to Step 3.

3. Strip off the MAC header.

4. Check TTL counter in the IP header and decrement it by one. Also, decrease TTL by one for every second that the packet stays in the router buffer. If TTL is 0, the packet is discarded and an ICMP "TTL expired" is sent to the source host.

5. Read the IP destination address and perform the routing algorithm (described in more detail later in this chapter).

6. If necessary, the packet is fragmented into smaller packets, to adjust to a smaller packet size of the underlying network. (The fragmentation process is described in detail later in this chapter.)

7. IP calculates a new checksum.

8. A new MAC header is placed on the packet, with the router's MAC address in the Source field.

9. IP forwards the packet.

This entire process is repeated at each router until the packet reaches its destination. At the final destination, the packet is passed to IP, if necessary, reassembled into the original packet, and then passed to the upper-layer protocol specified in the IP header.

Making the Route Decision

Every host in an IP network maintains a routing table. This also applies to clients. When a host needs to send a packet, it looks up its routing table. The routing table is updated by a routing protocol, such as RIP or OSPF. (Routing protocols are covered in detail in Chapter 7 and 8.) The routing table can also be updated by an ICMP redirect message.

The routing decision is based on the destination IP address. Figure 4.15 shows how the IP host examines its routing table.

In step one, after reading the destination IP address, the host has to determine whether this address is its own IP address. A router with multiple interfaces has to compare the address to the addresses of all of its logical interfaces.

If the datagram is not addressed to the router itself, the router looks for the best match in its routing table, according to the steps in Figure 4.15.

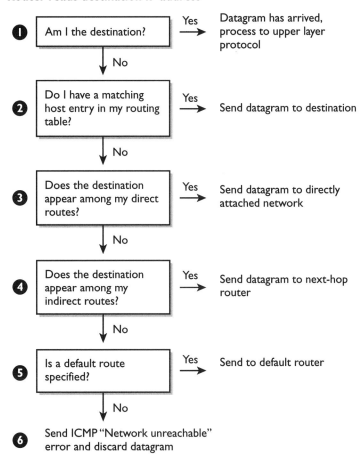

FIGURE 4.15

How the routing algorithm works

Router reads destination IP address

Table 4.7 shows what a routing table looks like. The Protocol column states how the route was learned. How the cost of the route is calculated depends on the routing protocol used.

T A B L E   4.7

Routing Table Entries

DESTINATION ADDRESS	MASK	PROTOCOL	COST	NEXT HOP	INTERFACE
130.1.128.50	255.255.255.255	RIP	2	200.1.1.193	A
160.4.4.50	255.255.255.255	local	0		C
130.1.128.0	255.255.248.0	RIP	2	200.1.1.193	A
130.1.224.0	255.255.248.0	RIP	2	200.1.1.193	A
160.4.1.0	255.255.255.0	RIP	2	160.4.2.20	D
160.4.2.0	255.255.255.0	local	0		D
160.4.4.0	255.255.255.0	local	0		C
200.1.1.192	255.255.255.252	local	0		A
200.1.1.224	255.255.255.252	local	0		B
0.0.0.0	0.0.0.0	static	1	160.4.2.20	D

This router has 4 interfaces:

 ▸ Interface A   200.1.1.194

 ▸ Interface B   200.1.1.226

 ▸ Interface C   160.4.4.40

 ▸ Interface D   160.4.2.40

The routing table is checked for the best match. If a packet comes in that is destined for a host in a directly connected network, the router sends an ARP request for that host's MAC address. If the packet is destined for a remote network, the router sends an ARP request for the next hop router's MAC address. The two entries in the table with the mask 255.255.255.255 are host entries.

According to the Host Requirements RFC, the IP layer must support multiple default routes. Many implementations, however, do not support this.

In the last step of the diagram in Figure 4.15, if the packet cannot be forwarded, an ICMP message is created. This can be a Host Unreachable or Network Unreachable message. Which of these two messages is created depends on the TCP/IP implementation of your host's operating system.

The Use of the TOS Field

The fastest route, the best route, and the shortest route can be three different paths through your network. Today, routers usually make decisions based on the hop count only. More advanced routing protocols, such as OSPF, can use configurable metrics for their routing decisions. The implementation of the TOS fields at the host and router would enable a future router generation to choose the route based on configurations made by an upper-layer protocol or an application. Here is an example:

Telnet	Low delay requested
Transaction Processing Application	High reliability requested
FTP, SNMP, Routing Protocols	High throughput requested
NNTP	Low cost requested

So each of the applications mentioned above would have a different TOS setting. RFC 1700 specifies how these bits should be set by all the standard applications. RFC 2474 contains some corrections to RFC 1700 and a more detailed description of the TOS feature.

Routing Protocols

Routing protocols are needed to maintain routing tables. IP uses the routing table for lookups. Some of the many different routing protocols available are covered in Chapters 7 (RIP), 8 (OSPF), and 18 (IGRP and EIGRP). They are called *dynamic* (or *adaptive*) routing protocols, because they build their tables based on real-time analysis of the network. Conversely, in *static routing*, routes are entered into static tables manually.

Two different types of routing protocols support dynamic routing:

- **Distance vector protocols:** RIP and Cisco's IGRP are examples of distance vector protocols. Routers using these protocols know only about their next hops and learn their information from their neighbors. (Details on distance vector protocols are covered in Chapters 7 and 18.)

▶ **Link state protocols:** OSPF, Novell's NLSP (NetWare Link Services Protocol) and ISO's IS-IS (Integrated Intermediate System to Intermediate System) are examples for link state routing protocols. Every router has a picture of the whole network; therefore, these protocols are less prone to routing loops than are distance vector protocols. But, maintaining the maps takes overhead on the router and creates more traffic on the network. (Learn more about link state protocols in Chapter 8, which discusses OSPF.)

Fragmentation

The physical network layer normally imposes an upper limit on the size of the frame that can be transmitted. For example, the Ethernet maximum transfer unit (MTU) size is 1,518 bytes, whereas Token Ring's MTU is about 4,202 bytes. Whenever IP receives a datagram to route, it determines the interface over which it has to send the datagram (see the routing algorithm, explained earlier in this chapter) and queries that interface for its MTU size. Then, it compares the datagram size with the MTU and, if necessary, performs fragmentation.

The MTU size usually refers to the total size of data plus the header.

NOTE

Fragmentation can take place at either the sending host or any intermediate router. A fragment of a datagram may be fragmented again at a subsequent router. When an IP datagram is fragmented, it isn't reassembled until it reaches its final destination. The IP layer at the receiving host has to perform reassembly of all the fragments. Figure 4.16 shows an example of how a datagram can be fragmented.

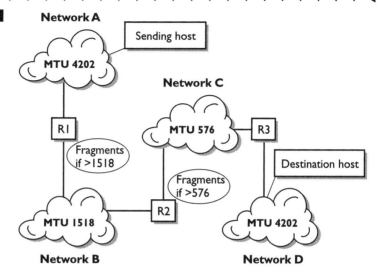

A datagram can be fragmented multiple times on its way through the network, and isn't reassembled until its final destination.

Figure 4.16 shows two hosts communicating. The host in Network A sends information to the host in Network D. Both hosts are on Token Ring networks with an MTU of 4,202 bytes. If the sending host sends a large datagram, router R1 fragments the datagram into fragments of 1,518 bytes and sends them to router R2. Because the interface to Network C has an MTU of 576 bytes, R2 further fragments the fragments to 576 bytes. Now, all of these fragments arrive at router R3, and although its interface connecting to Network D (where the destination host is) has an MTU of 4,202, R3 forwards all of the tiny 576-byte fragments over Network D. They are reassembled only by the destination host.

IMPORTANT

In the example in Figure 4.16, even though two hosts are communicating that both are on 4202 Token Ring networks, because of the network design, they can't use their MTU to talk to each other. This is an important point to watch when designing your network.

The trace file in Figure 4.17 shows a fragmented datagram that has five fragments. The *Identification* field for the datagram is 2052. This number can be found in the summary window and in the IP header of any of the fragments. In the first four fragments, the second Fragment Bit is set to 1, which tells the receiving host that more fragments will follow. Seeing this, the receiving host knows that it shouldn't deliver the datagram yet, but instead should keep the datagram in its buffer until it has received all the fragments. In the last fragment, the bit is set to 0, which indicates that this is the last fragment of the datagram. The receiving host now processes the datagram to the upper-layer protocol that is specified.

FIGURE 4.17

A fragmented datagram

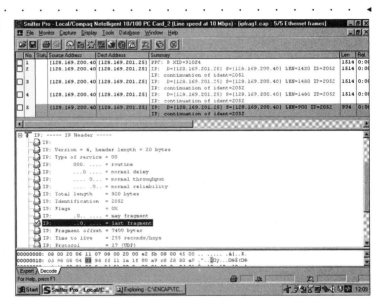

To summarize the fields in the IP header that apply to fragmentation (refer to Figure 4.1 for the fields in the IP header):

▶ **Identification field:** Contains a unique value for the datagram. This number is copied into the header of each fragment. Use this field to set a filter in your analyzer when you want to see all the fragments belonging to a datagram.

▸ **Flags field:** Consists of 3 bits. Bit 0 is not used and must be set to 0. Bit 1 is used to specify if a datagram should not be fragmented. If this bit is set to 1, IP doesn't fragment the datagram. The router discards the packet and should send an ICMP message stating Fragmentation needed but Don't Fragment Bit set. Bit 2 is the More Fragments bit. It is set to 1 in all fragments except the last. A setting of 1 tells the receiving IP stack that more fragments will follow. A setting of 0 means that this is the last fragment.

▸ **Fragment Offset field:** Contains the offset in 8-byte units from the beginning of the original datagram. If this field is 0, you are looking at the first fragment of a datagram. Also, when a datagram is fragmented, the Total Length field of each fragment is changed to the size of that fragment. The Fragment Offset field is used to reassemble the fragments in the correct order.

Each fragment gets its own IP header containing all the information needed. It is now a separate packet that can be routed independently of the other fragments belonging to the datagram. Therefore, the fragments can arrive out of order. The receiving host uses the Fragment Offset field to reassemble the fragments in the correct order. If one of the fragments gets lost, the whole datagram had to be resent. IP cannot ask for a specific fragment to be retransmitted.

NOTE

The IP stack should include a reassembly timer that defines how long IP waits for all the fragments. If that timer expires before all fragments have arrived, eventually, an ICMP message "Reassembly time exceeded" will be created. The configuration of that reassembly timer depends on what IP stack you are using. If that timer isn't configured, the host eventually gets stuck waiting for the last fragment.

Figure 4.18 explains the fragmentation process and the changes in the headers, and shows how a 1,518-byte datagram is fragmented into three packets of 512 bytes and then further fragmented into six packets of 256 bytes. The whole unit of data at the IP layer (before fragmentation) is called a *datagram*. A *packet* is the unit of data between the IP layer and the link layer. A packet can be either a complete IP datagram or only a fragment of an IP datagram.

▶ · ◀

FIGURE 4.18

How the fields in the IP header change when a datagram is fragmented

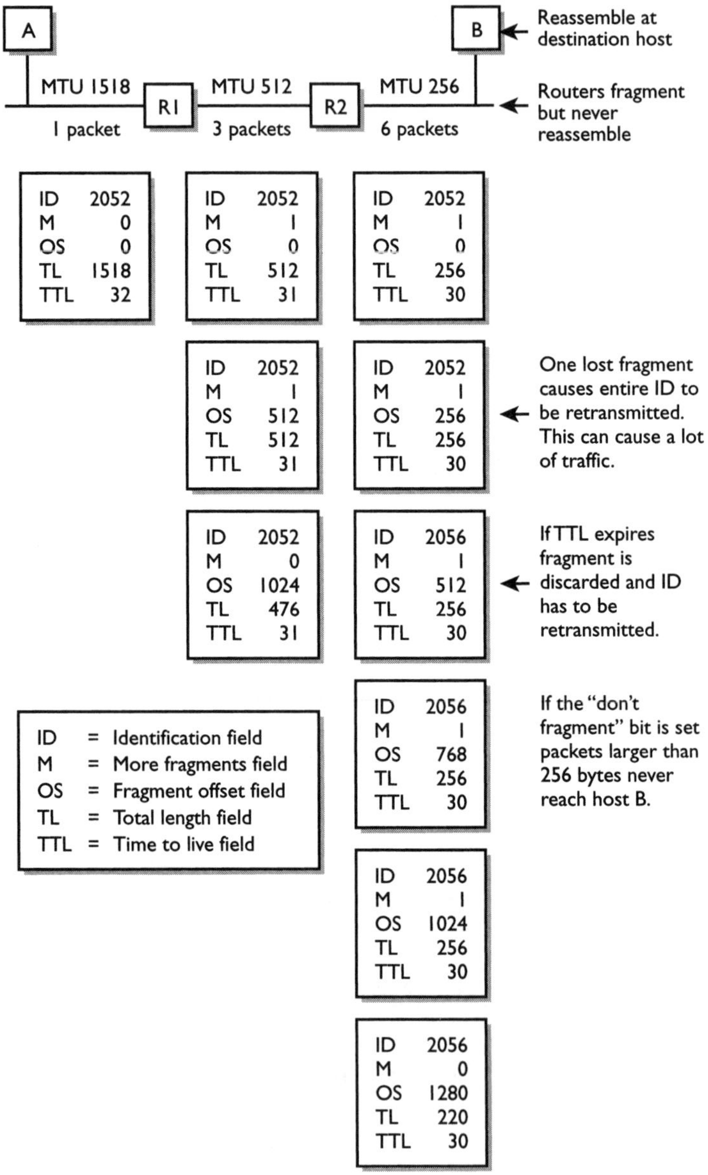

| A | | | | B | Reassemble at destination host |

MTU 1518 — R1 — MTU 512 — R2 — MTU 256 ← Routers fragment but never reassemble

1 packet   3 packets   6 packets

ID	2052
M	0
OS	0
TL	1518
TTL	32

ID	2052
M	1
OS	0
TL	512
TTL	31

ID	2052
M	1
OS	0
TL	256
TTL	30

ID	2052
M	1
OS	512
TL	512
TTL	31

ID	2052
M	1
OS	256
TL	256
TTL	30

← One lost fragment causes entire ID to be retransmitted. This can cause a lot of traffic.

ID	2052
M	0
OS	1024
TL	476
TTL	31

ID	2056
M	1
OS	512
TL	256
TTL	30

← If TTL expires fragment is discarded and ID has to be retransmitted.

ID	= Identification field
M	= More fragments field
OS	= Fragment offset field
TL	= Total length field
TTL	= Time to live field

ID	2056
M	1
OS	768
TL	256
TTL	30

If the "don't fragment" bit is set packets larger than 256 bytes never reach host B.

ID	2056
M	1
OS	1024
TL	256
TTL	30

ID	2056
M	0
OS	1280
TL	220
TTL	30

CHAPTER 4
· · · · ·
THE INTERNET PROTOCOL (IP)

Most of the current TCP/IP stacks support path MTU discovery, with the goal of reducing fragmentation in the internetwork. Path MTU discovery works as follows:

1. IP sends a datagram with the Don't Fragment bit set.

2. The router, which would have to fragment the datagram because the next segment doesn't support the bigger frame size, sends an ICMP message back to the source indicating that it can't forward the packet because fragmentation is needed but the Don't Fragment bit is set.

3. The datagram continues to be resent, with a lower size each time, until no fragmentation is needed and thus no ICMP message is created.

4. The sending host knows what the smallest MTU size on the path is. If the router supports path MTU discovery, it can include the next-hop MTU size in the ICMP header.

Check RFC 1191 if you are interested in more-detailed information.

Troubleshooting IP

This section discusses some common problems that you might find on the IP layer. It also describes the steps to follow to attempt to resolve the problems.

Host or Network Unreachable

Possible causes for the Host Unreachable or Network Unreachable error message include an improperly configured host or host table, improperly configured routing table, or improperly configured or inoperable router on the internetwork.

To identify whether this problem is IP-related or a higher-layer problem, try pinging the host by its IP address. If you can successfully ping the IP address but not the host name, then you may have a name resolution problem. In that case, check the troubleshooting tips in Chapter 12 for DNS and name resolution.

If you can ping successfully, you have verified IP communications between the network interface layer and the Internet layer. Ping uses ARP to resolve the IP address to a hardware address for each echo request and echo reply.

If your problem is on the Internet layer, use ping in the following order:

1. 127.0.0.1 (loopback address)

2. Your own IP address

3. Default gateway IP address

4. Router IP address

5. Remote host IP address

If Steps 1 and/or 2 don't work, something is wrong with your local TCP/IP configuration. You might have entered a wrong TCP/IP address or a wrong subnet mask. If you get your address from a DHCP server, check your DHCP configuration. Make sure that all the settings are correct, reboot, and try again.

If Steps 1 and 2 work, your next step is to check the default gateway IP address. Packets destined for remote networks are sent to the default gateway if no route to the destination network is configured on the local host. If a default gateway is not configured, communication is limited to the local network. Check your local route table and the configuration of your default gateway. Is it up and running? Again, make sure that your local settings or your DHCP server settings are correct and then try again. Consult the paragraph on the routing algorithm earlier in this chapter to make sure you understand how a host locates a remote host.

Are your router and the remote host functional? Also, verify the link between the hosts. Clear the ARP cache of your hosts and routers manually, if necessary.

Host *xxx* Unknown

The Host *xxx* Unknown message usually is a name resolution problem. Try pinging the IP address to verify communication on the IP layer. Then, check your name resolution configuration. Refer to Chapter 12 for further information on DNS and name resolution.

Connection Refused

The Connection Refused message very often results when either a daemon process isn't running or the remote server doesn't have the resources to service the request at that time. It isn't an IP layer problem.

Request Timed Out

The Request Timed Out message usually indicates that either the target host is offline or no route to the host is available. Excessive congestion at different points in the Internet can cause timeout problems. Especially check queues at your routers to determine whether you have a bottleneck somewhere.

Utilities to Verify IP Communication

To check local TCP/IP configuration, use the following utilities:

▶ **Windows 95/98:** Use WINIPCFG to check your IP configuration

▶ **Windows NT:** Use IPCONFIG /ALL — if a duplicate IP address is used, the IP address appears as configured, but the subnet mask appears as 0.0.0.0

▶ **Novell Server:** Use CONFIG on the server prompt to display your TCP/IP bindings, and use IPTRACE.NLM to make a traceroute and find out where the packet gets stuck

▶ **UNIX:** Use IFCONFIG *<interface>*

To check the route to find out where the packet gets stuck:

▶ **Windows NT:** Use TRACERT -D

▶ **Novell Server:** Use TCPCON, TPING.NLM, and IPTRACE.NLM

▶ **UNIX:** Use TRACEROUTE *<host>*

A PING utility is available on all operating systems.

TIP

**Ping has several options that are useful for troubleshooting.
Depending on the operating system, the parameters might be slightly
different.**

You can find options to ping a specified host until interrupted, to resolve
addresses to hostnames, to specify the number of echo requests to send, and to
specify the size of the datagram, to troubleshoot fragmentation problems. You can
set the Don't Fragment bit, specify the TTL, and, usually, record the route in the
header of the packet (up to nine hops). An option even exists that records the
timestamps for count hops. To check for specific routes, you can add parameters
for loose or strict source routes along a specified host list. Check the ping help file
of your operating system for details.

To check the routing table of your hosts along the path:

▸ **Windows NT:** Use ROUTE

▸ **Novell Server:** Use TCPCON.NLM

▸ **UNIX:** Use NETSTAT -R

To check IP communications in general:

▸ **Windows NT:** Use NETSTAT -S (displays statistics on TCP, UDP, and IP)

▸ **Novell Server:** Use TCPCON and look at the IP statistics

X-REF

**Chapter 6, on ICMP, provides an explanation of how traceroute and
ping work. They both use ICMP for communication.**

▸ · ◂

Case Study — What Can Go Wrong

This section analyzes some situations and trace files that show common
problems on the IP layer.

Problem 1: Duplicate IP Address

The following lists the background for the trace file that is being used in this example, which is shown in Figure 4.19:

▸ A reserved Class A network with a mask of 255.255.255.240

▸ A host Titan with the IP address of 10.10.10.4

▸ Another host boots up with the same address as the host Titan

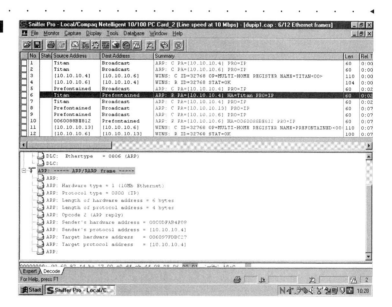

FIGURE 4.19

This host does a duplicate IP address test upon initializing its TCP/IP stack

This was a long trace file, so only the frames that apply to the duplicate IP address problem have been selected. Thus, a lot more was going on between the single datagrams shown in the trace. The following is the frame-by-frame analysis of the important frames in the trace:

Frame 1   Titan boots up and sends an ARP request for its IP address of 10.10.10.4. It receives no reply, so it decides that it can use that address, and thus goes on with its booting process.

Frame 2	Titan sends an ARP request for the IP address of its WINS Server.
Frame 4	Titan successfully registers with its WINS Server.
Frame 5	Host Prefontained boots up, claiming the same IP address of 10.10.10.4.
Frame 6	Host Prefontained receives an answer from Titan. Prefontained now knows that it can't use that address, because it's already being used. Prefontained tactfully stops using the address immediately and does not participate in network activity any more.
Frame 7	Titan does an ARP request for its own IP address again, to ensure that it can safely use that address. This is Microsoft TCP/IP stack behavior. Titan's ARP request ensures that all ARP tables refer to the correct MAC address for the specific IP address. Because Prefontained doesn't participate any more, no reply is made to Titan's ARP request. So, Titan knows that it can go on about its usual business.
Frame 8	Prefontained boots again and sends an ARP request for the IP address 10.10.10.13. The user has changed the TCP/IP configuration, and now Prefontained has a valid IP address. No reply is made to this ARP request, because nobody else is using that address.
Frame 9	Prefontained continues with its booting process, sending an ARP request for the IP address of its WINS Server.
Frames 11 and 12	Successful registration process with WINS.

The Analysis

In the preceding trace file, everything works out fine because Prefontained figures that it can't use the address. Windows NT does a duplicate IP address test, as do all the Microsoft TCP/IP stacks and Novell's TCP/IP stacks. HP UNIX, Sun Solaris, IBM, and Linux don't test for a duplicate IP address, which is why you can end up having trouble, as described in Figure 4.20.

The result of two hosts actively using the same IP address

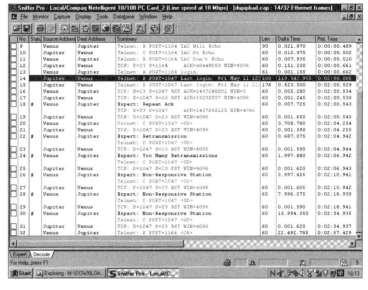

Up to frame 14, the trace shows how Jupiter sets up a TCP connection with Venus and then starts a Telnet session. Unfortunately, showing the whole trace in one screenshot is impossible. Thus, this figure shows the most important frames:

Frames 4 to 11	Show the Telnet option negotiation.
Frame 13	Shows the login.
Frame 15	Looks exactly the same as frame 14. If you could examine the DLC layer in the detail window (which isn't shown here), you would see that frame 15 goes to a different host with a different hardware address. But, that host obviously is using the same IP address as Venus.
Frame 16	The third host (named Pluto) sends a TCP reset.
Frame 18	Venus is repeating an ACK.
Frame 19	Venus sends another Reset to Pluto. This continues through the rest of the trace. Jupiter now is confused and keeps sending traffic to Pluto that should go to Venus.

Frames 20, 22, 24, 26, 28, 30 — Show how Venus sends a command to Jupiter. Jupiter sends a reset to each of them, believing the connection is closed. But, because Jupiter is confused, all of those resets go to Pluto and never reach Venus. Looking at the Delta Time column, you can see how Jupiter uses its backoff algorithm. It waits 2, 4, and 8 seconds after each reset before it resends its command.

The Solution

Avoid duplicate IP addresses! Different ways exist to eliminate this problem. If you statically configure your IP addresses for all hosts, you must be very careful that you don't assign the same address twice. If you have TCP/IP stacks that do a duplicate IP address test, *don't turn off* this feature. The best strategy for avoiding duplicate addresses is to use DHCP to configure your hosts. DHCP provides for central administration and allocation of your IP address range and makes sure that no address is given out twice.

Refer to Chapter 11 to learn about DHCP.

X-REF

Problem 2: Incorrect Address Mask

The network has been designed as diagrammed in Figure 4.21. The user on network 134.22.101.0 cannot establish a Telnet session to Host_2 on network 134.22.102.2.

The Analysis

The client wants to open a Telnet session with Host_2. It knows that the host's IP address is 134.22.102.2. Checking this against its subnet mask, it decides that Host_2 is on the same network. Therefore, it sends an ARP request for the host's hardware address. The analyzer sits on the same network as the user. All you can see in this trace are the ARPs for Host_2's IP address. But there is no answer (see Figure 4.22). IP broadcasts never cross an IP router. As you can see in the detail window of the trace file, the broadcast packet includes no IP header. It is ARP right on top of DLC.

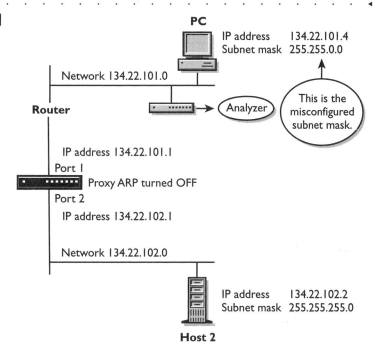

FIGURE 4.21

Network diagram for the trace file shown in Figure 4.22

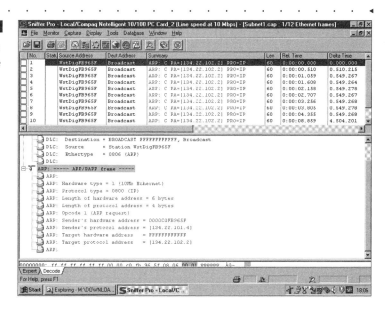

FIGURE 4.22

Because the client assumes that Host_2 is on the same network, it ARPs for that host's MAC address and never gets a reply.

If the router had Proxy ARP enabled, it would answer to this request. But, this option usually is disabled, by default, and you should deliberate before enabling it, because it puts unnecessary load on the router and thus usually isn't a good solution.

The Solution

In this case, the solution is to configure the client's subnet mask properly. Then, rather than ARPing for Host_2's MAC address in its local network, it will ARP for the router's MAC address (see Figure 4.23). It now knows that its destination host is on a different network.

FIGURE 4.23

After properly configuring the subnet mask, the user ARPs for the router's MAC address and gets a reply.

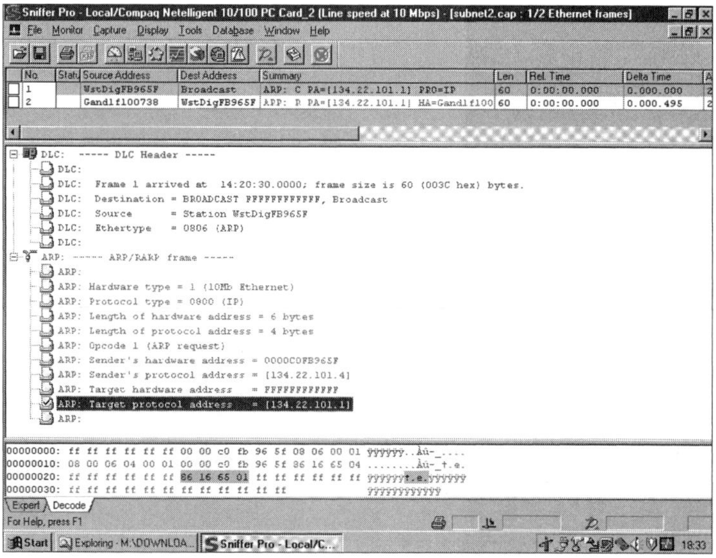

Figure 4.23 shows how the trace looks after properly configuring the client's subnet mask and setting it to 255.255.255.0. You can see the user ARP for the MAC address of 132.22.101.1, which is the router's interface. The next frame is the router's reply, including its MAC address.

Problem 3: Fragmentation Problems

A wide variety of fragmentation problems can occur in a network, and complete coverage of them all is beyond the scope of this book. Usually, the phenomenon that you'll encounter is that a host sends a request or data to another host but receives no reply. If this communication crosses a router, fragmentation is one thing to look at. Always carefully watch the position of your analyzer tool when interpreting your traces.

Assume that a host sends data to another host on another segment that has the Don't Fragment bit set. If the router has to fragment the datagram and finds that bit set, it can't forward the packet. Instead, it sends an ICMP message to the sending host stating Fragmentation needed and Don't Fragment bit set. You can see that communication only if you have your analyzer on the sending host's segment. Taking a trace on the other side of the router will not reveal anything, because the router has discarded the packet.

The Analysis

The network layout for this case study is described in Figures 4.24 and 4.25.

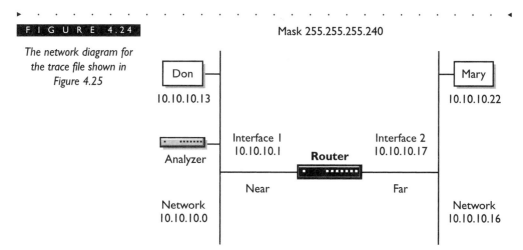

FIGURE 4.24

The network diagram for the trace file shown in Figure 4.25

Mask 255.255.255.240

Don — 10.10.10.13

Mary — 10.10.10.22

Analyzer

Interface 1 10.10.10.1

Router

Interface 2 10.10.10.17

Near

Far

Network 10.10.10.0

Network 10.10.10.16

▶ · ◀

FIGURE 4.25

The trace file with the fragmentation problem

This trace file was taken in a lab and ping was used with the Packet Size option to demonstrate the effect of a fragmentation problem. Don, the NT Workstation, tries to ping several hosts on the network. The addresses used are of Class A and the mask is 255.255.255.240. This means that the last octet's leftmost 4 bits belong to the subnet mask, and the rightmost 4 bits are reserved for host IDs. The router has two interfaces, named Router_Near for the interface to Don's subnet, and Router_Far for the interface to the other subnet. The following is the frame-by-frame analysis of the important frames:

Frame 1   Don pings Router_Near with the address of 10.10.10.1 and is successful.

Frame 2   The router's reply.

Frame 3   Don pings the other router interface with the address of 10.10.10.17. That ping is successful, too.

Frame 5   Don pings Mary with the address 10.10.10.22, a host that sits on the other subnet.

Frame 6   Mary's reply. So far so good. The communication from Don to Mary crossing the router is verified.

Frame 7   We set the TTL to 1 when pinging Mary.

Frame 8   The routers reply to the ping. Recall what happens on the router: one of the first things the router does is to decrement the TTL by one the moment the packet comes in. Because we set TTL to 1, the router now has a TTL of 0. It discards the datagram and sends an ICMP message back to the source. The ping never arrives at Mary and thus no reply is returned from Mary. If you watch the Packet Length column, you see that, so far, all pings have had a length of 74 bytes.

Frame 9   Don pings Mary again, but it sets the packet size to 2,048 bytes. We are on an Ethernet segment, so the ping is fragmented into two datagrams: frame 9 is 1,514 bytes; frame 10 is 610 bytes. No reply to that ping occurs.

The Solution

What conclusions can be drawn so far? Pinging with a small packet size (the default) is okay. Pinging with a packet size that causes fragmentation doesn't work. The source of the problem could be either the router, which could drop fragments, or the receiving host. To determine the problem, the following two options are available:

▸ Move the analyzer to the other subnet and find out whether we can see that ping. If not, the router is the problem; if yes, assume that Mary has a problem.

▸ Let Mary ping Don, without moving the analyzer.

Option 2 is what we did. Frame 11 shows Mary's first ping, with a size of 74 bytes. Don replies in frame 12. Frame 13 is Mary's next ping, now with a packet size of 3,096 bytes. The ping is fragmented into frames 13, 14, and 15. Frame 16 shows that Don replies to that ping. The conclusion is that the router seems to be working fine. Mary can send oversized pings but cannot respond to fragmented pings.

Problem 4: Local Router

A station wants to send a frame to a host on the same segment. Instead of sending the frame to the target host, the station addresses the frame to the router. All of those frames go to the router first, and the router must process them, only to send them back onto the same segment. This is a local router situation. It doubles the traffic on that segment and ties up valuable router processing time.

The Analysis

Figure 4.26 illustrates how Host A addresses the frame to the router.

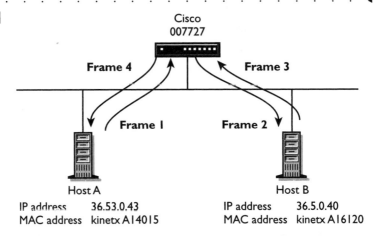

FIGURE 4.26

Instead of sending the frame to Host B, Host A addresses it to the router.

Host A
IP address 36.53.0.43
MAC address kinetx A14015

Host B
IP address 36.5.0.40
MAC address kinetx A16120

Frame 1 is the same as frame 2, except that frame 1 is addressed to the router's MAC address, and frame 2 has the router's MAC address in the Source field. The same is true for the frame pair 3 and 4. Figure 4.27 shows how the frame is addressed to the router's MAC address.

In frame 1, you can see that host 36.53.0.43 wants to communicate with host 36.5.0.40. The network diagram in Figure 4.26 shows that the hosts are on the same network. If you examine the DLC destination address in the detail window, you see that the packet is addressed to the Cisco router Cisco 007727. Frame 2 looks identical, except for the Sniffer Analyzer Expert System's comment on the local routing problem. Not every analyzer will comment on this.

Frame 2 is highlighted in Figure 4.28. The detail window shows that, on the IP layer, frame 2 is still a frame going from 36.53.0.43 to 36.53.0.40; but, in the DLC field, you can see that frame originates from the Cisco router. And, the same thing happens with the reply from 36.53.0.40 to 36.53.0.43.

FIGURE 4.27

The frame is addressed to the router's MAC address.

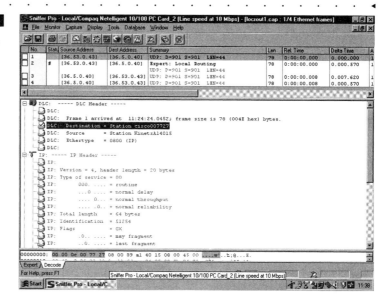

FIGURE 4.28

This frame originates from the router.

The Solution

This situation was caused by different subnet masks. The source host doesn't recognize that the destination host is on the same segment and, therefore, sends the packet to the router. This situation doesn't necessarily have to be a problem. In fact, in certain situations, you would configure this on purpose:

▶ **You have a segment that you want to split into two segments.**
Configure the new segment on the same interface of your router. Then, start migrating hosts to the new segment gradually. If a host on the old segment wants to talk to a host on the new segment, it has to go to the router to talk to the other host. When you are ready, you add the new interface to the router and configure the new segment. This way, you have a smooth migration.

▶ **You may want to use this as a permanent configuration for security reasons.** Create two subnets for your hosts on the same physical segment. Use the router's filtering options to secure the two subnets. If a host from one subnet wants to talk to a host on the other subnet, the frame goes through the router and is checked against the router's access list. But, be aware of the processing load that this may put on your router.

Possible reasons for unwanted local router situations can be one of the following:

▶ The router table might be configured improperly.

▶ The router might be performing gateway functions, such as protocol translation, at the application level.

▶ A device that is new to the network is sending frames through a router, either because it isn't aware of the direct route or because it has been configured to use that router.

How do you know that you have routing loops on your network? When you see the same packet repeatedly in your trace files, and the only thing that changes is the TTL, which is decreasing by one every time that the packet crosses a router. Also, if you have routing loops, you usually find ICMP Time Exceeded messages.

When the packet is discarded because the TTL has reached 0, this ICMP message should be created.

The main reasons for routing loops are the following:

▸ Misconfigured static routing entries (for example, default gateway)

▸ The use of RIP 1 in a meshed subnetted environment. Changes to the routing tables of adjacent routers, as a result of a common router resetting or powering off, may not propagate in a timely fashion to the adjacent routers if they are not running Split Horizon, Hold Down, Poison Reverse, or any of the other routing algorithms that were designed to overcome the deficiencies of RIP 1 in a meshed environment. In subnetted environments, RIP 2 or OSPF should be used. Refer to Chapter 7 for information on RIP 1 and 2, and refer to Chapter 8 for information on OSPF.

Summary

This chapter has covered IP communications, IP addressing, subnetting, and routing. The next chapter covers the ARP and RARP (Address Resolution Protocol and Reverse Address Resolution Protocol). To send datagrams, IP needs to map the IP address to the hardware address of the next hop or the destination host, which is what ARP/RARP is used for. It is like the link between the Internet layer and the network interface layer.

Address Resolution Protocol/Reverse Address Resolution Protocol (ARP/RARP)

All hosts in a TCP/IP network have at least two things in common: a 32-bit logical address (or IP address) and a physical hardware address (or MAC address). The physical address size can range from 8 bits (1 byte) for an Attached Resource Computing Network (ARCNET) to a 48-bit (6-byte) hardware address for an Ethernet address. For one host to communicate with another host, the originating host must know the destination host's MAC address. Sounds simple, right?

But, what if both hosts boot and know only their *own* logical and physical addresses? What if they don't even know their own IP address? Somehow, they must learn, which is where the Address Resolution Protocol (ARP) and Reverse Address Resolution Protocol (RARP) come to the rescue.

Overview of ARP/RARP Functionality

Address resolution refers to the process of finding the address of a computer in a network. Two hosts can communicate only if they know each other's hardware address, which defines the host uniquely throughout the network. (Theoretically, no two hosts should have the same hardware address.) ARP is used by the Internet Protocol (IP) layer through a broadcast to assist hosts in mapping 32-bit IP addresses to hardware (MAC) addresses. After these mappings are in place, normal communication between hosts can be established. This process is also known as *binding protocol addresses*.

ARP is used when the originating host knows its own IP address and the destination host's logical (IP) address. Reverse Address Resolution Protocol (RARP), conversely, is used by a host that knows its physical address, but needs to establish an IP address for itself. This is common on diskless workstations. When the diskless workstation boots, it issues a RARP broadcast command over the network, to obtain its IP address from a server. The most recent extensions to the RARP process are BOOTP and DHCP, discussed in other chapters. Figure 5.1 shows the data flow for the ARP and RARP protocols.

FIGURE 5.1

ARP and RARP data flow

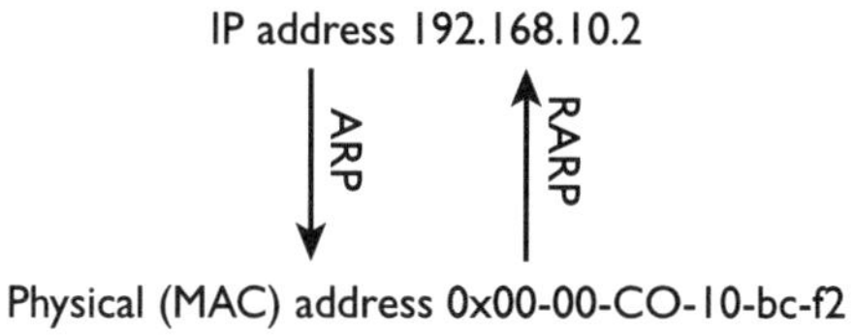

IP address 192.168.10.2

ARP

RARP

Physical (MAC) address 0x00-00-CO-10-bc-f2

Another, related ARP is called *Inverse Address Resolution Protocol (Inverse ARP)*. Inverse ARP enables a station to request a logical (IP) address that corresponds to a given hardware address, without using a broadcast method. Commonly seen in frame-relay networks, Inverse ARP enables a host to query a machine at the other end of a specific virtual circuit, rather than broadcast to every circuit available in the LAN or WAN. This is an efficient method for address resolution for frame-relay networks, and greatly reduces resolution traffic.

Why Do We Need Resolution?

Why do we even need resolution? In a TCP/IP network, all hosts begin with the same parameters and rules regarding communication:

▸ All hosts boot up knowing *only* their own MAC and IP addresses

▸ Hosts wanting to communicate on the network must do so by using the physical addresses of other hosts and networks

Using these two rules further clarifies that the mapping of IP addresses to physical addresses isn't just desired, but is required for network communication to occur. Figure 5.2 illustrates the mapping problem.

Resolution is performed through one of the methods described in the following sections.

ANALYZING AND TROUBLESHOOTING THE INTERNET LAYER

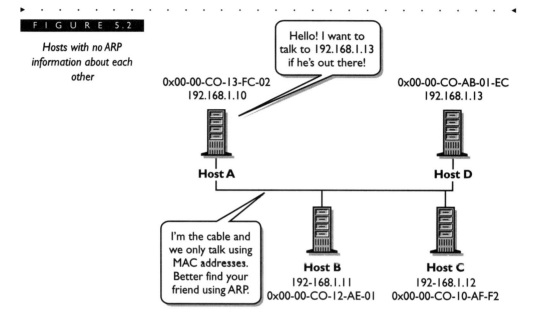

FIGURE 5.2

Hosts with no ARP information about each other

Table Lookup

Table lookup generally is used with Reverse ARP. All the IP addresses and corresponding hardware addresses are stored in a file on a RARP server. Figure 5.3 illustrates the RARP procedure, showing how a booting host obtains its IP address using RARP:

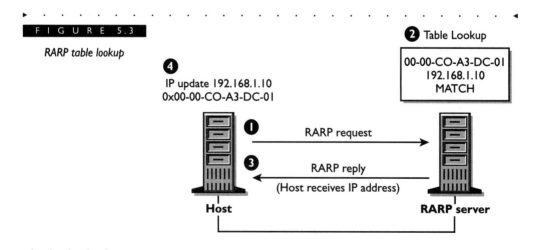

FIGURE 5.3

RARP table lookup

1. The host broadcasts a RARP request and uses its own physical (MAC) address for identification.

2. The RARP server receives the request and looks up the physical address in its database.

3. The RARP server replies to the host and fills in the appropriate IP address.

4. The host updates its own IP address and begins using TCP/IP communication.

NOTE

The host always had physical-level communication using its hardware address. It simply needed an IP address to use other resources on the network, such as Telnet or FTP.

Computation

Also known as *direct mapping*, computation is used in networks where hardware addresses are freely assigned when installing a network interface board in a computer. In this case, the installer assigns IP addresses with the host portion of the address equal to the physical address. Usually, host IP addresses are assigned in numerical sequence, such as 1, 2, 3, and so on, which makes choosing physical addresses easy. For example, with a Class C IP address of 192.168.12.5, the system administrator would choose a physical address of 5.

Broadcast Using the Network

By far the most popular resolution type, the broadcast method is used to map IP addresses to physical addresses. Because networks such as Ethernet have broadcast capability, this method of resolution requires no central database manipulation and no hardware address manipulation on the part of the system administrator. ARP uses this kind of resolution extensively, because it's reasonably efficient and easy to maintain.

The broadcast method enables a host to find the physical address of another host on the network simply by knowing its IP address. Figure 5.4 illustrates the broadcast resolution process.

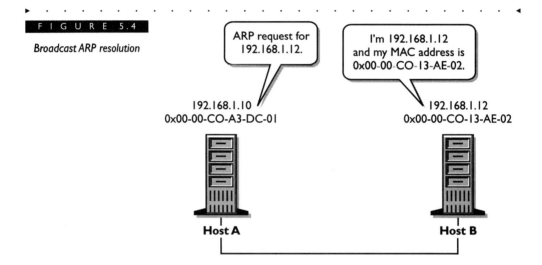

FIGURE 5.4

Broadcast ARP resolution

Host A wants to resolve the physical address for Host B. To accomplish this, Host A prepares an ARP packet requesting the physical address for Host B, which includes the specific IP address for Host B. All hosts on the local network, including Host B, receive the ARP request. Host B recognizes that the packet is addressed to it and prepares a reply. When A receives the reply, it uses the physical address and then begins sending packets directly to Host B.

Figure 5.5 illustrates the ARP request packet.

Notice that the requesting node, 192.168.1.102, fills in its own hardware address (sender) and its own IP (protocol) address. It also prefills the target IP address, but leaves the target hardware address blank, because this is the value that it's trying to resolve. The packet reply will have all fields filled in, as depicted in Figure 5.6.

ADDRESS RESOLUTION PROTOCOL/REVERSE ADDRESS RESOLUTION PROTOCOL (ARP/RARP)

F I G U R E 5.5

ARP request packet

F I G U R E 5.6

ARP reply packet

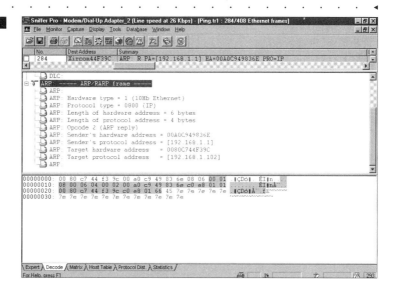

The ARP Cache

Doesn't it seem silly that every time a host wants to communicate with another it should send a broadcast? What if a host has just finished a communication with another host and wants to begin another session? Must it generate another broadcast? With all that broadcast traffic, how can anyone get anything done?

To reduce the amount of ARP traffic on the network, every host maintains an *ARP cache*. The ARP cache resides in host memory and keeps a list of recently acquired physical and IP address bindings. Earlier, Figure 5.5 illustrated the prefilled address fields sent with an ARP request. These fields are prefilled so that the receiver can update its ARP cache before sending a reply.

IMPORTANT

The sending host is required to fill in the hardware and protocol address when building an ARP request in a non-DHCP environment. However, in a DHCP environment in which a single computer assigns IP addresses to all hosts, the protocol address is *not* prefilled by the sender (instead, it's left as 0.0.0.0), to avoid confusing ARP caches in other hosts. Not all vendors' TCP/IP implementations adhere to this rule.

Whenever a host receives an ARP reply, it saves the sender's hardware and IP address in its cache for successive lookups. Figure 5.7 illustrates an ARP cache update in which a computer has just come onto the network and has no entries in its ARP cache. It knows only its own IP and hardware addresses, which require no ARP entries. The ARP cache is viewed on the Windows workstation by typing **ARP -a** at the command prompt.

IMPORTANT

All hosts begin knowing only their own IP and hardware addresses.

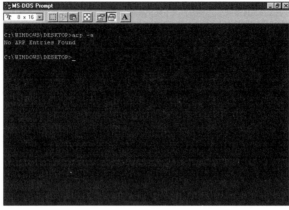

F I G U R E   5.7

ARP cache without entries

A host wants to communicate with another host on the network, but doesn't know the physical address. So, it sends an ARP request to the IP address of the destination host. After receiving an ARP reply, the ARP cache is updated, as shown in Figure 5.8.

F I G U R E   5.8

ARP cache update

Notice that the ARP cache now holds an entry for the physical and logical addresses of the destination device. The host may now use this information to send packets directly to the destination host instead of performing another ARP broadcast when it wants to communicate.

TIP

To find the physical address of a device quickly, simply go to a computer and PING for the IP address of the destination device. Then, use the ARP -a command to view the ARP cache of the local computer. Voilà! Quick and easy physical address identification.

Every host receiving and processing ARP broadcast requests must go through a sophisticated process to determine what to do with the packet and whether to update the cache. This process is illustrated in Figure 5.9.

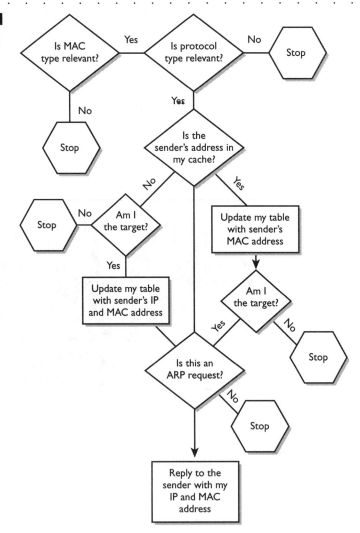

FIGURE 5.9

ARP packet receipt decision tree

As described in Figure 5.9, the host receiving the ARP packet must first determine whether the MAC address is relevant (it usually is fine). Then, it looks to the protocol type (0x0080 for IP) and checks its own cache to see whether the address already exists in the table. The host then updates the table, if necessary. Finally, just before the reply, it checks to see whether the ARP packet is a request. The manner in which this takes place may seem odd, but there is a reason: The process is based on the assumption that if Host A has reason to communicate with Host B, then, at some time in the future, Host B will probably want to talk to Host A. So, the ARP cache is updated "just in case," regardless of whether the future conversation ever takes place.

Static ARP Cache Entries

An entry can be placed into the ARP cache permanently, if you choose, by using the ARP -s command. Entries won't time out unless temp appears at the end of the command line. Figure 5.10 illustrates how permanent ARP cache entries may be placed in the ARP cache by using the ARP -s command.

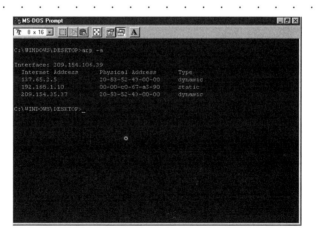

F I G U R E 5.10

Static ARP entries

Permanently setting entries in the ARP cache poses some dangers, and thus this method should be used sparingly. The ARP cache has a limited size, and setting too many entries in a permanent state does not leave enough room for learned broadcast entries, discussed next.

Learned ARP Cache Entries

When a host performs an ARP broadcast and receives a reply, it places the information from the destination host into its local ARP cache. This type of ARP entry placement is called a *learned entry,* which is a nonpermanent cache entry. Learned (nonpermanent) entries can be one of two types:

> ▸ **Complete entry:** A valid IP/physical address pair added to the ARP cache properly through the process previously described. This means that an ARP request was sent, and a reply from the appropriate host was received.

> ▸ **Incomplete entry:** An entry that is in the process of being resolved, but for which the host has not yet been able to receive a proper response.

Consider the scenario in Figure 5.11, in which a host tries to ARP to a nonexistent address, illustrating how a computer may build an ARP request for a nonexistent address. Hey, how would it know that the address was bad? Remember, though, that ARP is a local broadcast, and that everyone on the local segment of the network processes broadcasts.

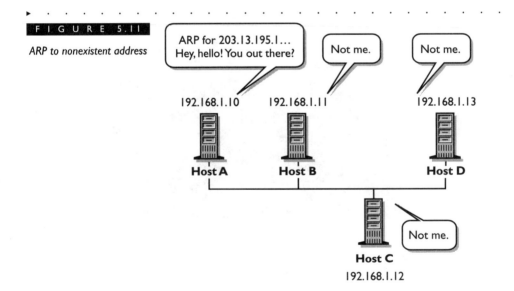

FIGURE 5.11

ARP to nonexistent address

Figure 5.12 shows the packets being sent when attempting communication with an invalid host. The user attempts to Telnet to a host with the IP number 192.168.1.10, which doesn't exist on the network. Notice that the first ARP command in packet 15 and subsequent ARP commands were issued until, finally, the application timed out. (Timeout is a TCP function, not an ARP issue. TCP is discussed in later chapters.)

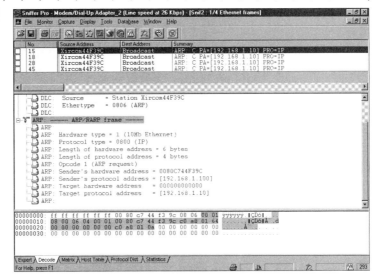

FIGURE 5.12

Telnet to invalid host

A closer look at the ARP cache after this invalid command shows a new entry with a type marked *invalid*. Figure 5.13 shows the ARP cache of the workstation after the invalid Telnet command.

ARP Cache Timeout

Each learned ARP cache entry is placed in the table, regardless of its complete or incomplete (invalid) status. As the ARP cache table grows, each entry takes up valuable host memory. To manage the table size, invalid or unused entries are purged from the cache by using a process called *ARP cache timeout*. The timeout value, as well as the total cache size, varies depending on both the manufacturer implementation of ARP and the amount of memory available in the host device.

▶ · ◀

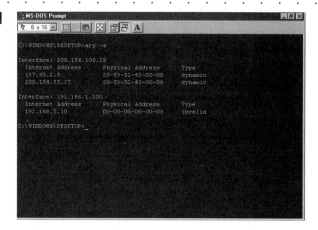

F I G U R E   5 . 1 3

*ARP cache with invalid
entries*

Another reason for the timeout process is simply to keep information current. For example, suppose that Host A has performed an ARP and caches the physical address for Host B. Host B's interface is replaced, which subsequently changes its MAC address, but Host A doesn't know that. If no timeout occurred, Host A would continue to use the old hardware address of Host B, which would result in an error.

A great way to force an update after an interface replacement is to simply PING the address of the local router interface. This accomplishes two things: It forces an update to the ARP cache in the router, and it verifies IP-level connectivity at the host.

TIP

With the timeout mechanism in place, the previously correct entry is flushed from the cache. Subsequent communication between Host A and B requires another ARP, which will place the correct information back into the cache.

The ARP timeout is not a requirement, simply a suggestion. Therefore, not all device manufacturers actually perform a timeout. This can mean some pretty large memory requirements, or a frequent device reset. Yuck!

NOTE

Analyzing ARP/RARP Packets

This section explores fields of the ARP/RARP packet, along with the definitions of each. First, it looks at how the ARP packet is sent within the TCP/IP network.

ARP Encapsulation

ARP packets are encapsulated within a physical frame. This is different than other diagnostic or informational protocols in the TCP/IP family, which are encapsulated into an IP datagram for routing purposes. With an ARP packet, the ARP information (or message) is actually sent in the frame data area. Figure 5.14 diagrams ARP encapsulation.

FIGURE 5.14

ARP encapsulation within a physical frame

ARP Message	
Frame header	Frame data area

Looking at the ARP packet from an analyzer, this encapsulation becomes a bit clearer. Figure 5.15 shows an ARP packet with the frame header (DLC) followed by the ARP packet and information. So, how does a receiver or sender know that this is an ARP packet? In a technology such as Ethernet, an ARP packet is designated by placing the Hex value 0x0806 in the Ethertype field of the frame header. This field tells the receiver and/or sender that it will be receiving ARP information next. The sender or receiver must still evaluate the ARP packet further, to see whether it is an ARP or RARP request or reply.

ARP/RARP Packet Structure

ARP and RARP packet structures are essentially the same. The major difference is in the Operation Code field, which tells the sender or receiver whether it needs to use ARP or RARP. Figure 5.16 depicts the fields in the ARP/RARP packet structure.

Ethernet Implementation

Hardware type
Protocol type
Hardware address length
Protocol address length
Operation code
Sender hardware address
Sender protocol address
Target hardware address
Target protocol address

The format depicted in Figure 5.16 is an Ethernet standard, which uses 48-bit (6-byte) hardware addresses. The ARP packet may be used to accommodate other protocol addresses that do not use 48-bit physical addresses, which would ultimately change the overall size of the packet. The fields in the packet are described in the following sections.

Hardware Type (2 Bytes)

This field identifies the hardware interface used by the sender. The value of 1 indicates an Ethernet hardware interface. Some other common hardware types are listed in Table 5.1.

TABLE 5.1	NUMBER	HARDWARE TYPE
Common Hardware Type Codes	1	Ethernet (10MB)
	2	Experimental Ethernet (3MB)
	3	Amateur Radio AX.25
	4	Proteon ProNET Token Ring
	5	Chaos
	6	IEEE 802.2 Networks
	7	ARCNET
	8	Hyperchannel
	9	Lanstar
	10	AutoNet Short Address
	11	LocalTalk
	12	LocalNet (IBM PCNet or SYTEK)
	13	Ultra link
	14	Switched Multimegabit Data Services (SMDS)
	15	Frame Relay
	16	Asynchronous Transmission Mode (ATM)
	17	High-level Data Link Control (HDLC)
	18	Fibre Channel
	19	ATM
	20	Serial Line
	21	ATM

Protocol Type (2 Bytes)

The protocol type field specifies the higher-layer protocol used by the sender. For an IP address, this value is hex 0x0800 (IP).

Hardware Address Length (1 Byte)

Specifies the length of the hardware address used with this ARP message. For an Ethernet network, the hardware length is 48 bits (6 bytes).

Protocol Address Length (1 Byte)

Specifies the length of the higher-level protocol, such as IP. Current IP addresses are 32 bits (4 bytes) long. Future IP implementations, such as IPv6, will be 128 bits (16 bytes) long, and will require modification of this field.

Operation Code (2 Bytes)

Defines the type of ARP packet being sent. Table 5.2 depicts common Operation codes.

TABLE 5.2	CODE NUMBER	CODE DESCRIPTION
ARP Operation Codes	1	ARP request
	2	ARP reply
	3	Reverse ARP request
	4	Reverse ARP reply
	8	Inverse ARP request
	9	Inverse ARP reply

Sender or Target Hardware Address (6 Bytes)

This is the actual physical address of the sender or target. In an Ethernet environment, the hardware address is the 6-byte MAC address.

Sender or Target Protocol Address (4 Bytes)

This is the IP address of the sender or target. In current IP, the protocol address is a 32-bit number shown in dotted decimal notation.

Finding Target Hosts on the LAN

You have already learned that a host communicates to other hosts on the LAN by using ARP broadcasts. However, ARP has a basic problem: the ARP request and reply are encapsulated within the frame header, which means that there is no protocol, such as IP, to directly route ARP broadcasts throughout the network. Therefore, ARP seemingly is a local-segment-only broadcast protocol, with no routing capability. But what if you need to find a host that is located on another segment? Two types of target host exist:

- Local targets

- Remote targets

The method that the requesting host uses to locate a target host differs depending on the location of the destination host. If the host is local (located on the same segment as the requesting host), all communication takes place between the nodes, as illustrated in Figure 5.17.

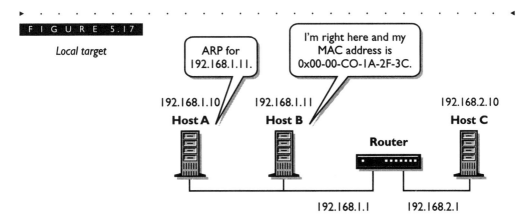

FIGURE 5.17

Local target

If a target is remote (located on a different segment), the requesting node follows a different series of steps to find the physical address of the remote node. When the originating host attempts to communicate with a remote host, the originating host realizes that the destination network isn't its own and, therefore, doesn't send an

ARP to the local segment. Instead, the originating host directs the ARP to the default router, with the expectation that the router will find the remote node on behalf of the requesting node, as shown in Figure 5.18.

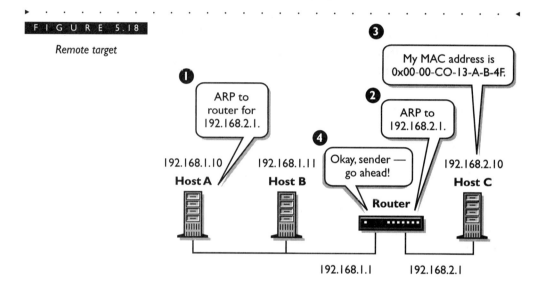

FIGURE 5.18

Remote target

In Figure 5.18, Host A wants to communicate with Host B. However, Host A knows that Host B isn't on its segment, so it passes an ARP request to the local router interface, Interface X. The router, connected to the other segment through Interface Y, performs an ARP request to locate Host B. Subsequent communication takes place through the router as it normally would.

Proxy ARP

In some cases, you may want to "hide" nodes beyond a router. This may be important if a single IP network address is shared between segments, or you simply don't want to have nodes on another segment respond to ARP requests, for security purposes. This is accomplished by using *Proxy ARP*. A *proxy* is simply a device that acts on behalf of another device. Figure 5.19 shows a simple network connected with a single router by using Proxy ARP.

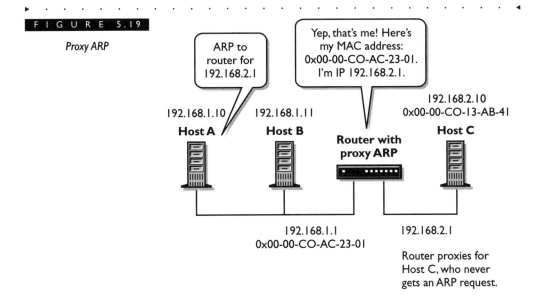

FIGURE 5.19

Proxy ARP

In this figure, Host A requests an ARP reply from Host C, located on another segment. Proxy ARP has been turned on at the router, so on receipt of the request, the router intercepts the packet and replies as if it were Host C, but using its own hardware address, not the address of Host C. Host C never receives an ARP request. Host A receives the reply and places the Host C entry in its ARP cache with the router's physical address. The router has successfully lied to Host A, and continues to do so for all communications in the future, unless Proxy ARP is turned off.

Using ARP for Troubleshooting

One of the methods used to check suspect duplicate IP addresses uses the ARP command. The following are the two ways that ARP may check for duplicate IP addresses:

▸ On device boot

▸ Using PING command

ARP for Duplicates on Bootup

Many vendors implement a duplicate address test during the initialization of a device. This process is known as *gratuitous ARP* and occurs when a host sends an ARP request looking for its own address. (If DHCP is in use, it assumes that an address was given to the host at some time in the past.) The implementation is actually quite simple: 1) Send out an ARP packet with the name of the last known good IP address and 2) Hope that no other device responds! All kidding aside, the gratuitous ARP process has two main features:

▸ **Determines IP address availability:** A booting host sends out an ARP request for its own address, but doesn't expect a reply, because it is preparing to use the address that it has configured manually or has had in the past. However, if a host is already configured with the same IP address as the booting host, a reply is sent. At that time, the booting host receives an error message, alerting the user that a duplicate IP address was found. Figure 5.20 shows a trace file of a host booting and looking for a duplicate address. Note that a host having IP address 192.168.1.66 boots up and sends the ARP packet. Inside the ARP packet, the sender and target protocol (IP) address are the same.

F I G U R E 5.20

Duplicate IP address test

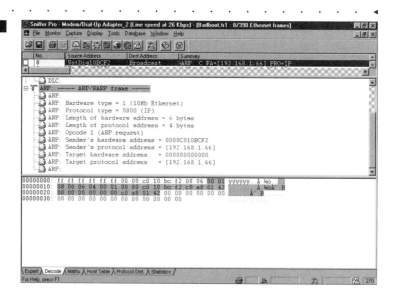

▸ **Alerts other nodes to a hardware change:** ARP can alert other nodes to a change in physical address. Consider a case in which a host is taken down and the network interface card (NIC) is replaced. The host still has the same IP address, but the cache tables in other hosts are wrong. When the host starts again and resends a gratuitous ARP packet, any other host on the segment that has an entry in its cache will be updated.

TIP

If a host receives an ARP request from an IP address that is already in the receiver's cache, that cache entry is updated with the sender's new hardware address. Remember, because ARP requests are broadcast, all hosts on the segment may receive an ARP cache update in this manner.

▸ · ◂

Case Study — What Can Go Wrong

This case study looks at what happens when a misconfigured ARP entry ends up in a router table, causing a communication problem on the network.

The Problem

Our customer called saying that a single workstation on the network was no longer able to communicate with another workstation on the network. The target workstation recently had its NIC replaced due to malfunction, but seemed to be working properly, except for its connection to the other computer. The devices in question are shown in Figure 5.21.

The Analysis

After reviewing the network setup, we realize that the router is performing a proxy function between segments. We take a trace and find an ARP response, as shown in Figure 5.22, which shows that the router has responded to Computer A's ARP request. Viewing the contents of the reply, we see that the router (10.3.16.3) has given Computer B's IP address as 10.3.21.74 and MAC address as 00-00-86-15-D2-9E. The router has obviously known about this device.

FIGURE 5.21

*Computer A cannot
communicate with
Computer B*

00-A0-C9-BB-16-66
10.3.16.10
Computer A

10.3.16.0

10.3.16.3
00-60-09-9C-SB-68

Proxy router

10.3.21.0

Computer B

10.3.21.74
00-00-86-15-EE-01

FIGURE 5.22

*Router responds to ARP
request*

However, a closer look at Computer B's configuration reveals that its hardware address is actually 00-00-86-15-EE-01, due to the fact that the NIC had been changed. The router has not updated its information, so Computer A is attempting a connection with a nonexistent MAC address.

We then took a closer look at the router. After consulting with the vendor, we determined that this vendor hasn't implemented an ARP timeout, which means all entries have stayed in the router's ARP table. Additionally, because the ARP table had gotten so big, the router had run out of memory and was unable to update its ARP table entries. This ultimately led to the router giving an invalid ARP reply.

The Solution

In this case, the vendor had an update to its TCP/IP software that implemented the ARP aging timeout. We updated the router with the new software, reset it to clear out the bad entries, and all was well.

Summary

The ARP protocol is a basic protocol that is used in almost every TCP/IP implementation. Normally, it does its work without any human intervention. You need to assist in resolving a host's IP address to its physical hardware address, which is required for any routing function to take place in the network. This chapter explained that an ARP is really a broadcast that is either a request or a reply for ARP or RARP services. Though the request may be broadcast, the reply is directed back to the originating host.

To reduce the number of ARP broadcasts on the network, each host uses an ARP cache to look up frequently used physical addresses. The ARP cache is efficiently cleared by using a timeout mechanism specific to each vendor.

Internet Control Message Protocol (ICMP)

In a TCP/IP network, devices such as routers use the Internet Protocol (IP) to deliver packets to the appropriate destination. In a perfect world, all machines operate correctly and maintain routes that are proper and complete. But, as you know, lines fail, routers can become congested, and data sometimes cannot be delivered. IP itself provides little help in diagnosing these types of unexpected errors. As discussed in Chapter 4, IP is considered to be an unreliable, connectionless datagram delivery service. "Unreliable" refers to the fact that no guarantees exist that an IP packet will successfully reach its destination.

Overview of ICMP Functionality

The unexpected situations that can arise on IP are reported by a mechanism known as *Internet Control Message Protocol (ICMP)*. When something goes wrong, such as a route becoming temporarily unreachable, the IP datagram is simply thrown away and an ICMP message is sent back to the source. It can then be analyzed to determine the cause of the discarded packet.

ICMP is designed to report communication or delivery errors and other messages relating to the IP datagrams (or packets) flowing within the network. We jokingly refer to ICMP as the "busybody" of the network, because it wants to tell about so many events happening during the network communication process. ICMP is often considered to be part of the Internet layer, but it's actually a required part of IP and must be implemented by any vendor wanting to support IP.

Consider the following situations in which a network device may report information, and ICMP messages may be generated:

► A host tries to connect to a remote device but uses the wrong router to reach its destination

► A user attempts to FTP to a nonexistent host

► A router cannot find the destination network requested by the program

In each of these cases, an ICMP error is reported, using a specific message type. Message types are discussed in detail later in this chapter.

Analyzing an ICMP Session

ICMP messages are contained within the IP datagram header, as detailed in Chapter 4. Additionally, the original IP datagram is contained in the data portion of the frame. Because part of the original data is always included in an ICMP error message, it is helpful for finding problem sources. Figure 6.1 illustrates the ICMP frame structure. Figure 6.2 shows what an ICMP message looks like when you use a network analyzer. Notice the ether frame type, the IP datagram portion, and the ICMP header. Within the IP header, notice the Protocol field. A value of 1 in this field indicates that the data following the IP header is ICMP data.

▶ · ◀

F I G U R E 6.1

ICMP is encapsulated within IP, which is sent in a frame for transmission.

ICMP header	ICMP data

IP header	Datagram data

Frame header	Frame data

▶ · ◀

F I G U R E 6.2

ICMP packet with IP header

Frame Header

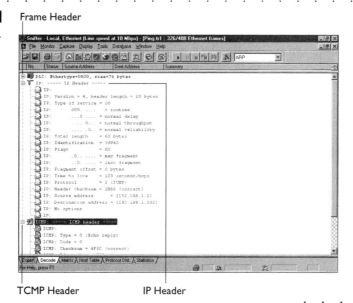

TCMP Header   IP Header

ICMP Message Classes

Not all ICMP messages are equal. Some must be handled specially. For this reason, ICMP messages can be divided into two categories:

▸ **ICMP error message:** Usually indicates that a device is malfunctioning or an action needs to be taken, and always contains the IP header and the first 8 bytes of the datagram that caused the error to be generated. This is helpful in determining which upper-layer protocol (such as UDP or TCP from the IP header) is causing the problem. Sometimes, generating an ICMP message isn't necessary, or isn't practical. For example, an ICMP error is *never* generated in response to an ICMP error, because this could cause a never-ending circle of error messages as one error goes back to the source, generates another error, goes back to the source, generates another error, and so on. Furthermore, generating an error message in response to a datagram destined for a broadcast address is unrealistic. These rules are designed to prevent broadcast storms that could be the result of too many error packets responding to other error packets.

TIP

ICMP error messages always include the IP header and the first 8 bytes of the datagram that caused the error to be generated.

▸ **ICMP query message:** A request for information, and doesn't necessarily indicate an error that requires corrective action. For example, a response to a PING command is a query message indicating that communication is active. An error message could be generated in response to a query message, however. For example, if a PING command is issued and no response is given, the result is an ICMP error message.

The ICMP Header Structure

Though each ICMP message has its own format, all ICMP message headers begin with the same three fields, as shown in Figure 6.3.

▶ . . . . ◀

FIGURE 6.3

ICMP header structure

ICMP Header Structure

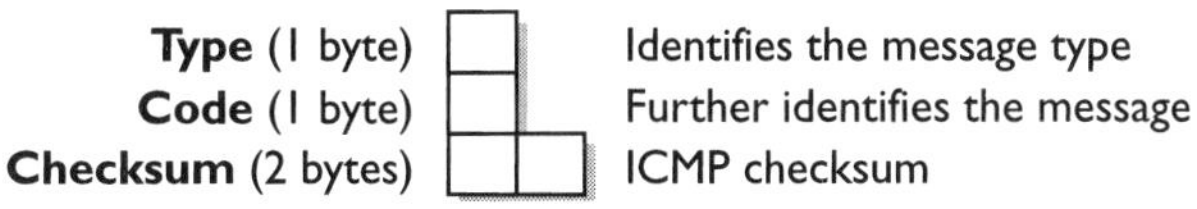

Type (1 byte)   Identifies the message type
Code (1 byte)   Further identifies the message
Checksum (2 bytes)   ICMP checksum

The following sections examine these common ICMP header fields and define the values and functions of each.

The ICMP Type and Code Fields

The first 2 bytes of an ICMP header define the ICMP message type and code. Table 6.1 lists the different ICMP message types, as determined by the Type field and the Code field in the ICMP message. The last two columns in the table specify whether the message is an error or a query message.

TABLE 6.1

Common ICMP Message Types and Codes

TYPE	CODE	DESCRIPTION	QUERY	ERROR
0	0	Echo Reply (Ping reply)	X	
1	-	Unassigned	-	-
2	-	Unassigned	-	-
3		Destination Unreachable		X
	0	Network Unreachable		X
	1	Host Unreachable		X
	2	Protocol Unreachable		X
	3	Port Unreachable		X
	4	Fragmentation Needed but Bit Not Set		X
	5	Source Route Failed		X
	6	Destination Network Unknown		X
	7	Destination Host Unknown		X

(Continued)

T A B L E 6.1

Common ICMP Message Types and Codes (continued)

TYPE	CODE	DESCRIPTION	QUERY	ERROR
	8	Source Host Isolated (obsolete)		X
	9	Destination Network Administratively Prohibited		X
	10	Destination Host Administratively Prohibited		X
	11	Network Unreachable for Type of Service		X
	12	Host Unreachable for Type of Service		X
4	0	Source Quench	X	
5		Redirect (change a route)		
	0	Redirect for Network (or subnet)		X
	1	Redirect Host		X
	2	Redirect Type of Service and Network		X
	3	Redirect Type of Service and Host		X
6	0	Alternate Host Address		X
7	-	Unassigned		
8	0	Echo Request (Ping request)	X	
9	0	Router Advertisement	X	
10	0	Router Selection	X	
11		Time Exceeded		
	0	Time to Live = 0 During Transit		X
	1	Time to Live = 0 During Reassembly		X
12		Parameter Problem		
	0	IP Header Bad		X
	1	Required Option Missing		X
13	0	Timestamp Request	X	
14	0	Timestamp Reply	X	

TYPE	CODE	DESCRIPTION	QUERY	ERROR
15	0	Information Request (obsolete)	X	
16	0	Information Reply (obsolete)	X	
17	0	Address Mask Request	X	
18	0	Address Mask Reply	X	
19	-	Reserved (for security)	-	-
20–29	-	Reserved (for Robustness Experiment)	-	-
30	-	Traceroute		X
31	-	Datagram Conversion Error		X
32	-	Mobile Host Redirect		X
33	-	IPv6 Where Are You	X	
34	-	IPv6 I Am Here	X	
35	-	Mobile Registration Request	X	
36	-	Mobile Registration Reply	X	
37–255	-	Reserved	-	-

ICMP Checksum Field

The Checksum field is 2 bytes. The checksum is an error-detection process designed to ensure integrity of the values in the ICMP message. To calculate the checksum, the message is first treated as a series of 16-bit words, or 2-byte increments. If the message does not contain an even number of 16-bit words, the data is padded with 1 byte to make it an even number. The value of the Checksum field is first set to 0 before calculation. An arithmetic process is then performed on the evened message, and the proper sum is placed in the Checksum field.

The checksum is calculated only for the ICMP message. The IP header checksum is calculated separately.

NOTE

The following sections of this chapter describe the most common ICMP messages, including details of the message format for each type.

ICMP Echo Test Request and Reply (PING)

One of the most frequently used utilities in the TCP/IP protocol suite is the PING command, which is used to determine whether a specified host is reachable and available to communicate on the network. A host invoking a PING command generates an ICMP Echo Request message to the specified destination. After receiving the Echo Request, the destination host formulates an ICMP Echo Reply to respond to the Request. The format of the ICMP Echo Request and Reply messages is shown in Figure 6.4.

Type (1 byte)　　(Must be type 8 or 0)
Code (1 byte)　0　(Must be 0)
Checksum (2 bytes)　　(ICMP checksum required)
Identifier (2 bytes)
Sequence number (2 bytes)
Optional data (variable length)

Identifier and Sequence Number Fields

The Identifier and Sequence Number fields may be used by the Echo sender to match Echo Replies with Echo Requests. Any data that is received in the Echo message must be returned in the Echo Reply. The *identifier* is used by the system to identify a session, whereas the *sequence number* is incremented for each Echo Request sent. An Echo Request packet is displayed in Figure 6.5.

Notice that the ICMP Request message has the number 512 in the Identifier field, and 256 in the Sequence Number field. The Reply packet, shown in Figure 6.6, has identical values, making this Request/Reply pair a perfect match.

FIGURE 6.5

ICMP Echo Request
Identifier and Sequence
Number

FIGURE 6.6

ICMP Echo Reply with
matching Identifier and
Sequence Number

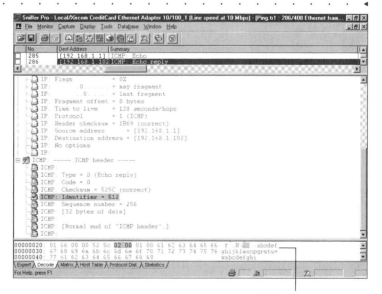

ICMP Echo Data

Optional Data Field

This field may be filled with different types of data, depending on the vendor's implementation of TCP/IP. Notice the letters of the alphabet located in the Data portion of the packet that is shown in Figure 6.6. This is the data that Microsoft Ping uses when issuing an Echo Request.

If the Echo Request is generated by a Novell client, the Ping data uses the send time of the originating host in the Data portion of the packet. Figure 6.7 shows a Ping generated by a Novell server.

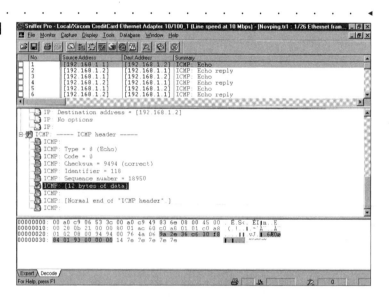

FIGURE 6.7

NetWare PING command used at the file server console

To generate this Ping, the PING utility was loaded at the NetWare console by typing LOAD PING. The Ping utility is discussed in detail in earlier chapters.

Sometimes, you can tell which TCP/IP is performing the ICMP Echo (PING) command. Fluke's LANMeter, for example, sends the words "Fluke LANMeter" in the Data field. Microtest's handheld COMPAS sends "To ping or not to ping, that is the question of the day." Don't spend too much time wondering why vendors choose specific ICMP data — it's just fun to read and doesn't really matter, as long as the Echo Request receives an Echo Reply.

▶ · ◀

ICMP Destination Unreachable

When an IP datagram is undeliverable, an ICMP Destination Unreachable message is generated. This is an error message with an ICMP Type 3 in the header portion of the packet. You need to look further into the header, to determine the exact code reported by the error. The format of this ICMP packet is shown in Figure 6.8.

▶ · ◀

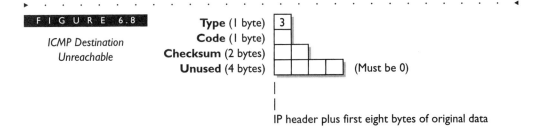

FIGURE 6.8

ICMP Destination Unreachable

Type (1 byte)   3
Code (1 byte)
Checksum (2 bytes)
Unused (4 bytes)   (Must be 0)

IP header plus first eight bytes of original data

Importantly, you must understand that whenever an error prevents a router from delivering a datagram, the Destination Unreachable message is sent back to the source, and the packet is dropped or discarded. Usually, a Network Unreachable message type is related to some kind of router misconfiguration. The Host Unreachable message tells you that delivery cannot be made to a host for some reason—it doesn't tell you whether it even reached the host network. The good news is that these error messages include the first 8 bytes of information about the datagram that caused the problem. By looking at this data, you will know exactly where to begin looking for problems on the network. Figure 6.9 shows an ICMP error Network Unreachable message.

Notice the ICMP Type 3 and Code 0, which is a Destination Unreachable/Network Unreachable error message. The top of the trace shows that the destination address (or host to which the error message is directed) is 128.104.170.17. The originator (or source address of 128.104.18.21) is the router that is unable to deliver the datagram. This does not mean that the router was the original destination—it simply was the error reporting device.

To find out where the original datagram was destined, you must look further into the ICMP area. Remember, all ICMP error messages such as these include the first 8 bytes of the *original* IP header. This is great, because you can determine the problem's actual location in the network. Figure 6.10 shows that the original destination network address was 128.104.0.0, which is the original IP network that the router was trying to reach.

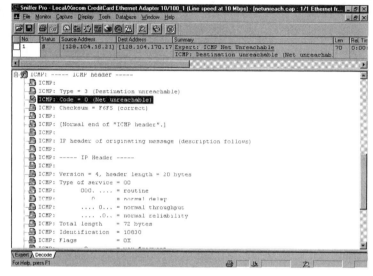

FIGURE 6.9

Network Unreachable

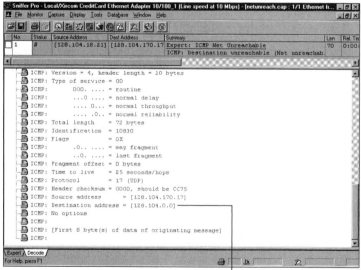

FIGURE 6.10

Original IP header data

Original Destination

ICMP Source Quench

The purpose of the Source Quench ICMP message is to notify data senders when a router overload occurs, a condition called *congestion*. Routers do not know when IP data will be coming, and because IP is connectionless, a router will not reserve any amount of memory or other resources to process those datagrams. Because no reserved resources exist, it is possible (and probable) that router congestion will occur.

Congestion may occur when datagrams are sent faster than they can be processed. This situation could occur when a fast computer generates traffic that crosses a slow link, such as a WAN link, even if the computer is connected to a fast network segment. Data leaves the computer, crosses the network wire, and lands at the router, which then queues the data for transmission across the slow link. Because the data is coming in faster than it is going out, the result is—you guessed it—congestion!

When a router is congested and begins to drop packets, it sends an ICMP Source Quench message for each datagram that it discards. An ICMP Source Quench message is identified by its Type 4 status. The fields in this message are described in Figure 6.11.

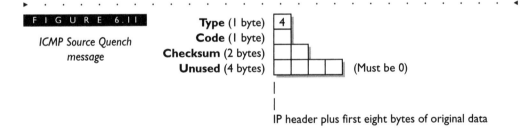

FIGURE 6.11

ICMP Source Quench message

Type (1 byte) 4
Code (1 byte)
Checksum (2 bytes)
Unused (4 bytes)   (Must be 0)

IP header plus first eight bytes of original data

Like any other ICMP error-class message, the IP header information included in the ICMP packet gives clues as to which host was the traffic generator, or the recipient of the Source Quench request.

When a host receives a Source Quench message, normally, the host has a field value in its IP module for *delaytime*, which usually starts out at 0. When IP is ready to send data to the network, it looks at that delay value before sending. When a Source Quench is received by the host, the delaytime value increases. Thus, the IP module waits the appropriate delay time before transmitting more data. Eventually, the delaytime value decreases and falls back to 0. Pretty tricky, huh? The actual delay value varies, but is documented in RFC 1016.

Basically, the IP module on the host is self-regulating. It responds and adapts to the receipt of Source Quench messages. Not all vendor implementations of IP are able to understand these ICMP Source Quench messages and, consequently, just keep sending data, even though the host is already congested.

ICMP Redirect

Although routing tables on end nodes usually remain static, a change in network topology can change the data flow in the network. An ICMP Redirect message is used to inform a sender that the IP destination to which it sent a datagram is not the appropriate one. The packet is sent to the destination, and the ICMP Redirect message is sent back to the sender to tell it how to direct packets in the future.

Figure 6.12 shows how a host is informed of an alternative (and more appropriate) route to take when attempting communication across a router. Host 1 attempts communication with Host 2. Host 1 sends its first request to IP Router 1, which generates an ICMP error informing Host 1 that using Router 2 is more efficient. Host 1 receives the ICMP error and executes its request a second time, using Router 2 to communicate with Host 2.

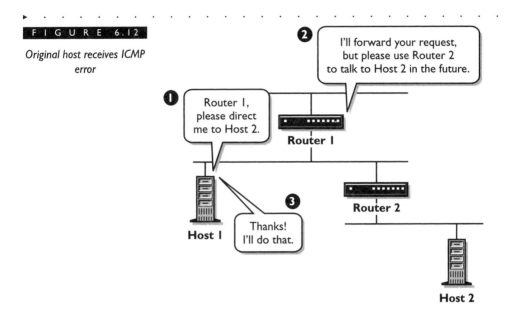

Original host receives ICMP error

The benefit of this Redirect capability is simplicity. When a host boots, it needs to know the address of only one router on the network. If the host sends data to a route that is not optimal, the router notifies the host. This eliminates the need for the host to know (and possibly have to guess) to which router data should be sent. A field in the ICMP Redirect message informs the host of the appropriate route. Figure 6.13 shows the ICMP Redirect packet structure. It is identified by an ICMP Type 5 in the first field.

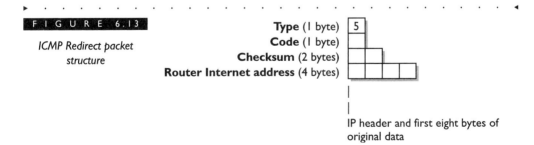

ICMP Redirect packet structure

Router Internet Address Field

The Router Internet Address field is used by the ICMP Redirect packet to hold the address of a router that the host is supposed to use when making future attempts to reach the original destination. Because this message class is an ICMP error, the original IP header plus first 64 bits (8 bytes) of original is also included. Figure 6.14 shows an ICMP Redirect message.

FIGURE 6.14

ICMP Redirect message

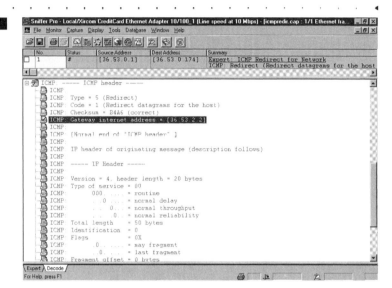

ICMP Redirect Communication

ICMP messages are limited to communication between a host and a router on the directly connected network, which means that, in some cases, an ICMP Redirect message may not be received and processed by the host.

Routers may not generate ICMP messages unless all of these conditions are met:

- ▶ The packet is being forwarded out the same physical interface from which it was received.

- ▶ The IP source address in the packet is on the same logical (sub) network as the next-hop IP address.

- ▶ The packet does not contain an IP source route option.

The following sections consider some ICMP Redirect situations.

Typical Redirect Scenario

In a normal IP network, the host knows about only one router, usually configured as its default gateway (also known as the *default route*). On bootup, most hosts perform the following steps to find the default gateway:

1. ARP request for data link address of the default gateway.

2. Receive reply.

3. Update host routing table to reflect default gateway address.

Figure 6.15 shows the host routing table update on bootup.

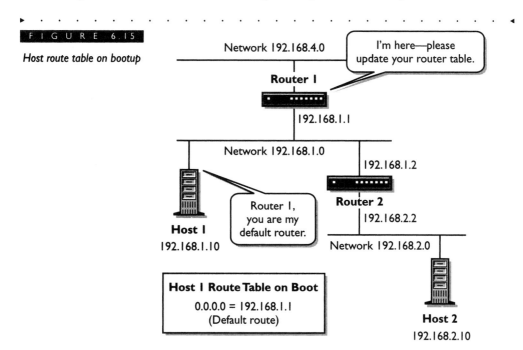

FIGURE   6.15

Host route table on bootup

Notice that the ARP request resolves the data link IP address *only* for that default gateway device. The ARP reply is kept in the host cache. In the normal course of operation, the host may request data that generates a Redirect message. Examine the host routing table in Figure 6.16 to see what happens when a host attempts to reach a resource through a nonoptimal route. The packet is forwarded but a Redirect message is sent to the host to update its routing tables.

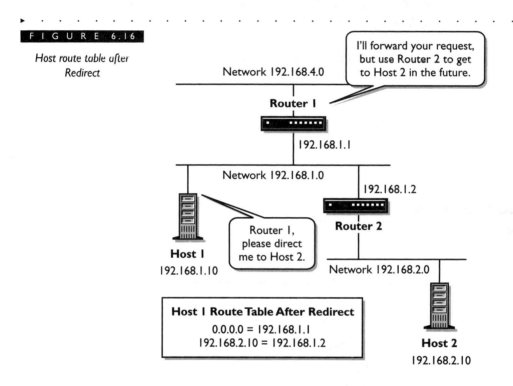

FIGURE 6.16

Host route table after Redirect

The host now knows that it must use an alternative route to communicate with this resource in the future. This type of communication is common, using only a single Redirect to establish proper communication. Like a good child, the host has to be told only once when it did something wrong. When the new route is entered into the routing table after an ICMP Redirect message, it expires after a certain period of time. When this route expires and a communication request packet is sent to the same host, another Redirect message is generated.

No Host Redirect Support

Not every IP vendor supports full ICMP functionality. Usually, you can assume that the basic ICMP messages, such as Echo Request and Reply (used with the

PING command) are available in a vendor's IP implementation. But, sometimes, Redirect messages are not understood by the host's IP module. This is the "bad child" on the network, resulting in a Redirect every time that it talks to the router. The communication path works in a triangle—the host talks to the router, the router sends a Redirect and forwards the packet anyway. The host ignores the Redirect and talks to the router again—this same thing happens over and over. Figure 6.17 depicts this triangular communication.

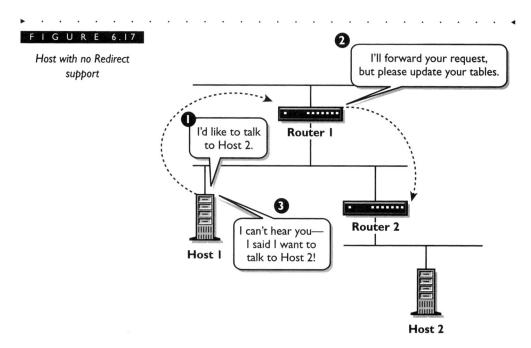

FIGURE 6.17

Host with no Redirect support

It really *is* like talking to a 2-year-old. This kind of scenario results in an unnecessary increased traffic load on the segment and, ultimately, a performance degradation. Generally, this problem may be solved by implementing an IP protocol stack that supports the complete ICMP message capability.

ICMP and Routers

ICMP is a type of communication that is limited to interaction between a router and a host. Routers use different protocols to communicate route information to each other, and routers do not receive ICMP messages. Routers may, however, use ICMP messages to advertise default routes to other nodes on a segment. This presents a potential problem—what if any one of multiple routes could be taken to a destination, but only one router is directly connected to the host? For example, Figure 6.18 shows how routers between a source and destination may be connected by multiple paths.

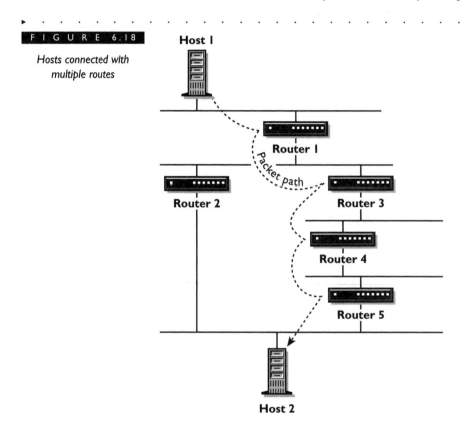

FIGURE 6.18

Hosts connected with multiple routes

In Figure 6.18, Host 1 wants to communicate with Host 2. Host 1 sends the message to the only router available to it on the connected network. Router 1 has two possible paths to take, and it incorrectly chooses a long path. When Router 5 receives the packet, it can't send an ICMP message to the original router, because it doesn't know Router 1's address. This is due to the fact that each time the packet crosses a router, the router updates the source address of the packet with its own address.

Sending a packet through an optimal route is called *propagation*. Making sure that the most optimal route between routers is used is not an ICMP issue, but is a routing protocol issue. Routing protocols, discussed later in this book, are responsible for establishing and maintaining proper IP routes.

ICMP Time Exceeded

Before a router sends a packet to the next-hop destination, it must look inside the IP header at the field called Time To Live (TTL), which is a timer that limits the amount of time that a datagram may live on the network. Why is a limit necessary? Consider the effect of a router that has an error in its routing tables. Router A passes the datagram to Router B, which passes it back to A, which passes it back to B, and so forth. Without a TTL value, the data could float around the network endlessly.

The TTL field in the IP header actually measures the units in seconds. Router rules state that each time the datagram crosses a router, the TTL field must be decremented by at least one before the packet is passed along. The router must decrement by at least one full second, even if forwarding the packet took less time. Because forwarding a packet very often takes less than one full second, the TTL really becomes a hop-count limit on how far the datagram can travel through the network. If the packet is held in the router for more than one second, the router may decrement the TTL by more than one.

NOTE

Routers must decrement the TTL field by at least one before forwarding the packet.

When the TTL field value is equal to 0, the packet is discarded and an ICMP Time Exceeded message is sent back to the source. Time Exceeded messages may be used when rebuilding fragmented packets. If a fragmented packet cannot be rebuilt within a specific time limit (which varies, depending on the vendor— NetWare time is two seconds), a Time Exceeded message is sent. The structure of the ICMP Time Exceeded message is identified by Type 11 in the Type field of the packet. Figure 6.19 shows the structure.

FIGURE 6.19

ICMP Time Exceeded message header

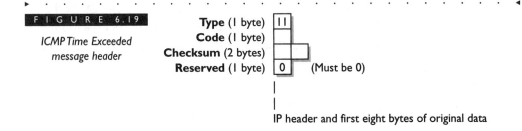

One of the most common utilities that generates these messages is the TRACEROUTE command, described in earlier chapters. If this message is generated without using this utility, then some sort of routing problem exists in the network. Figure 6.20 depicts an ICMP Time Exceeded message.

FIGURE 6.20

ICMP Time Exceeded message

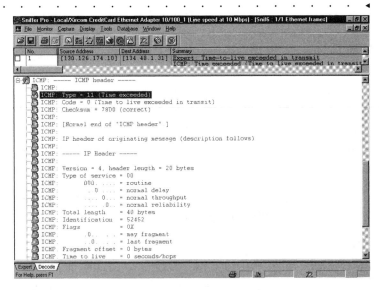

ICMP Parameter Problem

The ICMP Parameter Problem is a catchall error message. When a router or host finds a problem that it can't classify perfectly into another ICMP type, such as Destination Unreachable, the ICMP Parameter Problem message is sent to the source. The Parameter Problem message is identified by a Type 12 in the ICMP header. Figure 6.21 illustrates the format of this message.

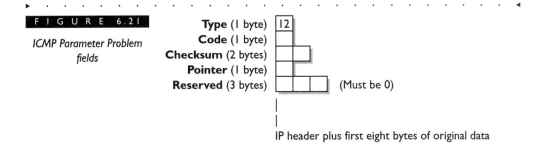

FIGURE 6.21

ICMP Parameter Problem fields

Type (1 byte) | 12 |
Code (1 byte)
Checksum (2 bytes)
Pointer (1 byte)
Reserved (3 bytes)   (Must be 0)

IP header plus first eight bytes of original data

Normally, you shouldn't see this type of message on the network. If it appears, it means that the packet header was discarded because the error was quite severe and processing couldn't continue.

The Pointer Field

The Pointer field is used in the ICMP Parameter Problem message header to identify where the error may be located. It identifies the octet of the original header where the datagram error was detected. This information is included in the ICMP error-class message.

ICMP Timestamp

When computers in a TCP/IP network operate, they generally have a sense of their own built-in time, but they don't necessarily know about the time on other computers. This can be a problem for those applications that rely on time, or large systems that need to maintain time between devices. The TCP/IP suite has several protocols that can be used for time management and synchronization. One of the simplest techniques uses an ICMP Timestamp message to request and obtain information from another host. A Timestamp request is identified by a Type 13 in the first ICMP header field, as Figure 6.22 illustrates.

FIGURE 6.22

ICMP Timestamp message header

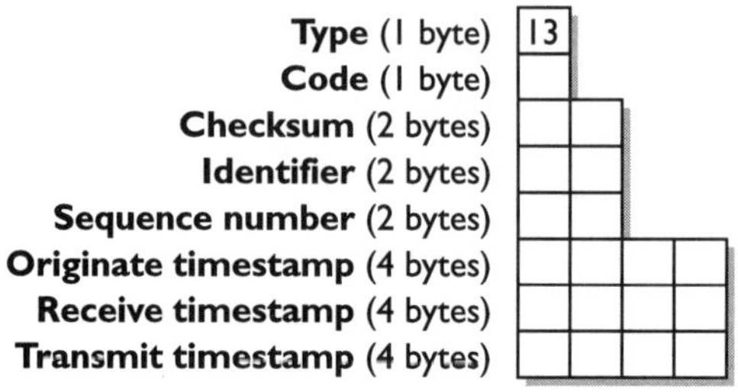

Type (1 byte) 13
Code (1 byte)
Checksum (2 bytes)
Identifier (2 bytes)
Sequence number (2 bytes)
Originate timestamp (4 bytes)
Receive timestamp (4 bytes)
Transmit timestamp (4 bytes)

The Identifier and Sequence Number Fields

The Identifier and Sequence Number fields may be used by the Timestamp sender to match Timestamp replies with Timestamp requests. Any data that is received in the Timestamp message must be returned in the Timestamp reply. The identifier is used by the system to identify a session, whereas the sequence number is incremented on each Echo Request sent.

The Timestamp Fields

ICMP uses three fields to compute estimates of the delay time between them. Ultimately, this information is used to synchronize the clocks of the computers involved in the timestamp session. These fields are shown in Table 6.2.

TABLE 6.2

Timestamp Field Values

TIMESTAMP FIELD TYPE	DESCRIPTION
Originate Timestamp	Filled in by the sender just before the message is sent
Receive Timestamp	Filled in by the receiver when it first touches the message during receipt
Transmit Time	Filled in by the receiver just before transmitting the packet back to the sender

The Transmit Time can be either calculated or filled in by the receiver. If the Transmit is calculated, the host simply uses this formula:

```
Originate Timestamp - Receive Timestamp = Transmit
(calculated)
```

The host uses the Originate Timestamp to determine how long the packet takes to travel from the sender to the receiver and back again. Conversely, the reply carries information about the time that the request entered and left the receiver. From those Timestamps, the original host can compute the network transit time and then estimate the differences in clock time.

The Timestamp data is actually 32 bits (4 bytes) of milliseconds since Midnight Universal Time (UT). If time isn't available for some reason, or if the computer doesn't provide time based on the Midnight UT time, another value may be placed in this field.

You need to understand that this method of time synchronization isn't always entirely accurate. Routers, switches, and other network devices all add delay to the Timestamp fields. The round trip packet return time can also vary greatly in a large network, depending on bandwidth utilization, router hops, and congestion.

Using ICMP As a Troubleshooting Tool

ICMP messages travel across the network just like other datagrams. The destination of an ICMP message is the IP software on the remote device—not the application, as some might expect. Setting the filter on your analyzer to capture ICMP packets is a great way to begin troubleshooting a TCP/IP network. This section examines how an ICMP error is reported.

As previously stated, ICMP is an error-reporting mechanism used by routers. When an error is discovered, it is reported back to the original source. The source is then responsible for taking appropriate action to resolve the error. The source may send an error to the application program or take other action based on the message type.

Route Discovery

Using the utility TRACERT (traceroute) from your Windows workstation is one way to determine the route that a packet takes on its way to communicate with another host. From a NetWare Server console, you would use the IPTRACE.NLM.

To use the workstation TRACERT.EXE utility, open a command line window from your Windows 3.1 or DOS computer, or click Start ➪ Run from the Windows 95/98 desktop. At the command line, type

```
TRACERT IP address or host name
```

You may use either a valid IP address (if you know it) or a valid host name, such as server1.abc123.com. The result is the route the packet takes, including each router it crosses on its journey. The packet can cross up to 30 routers (hops) with this utility.

Figure 6.23 shows the result of a TRACERT command.

FIGURE 6.23

A TRACERT command

Quite a few "visual" traceroute utilities are available on the Internet. A map is placed on the screen, and you can see how the packet travels throughout the world.

TIP

How a Route Is Discovered by Using Traceroute

All routes discovered through the traceroute utility use ICMP error messages. The process is kind of like detective work on the internetwork. Figure 6.24 illustrates the discovery process.

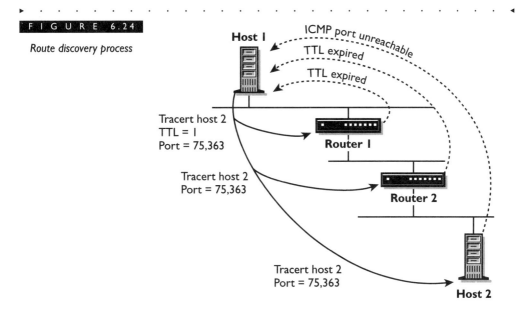

F I G U R E   6.24

Route discovery process

A Computer Needs to Discover a Route

Host 1 issues a TRACEROUTE command for Host 2, as shown in Figure 6.24, which travels through two routers before it can communicate with Host 2. However, Host 1 doesn't know that yet and sends its first request, with a TTL value of 1. The request hits the first router, which decrements the TTL by 1, resulting in a TTL value of 0. The router can't forward a packet with no TTL, so it discards the packet and sends an ICMP packet back to the host, telling the host that the TTL is 0.

The host now knows where the first router is located in the chain, and resends the packet, changing the TTL to 2 (the value of 1 plus the single hop count that it knows about). Router 1 receives the packet and checks the TTL, which is greater than 1, so it decrements the TTL by 1 (which is required every time that a packet crosses a router) and sends it on.

Router 2 receives the request, but the TTL is now set to 1. The router decrements the TTL by 1, again resulting in a value of 0. The router can't forward the packet, so it discards the packet. Once again, an ICMP message is generated and sent back to the original host, stating that the TTL has expired.

The host now knows that at least two routers stand between it and the destination. It resends another request, this time setting the TTL to 3 (1 plus the 2 hops that it knows about). This time, it crosses both routers and reaches its destination, Host 2. Host 2 replies with a different ICMP message, Port Unreachable, which is generated because the host software isn't listening on port 40001. The host now knows the full route to the destination.

Host 1 knew when to stop executing requests, because in the original packet, an unsupported TCP port number was used inside the ICMP request packet. Each of the routers, noticing that the TTL had expired, never looked at the port number to process the request. When the packet finally reached the correct computer, Host 2, the packet was opened and processing began. At that time, Host 2 reported that it didn't have that port available and thus returned a Port Unreachable ICMP error message to Host 1. So, Host 1 knew that it had reached the correct machine, and it never expected proper processing to occur anyway, because the port was invalid.

TCP port numbers are discussed in detail in Chapter 10.

X-REF

When Not to Use Traceroute

This type of ICMP troubleshooting works well in a corporate internal environment in which single routes are defined. However, in a mesh network, such as the Internet or a corporate network for which routes may be duplicated for redundancy, this isn't a good tool. For example, Figure 6.25 shows the result of a traceroute command to `www.novell.com`.

FIGURE 6.25

*Results of Traceroute to
www.novell.com*

```
Tracing route to www.novell.com [137.65.2.11]
over a maximum of 30 hops:

 1  228 ms  187 ms  226 ms  hil-dnptf-254.oh.compuserve.net [206.175.102.254]
 2  262 ms  228 ms  208 ms  hil-ppp-2-fe21.compuserve.net [209.154.35.350]
 3  209 ms  256 ms  181 ms  hil-core1-fe-4-1-0.compuserve.net [205.156.214.161]
 4  201 ms  226 ms  204 ms  atm1-03-core.hyt.compuserve.net [205.156.223.134]
 5  201 ms  232 ms  241 ms  fddi0-border1.hyt.compuserve.net [205.156.223.194]
 6  261 ms  247 ms  205 ms  hssi1-mae-east.hyt.compuserve.net [206.175.73.2]
 7  233 ms  240 ms  209 ms  maeeast2.bbnplanet.net [198.32.186.2]
 8  210 ms  196 ms  211 ms  p2-2.vienna1-nbr2.bbnplanet.net [4.0.1.93]
 9  239 ms  207 ms  222 ms  p1-0.vienna1.nbr3.bbnplanet.net [4.0.5.46]
10  264 ms  316 ms  258 ms  p3-1.paloalto-nbr2.bbnplanet.net [4.0.3.178]
11  258 ms  289 ms  265 ms  p1-0.paloalto-nbr1.bbnplanet.net [4.0.5.65]
12  267 ms  284 ms  265 ms  p1-0-0.paloalto-cr9.bbnplanet.net [4.0.2.214]
13  281 ms  357 ms  288 ms  h4-0.novellut5.bbnplanet.net [131.119.26.94]
14  336 ms  315 ms  372 ms  www.novell.com [137.65.2.11]

Trace complete.
```

Compare Figure 6.26, which is a traceroute command to the same place on a different day. On one day, the traceroute command took 14 hops, whereas it took 13 hops the other day. Additionally, it went through different routers entirely, even though the eventual ending point was the same.

FIGURE 6.26

*Traceroute results to
www.novell.com are
different on another day.*

```
Tracing route to www.novell.com [137.65.2.11]
over a maximum of 30 hops:

 1  436 ms  303 ms  338 ms  206.175.97.127
 2  285 ms  293 ms  333 ms  hil-ppp-1-fe20.compuserve.net [209.154.35.2]
 3  344 ms  322 ms  267 ms  fddi0-border1.hil.compuserve.net [205.156.223.82]
 4  311 ms  244 ms  267 ms  fddi0-core.hil.compuserve.net [205.156.223.83]
 5  515 ms  593 ms  523 ms  atm4-01-core.sf.compuserve.net [205.156.223.230]
 6  309 ms  361 ms  356 ms  fddi0-border1.sf.compuserve.net [205.156.223.146]
 7  331 ms  298 ms  335 ms  hssi1-mae-west.sf.compuserve.net [205.156.223.234]
 8  350 ms  305 ms  342 ms  sanjose1-br1.bbnplanet.net [198.32.136.19]
 9  363 ms  364 ms  369 ms  sanjose1-nbr1.bbnplanet.net [4.0.3.193]
10  392 ms  324 ms  347 ms  su-bfr.bbnplanet.net [4.0.1.1]
11  389 ms  358 ms  337 ms  paloalto-cr9.bbnplanet.net [4.0.2.214]
12  333 ms  452 ms  317 ms  131.119.26.94
13  429 ms  364 ms  362 ms  www.novell.com [137.65.2.11]

Trace complete.
```

Case Study—What Can Go Wrong

This case study looks at one of the ways in which ICMP is used to troubleshoot networks.

The Problem

A customer has an internetwork consisting of a small number of Ethernet segments connected by a router. Users are complaining of a slowdown in network performance on one of the segments, yet no one has installed anything new or is using a new program on the network. One user who has specifically noticed a slowdown is Sue. Figure 6.27 shows the network layout on which Sue resides.

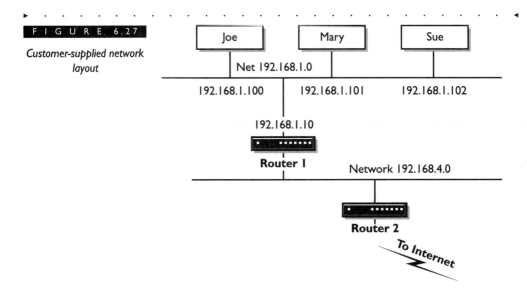

FIGURE 6.27

Customer-supplied network layout

The Analysis

Knowing that ICMP packets can reveal the source of many problems on the network, we first set up our analyzer to capture only ICMP packets. After capturing for a few minutes, we view the results, shown in Figure 6.28.

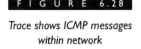

FIGURE 6.28

Trace shows ICMP messages within network

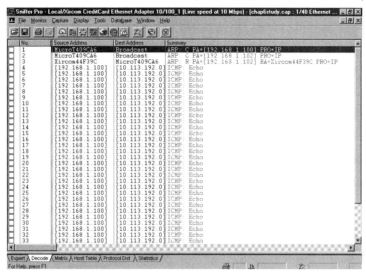

This initial trace is interesting, because a quick glance shows that at least three stations are involved in this problem, based on the IP numbers in the Source and Destination Address fields, and the ARP requests. This trace also shows a pattern of data in the form of an ICMP Echo Request, but no Echo Replies. The following steps dig a bit further into the trace:

1. Frame 1 shows a station performing an ARP request for IP number 192.168.1.100. No reply is forthcoming. Yet further in the trace, the 192.168.1.100 address is being used extensively, so we know that it exists. The true reason for the ARP is unknown, but we can make a guess. Many vendors implement a type of duplicate-IP-number testing on bootup of a device. The device does an ARP request for its own number, just to see whether another device with its address exists. In this case, no response is expected. Given that information, we may have caught a new device coming onto the network.

2. Frames 2 and 3 show an ARP request and reply to IP address 192.168.1.102. This address belongs to a workstation used by Sue. Why would the ARP request go to Sue?

3. Frames 4 through the end of the trace show a source computer, IP number 192.168.1.100, making an Echo Request (PING) to address 10.113.192.0. We can assume, given the IP numbers, that these are not on the same segment. Therefore, for an Echo Request/Reply (PING) to occur, a router must be used. Figure 6.28 shows that the router that should be used in this case is numbered 192.168.1.10. Why did the device look for Sue's address rather than the router address? The logical conclusion is that the device using IP address 192.168.1.100 has a misconfigured default gateway address.

4. Putting together all the information, we see that the device booted up and made an ARP request for its own number and for Sue's IP number, probably thinking that it was the router. Because Sue's workstation was turned on and IP was functioning, the device received an ARP reply. The device then began a series of PING commands, which went unanswered.

The Solution

Sue's complaints of a slowdown are now understandable. The device at IP number 192.168.1.100 was trying to use her computer as a router to get to another address. Because Sue's computer is not configured as a router, the originating device never received an Echo Reply, so it just kept trying. Though some PING commands stop after a certain number of Echo Replies, ways exist to make a PING request go on forever, as is the case here. A look at the device at 192.168.1.100 showed that, indeed, its default gateway address was set to Sue's IP number — 192.168.1.102, and it was issuing the PING command. Reconfiguring the host's default gateway solved this problem.

Summary

This chapter explored how the Internet Control Message Protocol is used in the TCP/IP environment. Common implementations of ICMP messages were defined. It also looked at how ICMP can be used as a great troubleshooting tool.

## CHAPTER 7

Routing Information Protocol

This chapter introduces and discusses the Routing Information Protocol (RIP). RIP is used by routers within an internetwork to learn how to send information to other networks within a system. When a router learns about another network, it stores this information as a *route*. A route is simply the path that network traffic must take to go between a source and a destination network or host. Ultimately, the stored routes are used by the routers to process and send network traffic to the appropriate places within the network.

Routing Protocol Types

Many types of routing protocols exist that may be used to assist routers in making proper decisions when forwarding packets. As an overview, this section first looks at two very different routing protocol classifications:

► Interior gateway protocols (IGPs)

► Exterior gateway protocols (EGPs)

Interior and Exterior Gateway Protocols

Interior gateway protocol is a classification for protocols that are used by routers to exchange routing information within a single system, or site location (also referred to as an *autonomous system*). One of the most popular interior gateway protocols is RIP, due to its efficiency and redundancy.

After all routers within a single, autonomous system have communicated with each other and exchanged routing information, an *exterior gateway protocol*, such as Border Gateway Protocol (BGP) or Exterior Gateway Protocol (EGP), is used to provide routing information advertisements for routers outside the autonomous system. A network consisting of three autonomous systems looks similar to the network shown in Figure 7.1.

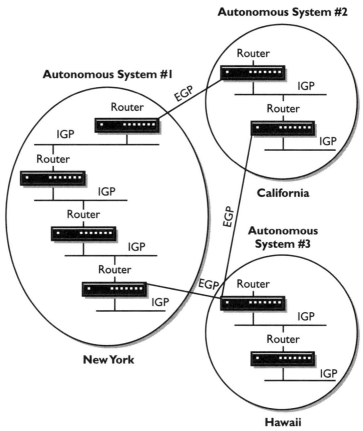

Autonomous System #2

Router

IGP

Router

IGP

California

Autonomous System #1

Router

IGP

Router

IGP

Router

IGP

Router

IGP

New York

Autonomous System #3

Router

IGP

Router

IGP

Hawaii

Internally, these three connected systems use an interior gateway protocol, such as RIP, to communicate information about other routers within the location. To communicate externally, the routers use an exterior gateway protocol.

In addition to these two major classifications, routing protocols may take on the characteristics associated with one of two major types of information exchange: *distance vector* and *link state*, which determine how, when, and what information will be exchanged between routers.

Distance Vector vs. Link State Protocols

As noted, two distinct types of protocols are in use between routers today:

▸ Distance vector

▸ Link state

RIP is a *distance vector* protocol, which is an *advertising* protocol. That is, routers using RIP advertise their routes and knowledge of other routers on a periodic basis. Other routers receive the advertisements and update their routing tables accordingly. Broadcasts are made every 30 seconds, sending out a message that contains information taken from the router's current routing table. All RIP messages contain the distance, also called the *hop count,* to the next router. Basically, RIP is like going to a party — every router on the network talks about every other router that they know, how they met, and where they live.

Link state protocols do not work in the same way as distance vector protocols. Link state routers know about their neighboring routers and test the link status to each of their neighbors on a periodic basis. Next, the link-status information it sent to each of their neighbors, which in turn send it throughout the autonomous network. Each router takes the information and builds a complete picture of the network. A popular link state protocol is the Open Shortest Path First (OSPF) protocol (discussed further in Chapter 8).

This chapter focuses on the Routing Information Protocol and its use in interior autonomous systems.

Routing Information Protocol Functionality

RIP is a very common interior gateway protocol. It is not a protocol you will see across the Internet. Imagine what might happen if all routers on the Internet broadcast their routing tables every 30 seconds! Of course, this should not happen, which is why RIP is kept inside the autonomous network.

IP RIP is not the same as IPX RIP — do not confuse the two.

IMPORTANT

As already mentioned, RIP routers actively broadcast their routing table every 30 seconds. Each message sent on the network contains the network IP address and the distance to another network, which is called a *hop count*. Generally, a hop is generated when a packet must cross a router to get to a destination. In a RIP network, a single hop indicates a directly connected network (or local network), two hops indicates that the network is reachable through one router, and so on, as shown in Figure 7.2.

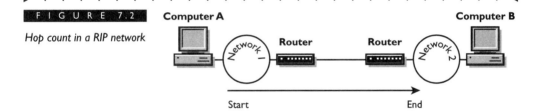

FIGURE 7.2

Hop count in a RIP network

In Figure 7.2, a packet traveling from Computer A on Network 1 to Computer B on Network 2 must cross two routers to reach its destination. Therefore, its hop count is two. When faced with a routing decision, a router generally takes the path with the lowest hop count to reach the destination. This is not always foolproof, however. Consider the example shown in Figure 7.3, in which a packet traveling from Computer A on Network 1 to Computer B on Network 2 reaches the router on Network 1. The router must now make a decision: send the packet on Path 1 or on Path 2.

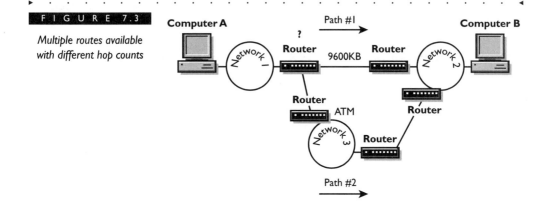

FIGURE 7.3

Multiple routes available with different hop counts

Path 1 poses a hop count of 2, and Path 2 poses a hop count of 4. Therefore, the router decides to send the packet down Path 1, ignoring the fact that Path 1 contains a very slow link, and that Path 2 probably is a better choice. To compensate for this scenario, many routers allow configuration of paths with higher hop counts, to deter routers from choosing slow link paths.

Broadcast, Aging, and Hold Down

The RIP protocol broadcasts its routing tables every 30 seconds. But what happens when a router stops broadcasting, due to failure? The RIP process must go through more steps, called *aging* and *hold down*.

When a router receives a route, it begins a timer for that table entry. Each router keeps an entry in its table for three minutes. When a router fails, its routing tables will not be broadcast during the normal time. After three minutes, a table entry expires. When a table entry expires and another broadcast is not received for that same route, the router begins to increase the cost (or hop count) of the route by one hop for each cycle (30 seconds) that it does not hear from the router.

Figure 7.4 shows a simple network consisting of four routed segments. A packet traveling from Router 1 to Router 4 has two possible paths. The preferred (and lowest hop count) path is to travel from Router 1 to Router 2 to Router 4.

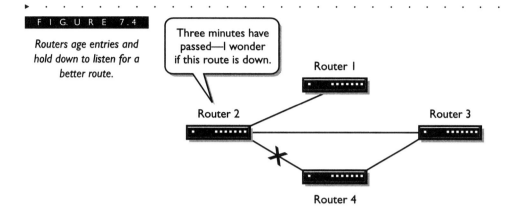

FIGURE 7.4

Routers age entries and hold down to listen for a better route.

Three minutes have passed—I wonder if this route is down.

Router 1

Router 2

Router 3

Router 4

Now, assume that the link is broken between Routers 2 and 4. After three minutes, the aging entry is discarded from Router 2's routing table, because it has not heard from Router 4. At the next broadcast time (30 seconds), Router 2 will begin to increase and broadcast the hop count by one during each subsequent 30-second cycle. At a certain point (in this case, after two cycles), the hop count of the original route will be greater than the hop count to Router 4 through Router 3.

This is good, except for one thing—we have no way of acknowledging whether the other routers in the network know about this new route. RIP broadcasts are assumed to be accepted and processed, but are not acknowledged. So, even though the routers now know a better route, they must use a *hold down* process before the route is valid. During a hold down, a router listens for the new route and ignores information about the unreachable route for 60 seconds. After a router has heard about a new route three times, it is free to use that new route.

Using this timing mechanism means that RIP networks take a long time to reconfigure, or *converge,* when a route is lost. The next section looks at how RIP attempts to correct these problems.

Solving Slow Convergence

RIP tables can become inconsistent, especially over a slow link, where data takes a long time to travel between routers. Likewise, because RIP only carries information about a route and its distance, any changes in topology may be broadcast slowly, and only after aging timers expire, again causing inconsistency in the RIP environment. This section explores several common issues relating to slow convergence:

- Count to infinity

- Routing loops

- Split horizon

- Poison reverse

- Triggered updates

Each of theses mechanisms assists in making RIP routing tables more consistent.

Count to Infinity

The last section explained how a router might begin to increase the hop count for a route that no longer advertises. But how long does that router count? Forever? Thankfully, this is not the case. The hop count limit for a route is 16 hops. When a route reaches 16 hops, it is considered no longer valid, which is also called *count to infinity*.

Routing Loops

A *routing loop* is a common occurrence in a RIP environment. In a network with more that one router, routers may advertise routes that lead back to themselves. Consider the inline router example in Figure 7.5.

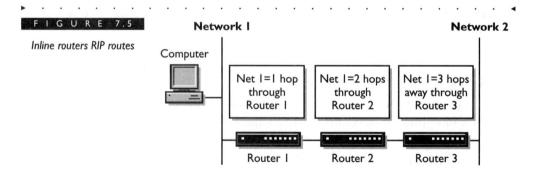

FIGURE 7.5

Inline routers RIP routes

In Figure 7.5, Router 1 advertises that it is directly connected to Network 1. Router 2 hears this broadcast, adds one hop, and broadcasts that Router 2 can get to Network 1 in two hops. Router 3 then broadcasts that it can get to Network 1 in three hops. This generally isn't a problem, *until* the link is broken between Routers 1 and 2. At this point, a routing loop occurs, as shown in Figure 7.6.

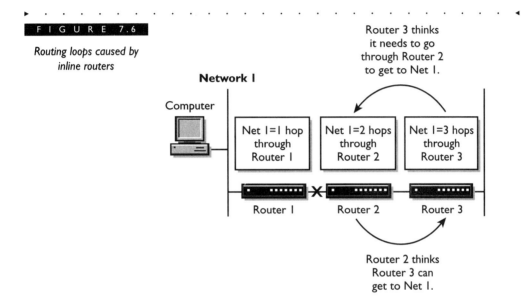

FIGURE 7.6

Routing loops caused by inline routers

In Figure 7.6, the link is broken between Router 1 and Router 2. Router 2 remembers that Router 3 said it could get to Network 1, even though it would take three hops. What Router 2 doesn't know is that the first hop is right back to itself. So, Router 2 passes the packet to Router 3, which passes it back to Router 2, and so on, until the packet's time-to-live timer expires, and the packet is lost. The routers will continue to have this problem until the route is finally counted to infinity.

Split Horizon, Poison Reverse, and Triggered Updates

Three methods currently are employed to assist with faster and more efficient RIP updating. To stop loops from happening and to get routers to agree on proper routes faster, the rule of *split horizon* should be used. Split horizon is a very simple rule that states that a device may not advertise a route back over the same interface from which it was learned.

Using the rule of split horizon, a device may not advertise a route back over the same interface from which it was learned.

IMPORTANT

If you were using split horizon in the example in Figure 7.6, Router 3 would not have told Router 2 that it could get back to Network 1. Therefore, the loop would not have happened. Though split horizon is useful in solving routing loops, it does not allow routers to broadcast a route that is considered to be down. Instead, RIP routers wait for several cycles to listen for down routes. To help routers learn about down routes faster, the rule of *poison reverse* is used.

Poison reverse really isn't as bad as it sounds. Once again, the concept is quite simple. When a route disappears, a router that was previously advertising the connection keeps the entry for several cycles, and includes a cost (or hop count) of 16 in its broadcasts. Using the cost of 16 causes the router to force a route to be down.

To make poison reverse efficient, it is combined with a process called *triggered updates*. Using a triggered update, a router will be forced to send an immediate broadcast when informed that a route is down.

RIP1 Packet Structure

Two versions of RIP are used today — RIP1 and RIP2. This section looks at the RIP1 specification and field values.

RIP is a UDP-based protocol, which uses port 520 directed to the router's routing process. RIP messages have both the source and the destination UDP port equal to 520.

The RIP1 packet structure is shown in Figure 7.7. Up to 25 RIP entries may be in one RIP packet.

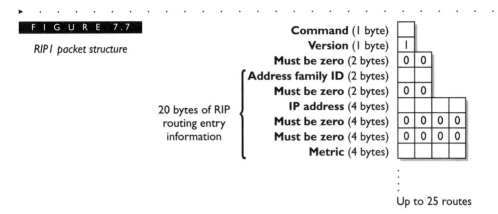

FIGURE 7.7

RIP1 packet structure

20 bytes of RIP routing entry information

Command (1 byte)
Version (1 byte)
Must be zero (2 bytes)
Address family ID (2 bytes)
Must be zero (2 bytes)
IP address (4 bytes)
Must be zero (4 bytes)
Must be zero (4 bytes)
Metric (4 bytes)

Up to 25 routes

Command

The Command field in the RIP1 packet may contain one of five values, as shown in Table 7.1.

TABLE 7.1

RIP1 Command Field Values

COMMAND VALUE	DESCRIPTION
1	Request for routing table information.
2	Response to request for routing table information.
3	Traceon command—obsolete and not used. Messages containing this command value are ignored.
4	Traceoff command—also obsolete and not used.
5	Reserved for Sun Microsystems only.

Version

The Version field contains the RIP protocol version number. For RIP1, this value is 1.

Address Family ID

The format of the RIP packet is intended to allow RIP to carry multiple routing protocols. For each message sent, a value is placed in this field to indicate the protocol family being used. The protocol Address Family ID for IP is 2.

IP Address

The IP Address field contains the IP address for the route. A special address, called the *default route,* may appear in this field. This IP address is 0.0.0.0 and, when broadcast, is used as the default path for the router to send data. This field may also include an IP address of a network or a host. When using the routing table, if no match exists for the host or network IP address, the configured default route will be used.

Metric

The Metric field contains the hop count for this routing entry. The field must contain a value of 1 through 15, or the value 16 if the route is considered to be unreachable. If a router receives an update to a route that is already in the table, the old route is replaced with the new route.

It may be a bit easier to look at this using an analyzer, as shown in Figure 7.8.

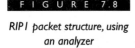

F I G U R E   7 . 8

RIP I packet structure, using an analyzer

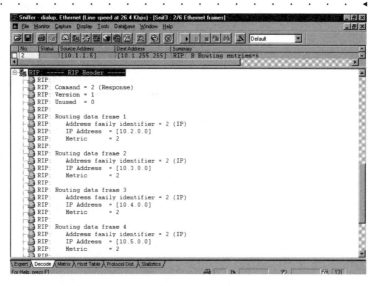

Notice in Figure 7.8 that the RIP command is a type 2 (Response) and the version is 1. For each RIP entry, the family ID (IP) value is 2, along with specific IP network information and hop count. This packet has six entries, but a maximum of 25 entries per packet is possible.

RIP1 Compared to RIP2

The original RIP specification was quite simple — cause a route to be advertised with basic IP information and a distance value. This original standard is called RIP1. Some extensions have been defined for RIP1 to assist with larger network configurations. This newer specification is called RIP2. Though RIP2 does not change the basic algorithms or processes of RIP1, it does add some features that enhance the overall functionality of the protocol.

Some of the newer features of RIP2 are the addition of a Subnet Mask field, for variable-length subnetting and routing domain information; external route tags, to allow propagation of information obtained from an external router; next-hop addresses, for route optimization; and password authentication.

RIP2 Packet Structure

The RIP2 packet header is exactly the same as RIP1, except for the Version field. However, the routing information entries have changed to include the new features, as shown in Figure 7.9.

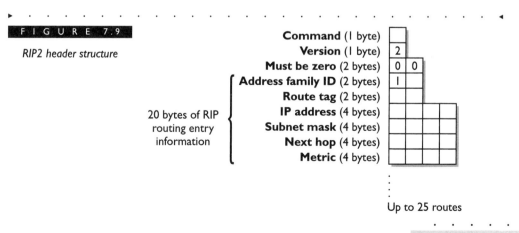

FIGURE 7.9

RIP2 header structure

20 bytes of RIP routing entry information

Command (1 byte)
Version (1 byte)
Must be zero (2 bytes)
Address family ID (2 bytes)
Route tag (2 bytes)
IP address (4 bytes)
Subnet mask (4 bytes)
Next hop (4 bytes)
Metric (4 bytes)

Up to 25 routes

The first three fields in the RIP2 header are exactly the same as those in the RIP1 header. However, the routing information entries for RIP2 contain extra field values — those fields that were all zeroes in RIP1. These field values are described in the following sections.

Address Family and Authentication

With a RIP1 message, the Address Family ID value was 2 for IP. With the RIP2 specification, password authentication may be used. However, looking at the available fields in the RIP2 message, only 2 bytes are available for use. That means the largest password you could use would be two characters, which is hardly enough for a password. So, the RIP2 specification uses an entire routing information entry for the password (if it is used), leaving 24 entries available in the rest of the packet. Additionally, the value of 0 is placed in the Address Family ID field, to indicate that the first routing entry is used for authentication.

Figure 7.10 shows what the first routing information entry would look like in a RIP2 packet with authentication.

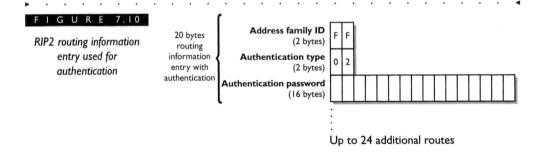

F I G U R E 7.10

RIP2 routing information entry used for authentication

20 bytes routing information entry with authentication

Address family ID (2 bytes)

Authentication type (2 bytes)

Authentication password (16 bytes)

Up to 24 additional routes

Currently, a password is the only authentication method available, and it carries an authentication value of 2. The Authentication Password is a 16-byte field that allows a clear-text password value.

Route Tag

The Route Tag field has an attribute assigned that is used when the route is readvertised. The Route Tag field is designed to provide a way to separate internal

RIP routes from external RIP routes that may have been imported through an exterior gateway protocol.

IP Address

As with RIP1, the IP address is the address for the advertised route.

Subnet Mask

Included with RIP2, the Subnet Mask field contains the value of the subnet mask for the advertised route. The subnet mask and IP address are applied together to form the network portion of the IP address. If the Subnet Mask field is 0, then the routing entry does not contain a subnet mask.

In a network where both RIP1 and RIP2 packets may be exchanged, backward-compatibility must be maintained. Therefore, RIP2 routing entries must adhere to the following rules:

▸ Internal information on one network must never be advertised into another network.

▸ The RIP2 route must not advertise a more specific subnet. This may cause a RIP1 router to consider the subnet a route to a host, not a network.

▸ A route with a subnet mask whose value is less than that of the true network mask (in other words, a *supernet* route) could be misinterpreted by a RIP1 router. Therefore, supernet routes must not be advertised.

Next Hop

The next hop address tells how packets sent to the destination of the route entry should be forwarded. In other words, it attempts to give an appropriate route rather than allow the router to simply guess the best direction for packet forwarding. This field was designed expressly for the purpose of eliminating the extra routing hops that could be taken by a packet when moving through a network.

The next hop address may be a value of 0.0.0.0, which indicates that routing should be performed through the originator of the RIP advertisement. It also tells other routers that the source of this RIP advertisement, the router, can directly reach the advertised segment.

Metric

Like RIP1, the Metric field contains the hop count for the routing entry. Using an analyzer, the differences in the RIP2 packet are shown in Figure 7.11.

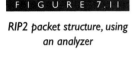

FIGURE 7.11

RIP2 packet structure, using an analyzer

Case Study — What Can Go Wrong

One common problem associated with RIP is broadcasts and table updates, which can very often lead to a routing loop. This section steps through an example where this may happen.

Figure 7.12 shows three networks connected with RIP routers. They are labeled Network 1, Network 2, and Network 3.

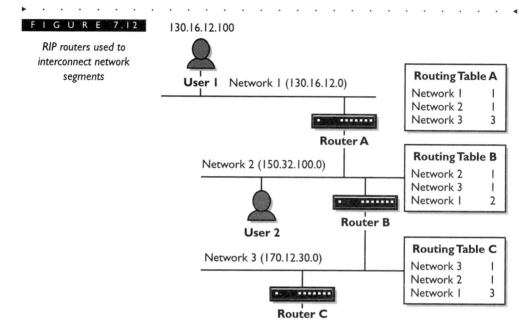

FIGURE 7.12

RIP routers used to interconnect network segments

On bootup, we can see the routing table entries for each of the routers in the network. Starting with Router A, we see that it is connected to two networks — Network 1 and Network 2. Router A updates its table to reflect that it is one hop away from either Network 1 or Network 2.

Also on bootup, Router B updates its table to reflect its connection to Networks 2 and 3. Router B places the entries in its table, to reflect that it is one hop away from either Network 2 or 3 through Router B. Router C reflects that it is directly connected to Network 3.

Soon, the first broadcast cycle occurs. Each router updates its table, as previously shown in Figure 7.12. Notice that this network is not using split horizon — Router C learned about Network 1 through Router B. Router C then updated its table to show that Network 1 was three hops away, through Router B. What happens next will cause a routing loop.

Assume that the connection between Router A and Network 1 is lost due to a cable break. Router A advertises that Network 1 is unreachable through itself. Router 2 updates its table to show that Network 1 is unreachable through Router A. However, Router B also sees that a route to Network 1 has been broadcast by

Router C. (He said he could get there!) So, a packet is sent to Router B for delivery to Network 1. Knowing that it can't get there through Router A, Router B sends the packet to Router C. Router C turns around and sends it right back to Router B, claiming that the next step should be to go through Router A. Router B, knowing this is impossible, sends the packet back to Router C, and so on.

· ·

Summary

In this chapter, you learned how the Routing Information Protocol (RIP) is used by routers to determine appropriate paths for traveling data. This chapter discussed the differences between interior and exterior routing protocols, along with the differences between distance vector and link state systems. Both RIP versions and their respective packet structures were examined.

## CHAPTER 8

Open Shortest Path First (OSPF)

Chapter 7 discusses the Routing Information Protocol (RIP), which uses a distance vector algorithm (Bellmann-Ford; see RFC 1058 for an explanation) to exchange routing information among gateways and hosts. A router using RIP announces all the networks in its routing table to its immediate neighbors. The neighbors add the cost of the receiving interface to the routing information, process the routing information, and add new or changed routes to their routing table. The neighbors then pass on their routing information to their neighbors. The information received cannot be verified for its reliability, and thus is only "hearsay" information.

Instead of using a distance vector algorithm, Open Shortest Path First (OSPF) uses a link-state algorithm. Every router has an identical database reflecting all the link information in the network. Every router issues its link-state information, which is passed on (flooded) to every other router. Every router uses this identical database to calculate the best paths to every other router and network.

This chapter discusses the contents of a link-state database, the process of building the shortest path first (SPF) tree to calculate the best paths, and the exchange of link-state information among the routers. It looks into all the packet types used by OSPF to establish connections to neighboring routers and to exchange database information.

For a glossary of specific terms and abbreviations used with OSPF, see Table 8.6 at the end of this chapter. Throughout the chapter, the same sample network is used to illustrate the operations of OSPF. Figure 8.1 shows this network, and you can always refer back to this figure.

OSPF Overview

OSPF is standardized in RFC 2328, which replaces RFC 2178 and RFC 1583. In addition to these documents, several extensions to OSPF have been defined. RFC 1584 describes multicast extensions to OSPF. RFC 1587 adds not-so-stubby areas (NSSAs) to OSPF. The latest extensions are specified in RFC 2370, which talks about the OSPF opaque LSA (link-state advertisement) option to be used for additional information sent through OSPF.

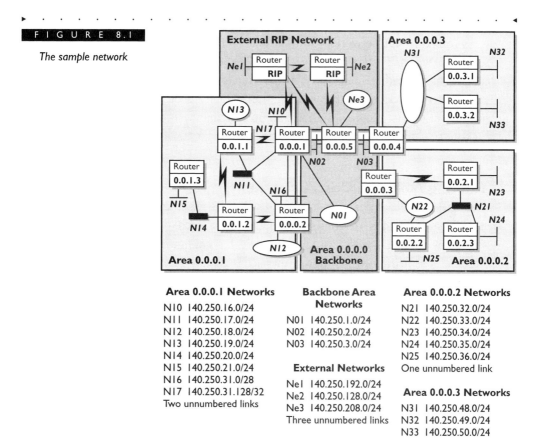

FIGURE 8.1

The sample network

Area 0.0.0.1 Networks
N10 140.250.16.0/24
N11 140.250.17.0/24
N12 140.250.18.0/24
N13 140.250.19.0/24
N14 140.250.20.0/24
N15 140.250.21.0/24
N16 140.250.31.0/28
N17 140.250.31.128/32
Two unnumbered links

Backbone Area Networks
N01 140.250.1.0/24
N02 140.250.2.0/24
N03 140.250.3.0/24

External Networks
Ne1 140.250.192.0/24
Ne2 140.250.128.0/24
Ne3 140.250.208.0/24
Three unnumbered links

Area 0.0.0.2 Networks
N21 140.250.32.0/24
N22 140.250.33.0/24
N23 140.250.34.0/24
N24 140.250.35.0/24
N25 140.250.36.0/24
One unnumbered link

Area 0.0.0.3 Networks
N31 140.250.48.0/24
N32 140.250.49.0/24
N33 140.250.50.0/24

OSPF is classified as an Interior Gateway Protocol (IGP). IGPs are used within autonomous systems (ASs). Other IGPs are RIP (Routing Information Protocol), and Cisco's IGRP (Interior Gateway Routing Protocol) and EIGRP (Enhanced Interior Gateway Routing Protocol). Routing information is dynamically distributed within a single AS governed by a single authority. OSPF has been developed by the OSPF working group of the IETF (Internet Engineering Task Force).

Link-State-Based Protocol

Each router maintains a database describing the link states of each participating router within the AS, and issues a *link-state advertisement (LSA)* advertising the local state of its interfaces. Additional LSAs are issued that describe networks with multiple routers (called *transit* networks), summary networks from other areas, or networks external to the OSPF autonomous system. All LSA types are described during this chapter (summarized in Table 8.2). The LSAs are flooded within the AS. The flooding mechanism is described in the section "Link-State Advertisements," later in this chapter. Every router receives all LSAs and puts them into its database of LSAs, called its *link-state database (LSDB)*. Therefore, the LSDB is identical on each router.

Routing Table and Cost Assignment

Using the LSDB as the source, each router runs the exact same algorithm to build a tree of least-cost paths (shortest-path first tree) to each destination. The cost is described by a single, dimensionless metric, which is configurable on each interface of the router. The metric assigned to the interface is usually inversely proportional to its line speed; in other words, the higher the bandwidth, the lower the cost. A common formula, according to the RFCs, is to divide 10^8 by the line speed (bits/sec). Customers can choose to use other formulas according to corporate standards. OSPF can put multiple equal cost paths to the same destination into the routing table. The forwarding mechanism of the router is responsible for distributing traffic among equal cost paths. For example, it can send traffic down multiple equal cost paths in a round-robin fashion, to optimize the use of the additional bandwidth. Using this method, however, bears a risk of packets arriving out of sequence at the destination. The out-of-sequence problem can be solved by choosing an IP-address-based distribution over multiple equal cost paths.

Support for TOS

RFC 1583 defines the support for metrics used for different types of services defined in the TOS field of the IP header. In addition to the metric for TOS 0 (normal), metric values can be assigned for TOS 2 (minimize monetary cost), TOS 4 (maximize reliability), TOS 8 (maximize throughput), and TOS 16 (minimize delay). RFCs 2178 and 2328 have withdrawn the TOS option. TOS information can still be distributed for backward-compatibility, but will no longer be used in the calculation of the routing table.

OSPF Areas

OSPF allows the link-state database to be partitioned into areas. This reduces routing traffic by replacing all routing information of one area with summary information to be distributed to the rest of the AS. The topology of an area, therefore, is hidden from the rest of the AS. Routing within the area is determined by the area's own LSDB. Areas are further discussed in the following section, "OSPF Areas."

Variable-Length Network Masks

OSPF enables the use of variable-length network masks. Each route distributed by OSPF consists of a destination address and its associated mask. Subnets with different masks are allowed within the same IP network. A packet is routed to the best match with the most specific (longest) mask.

Authentication

OSPF packets can be authenticated, similar to RIP2. A password can be configured for each interface. Authentication can be none (no authentication), simple (password in clear-text), or encrypted. Encryption has been added in RFC 2178.

Routes External to OSPF

In addition to distributing routing information configured with OSPF, OSPF can import routes derived from external sources (for example, RIP, BGP, static routes) into OSPF. Because the metrics of these external routes and OSPF metrics cannot be compared, external routes are kept separate in the LSDB. They are added to the routing table after the calculation of the SPF tree. OSPF will allow you to carry additional information about the external routes by using tags. This is discussed further in the section "Non-OSPF Routes."

OSPF Areas

Within an AS, routers can be grouped together to form areas. An OSPF area is a collection of networks and hosts. Each area is assigned a unique *area ID,* a 32-bit integer variable typically represented as a dotted decimal number. It looks very much like an IP address, but does not have to follow the same addressing rules. Each router in the area has its interfaces configured using the same area ID. Each area has its own LSDB from which every router internal to the area will calculate all the routes to all the networks and hosts within the area.

Routers with all interfaces belonging to a single area are called *internal routers*. Areas are linked together by using *area border routers* (ABRs). Each area must always be linked to a single common area, called a *backbone area* (the area ID is always 0.0.0.0). Therefore, an ABR must have at least one interface in the backbone area. ABRs advertise all networks and hosts of their area to the backbone area, which thereafter advertises these networks to all the other areas. In reverse, the ABR advertises all networks from the backbone area into its area.

Using multiple areas, all routers within the AS no longer necessarily have an identical LSDB. An internal router maintains only the LSDB of its own area. An ABR has an LSDB for each area it is connected to, including the backbone area. Routing within the AS takes place at two levels:

▸ **Intra-area routing:** If the source and destination IP address of a packet belong to the same area, the packet is routed based solely on information obtained from the area LSDB.

▸ **Inter-area routing:** If the destination address is within another area, the packet has to be routed to the ABR. From there, it is routed through the backbone to the ABR of the destination area. This ABR then routes the packet to the final destination within the destination area. The path is split into three parts: the intra-area route to the ABR, the inter-area route to the ABR of the destination area, and, finally, the intra-area route to the final destination.

The Backbone Area

The backbone area is a special area using area ID 0.0.0.0 (area 0). The backbone area contains all ABRs of the AS. If the AS is not split into areas, the backbone area will be the only area configured. If the AS is split into areas, the backbone area is responsible for distributing routing information between all nonbackbone areas. The backbone area has to be *contiguous*, meaning that each router within the same area has at least one direct link to another router in the same area, and this link belongs to the area. However, with the introduction of *virtual links*, a backbone area doesn't have to be physically contiguous. A transit area can be used to create a tunnel (virtual link) belonging to the backbone area. This is further discussed in the section "Virtual Links."

Nonbackbone Areas

Nonbackbone areas receive a unique area ID other than 0.0.0.0. They have to be physically contiguous. Each nonbackbone area must have an ABR connected to the backbone, using either a physical link or a virtual link. ABRs advertise all the networks known to the backbone into the nonbackbone area. In reverse, an ABR advertises all the networks of the nonbackbone area into the backbone. A nonbackbone area can have multiple ABRs.

Normally, the ABR uses a single LSA for each network found in the area. The ABR can be configured to summarize networks by using a summary network and summary mask, to reduce the amount of routing information advertised. It is important to plan the assignment of network addresses within the area to benefit most of the summarization of networks. The ABR assigns a metric to this summary. The whole summary is advertised by using a single summary LSA. If summarization is omitted, the ABR advertises every single network of the area by using a single summary LSA for each network. Note that the LSA issued by the ABR is always called a *summary LSA*.

Figure 8.2 explains summaries being advertised by ABRs. The ABR is summarizing nonbackbone routes into the backbone, and backbone routes into the nonbackbone area.

Virtual Links

Virtual links are logical links that tunnel backbone traffic through a nonbackbone area. They can be configured between two ABRs by using a common nonbackbone area called the *transit area*. Virtual links belong to the backbone and can only cross a single transit area. The transit area must not be a stub area (see the subsequent section "Stub Area"). A remote area that doesn't have a physical interface to the backbone area can be connected to the backbone by using virtual links. Virtual links can also be used to create redundant connections to the backbone. OSPF considers virtual links as numbered point-to-point links. Figure 8.3 shows an example of virtual links.

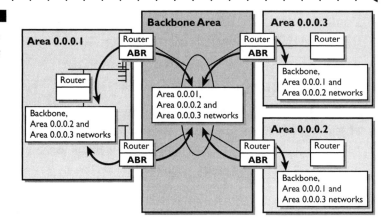

FIGURE 8.2

Area routes advertised by ABR, using summary LSAs

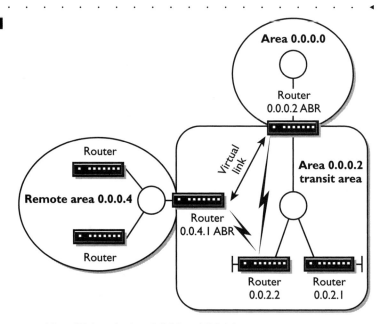

FIGURE 8.3

Virtual links

Virtual link endpoints: 0.0.0.2 and 0.0.4.1
Actual path according to the least cost path within area 0.0.0.2

▶ · ◀

Non-OSPF Routes (External Routes)

A router can learn about networks and hosts in many different ways, such as RIP, static routes, ICMP, BGP, IGRP, EIGRP, EGP, and so on. Every network and host from a non-OSPF source is considered to be an *OSPF external route* and can be imported into OSPF. To import external routes into OSPF, a router must have at least one interface configured with OSPF. This router is called an *autonomous system border router (ASBR)*. It runs OSPF and knows about at least one non-OSPF network. External routes are imported by using a single external LSA for each external network or host. Policies on the ASBR can summarize a range of external routes to be imported as a single external LSA.

Figure 8.4 explains how external routes are imported into OSPF.

External LSAs must be flooded throughout the AS. Each router within the AS will forward packets for external networks to the ASBR or a specific forwarding address advertised by the ASBR. Therefore, the ABR of the area having an ASBR needs to advertise the existence of the ASBR to all other areas, as shown in Figure 8.5.

▶ · ◀

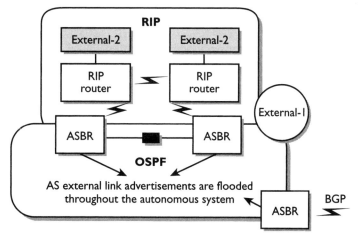

FIGURE 8.4

External routes imported into OSPF

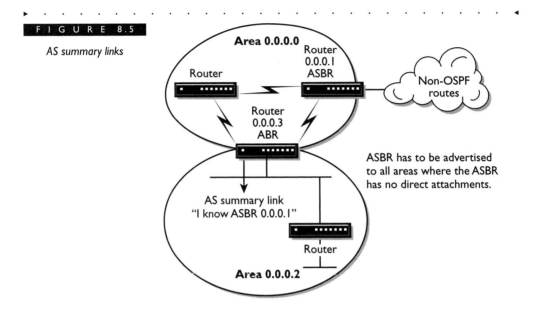

AS summary links

Metrics of external routes are not compatible with OSPF metrics. ASBRs advertise external routes by using one of two types of metrics:

▶ **External-1 routes:** Considered to be close to the ASBR. Routers within the AS calculate the OSPF cost to reach the ASBR or the advertised forwarding address for external-1 routes.

▶ **External-2 routes:** Considered to be further away from the ASBR. Therefore, a metric larger than the cost of any intra-AS path will be added to the metric already known by the ASBR.

If the same route is advertised as both an OSPF internal route and an external route, the path to the OSPF internal route is always chosen over the path to the external route. This can happen if multiple ASBRs are connected to the same external network. One ASBR is advertising an OSPF route to the external routing protocol, and another ASBR is importing the same route back to OSPF.

Stub Areas

The LSDB of a stub area is not allowed to maintain external routes. All external routes are instead represented by a single default route. External routes normally are flooded through the entire AS, which could result in quite a large LSDB, consisting of many external advertisements. To reduce the size of the LSDB, an ABR can prevent external routes from being flooded into an area. If the ABR does not advertise external routes into the area, it must replace the external routes with a single default route associated with a cost, called the *stub cost*. This default route is advertised as a summary LSA and flooded throughout the stub area, but no further. An area can be configured as a stub area when a single exit point (ABR) exists, or when multiple exit points (ABRs) exist with no need to find the best path on a per-external-destination basis. If multiple ABRs exist for a stub area, each internal router uses the default route with the least cost intra-area path to reach external destinations.

All routers within the stub area must be configured to be in the stub area by turning off the *external capability option*. This option is crucial to form adjacencies (see the later section "Bringing Up Adjacencies"), because all routers within an area have to agree on the same external capability option. Stub areas have some restrictions:

- ▸ They cannot be configured as transit areas for virtual links.

- ▸ No ASBR can be placed in a stub area, because all the routers in a stub area can't import external information.

- ▸ The backbone area can never be a stub area.

In addition to replacing all external routes with a single default route, the ABR of a stub area can be configured *not* to advertise summaries from other areas into a stub area, thereby replacing all possible destinations outside the area with a default route.

Figure 8.6 gives an example of stub areas.

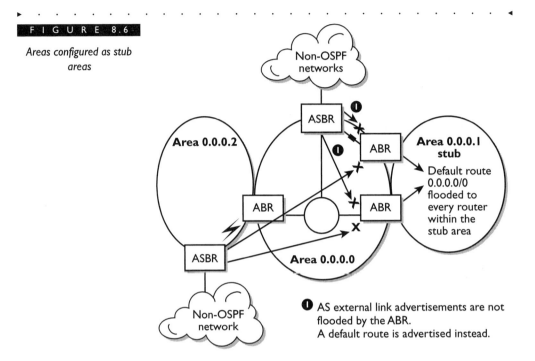

FIGURE 8.6

Areas configured as stub areas

Not-So-Stubby Areas

Consider a stub area consisting of multiple networks and hosts, as shown in Figure 8.7. Some of them are advertised using non-OSPF routing protocols. Nevertheless, these routes need to be known throughout the entire area. The OSPF specification forbids stub areas to import external routes. No external routes are allowed to exist within a stub area. RFC 1587 adds an additional type of area, humorously referred to as *not-so-stubby areas* (NSSAs). In an NSSA, external routes are imported by using a special link-state advertisement called an *NSSA external LSA*. These are very similar to external LSAs, except that they are flooded only within the NSSA and not throughout the entire AS. NSSA external LSAs are issued by an NSSA ASBR, using a single advertisement for each route.

Area border routers of the NSSA are called *NSSA area border routers*. They can translate an NSSA external LSA into an external LSA to be distributed to all the other areas. Therefore, NSSA ASBRs also need to be AS boundary routers. They may be configured to summarize several NSSA external LSAs into a single external

LSA. In addition, they advertise a default route into the NSSA (using NSSA external LSAs), allowing NSSA routers to reach all external routes outside the NSSA. Unlike stub areas, however, they aren't allowed to summarize OSPF routes from other areas into a default route.

All routers within the NSSA must be configured to be in an NSSA by turning on the NSSA capability option. This option must be set on all routers to form adjacencies (see the later section "Bringing Up Adjacencies"). The NSSA capability option automatically turns off the external capability option described in the previous section "Stub Areas."

The same restrictions that apply to the stub area apply to the NSSA. Figure 8.7 gives an example of an NSSA.

Not-so-stubby areas

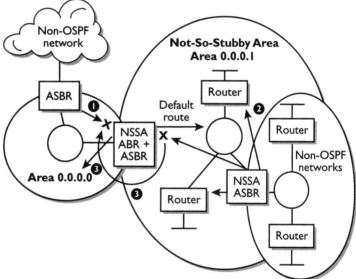

❶ AS external links are not flooded by the NSSA ASBR. A default route is sent to the NSSA.

❷ NSSA external links are advertised to all routes in the NSSA.

❸ NSSA external links are translated into AS external links.

OSPF Header Structure

The following sections discuss the information exchanged by OSPF routers. The routers use OSPF packets to exchange this information. By understanding the OSPF header structure, you will be able to troubleshoot your OSPF communications.

OSPF Encapsulation in IP Datagrams

Figure 8.8 shows an OSPF packet header. OSPF packets are directly encapsulated in IP by using IP protocol number 89. OSPF doesn't use fragmentation, therefore relying entirely on IP fragmentation when sending packets larger than the MTU (maximum transfer unit).

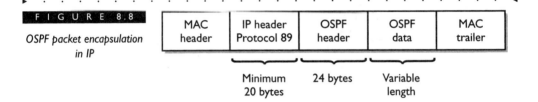

FIGURE 8.8

OSPF packet encapsulation in IP

Within the IP header, the following fields are worth mentioning:

- **Destination MAC Address (6 bytes):** Within the MAC header, OSPF uses either the broadcast address FFFFFFFF or the multicast MAC address used to send IP multicast packets.

- **Destination IP address (4 bytes):** OSPF uses a multicast destination IP address. Depending on the OSPF packet type, it will be either 224.0.0.5 (AllSPFRouters), 224.0.0.6 (AllDRouters), or unicast. (The sections "Bringing Up Adjacencies" and "Link-State Advertisements" explain the use of these addresses.)

▸ **TOS (1 byte):** Precedence is set to Internetwork Control. The TOS bits are set to 0 (normal).

▸ **Protocol (1 byte):** OSPF is using IP protocol number 89.

OSPF Header

OSPF uses five different packet types. All OSPF packets begin with a standard 24-byte header, shown in Figure 8.9.

 NOTE   **OSPF uses the word *type* in many instances. Carefully distinguish between OSPF packet types, LSA types, and link types. This document is using the name of a particular type rather than the type number.**

▶ · ◀

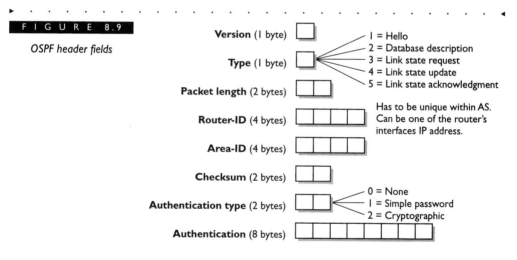

FIGURE 8.9

OSPF header fields

Version (1 byte)
The current version is 2.

Type (1 byte)
Important for troubleshooting, because it identifies the type of OSPF packet. Table 8.1 describes the OSPF packet types.

TABLE 8.1

OSPF Packet Types

PACKET TYPE	NAME	DESCRIPTION
I	Hello	Establish and maintain adjacencies, and elect DR and BDR. (See the section "Bringing Up Adjacencies.")
2	Database Description (DD)	Exchange of database description when bringing up adjacencies. (See the section "Bringing Up Adjacencies.")
3	Link-State Request	Request for missing or outdated link-state information. (See the section "Bringing Up Adjacencies.")
4	Link-State Update	Contains LSAs either to answer requests when bringing up adjacencies or to be flooded if a change occurs in the network. (See the sections "Bringing Up Adjacencies" and "Link-State Advertisements.")
5	Link-State Acknowledgment	Every Link-State Update has to be acknowledged. (See the section "Link-State Advertisements.")

Packet Length (2 bytes)

The length (in bytes) of the OSPF protocol packet, including the OSPF header.

Router ID (4 bytes)

The router ID of this router (source of the OSPF packet). Each router must have a unique router ID. This is a 32-bit number, normally represented in dotted decimal notation. The router ID has to be unique within the entire AS. In some cases, a valid IP address of one of the router's interfaces is used as the router ID. This field is important to identify the sending router.

Area ID (4 bytes)

Area ID of the interface originating this OSPF packet (see the section "OSPF Areas"). It is a 32-bit integer, normally represented in dotted decimal notation. All packets on the same network (transit or point-to-point) must use the same area ID.

Checksum (2 bytes)

The standard IP checksum of the entire packet, starting with the OSPF header, and excluding the 64-bit Authentication field. It is based on 16-bit complements.

If the packet's length is not an integral number of 16-bit words, the packet is padded with a byte of 0, before building the checksum.

Authentication Type — AuType (2 bytes)

Identifies which authentication method is used for the packet. Each OSPF packet must be authenticated by using this field and the checksum. Currently, the following three authentication mechanisms are defined. Neighboring routers must use the same authentication type to exchange packets.

- **Null authentication (AuType=0):** Only the Checksum field must be set (outgoing packets) or verified (incoming packets).

- **Simple password (AuType=1):** The Checksum field must be set (outgoing packets) or verified (incoming packets). In addition, the Authentication field is set (outgoing) or verified (incoming) by using the password configured for the interface. The Authentication field is sent in clear-text. A packet is authenticated when the interfaces of neighboring routers are configured with the same password.

- **Cryptographic authentication (AuType=2):** The Checksum is not calculated but is set to 0. The authentication algorithm sets and uses a Key ID field, Authentication Length field, and Cryptographic Sequence Number field. RFC 2178 introduced cryptic authentication. See Appendix D of this RFC for more details.

Authentication (8 bytes)

Depending on the AuType, this 64-bit field is set for authentication of the packet.

The Link-State Database (LSDB)

The LSDB is the most important component of OSPF. Figure 8.10 illustrates the components of OSPF.

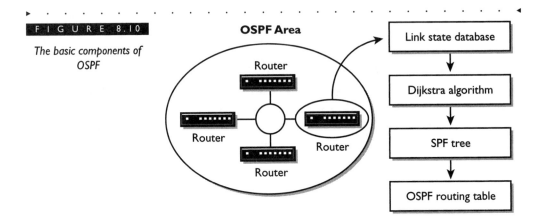

FIGURE 8.10

The basic components of OSPF

The LSDB is a data structure built by link-state information sent by each router in the AS. If the AS is split into multiple areas, the LSDB will only contain link-state information sent by each router within that particular area, including the ABR. The LSDB reflects the topology of the AS or the area.

A *shortest-path first (SPF)* algorithm is used by each router to calculate the *shortest-path tree (SPF tree)*. Most commonly, the routers use the algorithm developed by Dijkstra. The SPF tree is then used to build the OSPF routing table. The following sections describes each of these components, starting with analyzing the contents of the LSDB. Then, a description is presented of how the Dijkstra algorithm determines the shortest path, followed by an explanation of how the routing table is determined.

Contents of the LSDB

The LSDB describes the network topology by using directed graphs. A vertex is connected by using a graph edge pointing to another vertex, therefore allowing the Dijkstra algorithm to build a tree of least-cost connections to all vertices. The vertices represent either routers or networks. Each vertex has a unique vertex ID in OSPF, called its *link-state ID*.

A vertex can be one of two types describing the connection:

▸ **Point-to-point vertices:** Connect two routers directly (point-to-point link)

▸ **Network vertices:** Connect routers to a network.

A network having multiple routers is called a *transit network*. If only a single router is attached to the network, the network is called a *stub network*.

Point-to-point links identified by IP addresses are called *numbered links* and are represented by point-to-point vertices. In addition, the routers on both sides of the numbered point-to-point link declare the network of that numbered link as a stub. Virtual links are also represented that way, except that there isn't necessarily a single network connecting the two ends and therefore no stub is added.

Figure 8.11 shows the directed graphs for transit networks and point-to-point links. The rectangles represent router vertices, and circles represent network vertices.

The LSDB consists of different types of link information (see Table 8.2). To advertise the link information, the routers issue OSPF Link-State Update packets containing one or more Link State Advertisements or LSAs (refer to Table 8.1). LSAs are discussed later in the chapter, in the section "Link-State Advertisements".

Router links are advertised by routers, describing all the interfaces (graph edge) to either the next router or a transit network (next vertice). *Network links* are advertised for transit networks only, describing all routers (next vertices) connected to the transit network. A *designated router* advertises network links on behalf of the transit network. The designated router is elected when the transit network comes up. Stub network information will be part of the router link. *Host routes* (routes to a single host) are represented as stub networks.

In addition to network links and router links, the LSDB can contain information about external networks called *AS external links*. If the AS is partitioned into multiple areas, the ABR generates *summary links,* to summarize all networks and ASBRs from other areas. Table 8.2 describes all link-state information types that you can find in the LSDB.

*Examples for directed
graphs*

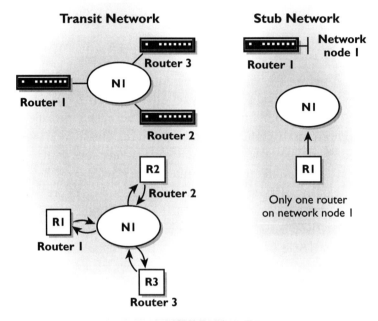

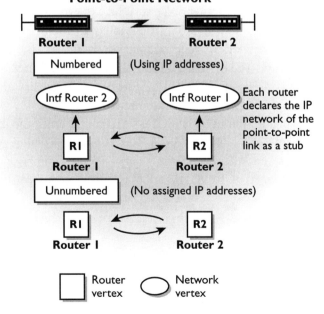

T A B L E   8.2

Link-State Types in LSDB

LS TYPE	NAME	ADVERTISED BY	FLOODED TO	LINK-STATE ID
1	Router link	Each router	Flooded to area only	Router ID
2	Network link	Designated router of each transit network	Flooded to area only	Interface IP address of the designated router
3	Summary link	Area border routers (ABRs)	Flooded to area only	Host or network IP address
4	AS summary link	ABRs	Flooded to area only	Router ID of AS border router (ASBR)
5	AS external link	ASBRs in nonstub areas	Flooded through AS	Host or network IP address of external network
6	Group-membership-link	Routers that have directly attached networks containing hosts belonging to the advertised multicast IP address		
		ABRs of areas containing routers belonging to this multicast IP address	Only flooded to multicast-capable routers	Multicast IP address
7	NSSA AS external link	NSSA ASBRs of external network	Flooded to area only	Host or network IP address
9, 10, or 11	Opaque link	Routers wanting to advertise additional information to OSPF	Only flooded to opaque-capable routers	Opaque type and opaque ID

Each entry in the LSDB is uniquely identified by its LS type, advertising router, and link-state ID. The link-state ID is used to build the nodes in the SPF tree. Each link type contains data specific to its LS type. The following sections explain the different types of links and their data.

Router Link (LSA Type 1)

Router links describe all the router's interfaces configured for OSPF. An ABR issues router links for each attached area containing only the interfaces belonging to that particular area. Virtual links always belong to area 0.0.0.0.

The data portion starts with a Flag field stating the type of router. The flags are explained in Table 8.3. The Flag field is followed by a Count field that determines the number of interfaces. After that, all the different interfaces (link types) are described. For every link type, a required metric for TOS 0 (normal) is included. Additional metrics for different types of services (TOSs) can be provided by specifying the TOS number and its corresponding metric (refer to "OSPF Overview").

TABLE 8.3	BIT	NAME
Flags in the Router Link	V-bit	This router is an endpoint of a virtual link using this area as a transit area.
	E-bit	This router is an ASBR.
	B-bit	This router is an ABR.
	W-bit	This router is a wildcard multicast receiver that receives all multicast datagrams.

Table 8.4 describes all the possible link types.

Figure 8.12 shows an example of a router link using router 0.0.0.1 of the sample network shown in Figure 8.1. Note the point-to-point link. One is numbered, declaring a stub as well, and the other is unnumbered.

TABLE 8.4

Description of Link Types (Interfaces) of the Router

LINK TYPE	NAME	LINK ID (4-BYTE)	LINK DATA (4-BYTE)
I	Point-to-point	Router ID of neighbor router, used to determine next node in SPF tree	IP address of router's interface to point-to-point link. If unnumbered, it contains the interface index according to MIB-II.
2	Transit	IP address of designated router, used to determine next node in SPF tree	IP address of router's interface to transit network.
3	Stub	IP address of stub network	Network mask of stub network.
4	Virtual	Router ID of router at the endpoint of the virtual link, used to determine next node in SPFNetwork Link (LS Type 2)	IP address of router's interface used for virtual links.

▶ . . . . ◀

FIGURE 8.12

An example of a router link

```
Area 0.0.0.1
Router-link header:
Link State id = 0.0.0.2          Age 0      Advertising Router 0.0.0.2
Seq.#(hex) 8000000d Xsum(hex)  d00b Len(hex)   54 Options  E   Type Router
Router-link data:
Flags(BEVW) B V  Count 5
Link 140.250.31.0     Data 255.255.255.240 Type Stub Net  cnt   0 tos   100
Link 0.0.0.1          Data 140.250.31.2    Type P-to-P    cnt   0 tos   100
Link 140.250.18.0     Data 255.255.255.0   Type Stub Net  cnt   0 tos    70
Link 140.250.17.3     Data 140.250.17.2    Type Trans Net cnt   0 tos    10
Link 0.0.1.2          Data 0.0.0.4         Type P-to-P    cnt   0 tos   500
```

Network Link (LS Type 2)

A network link describes a single transit network within a particular area. The data portion includes the network mask used for the routing table, and an entry for each router (using the router ID to reference the router links when building the SPF tree) on that transit network. No metric is used for network links, because the metric to the transit networks is part of the router-link information.

Figure 8.13 shows the transit network 140.250.17.0/24 in area 0.0.0.1. The router with the interface 140.250.17.3 is the designated router advertising this network link.

▶ · ◀

```
F I G U R E   8.13

An example of a network
        link
```

```
Area 0.0.0.1
Network-link header:
Link State id = 140.250.17.3    Age 5      Advertising Router 0.0.1.1
Seq.#(hex) 80000005 Xsum(hex) f8b6 Len(hex)   24 Options  E   Type Network
Network-link data:
netmask 255.255.255.0
link 0.0.1.1
link 0.0.0.1
link 0.0.0.2
```

Summary Link (LS Type 3)

ABRs advertise routes of other areas into the area using a single summary link for each advertised route. If the networks are contiguous, they can be summarized by the ABRs into a single summary link. This reduces the amount of information imported into the area. In a stub area, the ABR advertises the default route into the area.

The data sent along with summary links includes the network mask and the metric for TOS 0 (normal). Additional metrics for different types of services can be added.

Figure 8.14 shows a summary link of networks 140.250.32.0/20. The advertising router 0.0.0.1 is the ABR. This summary link summarizes all networks in area 0.0.0.2.

▶ · ◀

```
F I G U R E   8.14

An example of a summary
        link
```

```
Area 0.0.0.1
Summary-link header:
Link State id = 140.250.32.0    Age 0      Advertising Router 0.0.0.1
Seq.#(hex) 80000001 Xsum(hex) 5712 Len(hex)   1c Options  E   Type Sum Net
Summary-link data:
netmask 255.255.240.0 tos metric 140
```

Figure 8.15 shows the summary link sent into the stub area 0.0.0.2.

▶ · ◀

```
F I G U R E   8.15

An example of a summary
  link into a stub area
```

```
Area 0.0.0.2
Summary-link header:
Link State id = 0.0.0.0    Age 82      Advertising Router 0.0.0.3
Seq.#(hex) 80000001 Xsum(hex) cd74 Len(hex)   1c Options    Type Sum Net
Summary-link data:
netmask 0.0.0.0 tos0 metric 1
```

AS Summary Link (LS Type 4)

ABRs advertise the router ID of each ASBR in the area to other areas using a single AS summary link for each ASBR. AS summary links use the same format as summary links. The network mask, however, is not used. Figure 8.16 shows an AS summary link advertising ASBR 0.0.0.5 (which is in a different area) by the area border router 0.0.0.2.

FIGURE 8.16

An example of an AS summary link

```
Area 0.0.0.1
AS Summary-link header:
Link State id = 0.0.0.5         Age 10     Advertising Router 0.0.0.2
Seq.#(hex) 80000001 Xsum(hex) b9a5 Len(hex)   1c Options   E   Type Sum Asb
AS Summary-link data:
netmask 0.0.0.0 tos metric 170
```

AS External Links (LS Type 5)

AS external links are advertised by ASBRs. AS external links advertise the external route into OSPF. They are flooded throughout the entire AS and therefore are known to every router, with the exception of routers in a stub area. The data includes the network mask, the type of the external route, and a metric. The metric will depend on the external type (refer to the section "Non-OSPF Routes"). Additional metrics for a different TOS can be added. For each metric, a special forwarding address and tag can be passed along. If the forwarding address is 0.0.0.0, the external route can be reached via the advertising router (ASBR). Tag information will be used to pass external route information through the OSPF network. It has no significance for OSPF.

Figure 8.17 shows an example of an AS external type 1 network being advertised by 0.0.0.5. Metric 0 will be added to the OSPF metric to reach 0.0.0.5.

FIGURE 8.17

Example of an AS external link type 1

```
AS External-link header:
Link State id = 140.2.208.0      Age 106    Advertising Router 0.0.0.5
Seq.#(hex) 80000001 Xsum(hex) 2bc5 Len(hex)   24 Options      Type Extrn 1
AS External-link data:
mask 255.255.255.0 tos metric(hex)       0 fwd addr 0.0.0.0 tag(hex)    0
```

Figure 8.18 shows an example of an AS external type 2 network advertised by 0.0.0.1. Metric 2 will be added to a route weight, which is, by far, larger than any OSPF metric.

FIGURE 8.18

Example of an AS external link type 2

```
AS External-link header:
Link State id = 140.2.128.0      Age 3     Advertising Router 0.0.0.1
Seq.#(hex) 80000001 Xsum(hex) 625e Len(hex)   24 Options      Type Extrn 2
AS External-link data:
mask 255.255.255.0 tos metric(hex)       4 fwd addr 0.0.0.0 tag(hex)    0
```

Group-Membership Link (LS Type 6)

RFC 1584 adds multicast routing to OSPF. Multicast datagrams have to be forwarded to each member of the destination multicast group (IP addresses of class D 224.0.0.0-239.255.255.255). Multicast routing depends on the datagram's source address and its multicast destination address. The Internet Group Management Protocol (IGMP; RFC 2236) is used to register hosts as members of a particular multicast address (called a *multicast group*). A router supporting IGMP and OSPF can participate in the distribution of multicast datagrams. The router has to advertise each multicast IP address for which it has hosts on directly attached stub networks or transit networks for which the router is also the designated router. This is done by using group-membership LSAs. In addition, ABRs have to issue group-membership LSAs to inform other areas about hosts belonging to the multicast group. For each multicast group, the router has to calculate a separate SPF tree containing only routers belonging to that multicast group. This tree allows the router to forward packets to all hosts belonging to that multicast group.

X-REF

Refer to Chapter 4 to learn about multicast addressing; see Chapter 18 for information about IGMP (Internet Group Management Protocol).

NSSA AS External Link (LS Type 7)

NSSA AS external links are advertised by AS boundary routers in an NSSA. They are only flooded within the NSSA and use virtually the same syntax as AS external links (LS type 5). ABRs of NSSA are also ASBRs, to translate LS type 7 information into LS type 5 information to be distributed to other areas. NSSA ABRs issue an LS type 7 default route to be distributed within the NSSA. This allows all routers within the NSSA to reach routes external to OSPF.

Opaque Link (LS Types 9, 10, or 11)

Opaque links are used to distribute additional information within OSPF. Opaque information can contain information used by OSPF (such as quality of service routing) or by applications within the OSPF AS. The link-state ID contains the opaque type and opaque ID, to specify the type of information distributed. Opaque IDs 0 to 127 are allocated through IETF (Internet Engineering Task Force).

Currently three types of opaque links are defined (LS Types 9, 10, and 11):

▸ **Type 9 links (link-local):** Contain information destined only for the link. They are flooded only to local (sub) networks.

▸ **Type 10 links (area-local):** Contain information for the area. These area-local opaque links are flooded throughout the local area.

▸ **Type 11 links (AS-wide):** Contain information about the entire AS. They are flooded to all areas, much like LS type 5 links.

The discussion of opaque links is beyond the scope of this chapter. See RFC 2370 for further information.

Calculation of the Routing Table (Dijkstra Algorithm)

Using the LSDB as a base, the router calculates the SPF tree to find the shortest paths to all destination networks and hosts within the LSDB. The SPF tree is then used to build the routing table. The routing table contains the destination IP address, the address mask associated with it (all 1s in case of a host route), the next hop IP address (or next hop interface, in case of unnumbered links), and the metric associated with the route. Using the SPF tree, the router establishes intra-area routes (preference 4), inter-area routes (preference 3), external routes type 1 (preference 2), and external routes type 2 (preference 1). If multiple routes to networks or hosts within the LSDB exist, the router will place the route with the highest preference into the routing table (for example, preferring inter-area routes over external routes).

The rest of this section looks at the different steps to build the tree, We use the LSDB for area 0.0.0.1 of the sample networks (Figure 8.1) as an example to build the tree. This is shown in Figure 8.19. Note that the transit link (140.250.31.0/28) between router 0.0.0.1 and 0.0.0.2 is being declared as a numbered point-to-point link. This can be done to reduce the number of network links in the LSDB, but is only allowed in the case of two routers connected to a transit network.

▶ • ◀

```
Ospf Area: 0.0.0.1

Type    Link State ID  Adv Router
--------------------------------------------------------------------------
Router  0.0.0.1         0.0.0.1
   Link 140.250.31.128 Data 255.255.255.252 Type Stub Net  metric 500
   Link 0.0.1.1         Data 140.250.31.129 Type P-to-P    metric 500
   Link 140.250.31.0    Data 255.255.255.240 Type Stub Net  metric 100
   Link 0.0.0.2         Data 140.250.31.1    Type P-to-P    metric 100
   Link 140.250.17.3    Data 140.250.17.1    Type Trans Net metric  10
   Link 140.250.16.0    Data 255.255.255.0   Type Stub Net  metric  70
Router  0.0.0.2         0.0.0.2
   Link 140.250.31.0    Data 255.255.255.240 Type Stub Net  metric 100
   Link 0.0.0.1         Data 140.250.31.2    Type P-to-P    metric 100
   Link 140.250.18.0    Data 255.255.255.0   Type Stub Net  metric  70
   Link 140.250.17.3    Data 140.250.17.2    Type Trans Net metric  10
   Link 0.0.1.2         Data 0.0.0.5         Type P-to-P    metric 500
Router  0.0.1.1         0.0.1.1
   Link 140.250.31.128 Data 255.255.255.252 Type Stub Net  metric 500
   Link 0.0.0.1         Data 140.250.31.130 Type P-to-P    metric 500
   Link 140.250.19.0    Data 255.255.255.0   Type Stub Net  metric  70
   Link 0.0.1.2         Data 0.0.0.4         Type P-to-P    metric 500
   Link 140.250.17.3    Data 140.250.17.3    Type Trans Net metric  10
Router  0.0.1.2         0.0.1.2
   Link 140.250.20.2    Data 140.250.20.1    Type Trans Net metric  10
   Link 0.0.0.2         Data 0.0.0.2         Type P-to-P    metric 500
   Link 0.0.1.1         Data 0.0.0.3         Type P-to-P    metric 500
Router  0.0.1.3         0.0.1.3
   Link 140.250.21.0    Data 255.255.255.0   Type Stub Net  metric 100
   Link 140.250.20.2    Data 140.250.20.2    Type Trans      metric  10
Network 140.250.17.3    0.0.1.1         Netmask 255.255.255.0
   Link 0.0.1.1
   Link 0.0.0.1
   Link 0.0.0.2
Network 140.250.20.2    0.0.1.3         Netmask 255.255.255.0
   Link 0.0.1.3
   Link 0.0.1.2
Sum Net 140.250.0.0     0.0.0.1         Netmask 255.255.252.0 metric   70
Sum Net 140.250.0.0     0.0.0.2         Netmask 255.255.252.0 metric   70
Sum Net 140.250.32.0    0.0.0.1         Netmask 255.255.240.0 metric  140
Sum Net 140.250.32.0    0.0.0.2         Netmask 255.255.240.0 metric  140
Sum Net 140.250.48.0    0.0.0.1         Netmask 255.255.240.0 metric  270
Sum Net 140.250.48.0    0.0.0.2         Netmask 255.255.240.0 metric  340
Sum Asb 0.0.0.5         0.0.0.1         Netmask 0.0.0.0       metric  100
Sum Asb 0.0.0.5         0.0.0.2         Netmask 0.0.0.0       metric  170
Ext1    140.2.208.0     0.0.0.5         Netmask 255.255.255.0 metric    0
                                        fwd addr 0.0.0.0  tag(hex) 0
Ext2    140.2.128.0     0.0.0.1         Netmask 255.255.255.0 metric    3
                                        fwd addr 0.0.0.0  tag(hex) 0
Ext2    140.2.128.0     0.0.0.5         Netmask 255.255.255.0 metric    2
                                        fwd addr 0.0.0.0  tag(hex) 0
Ext2    140.2.192.0     0.0.0.1         Netmask 255.255.255.0 metric    2
                                        fwd addr 0.0.0.0  tag(hex) 0
Ext2    140.2.192.0     0.0.0.5         Netmask 255.255.255.0 metric    2
                                        fwd addr 0.0.0.0  tag(hex) 0
```

Building the SPF Tree to Determine Intra-Area Routes

Using the previously mentioned graph terminology, the router uses the *Dijkstra algorithm* to build the SPF tree in two stages. In the first stage, only router links (ignoring stub networks, at first) and network links are considered. In the second stage, stub networks are added to the tree. The link-state ID of router and network links is used as the vertex ID, and the link ID contained in router and network links is used as the edge pointing to the adjacent vertex or vertices.

Using area 0.0.0.1, the following description uses router 0.0.0.1 to build the SPF tree and the routing table. The router calculates the SPF tree by using its own router link as the root. Each link in the router link points to an adjacent vertex (router or network link), with the exception of stub links. Each adjacent vertex is temporarily placed in the tree. The vertex with the least cost is made a permanent branch of the tree. A shorter path will never exist to that destination. The process continues by adding all the adjacent vertices of this newly added vertex. If a vertex is already in the tree, it is ignored. Again, the best path is chosen according to the sum of the costs from the root, and the vertex is added as a permanent branch of the tree. This continues until all vertices have been examined. The permanently placed vertices (router and network links) make up the tree. At the end, all stub networks are added to the tree by adding them to the router links advertising the stub networks. Figure 8.20 explains the tree building for router 0.0.1.1.

After the calculation of the tree is finished, all intra-area routes can be determined. The next hop is derived from the branches starting at the root. Figure 8.21 shows the routing table for intra-area routes for area 0.0.0.1 on router 0.0.1.1. Note the equal cost paths. Some vendors support the configuration of a limited number of equal cost paths. The router then has to decide which path to put into the final routing table. The RFC doesn't specify the decision process any further.

If the router is an area border router, intra-area routes are derived from the LSDBs of each attached area.

In case of area 0.0.0.1 being a transit area (nonbackbone, no stub, and no NSSA), virtual links have to be considered, as well. Assume a virtual link exists between 0.0.0.1 and 0.0.0.2 (both being ABRs) to add a redundant backbone link in case connection to network 140.250.1.0/24 fails on router 0.0.0.2. For example, router 0.0.0.2 declares its interface 140.250.17.2 as the endpoint of the virtual link,

ANALYZING AND TROUBLESHOOTING THE INTERNET LAYER

because this interface represents the best path to router 0.0.0.1. The virtual link is advertised in router links for area 0.0.0.0 by routers 0.0.0.1 and 0.0.0.2.

FIGURE 8.20

Building the SPF tree for router 0.0.1.1

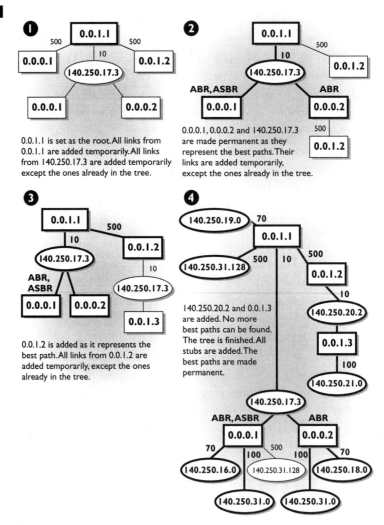

① 0.0.1.1 is set as the root. All links from 0.0.1.1 are added temporarily. All links from 140.250.17.3 are added temporarily except the ones already in the tree.

② 0.0.0.1, 0.0.0.2 and 140.250.17.3 are made permanent as they represent the best paths. Their links are added temporarily, except the ones already in the tree.

③ 0.0.1.2 is added as it represents the best path. All links from 0.0.1.2 are added temporarily, except the ones already in the tree.

④ 140.250.20.2 and 0.0.1.3 are added. No more best paths can be found. The tree is finished. All stubs are added. The best paths are made permanent.

FIGURE 8.21

Intra-area routes for area
0.0.0.1 on router 0.0.1.1

```
Router 0.0.1.1
Destination     Mask                   Metric Next Hop
-----------------------------------------------------------------
Intra-area routes
140.250.16.0/24     OSPF                80 140.250.17.1
140.250.17.0/24     Direct               0 140.250.17.3
140.250.18.0/24     OSPF                80 140.250.17.2
140.250.19.0/24     Direct               0 140.250.19.1
140.250.20.0/24     OSPF               510 0.0.0.4
140.250.21.0/24     OSPF               610 0.0.0.4
140.250.31.0/28     OSPF               110 140.250.17.1
140.250.31.0/28     OSPF               110 140.250.17.2
140.250.31.128/30   Direct               0 140.250.31.130
```

Adding Inter-Area Routes

The router identifies all summary links (LS type 3) and its advertising router, which must be an existing ABR in the SPF tree. The intra-area metric to the ABR is added to the metric advertised in the summary link. The least-cost summary networks are added to the routing table. The next hop is determined by examining the intra-area path to the ABR. Figure 8.22 shows the inter-area routes added to the routing table. Note the equal cost paths for 140.250.32.0/20 and 140.250.0.0/20. Both ABRs advertise this summary with the same cost, and both ABRs can be reached with the same intra-area costs.

FIGURE 8.22

Inter-area routes are added
to the routing table

```
Router 0.0.1.1
Destination     Mask                   Metric Next Hop
-----------------------------------------------------------------
Intra-area routes
140.250.16.0/24     OSPF                80 140.250.17.1
140.250.17.0/24     Direct               0 140.250.17.3
140.250.18.0/24     OSPF                80 140.250.17.2
140.250.19.0/24     Direct               0 140.250.19.1
140.250.20.0/24     OSPF               510 0.0.0.4
140.250.21.0/24     OSPF               610 0.0.0.4
140.250.31.0/28     OSPF               110 140.250.17.1
140.250.31.0/28     OSPF               110 140.250.17.2
140.250.31.128/30   Direct               0 140.250.31.130
Inter-area routes
140.250.0.0/22      OSPF                80 140.250.17.1
140.250.0.0/22      OSPF                80 140.250.17.2
140.250.32.0/20     OSPF               150 140.250.17.1
140.250.32.0/20     OSPF               150 140.250.17.2
140.250.48.0/20     OSPF               280 140.250.17.1
```

If the router itself is an ABR, only summaries of the backbone received by other backbone routers are considered. All summaries that represent routes in directly attached areas are ignored, because a (better) intra-area path always exists to that destination.

Adding External Routes

The router first examines external type 1 links and then type 2 links. If the forwarding address of the external link is specified, the router tries to find a match for this address in its existing intra- or inter-area routing table. In case of a match, the router takes the same next-hop IP address as the match found. Otherwise, the external link is ignored. If the forwarding address is set to 0.0.0.0, the router tries to find the least-cost path to the ASBR. If the ASBR is part of the area directly attached to the router, an intra-area route to the ASBR can be found. Otherwise, the ASBR should have been advertised as an inter-area route by the ABR using the AS summary link.

The calculation of the metric for external networks depends on the external link type. For external type 1 networks, the metric advertised by the external link is added to the OSPF metric to reach either the forwarding address or the ASBR. Metrics for external type 2 networks are considered as they are advertised by the external link. The OSPF cost to reach the forwarding address or the ASBR is assumed to be substantially higher than any intra- or inter-area routes and is not added to the overall metric for external type 2 networks. If the same external type 2 network is advertised by different ASBRs with the same cost, the best OSPF path to the ASBR or the forwarding address is used.

If the same network is advertised by different ASBRs as either external type 1 or external type 2, the route to the external type 1 network is always preferred.

Figure 8.23 shows external routes added to the routing table. External routes are advertised by ASBR 0.0.0.5 and ASBR 0.0.0.1. For router 0.0.1.1, only ASBR 0.0.0.1 can be reached using an intra-area route. It looks at the AS summary link to find out which ABR is advertising 0.0.0.5. The external type 2 route to 140.2.192.0/22 has two entries with the same metric. Therefore, the best path to ASBR (0.0.0.1) is chosen. The metric for external type 2 is set as advertised by the ASBR.

The calculation of the routing table is now finished. Arrivals of new LSAs and their effects on calculating the routing table is discussed later, in the section "Link-State Advertisements".

▶ . . . . ◀

FIGURE 8.23	
External routes are added to the routing table	

```
Router 0.0.1.1
Destination    Mask                 Metric Next Hop
--------------------------------------------------------------
Intra-area routes
140.250.16.0/24    OSPF              80 140.250.17.1
140.250.17.0/24    Direct             0 140.250.17.3
140.250.18.0/24    OSPF              80 140.250.17.2
140.250.19.0/24    Direct             0 140.250.19.1
140.250.20.0/24    OSPF             510 0.0.0.4
140.250.21.0/24    OSPF             610 0.0.0.4
140.250.31.0/28    OSPF             110 140.250.17.1
140.250.31.0/28    OSPF             110 140.250.17.2
140.250.31.128/30  Direct             0 140.250.31.130
Intrer-area routes
140.250.0.0/22     OSPF              80 140.250.17.1
140.250.0.0/22     OSPF              80 140.250.17.2
140.250.32.0/20    OSPF             150 140.250.17.1
140.250.32.0/20    OSPF             150 140.250.17.2
140.250.48.0/20    OSPF             280 140.250.17.1
External-1 routes
140.2.208.0/24     OSPF             110 140.250.17.1
External-2 routes
140.2.128.0/24     OSPF               2 140.250.17.1
140.2.192.0/24     OSPF               2 140.250.17.1
```

▶ . . . . ◀

Bringing Up Adjacencies

The routers must create "secure" channels, called *adjacencies,* on each interface, to flood LSAs throughout the AS and/or area. OSPF creates adjacencies between neighboring routers. On transit networks (networks with multiple routers), creating adjacencies between every router isn't necessary. Each transit network elects a *designated router* (DR) to keep adjacencies with all routers on behalf of the transit network. To ensure uninterrupted operation, a *backup designated router* (BDR) is elected as well. Figure 8.24 shows adjacencies on point-to-point links and transit networks.

The Hello Protocol

The Hello protocol is responsible for establishing and maintaining adjacencies as well as electing a DR/BDR on transit networks. It also ensures that communication between two routers is bidirectional. Hello packets are sent out through each interface in regular intervals. On point-to-point or broadcast-capable transit networks (such as Ethernet or Token Ring), OSPF Hello packets are sent to the multicast address 224.0.0.5, referred to as *AllSPFRouters*. The neighbors can be discovered dynamically.

FIGURE 8.24

Adjacencies formed on point-to-point links and transit networks

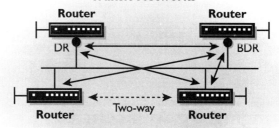

Point-to-Point Link

Router   Router

Adjacency is always formed

Transit Networks

Router   Router

DR   BDR

Two-way

Router   Router

Every router only forms an adjacency with the designated router and backup designated routes.

Transit networks not capable of transmitting broadcast or multicast packets (such as X.25, Frame Relay) are called *nonbroadcast multiaccess (NBMA) networks*. NBMA networks can be configured either as transit or point-to-multipoint networks.

In the case of point-to-multipoint networks, logical point-to-point links are created to each router. No DR has to be elected and no network link is issued. Point-to-multipoint links don't declare the whole network as a stub (as do ordinary point-to-point links), but instead declare a stub host route to the interface configured for point-to-multipoint.

NBMA networks configured as transit networks need to have all neighbors configured statically. A DR is elected and a network link is issued. All OSPF packets use the statically configured IP address to communicate with the neighbors.

Figure 8.25 shows the Hello packet format. It is an OSPF packet type 1, as explained earlier in Table 8.1. Its fields are the following:

▶ · ◀

FIGURE 8.25

Format of the Hello packet

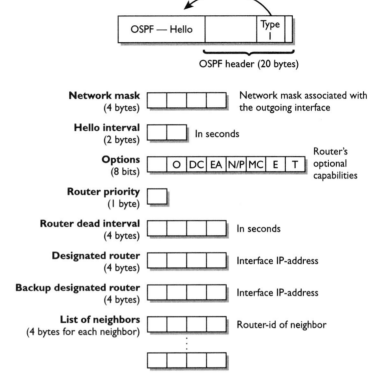

Network Mask (4 bytes)

The assigned 32-bit network mask of this router's interface sending the Hello packet.

Hello Interval (2 bytes)

The number of seconds between this router's Hello packets. Normally set to 10 seconds.

Options (1 byte)

Describes this router's optional capabilities. This field is set in OSPF Hello packets, Database Description packets, and all LSAs. Table 8.5 explains the bits used in the Options field.

TABLE 8.5

The Options Bits

BIT	NAME	DESCRIPTION
1	Not used	
2	O	Handling of opaque LSA, as described in RFC 2370.
3	DC	Handling of demand circuits, as described in RFC 1793.
4	EA	Handling of external attribute LSAs, as described in D. Ferguson's "The OSPF External Attributes LSA" work in progress.
5	N/P	All routers within an NSSA must set this bit. In addition, the E-bit must be cleared if this bit is set (see RFC 1587). The Hello protocol calls this bit the N-bit. Type 7 LSA calls this bit the P-bit.
6	MC	Multicast capability, as defined in RFC 1584.
7	E	External-routes capability of the sending router. All members of an area must agree on the external capability. In a stub area, all routers must clear this bit to achieve adjacency. The E-bit is meaningful only in Hello packets (similar to the N-bit).
8	T	TOS capability of the router. If cleared, only TOS 0 (normal) is allowed. RFC 2178 abandoned TOS capabilities for OSPF; therefore, this bit is set only for backward-compatibility.

Router Priority (1 byte)

A priority number given to this router for the election of the DR. This field is meaningful only on transit networks. The router with the highest priority becomes the DR or BDR. This is only true if a DR or BDR has not been elected. If set to 0, this router cannot become DR or BDR.

Router Dead Interval (4 bytes)

The number of seconds before this router declares a silent router down. A silent router is no longer sending Hello packets. Normally set to 40 seconds. This interval is also used to elect the DR or BDR on transit networks. Each transit interface (broadcast or NBMA) upon initialization enters a waiting state to determine whether a DR or BDR has already been declared. The duration of the waiting state is the Router Dead Interval.

Designated Router (4 bytes)

The identity of the DR, as seen from this router. The DR is identified not by its router ID but by the IP address of the interface. This field is only set on transit networks. Set to 0.0.0.0 in case no DR has been elected or on point-to-point links.

Backup Designated Router (4 bytes)

The identity of the BDR, as seen from this router. The BDR is identified not by its router ID but by the IP address of the interface. This field is only set on transit networks. Set to 0.0.0.0 in case no BDR has been elected or on point-to-point links.

List of Neighbors (4 bytes per neighbor)

The router ID of each router from whom valid Hello packets have been seen on this network in the last RouterDeadInterval seconds.

Figures 8.26 shows Hello packets being exchanged on the transit network 140.250.17.0 in area 0.0.0.1.

FIGURE 8.26

Hello packet exchange

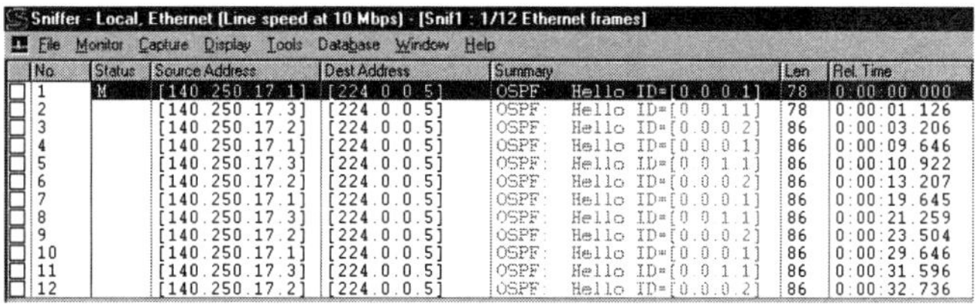
Sniffer - Local, Ethernet (Line speed at 10 Mbps) - [Snif1 : 1/12 Ethernet frames]

File Monitor Capture Display Tools Database Window Help

No.	Status	Source Address	Dest Address	Summary	Len	Rel. Time
1	M	[140.250.17.1]	[224.0.0.5]	OSPF: Hello ID=[0.0.0.1]	78	0:00:00.000
2		[140.250.17.3]	[224.0.0.5]	OSPF: Hello ID=[0.0.1.1]	78	0:00:01.126
3		[140.250.17.2]	[224.0.0.5]	OSPF: Hello ID=[0.0.0.2]	86	0:00:03.206
4		[140.250.17.1]	[224.0.0.5]	OSPF: Hello ID=[0.0.0.1]	86	0:00:09.646
5		[140.250.17.3]	[224.0.0.5]	OSPF: Hello ID=[0.0.1.1]	86	0:00:10.922
6		[140.250.17.2]	[224.0.0.5]	OSPF: Hello ID=[0.0.0.2]	86	0:00:13.207
7		[140.250.17.1]	[224.0.0.5]	OSPF: Hello ID=[0.0.0.1]	86	0:00:19.645
8		[140.250.17.3]	[224.0.0.5]	OSPF: Hello ID=[0.0.1.1]	86	0:00:21.259
9		[140.250.17.2]	[224.0.0.5]	OSPF: Hello ID=[0.0.0.2]	86	0:00:23.504
10		[140.250.17.1]	[224.0.0.5]	OSPF: Hello ID=[0.0.0.1]	86	0:00:29.646
11		[140.250.17.3]	[224.0.0.5]	OSPF: Hello ID=[0.0.1.1]	86	0:00:31.596
12		[140.250.17.2]	[224.0.0.5]	OSPF: Hello ID=[0.0.0.2]	86	0:00:32.736

Figure 8.27 shows the details of a Hello packet. In the beginning, you can see the router ID and the area ID. The Router Priority is set to 1. Note the Designated Router field and the list of neighbors at the bottom of the detail window.

Each transit network within the AS has to elect a DR and a BDR. On a transit network, the DR and BDR form adjacencies with all routers on that particular transit network. Each router having an interface to that transit network enters into a waiting state upon initialization. The duration of the waiting state is the RouterDeadInterval. During the waiting state, the DR and BDR listen to Hello packets and send Hello packets with no DR/BDR address set.

FIGURE 8.27

Detail decode of a Hello
packet

If a router already claims to be the DR, then no election of a DR takes place. If no router declares itself as the DR (all Hellos sent use 0.0.0.0 in the DR field), the router with the highest priority claims itself as the DR after its waiting period. If the configurable priority is set equal on all routers, the router with the highest router ID claims itself as the DR. Routers having a priority set to 0 never become DR.

The same process applies for the election of the BDR. If the DR is down (not sending Hellos for RouterDeadInterval), the BDR becomes the DR, and a new BDR has to be elected. Because the BDR already has all the adjacencies established, there is no disruption of OSPF LSAs distributed over that transit network. If the original DR is coming back online, it will not take over from the new DR. During its waiting state, it will recognize the new DR/BDR. If the BDR is down, a new BDR has to be elected and adjacencies to all other routers have to be formed.

If no Hello packets are received on a transit network during the waiting period, the router declares the interface to that network as a stub network.

Before a Hello packet is received and an adjacency is formed, a number of criteria must be met. Figure 8.28 shows the decision process to accept a Hello packet. The Hello packet received is authenticated first. Then, the area ID, network mask, Hello interval, and RouterDeadInterval are checked. They must match the values set on the receiving interface. Next, the E-bit in the option field is examined. If the interface is within an NSSA, the N-bit is examined. The setting of the E/N-bit must match the value set on the receiving interface.

At this point, if all the criteria match, the packet is accepted and the neighbor is identified by either the source IP address (transit networks) or the router ID (point-to-point or virtual links). If an adjacency already is established with that neighbor, the Hello timer is reset. Otherwise, the router examines the list of neighbors proclaimed in the received Hello packet. If the router sees itself listed as a neighbor, bidirectional communication has been established (state changes to two-way). Otherwise, the state of the interface is changed to Initialize (Init). On transit networks, the interface has to wait until the DR or BDR is determined.

Figure 8.29 explains the formation of adjacencies and the corresponding state of the interface. The process starts by synchronizing the LSDB. This is done by sending database description (DD) packets and requesting missing information from the neighbor. After the database is synchronized, the adjacency is known to be completed. Continuous sending of Hello packets ensures that the adjacency stays alive.

Database Description Exchange

Figure 8.29 illustrates the situations in which the router forms an adjacency with the neighboring router. On a point-to-point link, the routers on each end always form an adjacency. On a transit network, adjacencies are formed only between the DR and all other routers, and between the BDR and all routers. If the router itself is the DR or BDR, it forms an adjacency. Otherwise, looking at the Hello packet, the router checks whether the neighbor router is a DR or BDR and forms an adjacency. If none of the preceding is true, the router stays in a two-way state with that particular neighbor.

▶ · ◀

FIGURE 8.28

Processing incoming Hello packets

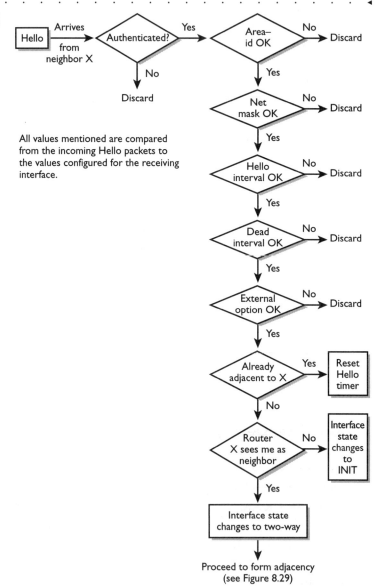

All values mentioned are compared from the incoming Hello packets to the values configured for the receiving interface.

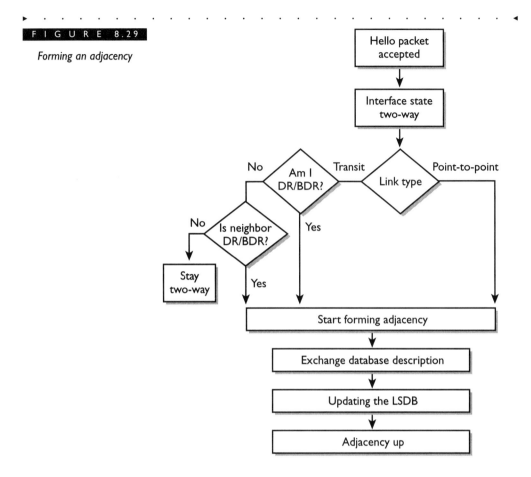

FIGURE 8.29

Forming an adjacency

Figure 8.30 describes all the packets exchanged to reach adjacency. The first step is the exchange of database descriptions. The router changes its state to Exchange Start and sends an initial database description (DD) packet without data. To achieve an orderly exchange of DD packets, the two routers forming an adjacency establish a master-slave relationship. Each router declares itself as the master in the initial DD packet. The only relevant information within the initial DD packet is the DD sequence number issued by each side. The router with the higher router ID declares itself as the master.

▸ · ◂

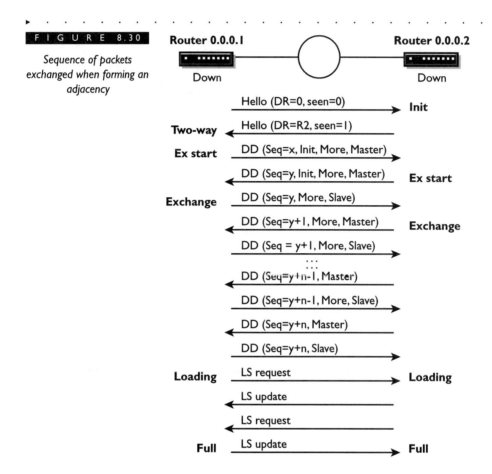

FIGURE 8.30

Sequence of packets exchanged when forming an adjacency

The routers then enter the Exchange state. Starting with the slave, routers are now exchanging a series of packets describing the contents of their respective LSDBs. The master always increments the sequence number, and the slave always uses the master's sequence number in its packet. Each router indicates that it has more data to send by setting the More bit (see Figure 8.31). If one router has sent all of its DD packets, but the other hasn't, the first router is obliged to send empty packets to keep the sequence numbers matched. As soon as both routers have nothing more to send, the routers enter the Loading state.

To describe the LSDB, the router only sends the database headers (LSA headers), consisting of link-state type, link-state ID, advertising router, link-state sequence number, link-state age, link-state checksum, link-state length, and optional capabilities. (The LSA header is discussed later in the chapter.)

In case of a DD sequence number mismatch, the exchange process is torn down and has to restart.

Figure 8.31 shows the format of the DD packet. All DD packets are sent to the IP address of the neighbor and not to the multicast addresses used by Hello. The following are the fields of the DD packet:

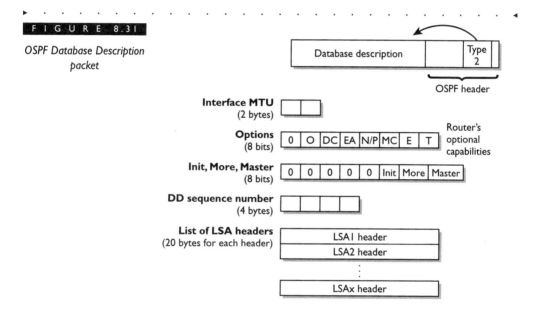

F I G U R E   8.31

OSPF Database Description packet

▶ **Interface MTU (2 bytes):** Largest frame size that can be sent through that interface without fragmentation. On virtual links, this should be set to 0.

▶ **Option (1 byte):** The router's optional capability. Refer to Table 8.4 for the list.

▶ **Init-bit (I-bit):** If set to 1, indicates the first DD packet sent by this router. This packet contains no data and starts the exchange process. The M/S-bit is also set.

- **More-bit (M-bit):** If set to 1, indicates that more DD packets are to follow. If set to 0, indicates all DD packets have been delivered.

- **Master/Slave-bit (M/S-bit):** If set to 1, indicates this router is the master; otherwise, it is the slave.

- **DD Sequence Number (4 bytes):** Used to sequence the exchange. The master increments the sequence number by 1 each time it sends a DD packet. The slave always uses the last sequence number sent by the master.

- **List of LSA headers (20 bytes for each header):** Describes the entry in the LSDB. (This is further explained later in the chapter.)

Figure 8.32 shows the details of an OSPF Database Description packet.

At this point, the master-slave relationship has been established. You can see the slave bit (set to 0) right above the sequence number. Note that the decode says Reserved where the interface MTU bytes are located. Some implementations of OSPF do not use this field. This setting should be 0 on virtual links. Otherwise, it states the largest frame size that can be sent through that interface without fragmentation (if used). Two LSAs are in that packet. Only the first part of the second LSA can be seen in Figure 8.32.

Updating the LSDB

During the loading state, each router is requesting the missing or out-of-date LSA learned during the exchange of the database description.

Link-State Request packets (OSPF packet type 3) identify the requesting LSA by its link-state type, link-state ID, and advertising router. Multiple requests can be sent by using a single packet. The router replies to the request by sending the corresponding and most recent LSA from its database. The LSA is sent by using Link-State Update packets (OSPF packet type 4). (Link-State Update packets are described in the next section.) Multiple LSAs can be sent in a single packet. Each Link-State Update packet must be acknowledged by a Link-State Acknowledge packet (OSPF packet type 5). The Link-State Update packet contains the LSA header to be acknowledged. Multiple LSAs can be acknowledged in a single packet. The Link-State Request and Acknowledge packets contain no new fields and, therefore, are not discussed in detail.

F I G U R E   8.32

*Details of an OSPF
Database Description
packet*

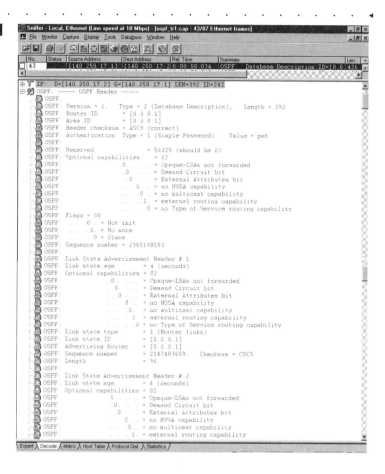

The adjacency is now up. Hello packets keep the adjacency alive. If a router on one side of the adjacency receives a new or changed LSA, the LSA is sent to the adjacent router, which in turn will acknowledge the received LSA with a Link-State Acknowledgment packet. The next section discusses the flooding of LSAs throughout the area and/or AS.

Figure 8.33 shows the sequence of packets seen during the forming of an adjacency.

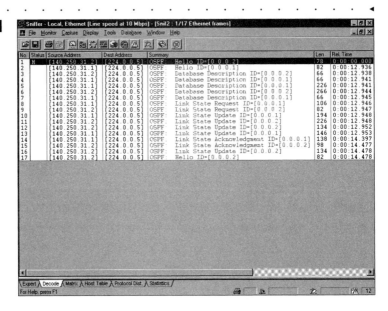

FIGURE 8.33

Packets exchanged during formation of an adjacency

In frames 3 to 7, the database description is exchanged. Frames 8 and 9 show the routers requesting missing or out-of-date LSAs. Frames 11 to 16 show the LSAs being exchanged. Now the adjacency is up.

Link-State Advertisements

Any change in the network causes a certain link-state information to change. Examples of such changes include:

- A router's interface goes down or comes up

- An area's summary information changes

- An external route is added or withdrawn at the ASBR

Depending on the change, new or changed LSAs are advertised using Link-State Update packets (OSPF packet type 4). Multiple LSAs can be sent in a single packet. LSAs are flooded, depending on the LSA type (refer to Table 8.2 for the list of types). These LSAs are sent to the following destinations:

- ▸ LSA types 1, 2, 3, 4, and 7 are only flooded throughout the area.

- ▸ LSA type 5 is flooded throughout the AS.

- ▸ LSA type 6 is flooded only to multicast-capable routers.

- ▸ LSA types 8, 9, 10 are flooded only to opaque-capable routers on the link, either in the area or throughout the entire AS (depending on the opaque type).

Flooding means that the LSA is passed from the advertising router to all of its adjacent neighbors. These neighbors pass it on to their neighbors, and so on. Each router receiving an LSA first evaluates whether the LSA is newer than the one already installed in the LSDB. An LSA is considered newer if it has a lower sequence number. In that case, it installs the LSA in the LSDB. Now the router considers the interfaces to be used for further flooding. It will not flood the LSA out the same interface it was received on. The exception to this rule is if the router is a DR for the interface receiving the LSA, and the LSA has not been sent by the BDR. The DR is responsible for sending LSAs to all of its neighbors. Another reason not to flood the LSA out of its interfaces is if the LSA is older or the same as the one already installed. This prevents LSAs from looping in the network. LSAs normally are sent to the multicast address 224.0.0.5 (AllSPFRouters), with the following exceptions:

- ▸ On transit networks, LSAs are sent to the address 224.0.0.6 (AllDRouters). Only DRs listen to and send out LSAs.

- ▸ If a router requests a link-state update by sending a Link-State Request packet, the LSA is sent using the unicast address of the requesting router.

- ▸ On NBMA networks, all LSAs are sent unicast to the statically configured neighbors.

- ▸ Retransmission of LSAs are always sent to the unicast address of the neighbor not acknowledging the receipt of the LSA.

Figure 8.34 describes the process of a designated router receiving new or changed LSAs and flooding them to all routers.

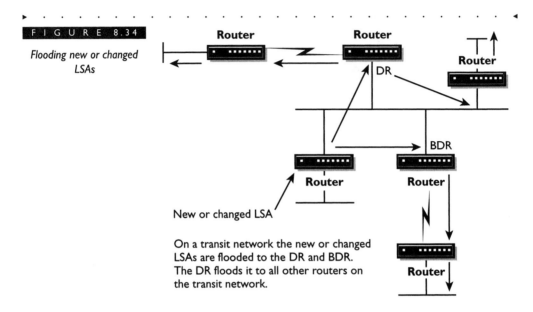

FIGURE 8.34

Flooding new or changed LSAs

Router **Router** **Router**

DR

BDR

Router **Router**

New or changed LSA

Router

On a transit network the new or changed LSAs are flooded to the DR and BDR. The DR floods it to all other routers on the transit network.

Each router receiving a new or changed LSA has to acknowledge this LSA. This is usually done by sending a Link-State Acknowledgment packet. It could also be acknowledged by sending back the LSA, if the received LSA is older or the same as the one already installed in the LSDB. In that case, the sequence number is set to the one already installed. Unacknowledged LSAs have to be retransmitted. Each router keeps track of which neighbor has acknowledged which LSA. Retransmissions are always sent to the unicast address of the neighboring router.

Flooding LSA

Three fields uniquely identify an LSA (for an explanation of the fields, refer to Table 8.2):

▸ Link State Type (1 byte)

▸ Link-State ID (4 bytes)

▸ Advertising Router (4 bytes)

A sequence number is assigned to the LSA by the advertising router to keep track of the most recent instance of this particular LSA. The sequence number is incremented by the advertising router each time the LSA is changed. When a new or changed LSA of type 1 or 2 (router or network links) is received and accepted according to the flooding mechanism, the router installs it in the LSDB. It then recalculates the SPF tree (explained earlier in the chapter, in "Calculation of the Routing Table").

If a new or changed LSA of type 3, 4, 5, or 7 (summary and external links) is received, recalculating the SPF tree is not necessary. The new information will be used to reevaluate the best path for the summary or external route by associating the information to the ASBR or ABR found in the SPF tree. If a new or changed LSA type 6 (group membership) is received, a new multicast datagram SPF tree has to be calculated for each area containing routers belonging to the multicast group described by the LSA. New or changed opaque LSAs (type 8, 9, or 10) don't cause a recalculation of the SPF tree, but have to be passed along to the application in need of the information contained in the opaque LSA.

Aging the LSA

In addition to the sequence number, each LSA maintains an Age field. The age is expressed in seconds. Each router increments the Age field of its LSA continuously. If an LSA is transmitted to the neighbor router, a transmit delay must be added to the Age field. An LSA can never age beyond a configurable maximum age (MaxAge). All routers must agree on the maximum age. Normally, it is set to 3600 seconds. Usually, a router is flooding a new instance (increment sequence number) of its own LSA when it has reached MaxAge/2. LSAs that have reached MaxAge are not considered for the SPF tree and are eventually deleted from the LSDB. The advertising router can prematurely age an LSA to flush it from the OSPF area or AS. This is used if, for example, an external route has been withdrawn. Another reason to prematurely age an LSA is if the LSA has reached the biggest sequence number possible. Before wrapping the sequence number (starting again), the LSA has to be flushed.

Self-Originating LSA

A router can receive an LSA that it has issued itself, such as when redundant links exist within the area, thus forming a loop. Self-originated LSAs normally are discarded, except if the self-originated LSA is newer. Obviously, this should not happen, because only the advertising router can increment the sequence number of the LSA. However, if the router has been rebooted, previously issued LSAs are still held in the other router's LSDB. If a newer, self-originated LSA is received, the router will prematurely age that LSA, thereby flushing it from the area or AS.

LSA Header Structure

Each LSA starts with a common, 20-byte header. Figure 8.35 shows the details of this header, which includes the following fields:

FIGURE 8.35

Link-state header

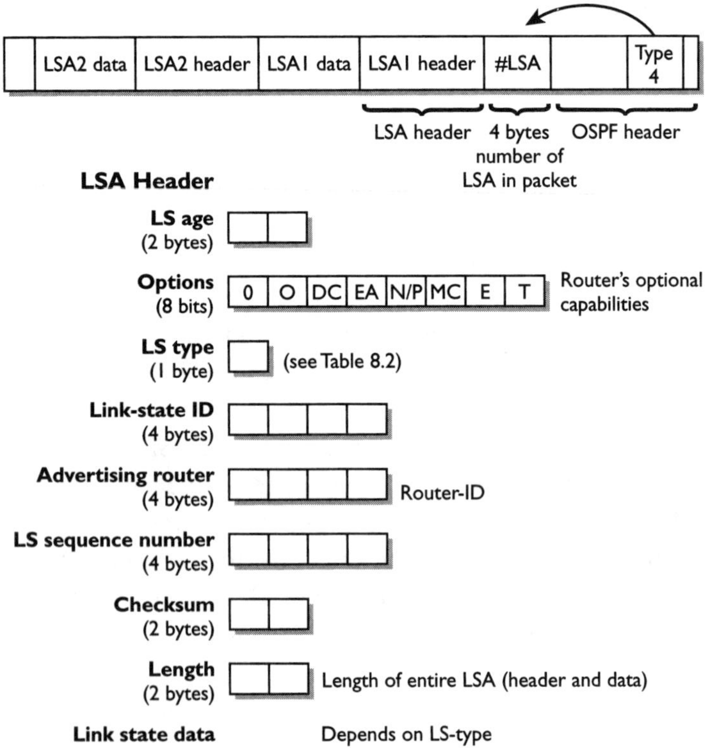
LSA2 data
LSA2 header
LSA1 data
LSA1 header
#LSA
Type 4
LSA header
4 bytes number of LSA in packet
OSPF header
LSA Header
LS age (2 bytes)
Options (8 bits)
0
O
DC
EA
N/P
MC
E
T
Router's optional capabilities
LS type (1 byte)
(see Table 8.2)
Link-state ID (4 bytes)
Advertising router (4 bytes)
Router-ID
LS sequence number (4 bytes)
Checksum (2 bytes)
Length (2 bytes)
Length of entire LSA (header and data)
Link state data
Depends on LS-type

▶ **LS Age (2 bytes):** The time, in seconds, since the LSA was originated. If it has reached MaxAge (normally 3600 seconds), the LSA is not considered for the routing table. The advertising router is renewing the LSA (incrementing the sequence number) when MaxAge/2 is reached.

▶ **Options (1 byte):** The router's optional capability (refer to Table 8.4).

▶ **LS Type (1 byte):** The type of LSA being advertised (refer to Table 8.2 for details on link-state types).

▶ **Link-State ID (4 bytes):** Identifies the LSA. In router and network links, it is used as the vertex ID when building the SPF tree. Represents the network on summary links, AS summary links, all external links, and group-membership links (refer to Table 8.2).

▶ **Advertising Router (4 bytes):** The router ID of the router originating this LSA. In summary links, AS summary links, all external links, and group-membership links, it is used to associate the link-state ID with the advertising routing (refer to Table 8.2).

▶ **LS Sequence Number (4 bytes):** Identifies the instance of this LSA. It is used to determine whether an LSA is newer. The starting sequence number is always 0x80000000. The highest sequence number possible is 0x7FFFFFFF. If this number is reached, the LSA is aged out (Age field equals MaxAge) and flooded before a new instance of the LSA (now using 0x80000000) is issued.

▶ **Checksum (2 bytes):** Checksum of the entire LSA, excluding the Age field. The checksum is used to validate the LSA. It has to be calculated.

▶ **Length (2 bytes):** The length of the entire LSA, in bytes.

▶ **Link-State Data:** Contains the data depending on the link-state type. Refer to Table 8.2 or RFC 2328 Appendix A.4 and its explanation for the detailed syntax of the LSA.

RFC 1793 describes the flooding procedures using demand circuits. RFC 1584 describes the configuration for frame relay networks.

Troubleshooting OSPF

To troubleshoot OSPF, you must understand how OSPF works. Always check the states of the OSPF interfaces and their adjacencies. The following section includes a checklist to perform on the router, and tips on what to look for in packet traces.

Checklist on the Router

To check proper operations of OSPF on a router, always check in the following order:

1. **Are all IP interfaces up?** Check whether all interfaces are up, which guarantees that OSPF can start adjacencies.

2. **Are OSPF interfaces up?** Check whether OSPF has recognized all interfaces and whether the interfaces are assigned to the proper areas. The interface is initialized as either broadcast, NBMA, point-to-point, or point-to-multipoint. This determines how the OSPF interface deals with its neighbors. Figure 8.36 shows an example of the OSPF interfaces on router 0.0.0.1. Interfaces 140.250.16.1 and 140.250.31.1 are down. This indicates that IP is not up on these interfaces. If the interface is of the wrong type, check your configuration.

   An interface being down indicates that IP is not up on that interface. If the interface is of the wrong type check your configuration.

FIGURE 8.36

State of OSPF interfaces

```
OSPF Interfaces
---------------
IP Address        Area ID          Type  State     Metric  Priority DR / BDR
---------------   ---------------  ----  --------  ------- -------- ------------
140.250.1.1       0.0.0.0          BCAST Down          70      1 0.0.0.0
                                                                  0.0.0.0
140.250.2.1       0.0.0.0          BCAST BDR          100      1 140.250.2.2
                                                                  140.250.2.1
140.250.16.1      0.0.0.1          BCAST DR            70      1 140.250.16.1
                                                                  0.0.0.0
140.250.17.1      0.0.0.1          BCAST DR Other      10      1 140.250.17.3
                                                                  140.250.17.2
140.250.31.1      0.0.0.1          P-P   Down         100      1 0.0.0.0
                                                                  0.0.0.0
140.250.31.129    0.0.0.1          P-P   P to P       500      1 0.0.0.0
                                                                  0.0.0.0
6 Entries

OSPF Virtual Interfaces
-----------------------
Area ID          Virtual Neighbor State
---------------  ---------------- -------------
0.0.0.1          0.0.0.2          Point to Point

1 entries
```

3. Are all expected adjacencies present? Check whether the router has found all of its neighbors. The state of the adjacency, as described in the section "Bringing Up Adjacencies," describes the different states. If the neighbor doesn't appear in the adjacency list, check your Hello packets, as described in the case study section.

If a neighbor on a multiaccess network appears in the table in a two-way state, it could mean that both this router and its neighbor are neither the designated router nor the BDR. Therefore, no need exists to form an adjacency. Figure 8.37 displays a list of neighbors on router 0.0.0.1. You can see the state of the adjacencies. Neighbor 0.0.0.5 is not in the list. Therefore, forming the adjacency to 0.0.0.5 is a problem. No statically configured neighbors exist on this router. It doesn't have an interface to an NBMA network. One virtual link is configured between 0.0.0.1 and 0.0.0.2. This virtual link is used as a redundant link in case router 0.0.0.2 or 0.0.0.1 loses the physical connection to the backbone. If adjacencies are full and all neighbors are recognized, you can safely assume that the LSDB contains all necessary entries.

Check the Log File

Most routers will report OSPF events to a log file. Take a close look at that log file. This is an excellent source to find problems on OSPF routers. Figure 8.38 shows some sample entries found in log files. You can see an adjacency coming up and going through all the phases. You can also see a problem with Hello packets.

▶ · ◀

FIGURE 8.37

List of OSPF neighbors on router 0.0.0.1

```
OSPF Neighbors
--------------
                                  Neighbor
     IP Interface    Router ID    IP Address     State      Type
     ------------    ---------    ----------     -----      ----
     140.250.1.1     0.0.0.2      140.250.1.2    Full       Dynamic
     140.250.1.1     0.0.0.3      140.250.1.3    Two Way    Dynamic
     140.250.17.1    0.0.0.2      140.250.17.2   Init       Dynamic
     140.250.17.1    0.0.1.1      140.250.17.3   ExStart    Dynamic
     140.250.31.1    0.0.0.2      140.250.31.2   Full       Dynamic
     140.250.31.129  0.0.1.1      140.250.31.130 Loading    Dynamic
6 dynamic neighbors

0 configured neighbors

OSPF Virtual Neighbors

----------------------

     Area Address    Router ID       State
     ------------    ---------       -----
     0.0.0.1         0.0.0.2         Full

1 virtual neighbors
```

▶ · ◀

FIGURE 8.38

Extracts from a log file on an OSPF router

```
# 159: 02/08/99 12:07:22 WARNING   SLOT  1 OSPF              Event Code:  54
C2: Hello Rejected: HELLO INTERVAL MISMATCH
    src 140.250.1.2(10)  interface 140.250.1.1(15)
-------------------------------------------------------------------------------
# 577: 02/08/99 15:22:53 WARNING   SLOT  1 OSPF              Event Code:  53
C2: Hello Rejected: NETMASK MISMATCH
    src 140.250.1.1:255.255.255.240 interface 140.250.1.3:255.255.255.0
-------------------------------------------------------------------------------
#   2: 02/08/99 12:46:25 WARNING   SLOT  1 OSPF              Event Code:  51
C1: Packet Rejected: AUTH TYPE(1)    src 140.250.17.1 dst 140.250.17.2 routerid 0.0.0.1
-------------------------------------------------------------------------------
# 384: 02/08/99 12:54:52 WARNING   SLOT  1 OSPF              Event Code:  52
C1: Packet Rejected: AUTH KEY(70:77:64:00:00:00:00:00)
    src 140.250.31.1 dst 224.0.0.5 routerid 0.0.0.1
-------------------------------------------------------------------------------
# 127: 02/08/99 12:06:47 TRACE     SLOT  1 OSPF              Event Code:  39
T2: Neighbor 140.250.31.2 Event: Hello Received   State change: Down->Init
# 128: 02/08/99 12:06:48 TRACE     SLOT  1 OSPF              Event Code:  39
T2: Neighbor 140.250.31.2 Event: Two Way Received  State change: Init->2 Way
# 129: 02/08/99 12:06:48 TRACE     SLOT  1 OSPF              Event Code:  39
T2: Neighbor 140.250.31.2 Event: Adjacency OK  State change: 2 Way->Exch Start
# 130: 02/08/99 12:06:48 TRACE     SLOT  1 OSPF              Event Code:  39
T2: Neighbor 140.250.31.2 Event: Negotiation Done  State change: Exch Start->Exch
# 131: 02/08/99 12:06:48 TRACE     SLOT  1 OSPF              Event Code:  39
T2: Neighbor 140.250.31.2 Event: Exchange Done   State change: Exchange->Loading
# 132: 02/08/99 12:06:48 TRACE     SLOT  1 OSPF              Event Code:  39
T2: Neighbor 140.250.31.2 Event: Loading Done  State change: Loading->Full
```

Table 8.6 gives a glossary of OSPF terms and abbreviations.

T A B L E   8.6

OSPF Terms and Abbreviations

ABBREVIATION	TERM
ABR	Area border router. Connects different areas; must be connected to the *backbone area.*
AllDRouters	All Designated Routers. The name of the multicast address 224.0.0.6, addressing DRs and BDRs.
AllSPFRouters	All Shortest Path First Routers. The name of the multicast address 224.0.0.5, addressing all routers running OSPF.
Area	A collection of networks and hosts with the same unique area ID. Routers within the area are called *internal routers.* Different areas can be linked by ABRs. Each area must always be linked to the backbone area through the ABR.
AS	Autonomous system. A network under the same administration. This can be one segment or can consist of multiple segments connected by routers using a common routing protocol (in this case OSPF).
ASBR	Autonomous system border router. A router that imports routing information derived from non OSPF routing protocols into OSPF.
Backbone	The Backbone Area must be logically contiguous and must be connected to each area. It must be assigned the address 0.0.0.0.
BDR	Backup designated router. Refer to DR.
DD	Database description. The first step in building an adjacency is the exchange of the database description, describing the content of the databases.
DR	Designated router: Each multiaccess OSPF network that has at least two attached routers has a DR that is elected by the Hello protocol. The DR enables a reduction in the number of adjacencies required on a multiaccess network, which in turn reduces the amount of routing protocol traffic. To keep the adjacencies redundant, a BDR is elected as well. The BDR takes over in case the DR fails, ensuring uninterrupted flooding of LSAs.
LS	Link state. The information sent out by each router in the LSA.
LSA	Link-state advertisement. Contain LS information according to the LSA type. LSAs are used to build the LSDB. LSAs are advertised using OSPF link-state update packets..
LSDB	Link-state database. Maintained by every OSPF router. It is filled with LSAs, and is identical on all routers within the same area or in case of a single area only within the AS. Every router runs the same algorithm to build the SPF tree.

Continued

ABBREVIATION	TERM
NBMA	Nonbroadcast multiaccess network. Network that isn't capable of transmitting broadcasts or multicasts. It can be configured in OSPF as a transit network or a point-to-point multipoint network.
NSSA	Not-so-stubby area. Similar to the existing OSPF stub area configuration option, but has the additional capability of importing AS external routes in a limited fashion.
SPF	Shortest path first. This algorithm is used by every router in an AS to calculate a tree of shortest paths (Dijkstra algorithm). The SPF tree is then used to build the routing table.
Stub area	A stub area is not allowed to import external routes. Each ABR of the stub area advertises a default route into the area to summarize all external routes.
Transit area	Area that can be used to set up virtual links between ABRs. The transit area cannot be a stub area.

Case Study — What Can Go Wrong

The most common case of something going wrong is while bringing up an adjacency. Routing loops created by external networks is another problem this section reviews.

Problem 1: Adjacencies Are Not Up

The most important thing for proper operation of OSPF is the forming and maintaining of adjacencies. Assume router 0.0.0.2 is not able to bring up the adjacency on the point-to-point link to 0.0.0.1.

The Analysis

To find the problem, look at the Hello packets being exchanged on that link. To trace for Hello packets, define a filter using an offset of 21 bytes from the IP header (if the IP header uses the standard 20 bytes), a length of 1 byte, and a pattern of 0x01. This represents the OSPF packet-type field using 1 for Hello packets.

Figures 8.39 and 8.40 each show a Hello packet, one sent by router 0.0.0.2 and the other sent by router 0.0.0.1.

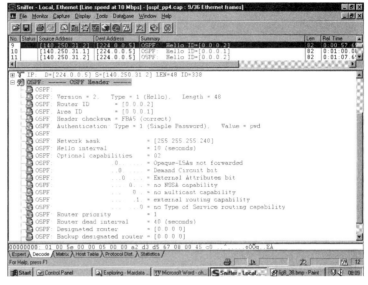

FIGURE 8.39

A Hello packet sent by 0.0.0.2

FIGURE 8.40

A Hello packet sent by 0.0.0.1

The Password, Area ID, Network Mask, and E-bit are set the same by both routers. The Hello Interval and Router Dead Interval, however, are set differently on the two routers. Thus, they will not be able to form an adjacency. Note that no DR or BDR is set in the Hello packets exchanged. On a point-to-point link, no DR or BDR is elected.

The Solution

On one of the routers, the timer has to be changed to be equal to the timer of the neighbor router. Refer to Figure 8.28 to determine all the settings that have to be equal on both neighboring routers.

Problem 2: Routing Loops

In your LSDB, you see OSPF networks being advertised as external routes using a more specific (longer) mask. Your router will always use this route to forward traffic to that destination. Packets will be forwarded to the ASBR, through the external network and back to OSPF. That will continue until the packet's TTL has expired.

The Analysis

Routing loops can occur when multiple ASBRs are connected to a contiguous external network. OSPF networks are sent into the external network governed by other routing protocols. Some routing protocols (such as RIP1) change network information by changing the subnet mask. The changed information is imported back into the OSPF network, suggesting a different network is present. If the new information is more specific (has a longer mask), packets are routed to the external network, which in turn routes them right back into OSPF.

Figure 8.41 shows network 140.250.16.0 with a mask of 255.255.240.0 being advertised by router 0.0.05 into the external network using RIP1. RIP1 changes the mask to 255.255.255.0, because the RIP networks use the same class B address range. Therefore, RIP1 is assuming the configured masks for all 140.250.x.x addresses. ASBR 0.0.0.1 imports 140.250.16.0 with a mask of 255.255.255.0 back to OSPF. This route is a new route to OSPF with a more specific mask. Each packet destined for 140.250.160.x will be routed to the ASBR 0.0.01. From there, it will be routed through the external network to router 0.0.0.5, which then forwards it to 0.0.0.1. The packet is routed in a loop until the TTL expires.

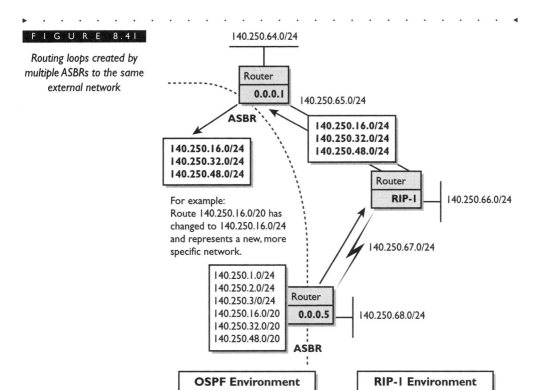

FIGURE 8.41

Routing loops created by multiple ASBRs to the same external network

The Solution

To solve the problem, you have to make sure that the network mask changed by the external network is corrected before importing the network back to OSPF. You could configure RIP Policies on the ASBR, to correct the network masks or to block OSPF-learned networks from being imported back to OSPF. Using RIP2 for the external network would, however, be a much better solution. RIP2 doesn't change the masks at all.

▶ · ◀

Summary

This chapter discussed the functionality of OSPF. OSPF distributes routing information to all routers in an autonomous system. Only changes in topology are advertised by OSPF. All topology information about an AS is kept in a link-state database called the LSDB. The LSDB is the base for calculating the routing table on each router. This chapter gave an insight into the LSDB, the calculation of the routing table, and all the information exchanged between OSPF routers.

You have now covered the protocols residing on the Internet layer of the DOD model. You are ready to go one step further and find out what's happening on the host-to-host layer.

Troubleshooting and Analyzing the Host-to-Host (Transport) Layer

## CHAPTER 9

User Datagram Protocol (UDP)

IP receives a datagram, strips off the IP header, and processes the datagram according to the information in the IP header. If it does not have to route the datagram, it processes it to the Upper Layer Protocol specified in the IP header. This is either TCP or UDP, the two protocols residing on the host-to-host layer, which corresponds to the transport layer in the OSI model. The responsibility of the host-to-host layer is to control the flow of data between two hosts. After the datagram arrives at the destination host, it has to be forwarded to the correct process or application on this host. UDP and TCP are responsible for this forwarding mechanism.

This chapter describes the User Datagram Protocol (UDP). It examines the UDP header, explains what the pseudo-header is used for, describes how UDP communicates, and discusses where UDP can cause problems in your network.

Overview of UDP Functionality

UDP is often compared to sending a postcard. You put an address on the postcard and throw it into the mailbox. Now, just from experience, you know that most postcards arrive at their destination. However, no confirmation comes back to inform you that delivery has been successful. UDP is a simple, connectionless protocol that provides no reliability. It provides no guarantee that the datagram ever reaches its destination. Messages can be lost, duplicated, or arrive out of order. Also packets can arrive faster than the recipient can handle them. Timeout and retransmission algorithms must be provided by the application.

The advantage that UDP has over TCP is a smaller header with less overhead. UDP is connectionless, whereas TCP is connection-oriented. A UDP header has 8 bytes, a TCP header contains 20 bytes minimum. TCP is more reliable, but UDP is much faster. UDP provides no ordering of incoming messages nor flow control — this is typically handled, if at all, by the Upper Layer Protocol.

UDP is used in environments where applications frequently send short or single messages between hosts on the same network. Often, these messages are requests for time-critical information. Routing protocol updates often use UDP for regularly repeated communications. Broadcasts also use UDP. RFC 768 describes UDP.

UDP messages are called *datagrams*, whereas TCP messages are called *segments*. Every output operation by a process produces one UDP datagram. This causes one

IP datagram to be sent over the network (if IP does not have to fragment the datagram). This behavior is different from TCP, which is a streaming protocol. With TCP the application data is broken into whatever TCP considers to be the best-sized chunks to send.

X-REF

To learn how TCP works, refer to Chapter 10.

Using Ports

UDP uses IP to carry messages. IP delivers the datagram to the destination host, at which point the datagram has to be forwarded to the correct process or application on that host. This is exactly what UDP does: it adds the ability to distinguish among multiple destinations on a host computer. A host usually has different processes and applications running on it. To allow them to communicate independently from each other, the operating system assigns a port to each process or application. It is like an internal address to identify the destination process. The application negotiates a port with the operating system. The operating system creates an internal queue that can hold incoming messages destined for that application. Figure 9.1 illustrates this procedure. If the desired service is not loaded on the destination host, an ICMP *Port Unreachable* message is created. If the port queue is full, the host may create an ICMP *Source Quench* message (RFC 792).

FIGURE 9.1

How ports are used to address a destination process on a host

| TFTP port 69 | DNS port 53 | NTP port 123 | Application layer |

UDP — UDP forwards to applications based on the port number in the UDP header. — Host-to-host layer

IP — Internet layer

The following are the two approaches to port assignment:

▸ **Well-known port numbers:** Assigned by the IANA (Internet Assigned Numbers Authority). Their range is from 0 to 1023.

▸ **Registered port numbers**: Range from 1024 to 65535.

IANA does not control the assignment of the registered ports. If you check RFC 1700 you can see that some of those port numbers have duplicate assignments. Examples of this are port 1525 and port 1992. If two applications using the same port are loaded on one server, a port conflict is inevitable. Clients usually use dynamically assigned port numbers, very often in the range of 1024 to 5000. Because client ports are in the same range as registered ports, they can conflict, too.

A vendor's TCP/IP stack determines which random ports are chosen. Usually, the software selects a first port and then increases the number sequentially. Most vendors choose the first port low around 1030.

Check RFC 1700, the Assigned Numbers Document, for a list of all the well-known and registered port numbers.

NOTE

Until 1992, the well-known ports were between 0 to 255. The UNIX world used 256 to 1023 for UNIX-specific services usually not found on other operating systems.

TCP port numbers are independent of UDP port numbers. Remember that IP has de-multiplexed the IP datagram to either TCP or UDP (based on the protocol value in the IP header). This means that TCP looks at the TCP port numbers, and UDP looks at the UDP port numbers. In practice, if a well-known service is provided by TCP and UDP, the same port number usually is chosen for both transport protocols. This is not a requirement of the protocols, though, but is purely for convenience.

UDP Header Structure

We are moving up through the layers of the protocol stack. Recalling what you have learned regarding the network layer (Chapter 3) and IP (Chapter 4), this section looks at the packet structure in general and the addressing schemes on the different layers (see Figure 9.2), before examining the UDP header structure.

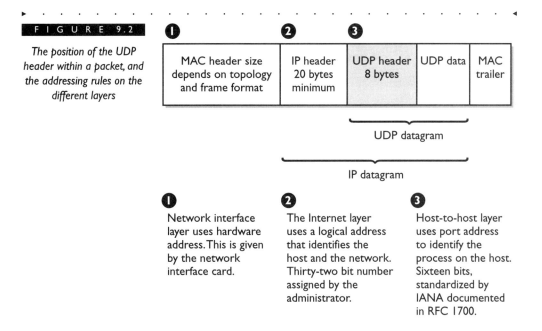

FIGURE 9.2

The position of the UDP header within a packet, and the addressing rules on the different layers

①
Network interface layer uses hardware address. This is given by the network interface card.

②
The Internet layer uses a logical address that identifies the host and the network. Thirty-two bit number assigned by the administrator.

③
Host-to-host layer uses port address to identify the process on the host. Sixteen bits, standardized by IANA documented in RFC 1700.

The combination of a port address and an IP address is referred to as a *socket*.

NOTE

Figure 9.3 shows the format of the UDP header. Each field is discussed in detail later in this chapter. The size of the UDP header is 8 bytes. A *pseudo-header* also is created, which includes information about the source and destination IP addresses. The purpose of the pseudo-header is to verify that the datagram has reached its correct destination, which is why it has to include the IP addresses of the source and destination hosts. The pseudo-header is used to calculate the checksum that will be placed into the UDP header. After that, the pseudo-header is discarded. It is not transmitted with the datagram, nor are its fields included in the datagram size field.

▶ · ◀

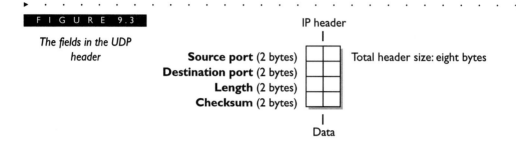

FIGURE 9.3

The fields in the UDP header

IP header

Source port (2 bytes)
Destination port (2 bytes)
Length (2 bytes)
Checksum (2 bytes)

Total header size: eight bytes

Data

Source Port

This is a 2-byte field that contains the port number for the sending process or application. Indication of the source port is optional. If it is not used, it should be 0.

Destination Port

This 2-byte field contains the destination port number.

Length

This 2-byte field contains the length of the UDP datagram. It is a count of bytes of the datagram, including the UDP header and the data. The minimum value for this field is 8, which is the length of the header alone if no user data is included.

Checksum

This 2-byte field contains the UDP checksum. The UDP checksum is optional, whereas the TCP checksum is mandatory. A value of 0 means that the checksum has not been computed. If the receiving host finds a 0 in this field, it will not do a checksum test. If the checksum computation returns 0, the Checksum field is set to all ones. If the checksum has been used and the receiving host detects a checksum error, the datagram is silently discarded (the sender will not be notified). The checksum covers the pseudo-header, the UDP header, and UDP data. Remember that the checksum in the IP header only covers the IP header, and not any data

Notice that by not using the checksum, the header does not get smaller. The UDP datagram is the same length either way.

The Pseudo-Header

Figure 9.4 shows the fields of the pseudo-header.

▶ · ◀

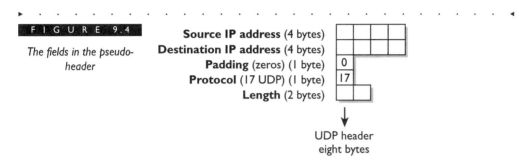

FIGURE 9.4

The fields in the pseudo-header

Source IP address (4 bytes)
Destination IP address (4 bytes)
Padding (zeros) (1 byte)   0
Protocol (17 UDP) (1 byte)   17
Length (2 bytes)

↓

UDP header
eight bytes

The pseudo-header has 12 bytes and contains the source and destination IP addresses, the Protocol field, which is 17 for UDP (RFC 1700), and the length of the UDP datagram. One byte of 0s is used to round out the 32-bit word. (Remember that headers are extended in units of 32 bits. After adding this 1 byte of 0s, the header is 12 bytes, which is 3 times 32 bits.)

Calculating the checksum over the source and destination IP addresses protects against misrouted datagrams. It ensures that both host IP addresses and port addresses are correct. To calculate the checksum, UDP needs information from the IP layer. After the checksum is calculated and placed into the UDP header, the pseudo-header is discarded and the UDP datagram is sent to the IP destination host, where the checksum is recalculated to be checked against the checksum in the header. Notice that in the checksum calculation, the length of the UDP datagram is contained twice (once in the pseudo-header and once in the UDP header).

Figure 9.5 shows the UDP header in a protocol decode.

In the Summary window, you can see the different layers (DLC, IP, UDP, and RIP), as previously described in Figure 9.2. The UDP header is highlighted in the detail window. In this case, port 520 is used, which is RIP. The checksum has been used, and 15 routing entries are in the data portion of the datagram. Because the UDP header is highlighted in the detail window, the 8 bytes that make up the UDP header are also highlighted in the hexadecimal window in the lower portion of the screen.

FIGURE 9.5

The UDP header in a
protocol decode

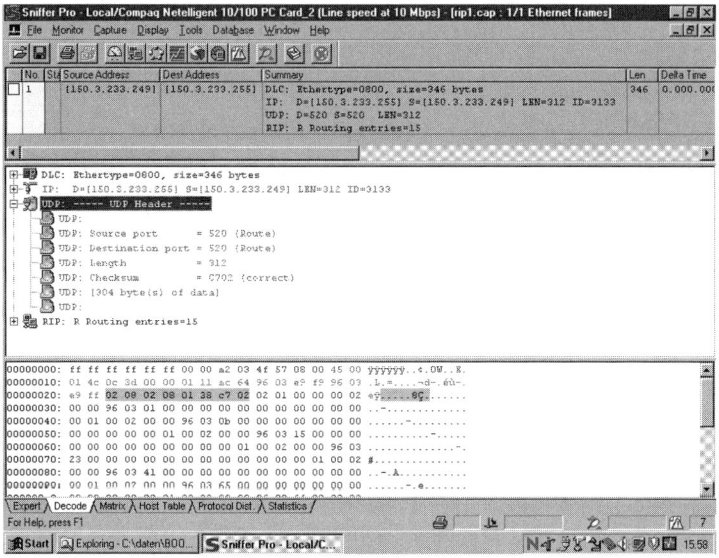

Applications That Use UDP

Applications that use UDP are usually applications that need to get data to the target host as quickly as possible. By using UDP, we are willing to take the chance of losing some datagrams, because performance is more important. UDP is also a convenient protocol for applications that frequently send short messages. Broadcasts use UDP. Another reason to use UDP is when the Upper Layer Protocol already provides TCP-like functionality. For example, Sun's RPC has streaming functions like TCP, so using UDP for the transport is more effective in this case.

The following list shows some examples of common port numbers:

DNS	Port 53
TFTP	Port 69
BootP (DHCP)	Port 67 server; port 68 client
Sun RPC	Port 111
NTP (Network Time Protocol)	Port 123

NetBIOS name service	Port 137
NetBIOS datagram service	Port 138
SNMP	Port 161 monitor; port 162 traps
IPX (IP Tunnel, VPN)	Port 213 (control channel)
DSS (Domain SAP/RIP Server)	Port 396
SLP (Service Location Protocol)	Port 427
RIP	Port 520
NCP (NetWare Core Protocol)	Port 524 (NetWare 5 Pure IP)
IP Tunnel, IP Relay	Port 2010 (data channel)
VPN (Virtual Private Network)	Port 2010 (BorderManager)
SCMD (Compatibility Mode Driver)	Port 2645 (NetWare 5 Migration Agent)
NetWare IP	Port 43981 (for SAP/RIP queries)
	Port 43982 (for NCP calls)
	Default ports, configurable in Unicon
NAT (network address translation)	Port 55000 – 59999 (BorderManager)

TIP

A good rule for preventing port allocation problems is to start services that run continuously and use assigned ports first. Start services that dynamically assign port numbers last. Have your port lists ready when you configure your firewalls, to make sure you only allow the ports for services that you want to go through.

Troubleshooting UDP

If your host-to-host communication fails and you receive an ICMP Port Unreachable message, the first question to ask is whether the communication uses UDP or TCP. If it is TCP, then refer to Chapter 10 for troubleshooting information.

If the communication uses UDP, the first check is to find out whether the application or the service required is running. If this is the case, examine the ports being used by the application. Is there a port conflict? Are two processes or applications on one host using the same port number?

If you have too many retransmissions, then you have to look at the application's configuration regarding the transport mechanism. Does the application have timeout parameters that are unreasonable? Check your application's documentation for information on those parameters.

A general question to look at is whether using UDP for transport is adequate for this application.

TIP

Whenever you install new services or applications, the ports being used by that application are entered into the Services file. So, after installation, it is a good idea to check this file for the entries that the new application has made. This way, you can easily spot duplicate entries. Compare the ports added by the new application to the ports already in the file. This is proactive work, which is preferable to reactive work.

The following listing shows the output of the Services file of a NetWare Server. The location of the Services file depends on your host's operating system. The end of this section provides a list of locations for Services files for different operation systems. Try to find within this file the services and applications previously mentioned. Notice that, as explained earlier in the chapter, the port number for a service very often is the same for UDP as for TCP, although the ports are independent of each other.

```
#

# SYS:ETC\SERVICES

#

#      Network service mappings.  Maps service names to
transport

#      protocol and transport protocol ports.

#

echo           7/udp

echo           7/tcp

discard        9/udp              sink null
```

```
discard        9/tcp           sink null

systat         11/tcp

daytime        13/udp

daytime        13/tcp

netstat        15/tcp

ftp-data            20/tcp

ftp            21/tcp

telnet         23/tcp

smtp           25/tcp       mail

time           37/tcp       timserver

time           37/udp       timserver

name           42/udp       nameserver

whois          43/tcp       nicname # usually to sri-nic

domain         53/udp

domain         53/tcp

hostnames      101/tcp      hostname # usually to sri-nic

sunrpc         111/udp

sunrpc         111/tcp

#

#

# Host specific functions

#

tftp           69/udp

rje            77/tcp

finger         79/tcp
```

```
link         87/tcp          ttylink

supdup       95/tcp

iso-tsap     102/tcp

x400         103/tcp         # ISO Mail

x400-snd     104/tcp

csnet-ns     105/tcp

pop-2        109/tcp         # Post Office

uucp-path    117/tcp

nntp         119/tcp     usenet # Network News Transfer

ntp          123/tcp             # Network Time Protocol

NeWS         144/tcp     news # Window System

#

# UNIX specific services

#

# these are NOT officially assigned

#

exec         512/tcp

login        513/tcp

shell        514/tcp     cmd    # no passwords used

printer      515/tcp     spooler  # experimental

courier      530/tcp     rpc   # experimental

biff         512/udp     comsat

who          513/udp     whod

syslog       514/udp

talk         517/udp
```

```
route          520/udp       router routed

new-rwho       550/udp       new-who    # experimental

rmonitor       560/udp       rmonitord  # experimental

monitor        561/udp                  # experimental

ingreslock     1524/tcp

snmp           161/udp       # Simple Network Mgmt Protocol

snmp-trap      162/udp       snmptrap # SNMP trap (event)
messages
```

An application that uses UDP is responsible for handling reliability. Often, application programmers ignore this when they design software. And, very often, they test their applications on highly reliable, low-delay local area networks. Testing might be okay in this reliable environment, but then fail when used in a larger, less-reliable internetwork. In this case, your problem is not UDP, but rather the application, and you need to ask the application's vendor for a solution. In such a case, you get into a situation in which you have to prove that the problem is within the application. Your best help for proving this will be your analyzer trace files.

Utilities Used to Check on Port Numbers

The following utilities can be useful when checking on port numbers:

▸ On Windows 95 and Windows NT, use NETSTAT -a to display the ports currently in use.

▸ On a Novell NetWare Server, load TCPCON, go to Protocol Information, choose UDP, and then get the list for the UDP listeners. By using the Tab key, you can switch to have the port number displayed in decimal.

▸ On UNIX systems, use NETSTAT -A to view the ports currently in use.

Figure 9.6 shows the screen in TCPCON when you view the UDP listeners. Port 524 is shown in decimal. It is used for NCP over UDP.

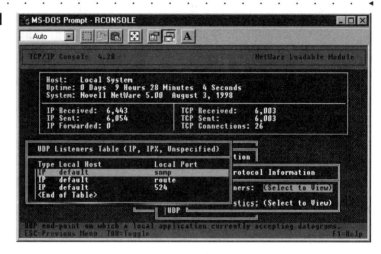

Get a List of Known Services

To get a list of the known services that a machine recognizes, check the Services file in the etc directory, the location of which is listed next for various operating systems. Notice, though, that the services and ports listed there are not necessarily currently in use.

- **Novell NetWare Server:** Sys:etc\services

- **Windows NT:**
  Windowsdrive:\winnt\system32\drivers\etc\services

- **Windows 95:** Windowsdrive:\Windows\services

- **UNIX systems:** /etc/services

Case Study—What Can Go Wrong

The following case study demonstrates why using checksums can be important.

The Problem

We have a misbehaving router in our network. A corrupted IP header checksum prevented the worst case (which would have been wrong information in the routing table propagated through the network). The trace file reveals what is going on.

The Analysis

We have a router connecting two networks, network 134.122.0.0 and network 134.123.0.0. Its interface address to network 134.123.0.0 is 134.123.1.1. This router has just been booted. The analyzer was on network 134.123.0.0. Figure 9.7 shows the network layout.

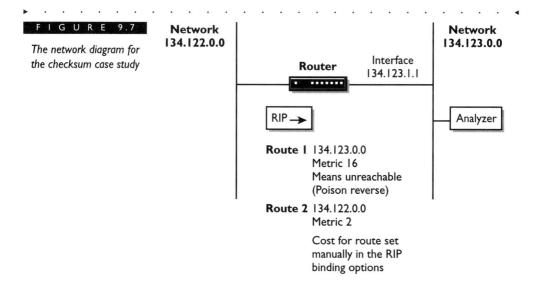

FIGURE 9.7

The network diagram for the checksum case study

Network 134.122.0.0

Router

Interface 134.123.1.1

Network 134.123.0.0

Analyzer

RIP →

Route 1 134.123.0.0
Metric 16
Means unreachable
(Poison reverse)

Route 2 134.122.0.0
Metric 2

Cost for route set manually in the RIP binding options

Now look at the trace file in Figure 9.8. The first two frames show multicasts to an unknown Ethertype (7031) with a bad CRC (cyclic redundancy check). Don't worry about these frames. They come from a Mycom Card. This was an older,

TROUBLESHOOTING AND ANALYZING THE HOST-TO-HOST (TRANSPORT) LAYER

intelligent LAN card with an onboard processor. Those frames are sent out on purpose to test the wire for shorts and opens. The bad CRC makes sure that no other host will process that frame.

Frame 3 is a RIP request originating from 134.123.1.1 for the entire routing table. It is sent out as a broadcast to UDP port 520. In frame 4, the router advertises its own routes. Interface 134.123.0.0 is advertised with a metric of 16 (hops) which means *Unreachable*. This is RIP's poison reverse, which tells the receiver not to enter this route into the routing table, because the route is considered to be unreachable through this router. The route is considered unreachable because the advertisement goes out to that same network. The route to 134.122.0.0 is advertised with a metric of 2 (not seen in the figure).

F I G U R E   9.8

A router advertising its routes by using RIP port 520

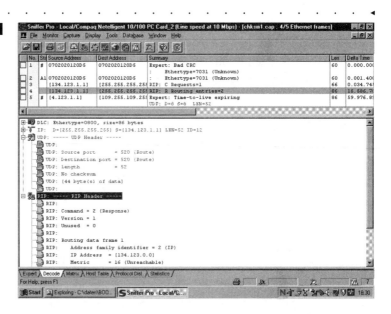

So far, everything looks good. But something interesting occurs in frame number 5. Figure 9.9 shows the details of that frame. This frame is supposed to be the same as frame 4, but the router seems to be in trouble. The frame is a good Ethernet frame, but the source and destination IP address in the IP header are rather strange. They are in no relation to the networks to which this router is connected, nor to the interfaces it has. Also notice that the IP header checksum is bad. It has caught the problem with the wrong IP addresses. The TTL is set to 0. The IP header has no way to tell whether problems exist within UDP data. The UDP checksum is disabled. But the UDP information is also bad because it is addressed to port 8 instead of 520.

In this case, the bad IP header will cause the datagram to be discarded. But imagine the situation in which the IP header is fine, the UDP port is correct, and only the UDP data is bad. Not using the UDP checksum would allow this problem to go undetected. Consequently, bad routing information would be propagated to all routers. As you know, this can cause quite some confusion in your network.

FIGURE 9.9

The bad IP header checksum saves this bad UDP data from being propagated through the network.

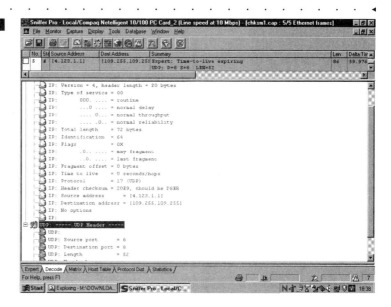

The Solution

The reason for that bad UDP datagram was a TCP/IP stack with a bug that has been fixed in a later release of that stack.

The UDP checksum is designed to catch any modifications of the UDP header or UDP data anywhere between the sender and the receiver. Checksums should always be enabled, because no other way exists to find out whether a device on the path has a corrupted UDP header or data. The Host Requirements RFC states that UDP checksums should be enabled by default. It also requires that an implementation verify a received checksum if the sender has calculated one for the datagram. Many implementations, though, verify a received checksum only if outgoing checksums are enabled. So much for standards.

Refer to Chapters 7 and 8 to learn about RIP, OSPF (Open Shortest Path First), metrics, and poison reverse.

X-REF

Summary

This chapter explained the functionality of UDP. It is a simple, connectionless transport layer protocol. By using port numbers, UDP makes it possible to distinguish between multiple processes running on a host.

The next chapter introduces TCP, the connection-oriented protocol on the transport layer.

## CHAPTER 10

Transmission Control Protocol (TCP)

Chapter 9 discussed the User Datagram Protocol (UDP) and transport service function within the TCP/IP protocol stack. You learned that UDP is a simple, connectionless protocol that does not guarantee delivery of service. In contrast, the Transmission Control Protocol (TCP) provides connection-oriented, reliable delivery of data within the network.

Overview of TCP Functionality

Within the host-to-host (or transport) layer of the TCP/IP model, two transport protocols generally are used: User Datagram Protocol and Transmission Control Protocol. Though they both reside in the same layer, they each provide a very different method of service. The purpose of TCP is to provide a connection-oriented, reliable service.

The term *connection-oriented* means that two applications using TCP must establish a TCP connection with each other before data exchange may occur. A TCP connection is very similar to a telephone call. When you pick up the phone to make a call, you dial the number for the other person. As the connection is attempted, you hear the ringing of the telephone on the other end. If the person answers, the information exchange may take place and you both may speak. If the person does not answer, no communication may take place. (Sorry, no answering machines in the TCP world.)

TCP provides support in several ways for applications that require communication reliability. Some of the characteristics of TCP's reliable service are the following:

> **Streaming service:** Two application programs generally send large amounts of data between computers, which is called a stream. A *stream* is a large amount of data sent in 8-bit (or 1-byte) increments across the TCP connection. Data is passed through TCP from one computer to another exactly as it was sent. TCP does not interpret the information, and has no idea of the type of data being sent. The interpretation is left up to the application itself. TCP data is called a *segment,* and segments are transmitted within IP *datagrams.* The nature of IP datagrams is such that datagrams may arrive out of order. Because TCP is sent within an IP datagram, TCP

segments may also arrive out of order. If this happens, the receiving computer's TCP protocol simply resequences the data, if necessary, and passes it to the application.

▸ **Acknowledged communication:** When TCP sends a segment, it begins a timer-and-wait process, waiting for the other end to acknowledge the receipt of the segment. If an acknowledgment is not received within a certain period of time, the segment is retransmitted. Likewise, when a TCP segment is received, an acknowledgment is returned to the sender.

▸ **TCP connections**: When a TCP application makes a request for communication of a data stream with another computer, it must first make a request (much like placing that telephone call). When a reply is received, the two applications exchange protocol information and begin communication through a single channel, called a *connection*. This single connection is maintained between the two computers until the link is broken. This may be a voluntary application end, or a loss of communication due to a hardware failure somewhere in the data path.

▸ **Segment sizes:** TCP breaks up the application data into what TCP considers to be the best size to send (discussed later in this chapter).

▸ **Checksum:** TCP maintains a checksum on both the TCP header and the data. The purpose of the checksum is to detect any kind of change in transmission from the beginning to the end point. If a segment arrives with an invalid checksum, TCP simply throws away the segment and does not provide acknowledgment. In this situation, the sender should be aware that no acknowledgment was received and thus retransmit the segment.

▸ **Flow control:** Each end of the TCP connection has a set amount of buffer space allotted to receive segments. Using flow control, a receiving TCP station allows the other end to send only as much data as can be received by the available buffers. This prevents a TCP sender from taking up all the buffers on another host, which could cause it to malfunction.

TCP Header Structure

The TCP header is part of the host-to-host layer (or transport layer), which is the third layer of the TCP/IP model. TCP data is encapsulated into an IP datagram, as shown in Figure 10.1.

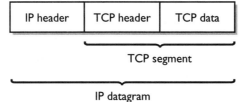

F I G U R E   10.1

TCP header and data is encapsulated within an IP datagram

Figure 10.2 depicts the fields of the TCP header, which is normally a 20-byte header.

F I G U R E   10.2

TCP header field structure

The following sections describe each of these fields in more detail.

Source Port Number

This field is used to identify the *port number* used by the sending application. Like the UDP transport protocol, TCP also uses these special numbers to identify specific applications, such as FTP or Telnet.

Destination Port Number

The destination port number identifies the application port for which TCP is attempting to make a connection. If the destination computer does not have this port available, the sending computer receives an error message.

Well-Known Application Port Numbers

Most of the well-known application port numbers are located in RFC 1700 and detailed in Appendix C of this book. Table 10.1 depicts many of these well-known ports, along with many new Novell port numbers.

T A B L E 10.1 *Well-Known Application Port Numbers*	DESCRIPTION	TCP PORT NUMBER
	File Transfer Protocol (FTP-DATA)	20
	File Transfer Protocol (FTP-Control)	21
	Telnet (TELNET)	23
	Simple Mail Transfer Protocol (SMTP)	25
	Domain Name Server (DNS)	53
	Bootstrap Protocol Server (BOOTPS)	67
	Bootstrap Protocol Client (BOOTPC)	68
	Trivial File Transfer Protocol (TFTP)	69
	Gopher	70
	Finger	79
	Hypertext Transfer Protocol (HTTP)	80
	Post Office Protocol (POP3)	110
	Network Time Protocol (NTP)	123
	NetBIOS Name Service (NETBIOS-NS)	137
	Simple Network Management Protocol (SNMP)	161
	SNMP traps	162
	Internet Relay Chat Protocol (IRC)	194
	NetWare Virtual Private Network (VPN), IP Tunnel, and IP Relay	213
	AppleTalk Routing Maintenance (RTMP)	201

Continued

TABLE 10.1	DESCRIPTION	TCP PORT NUMBER
Well-Known Application Port Numbers (continued)	AppleTalk Zone Information (ZIS)	206
	Lightweight Directory Access Protocol (LDAP)	389
	NetWare/IP	396
	NetWare Service Location Protocol	427
	NetWare Core Protocol (over TCP/IP)	524

A Word About Ports

Each TCP segment contains the source and destination port numbers, to identify the sending and receiving application. In addition to these port numbers, the source and destination IP addresses are located within the IP header. The combination of these values (port number and IP address) uniquely identifies each side of the TCP connection and is sometimes referred to as a *socket*. When two devices begin a communication, the socket of the source and destination devices combine to form what is sometimes referred to as a *socket pair*. The socket pair (source IP address, source port address, destination IP address, and destination port address) defines the end points of a particular connection at any given time.

Sequence Number

The sequence number identifies the position of the first byte in the data stream. It is a 4-byte number that increments as data is passed through the TCP connection. When a new connection is established, an initial sequence number is placed in this field. The initial sequence number is sometimes generated by the sender's clock, with an update every four microseconds, though this may vary in different implementations.

Acknowledgment Number

The Acknowledgment Number field contains the value of the next sequence number expected by the sender. Each TCP segment contains both a sequence and acknowledgment number. Upon receipt of a sequence number, TCP calculates the outgoing acknowledgment number by using the following formula:

```
Incoming Sequence # + # of Data Bytes = New Acknowledgment #
```

The last acknowledgment becomes the new sequence number for the next packet. You need to understand how this process works, especially when troubleshooting misbehaving networks. Figure 10.3 shows how sequence and acknowledgment numbers work during data transmission.

▶ · ◀

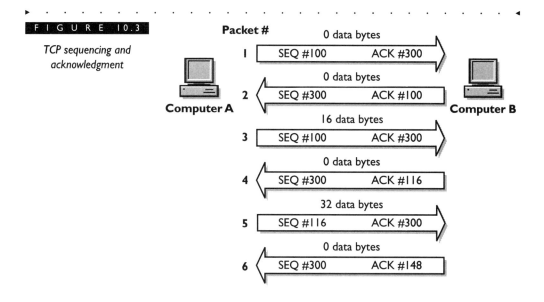

FIGURE 10.3

TCP sequencing and acknowledgment

In Figure 10.3, Computer A makes a transmission with a sequence number of 100 and 0 TCP data bytes (Packet #1). Computer B calculates the acknowledgment number (100 + 0 = 100), takes the acknowledgment number from Computer A (300), and returns the packet (Packet #2). Computer A then sends a packet with 16 data bytes (Packet #3), using the proper sequence number (100, from Packet #2) and acknowledgment number (300) received from Packet #2. Computer B calculates the acknowledgment number (100 + 16 =116) and returns Packet #4 with a new acknowledgment number of 116 and a sequence number of 300. (This number has not changed, because no data has been transmitted from Computer B to Computer A.) The next packet, Packet #5, is sent from Computer A to Computer B and contains 32 bytes of data. The new acknowledgment number sent back from Computer B would be 148 (116 + 32=148).

The example in Figure 10.3 does not represent what could happen in everyday communication. In that example, only Computer A is sending data, causing the acknowledgment number to change in Packets #4 and #6. In reality, both computers may send data back and forth, which would cause the acknowledgment number to change for every packet. For this reason, troubleshooting TCP sequencing problems is best done using only one communication path at a time.

Header Length (Data Offset), Reserved, and Codes Fields

This 2-byte field actually serves three purposes. The first purpose is to provide the header length (also called the data offset), which consists of the first 4 bits of this field. These bits give the length of the TCP header. These bits are needed because the Options field can change the overall length of the header if options are present. Without options, the header length is 20 bytes.

The next 6 bits of this 2-byte field are reserved for future use.

The Codes field is a 6-bit field used to tell TCP how to handle the incoming segment. Some segments might tell TCP to open or close a connection, while other segments may carry data. Codes are turned on and off by placing a 1 or a 0 in the bit placeholder. Table 10.2 shows the codes and their meanings.

TABLE 10.2	CODE NAME	DESCRIPTION
TCP Codes	URG	The Urgent Pointer Field is Valid. Placed in the data stream by the application to let the other end know that some sort of urgency is required in processing.
	ACK	Shows that the acknowledgment field is valid.
	PSH	This segment requests a *push*, which is used to tell the receiver to send all of its data to the receiving process or application. The data involved includes any data received in the segment with the PUSH code, along with any other data collected by TCP for the receiving process.
	RST	A connection reset request.
	SYN	Synchronize sequence numbers when initiating a connection.
	FIN	The sender has finished sending the byte stream.

Window Size

When a segment is sent, TCP can advertise how much data it is willing to accept. The *window size* is the number of bytes that will be accepted. The window size may change during transmission, because buffers may either fill up, causing the window size to decrease, or become available, causing the window size to increase.

Checksum

The checksum is used to verify the validity of the TCP segment as well as the TCP data. Unlike the optional UDP checksum, with TCP, this is mandatory. The Checksum field is calculated and stored by the sender and then verified by the receiver. To calculate the checksum, TCP software on the sending machine attaches a *pseudo header* to the segment, much like that described in Chapter 9 for UDP. The purpose of the pseudo header is to allow the receiver to verify that the segment has reached its correct destination using both an IP address and a port number. The pseudo-header fields are shown in Figure 10.4.

▶ · ◀

F I G U R E   10.4

TCP pseudo-header fields used in the checksum process

Source IP address (4 bytes)
Destination IP address (4 bytes)
Zero (1 byte)
Protocol (1 byte)
TCP length (2 bytes)

When the pseudo header is placed on the segment, zeroes are appended to make the segment a multiple of 16 bits. The 16-bit checksum is then computed over the entire result. The sending TCP device assigns a value to the Protocol field to indicate how the underlying protocol will use the upper-layer protocols. When IP datagrams carry TCP segments, the value for this field is 6. The TCP Length field identifies the total length of the TCP segment, which does include the TCP header.

Urgent Pointer

The Urgent Pointer field is activated when the URG code is set within the TCP segment. This field is used to indicate that the receiving device should be notified of its arrival immediately and that the segment should be processed before all others. When all the urgent data segments have been processed, the device will return to normal operation.

One example of the use of the Urgent Pointer field might be this: Assume a user sits down at a computer and makes a request for data to another device. Suppose that the user is beginning an FTP session to transfer data. As the user makes the request, segments are sent into the data stream, without waiting for the device at the other end to process all the segments being sent. Sometime during the process, the user wants to stop the process and thus types a keyboard command that should stop the FTP data transfer. At this time, the receiving device may receive an urgent command to abort the transfer. Without this urgent pointer, the user may not be able to stop the transfer once it has started.

Options

TCP uses the Options field to negotiate with the TCP software on the other end of the connection. Some codes have a length value, which is the representation of the total length, including the code and length value. Table 10.3 shows some of the available option codes that are available.

TABLE 10.3	CODE	LENGTH	DESCRIPTION
Common TCP Option Codes	0	-	End of option list
	1	-	No operation involved
	2	4	Indicates a maximum segment size value in the next 4 bytes
	3	3	Indicates a window scale size value in the next 3 bytes
	6	6	Echo (option 8 has made this obsolete)
	7	6	Echo Reply (option 8 has made this obsolete)
	8	10	TSOPT — Time Stamp Option

By far the most common option code is code 2 — the Maximum Segment Size (MSS) option. The MSS is the largest amount of data that TCP will send. The MSS is generally established during the connection setup. During this process, as the sequence numbers are established, the MSS is announced. If one end does not receive an MSS announcement from the other end, a default MSS of 536 bytes is assumed. Using this default, a 20-byte IP header and a 20-byte TCP header can be placed and fit into a single 576-byte IP datagram.

Generally, the larger the MSS the better. At some point, however, fragmentation may occur. During the connection process, a sending and receiving device may send an MSS value that is as large as the maximum transfer unit (MTU) available on the outgoing network interface. For an Ethernet system, this value can be up to 1,460 bytes. Some systems require the MSS to be a multiple of 512. This means that you may see MSS values of 512 or 1024, but not 1460.

Padding

The Padding field is used to ensure that the TCP header ends on a 32-bit boundary. The Padding field is filled with zeroes, if needed.

To help put it all together, take a look at a TCP packet in the analyzer, shown in Figure 10.5.

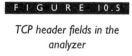

FIGURE 10.5

TCP header fields in the analyzer

In Figure 10.5, the TCP header appears as described throughout this section. Beginning with the Source Port and Destination Port fields, you can see that this segment is used for Web (Port 80) communication. Sequence and acknowledgment numbers are next, followed by the data offset and codes. The data offset is 28 bytes rather than an even 20 bytes, because of the option codes at the end of the header (4 bytes for the Maximum Segment Size field, 1 byte for the No-Operation code, and 3 bytes for the Window Scale Option field).

Now that you know about the fields in the TCP header, you are ready to look further at how TCP communication takes place.

▶ · ◀

Establishing a TCP Connection

The TCP protocol is a *connection-oriented* protocol, which means that a connection must be established before one device begins sending data to another device. This section explores the methods used by TCP to establish a connection.

Opening a TCP Connection

The method used to establish a TCP connection is called the *three-way handshake*. It uses the TCP codes defined earlier in this chapter to establish communication. The three-way handshake is a three-packet exchange between devices that performs the following steps:

Step 1: Client Sends SYN Packet

The originating device (the *client*) sends a SYN (Synchronize sequence number request) to the receiver (the *server*). This packet contains the port number requested on the server by the client, along with the client's initial sequence number, as shown in Figure 10.6.

In Figure 10.6, the client sends a segment to the server with an initial sequence number of 10054381 and a destination port of 23 (Telnet). This begins the connection sequence with the server.

Step 2: Server Responds with SYN ACK Packet

The server receives the SYN segment and responds with its own SYN segment. The response contains the server's initial sequence number, along with an acknowledgment of the client's sequence number (SYN ACK).

NOTE

The SYN ACK is the client's original sequence number plus one because the SYN itself takes up a sequence number.

Figure 10.7 illustrates the sequence process.

Notice in Figure 10.7 that the server has created its own initial sequence number (3097284) and has acknowledged the original client's sequence number plus one (10054382).

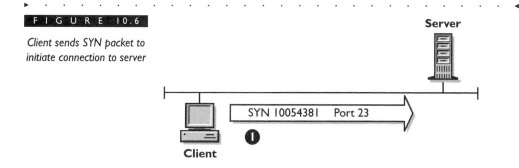

FIGURE 10.6

Client sends SYN packet to initiate connection to server

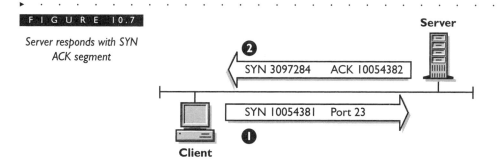

FIGURE 10.7

Server responds with SYN ACK segment

Step 3: Client Sends ACK Segment to Server

The last step in the three-way handshake is for the client to acknowledge the server's sequence number. This is an acknowledgment segment sent from the client to the server, using the ACK TCP code. The client responds by acknowledging the server's initial sequence number plus one. (Remember, the SYN segment takes up a sequence number.) Figure 10.8 illustrates this exchange.

In Figure 10.8, the client has used the server's acknowledgment number as its new sequence number (10054382). The client then acknowledges the server's initial sequence number plus one (3097285). At this point, communication may take place.

Looking at an analyzer, you can see this process happening during the beginning of an FTP session. In Figure 10.9, the SYN, SYN ACK, and ACK packets are located in the top of the analyzer window. This is what the three-way handshake should look like.

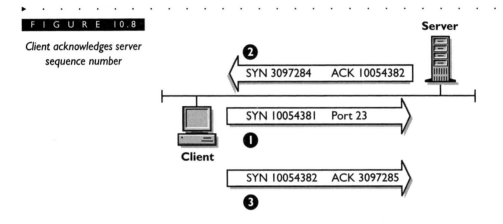

FIGURE 10.8

Client acknowledges server sequence number

FIGURE 10.9

Three-way handshake

Figure 10.9 shows the contents of the first SYN segment sent by the client to the server. Notice the TCP codes — SYN is active. Also, notice the options list for Maximum Segment Size set to 1024, and initial SYN of 46336000 sent by the client.

Next, the SYN ACK segment is sent from the server to the client, as shown in Figure 10.10. The server has returned a SYN number of its own (1541568000). Additionally, the server has acknowledged the client's initial sequence number plus one, and returned a value of 46336001. The TCP codes in this segment are set to SYN and ACK, and the maximum window size of 1024 has been announced.

The final step of the three-way handshake is shown in Figure 10.11. The client has taken the server's sequence number acknowledgment value of 46336001 and used it as its new sequence number. The client has also acknowledged the server's initial sequence number plus one, and returned a value of 1541568001. No more TCP options remain in this segment, because TCP options may only be used in a SYN segment.

▶ • ◀

FIGURE 10.11

Client acknowledges server's
initial sequence number

 TCP options are only set in a SYN segment.

NOTE

At this point, the connection has been established and data may be transmitted for this session.

Active vs. Passive Opens

TCP is considered to be a *full-duplex, connection-oriented* protocol, which means that each side of the connection can send and receive simultaneously and must participate in the connection. When a client sends an initial SYN segment to a server, the process is known as an *active open*. The active open occurs when a device makes a connection request of the device at the other end.

Conversely, the device receiving the request establishes a *passive open* function during the connection sequence. In a passive open mode, the device makes itself available to accept incoming connections. During the passive open, the receiving device makes a port available to the sending device for communication. Figure 10.12 shows the three-way handshake, with the client requesting FTP data transmission on port 2918 from the server. After the three-way handshake is established, the FTP session occurs on port 2918 and the data transfer takes place.

Client requests data on port 2918

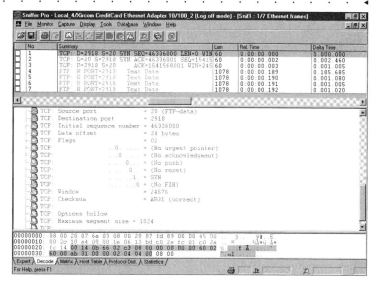

Multiple Simultaneous Connections

More than one device may request services of another device simultaneously, especially in the case of an FTP server or a Web server, as shown in Figure 10.13. TCP communication is taking place between a single computer and server. A different port number is defined during each three-way handshake, which indicates that this device is making many requests.

Half-Open Connections

Because TCP is a protocol that requires a connection establishment on both ends of the link, what happens when one side unexpectedly shuts down? This is called a *half-open connection*. A half-open connection can occur any time one of the two hosts stops communicating for some reason. That reason might be a malfunctioning network card, overloaded system, bad cable, or simply a machine that has been powered off improperly. A half-open connection will be detected when one end attempts to send data. If no attempt to send data is made, the half-open connection will not be detected.

Many scenarios may occur during the detection of a half-open connection. For a simple example, suppose that you have a network with two computers, Computer A and Computer B. Assume that Computer A has crashed. Either Computer A or Computer B may attempt to send data, which then required that computer to detect the half-open connection. For the first scenario, look at what happens when Computer A tries to send data on the half-open connection, as shown in Figure 10.14.

FIGURE 10.13

Multiple simultaneous
connections

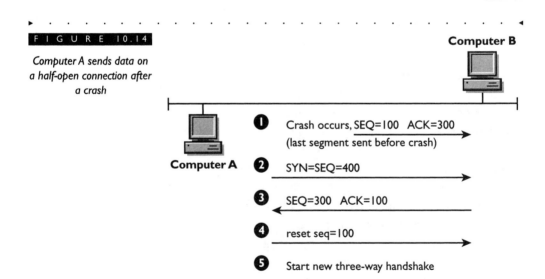

FIGURE 10.14

Computer A sends data on
a half-open connection after
a crash

Computer B

Computer A

❶ Crash occurs, SEQ=100   ACK=300
(last segment sent before crash)

❷ SYN=SEQ=400

❸ SEQ=300   ACK=100

❹ reset seq=100

❺ Start new three-way handshake

In Figure 10.14, Computers A and B are communicating when Computer A experiences a crash and loss of memory in its TCP software. The last segment sent to Computer B contained a sequence number of 300 and an acknowledgment of 100. Computer B is unaware that Computer A has crashed, causing a half-open connection. Computer A has lost its mind, so it is also unaware that a half-open connection exists at this point.

When Computer A returns to normal operation, it may begin some sort of recovery state. Computer A will either try to reopen the connection or try to send on the connection that it thinks is already open. When it tries to send on the "open" connection, Computer A is notified by its own TCP software that the connection is not open. Computer A then sends a segment containing a SYN request, shown in Step 2 in Figure 10.14. It generates a new sequence number and sends it to Computer B.

Computer B receives the SYN request and is confused, having thought that the connection was open the whole time. Computer B responds with the acknowledgment number that it expects to hear next (ACK=100) in Step 3 of Figure 10.14.

In Step 4, Computer A sees that the response does not acknowledge anything that it sent to Computer B, and thus recognizes the half-open connection. Computer A then sends a RESET command to Computer B, and Computer B aborts its operation.

In Step 5, Computer A reestablishes the connection by using a standard three-way handshake.

Another interesting scenario in a half-open connection occurs when Computer B is the first to send data after a crash, as shown in Figure 10.15.

FIGURE 10.15

Computer B sends data on a half-open connection after a crash

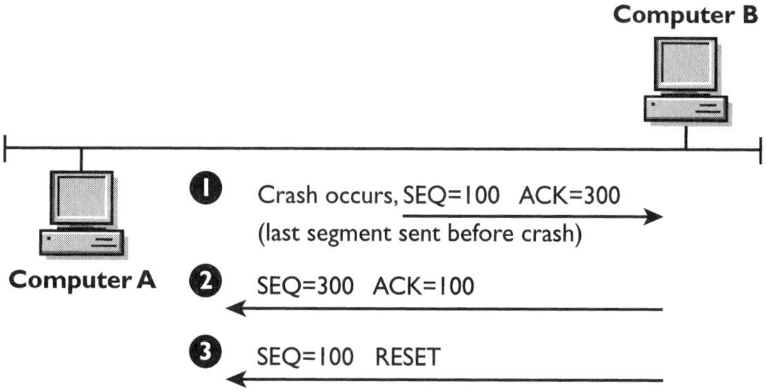

Computer B

① Crash occurs, SEQ=100 ACK=300
(last segment sent before crash)

Computer A

② SEQ=300 ACK=100

③ SEQ=100 RESET

In Figure 10.15, Computer A sends a segment and then crashes (Step 1). In Step 2, Computer B attempts to send data on the connection it believes to be open. Computer A has crashed and returned to a normal operational state by this time, but has completely forgotten about the last segment it sent. Computer A receives the segment from Computer B and assumes Computer B has gone crazy. Computer A then returns a RESET request to Computer B. Computer B simply resets its connection and waits.

Many other scenarios exist in which a half-open connection may be detected, but in every scenario, reset rules are followed to assist the devices with reconnection of the TCP software. Connection resets are discussed later in this chapter.

Several references have been made in this section to the state of TCP at any given time. A TCP connection is not simply open or closed — at any point in time, it may be waiting for a response to a SYN request, listening, finishing a data transfer, and many other items. These connection types are called *TCP transition states*. They are used to determine the exact status of TCP at any given time. The next section explores some of the TCP transition states.

TCP Transition States

When opening, closing, or using a TCP connection, TCP goes through a series of *transition states*. A connection may use any of 11 possible transition states during the life of that connection. Table 10.4 lists the possible TCP transition states and their meanings.

TABLE 10.4

TCP Transition States

TRANSITION STATE NAME	TRANSITION STATE DESCRIPTION
LISTEN	Device is waiting for a connection from any remote TCP and port.
SYN-SENT	Device is waiting for a response to a synchronization request that was sent.
SYN-RECEIVED	Device is waiting for an acknowledgment after having received and sent a reply to a connection request.
ESTABLISHED	An open connection. This is a normal state for data transfer between TCP devices.

TRANSITION STATE NAME	TRANSITION STATE DESCRIPTION
FIN-WAIT-1	Device is either waiting for a connection termination request from the remote TCP or waiting for an acknowledgment of a termination request previously sent.
FIN-WAIT-2	Device is waiting for a termination request from the remote TCP.
CLOSE-WAIT	Device is waiting for a termination request from the local user.
CLOSING	Device is waiting for a termination request acknowledgment from the remote TCP.
LAST-ACK	Device is waiting for an acknowledgment of the connection termination request sent previously to the remote TCP.
TIME-WAIT	Device is waiting for enough time to pass to make sure that the remote TCP received the acknowledgment of its connection termination request. This state is entered after the connection is closed to prevent segment interference from another connection.
CLOSED	No connection.

A Word About the TIME-WAIT State   The TIME-WAIT state is sometimes referred to as the *2MSL wait state*. The acronym *MSL* stands for Maximum Segment Lifetime. The MSL value is the maximum amount of time that any segment may exist in the network before being discarded. The definition of the time allowed is two minutes; however, many vendors implement the MSL with different time values.

 A computer entering the TIME-WAIT state waits twice the MSL value before it destroys its record of the connection.

NOTE

While the TIME-WAIT state is active, the socket pair that uniquely identifies the connection may not be reused. When the wait time is over, the connection may then be used.

It is also very possible that different connections may be in different states at different times. One great way to check the connection state of any TCP connection is to use the NETSTAT command, which shows each connection and real time state, as shown in Figure 10.16.

▶ · ◀

NETSTAT and TCP transition states

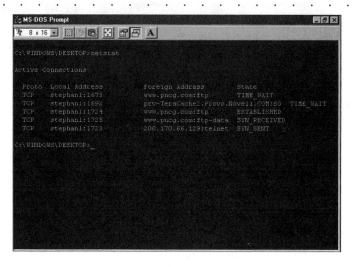

In Figure 10.16, the user has initiated several TCP connections at one time. The Foreign Address column of the NETSTAT command shows that the user has attempted an FTP and Telnet connection, along with a browser connection, which is identified by the port 80 at the end of the World Wide Web address. Additionally, each of these TCP connections is currently in a different state. The first two states are TIME-WAIT states, which indicates a closing of a connection. Next is an ESTABLISHED connection to an FTP site, followed by a data transfer connection in the SYN_RECEIVED state, indicating that a synchronization sequence has been sent and returned, and that the client is waiting for the final acknowledgment in the three-way handshake. The final entry shows a SYN_SENT state, indicating that the client is waiting for the synchronization acknowledgment, which is the second step in the three-way handshake.

You may also notice that these TCP states work in conjunction with the TCP codes defined earlier in this chapter. For example, a client sending a SYN segment would move to a SYN_SENT TCP transition state and then, after receiving the SYN ACK segment, move into a SYN_RECEIVED transition state. Upon receipt of the third and final handshake segment containing the ACK code, the client would move to the ESTABLISHED connection state. Figure 10.17 will help you to understand how different TCP codes affect transition states.

· · · · ·

FIGURE 10.17

TCP transition state diagram

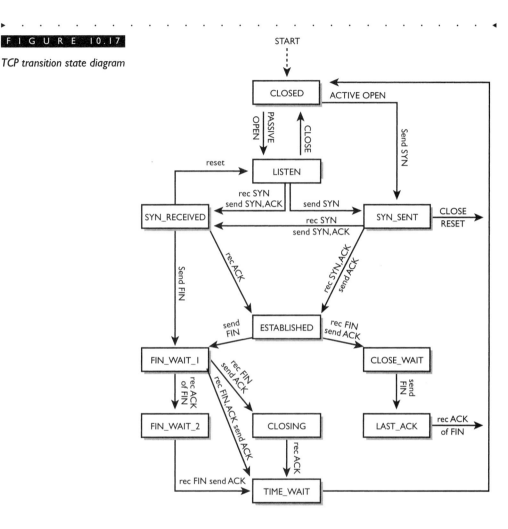

Transition State Example   This example uses Figure 10.17 to follow the steps that a connection may take to open an application. Assume that a user is attempting to make an FTP connection to another host. After the connection is made, the user performs a proper application close (discussed in the next section). The following are the steps taken by the TCP transition to open a connection:

1. Client computer begins in the CLOSED state.

2. SYN is sent by the client to the server to initiate three-way handshake (active open). Client device moves to SYN_SENT state.

3. The SYN is received by the server and a SYN-ACK is sent to the client. The client computer moves into the SYN_RECEIVED state.

4. An ACK (last segment of the three-way handshake) is received by the client. The client computer moves into the ESTABLISHED state.

At this point, the user is free to do whatever they want within the FTP application. At some point, the user wishes to terminate the connection. Before continuing with this example, the next section explores how a connection may be closed.

Closing a TCP Connection

You have already learned that three segments are required to initiate a TCP connection. To close a TCP connection properly, the process actually takes four segments. The reason for this type of close sequence is the full duplex nature of TCP. Because it is a full duplex protocol, it considers each end of the data stream to be independent of the other, with data flowing in two directions. Therefore, each end must initiate a close sequence consisting of two segments: a FIN (which closes the flow of data) and an ACK (acknowledgment of the FIN close) for each end of the connection, as shown in Figure 10.18.

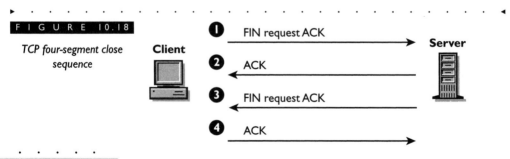

FIGURE 10.18

TCP four-segment close sequence

① FIN request ACK

② ACK

③ FIN request ACK

④ ACK

Client

Server

This may make more sense by looking at it with an analyzer. Figure 10.19 shows a normal TCP close of an FTP application using the four-way disconnect. Two computers are involved in this connection. The client first requests a FIN application close. The server acknowledges. Then, the server requests a FIN close from the client, and the client acknowledges.

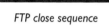
FIGURE 10.19

FTP close sequence

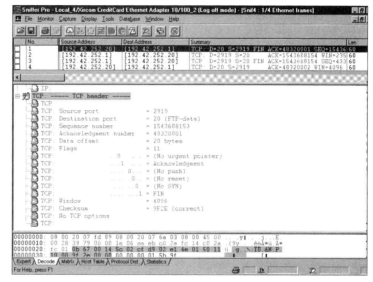

Looking at this normal closing sequence from a TCP transition state perspective, the computer follows this procedure when making the close shown in Figure 10.19 (refer to Figure 10.17 for the transition state diagram).

Transition States While Closing an FTP Connection

To close an FTP connection, the computers go through different transition states. This example uses the terms *client* and *server* to help define the sequence. The following sequence shows the client states:

1. Client computer in ESTABLISHED state sends a FIN request to server to close the application. Client computer moves into FIN_WAIT_1 state.

2. Client computer receives an ACK from the server responding to original FIN request. Client moves into FIN_WAIT_2 state.

3. Client computer in FIN_WAIT_2 state receives FIN request from the server.

4. Client computer sends an ACK and moves into TIME-WAIT state.

The preceding four steps complete the connection close exchange.

5. After twice the maximum segment lifetime, the client connection moves into a CLOSED state.

From the server view, the transition states are a bit different. The following sequence explains what the server does when it receives an application close request from a client:

1. Server in ESTABLISHED state receives a FIN request from a client.

2. Server sends ACK to client and moves into CLOSE_WAIT state.

3. Server sends a FIN to client requesting a connection close and moves into LAST_ACK state.

4. Server receives ACK from client and moves to CLOSED state.

All the processes described thus far are examples of normal closing procedures within the TCP protocol. But, as you know, everything is not always perfect — computers crash and people make mistakes when trying to connect to another computer. To enable TCP to recover from failures such as these, a special segment called a *reset segment* is used. The reset segment is simply a TCP segment that uses the RST (Reset) code to inform the other end of the connection that a connection must be terminated. The next section discusses resets in detail.

Connection Resets

A connection reset is a useful and necessary component of the TCP protocol. Without resets, devices would be unable to recover from catastrophic (or even not-so-catastrophic) problems on the network. A reset is used when a user types the wrong IP address for a Telnet or FTP session, for example, or to abort a connection that was created by mistake.

TCP requires a reset to be sent whenever a segment arrives that is not intended for the current connection. If it is not clear whether the segment is intended for the connection, then a reset must not be sent.

Figure 10.20 shows an example of a connection reset using an analyzer. Notice that the RST TCP code (flag) is set to 1, meaning that a reset is requested. Also notice that the TCP window size has been set to 0, announcing that the source computer (the device requesting the reset) will not accept any more data on this connection.

FIGURE 10.20

TCP connection reset

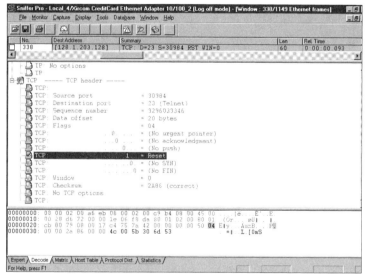

The following are the three general rules for resetting a connection:

▸ **Rule 1: Reset all nonexisting (half-open) connections.** If a device receives a segment on a connection that is closed (or undetected half-open), then it returns a reset to the originator. The acknowledgment number from the incoming segment is used as the sequence number for the outgoing packet. If the incoming segment does not have an acknowledgment number, the outgoing segment uses 0 as the sequence number and calculates an acknowledgment number equal to the sum of the sequence number and the segment length of the incoming segment.

▸ **Rule 2: Reset invalid acknowledgments when waiting for connection.** This reset occurs when a device is listening for incoming segments containing connection requests. If a segment arrives with an acknowledgment number equal to something that has not yet been received (such as a SYN request), it is considered to be an unacceptable acknowledgment segment. At this point, the connection will be reset.

▸ **Rule 3: Reset any unacceptable segments while connected and synchronized.** When a connection is established and synchronized, a reset may occur if a device receives an unacceptable segment. This could be an invalid sequence number or a bad acknowledgment number.

Receiving and Processing a Reset

When a device receives a RST segment, it must perform these steps:

1. **Validate the RST segment.** The reset command is validated by checking the sequence fields in the packet. The reset is considered to be valid if the sequence number is in the data window. If a computer receives a reset response to a synchronization request (SYN), it checks the Acknowledgment field. If the Acknowledgment field in the RST segment acknowledges the SYN just sent, then the device resets.

2. **Change connection state.** When a device receives and validates an RST segment, it must change operating states. At the time of the reset, the device may be listening for incoming connection requests or may be already connected. Upon receipt of a reset, if the device is listening for a connection, it ignores the reset. If it is receiving a SYN request, it goes back to listening. If it is connected, it aborts the connection.

In addition to recovering from half-open connections, one of the most common causes for a reset is a connection request to a nonexistent port on a host. In Figure 10.21, an FTP request is made to `ftp.microsoft.com`. The client has received an error message, Connection Refused, on the application screen. A closer look at the trace screen reveals the problem: the RST segment has been sent to the client. Looking further into the packet at the source and destination ports, you see that the original request was made in packet 11 from source port 1075 to destination port 2000. Checking the proper port value for FTP indicates that the proper port should be port 21 (refer to Table 10.1). The client software is checked and the misconfigured port is restored to port 21.

FIGURE 10.21

FTP Connection Reset

HTTP Connections and Resets

The Hypertext Transfer Protocol (HTTP) used with Web browsers does some interesting things with connections. To keep up with all the clicking that users do on a Web page, a new connection is opened for each request. As connections become invalid (users leave Web pages), they are reset by the server. Figure 10.22 shows an example of a server setting up and destroying connections. Though the three-way handshake is used to create each connection, notice that a simple reset is used to destroy it.

Figure 10.22 shows a trace of information sent to and from the client to a Web server. (This trace has been filtered to show the connection relationships better.) First, notice that four connections are being set up in this trace. They are identified by the client making the request as ports 1126, 1127, 1128, and 1129. These are arbitrary and valid for the client's purpose. Notice that the SYN, SYN ACK, and ACK (three-way handshake) occur for each connection request, but not necessarily in order. The last four packets in the trace tear down the connections for ports 1126 through 1129 by using a RST command and a window size of 0, indicating that no more data will be accepted by the client.

Now that you have seen how connections are created and closed, you are ready to learn how data is transmitted using a TCP connection.

▶ . . . . ◀

FIGURE 10.22

HTTP connection and resets

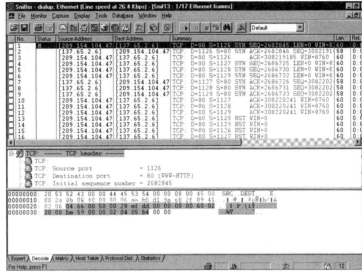

▶ . . . . ◀

Maintaining a TCP Connection

You have already learned that TCP sends data in a stream of segments for transmission. For efficient data flow to occur, TCP uses several mechanisms to assist in this process. This section looks at how data flow occurs within TCP, the sliding window process, and other mechanisms for efficient transmission and flow control. First, take a look at what normal data flow should look like. The following are the two types of normal data transfers that may be used in a TCP environment, each of which is described in the next two sections, respectively:

▶ Interactive data transfer

▶ Standard or bulk data transfer

Interactive Data Transfer

Interactive data transfer programs, such as a login process, require user input. A segment is transmitted and acknowledged for each keystroke sent from the client to the server. Telnet, which uses several modes of transmission, is used in this section as an example of a program that uses interactive data transfer. Figure 10.23 illustrates the Telnet interactive process, using the Sniffer analyzer.

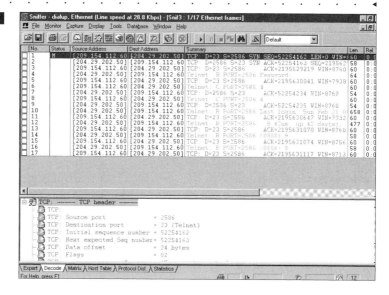

Telnet login interactive process

Figure 10.23 shows a user beginning a Telnet session. The first three packets identify the three-way handshake. Next, the Telnet session requests a password in packet 4. An immediate acknowledgment is made in packet 5. Packets 6 and 7 are the first character of the password and the acknowledgment, packets 8 and 9 are the second character of the password and the acknowledgment, and so on. People sometimes find it surprising that during Telnet, data is transmitted one byte at a time. Even more surprising is that the Telnet data is in clear text.

The interactive process can involve up to four segments per keystroke, because the server will echo back each character that the client types. The four generated segments are shown in Figure 10.24.

The client first sends a byte of data, which is acknowledged by the server. The server then echoes the byte back to the client. When the client receives the echoed data, an acknowledgment of the echo is returned to the server. Generally, Steps 2 and 3 are combined, as shown in Figure 10.25. Packet 1 contains 1 byte sent from the client to the server. The client data is the letter *e*. Packet 2 shows the echo of the data (the letter *e*). Notice also in packet 2 that the ACK code is set in the TCP header. This is the combined echo/acknowledgment. The last packet is the acknowledgment of the echo.

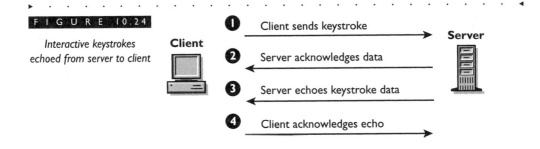

FIGURE 10.24

Interactive keystrokes echoed from server to client

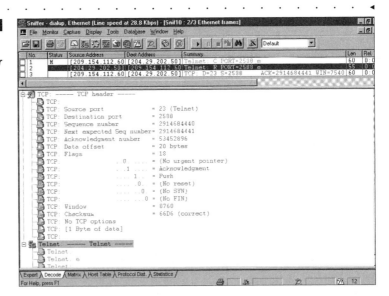

FIGURE 10.25

Received data is echoed and acknowledged by server

Many different types of TCP programs use this interactive method of data transfer. However, acknowledging all data bytes immediately is inefficient.

Imagine how long a Web page might take to load if every character had to be acknowledged.

Delayed Acknowledgment

TCP is not required to send an acknowledgment the second that it receives data. Instead, it is capable of delaying the acknowledgment for up to 200ms (milliseconds) before sending an acknowledgment. This allows the TCP software to wait up to 200ms for more data before sending the ACK along with the data. When a packet contains only 41 bytes (20 bytes for the IP header, 20 bytes for the TCP header, and 1 byte of data), as in the earlier examples, these segments are called *tinygrams*. These tinygrams can be a great nuisance on the network and can cause quite a bit of congestion. To help eliminate that congestion, an algorithm, called the *Nagle algorithm,* has been put in place (RFC 896) to solve the problem of congestion due to tinygrams.

Nagle Algorithm and the Silly Window Syndrome

The Nagle algorithm states the following:

▶ Only one tinygram can be outstanding on a connection at any given time.

▶ The receiver must *not* acknowledge the tinygram until:

- It is able to advertise a window at least as large as the smaller of half of its total buffer space.

- It can advertise a window equal to its full maximum segment size (MSS).

▶ The sender must not transmit until:

- It can send a full-sized maximum segment size (MSS) segment.

- It can send a half or more of the largest window ever advertised by the other device.

- No acknowledgments are outstanding.

The Nagle algorithm is used to reduce the number of tinygrams so that fewer segments are sent and the network bandwidth is better utilized. By applying the

Nagle algorithm, many potential congestion problems are solved. Some existing rules state that all TCP implementations must apply the Nagle algorithm. However, the algorithm is turned off in a few instances, such as when a client is sending small segments containing input from other than the keyboard (such as the mouse). If a delayed acknowledgment were sent, the client would experience jerky and slow mouse response to a TCP application.

Some networks suffer from the effects of a condition known to TCP as the *silly window syndrome*. This occurs when a sender and receiver generate more and more segments with smaller and smaller amounts of data.

For example, an application that generates data quickly, such as a running ticker tape process, may cause the silly window syndrome to occur. Either side of the connection may trigger the syndrome. Suppose that you have two computers — a client and a server. The client begins the connection and sends data to the server. At the beginning of the session, the server allocates buffer space for the client application. Because the client application sends data very quickly, it fills the buffer space on the server, causing the server to advertise a window size of 0. Now suppose that 1 byte of buffer space opens on the server. The server advertises a window size of 1 byte and the client fills the buffer. This process continues, with the server advertising a window size of 1, the client filling the space 1 byte at a time, and the server acknowledging 1 byte at a time. This results in a decrease in performance on one or both ends of the connection, almost to the point where one device can be brought to its knees.

When the smaller window size value is advertised, future transmissions will occur using that window size during the course of the connection. If either device stops sending data (or closes the connection), the buffers will be emptied and eventually the window size will increase.

You now have seen one way that data is transmitted in a TCP environment. The next section looks at another method. Generally used with FTP and other data-movement-intensive applications, the standard, or bulk, method is a common transmission method.

Bulk Data Transfer

The last section demonstrated how data segments are acknowledged as they are sent from the client to the server. To transfer larger amounts of data (perform a file transfer, perhaps), a flow control process known as the *sliding window protocol* is used. The sliding window protocol allows a sender to transmit multiple data segments before waiting for an acknowledgment. This section explores the sliding window protocol process and how data delivery is forced using the PSH TCP code. First, take a look at what normal bulk data flow looks like.

Normal Bulk Data Flow

Unlike the interactive processes already discussed, bulk data flow allows multiple packets to be sent before an acknowledgment is generated. Consider the example in Figure 10.26, which shows a simple bulk data flow. The client sends three segments to the server with a window size of 4096. The first three segments are placed into the TCP input queue for processing. They are sent to TCP in the same order in which they are received. When TCP processes segment 1, it is marked for delayed acknowledgment. Then, TCP processes segment 2 and notices that two segments now can be acknowledged. It sends an acknowledgment in segment 4 of 5000, which acknowledges the first two segments. TCP next processes segment 3, holds it, and places a delayed acknowledgment code on it. In segment 5, an acknowledgment has been sent with a modified window size, indicating two very important things:

▸ The TCP acknowledgment has been held too long and the delayed ACK must be sent.

▸ The server has data in its buffers that it has yet to read, which is indicated by the window size of 2048.

This scenario is a very common method for generating acknowledgments in a TCP network.

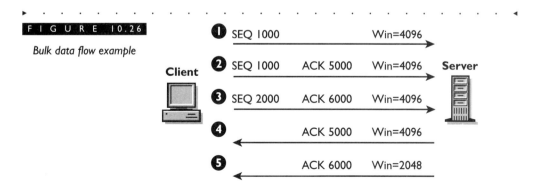

FIGURE 10.26

Bulk data flow example

With TCP, the acknowledgments are *cumulative*, which means that for each acknowledgment sent by the receiver, the receiver has correctly received all bytes up through the acknowledged sequence number in the segment. Additionally, through the use of the sliding window protocol, it means that not all packets must be individually acknowledged.

TCP Sliding Window Process

You have learned that TCP uses segments in its transmission, and that TCP segments are encapsulated into IP datagrams to travel across internetworks. To provide efficient and proper TCP data flow with large amounts of data, the *sliding window protocol* is implemented, shown in Figure 10.27. This process makes it possible to send multiple segments before an acknowledgment arrives. Additionally, the sliding window protocol allows an overloaded receiver to restrict transmission until it has buffer space available to accommodate more incoming data. TCP uses a variable window size (discussed later in this section) to provide for proper data-flow control.

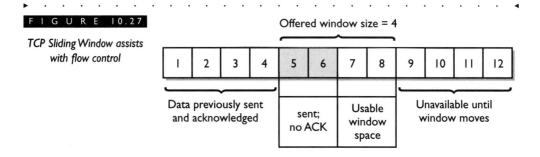

FIGURE 10.27

TCP Sliding Window assists with flow control

The sliding window uses actual bytes, not segments, to identify how much data is being transmitted. In Figure 10.27, the process is simplified. The TCP-offered window is 4 bytes (using bytes 5 through 8). Bytes 1 through 4 have already been sent and acknowledged, which caused the window to move to the right, framing bytes 5 through 8. In this diagram, bytes 5 and 6 have been sent but not acknowledged, and bytes 7 and 8 can be sent any time. As the acknowledgments are received, the window will move to the right, allowing data bytes 9 through 12 to be used. Both the sender and receiver must maintain a similar window, to allow data streams to be put together at the other end of the connection.

Window Size Announcement

TCP window sizing was briefly discussed earlier in this chapter. As TCP communication takes place, the window size increases and decreases, depending on the total amount of buffer space available to the device. Generally, the window size is the same as the receiver's buffer size. The size of the window is offered by the receiver and is most often controlled by the receiving process. For example, a sender establishes a connection with another device, which advertises a window of 4,096 bytes. The sender begins to send data, but the receiving device has a slow processor, which makes reading the data slower for the receiver. It receives the data, sends an acknowledgment, and reduces its window size, indicating that it still has data to read in its buffer. After the receiver reads all the data in its buffer, it again announces a larger window size.

Figure 10.28 shows how window size changes during an FTP file transfer.

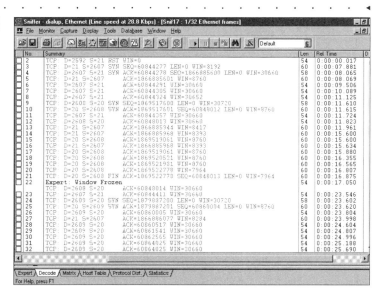

F I G U R E 10.28

Window size advertisement is controlled by the receiver

In Figure 10.28, the user performs an FTP file transfer. (This trace is modified to show only the receiver acknowledgments and window size adjustments.) Beginning with a window advertisement of 30660, the connection is made. Sometime during the file transfer, in packets 11 through 21, the receiver is beginning to slow down and advertise smaller window sizes. Toward the end of the file transfer, the window size increases. This shows the dynamic nature of the window size. In packet 22, the Sniffer indicates that the window is in a *frozen* state. This means that the advertised window size has not changed for some period of time, which could result in poor performance. A frozen (sometimes called *stuck*) window is generally the result of an overloaded receiver that is out of buffer space.

Data Delivery Using the PSH Code

To notify a server that it should process all the received data, the sending application uses a TCP code called PSH (push), literally to push the received data to be processed. When a receiver buffers segments, it may not know that the sender is through sending, and thus may continue to wait for more data. To avoid this situation, the sender simply sends a PSH code through a TCP segment to notify the receiver that it is through sending data and to tell the server to process its buffers.

TCP Timers

The TCP protocol has several mechanisms that assist with reliable and proper communication. What happens when a segment is lost or a connection is stuck? TCP timers keep both ends of a connection working together to make sure data transmission is complete. For each connection, TCP keeps these four timers:

- Retransmission timer

- Persist timer

- Keepalive timer

- 2MSL timer

The following sections look at each of these timers and how they affect TCP operation.

Retransmission Timer

The retransmission timer is used by a sending TCP device when it is expecting an acknowledgment. After a TCP segment is sent, the sending device starts a timer and waits. If an acknowledgment isn't received before the timer expires, the sent segment is retransmitted. The retransmission timer is not a static value — that is, it changes depending on the speed of the connection, the number of routers the segment must cross, and so on.

To calculate the retransmission time, the TCP protocol uses an *adaptive transmission algorithm,* which is based on a round-trip time for segment delivery for each connection. Basically, TCP is able to monitor each connection and modify its retransmission time to accommodate the fluctuating nature of the Internet.

To calculate the value for the retransmission timer, the TCP protocol must go through several steps:

1. **Collect data needed to calculate the *round-trip sample* time.** TCP records the time the segment was sent and the time at which an acknowledgment arrives for that segment.

2. **Calculate the *round-trip sample* time.** TCP subtracts the send from the receive ACK times, which results in a round-trip sample time.

3. **Calculate the TCP *average* round-trip time.** TCP generally stores an *average* round-trip time based on the round-trip samples. As the round-trip sample changes, so does the stored average round-trip time. One of the calculations used to calculate the average round-trip time is a weighted calculation:

   ```
   ART (average round trip) =(x*Old_ART)+(1-x) * new round
   trip sample
   ```

   In this calculation, the value of x is a weighting factor. The recommended value for this variable is 1 (or .9 in the original specification).

4. **Calculate the retransmission timeout time.** This is the value that is used to retransmit unacknowledged packets. The calculation used is the following:

   ```
   Timeout=y*ART
   ```

   The recommended value for y is 2, according to specification.

This seems to be a pretty good way to calculate a retransmission timer. But, consider what may happen in the following example, shown in Figure 10.29.

1. The client sends a segment to the server, but receives no acknowledgment.

2. The client's retransmission timer expires.

3. The segment is retransmitted.

4. The server acknowledges the segment.

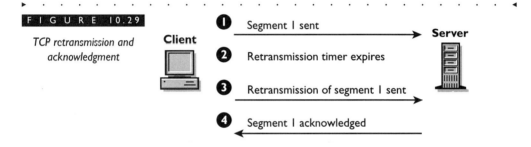

F I G U R E 10.29

TCP retransmission and acknowledgment

Client

Server

① Segment 1 sent

② Retransmission timer expires

③ Retransmission of segment 1 sent

④ Segment 1 acknowledged

Now the problem occurs—because both the original segment and retransmission contain *exactly* the same data, how should the client calculate the new round-trip sample time? If the client uses the *original* segment send time with the acknowledgment time, the sample round-trip time may be way too long. Conversely, if the client uses the *retransmission* segment time and the acknowledgment time to calculate the round-trip sample, the timeout will be too small for the next segment.

This is known as an *ambiguous acknowledgment* and is corrected by a process known as *Karn's algorithm*. Simply put, Karn's algorithm states: When computing the round-trip estimate, do not calculate based on an acknowledgment for retransmitted data. Use a backoff strategy for future transmissions until a new valid sample is obtained.

Using this algorithm, TCP simply chooses not to update the round-trip estimate for retransmitted segments. However, if retransmitted segments are ignored for calculating timeouts, the retransmission cycle could continue and a new timeout value may never be implemented. Therefore, the following calculation is used in conjunction with the existing timeout value until a new and proper timeout can be established:

```
new_timeout=y*timeout
```

Typically, the value of y is 2, though several implementations of this calculation exist. Using Karn's algorithm, TCP uses the round-trip estimate to calculate an initial timeout value. It then backs off the timeout on each retransmission until a segment is finally sent successfully. When the acknowledgment arrives that corresponds to a segment that was not retransmitted, TCP recalculates the true round-trip estimate and resets the timeout.

Persist Timer

The persist timer is used by TCP to query the device at the other end of the connection during a connection. The most common example of the need to use a persist timer is when a connection is established and one side of the connection suddenly either stops sending/receiving or advertises a window size of 0. Assume the latter has happened in the example. At this point, a sender seeing a window size of 0 stops transmitting data. However, using the persist timer, the client continues to make 1-byte requests to the server to see whether the window size has been increased. The persist timer timeout begins after 1.5 seconds and uses exponential values to determine future timeout values. After the first timeout at 1.5 seconds, future calculations are determined as shown in Table 10.5.

TABLE 10.5	MULTIPLIER	TIMEOUT OCCURRENCE	ACTUAL TIME
Persist Timeout Value Calculations		First	1.5 Seconds
	2	Second	3 Seconds
	4	Third	6 Seconds
	8	Fourth	12 Seconds
	16	Fifth	24 Seconds

The values in Table 10.5 continue until 60 seconds has elapsed. After that, probes are sent out at 60-second intervals until the window reopens or the connection is terminated, which is why this timer is called persistent.

Keepalive Timer

Within TCP communications, you need to understand that when a connection is idle (connected, but no data flowing through it), the devices on each end do not send any information about the connection. No active polling or broadcasts occur to check on the other end. Thus, using a TCP application, a user may establish a connection and then walk away for an extended period of time. Unless one of the ends of the connection restarts, the connection can remain up forever, even if a device in the path fails and comes back online.

The keepalive timer usually is used by a server to detect whether the client at the other end of the connection is still "alive and well." The keepalive timer is not specifically part of the TCP specification, yet many vendor implementations use this feature.

A keepalive probe is sent whenever a connection is inactive for two hours. When a keepalive probe is sent (again, usually from the server to the client), it may find the client in one of several conditions. Table 10.6 describes what happens in response to a keepalive probe under various circumstances.

TABLE 10.6

Keepalive Probe Responses

IF THE CLIENT...	THE SERVER...
Is up and running and reachable by the server	Resets its keepalive timer for two hours into the future.
Has crashed and is down	Attempts to reach the client ten times. Each attempt is made at 75-second intervals. If the server cannot contact the client after ten attempts, the server resets the client connection.
Has crashed and rebooted, and is back up again	Receives a RST response from the client, causing the connection to be terminated.
Is up and running, but unreachable (due to a software malfunction)	Attempts to reach the client ten times. Each attempt is made at 75-second intervals. If the server cannot contact the client after ten attempts, the server resets the client connection.

When an operator shuts down a computer properly, a normal RST is sent to the server. This type of shutdown will not generate a keepalive probe at any time.

2MSL Timer

TCP wait states were discussed earlier in this chapter. The TIME_WAIT state is the state in which TCP waits after an active close request. The TIME_WAIT state is sometimes referred to as the *2MSL wait state*. In this state, the TCP process must decide how long it has to stay in the TIME_WAIT state until it can safely close the connection. Remember from earlier in the chapter that during this state, the sockets that define this unique TCP connection (sockets consist of the client IP address, client port number, the server IP address, and server port number) may not be reused.

To determine the amount of time that a device remains in the TIME_WAIT state, it must call upon the *maximum segment lifetime (MSL)* value. Every implementation of TCP must choose an MSL value.

NOTE

The standard specification for the MSL value is two minutes. However, some TCP implementation values can be thirty seconds, one minute, or two minutes.

After the MSL value is chosen by TCP and a connection close request is made, TCP moves into the TIME_WAIT state. From there, the 2MSL timer runs out and the connection is then considered closed.

Now that you've explored some of the timers used by TCP during transmission, you are ready to explore the four common flow control mechanisms used for reliability.

Controlling Data Flow

So far, you have seen how the TCP connection is established, maintained, and torn down. To keep the client/server nature of TCP as functional as possible, *flow control* is implemented within the TCP software. Flow control is defined as the management of transmissions between two devices. Flow control is concerned with the timing of signals and enables slower-speed devices to communicate with higher-speed ones. Various flow control techniques exist, but all are designed to ensure that the receiving station is able to accept the next block of data before the sending station sends.

Through the use of flow control, a single device can't just "throw up" on the network and overload another device just because it feels like doing so. Several methods have been established to make sure that TCP devices are more polite. Four of these common methods are the following:

▸ Slow start

▸ Congestion avoidance

▸ Fast retransmit

▸ Fast recovery

The following sections review each type of flow control and explain how each helps TCP to communicate effectively.

Slow Start

Rather than just spitting out packets onto the network blindly and hoping for the best, TCP communication is required to use the slow start algorithm. Using the slow start algorithm, TCP is allowed to send new packets to the network at the same rate at which it receives acknowledgments from the other end of the connection. To accommodate the slow start algorithm, another window, called the *congestion window*, is added to the *sender's* TCP. This is different from the *advertised window*, which is imposed and controlled by the receiver.

IMPORTANT

> **The congestion window is controlled by the sender, whereas the advertised window is controlled by the receiver.**

The slow start algorithm sequence begins when a connection is made to another computer on the network, as shown in Figure 10.30.

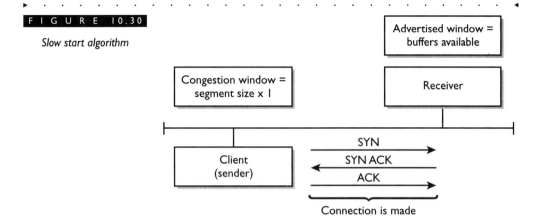

FIGURE 10.30

Slow start algorithm

Initially, the client begins with a congestion window equal to 1 times the segment size of the packets. Each time an acknowledgment is received by the client, the congestion window is increased by one segment size (in bytes). The first segment sent and acknowledged causes the congestion window to increase by one segment. The client then sends two segments. Upon acknowledgment, the congestion window is increased to four segments. After receipt of the four segments, the congestion window is increased to eight segments, and so on. This begins an exponential size increase of the congestion window, as shown in Figure 10.31.

Given the exponential nature of the increase in the congestion window, a problem is bound to occur. Eventually, the window size becomes too large, congestion occurs, and segments are dropped by intermediate devices, such as routers.

Congestion Avoidance

Given the nature of the fast start process, *congestion* is bound to appear somewhere in the network. Congestion occurs when too much data is on the network to be handled in a timely manner. During a congestion period, packets are dropped or discarded, causing performance and retransmission issues.

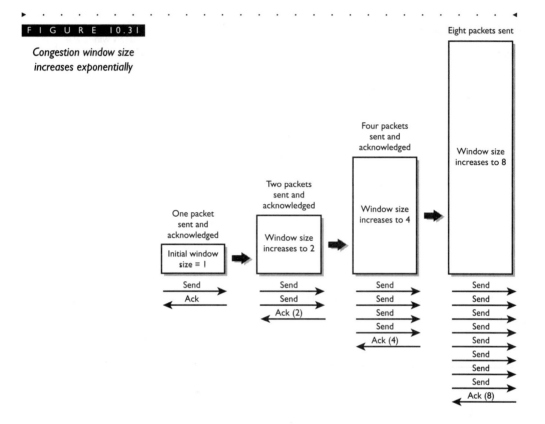

FIGURE 10.31

*Congestion window size
increases exponentially*

Think of congestion as taking your car for a drive. During that drive, you find yourself on the toll highway, which requires you to stop at several points along the way to deposit money—a process that takes time. If you are traveling on the highway during a nonpeak time, such as lunch hour, you simply drive right up to the toll booth and deposit your coins. During a peak period, such as early morning or late afternoon when people are going to and from work, stopping at the toll booth is quite a different story. During this time, you have to stop completely, merge into a lane along with other traffic, and wait until it is your turn to deposit your coins. After you make it through the toll booth, you must once again deal with traffic to get into the proper highway lanes for traveling.

The congestion avoidance algorithm helps TCP to slow the rate of new packets being sent on the network during periods of congestion, and then uses the fast start process to get TCP back up to speed.

The congestion algorithm makes a very important assumption. It assumes that packet loss caused by damage is very small (less than 1 percent). Therefore, the loss of a packet signals congestion somewhere in the network between the source and the destination. Evidence of congestion includes timeouts, retransmissions, and duplicate acknowledgments on the network.

The congestion algorithm works together with the fast start process, though they are different algorithms. The fast start process uses the congestion avoidance window. The congestion avoidance algorithm uses another variable, called a *slow start threshold size*. The slow start threshold size is measured in bytes. Initially, the variable is set to 65,535 bytes.

The slow start threshold is initialized at 65,535 bytes, by default.

NOTE

To see how these two processes work together, the following steps show how congestion and slow start thresholds are used:

1. **The TCP connection is initialized.** The congestion window (for slow start) is set to one segment and the slow start threshold size (for congestion avoidance) is set to 65,535 bytes, as shown in Figure 10.32.

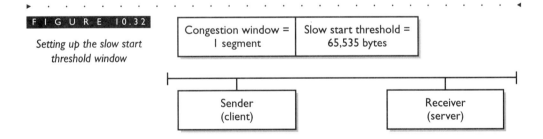

F I G U R E   10.32

Setting up the slow start threshold window

2. **Congestion occurs.** Somewhere on the network, a timeout or duplication acknowledgment (congestion) occurs. When this happens, the slow start threshold value is reset and the congestion window may also be reset.

3. **Calculate the new value of the slow start threshold.** To calculate the new value of the threshold, TCP takes one half of the current window size (which is the value of the congestion window and the receiver's advertised window size) and places that value in the threshold variable. The congestion window size increases with congestion avoidance, as you saw with the slow start, but in a different way. With a slow start, the congestion window increases exponentially. With congestion avoidance, the congestion window increases incrementally by only one segment at a time, as shown in Figure 10.33.

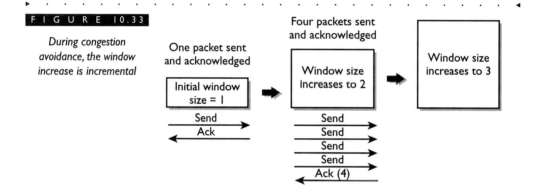

FIGURE 10.33

During congestion avoidance, the window increase is incremental

As Figure 10.33 indicates, by using the congestion avoidance algorithm, the congestion window increases by only one segment per acknowledgment. It does not matter how many acknowledgments are actually received — the window increases by one segment each time.

Fast Retransmit

The fast retransmit process is used by TCP when it believes that a segment is lost in transmission. But, how does TCP know that a segment is lost? It doesn't really know, but it has a strong indicator, as explained next.

Remember, the TCP specification states that all TCP segments must be acknowledged. Sometimes, segments may be received out of order or may be lost. When this happens, TCP sends an immediate duplicate acknowledgment, which notifies the other device that a segment was received out of order. When a duplicate acknowledgment is received, TCP has no way of knowing whether the segment was lost in transmission or just received on the other end out of order.

So, TCP waits to see how many duplicate acknowledgments are received. If the segments have simply arrived out of order at the destination, only one or two duplicate acknowledgments should be sent back to the sender during the processing and reordering of the segments in the receiver's buffer. However, if three or more duplicate acknowledgments are sent back to the sender, TCP uses fast retransmit to resend the apparently lost segment. TCP does not wait for the retransmission timer to expire, which is why this process is called *fast retransmit*.

Fast Recovery

TCP may use a fast recovery method after completing the fast retransmit process. The fast recovery algorithm states that, after a fast retransmit, TCP should use the congestion avoidance algorithm and recalculate its congestion window size, but should *not* perform a slow start. The reason for this is quite simple.

Assume that you have two computers participating in a TCP connection. Suddenly, several segments are lost, duplicate acknowledgments are sent, and fast retransmit occurs. Because data is still moving across the connection, in this case, you don't want the computers to stop what they are doing and you don't want the sender to reinstitute a slow start. This would cause severe performance degradation within the connection.

▸ · ◂

Case Study — What Can Go Wrong

The most common problems associated with TCP communication seem to be associated with slow response. Several things can cause slow response. Remember, an overloaded network device, such as a router or server, may discard packets silently, requiring TCP clients to retransmit data. Here is another example of a slow response.

The Problem

The network in this case has a single main site and several outside access sites and users. All users on the network at some point must use the FTP server located at the main site. Suddenly, several users at the remote sites call to report slow response with the FTP server when transferring files, frequent disconnections, and, sometimes, the inability to transfer files at all. The general layout of the network is shown in Figure 10.34.

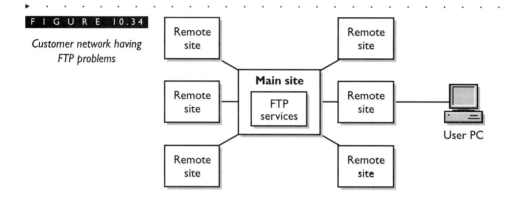

F I G U R E   10.34

Customer network having FTP problems

We have been called in to determine the source of this problem.

The Analysis

As previously stated, slow TCP response is often caused by dropped packets due to buffer overload in a device, such as a router or server. So, of course, this is the first place to look. We have access to the main site, but the routers seem to have plenty of buffer space. We ask whether more than one site is having the FTP-slowness problem. The response is a resounding "Yes!" Because more than one site is having the problem, we can begin to look at the main site. We take a trace of an FTP transfer between a computer on the local segment and the main FTP server. We filter the trace to show TCP data only, as shown in Figure 10.35.

The trace in Figure 10.35 shows an interesting pattern. Notice how the TCP window size is a respectable 8760 for a short period of time, but then drops unexpectedly to 0. At the end of the trace, the connection is just dropped, again for no apparent reason. We look at the FTP server — no lockups, no apparent problem at all. But, the data flow pattern with the 0 window size clearly is not right. We look for error packets on the network — none exist.

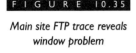

FIGURE 10.35

Main site FTP trace reveals
window problem

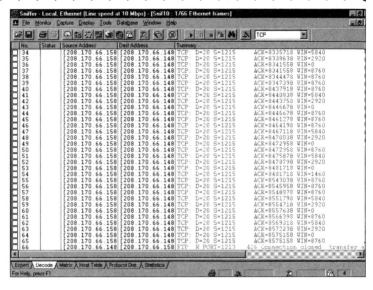

At this point, we know that we must dig into the FTP server a bit more. We perform tests on the network card—no failure, no problems. We do memory tests on the FTP server—again, no problems. Finally, we check the network patch cable itself. We run two tests on the cable (as we do with all hardware components) and find that one test passes the cable and one test says the cable test fails. We replace the patch cable and perform another FTP file transfer. This time, the transfer looks great, as shown in Figure 10.36.

What a difference! At this point, the users no longer complain of slow FTP response and are able to transfer their files with ease.

The Solution

After we replaced the patch cable, we took the suspect cable along with us for further testing. We found that when the cable end connector had been put on the cable, two of the wires had been nicked by the wire cutter, causing an intermittent ground in the cable. Just one more reason to make sure that your cabling is up to specification. If this cable had been tested and certified prior to the installation of the network, this marginal cable would have been caught and replaced before it caused problems on the network.

FIGURE 10.36

FTP file transfer with new patch cable

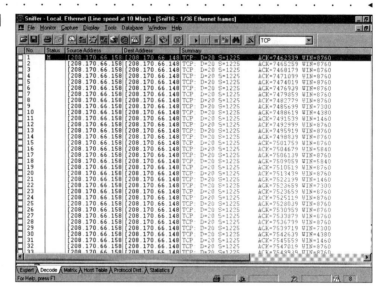

Summary

In this chapter, you learned how the Transmission Control Protocol (TCP) works within the host-to-host layer of the TCP/IP model. You found out how the reliability of the TCP protocol is established, and how TCP connections are created, established, and torn down by either device at the two ends of a connection. You also learned how connections are maintained by using TCP and the algorithms used to avoid network congestion, dropped packets, or lost packets. You also examined how retransmission takes place.

## PART IV

Analyzing and Troubleshooting the Application Layer

## CHAPTER 11

Dynamic Host Configuration Protocol (DHCP) and BOOTP

Chapter 4 discussed IP addressing rules, including the importance of controlling address assignments and avoiding duplicate IP addresses. Chapter 5 on ARP/RARP (Address Resolution Protocol/Reverse Address Resolution Protocol) explained how a bootstrapped client can use RARP to get its IP address from a RARP server by providing its hardware address in a RARP request. This is important in the case in which the client is a diskless system that does not have local disk space to store its TCP/IP configuration.

This chapter introduces the Bootstrap Protocol (BOOTP) and the Dynamic Host Configuration Protocol (DHCP), both of which have been developed to overcome the limitations of RARP, by offering much more functionality than RARP. They are used not only to configure diskless clients with their IP address, but also to provide much more information, especially in regard to helping administrators manage the task of controlling IP address assignments from a central location.

BOOTP and DHCP are closely related protocols. DHCP is newer and is an extension to the BOOTP protocol. Many descriptions in this chapter will apply to both, and any important distinctions between the two will be made where necessary.

▶ · ◀

Overview of DHCP/BOOTP Functionality

BOOTP is described in RFC 951 and updated in RFC 1532. DHCP is described in RFCs 2132 (formerly 1533), 1534, 2131 (formerly 1541), and 1542. RFC 2241 describes the new DHCP options for Novell Directory Services (NDS).

A diskless workstation uses BOOTP to obtain its IP address from a BOOTP server. BOOTP uses UDP for transport. The UDP datagrams are encapsulated in IP datagrams for delivery. Figure 11.1 shows the format of a BOOTP/DHCP message.

How can a workstation use IP to send a datagram before it even knows its IP address? IP allows a host to accept and broadcast datagrams addressed to the limited broadcast address of 255.255.255.255. The server can reply in one of two ways. It can either broadcast the reply or use the information in the request to update its ARP cache with the workstation's hardware address. Usually, the server replies with a broadcast. When the header fields are discussed in detail later in the chapter, you'll see how, when using DHCP, the client can request the reply to be a broadcast.

How a BOOTP/DHCP message is encapsulated in an IP datagram

MAC header	IP header 20 bytes	UDP header 8 bytes	BOOTP/DHCP message Request/Reply	MAC trailer

The BOOTP message has a fixed length of 300 bytes and can be a request or a reply. A DHCP message has a variable length format.

BOOTP/DHCP message

UDP port 67 for BOOTP/DHCP server
UDP port 68 for BOOTP/DHCP client

UDP datagram

IP datagram

BOOTP requires UDP to use checksums and to set the Don't Fragment bit. The latter requirement allows clients that don't have enough memory for reassembly to still use BOOTP. If a client sending a request receives multiple replies, it will accept and process the first one. Possible datagram loss (remember, UDP is unreliable) is handled by timeout and retransmission parameters. When the client sends out a request, it starts a timer. Retransmission occurs when the timer expires before a reply has been received. After each retransmission, the timer value is doubled to keep BOOTP from adding excessive traffic to a probably already congested network.

BOOTP/DHCP Header Structure

BOOTP/DHCP requests and BOOTP/DHCP replies have the same format. One field in the header differentiates them from each other. The fields in the BOOTP header are all fixed-length fields. This is different with DHCP. With DHCP, much more configuration information can be passed down to the client. Figure 11.2 shows the BOOTP/DHCP header fields. Where nothing is mentioned, the fields are the same for BOOTP and DHCP.

FIGURE 11.2

The header fields in a BOOTP/DHCP message

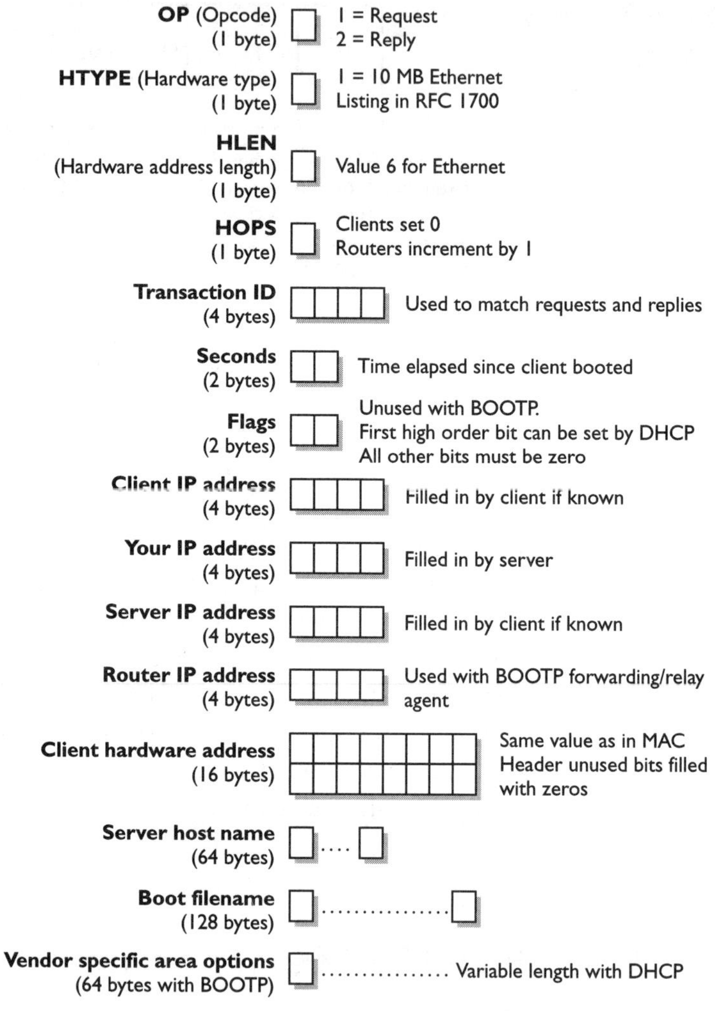

OP (Opcode) (1 byte)	1 = Request 2 = Reply
HTYPE (Hardware type) (1 byte)	1 = 10 MB Ethernet Listing in RFC 1700
HLEN (Hardware address length) (1 byte)	Value 6 for Ethernet
HOPS (1 byte)	Clients set 0 Routers increment by 1
Transaction ID (4 bytes)	Used to match requests and replies
Seconds (2 bytes)	Time elapsed since client booted
Flags (2 bytes)	Unused with BOOTP. First high order bit can be set by DHCP All other bits must be zero
Client IP address (4 bytes)	Filled in by client if known
Your IP address (4 bytes)	Filled in by server
Server IP address (4 bytes)	Filled in by client if known
Router IP address (4 bytes)	Used with BOOTP forwarding/relay agent
Client hardware address (16 bytes)	Same value as in MAC Header unused bits filled with zeros
Server host name (64 bytes)	
Boot filename (128 bytes)	
Vendor specific area options (64 bytes with BOOTP)	Variable length with DHCP

Opcode (OP)

This field has 8 bits and specifies whether the message is a request or a reply. Opcode 1 implies a request, and Opcode 2 implies a reply.

Hardware Type (HTYPE)

This field has 8 bits and specifies the type of the underlying network hardware. A value of 1 is for a 10MB Ethernet. These hardware codes are defined in RFC 1700, the "Assigned Numbers Document." They are the same codes that are used for the ARP/RARP protocol.

Hardware Address Length (HLEN)

This field has 8 bits and specifies the length of the hardware address. For Ethernet, this field is set to 6 (bytes).

Hops

This field has 8 bits. When the packet is sent out by a client, it puts 0 in this field. A BOOTP/DHCP relay agent that receives the message and decides to forward it to another server will increment this count by 1. This process is discussed in more detail in the section "BOOTP Forwarding/DHCP Relay Agents," later in the chapter.

Transaction ID

This 32-bit field contains an integer value that is set by the client and returned by the server. It is used to match requests and replies. It should be set to a random number for each request.

Use the Transaction ID field to set a filter in your analyzer to view all frames relating to a DHCP communication for a certain client.

TIP

Seconds

This 16-bit field reports the number of seconds that have elapsed since the client booted. If the number of seconds is high, it can be assumed that the client's primary DHCP server is unreachable. A secondary DHCP server may then decide to service the client. This field is also used by BOOTP Forwarders (DHCP relay agents). Check the section "BOOTP Forwarding/DHCP Relay Agents," later in the chapter, to learn more about how the router uses this field.

Flags

This 16-bit field isn't used with BOOTP. DHCP only uses the first High Order bit. All other bits must be 0. The BOOTP/DHCP message contains the client's hardware address. The server can respond by sending a unicast reply. If the DHCP client sets this first bit in the Flags field to 1, it requests the server to answer with a hardware broadcast.

Client IP Address

In this field and in the following fields, the client fills in as much information as it has. All other fields are left set to 0. The client IP address has — you guessed it — 32 bits. If the client already knows its IP address, it fills it in. Otherwise, it leaves this field with a value of 0.

Your IP Address

This 32-bit field is filled in by the server in cases in which the client requests its IP address.

Server IP Address

Again, this is a 32-bit field. If the client knows the IP address of a server from which it wants information, it puts that server's IP address in this field. Only the server with a matching address will reply to this request.

Router IP Address

This is a 32-bit field. If a BOOTP forwarder (also called *relay agent*) is used, that forwarder fills in its own router IP address. If the packet travels over more than one router, the address of the first router will be in this field. See "BOOTP Forwarding/DHCP Relay Agents," later in the chapter, to learn more about this process.

Client Hardware Address

This 16-byte field is filled in by the client. This is the same value as in the MAC header. By placing this field within the BOOTP message, it is easily available to any user process (such as the BOOTP/DHCP server). A MAC address could use this information to update its ARP cache (if the operating system allows this) with the client's hardware address and reply with a unicast instead of a broadcast. This field is not truncated but is filled with zeros if the hardware address is shorter than 16 bytes.

Server Host Name

This is a 64-byte field. If the client knows the name of the server from which it wants information, it can fill in this field. That way, only that specific server will reply to the request. If the client does not know the name of the server, this field will be 0.

Boot File Name

This is a 128-byte field. The client can either fill in a boot filename or leave the field set to 0, which lets the BOOTP server choose the boot file.

The bootstrap process takes place in two stages. The BOOTP server provides the client only with the information needed to obtain a boot file. Then, the client uses the TFTP (Trivial File Transfer Protocol) to obtain the boot file. The advantage of this is that the configuration of the BOOTP server and the storage space for the boot files are independent and can be on different hosts. The BOOTP server holds only a simple database that contains the names of the boot files.

A client may have multiple operating systems installed. When it boots, the user decides which of the operating systems to use. Depending on the choice made, a different boot file is needed, which can be specified by the client in the Boot File Name field. The client can also specify a generic name in this field, to designate the operating system. For example, if the client puts *UNIX* in the Boot File Name field, it means "I want to boot the UNIX configuration for this machine." Now, the BOOTP server consults its database to find the filename that contains the UNIX memory image for this client.

Vendor Specific Area/DHCP Options

With BOOTP, this field has a fixed length of 64 bytes. With DHCP, it is a variable-length field. A DHCP client must be able to accept at least 312 bytes of options. This field contains optional information that can be passed from the server to the client.

 A common choice of options is described in Table 11.1. RFC 2132 includes all the BOOTP vendor extensions that were described in RFCs 1497 and 1533, and contains the new DHCP extensions. Novell's new DHCP options for Novell Directory Services (NDS) are described in RFC 2241.

The length of options can be either fixed or variable. DHCP options have the same format as BOOTP vendor extensions. The first 4 bytes of the Vendor Information field have been assigned to the Magic Cookie (as suggested in RFC 951). The value of the Magic Cookie is 99.130.83.99 in dotted decimal notation. If this value is set, it basically means that information is contained in the following fields. Options 0 and 255 are the two fixed-length options. They have only 1 byte and contain no data. All other options have a variable length. Many of these options have default values specified in other RFCs. RFC 1122 (the "Host Requirements Document") specifies default values for most IP and TCP configuration parameters. Figure 11.3 illustrates the format of the Vendor Specific Area.

The first 4 bytes contain the Magic Cookie. The rest of the area is a list of items. Each item starts with a 1-byte Tag field. A Tag field with the value of 0 is a pad byte. The Tag field with the value of 255 marks the end of all the items. These are the two fixed-length options. All the remaining items consist of a 1-byte Tag field and a 1-byte Length field, followed by the information.

Table 11.1 shows some examples from RFC 2132 that help to explain the concept.

FIGURE 11.3

Format of the Vendor Specific Area in the BOOTP/DHCP header

Magic Cookie (4 bytes)

99.130.83.99 dotted decimal notation means there is information in these fields.

The two fixed length options:

Pad (1 byte)   0

End (1 byte)   255   Always has to come at the end of all the options.

Some examples for variable length options:

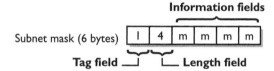

Subnet mask (6 bytes)

Information fields

Tag field ⏝ ⏝ **Length field**

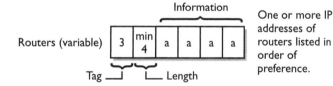

Routers (variable)

Information

Tag ⏝ ⏝ Length

One or more IP addresses of routers listed in order of preference.

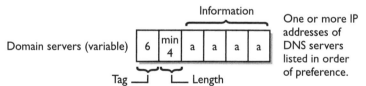

Domain servers (variable)

Information

Tag ⏝ ⏝ Length

One or more IP addresses of DNS servers listed in order of preference.

TABLE 11.1

Data Types in the Vendor Specific Area of a BOOTP/DHCP Header

TAG	DATA TYPE	LENGTH IN BYTES	DESCRIPTION
0	Padding	1	Used to align subsequent fields to word boundaries.
255	End	1	Marks the end of valid information in the Vendor Specific Area.

Continued

TABLE 11.1

*Data Types in the Vendor
Specific Area of a
BOOTP/DHCP Header
(continued)*

TAG	DATA TYPE	LENGTH IN BYTES	DESCRIPTION
1	Subnet Mask	4	Specifies the subnet mask for the local network. If both the Subnet Mask and the Routers option are specified in a DHCP header, the Subnet Mask option must be first.
2	Time of Day	4	Provides the time offset of the local network in seconds and specified in UTC (Universal Time Coordinated).
3	Routers	Variable	Specifies the IP addresses of one or more routers. They should be listed in order of preference. The minimum length for this field is 4 bytes and the total length must always be a multiple of 4.
4	Time Servers	Variable	Specifies a list of IP addresses of time servers available to the client. They should be listed in order of preference. The minimum length for this field is 4 bytes and the total length must always be a multiple of 4.
6	Domain Servers	Variable	Specifies a list of IP addresses for DNS (Domain Name System) name servers available to the client. They should be listed in order of preference. The minimum length for this field is 4 bytes and the total length must always be a multiple of 4.
12	Host Name	Variable	Specifies the name of the client. The name may or may not be qualified with the local domain name. The minimum length is 1 byte.
13	Boot File Size	2	A 2-byte value that specifies the size of the boot file, expressed in 512-byte blocks.

TAG	DATA TYPE	LENGTH IN BYTES	DESCRIPTION
2	Overload Option	1	If this option is used, it indicates to the client that no values exist for the Host Name and the Boot File Name fields. It tells the client to interpret those fields as regular DHCP options. This way, if a hostname and a boot file name are not specified, their corresponding fields' space in the header can be used for other information instead of being wasted. Possible values: 1 — The Boot File Size field is used to hold options 2 — The Host Name field is used to hold options 3 — Both fields are used to hold options
53	Message Type	3	Specifies the DHCP message type. The value can be any number between 1 and 8. These message types are explained later in the chapter and illustrated in Figure 11.4.
128 – 254	Reserved	-	Reserved for site-specific information.

These are just a few examples. For a complete list, refer to RFC 2132, which contains further options for IP layer parameters (such as IP forwarding, IP source routing, datagram reassembly options, TTL values, MTU options, subnet options, broadcast address options, and static route options), link layer parameters (such as ARP cache options and encapsulation options), TCP layer parameters, NetBIOS-over-TCP/IP options, and X-Windows options.

DHCP Message Types

Every DHCP header includes information about the type of message. Figure 11.4 shows that the option used to define a message type has 3 bytes. The first field, Tag, is set to 53, which states that the following option will define the message type. The second field, Length, is set to 1, for the length of the option. The third field, Type, states the type and can have a value between 1 and 8. Type 8 is a DHCP Inform message, added in RFC 2132.

► · ◄

FIGURE 11.4

The option fields that define the DHCP message type

Tag (I byte) [53]   The tag field contains the value 53 if this option defines the message type.

Length (I byte) [I]   The DHCP message option is fixed length. The length field indicates that one byte of options will follow.

Type (I byte) [I–8]   This field specifies the message type.

Type Field	DHCP Message Types
I	DHCPDISCOVER
2	DHCPOFFER
3	DHCPREQUEST
4	DHCPDECLINE
5	DHCPACK
6	DHCPNACK
7	DHCPRELEASE
8	DHCPINFORM (added with RFC2132)

Figure 11.5 shows how a DHCP header presents itself in the detail window of a protocol decode.

► · ◄

FIGURE 11.5

A DHCP header in a protocol decode

The Opcode field is set to 1, which indicates a request. Sniffer Pro decodes this as Boot Record Type. This example is on a 10MB Ethernet network, so the Hardware Address Length is set to 6 bytes. The Hops field would be set only by a forwarding router. This is a client issuing a request, so the value is 0. The client has assigned a random transaction ID, and 0 seconds have elapsed since it booted. The Flags field has not been set and the server will reply with a unicast to the hardware address of the client. Remember that this Flag field is not used with BOOTP. The Client Self-Assigned IP Address field is filled in by the client. This is a DHCPInform message, used by the client to get additional information. It does not need an IP address. The next three fields are all set to 0, which means the client does not have any specific information yet. The Vendor Information Tag field with the value of 63825363 is the hexadecimal representation of the Magic Cookie. The dotted decimal representation would be 99.130.83.99, as mentioned earlier. The Message Type is set to 8, which indicates that this is a DHCP Inform message.

The client requests two specific parameters: a directory agent (option 78) and a service scope (option 79). (These two options are used with the Service Location Protocol. Refer to Chapter 14 to learn about SLP.) To interpret such a trace, make sure that you have RFC 2132 within reach to interpret the option codes. If you are interested in learning more about those NetBIOS-over-TCP/IP codes, refer to RFC 1001 and RFC 1002.

DHCP Versus BOOTP

BOOTP is the older protocol. It is primarily used for diskless workstations that do not have local storage to store their configuration. Thus, they use BOOTP to get their configuration from a boot file stored on a central BOOTP server. BOOTP was designed for a rather static environment. It can't be used to configure a workstation dynamically. All the settings for the client have to be predetermined by the administrator and entered into the boot file. If anything changes, the administrator has to change the content of the boot file.

Today's networks need much more flexibility. A user may have different operating systems on his/her workstation that require different configuration settings. Also, users may move from one network segment to another, which calls for changes in the IP address assignment. Another case in which dynamic address assignment is needed is where the total number of possible clients exceeds the number of IP addresses available. Assuming that not all users are logged in concurrently, the address space may work well. But dynamic IP address allocation is necessary, which is what DHCP has been developed for. It extends BOOTP in two ways:

▸ Allows a client to receive all necessary configuration information in one message (because it does not have a fixed length).

▸ Allows a client to receive an IP address dynamically. To use this dynamic feature, you must have a DHCP server configured with a set of IP addresses that it can use for allocation to client requests.

DHCP supports three different configurations for allocating addresses:

▸ **Manual:** You assign a specific IP address to a specific workstation.

▸ **Automatic:** The DHCP server assigns a permanent address to a host on first request.

▸ **Dynamic:** The DHCP server loans an IP address to a computer for a limited time (Lease Time).

DHCP servers are flexible in their configuration. The client identifies itself to the server, usually by the hardware address (see the Client Identifier field in Figure 11.8 and compare it to the hardware address). The DHCP server can be configured to assign a permanent address to some clients, but dynamically assign IP addresses to other clients.

DHCP can do much more than just assign IP addresses. It has a tremendous functionality built in. Refer to the related section "Vendor specific area/DHCP Options" on DHCP options, which explains this in more detail.

 NOTE **Most DHCP servers can be configured to answer BOOTP requests as well as DHCP requests. If you configure a DHCP server to reply to BOOTP requests, it can service both clients that request IP address information and BOOTP clients that request boot file information. In the case where BOOTP clients require boot file information, you also need to have a TFTP service running, because that's how clients get**

their boot file. Refer to your vendor's product documentation to
learn how to configure your DHCP/BOOTP server.

Analyzing a DHCP Session

DHCP has several frequently used forms of communication patterns. The
following sections explain these different communication patterns and show how
they look in trace files.

IP Address Initialization

DHCP uses a four-phase process to configure a DHCP client. Figure 11.6
summarizes the four frames and their specific information. The bottom of the
figure includes a hint to memorize this process, D-O-R-A, which represents
Discover, *Offer*, *Request*, *Ack*.

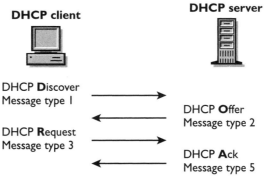

FIGURE 11.6

*Overview of the four-phase
DHCP initialization process*

DHCP client

DHCP server

DHCP **D**iscover
Message type 1

DHCP **O**ffer
Message type 2

DHCP **R**equest
Message type 3

DHCP **A**ck
Message type 5

Always look for these four frames in the IP address
initialization process. Call them **D-O-R-A**:

D	Discover	Client:	I need an IP address.
O	Offer	Server:	Here's one.
R	Request	Client:	Can I use it with these parameters?
A	Ack	Server:	Yes, you can.

Figure 11.7 presents the information as you would find it in your analyzer's trace file.

FIGURE 11.7

The DHCP initialization process in a trace file

Note that the source IP address of the frames originating from the client is 0.0.0.0, which means that the client does not know its IP address yet. The destination IP address is 255.255.255.255, which is the limited broadcast address. In frame 18, the server replies by using the client's MAC address in the DLC layer and the client's future IP address in the IP header, because, in frame 14, the client hasn't set the Flags bit to indicate that it wants the reply to be a broadcast. The UDP summary shows source port 68 for the client, and destination port 67 for the server.

DHCP Discover Frames

When the client first boots, it initializes a limited IP stack and broadcasts a request for the location of a DHCP server. The request goes to the IP broadcast address of 255.255.255.255 and to UDP port 67. This request is called Discover and goes out to the local network. Figure 11.8 shows the details of a Discover message.

The Opcode field is set to 1, which means that it is a request. The Transaction ID is randomly assigned by the client. The Flags field is not set to 1, which means the server will reply with a unicast. The next four fields are set to 0, because the client doesn't have any specific information yet. The Vendor Information tag is the Magic Cookie in hexadecimal representation. The dotted decimal notation would be 99.130.83.99. The Message Type option (code 53) is set to 1, which indicates DHCP Discover (refer to Figure 11.4 for the message type values). The Client Identifier field is used by the server to find the configuration for that workstation. It usually includes the Ethernet hardware address of the client. The client requests a specific IP address — the one that it used in its last session. It also supplies its hostname. What follows is the list with the requested parameters, bounded by the End field of 255 (not shown in the picture). The parameters that the client is requesting are, in this case, the subnet mask (1), a list of routers (3), a list of DNS servers (6), the name of its domain (15), its IP address lease time (51), and the IP address of its WINS server (44).

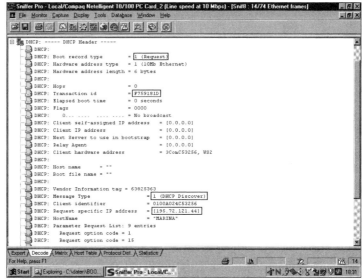

F I G U R E   1 1 . 8

The DHCP Discover frame
in a protocol decode

DHCP Offer Frames

All DHCP servers on the local network (in other words, all servers that listen on UDP port 67) send an Offer to the client. The Offer is broadcast onto the local network and contains valid configuration information. Because the client has a limited IP stack running, it can receive the broadcast. Thus, the client may receive zero or more Offers. To learn how this works in the case where the DHCP server is in a remote network, refer to "BOOTP Forwarding/DHCP Relay Agents," later in the chapter. Figure 11.9 shows the details of the DHCP header in the server's Offer, which is the detail window of frame 18 in Figure 11.7, shown earlier.

▶ · ◀

FIGURE 11.9

The detail window of the server's DHCP Offer

The Opcode field is set to 2, indicating that this is a reply. The transaction ID matches the one the client assigned in frame 14. The client is assigned the IP address of 192.168.0.101. The Message Type option 2 shows that it is a DHCP Offer. The additional configuration information includes the subnet mask, the server's IP address, and the lease time. The lease time plays an important role and is discussed soon in the section "IP Address Renewal."

DHCP Request Frames

The client chooses the first DHCP Offer coming in and replies to it by broadcasting a Request for the offered parameters from one server. By explicitly requesting them from a specific server (by stating its IP address), all other servers know that their Offers have been declined by the client. They can now reuse the offered IP address when new Discover Requests arrive from other clients.

Frame 19 in Figure 11.7 is the client's answer to the DHCP Offer. It includes all the configuration information from the Offer and specifies the server IP address and the offered client IP address.

If the client does not receive any Offers within 1 second, it rebroadcasts the Request three times (at 9-, 13- and 16-second intervals which include an additional random length of time between 0 and 1000 milliseconds). If an Offer is not received after four Requests, the client retries every five minutes. These are Microsoft Windows NT defaults. Other operating systems may have other defaults (for example, MSNet v3.0 uses timers of 4, 8, 16, 32, and 64 seconds).

DHCP Ack Frames

The server, who's DHCP Offer has now been accepted, sends an acknowledgment (Ack) to the client that contains an IP address and all additional configuration parameters.

Upon receiving the server's Ack, the client finishes initializing its TCP/IP stack and binds the protocol.

The DHCP server's Ack is a broadcast using UDP. If that frame gets lost on its way to the client, the server will not know and will not release the IP address acknowledged in that frame.

NOTE

This four-step, IP-address-initialization process (remember D-O-R-A from Figure 11.6) is used when one of the following occurs:

▸ TCP/IP is initialized for the first time as a DHCP client.

▸ The client requests a specific address and is denied (the server sends NAck). Possible reasons for this occurring are that the server dropped the current lease and gave the address to another client, or the client has moved to another subnet and the previous address is not valid for that subnet.

▸ The client has released an IP address and now requires a new lease.

IP Address Renewal

The address renewal process consists of two frames. They are the same frames as in the IP address initialization process: Request and Ack.

To understand when the renewal of an address takes place and what happens if a client cannot renew its address, you have to understand what the lease time is. As mentioned earlier, when the DHCP server sends an Offer to a client, it includes the *lease time*, which specifies how long the client can use the address. The lease time can be configured on the DHCP server. The lease time has three timers associated with it, as listed in Table 11.2.

TABLE 11.2

DHCP Timers

NAME	REFERRED TO AS	DESCRIPTION
Renewal Timer	T1	At 50 percent of lease time
Rebinding Timer	T2	At 87.5 percent of lease time
Lease Timer	T3	At 100 percent of lease time

The detail window shown in Figure 11.10 is a DHCP Offer. You can see all the timers discussed in Table 11.2. You can also see that we had some fun playing around in the lab. We have modified the lease time on our DHCP server to be 120 seconds.

Figure 11.11 illustrates the frames issued during an address renewal. The client does not have to send another DHCP Discover frame for the renewal. Instead, the client just sends out a new Request asking to renew the IP address that it already has.

When 50 percent of the lease time has expired (T1), the client sends out the Renewal Request to the server from which it received the IP address.

If the DHCP server is available, it replies with a DHCP Ack, including the new lease time and any updated configuration parameters. If the server is unavailable, the client continues to use its address until T2, the address Rebinding Timer. It does this by broadcasting a DHCP Request, specifying the last IP address that it leased. If the DHCP server is unavailable, the client continues using the address until T2.

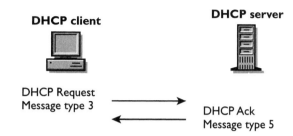

DHCP client **DHCP server**

DHCP Request
Message type 3 →

← DHCP Ack
Message type 5

T1: First renewal request to DHCP server it obtained the address from. If there is no Ack it will use the address until T2 and keep requesting in the background.

T2: If there was no Ack from the DHCP server until T2, the client sends a request to any DHCP server to renew its address.

T3: If the client did not receive an Ack until T3 (lease time), it cannot use its IP address any more and has to restart with the address initialization process.

NOTE

When a DHCP client reboots, you may see this same two-frame communication. Instead of going through the whole address initialization process (DORA), the client may try to use the same address that it had on its last session. It can do this only if it can store its configuration information locally.

If an address lease could not be renewed at the 50-percent lease time interval (T1), the client will try to contact *any* DHCP server on the local network at T2, the Rebinding Timer, which is at 87.5-percent expiration of the lease time. It will broadcast a DHCP Request to renew its address. This Request can be answered by a DHCP Ack (renewing the address) or DHCP NAck (which forces the client to restart the DHCP Discover process).

If the lease time expires (T3) and the client did not get an Ack from a DHCP server, it cannot use the IP address any longer and has to restart the address initialization process (DORA).

TIP

The lease time usually has default values that can be changed. The default lease time for Windows NT is three days, which is a common value. Choose the lease time carefully for your environment. If you are short on IP addresses and your users change a lot, you might choose a shorter lease time. My ISP (Internet service provider) has a lease time of one hour. If your users usually remain the same, requiring the same address again, the default might work well for you. When deciding on the default lease time, consider that if your DHCP server has a problem and you need to troubleshoot it, the users can continue using their last leased address until the lease time expires (T3). Having a lease time of three to four days gives you that much time to troubleshoot your DHCP server.

IP Address Release

Only one frame goes out for the IP address release, a DHCP Release message type 7 sent from the client to the server. It includes the common header values, such as a transaction ID, the client's IP address to be released, the client's hardware address, the message type 7, the server's IP address, and the client ID. Figure 11.12 shows the process of an address release.

FIGURE 11.12

The DHCP address release process

If a client needs an IP address after the DHCP Release, it has to restart the address initialization process with a DHCP Discover frame.

NOTE

If the DHCP Release message gets lost on its travel to the DHCP server, the server will not release the address. The client will not know that the packet got lost because this is connectionless UDP communication.

DHCP Inform Frames

This is a new message type (described in RFC 2131) that is used if a client has already obtained a network address through some other means (such as via manual configuration). It may use a DHCP Inform request message to obtain other local configuration parameters. Servers receiving a DHCP Inform message construct a DHCP Ack message with any local configuration parameters appropriate for the client, without allocating a new address, checking for an existing binding, or including lease time parameters. The server should check the network address in a DHCP Inform message, for consistency, but must not check for an existing lease. The server forms and sends directly to the client a DHCP Ack message containing the configuration parameters for the requesting client.

Refer to Chapter 15 on Novell's implementation of TCP/IP. The Novell Client software for Microsoft Windows uses DHCP Inform frames to get SLP (Service Location Protocol) and NDS (Novell Directory Services) information.

X-REF

BOOTP Forwarding/DHCP Relay Agents

Several terms are used to describe what is now commonly called a DHCP relay agent. In earlier days, the term *BOOTP forwarding agent* was common. The Cisco world calls it an *IP Helper* address. Routers must support RFC 1542 (this is a clarification and an update to RFC 1532). If they don't, you have to implement a DHCP server on each subnet.

When you configure a router to be a DHCP relay agent, it will listen for DHCP Requests on the well-known UDP port number 67. When the router receives a DHCP Request, it puts its own IP address into the Router IP Address field of the DHCP header (the address of the interface on which it received the Request), increments the Hops field in the DHCP header, and sends the Request to the DHCP server. Because this outgoing DHCP Request is usually a unicast datagram, it can follow any route to the DHCP server and possibly cross more routers. The DHCP server sends its Offer back to the relay agent, and the relay agent forwards it to the client.

Figure 11.13 shows the network layout for the following example to explain the relay agent.

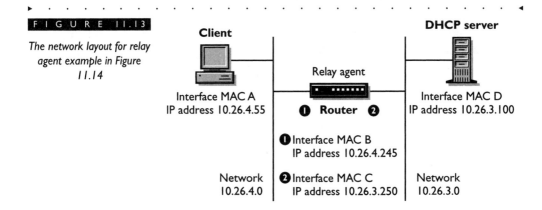

FIGURE 11.13

The network layout for relay agent example in Figure 11.14

Client

DHCP server

Relay agent

Interface MAC A
IP address 10.26.4.55

❶ **Router** ❷

Interface MAC D
IP address 10.26.3.100

❶ Interface MAC B
IP address 10.26.4.245

Network
10.26.4.0

❷ Interface MAC C
IP address 10.26.3.250

Network
10.26.3.0

Figure 11.14 shows how the header fields change when a Discover and an Offer are forwarded by a relay agent. If you put an analyzer on both sides of the router, you see the four frames (Discover, Offer, Request, Ack) on both sides. Depending on which side of the router your analyzer sits, the information in the headers looks different.

On the MAC layer, the source and destination information always show the actual interface from which the frame originates and to which it is sent. When you look at frame 2, the forwarded Discover, on the IP layer the relay agent puts in its IP address (the one of the interface on which it received the frame) and puts the DHCP server's IP address in the Destination Address field (this address was configured on the relay agent). It also decreases the IP TTL by 1, which is part of normal frame forwarding. The UDP source and destination ports do not change. Note that the transaction ID is the same in all four frames. So, when you troubleshoot and analyze DHCP communications, always check whether the transaction IDs match. The Hops field is incremented when the relay agent forwards the frame, and it also puts its IP address in the Relay Agent field.

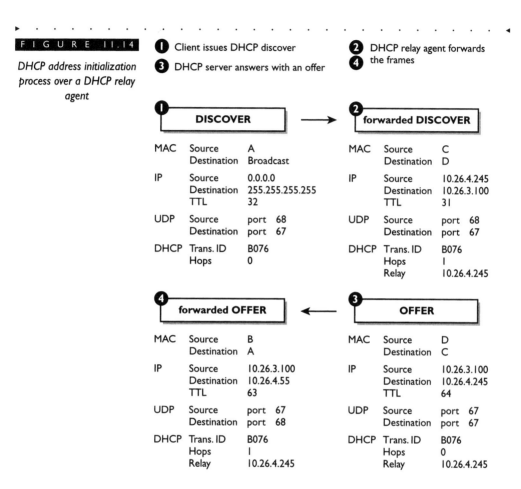

FIGURE 11.14

DHCP address initialization process over a DHCP relay agent

❶ Client issues DHCP discover
❸ DHCP server answers with an offer
❷ DHCP relay agent forwards
❹ the frames

❶ **DISCOVER** → ❷ **forwarded DISCOVER**

MAC	Source	A
	Destination	Broadcast
IP	Source	0.0.0.0
	Destination	255.255.255.255
	TTL	32
UDP	Source	port 68
	Destination	port 67
DHCP	Trans. ID	B076
	Hops	0

MAC	Source	C
	Destination	D
IP	Source	10.26.4.245
	Destination	10.26.3.100
	TTL	31
UDP	Source	port 68
	Destination	port 67
DHCP	Trans. ID	B076
	Hops	1
	Relay	10.26.4.245

❹ **forwarded OFFER** ← ❸ **OFFER**

MAC	Source	B
	Destination	A
IP	Source	10.26.3.100
	Destination	10.26.4.55
	TTL	63
UDP	Source	port 67
	Destination	port 68
DHCP	Trans. ID	B076
	Hops	1
	Relay	10.26.4.245

MAC	Source	D
	Destination	C
IP	Source	10.26.3.100
	Destination	10.26.4.245
	TTL	64
UDP	Source	port 67
	Destination	port 67
DHCP	Trans. ID	B076
	Hops	0
	Relay	10.26.4.245

The DHCP server receives the Discover frame and answers with an Offer. The source IP address is its own address. The destination IP address is the interface of the router on which the router received the Discover. The DHCP server sets the TTL according to its configuration. Note that in this frame, the UDP source and destination port both are set to 67. A relay agent listens on port 67, so this frame needs to be addressed to 67 in order to be forwarded by the relay agent. When the relay agent forwards the Offer, it changes the MAC source and destination address, addresses the frame to the client's IP address (or to the broadcast address, depending on the configuration), decreases the IP TTL by 1, sets the UDP destination port to

68, increments the hop count in the DHCP header by 1, and forwards the frame to the client.

The same changes will occur when the client now issues a Request, which again will be forwarded by the relay agent, answered by the DHCP server with an Ack, and forwarded to the client by the relay agent.

IMPORTANT

Relay agents usually have multiple configuration parameters that define how they will react to client Requests. One parameter is the *Minimum Seconds to Wait*. The relay agent can be configured with a minimum time to wait. It compares the value in the Seconds field of the DHCP header with its configured Minimum Seconds to Wait, and then forwards the Request only if the value in the header is higher than its minimum time to wait. This gives local DHCP servers time to answer the Request. The relay agent will forward the Request only if the local DHCP server is unreachable.

The "DHCP Troubleshooting" section looks at a trace file where a relay agent forwards client requests to a DHCP server sitting on the same segment as the client, because the "minimum time to wait has not been configured properly."

Another common parameter is the hop count. If the packet has a higher hop count than the value of the hops parameter on the relay agent, the relay agent will not forward the packet. This restricts endless forwarding of DHCP Requests. RFC 1542 states that a relay agent *must* discard a packet with a hop count greater than 16. It also recommends that the configurable option on the relay agent should default to four hops. Relay agents usually can be configured as to how to forward DHCP Requests. You can configure which interface(s) it should use for forwarding and whether it should forward the Request as a broadcast or a unicast to a specific IP address.

Multiple DHCP Servers

If your network requires multiple DHCP servers, you have to create separate and unique scopes for each subnet. A *scope* is a range of IP addresses available to be leased or assigned to clients.

DYNAMIC HOST CONFIGURATION PROTOCOL (DHCP) AND BOOTP

To ensure that clients can lease IP addresses, even if one DHCP server is down, you have to distribute the scopes to more than one DHCP server. For example, each DHCP server should have a scope containing the following:

▸ Approximately 75 percent of the available IP addresses for the local subnet.

▸ Approximately 25 percent of the available IP addresses of the remote networks.

This way, even if a client's local DHCP server is unavailable, it can still receive an IP address from a remote DHCP server. However, this is possible only if the router is configured as a DHCP relay agent.

Figure 11.15 gives you an example for setting up two DHCP servers in two subnets.

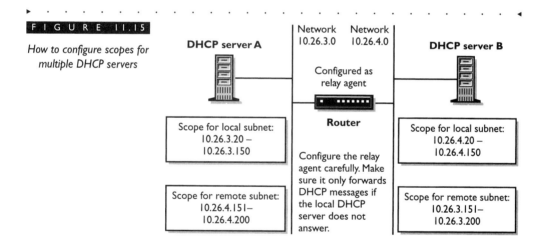

FIGURE 11.15

How to configure scopes for multiple DHCP servers

Server A has a scope for the local subnet with an address range of 10.26.3.20 to 10.26.3.150, and Server B has a scope for its local subnet with a range of 10.26.4.20 to 10.26.4.150. Each server can lease addresses to clients on its subnet.

Additionally, each server has a scope containing a small range of IP addresses for the remote subnet. Server A has a scope for Subnet B of 10.26.4.151 to 10.26.4.200, and Server B has a scope for Subnet A of 10.26.3.151 to 10.26.3.250. Now, when a client on Subnet A is unable to lease an address from Server A, it can lease an address for its subnet from Server B, and vice versa.

Before you use a design like this, consider the following: do you really need that much redundancy?

IMPORTANT

The crash of a DHCP server becomes a problem the moment your client's IP address lease time expires. If your lease times are not too short, you might as well do without a redundant DHCP server. In the preceding design, the relay agent must be properly configured. Its waiting time before forwarding a Request should be high enough so that it will not forward the Request if the local DHCP server is up and answering it already.

Multihomed DHCP Server

A *multihomed* server is a server with more than one logical interface. Setting up a multihomed DHCP server could save you the cost of having multiple DHCP servers to serve multiple subnets. This server would be set up at a central location in your network, with a logical interface to each of the subnets. Setting it up as a DHCP server would provide a local DHCP server for each subnet. You have to configure it with address scopes for each subnet. In this case, you do not need to enable a DHCP relay agent. Consider turning off routing on this server so that it can use its resources for the DHCP communications. Make sure that the DHCP server product you are using can deal with this configuration.

Troubleshooting DHCP

DHCP provides a central administration point for TCP/IP addresses. It helps to control the assignment of IP addresses, which should help to avoid duplicate IP addresses and incorrect TCP/IP subnet masks, and is much easier in case we need to change our IP addressing scheme or other global parameters. Some common problems that can arise are discussed in this section.

Generally, we can say that the client side does not impose many problems— most of the problems are on the server side. Very often, they are related to bugs in the server programming code. What kind of problems you may encounter depends on the product you are using. You have to make sure that you have updated your server with the latest patches, and refer to support information from your vendor to solve these problems.

Client Can't Get an IP Address

When a client first initializes its TCP/IP stack, it has to go through the D-O-R-A process. Send a Discover broadcast, receive an Offer, broadcast a Request, and receive an Ack. On subsequent connections, the client will broadcast a Request asking for the TCP/IP address that it had on its last session. The server will answer with an Ack.

This is your troubleshooting path. Does the client issue a DHCP Discover? If no, check the client's TCP/IP configuration. Is it configured to use a DHCP server and obtain its IP address automatically?

If the client broadcasts its Discover frame but receives no answer, you have to check on the server side. Is the server on the local network? Is it up, and is the DHCP server service running (listening on port 67)? Check the server's DHCP configuration for errors. Check the DHCP server for overload or high utilization. Although it's running, it may be flooded with requests or too busy with other processes and, therefore, unable to reply.

If the DHCP server is on a remote subnet, then you have to check whether the router is configured properly as a relay agent. The relay agent must know the address of the DHCP server and listen on port 67 for incoming DHCP broadcasts. Can you see the Discover frame on the other side of the router? If no, the problem is on the relay agent. If you can see the frame on the other side, you have to check the DHCP server's configuration.

Compare your trace files with the traces in this book to find out where things do not work the way they are supposed to. This will lead you to the troubleshooting area. The subject of troubleshooting the DHCP server configuration is beyond the scope of this book. Many different DHCP products are available on the market and they all differ in their features and functionality. Use your DHCP server's error log file to get detailed troubleshooting information.

Most products include options to set global defaults and to make exceptions for a group of clients or even a single client. The more complex your configuration, the more carefully you should check that you do not have configurations that don't work together.

TIP

A common problem is the following: You make exclusions for a certain MAC address and then change the network adapter in that client, but you forget about your DHCP configuration. The exclusion won't work anymore because the DHCP server can't recognize the client with the new MAC address.

Duplicate IP Addresses

Many problems arise from improperly configured scopes (address ranges). The DHCP server itself needs a statically configured unique IP address. It cannot be a DHCP client. Be careful with hosts that always use a specific address. Hosts such as routers and DNS servers (and my favorite components, printers) should have a permanent IP address, which can either be manually configured or assigned through DHCP. However, you have to exclude those addresses from your DHCP scope; otherwise, you will have duplicate IP addresses on your network.

In some cases, we have found duplicate IP address problems that weren't due to misconfiguration of the address ranges, but instead were due to problems in either the client's TCP/IP stack (apply the latest patches and refer to the vendor's support knowledge base for information) or the database of the DHCP server that was not working as intended.

X-REF

Refer to Chapter 16 to learn about Microsoft's DHCP support.

Another issue arises if multiple routes exist between the DHCP client and the DHCP server. Obviously, this situation can occur only if you are using a DHCP relay agent. It can lead to multiple Discover or Request packets with identical client ID and client MAC addresses arriving at the server. Again, the behavior of your specific DHCP server product determines whether it can handle that situation. If not, it will send an Offer to each Request, and the client probably won't be able to initialize its TCP/IP stack (or will be able to only for a short period of time). To find that problem, check your trace files for multiple Requests from the same client arriving at your remote DHCP server and multiple Offers from the same server arriving at the client.

X-REF

The "Case Study" later in this chapter covers a similar situation in which multiple requests and replies with the same transaction ID turn up because a relay agent is improperly configured.

If you have multiple DHCP servers on your subnet, make sure they have scopes that don't overlap. Again, if they do overlap, you may have duplicate IP address assignments. But, troubleshooting these problems is much easier these days, because you don't have to consult possibly outdated spreadsheets to find out where you assigned duplicate IP addresses. All configuration can be done centrally on the DHCP server(s).

IMPORTANT

Make sure to exclude broadcast addresses from your address ranges on the DHCP server. If you work with Class A, B, or C addresses, excluding 255 from your address range might be obvious. But, if your network is subnetted, the broadcast address isn't so obvious. If a client is assigned the broadcast address for its local network, it will not be able to communicate. Refer to Chapter 4 to learn about subnets and broadcast addresses.

To provide for redundancy, you can have a design similar to that described earlier in "Multiple DHCP Servers." However, this works only if the scopes are defined properly.

TIP

Some DHCP servers can be configured to PING an IP address before giving it out for a lease. The new DHCP server that comes with NetWare 5 and Windows NT DHCP Server (NT 4 with Service Pack 2 or higher) can do this.

IP Helper Configuration

The Cisco world refers to a DHCP relay agent as an IP Helper. If an IP Helper address is specified on a Cisco router, and UDP forwarding is enabled, broadcast packets to the following destinations will be forwarded:

- Time Service (port 37)

- TACACS (TAC Access Control System, used with Telnet, port 49)

- DNS (port 53)

- TFTP (Trivial File Transfer Protocol, port 69)

- DHCP (ports 67 and 68)

- NetBIOS Name Server (port 137); NetBIOS Datagram Server (port 138)

This can cause problems in Microsoft Windows NT networks. The forwarding of NetBIOS broadcasts on UDP port 138 can impact the ability of the Microsoft Browser Service to elect properly a segment master browser or a domain master browser. You don't want to disable UDP forwarding completely, because your DHCP server is on a remote network. Note that you can disable the forwarding of UDP on a per-port basis. Therefore, this problem can be solved by disabling UDP forwarding on ports 137 and 138. (See Microsoft Support, Article ID Q190930.)

Default Gateway Not Assigned

If your clients get all the information they need from the DHCP server, except the default gateway, check your DHCP server's configuration. The default gateway must be on the local segment of the client. If your DHCP server tries to hand out a default gateway that is not on the client's local network, the client will not be configured with a default gateway, or will have an invalid entry.

Utilities

The following is a list of utilities that can be helpful in troubleshooting DHCP:

▸ On Windows 95/98, use WINIPCFG to view your IP configuration and to release and renew an IP address.

▸ On Windows NT, use IPCONFIG. You can use the /ALL parameter to view your IP configuration, and use the /RENEW or /RELEASE parameter, respectively, to renew or release your IP address.

▸ On UNIX, use IFCONFIG.

▸ For the configuration and log files of your DHCP server, refer to the product documentation of your vendor.

Case Study — What Can Go Wrong

This case study explains the problems that you will have if a relay agent is not properly configured. It also provides an opportunity to review what you have learned about DHCP communication patterns.

The Problem

The network administrator, after reading this book, is eager to make a trace file in his network. What he finds looks nothing like he expected, as described next.

The Analysis

Figure 11.16 shows the trace file summary screen of a DHCP communication. A filter was set to display only DHCP frames. The trace doesn't look correct. The following list is a frame-by-frame analysis of this DHCP communication:

▶ · ◀

F I G U R E I I . I 6

A DHCP communication

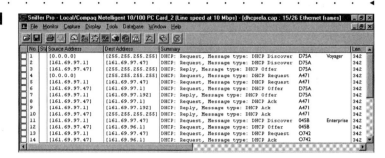

▸ **Frame 1:** The client issues a DHCP Discover. It requests the address 161.69.97.192 (not shown in Figure 11.16). The transaction ID is D75A.

▸ **Frame 2:** A copy of frame 1. It originates from a DHCP relay agent configured with the address of 161.69.97.1. It forwards the Discover to the DHCP server with the IP address of 161.69.97.47. Note that this DHCP server is on the same subnet as the client, so the relay agent doesn't need to forward this frame, but it does. The transaction ID is the same, D75A. Now, the DHCP server with the address 161.69.97.47 has received the same Discover frame with the same transaction ID twice.

▸ **Frame 3:** The DHCP server's Offer to frame 1. It is addressed to the broadcast address 255.255.255.255. Again, this transaction ID is D75A.

▸ **Frame 4:** The client's Request for the offered address, and the answer to frame 3.

▸ **Frame 5:** The relay agent is forwarding the client's Request.

▸ **Frame 6:** is the DHCP server's Offer as answer to frame number 2. Both Offers, the one in frame 3 and the one in frame 6, offer the same IP address of 161.69.97.192. Because the DHCP server has not ACKed the address initialization process, it considers the address to be available.

▸ **Frame 7:** the relay agent forwards frame number 6 to the client.

► **Frame 8:** The DHCP server Acks as an answer to frame 5. Note that this frame is addressed to the relay agent.

► **Frame 9:** The relay agent forwards the Ack to the client.

► **Frame 10:** The DHCP server's Ack as an answer to frame 4.

► **Frames 11 through 14:** Show a DHCP communication with a client from another subnet: 161.69.96.0. An interesting thing happens in these frames that explains why a relay agent is configured. Frame 11 shows the Relay Agent field in the DHCP header with the address of 161.69.96.1. Recall that the relay agent puts the address in there, and it is always the address of the interface on which the relay agent received the Request. The relay agent forwards this Requests to the DHCP server, which replies in frame 12. This frame shows that the destination IP address is the address of the relay agent's interface to the other subnet.

Figure 11.17 shows the network layout for this trace.

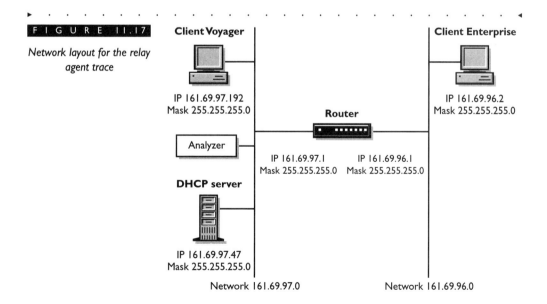

FIGURE 11.17

Network layout for the relay agent trace

Client Voyager

IP 161.69.97.192
Mask 255.255.255.0

Analyzer

DHCP server

IP 161.69.97.47
Mask 255.255.255.0

Router

IP 161.69.97.1   IP 161.69.96.1
Mask 255.255.255.0 Mask 255.255.255.0

Client Enterprise

IP 161.69.96.2
Mask 255.255.255.0

Network 161.69.97.0   Network 161.69.96.0

This is quite a confusing trace, so the following solution explains what's going on and how you can make things work better.

The Solution

First, why is a relay agent present? Looking at frames 1 through 10, everything would be perfect if no relay agent was present. Client Voyager does not need a relay agent to contact a DHCP server, because the DHCP server is on the same subnet.

Frames 11 through 14 provide the answer. Another subnet exists, with the number 161.69.96.0. That subnet does not have a DHCP server. Our DHCP server not only serves subnet 161.69.97.0, but also subnet 161.69.96.0. The relay agent has been configured on the router so that clients from that other subnet can contact a DHCP server.

To avoid all the unnecessary frames in subnet 161.69.97.0, the relay agent should be configured so that it does not forward local frames to the DHCP server on the same segment. This can be done in one of two ways:

▸ Set up a filter on the router to filter out local packets destined for port 67.

▸ Configure the relay agent for a certain Waiting Time (Minimum Seconds to Wait). If you do so, it doesn't forward DHCP communication that can be answered locally. This was discussed earlier, in the section "BOOTP Forwarding/DHCP Relay Agents."

One other strange thing exists in this trace that is worth mentioning. Usually, the transaction ID should be the same throughout the whole D-O-R-A process. In this case, though, both clients issue a new transaction ID for the Request. This must be a problem in the client's DHCP stack. We put the transaction ID into the summary display manually.

Summary

This chapter discussed the functionality of DHCP. The protocol becomes more and more important with the growth of networks. It provides flexible and dynamic management of IP hosts. As discussed in this chapter, DHCP is used not only for dynamic IP address assignment, but also to configure client hosts with many additional parameters. It makes the network administrator's job so much easier.

The next chapter covers the Domain Name System. DNS provides for name-to-address translation. Newer products even provide dynamic DNS (DDNS), which can interact with DHCP and dynamically update the name tables.

Domain Name System (DNS)

We have learned that any host in a TCP/IP network needs a unique address. The format of the address is a 32-bit integer, which is usually represented in the familiar dotted-decimal notation. Every host can be found and reached by addressing it with its IP address. Wouldn't it be much nicer to be able to address a host by a meaningful name? Names are so much easier to remember.

This chapter introduces the Domain Name System (DNS), which does exactly that — it enables you to assign hosts easy-to-remember, meaningful names, and provides a mechanism that maps between those names and the IP addresses of the hosts. It considers both the translation of names to IP addresses and the translation of IP addresses to names. DNS is a distributed database that uses a hierarchical name structure.

It is especially interesting to understand DNS, because it is used to assign machine names throughout the global Internet.

Overview of DNS Functionality

DNS is described in RFCs 1034 and 1035. RFC 2065 contains the description of security extensions to DNS.

DNS is a hierarchical client/server-based distributed database management system. It belongs to the application layer of the DOD (Department of Defense) model and uses UDP and TCP for transport (both on port 53).

A *name server* is a server program that supplies the name-to-address translation. If a name server is not able to resolve a request, it may forward it to a name server that can resolve it. The client software is called *resolver*. It passes name requests between applications and name servers. The resolver is often built into the application or runs on the host computer as a library routine. Notice that a name server has a built-in resolver function, too. If the resolver cannot resolve a name, it can resolve the query with another name server. In that case, it behaves like a resolver (client) to the other name server. So, when referring to a *resolver,* it can be a client or a server.

The most commonly used implementation of DNS is called *BIND (Berkeley Internet Name Domain Server).* The most current versions at the time of writing are BIND 4.9.7, which will not be developed further, and 8.1.2, which contains many improvements over 4.9.7, including dynamic DNS (DDNS) and more efficient zone transfers.

 Two cool Internet sites for DNS and BIND information are `http://www.isc.org` **and** `http://www.dns.net/dnsrd`**.**

Fully understanding the workings of DNS requires a discussion not only of headers and frames, but also of the organizational DNS hierarchy, which is reviewed next.

Proposition: To fully understand the workings of DNS it is not sufficient to just discuss headers and frames. We need to understand the organizational DNS hierarchy too. So let us review this part first.

▶ · ◀

DNS Hierarchy and Authorities

DNS is a database of host information. Domains define different levels of authority in a hierarchical structure. They are a subtree of the domain name space. The domain name of a domain is the same as the domain name of the node at the very top of the domain. The top of the hierarchy is called the *root domain*. Just below the root are the *top-level domains*. The Internet Authority has chosen to divide the top-level domains into the domains listed in Table 12.1.

TABLE 12.1

The Top-Level Internet Domains

DOMAIN NAME	DOMAIN DESCRIPTION
COM	For commercial organizations. It has grown very large, thus raising concerns regarding the administrative load and performance.
EDU	Originally intended for all educational organizations. Many universities, colleges, schools, and other educational institutions have registered here. A decision has been made to restrict further registration to four-year colleges and universities. Other educational institutes will have to register below the country domain.

Continued

T A B L E   1 2 . 1

The Top-Level Internet Domains (continued)

DOMAIN NAME	DOMAIN DESCRIPTION
GOV	For government institutions (nonmilitary).
MIL	For U.S. government military organizations.
NET	For providers of the Internet backbone; in other words, major network-support centers.
ORG	For organizations other than those previously listed (nonprofit).
ARPA	For reverse DNS.
INT	For international organizations.
country code	The two-letter abbreviation for each country (according to ISO 3166 standard).

These top-level domains can contain *second-level domains* and hosts. Second-level domains can contain both hosts and further subdomains.

You may have heard that the domain structure might be changed to accommodate for the rapid growth of the Internet. In the near future, many more top-level domains may exist, such as firm, shop, arts, or info.

 If you want more information on what's going on with the top-level of DNS, an interesting site is http://www.gtld-mou.org. **Another place to go is** http://nic.ddn.mil/DNS.

To understand how name servers work, imagine a tree structure that corresponds to the naming hierarchy. Figure 12.1 illustrates the tree.

At the root of the tree is a name server that recognizes the top-level domains and knows the name servers for each domain just below the root. This name server is *authoritative* for the root. When a client requests a name resolution, the root server chooses the correct server for that name. At the next level, a set of name servers provide answers for each top-level domain. So, one name server is authoritative (responsible) for the com domain, another for the edu domain, and so forth. A server at this level knows which name servers can resolve each of the subdomains under its domain. At the third level down, name servers provide translation for subdomains. For example, the name server that is authoritative for the com domain knows the name server that is authoritative for the novell.com domain. All the possible domains are not listed in Table 12.1, just some examples to illustrate the concept. As Table 12.1 shows, a country code exists for each country in the top-level domains. Each country then has its own structure below that. For example, in the uk domain (United Kingdom), you will find the co.uk domain for all commercial domains and the ac.uk domain for academic institutions. The United States has a code for every state below the us domain.

FIGURE 12.1

Name server hierarchy

Name server for the root

Root (unnamed) — Knows the name servers for each domain below (see NS records)

Top-level domains

com — Name server for com domain — Knows name servers for all subdomains

mil — Name server for mil domain — Knows name servers for all subdomains

uk — Name server for uk domain — Knows name servers for all subdomains

Second-level domains

novell — Name server for novell.com

ddn — Name server for ddn.mil domain — Knows name servers for all subdomains

co — Commercial domain for the UK

nic — Name server for nic.ddn.mil domain

Company names

nic.ddn.mil   The network information center

NOTE

It is important to understand that this tree in no way represents a physical network structure. All of these name servers may be located at any location within the physical Internet. It is a purely organizational and administrative schema.

A *zone of authority* is the portion of the name space for which a name server is responsible. A zone encompasses at least one domain. This topmost domain is referred to as the zone's *root domain*. The name server is said to be authoritative for that zone.

In reality, the relationship between the hierarchy and the tree of name servers is not as simple as in the preceding model. For example, instead of just one root server, as shown in Figure 12.1, 13 root servers currently exist. Also, a physical name server can contain all the information for large parts of the naming hierarchy. Information from multiple subdomains can be collected onto one name server, if desired. This name server then needs to know how to contact the root name servers, so that it can resolve names outside of its own zone, if required.

 You can find a list of the current root servers at
`ftp://nic.mil/netinfo/root-servers.txt.`

The top-level domains permit two completely different approaches to naming: either organizational or geographical. For example, a company can choose to be registered as an organization in the commercial domain, which leads to a name such as `novell.com`. Or, it can choose to be positioned in the geographical domain, which leads to a name such as `novell.ut.us`. Most companies choose the organizational approach, primarily because such names are much easier for users to guess. Another reason is that the geographical name is usually longer than the organizational name. For example, the `us` domain is subdivided into second-level domains, per state. Thus, a user who doesn't know the DNS name of a company has to know both the state in which the company is located and the abbreviation for that state to be able to guess that company's name.

▶ · ◀

Name Server Roles

DNS servers can be configured to perform different roles for each zone. Each *role* describes a different way the name server can store its zone data. Table 12.2 lists the roles.

DNS Name Server Roles

DNS NAME SERVER ROLE	DESCRIPTION
Primary master server	Obtains zone data from local files. Changes to a zone, such as name adding domains or hosts, are done at the primary master name server level. Per definition, only one primary name server exists per zone, although, in practice, multiple primary master name servers can be run for a zone and be synchronized manually. A primary master name server is said to be authoritative for its zone.
Secondary name server	Receives the data for its zones from another name server, called its *master name server*. The process by which this information is retrieved is referred to as a *zone transfer*. A secondary server queries the master for its zone in regular intervals, to receive new data. The interval can be configured by the administrator. The data can be stored locally if a backup file is configured. The master listed can be a primary or a secondary name server. When a secondary name server starts up, it contacts its master name server and initiates a zone transfer. A secondary name server is said to be authoritative for its zone.
Master name servers	When you define a zone on a name server as a secondary zone, you have to specify another name server from which to obtain the zone information. This source of zone information for a secondary name server is referred to as master name server. The master can either be a primary or a secondary name server for the requested zone.
Caching-only servers	All name servers cache queries that they have resolved. But, caching-only servers are not authoritative for any zone (meaning they have no zone data stored locally) and only have information that they have cached while resolving queries. A caching-only server might be used when dealing with a slow link between sites. When you boot this server, it will not do a complete zone transfer. It resolves names only as needed, and slowly build its DNS information table.

NOTE

The terms in Table 12.2 are not used consistently. In some documentation, a primary name server is called a "master" and a secondary name server is called a "slave." RFCs 1996 and 2136 contain definitions for these terms. When you read documentation, verify what terminology the author uses.

Secondary name servers are important for the reasons listed next. You can find information on this in RFC 2182, "Selection and Operation of Secondary DNS Servers (Best Current Practice Track)."

- Provide redundancy of the zone data.

- Provide faster DNS access for remote locations — if your users are in different locations, and you place a secondary server at each location, names will be resolved locally rather than across the WAN link.

- Reduce the load on the primary name server, by distributing name resolutions over multiple name servers.

NOTE

Information for each zone is stored in separate files. The primary or secondary designation is defined at the zone level. Therefore, a name server can be primary for one zone and secondary for another zone.

► . . . . ◄

DNS Records and Names

DNS data is stored in *resource records (RRs)*. Each name stored in DNS is assigned a *type* that specifies whether it is the address of a host, a mailbox, a user, and so on. When a client asks DNS to resolve a name, it must specify the type of resource record (RR) desired. A given name can map to more than one item in DNS. When the client asks for a name and a specific type of object, DNS returns objects only of that type.

The syntax of a name does not determine what type of object it names or the class of the protocol suite. Also, the number of *labels* (names) does not determine whether a name is a domain name or a hostname. For example, in the name edu.novell.com, edu can refer to either a third-level domain name within the novell domain or a host in the novell domain.

Hostnames are often referred to by their *Fully Qualified Domain Name (FQDN)*. An example is a host called ntserver within the domain universe.com and the subdomain dev (for *development*). Its FQDN would be ntserver dev. universe.com. The FQDN ends with a period. If a name does not end with a period, it is assumed that it has to be completed. Building the FQDN is a function of the resolver software. Name servers always use

FQDNs for a lookup. How a name is completed depends on the DNS resolver software being used.

Every node has a *label* (name) of up to 63 characters. The root of the tree is a special node with a null label. Uppercase and lowercase characters are considered the same.

Table 12.3 lists some common resource records. They are specified in RFC 1035. New types may be added over time. For example, RFC 1183 contains new RR definitions.

TABLE 12.3

DNS Resource Record Types

TYPE	MEANING	VALUE	CONTENT
A	Host address	1	Defines a 32-bit IP address. If a host has multiple IP addresses, there will be multiple A type records.
AAAA	Host address IPv6	28	New record type defined in RFC 1886 to store a 128-bit IPv6 address.
CNAME	Canonical name	5	A canonical domain name, used to provide an easy-to-remember *alias* for another host. A common use of this type of record is for FTP sites. A user can refer to an FTP site with a name such as `ftp.novell.com`. The CNAME record associates this with a certain host. The archive can be moved to another host, and only the CNAME record has to be changed to refer the user to the correct host.
			Note that a CNAME record can't coexist with another record of the same name. For example, if you have a CNAME of `maria.universe.com`, you can't have another record, such as A or MX, with the same name.
HINFO	CPU and OS	13	Name of CPU and operating system. Note that not all sites provide HINFO records for all of their systems, and the information provided may not be up to date. Many companies do not use the HINFO record, for security reasons.

Continued

T A B L E   12.3

DNS Resource Record Types (continued)

TYPE	MEANING	VALUE	CONTENT
MINFO	Mailbox information	14	Information about a mailbox or a mail list.
MX	Mail exchanger	15	The 16-bit preference and name of the host that acts as mail exchanger for the domain. Refer to the description of this record later in this section. Other mail type records are in the definition. Some of them are obsolete, and some are in an experimental state. Refer to RFC 1035 for the list.
NS	Name server	2	Used to specify the name of the authoritative server for the domain specified. Make sure this record never points to a CNAME record. Some implementations will ignore this record, whereas others might go into infinite loops trying to resolve the address of the name server.
PTR	Pointer	12	Used to point to other areas of the name space. It is used for inverse queries of the `in-addr.arpa` domain. To resolve an IP address to a hostname, a PTR record is required. The next bulleted list in this section includes more information on inverse queries.
SOA	Start of authority	6	Used to define zone management parameters. It denotes the beginning of the zone of authority. The different fields of this record are described in more detail in Table 12.4.
TXT	Arbitrary text	16	Contains an uninterpreted string of ASCII text. TXT records have no specific definition. You can put anything in them. Some use this record type for a generic description of the host, whereas others put specific information in it, such as location, primary user, or maybe even a phone number.
WKS	Well-known service	11	Used to supply additional information about hosts by providing information about well-known services supported by a protocol on a particular host. A WKS record will exist per protocol for a certain host. For example, UDP has a corresponding WKS record, listing all the ports that the server is listening on. If the host uses TCP too, another WKS record lists all the TCP ports for that host. If the server has multiple IP addresses, a WKS record will exist per address and protocol. RFC 1123 deprecates the use of WKS records.

The SOA record contains several important configuration parameters for the zone. Table 12.4 lists the different fields.

TABLE 12.4

The Fields of the SOA Record

FIELD NAME	DESCRIPTION
MName	Specifies the name of the primary server for the zone identified by the SOA.
RName	Specifies the mailbox address of the person responsible for the zone.
Serial	Specifies the serial number for the database. It has to be incremented each time the database changes. It is used by secondary servers to determine whether a zone transfer is necessary. This is an area to look at if zone transfers do not happen.
Refresh	Determines how often (in seconds) a secondary server polls the master server to check whether the serial number for the zone has increased. If the serial number has increased, the secondary server requests a new copy of the data for the zone.
Retry	Defines the time, in seconds, that should elapse before a failed refresh is retried.
Expire	Specifies the time, in seconds, after which the zone is no longer authoritative. If that time expires and the master cannot be reached, the server stops responding to queries. Make sure this interval is higher than the refresh interval. Otherwise, the name server will expire its data before it has a chance to get a new copy.
Minimum TTL	Specifies the minimum Time to Live (TTL) value that should be exported with any RRs from this zone. The TTL defines how long the resolver keeps the record in its cache.

When you create a zone on your name server, you can configure all of these fields. RFC 1912 contains a lot of tips of how to configure the timers. Later in this chapter, we will analyze trace files, and you will find all those entries in the details of the DNS answer section (part of the DNS header).

Most DNS records are of type A, consisting of the name of a host and its IP address. Another useful record is the *MX record*, which is assigned to names used for e-mail exchangers. It can be used to specify multiple hosts that are each capable of accepting mail. The user sends mail specifying an e-mail address in the form of, for example, user@novell.com. The mail system uses DNS to resolve the domain part of the address (novell.com) with query type MX. DNS returns a set of RRs, each of which contains a host's domain name and a preference field. The mail system steps through the set, starting with the highest preference field (a low number is a high preference). For each MX record, the mailer extracts the domain name and uses a type A query to resolve that name to an IP address. Based on this information, it tries to contact that host and deliver the mail. If the host is not available, the mailer will try to contact the host with the next-highest preference level in its list of MX records.

Name Resolution Query Types

A resolver can make the following three types of queries to a DNS server:

▶ **Recursive queries:** Means that the resolver requires complete translation. If the name server cannot locally resolve the name, it contacts another name server that can resolve the name and returns the answer to the client. Recursive operation therefore reduces the load on the client and the network. It allows for larger and fewer centrally located caches, which increases the hit ratio.

▶ **Iterative queries:** The queried name server gives the best answer it currently has back to the resolver (also called *nonrecursive queries*). This answer can be either the resolved name or a referral to another name server that may be able to answer the client's original request. The resolver then has to pursue the request with the name server it was referred to. This type of query is often used when a name server resolves a name with another name server to answer a recursive client query.

▶ **Inverse queries:** The client has an IP address and wants to resolve it to a hostname (also called *pointer queries*). No correlation exists between hostnames and IP addresses in the DNS name space. Therefore, only a thorough search of all domains would guarantee a correct answer. To prevent such an exhaustive search, a special domain called `in-addr.arpa` was created. Nodes in the `in-addr.arpa` domain are named after the numbers in the dotted-decimal representation of IP addresses. IP addresses get more specific from left to right (the rightmost part being the host ID). Conversely, domain names get more specific from right to left (the leftmost part being the name of the host or the lowest domain in the hierarchy).

For this reason, the order of the IP address octets (bytes) must be reversed when building the `in-addr.arpa` domain.

Pointer queries are built as follows:

The resolver wants to find the hostname for the IP address of `aa.bb.cc.dd`. To form a pointer query, it rearranges the order of the bytes in the IP address and forms a query string of `dd.cc.bb.aa.in-addr.arpa`. If the local name server queried is not authoritative for either `arpa` or `in-addr.arpa`, it contacts other name servers to complete the resolution.

The RR type PTR (pointer) is used for this type of name resolution. PTR records are added to the DNS database, to associate IP addresses and the corresponding hostname. To find the hostname for 197.240.38.32, the client queries the name server for a PTR record of `32.38.240.197.in-addr.arpa`. This PTR record, if found, contains the hostname. This information is sent back to the client.

NOTE

If you do a `PING -A <IP Address>`**, it will return the hostname for the given IP address by doing an inverse query.**

This explanation of how pointer queries are built is given simply to describe the concept. In reality, you don't have to worry about how a pointer query is built. It is a function of the resolver and is done for you automatically.

Caching and TTL

A resolver caches all results of name resolution queries. For example, if a name server is processing a recursive query on behalf of a client, it may have to send out multiple iterative requests to other name servers to find the answer. The name server caches all the information it receives during this process for a time specified in the returned data. This amount of time is referred to as *Time to Live (TTL)*. The name server administrator of the zone that contains the data decides and configures the TTL value for the zone (refer to Table 12.4, which lists the fields of the SOA record). The name server administrator can also specify TTLs for individual RRs, which then override the zone's default TTL. Smaller TTL values ensure that data about the domain is more consistent across the network, if this data changes often. However, this also increases the load on the name server, because it has to reverify the consistency of the data more often.

After data is cached by a DNS server, the server starts decreasing the TTL from its original value, so that it knows when to flush that data from its cache. If a query comes in that can be answered from this cache, the TTL that is returned is the current amount of time left before the data is flushed from the DNS server cache. Client resolvers also have data caches and honor the TTL value so that they know when to expire the data.

 Usually, DNS replies containing errors are also cached. If a client queries for a host and DNS replies with a name error (for example, the record does not exist), this negative answer will be cached. This process, called *negative caching*, is specified in RFC 2308, which is an update to RFC 1034.

NOTE

Whether your name server caches negative answers or not depends on the product you are using. All versions of BIND 4.9 and higher and all versions of BIND 8 implement negative caching. However, the TTL for negative caching is not configurable. It is hard-coded to ten minutes (600 seconds). Negative caching is useful, because it reduces the response time for negative answers, and reduces the number of messages that have to be sent between resolvers and name servers. A large portion of DNS traffic on the Internet could be eliminated if all resolvers implemented negative caching.

► . . . . ◄

DNS Header Structure

One DNS message format exists for both queries and responses. Figure 12.2 gives an overview of the fields in a DNS message. The message has a fixed, 12-byte header, which is always present. It is followed by four variable-length fields.

FIGURE 12.2

Overview of the DNS message format

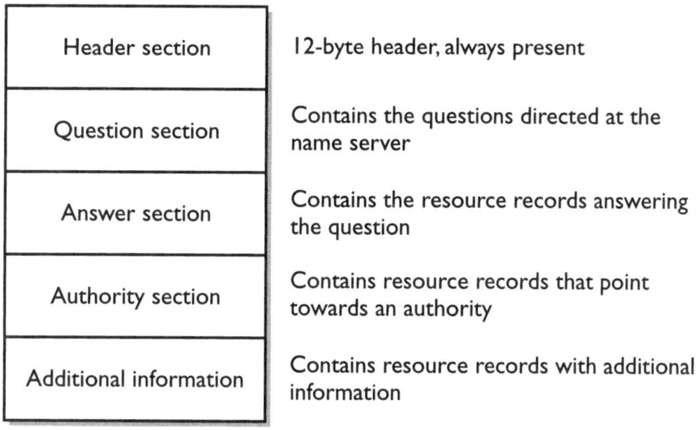

Header section	12-byte header, always present
Question section	Contains the questions directed at the name server
Answer section	Contains the resource records answering the question
Authority section	Contains resource records that point towards an authority
Additional information	Contains resource records with additional information

The header section has a fixed length of 12 bytes. All other sections are variable length.

The Header Section

Figure 12.3 shows the details of the 12-byte DNS Header, which is always present.

FIGURE 12.3

Details of the DNS Header section

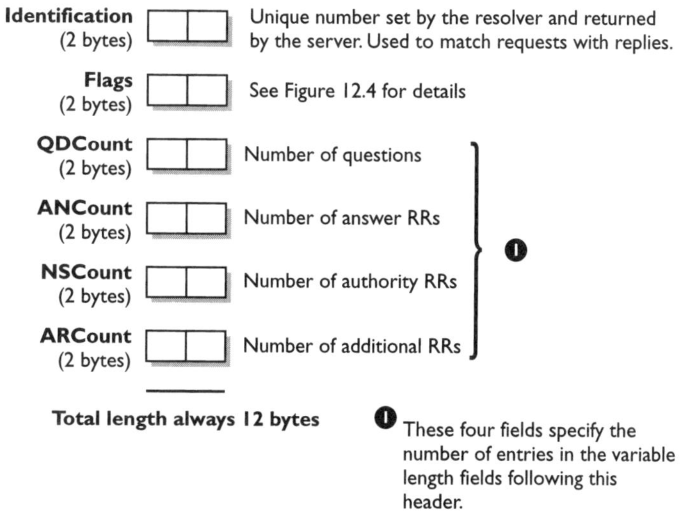

Identification (2 bytes) — Unique number set by the resolver and returned by the server. Used to match requests with replies.

Flags (2 bytes) — See Figure 12.4 for details

QDCount (2 bytes) — Number of questions

ANCount (2 bytes) — Number of answer RRs

NSCount (2 bytes) — Number of authority RRs

ARCount (2 bytes) — Number of additional RRs

Total length always 12 bytes

❶ These four fields specify the number of entries in the variable length fields following this header.

Identification (ID)

The DNS Header section's 2-byte Identification (ID) field is a unique number set by the system issuing the request and returned by the server. It is used to match requests and replies.

Flags

The 2-byte Flags field is divided into different pieces, as shown in Figure 12.4. Each part is described in Table 12.5.

FIGURE 12.4

Details of the Flags field in a DNS header

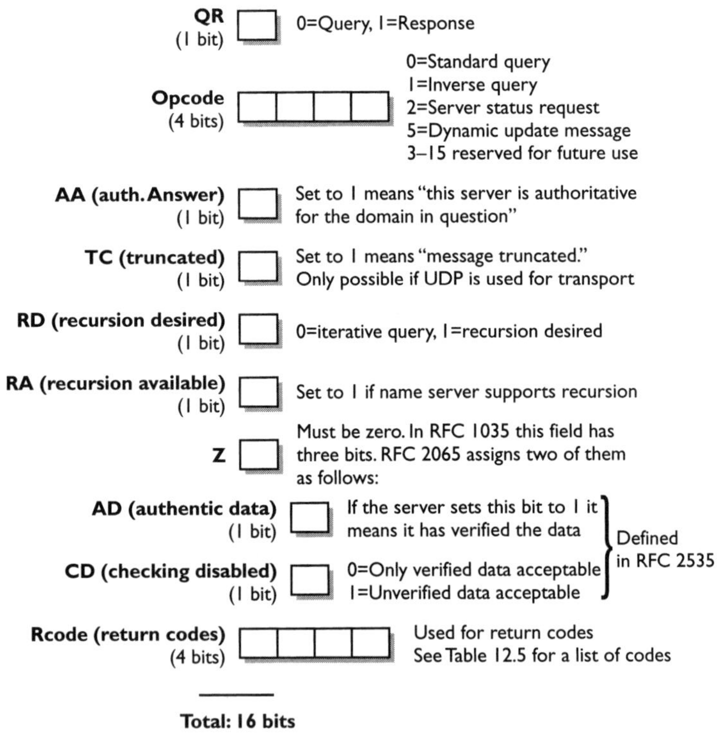

QR (1 bit) — 0=Query, 1=Response

Opcode (4 bits) —
0=Standard query
1=Inverse query
2=Server status request
5=Dynamic update message
3–15 reserved for future use

AA (auth. Answer) (1 bit) — Set to 1 means "this server is authoritative for the domain in question"

TC (truncated) (1 bit) — Set to 1 means "message truncated." Only possible if UDP is used for transport

RD (recursion desired) (1 bit) — 0=iterative query, 1=recursion desired

RA (recursion available) (1 bit) — Set to 1 if name server supports recursion

Z — Must be zero. In RFC 1035 this field has three bits. RFC 2065 assigns two of them as follows:

AD (authentic data) (1 bit) — If the server sets this bit to 1 it means it has verified the data

CD (checking disabled) (1 bit) — 0=Only verified data acceptable 1=Unverified data acceptable

Defined in RFC 2535

Rcode (return codes) (4 bits) — Used for return codes See Table 12.5 for a list of codes

Total: 16 bits

T A B L E 12.5

Description of the Flags Field

BIT POSITION	DESCRIPTION
QR, 1 bit	0 — Indicates a query 1 — Indicates a reply
Opcode, 4 bits	0 — Standard query 1 — Inverse query 2 — Server status request 5 — Dynamic DNS update (see RFC 2136) Values 3 through 15 are reserved for future use.
AA (Authoritative Answer), 1 bit	Authoritative Answer — If set to 1, the server is authoritative for the domain in the Question section.
TC (Truncated), 1 bit	Truncated — This field is set if UDP is used and the reply exceeds 512 bytes. The message is truncated and only the first 512 bytes are sent. The resolver then rerequests the data, using TCP for transport.
RD (Recursion Desired), 1 bit	If set to 1 it means *recursion desired*. This bit can be set in a query and will be returned in the reply. If this bit is set, the server resolves the name on behalf of the client. If the bit is not set and the name server does not have an authoritative answer, it returns a list of other name servers to contact for the answer. This is the *iterative query*. (For an explanation of query types, see the earlier section "Name Resolution Query Types.")
RA (Recursion Available), 1 bit	If set to 1 it means *recursion available*. The server sets this bit to 1 in its reply if it supports recursion. Most servers support recursion.
zero, 3 bits	According to RFC 1035, this field has 3 bits and is a reserved field that is always set to 0. RFC 2065 assigns 2 bits for security features. The bits are assigned as follows: bit 0 — Must be zero bit 1 — AD bit (set to 1 if data has been verified by server) bit 2 — CD bit (set to 1 if unverified data is acceptable)

Continued

TABLE 12.5

*Description of the Flags
Field (continued)*

BIT POSITION	DESCRIPTION
Rcode, 4 bits	Used for return codes. Possible values are the following: 0 — No error 1 — Format error; the server can't interpret the query 2 — Server failure 3 — Name error; returned only from an authoritative name server, and means that the domain name specified in the query doesn't exist 4 — Not implemented; the server doesn't support the requested query type 5 — Refused; issued if, for example, a policy exists that doesn't allow the server to answer a request for a certain resolver Values 6 to 10 are used for DDNS update messages, as follows: 6 — Some name exists that should not exist 7 — Some RRset exists that should not exist 8 — Some RR set that should exist does not exist 9 — This server is not authoritative for the zone mentioned 10 — A name used in the Prerequisite or Update section is not within the zone in the Zone section Values 11 through 15 are reserved for future use.

The next four 2-byte fields in the Header section are Number of Questions, Number of Answer RRs, Number of Authority RRs, and Number of Additional RRs. These fields specify the number of entries in the four variable-length fields of the message. In a query, the Number of Questions field is usually set to 1, and the other three counts are zero. For a reply, the Number of Answers field is usually at least 1, and the remaining two counts can be zero or nonzero.

The Question Section

The format of the Question section is shown in Figure 12.5. Usually, just one question exists per DNS query.

▶ • ◀

FIGURE 12.5

Format of the Question section

Query name [□ □] • • • [0] Variable length depending on the number of questions and the length of the names being queried

Query type (2 bytes) [□ □] Specifies the type of RR See Table 12.3 for a list of values on RFC 1035

Query class (2 bytes) [□ | 1] Specifies the protocol family used Usually set to 1 for Internet class

The Query Name field is the name being looked up. It is a variable-length field. Usually, one name is in this field. The Number of Questions field in the Header section specifies how many questions are in the message. The Query Name field contains a sequence of one or more labels, each beginning with an 8-bit count that specifies the number of bytes that follow. The name is terminated with a byte of zero, which is a label with a length of zero. This is the null label that represents the root. Each count byte must be in the range of 0 to 63, because labels are limited to 63 bytes. The total length of a name is limited to 255 bytes. Therefore, this field can be of any length up to the maximum permitted, and can end on a boundary other than 32-bit. No padding is used. Figure 12.6 illustrates how the domain name `ftp.novell.com` would be stored.

▶ • ◀

FIGURE 12.6

Representation of a domain name in the Question section

This is how the domain name ftp.novell.com would be stored in the "query name" field:

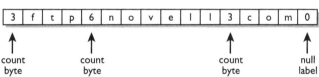

| 3 | f | t | p | 6 | n | o | v | e | l | l | 3 | c | o | m | 0 |

↑ count byte   ↑ count byte   ↑ count byte   ↑ null label

Count bytes are in the range of 0–63
Maximum length of name: 255 bytes

In the 2-byte Query Type field (shown in Figure 12.5), the type of RR is specified. Remember that the server returns records only of the requested type. The numbers for the values that you find here are the same as listed earlier in Table 12.3. The most common Query Type is an A type (value 1), which asks for an IP address for a given hostname. A PTR record (value 12) requests a hostname for a given IP address. Other query types exist, such as the AXFR record with a value of 252, which is a request for a zone transfer. Refer to RFC 1035 for the complete list. RFC 1995 mentions the IXFR query, with a Query Type value of 251 for incremental zone transfers.

The 2-byte Query Class field specifies the class. Normally, you find the value 1 here, which is the value for the Internet class. Again, RFC 1035 lists the classes. Value 3 is the Chaos class (this class has more-historic significance) and value 4 is the Hesiod class. Hesiod, besides being one of the earliest Greek poets, is an information service that was built upon BIND and is used for furnishing information about users, groups, file systems, and so forth in the MIT (Massachusetts Institute of Technology) world.

The Answer, Authority, and Additional Information Sections

The final three sections in the DNS message share a common format. They contain resource record information. Figure 12.7 shows the format of these sections. The following are the fields in these sections:

FIGURE 12.7

Format of the DNS resource record fields

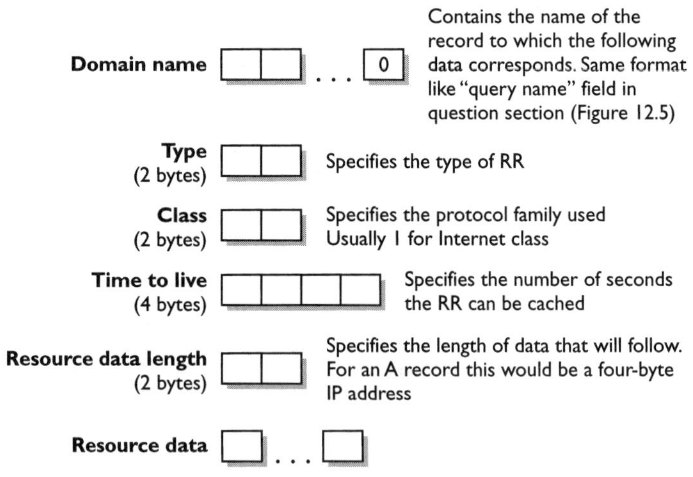

Domain name — Contains the name of the record to which the following data corresponds. Same format like "query name" field in question section (Figure 12.5)

Type (2 bytes) — Specifies the type of RR

Class (2 bytes) — Specifies the protocol family used Usually 1 for Internet class

Time to live (4 bytes) — Specifies the number of seconds the RR can be cached

Resource data length (2 bytes) — Specifies the length of data that will follow. For an A record this would be a four-byte IP address

Resource data

▸ **Domain Name:** Contains the name to which the following resource data corresponds (variable length). It has the same format as the Query Name field in the Question section, discussed earlier (refer to Figure 12.5).

▶ **Type:** Specifies one of the RR type codes (2 bytes). These codes are the same as the query type values in Table 12.3.

▶ **Class:** Contains the value for the class, usually 1, for Internet (2 bytes).

▶ **Time to Live:** The number of seconds that the RR can be cached by the resolver (4 bytes).

▶ **Resource Data Length:** Specifies the amount of resource data that will follow in the data section (2 bytes).

▶ **Resource Data:** Contains the actual resource data (variable length). The format of the data depends on the type. For example, for a type A record (value 1), the resource data is a 32-bit IP address.

Dynamic DNS (DDNS)

DNS servers were originally designed to query a static database. Updates have to be entered by editing zone master files. This works fine, as long as you don't have too many changes. Because changes are very frequent in today's networks, a lot of work has been done to make DNS dynamic. RFC 2136 explains how to add, update, or delete RRs to DNS automatically. RFC 2137 discusses security issues regarding DDNS. Many vendors are already implementing DDNS.

The overall format of a DDNS update message is shown in Figure 12.8.

FIGURE 12.8

Format of a DDNS update message

Header 12 bytes Opcode 5	Header as defined in RFC 1035 Update uses only one of the bits in the flag field Opcode 5 means "this is an update message"
Zone	Specifies the zone to be updated
Prerequisite	RRs which must (or must not) preexist
Update	RRs to be added or deleted
Additional data	

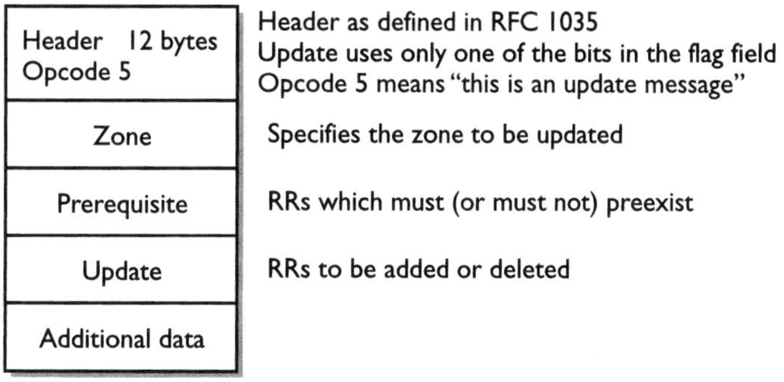

In the Flags field of the DNS Header section, the Opcode bit will be set to 5, which means *this is an update message*. DDNS has new return codes (refer to Table 12.5). The four sections for the record count (Question, Answer, Authority, and Additional) are present in the update message, but they have a different meaning. The header of an update message is shown in Figure 12.9. (Compare this header to the one shown in Figure 12.3.)

▶ . . . . ◀

FIGURE 12.9	**Identification** (2 bytes) ▢▢ Same as other messages
Header structure of a Dynamic DNS update message	**Flags** (2 bytes) ▢▢ Opcode bit set to 5 / New return codes, see Table 12.5
	ZOCOUNT (2 bytes) ▢▢ Number of RRs in the zone section
	PRCOUNT (2 bytes) ▢▢ Number of RRs in the prerequisite section
	UPCOUNT (2 bytes) ▢▢ Number of RRs in the update section
	ADCOUNT (2 bytes) ▢▢ Number of RRs in the additional data section

With the current release of the protocol, you cannot create or delete a zone with an update. Future versions will probably implement this.

IMPORTANT

Notice that this protocol makes your DNS servers more vulnerable. Anyone who can reach an authoritative DNS server can alter the contents of the zone files on that server. The security mechanisms discussed in RFC 2137 should be used.

▶ . . . . ◀

Analyzing a DNS Session

This section shows trace files for different DNS communications, such as DNS request, DNS reply, and zone transfer. They provide a picture of how communication looks if it works fine.

TCP or UDP

As previously mentioned, DNS uses both TCP and UDP. The well-known port number is port 53 for both protocols. Analyzing DNS communication in trace files will reveal that UDP is used most of the time. Remember that TCP is much more effective in transporting large amounts of data, because of its streaming capability. So, to perform a zone transfer, which usually includes quite a lot of data, TCP is used. Another case where TCP is used is when a client issues a query, and the response comes back with the TC bit set (Truncated). This means that the response was bigger than 512 bytes. In this case, the server returns only the 512 bytes. The client usually re-requests the data, using TCP.

A DNS Query

Figure 12.10 shows two frames pertaining to a DNS query. Frame 1 is the client's request for the address marina.sunny.ch. Frame 2 is the server's reply. Note that the ID is 3 in both frames, indicating that this reply is the answer to frame 1.

FIGURE 12.10

A DNS query in a trace file

Figure 12.10 shows the DNS Header section of frame 1 in detail. The Identification field is set to 3, as previously mentioned. It is used to match requests with replies.

You can use this field for filtering in your analyzer, if you want to trace a specific DNS communication.

The Flags field, which is 2 bytes, is decoded in two steps by Sniffer Pro. The first byte is set to 01. Sniffer Pro decodes the fields as follows: The first bit is the QR bit from Table 12.5. It is 0 for a query and 1 for a reply. The next field, called *Query* by Sniffer Pro, is the 4-bit Opcode field. Zero implies a standard query, whereas 1 would be an inverse query, and 2 would be a server status request. The next field is omitted in the decode. It is the AA bit that would be filled out in the reply from the name server. It states whether or not the answer is authoritative. Thus, it wouldn't make sense in the client's request. The next bit is the TC bit, which would be set to 1 if the server's answer was too long and had to be truncated. The last bit of byte 1 is the Recursion Desired bit (RD bit), which tells the server that the client expects recursion. This means that if the server does not have the answer to the request it will go out and resolve the name on behalf of the client. Later in this chapter we will discuss a trace that shows how recursion works.

The second byte of the Flags field is decoded as follows: The RA (Recursion Available) bit is not set. Again, this does not make sense in a client's request. A name server will fill that field if it supports recursion. The next 3 bits are the bits that were reserved and had to be 0. Two of them are now used for data-verification features (RFC 2065). Sniffer decodes the second bit as "Non Verified data NOT acceptable." You'll see in the next frame that the server answers with unverified data, and the client still accepts it. This behavior is explained in RFC 2065 and is necessary during the transition period when not all clients and name servers support the new definitions. The last 4 bits of the Flags field are used for return codes. A client request has no return code.

Next is the Question Count field, which is set to 1. All other counts are set to 0, which is normal for a query. They will be filled out by the name server in its reply. The Question section contains the name to be resolved, in this case `marina.sunny.ch`. Sniffer Pro calls the Question section *ZONE Section*. As discussed earlier, the type of record requested has to be stated (in this case, type A). The name server will only return objects of that type. The class is listed, too.

Figure 12.11 shows the details of the DNS header in the server's reply (frame 2 from Figure 12.10).

FIGURE 12.11

*Details of the DNS header
in frame 2*

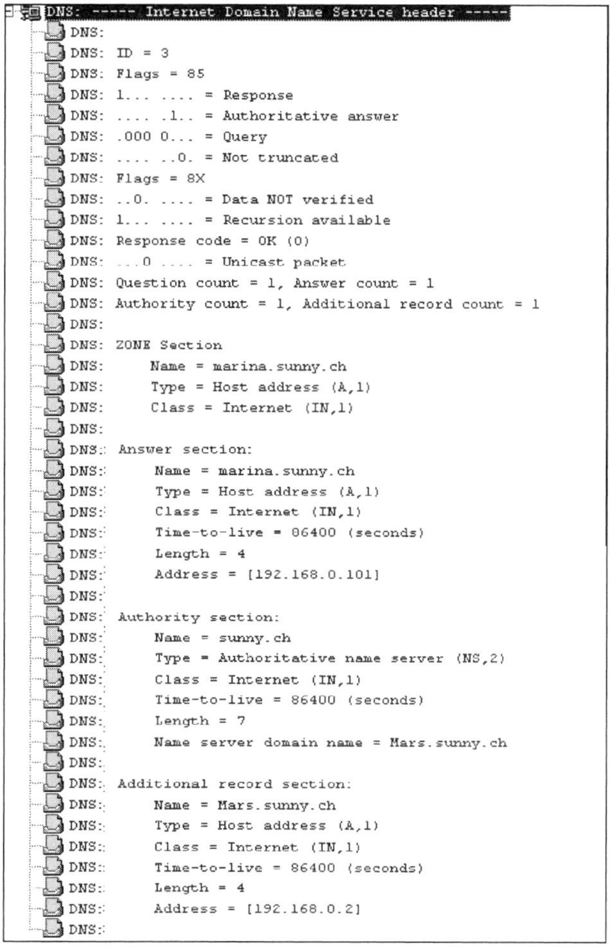

```
DNS: ----- Internet Domain Name Service header -----
DNS:
DNS: ID = 3
DNS: Flags = 85
DNS: 1... .... = Response
DNS: .... .1.. = Authoritative answer
DNS: .000 0... = Query
DNS: .... ..0. = Not truncated
DNS: Flags = 8X
DNS: ..0. .... = Data NOT verified
DNS: 1... .... = Recursion available
DNS: Response code = OK (0)
DNS: ...0 .... = Unicast packet
DNS: Question count = 1, Answer count = 1
DNS: Authority count = 1, Additional record count = 1
DNS:
DNS: ZONE Section
DNS:     Name = marina.sunny.ch
DNS:     Type = Host address (A,1)
DNS:     Class = Internet (IN,1)
DNS:
DNS: Answer section:
DNS:     Name = marina.sunny.ch
DNS:     Type = Host address (A,1)
DNS:     Class = Internet (IN,1)
DNS:     Time-to-live = 86400 (seconds)
DNS:     Length = 4
DNS:     Address = [192.168.0.101]
DNS:
DNS: Authority section:
DNS:     Name = sunny.ch
DNS:     Type = Authoritative name server (NS,2)
DNS:     Class = Internet (IN,1)
DNS:     Time-to-live = 86400 (seconds)
DNS:     Length = 7
DNS:     Name server domain name = Mars.sunny.ch
DNS:
DNS: Additional record section:
DNS:     Name = Mars.sunny.ch
DNS:     Type = Host address (A,1)
DNS:     Class = Internet (IN,1)
DNS:     Time-to-live = 86400 (seconds)
DNS:     Length = 4
DNS:     Address = [192.168.0.2]
DNS:
```

As the summary line in Figure 12.10 shows, the ID is set to 3, which identifies this frame as the answer to the request in frame 1. The first Flags byte is 85. The server is giving an authoritative answer, which means it is authoritative for the domain requested (sunny.ch). The second byte shows that the data is not verified and the server supports recursion. But, in this case, recursion is not necessary. The response code is OK. The next line decodes zero as a *unicast packet*. This looks like the Network Associates decode for the CD bit (refer to Figure 12.4). The Counts fields show that the server returns three answer records: an Answer record, an Authority record, and an Additional record. In the Question section, the question from the request is stated. Then, you see the three Answer sections. Note that each record has a TTL associated with it, which is the time that the record can be cached by the resolver. The server returns not only the required record, but also the NS record for the domain in question, and the A record for the name server. All of these entries will be cached at the resolver, which optimizes lookup performance and reduces traffic on the network.

NOTE **Most DNS clients expect the address from which a reply is received to be the same address as that to which the query was sent. This is true for servers acting as clients for the purposes of recursive query resolution, as well as simple resolver clients. Some multihomed hosts running DNS servers generate a reply using a source address that is not the same as the destination address from the client's request packet. The client will discard such an answer, because it seems to be an unsolicited response (RFC 2181, "Clarifications to the DNS Specifications").**

A Recursive Query

If the client requests recursion and the server does not have information about the record requested, the server will query other name servers for the answer and return the answer to the client. Figure 12.12 shows a trace file with two recursive queries.

This is the same client making two requests to its name server. The client has an IP address of 192.168.0.150 and queries its name server with the IP address of 192.168.0.1 in frames 3 and 7. In these two frames, the Recursion Desired bit is set, as shown in the detail window of frame 3. The name server does not know the object and queries the name server mars.moon.universe.com in frames 4 and 8. In these two frames, no recursion is desired; it is an iterative query. Mars replies to the first name server with a return code of 0, meaning that it found the entry, and returns the answer (frames 5 and 9). The first name server passes the reply to the client in frames 6 and 10. Note that when the initial name server sends the request to the mars name server, it uses a new ID. Mars replies with that ID, and then the initial name server, when it forwards the reply to the client, uses the initial client ID.

FIGURE 12.12

A recursive query in a trace file

Another interesting point in this trace is the query in frame 7. The query for alias.moon.universe.com is the request for a CNAME record that points to lilith.moon.universe.com. In frames 5 and 6, the name server returns the entries, as discussed in regard to Figure 12.11. That reply frame contains the A record requested, together with the NS record and the A record for the name server. Figure 12.13 shows the DNS Answer section in frame 9.

▶ . . . . ◀

F I G U R E   12.13

The DNS Answer section for a CNAME record

```
DNS: Answer section 1:
DNS:     Name = alias.moon.universe.com
DNS:     Type = Canonical name for alias (CNAME,5)
DNS:     Class = Internet (IN,1)
DNS:     Time-to-live = 86400 (seconds)
DNS:     Length = 26
DNS:     Canonical name = lilith.moon.universe.com
DNS: Answer section 2:
DNS:     Name = lilith.moon.universe.com
DNS:     Type = Host address (A,1)
DNS:     Class = Internet (IN,1)
DNS:     Time-to-live = 86400 (seconds)
DNS:     Length = 4
DNS:     Address = [192.168.0.11]
DNS:
DNS: Authority section:
DNS:     Name = moon.universe.com
DNS:     Type = Authoritative name server (NS,2)
DNS:     Class = Internet (IN,1)
DNS:     Time-to-live = 86400 (seconds)
DNS:     Length = 7
DNS:     Name server domain name = mars.moon.universe.com
DNS:
DNS: Additional record section:
DNS:     Name = mars.moon.universe.com
DNS:     Type = Host address (A,1)
DNS:     Class = Internet (IN,1)
DNS:     Time-to-live = 86400 (seconds)
```

The first Answer section contains the name that was requested. In its request, the client specifies the hostname as `alias.moon.universe.com` and asks for an A record. The name server returns the CNAME record with reference to the canonical name `lilith.moon.universe.com`. The second Answer section contains the A record for this host. The Authority and Additional Record sections are the same as in any reply. They contain the NS record and the A record for the name server. Again, remember that all of these entries are cached at the first name server and at the client. A next lookup will be answered out of cache, if the Time to Live has not expired by that time.

An Inverse Query

Figure 12.14 is a trace of an inverse query. The client wants to resolve the IP address of 192.168.0.1 to a hostname. The figure shows the Question and Answer sections in the DNS header. The Question section shows that a record of type PTR is requested. The Answer section contains the hostname for that IP address. Again, the Answer section is followed by the Authority section containing the information about the SOA record.

FIGURE 12.14

An inverse query in
a trace file

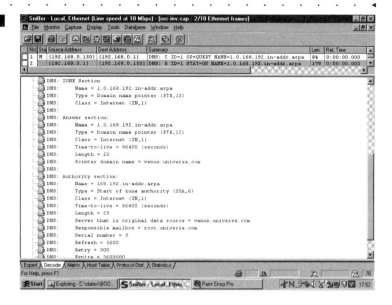

FIGURE 12.14

An inverse query in
a trace file

A Zone Transfer

A secondary name server receives its zone data by zone transfer from its master server. It contacts the master server and checks the serial number for the zone. If it has incremented since the last zone transfer, it will request the data from the master. Figure 12.15 shows a zone transfer traced in my lab, using LANalyzer for Windows. This is the best trace I could make for a zone transfer, which is why I used LANalyzer for Windows for this screen shot.

Frames 6 to 8 show the TCP handshake between the two name servers. Remember that for zone transfers, TCP is used for transport. In the detail window, you can see that the Destination Port is 53 (decoded as DOMAIN; the hex part at the bottom of the figure shows the port number highlighted). Unfortunately, the decode does not go any further, because I have not managed to find a proper decode of a zone transfer. Send me your trace file, if you have one. The secondary name server does a query for `moon.universe.com` of record type AXFR. Figure 12.16 shows the DNS server's log file for the same transfer.

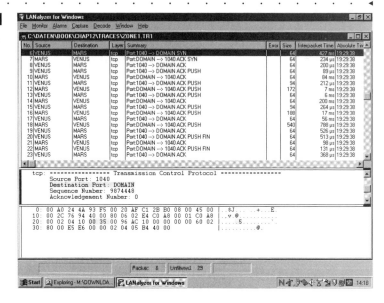

F I G U R E   12.15

A zone transfer traced with
LANalyzer for Windows

F I G U R E   12.16

The DNS server's log file for
the zone transfer

The log file shows that the name server receives a query for the zone moon.universe.com. You can see how the serial number is checked, followed by the request for the AXFR record and the beginning and successful completion of the zone transfer.

Using Multiple DNS Servers

If you are using multiple DNS servers, a wide variety of configurations are possible:

- **Use a secondary DNS server just for redundancy and load-balancing reasons.** The database of the primary name server will be downloaded to the secondary name server with a zone transfer.

- **Use multiple name servers for subdomains within your domain structure.** Each name server would service a separate subdomain. In this case, you have an NS record for each subdomain in your DNS databases. They have to point to the respective name servers servicing those subdomains. If those name servers are not in your current domain, you will also have to configure so-called *glue records*. They are A-type entries that provide the IP addresses for the name servers mentioned in the NS records.

- **Use a local DNS (which might consist of multiple local DNS servers), with this local name space linked to the Internet.** Many companies split their DNS name space. They have a DNS that is shown to the outside world, and a DNS for internal use, which is not shown outside. The configuration of such a scenario is outside the scope of this book.

Figure 12.17 shows a simple scenario for setting up multiple name servers (the main entries in the database are shown).

DNS1 needs the SOA record for the domain for which it is authoritative, an NS record that points to DNS1 for its zone, and an A record that provides the IP address for that name server. To answer queries for the subdomain `moon.universe.com`, another NS record is necessary. It points to server DNS2 in the `moon` subdomain. Because DNS2 is in the subdomain, it needs an A record, too (*glue record*).

▶ . . . . ◀

Multiple name server configuration

universe.com

Your company

Name server DNS1, IP address 192.168.0.1

Entries in the DNS database:

universe.com.	SOA	DNS1.universe.com.
universe.com.	NS	DNS1.universe.com.
DNS1.universe.com.	A	192.168.0.1
moon.universe.com.	NS	DNS2.moon.universe.com
❶ DNS2.moon.universe.com.	A	192.168.0.2

❶ This is called a "glue record"

moon.universe.com

subdomain

Name server DNS2, IP address 192.168.0.2

Entries in the DNS database:

moon.universe.com.	SOA	DNS2.moon.universe.com.
moon.universe.com.	NS	DNS2.moon.universe.com.
DNS2.moon.universe.com	A	192.168.0.2

Both name servers need to know how to contact the root name servers.

On DNS2, you need an SOA record for the domain `moon.universe.com` and the corresponding NS and A records. Usually, the entries in the zone databases are just shortcuts. For example, on DNS1, the entry for the A record would be DNS1. Then, the name server would add the default domain configured in the bootup file (which varies, depending on what DNS you are using). If you are stating FQDNs, make sure to type the trailing period so that DNS knows this is an absolute name. Otherwise, it might append the default domain again. To explain the concept, the FQDNs are used in Figure 12.17.

All name servers need to know how to find a root server. This can be accomplished in one of two ways:

▸ **Make an entry on both name servers that points to root name servers.** This is usually done in the cache file (depends on the DNS product you are using). The first time that one of the name servers is queried for a name outside of its own domain, it will contact a root name server and resolution will continue down the tree from there. The second query will then be answered out of cache, if the TTL has not expired yet.

▸ **Define a forward link on DNS2 that points to DNS1.** In this case, if a client makes a recursive query that cannot be answered from cache, DNS2 will query DNS1. If it does not receive an answer from DNS1 within a certain time, DNS2 will try to contact a root name server directly. DNS1 would then have the entries in the cache file that point to the root name servers.

Troubleshooting DNS

Now that you understand how DNS communication is *supposed* to work, you can use that understanding to troubleshoot. Analyze your trace files and look for irregularities. Is the packet sequence the way that it should be? Can you see the queries go out? Do unanswered requests exist? Where does a query get stuck?

If requests are not answered by a DNS server, check the following:

▸ Is the DNS server running?

▸ Is the route to the DNS server okay?

▸ Does a firewall exist between the client and the DNS server? If yes, check the firewall filters.

▸ Is the resolver configured properly? Does it know its DNS server?

If the name server replies but can't find the record (it will answer with a return code; refer to Table 12.5), ask the following questions:

▸ Is the client mistyping the hostname or looking for a host that does not exist?

▸ Is the record in the database?

▸ Is the name server properly configured?

▸ Is the client doing a recursive query and the name server does not know who to contact?

▸ Are the zones properly configured?

▸ Is the information in the primary name server's database consistent with the secondary name server's database? When was the last zone transfer and was it successful?

General questions to ask include the following:

▸ Do you have an internal or an external DNS problem? Is the name that cannot be resolved part of your local domain or part of the Internet domain?

▸ Does your DNS server resolve queries to the outside world? If not, then check the configuration of forwarding links to root servers. Talk to your ISP (Internet service provider) to find out whether its configuration is working properly.

▸ Does your DNS server not resolve queries to subdomains within your local domain? In this case, check the links between your local name servers (check the NS records).

▸ Check the fields in the headers and in the Question and Answer sections. Do IDs match?

▸ In the Question section, you can see the hostname the resolver is looking for. Is it correct?

▶ Do your A records and PTR records match? For multihomed hosts, make sure a PTR record exists for every address.

▶ Have you changed the configuration but the name server still answers with old entries residing in its cache?

TIP

Remember the caching rules when you troubleshoot. When a lookup is made, the reply is stored in cache. This is also true for negative answers (see negative caching). Whenever you change your DNS configuration and want to test whether it works, make sure that the name server does not reply with old entries still residing in its cache. Your DNS product should have options to view cache entries and a log to find out what's going on.

Client Configuration Problems

A common issue is the client configuration. Remember that DNS only uses FQDNs. The building of that name is a resolver function. Does the client use short names? How are its resolvers configured? Does the resolver append the correct default domain? Or does the user or application enter the name using the FQDN? Check the hostname in the Question section of the DNS request to see whether the entry is correct. If the client is configured to append the default domain, and then the FQDN is entered without a trailing period, the result is an invalid name.

The following is an example of this situation. The resolver is configured with a default domain of universe.com. If the client requests venus, the resolver software will add universe.com, which results in the correct FQDN of venus.universe.com. With the same configuration, if venus.universe.com is entered (without a trailing period), the result will be venus.universe.com.universe.com. Obviously, the name server will not be able to resolve that name, because it is invalid.

With regard to the configuration of your DNS server, you have to consult your vendor's documentation. Many problems can arise from an incomplete or wrong configuration. It is not within the scope of this book to discuss the server configuration. Many different products are on the market, and each one behaves differently and needs different configuration options.

TIP

A very good reference for information on how to design your DNS, name your domains and subdomains, and configure and troubleshoot your name servers is *DNS and BIND,* by Paul Albitz and Cricket Liu.

The next two sections describe how to configure your firewall to let DNS communication go through.

DNS Name Server Unreachable

Obviously, when you receive the DNS Name Server Unreachable message, the first thing that you have to check is whether the DNS server is running and the route to the DNS server is okay. The problem that can arise here comes from having a firewall or proxy server between the resolver and the DNS server.

When a client issues a DNS request, it uses UDP to port 53. It does several retries if it receives no answer. If it cannot reach the name server, it will try to reach it using TCP to port 53. In most cases, a firewall is configured to allow only DNS resolvers to use UDP. In this case, a request over TCP will not go out. If you want this to occur, you have to enable the forwarding of requests over TCP to port 53.

So, in order for your requests to go out through the firewall, the firewall has to be configured to allow packets over UDP (and TCP) from source port 1024 to 65535, with a destination of port 53. If a local DNS server is linked to the Internet through a firewall, this is usually configured to allow TCP requests to port 53, because that name servers use TCP to do recursive queries to other DNS servers.

Another way of resolving this issue would be to have a second name server outside the firewall. Then, you would configure a link on your internal name server to the external name server and allow that communication to go through the firewall. Your internal clients then query the internal server, and the internal server queries the external server on behalf of the client (recursive query).

No DNS Response

Your DNS request goes out but you don't receive an answer? Again, after you make sure the DNS server is running and the route is fine, check your firewall. A response coming back from a name server will be using UDP and will come from source port 53 to the dynamic destination port used by the resolver. So, your firewall has to be configured like this: allow packets over UDP (and TCP) from source port 53 to a destination port between 1024 and 65535.

Lame Delegation

A common error in DNS configuration is Lame Delegation. It happens when a name server is listed in the NS records for some domain, but it is not a name server for that domain. Queries are thus sent to the wrong servers. Either that host knows nothing about the queried domain or it doesn't even run a name server. Sometimes, NS records point to servers that don't exist anymore. As a result, queries are timed out and resent, only to fail, thus creating unnecessary traffic.

It's easy to create a lame delegation: the most common case happens when an administrator changes the NS list for his domain, dropping one or more servers from that list, without informing the parent domain administrator, who delegated authority over the domain. From that point on, the parent name server announces one or more servers for the domain, which then receive queries for something they don't know about.

On the other hand, servers may be added to the list without the parent's servers knowing, thus hiding valuable information from them—this is not a lame delegation, but shouldn't happen either. Other lame-delegation examples are when a name is included in an NS list without telling the administrator of that host, or when a server suddenly stops providing name service for a domain.

TIP

Check RFC 1713, "Tools for DNS Debugging," and RFC 1912, "Common DNS Operational and Configuration Errors." They contain a lot of useful information on DNS operations and troubleshooting.

Utilities for Troubleshooting

The following is a list of utilities that you can use on various operating systems to troubleshoot DNS communications:

- **UNIX:** Use TCPDUMP, HOST, and NSLOOKUP.

- **Novell NetWare (up to version 4.x):** Use UNICON, which enables you to, among other things, query RR records on remote DNS servers. Load DNSUTIL.NLM, which enables you to view the DNS cache and to synchronize the DNS database.

- **Novell NetWare 5:** Use DNS/DHCP Management Console. (Refer to Chapter 15 for more information on this utility.)

▶ **Windows NT:** Use `NSLOOKUP`; check the Microsoft documentation for all available parameters. Use IPCONFIG /ALL to view your IP configuration and to check whether the DNS server is known.

▶ **Windows 95/98:** Use WINIPCFG to view your TCP/IP configuration.

The best troubleshooting tool on UNIX and Windows NT is NSLOOKUP. Familiarize yourself with it because it has many options that you can use. Consult your UNIX help file or the Microsoft documentation to get a list of all parameters.

TIP

Figure 12.18 shows a sample output generated with `NSLOOKUP`. The first two lines of information you get is the name and the address of the name server queried. If you do not specify any name server, your default name server is contacted. To view which server you are using, type **IPCONFIG /ALL**. A different name server can be specified on the `NSLOOKUP` command line for troubleshooting.

▶ . . . . ◀

F I G U R E   12.18

A sample NSLOOKUP output — noninteractive mode

```
D:\WINNT\System32\command.com

D:\>nslookup mars.moon.universe.com
Server:  venus.universe.com
Address:  192.168.0.1

Name:     mars.moon.universe.com
Address:  192.168.0.2

D:\>nslookup alias.moon.universe.com
Server:  venus.universe.com
Address:  192.168.0.1

Name:     lilith.moon.universe.com
Address:  192.168.0.11
Aliases:  alias.moon.universe.com

D:\>_
```

`NSLOOKUP` is a very powerful tool. It has both *noninteractive* and *interactive* mode. For a single lookup, noninteractive mode is perfect. If you want to do extensive lookups, use interactive mode. To enter interactive mode, simply type **NSLOOKUP** to get the interactive prompt. Then, type **set all** to view the current option settings. They all can be changed. Refer to your documentation to get a list of all options. A very good description of the use of `NSLOOKUP` for troubleshooting can be found in *DNS and BIND,* by Paul Albitz and Cricket Liu. Figure 12.19 shows how to get into interactive mode and check the current options.

F I G U R E   12.19

*NSLOOKUP in interactive
mode*

The first two lines indicate that the name server being used for this lookup is venus.universe.com at IP address 192.168.0.1. Options that do not have an equal sign after them are Boolean options. They can be either On or Off. If a Boolean option is Off, it is preceded by *no.* So, *nodebug* means that debugging is Off. In Figure 12.19, for example, debug is Off and recursion (recurse) is On.

Table 12.6 explains the options. Knowing how you can configure NSLOOKUP will give you hints of how to troubleshoot your DNS communications.

T A B L E   12.6

NSLOOKUP Options

OPTION	DESCRIPTION
[no]debug	Debugging is turned off, by default. If you turn it on, the name server shows timeouts and displays the response packets.
[no]defname	By default, NSLOOKUP adds the default domain name to names without a dot in them.
[no]search	If set and the lookup request contains at least one period but does not end with a trailing period, this option appends the DNS domain names in the NDS domain search list to the request until an answer is received. (The search list is a configuration property of the resolver.)
[no]recurse	By default NSLOOKUP requests recursive queries. If set to recurse, the Recursion Desired bit is set in the request packet.

Continued

TABLE 12.6

NSLOOKUP Options
(continued)

OPTION	DESCRIPTION
[no]d2	Debugging at level 2 is turned off by default. If you turn it on, you see the query packets sent out in addition to the regular debugging output. If you turn on d2, debug will be turned on also. If you turn off debug, d2 is turned off, too. If you turn off d2, debug is left on. Simple, isn't it?
[no]vc	*vc* stands for *virtual circuit,* and means communication over TCP. By default, this option is set to no, meaning that NSLOOKUP uses UDP for queries, as resolvers usually do. But, you can configure NSLOOKUP to use TCP.
[no]ignoreetc	By default, NSLOOKUP does not ignore truncated packets. If the name server sets the *Truncated bit,* indicating that it could not fit all the information in a UDP packet, NSLOOKUP will rerequest the data using TCP. Again, this is normal resolver behavior.
port=53	DNS listens on port 53. If you start your DNS service on another port — perhaps for troubleshooting reasons — NSLOOKUP can be configured to address that port.
querytype=A	By default, NSLOOKUP looks for A-type RRs. You can change this value to any record type you desire.
class=IN	The only class that matters is Internet. The Hesiod class is used at MIT.
timeout=2	If the name server does not respond within two seconds, NSLOOKUP resends its query and doubles the timeout value. The number of times it will retry is configured with the retry option.
retry=3	NSLOOKUP resends a query three times if it doesn't receive an answer. Each time, it doubles the timeout value specified with the timeout option.
root=ns.nic.ddn.mil.	Changes the name of the root server. Affects the *root* command. Root switches your default server to the server named here.
domain=	The default domain name appended if the defname option is set to on.
srchlist=	If search is turned on, all domains listed here are appended to names that do not end with a trailing period.

Case Study — What Can Go Wrong

When writing this chapter, I had two DNS servers running in my lab. As you can imagine, things did not always work as they were supposed to. Because this is not a production network and I am writing a book on troubleshooting, I was not too sad about those problems. As you know, experience is what you get if you don't get what you wanted. This chapter presents some trace files showing how DNS communication looks if it does not work.

Problem 1: Recursive Query Does Not Work

I had two name servers running in my lab when I took the following trace. The name server on server venus (NetWare 4) was configured as shown in Figure 12.20.

FIGURE 12.20

My DNS server's database for the trace files in Figures 12.12 to 12.14 and 12.21

It has an NS record for the subdomain moon.universe.com pointing to server mars.moon.universe.com. It also has an A record for server mars (glue record). My NT client was configured to use server Venus with the address of 192.168.0.1 as its name server. I typed nslookup lame.moon.universe.com. Venus should now contact server Mars and get the address for that host. Server Mars was a DNS server that was running on NetWare 5. I had just created the entry for lame.moon.universe.com, so I could be sure Venus had not cached this entry yet. Figure 12.21 shows the trace file for this lookup.

▶ . . . . ◀

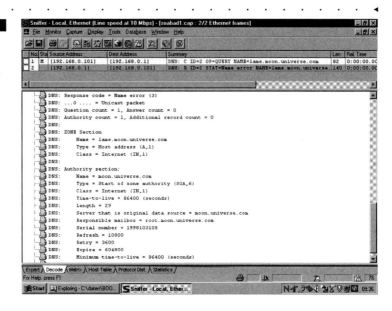

In frame 1, you see the client's query for `lame.moon.universe.com`. It is a regular query, with the Recursion Desired bit set (not shown in the figure). The client asks for an object of type A. Server Venus responds with a *name error* (return code 3) without trying to contact server Mars.

The Analysis

Figure 12.21 shows the details of the DNS message of frame 2, the server's response. The Authority section reveals the source of the problem. Everything is fine except one line: `Server that is original data source = moon.universe.com`. This is the information read from the NS record for the domain `moon.universe.com`. The server name is wrong. It should be `mars.moon.universe.com`. I then checked my server's DNS configuration, but it looked just as in Figure 12.20, with the correct entry for the NS record. Next, I used DNSUTIL.NLM on the server and created a dump file of the cache. The following is part of this dump file:

```
; Zone Origin moon.universe.com

;

$ORIGIN moon.universe.com.
```

```
moon.universe.com.        in    soa    moon.universe.com.
root.moon.universe.com. ( 1998103105 10800 3600 604800 86400 )

             in    ns    mars.moon.universe.com.

$ORIGIN moon.universe.com.

urs          in    a     192.168.0.255

blabla       in    a     192.168.0.151

lilith       in    a     192.168.0.11

marina       in    a     192.168.0.101

alias        in    cname lilith.moon.universe.com.

mars         in    a     192.168.0.2

notebook     in    a     192.168.0.100
```

At the top of the dump file, you can see the entry pointing to
moon.universe.com for the domain with the same name. It is an SOA record.
Looking at this, I learned that someone had configured server Venus to be a
secondary name server for the moon.universe.com domain without telling me.
(Did that ever happen to you?) Because of this, Venus did not contact Mars for
resolving the name. Why did Venus not resolve the query, being a secondary name
server for the domain? Venus did not have the information yet, because the zone
transfer with the updated records had not taken place yet. As you can see in the
cache dump file there are entries from the moon.universe.com domain which
are already cached. Doing an NSLOOKUP for these entries is successful, because
Venus can answer them from cache.

The Solution

After a zone transfer had taken place the lookup was successful. Then I
removed the secondary zone for moon.universe.com from Venus. The
NSLOOKUP worked fine again because now Venus contacted Mars to resolve
names of the child domain.

Problem 2: Lame Delegation

This is another case in which a recursive query is not resolved, but for a different reason.

The Analysis

The NSLOOKUP on my NT Workstation was for `silvia.moon.universe.com` when I created the trace file shown in Figure 12.22. Again, I had just created a new entry in DNS to make sure Venus would not have it in cache yet.

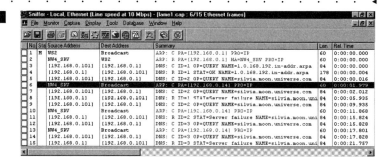

Frame 1 shows how the client broadcasts for its DNS server's IP address. Venus, the NetWare 4 Server with DNS running, responds in frame 2. In frames 3 and 4, the client gets the hostname for its DNS server by doing an inverse query. In frame 5, the problem begins. The client does a lookup for `silvia.moon.universe.com`. In frame 6, you can see server Venus ask for the IP address of 192.168.0.14. Venus is trying to do a recursive query and thinks that this is the name server to contact for the domain in question. But, no reply is made to this ARP broadcast. You can see Venus ARPing again in frames 10 and 13. No answers. In frame 7, the client repeats its request. Venus answers the client with a return code of 2, Server Failure.

The Solution

This situation is described as *lame delegation*. In this case, the NS record for the domain `moon.universe.com` points to a server that does not exist. The section "Troubleshooting DNS," earlier in this chapter, describes this problem in more detail.

Summary

DNS is a protocol that makes our lives so much easier. Instead of having to remember 32-bit IP addresses, we can use easy-to-remember hostnames. DNS resolves hostnames to IP addresses. DNS is especially interesting to understand because it is used in the global Internet.

DNS is a client/server-based protocol. The server side is called a *name server*, and the client side is called a *resolver*. This chapter has explained how DNS communication works and how it looks in trace files. It also explained DNS concepts and DNS configuration options, as far as possible within the scope of this book to help you interpret your trace files and find troubleshooting information there.

## CHAPTER 13

Simple Network Management Protocol (SNMP)

As networks grow, many managers run around trying unsuccessfully to manage the increasing number of devices on the network. Within the TCP/IP network, the *Simple Network Management Protocol (SNMP)* gives managers a much needed method to monitor and manage the ever-growing multivendor environment. This chapter focuses on the methods and standards used within the TCP/IP protocol suite to manage the network.

► · ◄

Overview of SNMP Functionality

The Internet Activities Board (IAB) recommends that any device using TCP/IP should be manageable. By using SNMP, a host running the TCP/IP protocol suite can participate in network management in one of two distinct ways: as an *agent* or as a *manager.* An agent device, such as a router, server, or workstation that takes part in the management process, runs software that can be called by the manager at any time. The management device is usually a workstation that is used to contact the agents to request specific information, such as link status or traffic volume. A manager may also issue commands to an agent to change conditions. For example, a manager may want to reinitialize an interface in a router. Rather than physically powering down the device, a network administrator can sit at a management workstation and issue the appropriate commands to the router. Figure 13.1 demonstrates how agents and managers might work together in a TCP/IP network.

Notice in Figure 13.1 that the internetwork has several management stations within it. In a large network, not all managers are allowed to control all agents. Several levels of authorization or security access may exist. Security and access control are discussed later in this chapter.

Communication between the manager and the agent can go in both directions. Consider the example in Figure 13.2. The manager requests ICMP statistics from a router interface and simultaneously receives information from an agent about an interface that has failed. Both pieces of information are received and processed by the management workstation, giving the network administrator an overall picture of the state of the network at any given time.

▶ . . . . ◀

FIGURE 13.1

Agents and managers within an internetwork assist in network management.

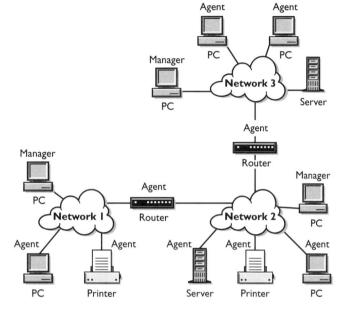

▶ . . . . ◀

FIGURE 13.2

Management communication can be bidirectional

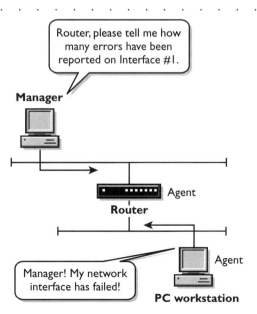

Of course, the description just given is simply a brief overview of how the management system really works. To really understand network management, you must explore the three major standards that define how management information is stored, referenced, and exchanged:

▸ **Management Information Base (MIB):** Specifies the informational elements specific to the device that may be queried or set by the manager.

▸ **Structure of Management Information (SMI):** The defined standard reference and modify the variables set in the MIB.

▸ **Simple Network Management Protocol (SNMP):** The protocol used between the manager and agent that carries out the actual requests sent to and from the manager and agent.

Management Information Base

MIB is the database of information stored within an agent that defines information about the agent that can be managed, queried, or controlled. For example, a router might store information about routing entries, whereas a file server may contain utilization statistics.

MIB has two versions: MIB I (RFC 1156) and MIB II (RFC 1213). Within each MIB standard, various major management information categories are defined. Table 13.1 illustrates the major TCP/IP MIB-II category standards.

TABLE 13.1

Major MIB-II Categories

MIB CATEGORY	DESCRIPTION
System Group	The host or router vendor identification
Interfaces Group	The number of network interfaces that can send or receive IP datagrams

MIB CATEGORY	DESCRIPTION
Address Translation Group (supported in MIB-II but will probably be removed from future mandatory MIB standards support)	Contains the translation tables (the same as the ARP cache in broadcast networks)
IP Group	Internet Protocol statistics
ICMP Group	Internet Control Message Protocol statistics
TCP Group	Transmission Control Protocol statistics
UDP Group	User Datagram Protocol statistics
EGP Group	Exterior Gateway Protocol statistics
Transmission Group (new in MIB-II)	Distinguishes between different types of transmission media
SNMP Group (new in MIB-II)	Simple Network Management Protocol statistics

By using these major groups, network administrators and vendors have a distinct advantage when managing the network. A vendor can include SNMP agent software in a product, knowing that the product can be managed even though a new device may have been defined. The network manager can use the existing management agent to query and manage the new device without having to change the existing infrastructure.

Within each of these groups, additional data elements are found for each major category. To help you fully understand the types of TCP/IP information that can be queried within a managed network, the individual data items are further discussed and listed next.

The following are the two types of data that can be defined within a MIB group:

▸ **Simple variables:** A value that can be stored in a single integer.

▸ **Tables:** The form in which most complex values are stored. A good example of a table is a query for a router's address table. When you make a request to a router for its address table, you expect all values for that router to be returned from that query. Additionally, you may request multiple values for each router, such as IP address, network mask, and so on.

The characteristics for multiple interfaces are another example of using simple variables and tables. A simple variable may be the interface number, such as 1, 2, or 3. After an interface number is chosen for a query, multiple characteristics for that single variable may be requested from a table, such as errors, physical address, or IP address. The query from the table would change as the interface number requested changes.

The System Group

The System Group is mandatory for all TCP/IP systems, although the agent is not required to be configured to provide this information. This group has seven variable data items, defined in Table 13.2, each of which identifies some element of the physical device itself.

TABLE 13.2

Data Items in the MIB-II System Group

DATA ITEM	DESCRIPTION
sysDescr	An ASCII description of the hardware type, software operating system, and networking software
sysObjectID	The vendor's authoritative identification of the device
sysUpTime	The time, in hundredths of a second, since the network management portion was last reinitialized
sysContact	Identifies the contact person for this node
sysName	The node's fully qualified domain name
sysLocation	The description of the physical location of the node
sysServices	A value that indicates the set of services that a node offers

Geek Alert!

The value of the sysServices item initially is zero. For each layer in which the node performs a transaction, a calculation is performed. To determine the value in this field, take the value L (for layer) and plug it into this formula:

2 raised to $(L-1)$ = *sysServices field value*

The possible functions available for this field are the following:

LAYER	FUNCTIONALITY
1	Physical (for example, repeaters)
2	Datalink (for example, bridges)
3	Internet (for example, IP gateway)
4	End to End (for example, IP hosts)
7	Applications (for example, mail relays)

For example, a router would have a value of 4. To calculate this value, take the layer where the service is performed (3) and plug it into the formula:

$2^{(3-1)} = 4$

Didn't you always want to know where that value came from?

The Interfaces Group

The implementation of the Interfaces Group is mandatory for all systems. The information provided by this group is specific to network hardware (or interfaces) found in the managed system. The Interfaces Group consists of a single variable and a table called the *Interfaces table*. The data items specified by the Interfaces Group are detailed in Table 13.3.

TABLE 13.3	DATA ITEM	DESCRIPTION
Variable Items in the MIB-II Interfaces Group	ifNumber	Number of interfaces on the device

The Interfaces table contains information on the device's interfaces. Each interface is considered to be attached to its own segment. Each interface has 22 characteristics available, as shown in Table 13.4.

TABLE 13.4	DATA ITEM	DESCRIPTION
Interfaces Table Items in the MIB-II Interfaces Group	ifIndex	The unique value for each interface. Values range between 1 and ifNumber.
	ifDescr	Text description of the interface

Continued

TABLE 13.4	DATA ITEM	DESCRIPTION
Interfaces Table Items in the MIB-II Interfaces Group (continued)	ifType	Interface type. Common values are: Ethernet (6), 802.3 Ethernet (7), 802.5 Token Ring (9), FDDI (15), PPP (23), and many other types.
	ifMtu	The size of the largest datagram that can be sent/received on the interface. This value is specified in octets (e.g., IPv4 value is 4 octets).
	ifSpeed	Current bandwidth estimate, measured in bits per second (bps)
	ifPhysAddress	The protocol address of the interface. Interfaces without an address, such as a serial line, contain an octet string of zero length.
	ifAdminStatus	The state of the interface: 1=Up, 2=Down, 3=Testing
	ifOperStatus	Current operational state of the interface: 1=Up, 2=Down, 3=Testing
	ifLastChange	The value of sysUpTime at the time the interface entered its current operational state
	ifInOctets	Total number of octets received, including framing characters
	ifInUcastPkts	Number of unicast packets sent
	ifInNUcastPkts	Number of non-unicast packets (such as broadcast or multicast) sent
	ifInDiscards	Number of packets discarded even though no errors were detected, such as in a buffer-overflow situation
	ifInErrors	Number of inbound packets that contained errors
	ifInUnknownProtos	Number of packets discarded due to an unknown or unsupported protocol
	ifOutOctets	Number of octets sent, including framing characters

DATA ITEM	DESCRIPTION
ifOutUcastPkts	Number of packets requested for transmission to a unicast address, including those that were discarded or not sent
ifOutNUcastPkts	Number of packets requested for transmission to a non-unicast (broadcast or multicast address), including those that were discarded or not sent
ifOutDiscards	Number of outbound packets discarded even though no errors were detected, possibly to free up buffer space
ifOutErrors	Number of packets discarded due to errors
ifOutQLen	Length of the output packet queue. This value is displayed in packets
ifSpecific	References MIB definitions specific to the particular media being used

The Address Translation Group

The Address Translation Group implementation is mandatory for all systems. This group is supported by MIB-II solely for compatibility with MIB-I nodes. This group will most likely be excluded from future (MIB-III) specifications.

The purpose of the Address Translation Group is simply to provide the management console with all the IP-to-network-specific addresses (previously referred to as the *physical address*). The translation table is equivalent to the ARP cache in a broadcast system, such as Ethernet. A single table is defined for the Address Translation Group. The data items available with the Address Translation Group table are shown in Table 13.5.

TABLE 13.5

Table Items in the MIB-II Address Translation Group

DATA ITEM	DESCRIPTION
atIfIndex	The interface number
atPhysAddress	The physical address (setting this object to a string of 0 invalidates the interface entry)
atNetAddress	The IP address of the interface

From the MIB-II specification forward, each network protocol group will contain its own address translation tables.

The IP Group

The IP Group is a mandatory group for all systems and is a large part of the MIB. This group provides valuable statistics relating to IP. The IP Group consists of quite a few elements, including numerous variables and three tables. Table 13.6 depicts the simple variables used in the IP Group.

TABLE 13.6

Variable Items in the MIB-II Internet Protocol Group

DATA ITEM	DESCRIPTION
ipForwarding	Determines whether IP forwarding is on or off. 1=forwarding (acting as a gateway), 2=nonforwarding (not acting as a gateway).
ipDefaultTTL	Default Time To Live (TTL) value.
ipInReceives	Total datagrams received, including errors.
ipInHdrErrors	Total discarded datagrams due to IP header errors.
ipInAddrErrors	Total discarded datagrams due to invalid IP addresses.
ipForwDatagrams	Total attempts to route datagrams. If the device is not a gateway, this value will include only successfully source-routed packets.
ipInUnknownProtos	Total locally addressed datagrams received but discarded due to an unknown or unsupported protocol.
ipInDiscards	Number of IP datagrams without errors discarded. Usually due to lack of buffer space.
ipInDelivers	Total datagrams successfully delivered.
ipOutRequests	Total requested datagrams passed to IP for transmission.
ipOutDiscards	Number of datagrams without errors that were discarded.
ipOutNoRoutes	Number of datagrams discarded because no route could be found for transmission.
ipReasmTimeout	Maximum number of seconds that received fragments are held while waiting for reassembly.
ipReasmReqds	Number of IP fragments received that needed reassembly.
ipReasmOKs	Number of IP datagrams successfully reassembled.

DATA ITEM	DESCRIPTION
ipReasmFails	Number of failures detected by the IP reassembly process.
ipFragOKs	Number of successfully fragmented IP datagrams.
ipFragFails	Number of discarded datagrams requiring fragmentation but where fragmentation was disallowed.
ipFragCreates	Number of fragments that have been generated.
ipRoutingDiscards	Number of valid entries discarded, usually to free up buffer space.

The first of the three tables in the IP Group is the IP Address table, which contains the device's IP addressing information. This table has five variables, as shown in Table 13.7.

TABLE 13.7 — IP Address Table Items in the MIB-II Internet Protocol Group	DATA ITEM	DESCRIPTION
	ipAdEntAddr	The IP address of the item
	ipAdEntIfIndex	Unique interface number
	ipAdEntNetMask	Subnet mask associated with the IP address of this entry
	ipAdEntBcastAddr	Value of the least significant bit in the IP broadcast address
	ipAdEntReasmMaxSize	The size of the largest IP datagram that can be created from the incoming IP fragments on this interface

The second table in the IP Group is the IP Routing table. This table consists of 13 variables, as shown in Table 13.8, and contains an entry for each route known to the device.

TABLE 13.8 — Routing Table Items in the MIB-II Internet Protocol Group	DATA ITEM	DESCRIPTION
	ipRouteDest	The destination IP address of this route
	ipRouteIfIndex	Unique interface value — same as ifIndex
	ipRouteMetric1	Primary routing metric for this route
	ipRouteMetric2	Alternate routing metric for this route

Continued

TABLE 13.8	DATA ITEM	DESCRIPTION
Routing Table Items in the MIB-II Internet Protocol Group (continued)	ipRouteMetric3	Alternate routing metric for this route
	ipRouteMetric4	Alternate routing metric for this route
	ipRouteNextHop	The IP address of the next hop in this route
	ipRouteType	The type of route. Possible values are 1=Other, 2=Invalid route, 3=Route to directly connected network or subnet, 4=Route to a nonlocal network or subnet
	ipRouteProto	How the route was learned. Several values exist, but the most common are 2=Local, 3=Netmgmt, 4=ICMP, 5=EGP, 6=GGP, 7=Hello, 8=RIP and many other routing protocols
	ipRouteAge	Number of seconds since this route was last updated
	ipRouteMask	The mask used to decide whether to route the datagram
	ipRouteMetric5	Alternate routing metric for this route
	ipRouteInfo	Specific MIB reference depending on the value of the ipRouteProto

The final table in the IP Group is the IP Address Translation table, which contains the IP-address-to-physical-address mappings, as shown in Table 13.9.

TABLE 13.9	DATA ITEM	DESCRIPTION
Address Translation Table Items in the MIB-II Internet Protocol Group	ipNetToMediaIfIndex	The interface number (same as ifIndex)
	ipNetToMediaPhysAddress	The physical address
	ipNetToMediaNetAddress	The IP address of this interface
	ipNetToMediaType	The type of address mapping: 1=Other, 2=Invalid, 3=Dynamic, 4=Static

This IP Address Translation table replaces the Address Translation Major Group previously used with the MIB-I specification.

NOTE

The ICMP Group

The ICMP Group is mandatory in its implementation. ICMP is the error and status reporting mechanism for routing errors, such as Destination or Port Unreachable, Route Redirection, and Echo Requests and Replies. The group is defined by 26 variables, as shown in Table 13.10.

TABLE 13.10

ICMP Variable Items in the MIB-II ICMP Group

DATA ITEM	DESCRIPTION
icmpInMsgs	Total number of ICMP messages received
icmpInErrors	Number of ICMP messages received with ICMP-specific errors, such as Bad Checksum or Length
icmpInDestUnreachs	Number of ICMP Destination Unreachable messages received
icmpInTimeExcds	Number of ICMP Time Exceeded messages received
icmpInParmProbs	Number of ICMP Parameter Problem messages received
icmpInSrcQuenchs	Number of ICMP Source Quench messages received
icmpInRedirects	Number of ICMP Redirect messages received
icmpInEchos	Number of ICMP Echo Request messages received
icmpInEchoReps	Number of ICMP Echo Reply messages received
icmpInTimestamps	Number of ICMP Timestamp Request messages received
icmpInTimestampReps	Number of ICMP Timestamp Reply messages received
icmpInAddrMasks	Number of ICMP Address Mask Request messages received
icmpInAddrMaskReps	Number of ICMP Address Mask Replies received
icmpOutMsgs	Number of ICMP message attempts sent (includes icmpOutErrors)
icmpOutErrors	Number of ICMP messages not sent due to problems within ICMP, such as a lack of buffers
icmpOutDestUnreachs	Number of ICMP Destination Unreachable messages sent
icmpOutTimeExcds	Number of ICMP Time Exceeded messages sent
icmpOutParmProbs	Number of ICMP Parameter Problem messages sent
icmpOutSrcQuenchs	Number of ICMP Source Quench messages sent
icmpOutRedirects	Number of ICMP Redirect messages sent

Continued

T A B L E   1 3 . 1 0

ICMP Variable Items in the MIB-II ICMP Group (continued)

DATA ITEM	DESCRIPTION
icmpOutEchos	Number of ICMP Echo Request messages sent
icmpOutEchoReps	Number of ICMP Echo Reply messages sent
icmpOutTimestamps	Number of ICMP Timestamp Request messages sent
icmpOutTimestampReps	Number of ICMP Timestamp Reply messages sent
icmpOutAddrMasks	Number of ICMP Address Mask Request messages sent
icmpOutAddrMaskReps	Number of ICMP Address Mask Replies sent

ICMP message types and their values are described in detail in Chapter 6.

X-REF

The TCP Group

The TCP Group is mandatory for any device that uses the TCP protocol stack. It consists of 14 variables and a table called the TCP Connection table. Importantly, the information represented within the data fields is transient in nature — that is, the data is available only when the TCP connection is present. Table 13.11 describes the 14 variables used in MIB-II for TCP.

T A B L E   1 3 . 1 1

TCP Variable Items in the MIB-II TCP Group

DATA ITEM	DESCRIPTION
tcpRtoAlgorithm	The algorithm used to determine the timeout value for retransmission. Values are 1=Other, 2=Constant rto, 3=Rsre (MIL-STD-1778, 4=Vanj (Van Jacobson's algorithm)).
tcpRtoMin	Minimum value permitted for the retransmission timeout, measured in milliseconds
tcpRtoMax	Maximum value permitted for the retransmission timeout, measured in milliseconds
tcpMaxConn	Total number of TCP connections supported by the device

DATA ITEM	DESCRIPTION
tcpActiveOpens	Number of times TCP opens a connection. (Transition from CLOSED to SYN-SENT state.)
tcpPassiveOpens	Number of times TCP opens a connection. (Transition from LISTEN to SYN-RCVD state.)
tcpAttemptFails	Number of times TCP has entered a CLOSED or LISTEN state after being in a SYN-SENT or SYN-RCVD state
tcpEstabResets	Number of times TCP closes a connection. (Transition from ESTABLISHED or CLOSE-WAIT to CLOSED state.)
tcpCurrEstab	Number of TCP connections in the ESTABLISHED or CLOSE-WAIT state
tcpInSegs	Total number of segments received on established connections (includes errors)
tcpOutSegs	Total number of segments sent on established (current) connections (excludes retransmissions).
tcpRetransSegs	Total number of segments retransmitted.
tcpInErrs	Total number of segments with errors received.
tcpOutRsts	Total number of TCP segments sent that contain the RST flag.

To retrieve information about an existing TCP connection, the TCP Connection table is used. The table consists of five variables, as shown in Table 13.12.

TABLE 13.12

TCP Connection Table Items in the MIB-II TCP Group

DATA ITEM	DESCRIPTION
tcpConnState	State of the TCP connection. Possible values are 1=Closed, 2=Listen, 3=SynSent, 4=SynReceived, 5=Established, 6=FinWait1, 7=FinWait2, 8=CloseWait, 9=LastAck, 10=Closing, 11=TimeWait, 12=DeleteTCB. DeleteTCB is the only value that may be set by a management station. Setting this value results in an immediate termination of the connection on the node.
tcpConnLocalAddress	The local IP address for the TCP connection. A value of 0.0.0.0 is used if the connection is in a listen state and willing to accept connections for any interface.
tcpConnLocalPort	The local port number for the TCP connection.

Continued

TCP Connection Table Items in the MIB-II TCP Group (continued)

DATA ITEM	DESCRIPTION
tcpConnRemAddress	The remote IP address for this TCP connection.
tcpConnRemPort	The remote port number for this TCP connection.

The UDP Group

The UDP Group is mandatory for any device that uses the TCP protocol stack. It consists of four variables and a table called the UDP Listener table. Importantly, the information represented within the data fields is *transient* in nature — that is, the data is available only when the UDP connection is present. Table 13.13 describes the four variables used in the MIB-II for UDP.

T A B L E   1 3 . 1 3

UDP Variable Items in the MIB-II UDP Group

DATA ITEM	DESCRIPTION
udpInDatagrams	Total number of UDP datagrams delivered to users
udpNoPorts	Total number of UDP datagrams received for which no application existed at the required port
udpInErrors	Number of UDP errors other than udpNoPorts
udpOutDatagrams	Total number of UDP datagrams sent from this device

To retrieve information about an existing UDP connection, the UDP Listener table is used. The table consists of only two variables, as shown in Table 13.14.

T A B L E   1 3 . 1 4

UDP Listener Table Items in the MIB-II UDP Group

DATA ITEM	DESCRIPTION
ucpLocalAddress	The local IP address for the listening device. If the device is listening and will accept datagrams for an interface, the value should be 0.0.0.0.
udpLocalPort	The local port number for this UDP listening device.

For a list of commonly used UDP port numbers, refer to RFC 1700, or to Chapter 13 or Appendix C in this book.

X-REF

The EGP Group

If a system uses the Exterior Gateway Protocol, then it must use the EGP Group data items defined in the MIB-II specification. The EGP Group consists of a set of five variables, shown in Table 13.15, and a single table called the EGP Neighbor table.

T A B L E   13.15

EGP Variable Items in the MIB-II EGP Group

DATA ITEM	DESCRIPTION
egpInMsgs	Number of EGP messages received without any errors
egpInErrors	Number of EGP messages received with errors
egpOutMsgs	Total number of locally generated EGP messages
egpOutErrors	Number of EGP messages not sent due to resource limitations within an EGP device
egpAs	The autonomous system number of this EGP device

Because EGP is a routing protocol, it makes sense that the MIB must contain routing entries. The EGP protocol uses the term "neighbors" to refer to systems known by the EGP routing device. These entries are stored in the EGP Neighbor table, as shown in Table 13.16.

T A B L E   13.16

EGP Neighbor Table Items in the MIB-II EGP Group

DATA ITEM	DESCRIPTION
egpNeighState	State of the local system with respect to the EGP neighbor. Possible values include 1=Idle, 2=Acquisition, 3=Down, 4=Up, 5=Cease.
egpNeighAddr	The IP address of the device's EGP neighbor
egpNeighAs	The autonomous system number of this EGP member (value will be 0 if the autonomous system number is not yet known)

Continued

TABLE 13.16

EGP Neighbor Table Items in the MIB-II EGP Group (continued)

DATA ITEM	DESCRIPTION
egpNeighInMsgs	Number of EGP messages received without errors
egpNeighInErrs	Number of EGP messages received with errors
egpNeighOutMsgs	Number of locally generated EGP messages to this device
egpNeighOutErrs	Number of locally generated EGP messages not sent to this device due to resource limitations
egpNeighInErrMsgs	Number of EGP-defined error messages received by this device
egpNeighOutErrMsgs	Number of EGP-defined error messages sent to this device
egpNeighStateUps	Number of EGP state transitions to the UP state with this EGP member
egpNeighStateDowns	Number of EGP state transitions from the UP state to any other state
egpNeighIntervalHello	Interval between the EGP Hello command retransmissions, measured in hundredths of a second
egpNeighIntervalPoll	Interval between EGP Poll command retransmissions, measured in hundredths of a second
egpNeighMode	Polling mode of this EGP device; possible values are 1=Active, 2=Passive
egpNeighEventTrigger	Variable used to trigger operator-initiated start and stop events; possible values are 1=Start, 2=Stop

X-REF

For more information on routing protocols, refer to Chapter 18.

The Transmission Group

New to the MIB-II specification, the Transmission Group is still in the experimental stage and currently isn't yet a proven standard. However, when Internet-
standard definitions for managing the transmission media are defined, the
Transmission Group will be used to provide a prefix for the names of objects, such
as Ethernet or Token Ring.

The SNMP Group

If a system supports the SNMP protocol, implementation of the SNMP Group is mandated in the MIB-II standard. The SNMP Group includes all devices, whether they are a management agent or a management station, though some variable items refer to either one type or the other. A management station may possibly also be a management agent, which would mean that certain variables pertain to both groups simultaneously for that node. The SNMP Group consists of 30 variable items, as listed in Table 13.17.

TABLE 13.17

SNMP Variable Items in the MIB-II EGP Group

DATA ITEM	DESCRIPTION
snmpInPkts	Total number of messages delivered to SNMP
snmpOutPkts	Total number of messages sent
snmpInBadVersions	Total number of incoming messages using an unsupported SNMP version
snmpInBadCommunityNames	Total number of incoming messages using an unknown community name
snmpInBadCommunityUses	Total number of messages requesting an operation not allowed by the community
snmpInASNParseErrs	Total number of ASN.1 errors found when decoding received SNMP messages
snmpInTooBigs	Total number of incoming messages in which the value of the Error Status field is Too Big
snmpInNoSuchNames	Total number of incoming messages in which the value of the Error Status field is noSuchName
snmpInBadValues	Total number of incoming messages in which the value of the Error Status field is badValue
snmpInReadOnlys	Total number of valid deliveries in which the value of the Error Status field is readOnly
snmpInGenErrs	Total number of incoming messages in which the value of the Error Status field is genErr
snmpInTotalReqVars	Total number of MIB objects that have been retrieved successfully

Continued

SNMP Variable Items in the MIB-II EGP Group (continued)

DATA ITEM	DESCRIPTION
snmpInTotalSetVars	Total number of MIB objects that have been altered successfully
snmpInGetRequests	Total number of Get-Request messages that have been accepted and processed
snmpInGetNexts	Total number of Get-Next messages that have been accepted and processed
snmpInSetRequests	Total number of Set-Request messages that have been accepted and processed
snmpInGetResponses	Total number of Get-Response messages that have been accepted and processed
snmpInTraps	Total number of Trap messages that have been accepted and processed
snmpOutTooBigs	Total number of outgoing messages in which the value of the Error Status field is tooBig
snmpOutNoSuchNames	Total number of outgoing messages in which the value of the Error Status field is noSuchName
snmpOutBadValues	Total number of outgoing messages in which the value of the Error Status field is badValue
snmpOutGenErrs	Total number of outgoing messages in which the value of the Error Status field is genErr
snmpOutGetRequests	Total number of outgoing Get-Request messages
snmpOutGetNexts	Total number of outgoing Get-Next messages
snmpOutSetRequests	Total number of outgoing Set-Request messages
snmpOutGetResponses	Total number of outgoing Get-Response messages
snmpOutTraps	Total number of outgoing Trap messages
snmpEnableAuthenTraps	Determines whether the SNMP agent process is allowed to generate authentication-failure traps; possible values are 1=Enabled, 2=Disabled

Many other MIBs have been developed, either as standards or by specific vendors, that aid in overall network management. All the descriptions in the preceding tables are specific to TCP/IP-based internets. But, what if a vendor wants to manage something else, such as a mail application? Could a vendor write a MIB to accommodate the management station?

The answer is yes. However, the vendor must adhere to a very strict method of addressing the data that will be contained in the MIB — it can't just add new fields and data as it pleases, wherever it pleases. Remember, this is a standards-based management system, so the next section looks at how the MIB data is structured and addressed by the management system.

Structure of Management Information (SMI)

The last section discussed the MIB standard, which is responsible for specifying management variables and their meanings. Variables are available both for the TCP/IP protocol suite and for individual devices. However, for a vendor to be able to define and implement new MIB variables, a specific set of rules must be followed to make those MIBs compatible with management systems available worldwide. Those rules are called the *Structure of Management Information (SMI)*. Where the MIB defines the variables themselves, the SMI specification defines the structure of the data contained in the MIB and creates rules for the definition of the types of variables, much like field definitions in a database.

Simply put, the SMI rules provide a method of organization and naming for objects, whereas the MIB stores the information about the object. The SMI also defines the few types of data that may be present in the MIB, such as IpAddress, which is defined as a 32-bit Internet address, or a Counter, which is simply a field that counts instances, such as an error count. A Counter field is defined as a nonnegative integer with a value in the range from 0 to $2^{32}-1$ (4,294,967,295), which wraps back to 0.

Object Representation and Naming

The SMI standard uses a tree-type concept to give visualization to the structure of the Internet-managed objects. Much like a NetWare NDS tree, objects flowing down each branch are called *leaf objects*. The SMI standards refer to the object names as object identifiers, each of which is an administratively assigned name that is specific to a single portion of the tree, or object name space. The object tree begins with a root object, which has no official name. From that level, three children are defined by RFC 1155, each of which is managed individually by the International Standards Organization (ISO), the International Telegraph and Telephone Consultative Committee (CCITT), and a joint ISO-CCITT affiliation. Therefore, the root of the tree is represented by four objects—the unnamed root and three child objects, as shown in Figure 13.3.

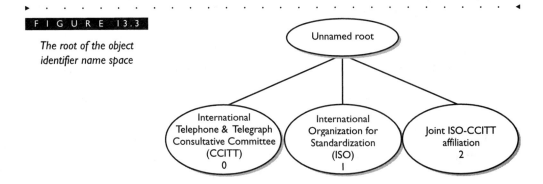

FIGURE 13.3

The root of the object identifier name space

Each child object may also have other child objects. For TCP/IP, the managing entity is the ISO (1) object, down to the Internet (1) object, as represented in Figure 13.4.

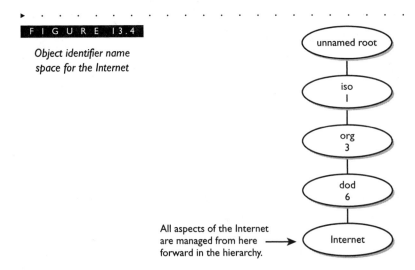

FIGURE 13.4

Object identifier name space for the Internet

Notice that, in addition to a unique name, each child also has a number assignment. These numbers are used as part of the SMI reference language, called *Abstract Syntax Notation 1 (ASN.1)*. ASN.1 is a formal language designed to provide two methods to communicate namespace information — via a natural language name and via an encoding method that can be used in place of words within communication protocols. For example, Figure 13.4 defines the name space to the Internet object identifier. This information can be expressed in one of two ways:

```
iso.org.dod.internet   OR   1.3.6.1
```

Usually, humans use the character-based method of communication when speaking about the name space, but to the computer, the numbers 1.3.6.1 make more sense and thus are processed quicker and easier.

Further down the tree is the Internet namespace assignment, the area in which all aspects of the Internet, including management and MIBs, are defined, as shown in Figure 13.5.

The Internet has six defined areas. Network management falls under the mgmt (2) category. Further defining the management area is the mib (1) object. Notice that under the MIB object, all categories defined earlier in this chapter are represented. Using ASN notation, a manager would refer to the objects by using either the character or numeric representation. The computer would simply refer to a specific object by number. For example, the definition of the icmp object using ASN.1 notation would be the following:

```
iso.org.dod.internet.mgmt.mib-2.icmp    OR 1.3.6.1.2.1.5
```

Using ASN.1, a manager can get even further into the name space and uniquely identify a specific MIB value simply by using ASN notation. Using the preceding example, suppose that a manager wanted to know a specific icmp value, such as icmpInMsgs (total number of ICMP messages received by the entity). Each of the data items also has a number that can be addressed by ASN.1. The number for icmpInMsgs is (1) under the ICMP name space, as shown in Figure 13.6.

Using ASN notation, the definition for the icmpInMsgs would be as follows:

```
iso.org.dod.internet.mgmt.mib.icmp-2.icmpInMsgs OR
1.3.6.1.2.1.5.1
```

This method of notation makes it very easy for network vendors to implement new MIBs, as needed, for management of their devices.

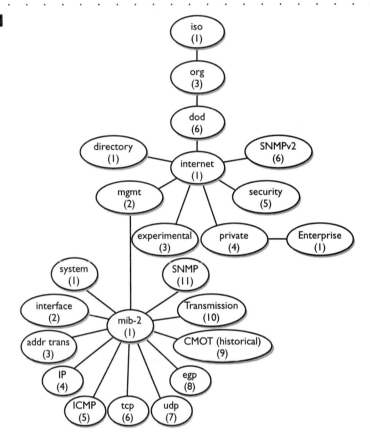

FIGURE 13.5

Object identifier name space under the Internet node

Simple Network Management Protocol (SNMP)

Having defined the MIB and the SMI standards used to define the structure of the data, the third component of the network management magic now needs to be explained — SNMP, the communication protocol that performs the actual task of retrieving and modifying the MIB items. SNMP is a component of the TCP/IP protocol stack. Two versions of SNMP are used today — SNMPv1 (Version 1) and

SNMPv2 (Version 2). A SNMPv3 developing standard exists, but it currently isn't complete. This book focuses mostly on SNMPv2 standards, but version 1 standards will be indicated as well.

FIGURE 13.6

ICMP name space

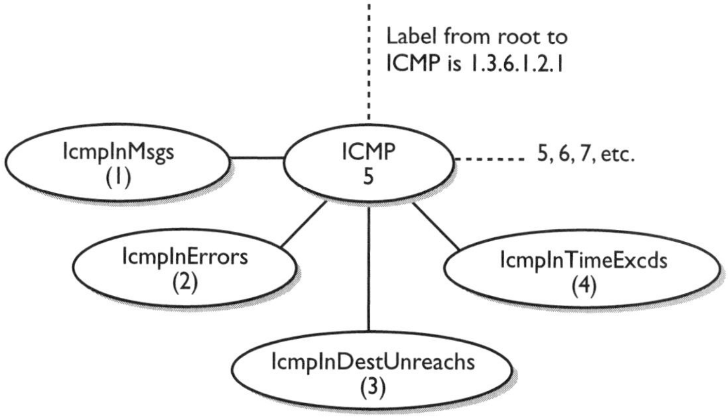
Label from root to
ICMP is 1.3.6.1.2.1
IcmpInMsgs
(1)
ICMP
5
5, 6, 7, etc.
IcmpInErrors
(2)
IcmpInTimeExcds
(4)
IcmpInDestUnreachs
(3)

The SNMP protocol simply specifies the communication between the network management agent and the manager. SNMP uses a *message* to request or reply to information sent between agents and managers. The nine types of SNMP messages are shown in Table 13.18.

TABLE 13.18

SNMPv2 Message Types

SNMPV2 MESSAGE TYPE	DESCRIPTION
Get-Request	Request the value of one or more variables
Get-Next-Request	Get the next value in a table
Get-Response	Return the value of one or more variables
Set-Request	Set the value of one or more variables
Trap	Notify the manager when an event is triggered on an agent (SNMPv1 only)
Get-Bulk-Request	New to SNMPv2 — used in place of get-next-request
Inform-Request	New to SNMPv2 — provide manager-to-manager communication

Continued

T A B L E   1 3 . 1 8

SNMPv2 Message Types (continued)

SNMPV2 MESSAGE TYPE	DESCRIPTION
SNMPv2-Trap	SNMPv2 trap message — follow same structure as other message types
Report-PDU	Usage and semantics are not presently defined

These nine SNMP message types fall into three general categories, depending on the version of SNMP being used:

▸ **Simple request-reply messages:** Most of the message types (get-request, get-next-request, get-response, set-request, inform-request, SNMPv2-Trap, and Report-PDU) fall within this category. A manager makes a request that is answered by the agent. Answers are provided in the variable portion of the packet.

▸ **SNMPv1 trap messages:** A *trap* is a simple message that contains a notification sent to the manager that a device needs attention.

▸ **The get-bulk-request message:** Specific to SNMPv2.

All SNMP message categories in TCP/IP are encapsulated within a UDP datagram, and an IP header for transmission on the wire. SNMP can be used with other transport protocols, such as IPX, to manage non-TCP/IP networks.

NOTE   **SNMP messages can be used with several transports, including UDP, IPX, and any other unacknowledged transport. This makes SNMP a perfect higher-level protocol for network management of multivendor systems.**

All SNMP messages share a common SNMP header. However, the actual format of the packet is different for the three message categories, as shown in Figures 13.7, 13.8, and 13.9. In addition, all the fields in an SNMP message are variable, with the exception of the IP and UDP headers that are placed on the messages. The IP and UDP headers are 20-bytes and 8-bytes long, respectively.

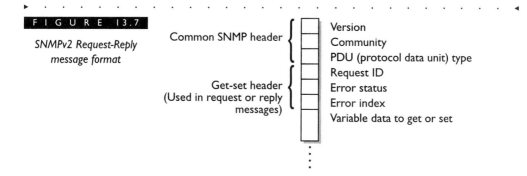

FIGURE 13.7

SNMPv2 Request-Reply message format

Common SNMP header { Version, Community, PDU (protocol data unit) type

Get-set header { Request ID, Error status, Error index, Variable data to get or set
(Used in request or reply messages)

Figure 13.7 shows a simple request message type. Notice the Request-Reply header (also called a Get/Set header) on this message, followed by variable data.

The SNMP v1 trap message shares a common SNMP header with the request-reply messages. With a trap message, however, the remaining packet structure includes a trap header and variable information, as shown in Figure 13.8.

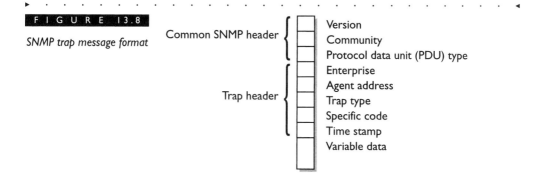

FIGURE 13.8

SNMP trap message format

Common SNMP header { Version, Community, Protocol data unit (PDU) type

Trap header { Enterprise, Agent address, Trap type, Specific code, Time stamp, Variable data

As mentioned, a message format is defined for the get-bulk operation in SNMPv2. The purpose of the get-bulk-request message is to allow the manager to make a looping request for data, instead of making multiple requests and receiving replies until no more data is requested. This message type will eventually replace the get-next-request message type, due to its efficiency and bandwidth-saving features. Figure 13.9 shows the get-bulk data message format.

FIGURE 13.9

SNMPv2 get-bulk PDU message format

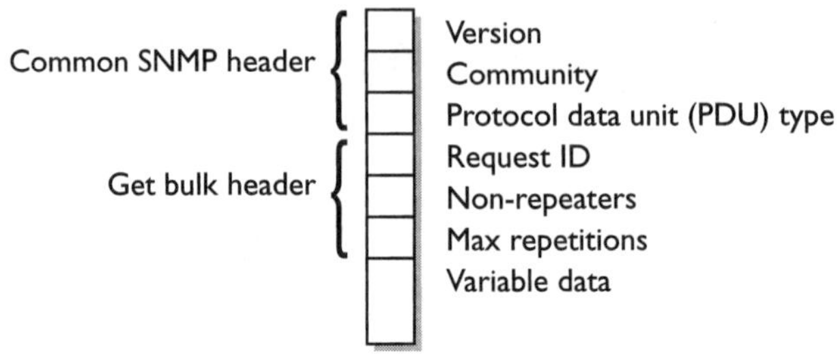

Common SNMP header { Version / Community / Protocol data unit (PDU) type

Get bulk header { Request ID / Non-repeaters / Max repetitions / Variable data

Unlike most of the other TCP/IP protocols, SNMP messages do not have fixed field lengths, except for the UDP and IP headers. This is due to the ASN.1 encoding method used by SNMP, which varies greatly in the length and quantity of data. The common SNMP header is described next.

SNMP Common Header Field Values

Three fields are common to all SNMP messages: Version, Community, and PDU Type.

Version

The value of the Version field today is 0. This is calculated by taking the SNMP version number minus one, as in SNMPv1. As SNMPv2 is adopted, this value may change.

Community

The Community field is a string that is a clear-text password between the manager and the agent. Community is also used as an identifier to group devices together for management by a specific manager. The default of this field is *public*, though the name may be changed by a manager. Many SNMP implementations, including Novell's, define three types of communities:

- **Monitor Community:** Grants read access to the MIB to anyone within this community, with the default set to public.

- **Control Community:** Members are able to read and modify the MIB components, provided that the MIB fields are modifiable. Members of the

Control Community may, for example, modify router tables, take interfaces up and down, and change the status of the routing provided by the server. However, variable counters, such as those containing number of errors, may not be modified.

▶ **Trap Community:** Accompanies all error (or trap) messages sent from an agent to a manager. The use of the Trap Community helps managers to define how traps are sent, and helps to ensure that no manager is overloaded.

PDU Type

The acronym *PDU* stands for *Protocol Data Unit*, which is essentially another name for a packet. The possible PDU Types are shown in Table 13.19.

TABLE 13.19 *SNMPv2 PDU Data Types*	PDU TYPE	DESCRIPTION
	0	get-request
	1	get-next-request
	2	get-response
	3	set request
	4	SNMP trap (obsolete in SNMPv2)
	5	get-bulk-request (used in SNMPv2 to get bulk information)
	6	inform-request (manager-to-manager communications)
	7	SNMPv2 trap
	8	Report PDU (not specifically defined; anyone wishing to use this must define it)

SNMP Request-Reply Message FormatWithin the Get/Set header of a request-reply SNMP packet, three more fields will be defined and used: Request ID, Error Status, and Error Index.

Request ID

The Request ID is a variable set by the manager during a Get, Get-Next-Request, or Set SNMP command. It is answered by the agent in a `get-response` message. It is similar to a transaction ID and allows the manager and agent to match request-response pairs.

Error Status

The Error Status is a number returned by the agent, specifying an error. It may be one of the types shown in Table 13.20.

TABLE 13.20	PDU TYPE	DESCRIPTION
Error Status Data Types	0	No Error
	1	SNMP message is too small for agent to fit reply
	2	Nonexistent variable specified
	3	Invalid value or syntax
	4	Attempt was made by manager to modify read-only variable
	5	General or unknown error
	6	No Access
	7	Wrong Type
	8	Wrong Length
	9	Wrong Encoding
	10	Wrong Value
	11	No Creation
	12	Inconsistent Value
	13	Resource Unavailable
	14	Commit Failed
	15	Undo Failed
	16	Authorization Error
	17	Not Writable
	18	Inconsistent Name

Error Index

The Error Index is an offset specifying which variable was in error (if that variable exists). The Error Index is set by the agent and will be set if an error occurs, so that the error may be found in the appropriate variable portion of the packet.

Examining an SNMP Request Message

The trace in Figure 13.10 depicts a normal SNMP get-next-request.

FIGURE 13.10

SNMP get-next-request

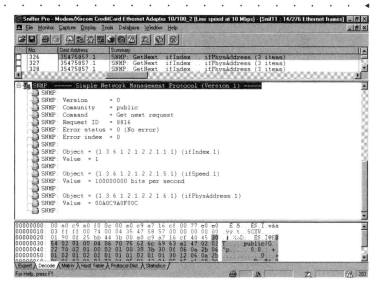

Notice in packet 326 that the SNMP manager has requested three items from the ifIndex data item in the device. The variable data shows that it received the values, indicating an interface number (1), an interface speed (100000000 bps), and a MAC address (00A0C9A0F00C).

SNMPv1 Trap Message Field Values

A trap message is sent to a manager (or group of managers) when something goes wrong at an agent, as shown in Figure 13.11.

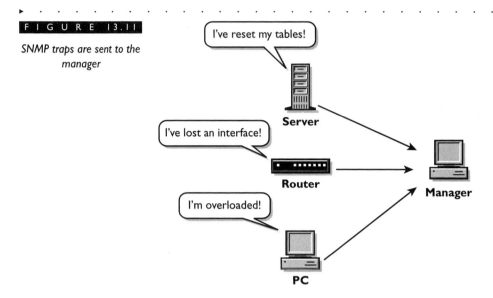

FIGURE 13.11

SNMP traps are sent to the manager

The trap message contains information (in an SNMPv1 format) about the type of error or warning that has occurred at an agent, as well as identification information for the agent. SNMPv2 uses the variable data portion of the packet to deliver this information. The following are the SNMPv1 trap message header fields and a description of the possible variable data that might fill them:

► **Enterprise:** The agent's sysObjectID (manufacturer ID).

► **Agent Address:** The IP address of the agent. The address scheme may change, due to the differences in the transport. For example, an IPX address would be the MAC address of the node instead of the IP address.

► **Trap Type:** A field that defines the specific error received. Possible trap type values are shown in Table 13.21. Six types are defined, with a seventh (number 6) available for vendor-specific implementations. The vendor-specific trap type is used in conjunction with the specific code field to determine the error.

► **Specific Code:** Enterprise-specific code used with vendor implementations of trap messages not previously specified.

- **Time Stamp:** A number representing a time since the agent last initialized. Values are shown in hundredths of a second.

TABLE 13.21

Trap Error Types

PDU TYPE	DESCRIPTION
0	Agent is initializing (cold start)
1	Agent is reinitializing (warm start)
2	Interface has entered the *down* state after having been in the *up* state
3	Interface has entered the *up* state after having been in the *down* state
4	Invalid community name was specified in an SNMP message (authentication failure)
5	EGP peer has moved into the *down* state
6	Vendor specific — look in the specific code field for more information

Get-Bulk-Request Field Values

The SNMPv2 get-bulk-request message type has two fields defined that tell the management computer how to request data from a table. Instead of making multiple requests until no more data is present, as in a get-next-request message, the get-bulk-request message can loop multiple times. The following are the field values specific to this message type:

- **Non-Repeaters:** The number of nonrepeating devices in the request.

- **Max-Repetitions:** The number of times the looping request should be made for this message.

Using SNMP Communication Ports

SNMP messages use ports to communicate information to and from managers and agents. Sometimes, a manager wants to have both management and agent software running on a management station. However, if all SNMP information (including management and trap information) is sent to the same port, how does a manager easily decipher which information was request information and which messages were traps that need attention?

SNMP separates the messages by allowing messages to communicate on two ports: 161 and 162. All SNMP Request and Set messages are sent to the agent on UDP port 161, while Trap information is sent to the manager on UDP port 162. This allows a workstation to have both management and agent software loaded and running properly, as shown in Figure 13.12.

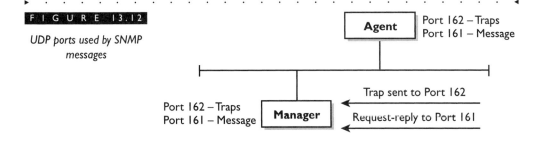

FIGURE 13.12

UDP ports used by SNMP messages

Request and Set messages are sent to the agent on UDP Port 161. Trap messages are sent to the manager on UDP Port 162.

NOTE

Built-In Novell Tools for Network Management

Tools such as Novell's ManageWise do an excellent job of trending, trapping, viewing, and managing networks using SNMP. This is not built in to NetWare, but is purchased as a separate product. However, Novell does provide a management agent and simple manager for servers and other network devices using four NetWare Loadable Modules (NLMs):

- ▸ SNMP.NLM

- ▸ SNMPLOG.NLM

- ▸ INETCFG.NLM

- ▸ TCPCON.NLM

SNMP.NLM

SNMP.NLM is the agent NLM uses with NetWare servers. This NLM is loaded automatically whenever the TCPIP.NLM is loaded at the server and provides SNMP services. To verify that SNMP.NLM is loaded, simply type MODULES SNMP at the server console, as shown in Figure 13.13.

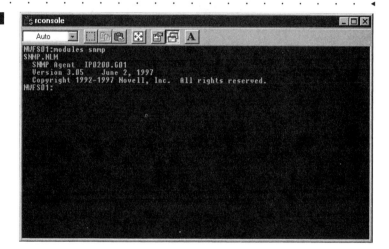

Type MODULES SNMP to verify SNMP module is loaded

SNMPLOG.NLM

The SNMPLOG.NLM module is loaded to enable the TCPCON utility to view the SNMP traps sent. SNMPLOG is a background process that collects trap messages and stores them in the local server, in the file sys:\etc\snmp$log.bin. The trap messages are read by TCPCON.NLM. SNMPLOG.NLM reads configuration information from the sys:\etc\traptarg.cfg file to determine where the traps should be sent.

INETCFG.NLM

Use the INETCFG.NLM module to configure SNMP communities, trap settings, and other SNMP values. All SNMP settings for the NetWare SNMP agent are configured through this module. Type **LOAD INETCFG** to start the configuration tool. From the main menu, choose Manage Configuration and then choose Configure SNMP Parameters (see Figure 13.14).

F I G U R E   13.14

SNMP Community
configuration for NetWare

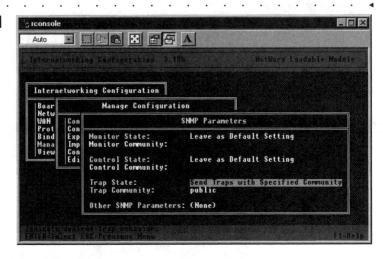

Figure 13.14 depicts the Community configuration options for the SNMP agent. For NetWare, the default setting for all communities is public. The administrator may set different communities and control and change trap community settings from this screen. Community information is initially loaded as SNMP.NLM arguments in the sys:etc\netinfo.cfg file. Information relating to hardware settings or human contact inserted through INETCFG is stored in the sys:\etc\snmp.cfg file. Specific manager IP addresses may be configured through the TCP/IP option of the INETCFG module, as shown in Figure 13.15.

By default, NetWare traps are sent to the local system (IP address 127.0.0.1). Additional managers may be added to the table by pressing the Insert key and specifying the manager's IP address while in the INETCFG module. This modifies the sys:\etc\traptarg.cfg file.

TCPCON.NLM

The TCPCON.NLM module is a simple SNMP manager that can be used to monitor SNMP statistics and change MIB data. Because it is a simple manager, TCPCON does not monitor MIBs that do not conform to the TCP/IP MIB-II specification, and does not provide trending.

To use the TCPCON manager, type **LOAD TCPCON** at the file server console. The manager appears, and current statistics are available, as shown in Figure 13.16.

FIGURE 13.15

SNMP Manager Table of IP addresses

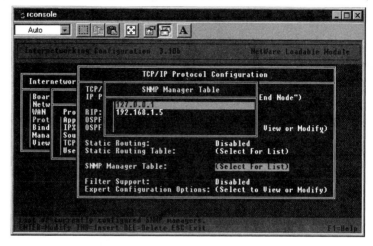

FIGURE 13.16

TCPCON Main menu provides SNMP statistics

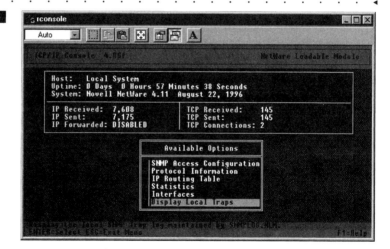

The default SNMP statistics shown are for the local system. The administrator may view statistics for another computer by choosing the SNMP Access Configuration menu choice. From there, the manager may type an IP address or hostname of an agent, followed by the transport desired. A manager may also view or modify the values of the agent MIB (if modification is allowed). A manager may also want to view the local Trap Log, as shown in Figure 13.17. Two type 6 traps have been sent to this server. The local Trap Log stays intact until you choose to clear it.

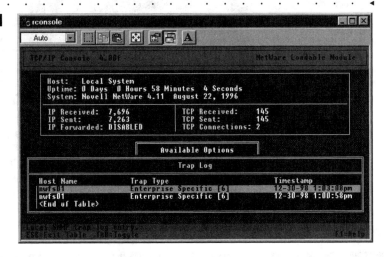

FIGURE 13.17

NetWare server local Trap Log

SNMP Security

SNMP has several versions, starting with the SNMPv1 standard, moving to the current (though not always implemented) SNMPv2 standard, and a developing third standard, SNMPv3.

Several threats to SNMP security exist when using the SNMP management system. Of greatest concern is that the nature of using SNMP management requires that agent software be installed on every managed node. Each of those nodes has access to the manager at some point in time.

In the original SNMP specification, a very simple and clear-text method existed for requesting and accessing SNMP information from an agent, using the community string for authentication. This leaves the door wide open for the unauthorized modification of information contained in the MIB. Anyone with access to a manager could potentially do harm to the network by taking interfaces up and down, changing router values, and rebooting devices.

Next was the trusting nature of the access authority given to the manager by an agent. No controls really existed to determine whether the originator of a message really was the authorized party, and not a manager taking on the identity of an authorized manager. Another security concern was the threat that a message could be modified, and falsified packets could be transmitted and received/processed by the agent.

With the SNMPv2 specification, new authentication and privacy protocols were defined to eliminate the possibility of malicious attacks on the system:

▸ **Authentication protocol:** Provides a mechanism by which SNMPv2 management communications transmitted by the party may be reliably identified as having originated from that party. It also reliably determines that the message received is the message that was sent.

▸ **Privacy protocol:** Provides a secret method of communication between an agent and a manager, and specifies that only authenticated messages are to be privacy protected.

Using more sophisticated encryption methods and the development of newer, more efficient security protocols has helped network managers eliminate the worries that their network SNMP devices may be compromised.

Analyzing SNMP Communication

You've learned about MIBs and how they work. Now, you're ready to look in depth at the packet to see how all of these concepts—SMI, MIB, and SNMP, work together. You learned earlier in the chapter that every device running TCP/IP has a standard MIB built in. Figure 13.18 shows a simple request/reply pair generated in frames 1 and 2.

In Figure 13.18, frame 1 shows an SNMP request sent from 130.128.1.40 to 192.9.11.44. The request is for the TCP/IP Interfaces Group (shown in the summary decode at the attribute ifOperStatus) and is requesting the value of the Operational Status of the interface. In other words, the request is attempting to determine whether the interface is working.

F I G U R E   13.18

TCP/IP MIB interface status request

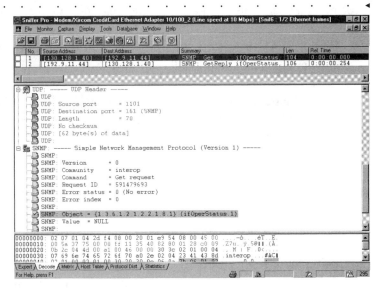

Notice that the UDP header Destination Port shows a value of 161. This indicates the SNMP message as something other than a trap message. So far so good. The SNMP portion of the packet indicates the actual command, Get Request. Also notice the unique Request ID value of 591479693, and the Error Status of 0. After the Error Index comes the variable portion of the packet. In this SNMP request, the actual request shows the SMI information (1.3.6.1.2.1.2.2.1.8.1). This is a designation of the particular interface group field ifOperStatus using ASN.1 notation.

To find the ASN.1 notation for all TCP/IP MIB field and table values, refer to RFC 1213.

NOTE

The last field to explore is also in the variable section. It lists the current value of the ifOperStatus field as NULL, which makes sense, because this is a request, not a reply.

Figure 13.19 shows receipt of a reply to the interface status request.

FIGURE 13.19

TCP/IP MIB interface status reply

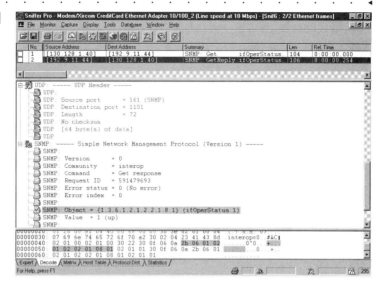

This time, the Source Address is 192.9.11.144 and the Destination Address is 130.128.1.40. This is to be expected, because this is a reply to a request. Notice also that in the Sniffer summary, the message is listed as a GetReply message.

Once again, in the UDP header, the Source Port listed is 161, designating a request/reply message rather than an error or trap message. Within the SNMP header, notice the Command field value has changed to Get Response, because this is a reply. Additionally, the Request ID, 591479693, is the same as the previous frame, showing that this is a reply to that specific request.

The variable portion of the packet begins, again, with the Object field, which comes just after the Error Index. Once again, the ASN.1 notation for the ifOperStatus field is designated, just like the request packet. However, notice the data in the Value field. This time, instead of a NULL value, the actual status (up or down) of the interface is listed. Thus, you have just discovered that the interface card in computer 192.9.11.44 is working properly, because the Value field is set to (up).

Case Study—Learning to Read the MIBs

This chapter has focused on reading the statistics coming from the TCP/IP MIB. However, in a real-world environment, TCP/IP is not the only manageable portion of a network. What about hubs, routers, and other protocols, such as IPX? (Remember, SNMP can run on protocols other than TCP/IP).

The Problem

We are presented with the trace shown in Figure 13.20.

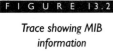

FIGURE 13.20

Trace showing MIB information

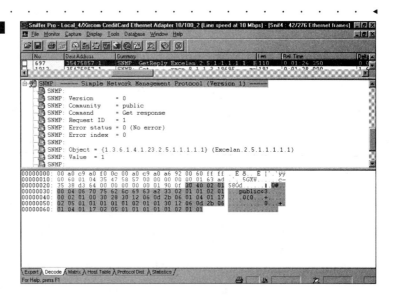

The question asked by the person presenting the trace is: what am I looking at? More specifically, what information is being delivered by this reply packet? To answer this question, we must dig a bit deeper.

The Analysis

The first step is to determine who the MIB belongs to. In Figure 13.20, we see the full ASN.1 number in the Object field of the trace. The Object field contains 1.3.6.1.4.1.23.2.5.1.1.1.1.1. We know already that the 1.3.6.1. belongs to iso.org.dod.internet. The .4.1 belongs to private.enterprise. (Refer to Figure 13.5, earlier in this chapter, for verification.) So now what? How do we find the number 23? What does it mean?

Private enterprises can have their MIB data represented in the SMI structure by applying for a Private Enterprise Code from the Internet Assigned Numbers Authority (IANA). The list is available on the Web and is shown in Figure 13.21.

Go to ftp://ftp.isi.edu/in-notes/iana/assignments/enterprise-numbers with your browser for a list of all Private Enterprise Codes.

FIGURE 13.21

IANA Private Enterprise Codes

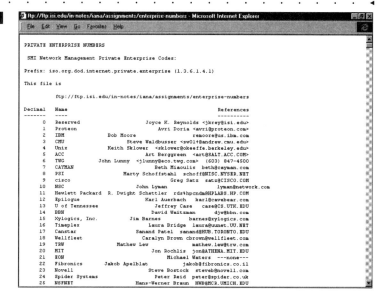

We have already identified 1.3.6.1.4.1, so we look on the Private Enterprise Code list to help define the owner of the next number, which is 23. Figure 13.21

shows that number 23 is assigned to Novell. If we were to draw the SMI tree to this point, it would look like that shown in Figure 13.22.

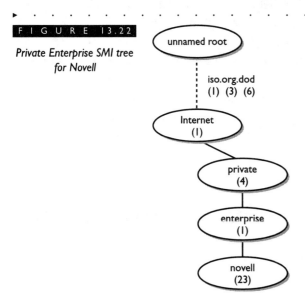

Private Enterprise SMI tree for Novell

Now, we must find the MIB that defines the rest of the numbers. We know that the MIB information belongs to Novell, so we look to it to supply the MIB files. (Most manufacturers provide MIB files with their devices — Novell supplies many with the ManageWise management system.) The network used for this trace uses ManageWise, so we start looking there. MIB files are text files. We know that we are looking for the next number, which is 2, so we to do a text search within the MIB files for the words **novell 2**. This is important, because it describes exactly what we are looking for — the SMI meaning of number 2 under number 23 assigned to Novell.

We find a MIB file called IPX that contains the text we are looking for, and then open it in a word processor, as shown in Figure 13.23.

FIGURE 13.23

IPX MIB file

```
Ipx - Notepad
File  Edit  Search  Help
-- This MIB defines the management information for a system using the IPX
-- protocol.  The MIB consists of four groups:
--
--    1.  System Group - contains general information about all instances
--                       of IPX on the system
--
--    2.  Circuit Group - contains information about all circuits used by
--                        IPX on the system
--
--    3.  Forwarding Group - contains generic routing information that
--                           must be provided by any IPX routing protocol.
--
--    4.  Services Group - contains information about all known services.
IMPORTS
           enterprises, Counter
                  FROM RFC1155-SMI
           OBJECT-TYPE
                  FROM RFC-1212
           TRAP-TYPE
                  FROM RFC-1215
           PhysAddress
                  FROM RFC1213-MIB;

novell  OBJECT IDENTIFIER ::= { enterprises 23 }
mibDoc  OBJECT IDENTIFIER ::= { novell 2 }
ipx     OBJECT IDENTIFIER ::= { mibDoc 5 }

-- Groups

ipxSystem OBJECT IDENTIFIER ::= {ipx 1}
ipxCircuit OBJECT IDENTIFIER ::= {ipx 2}
ipxForwarding OBJECT IDENTIFIER ::= {ipx 3}
ipxServices OBJECT IDENTIFIER ::= {ipx 4}
ipxTraps OBJECT IDENTIFIER ::= {ipx 5}
```

SMI Namespace Information

The important thing about this MIB file is that it defines another major portion of the SMI structure, right at the beginning. Notice in Figure 13.23 the words OBJECT IDENTIFIER and more words in parentheses, which indicate a category, along with a specific instance within each category. For example, novell OBJECT IDENTIFIER ::= { enterprises 23 } documents the fact that the novell object is labeled number 23 and sits under the enterprises SMI object. Figure 13.22 shows that we have already verified this information. Looking further into the file, we see the following text:

```
novell  OBJECT IDENTIFIER ::= { enterprises 23 }

mibDoc  OBJECT IDENTIFIER ::= { novell 2 }

ipx     OBJECT IDENTIFIER ::= { mibDoc 5 }


— Groups


ipxSystem OBJECT IDENTIFIER ::= {ipx 1}
```

```
ipxCircuit OBJECT IDENTIFIER ::= {ipx 2}

ipxForwarding OBJECT IDENTIFIER ::= {ipx 3}

ipxServices OBJECT IDENTIFIER ::= {ipx 4}

ipxTraps OBJECT IDENTIFIER ::= {ipx 5}
```

If we were to use this information to map out more of the SMI tree, it would now look like Figure 13.24:

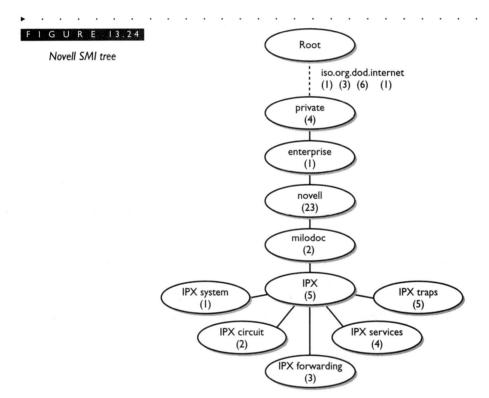

FIGURE 13.24

Novell SMI tree

At this point, we have identified the request of 1.3.6.1.4.1.23.2.5.1 as `iso.org.dod.internet.private.enterprise.novell.mibdoc.ipx.ipxSystem`. Look at the MIB again to define the rest of the numbers, given as 1.1.1.1.

Moving further down in the MIB text, we are trying to identify the field that carries an identifier of {1} under the ipxSystem object. Within the MIB, we see the following text:

```
ipxBasicSysTable OBJECT-TYPE

    SYNTAX       SEQUENCE OF IPXBasicSysEntry

    ACCESS       not-accessible

    STATUS       mandatory

    DESCRIPTION "The IPX System table - basic information."

    ::= {ipxSystem 1}
```

Looking at this text, we can now see that the ipxBasicSysTable object is described at {ipxSystem 1}, which is also the the object named 1 that is found directly under the ipxSystem object. We see that this is a table of information. The next entry in the MIB looks like this:

```
ipxBasicSysEntry OBJECT-TYPE

    SYNTAX       IPXBasicSysEntry

    ACCESS       not-accessible

    STATUS       mandatory

    DESCRIPTION "Each entry corresponds to one instance of IPX
running

                 on the system."

    INDEX        {ipxBasicSysInstance}

    ::= {ipxBasicSysTable 1}
```

And the next entry appears as follows:

```
ipxBasicSysInstance OBJECT-TYPE

    SYNTAX       INTEGER

    ACCESS       read-write

    STATUS       mandatory
```

```
    DESCRIPTION "The unique identifier of the instance of IPX
    to which this row corresponds.  This value may be written
    only when creating a new entry in the table."

    ::= {ipxBasicSysEntry 1}
```

We have now defined the entire SMI name space by using ASN.1 notation, with the exception of the final entry, 1, because it is actually a data value, not a MIB object. In this case, the final number identifies the instance of IPX that is loaded on the computer in question. If two IPX stacks were loaded, the final number would be 2. So, overall, we have identified the name space 1.3.6.1.4.1.23.2.5.1.1.1.1.1 as iso.org. dod.internet.private.enterprise.novell.mibdoc.ipx.ipxSystem. ipsBasicSysTable.ipxBasicSysEntry.ipxBasicSysInstance.1.

If we were to draw the Novell portion of the SMI name space now, it would look like that shown in Figure 13.25.

FIGURE 13.25

Full Novell SMI name space

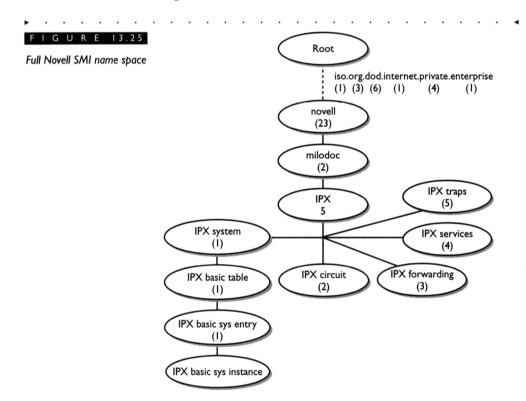

The Solution

We now understand how MIB information is read. This trace tells us that one instance of IPX is loaded on a server, and it is supplying SNMP information over IPX for management. Other manufacturers may have different MIB information. For example, a hub manufacturer may write a MIB that can get port speed, link status, and collision rates. Each of these MIBs assists in the daily management of the network, by adding features not available in the TCP/IP MIB.

Summary

This chapter discussed how network management protocols assist in managing network devices. A network program running on the device, called an *agent*, is queried by the software on the management device, called the *manager*. The manager may request or change data within the Management Information Base (MIB) located on the agent device.

The Structure of Management Information (SMI) is the naming mechanism for storing managed objects. Objects are referenced by using a special language, called *Abstract Syntax Notation* (ASN.1)

The TCP/IP protocol defined for network management is the Simple Network Management Protocol (SNMP), which is a request and reply protocol. A special message is defined within SNMP, called a *trap*, that can be used to alert network managers to triggered events within an agent device.

## CHAPTER 14

Service Location Protocol (SLP)

The Service Location Protocol (SLP) is a new standards-track protocol. It is designed to simplify the discovery and use of network resources. In the future, a wide variety of services, such as printers, Web servers, fax machines, video cameras, file systems, backup devices, databases, mail servers, calendars, coffee machines, and whatever else you can think of will be part of our networks. Accessing services by manual configuration or administrative procedures will no longer be manageable. Providing for the dynamic nature of service availability is an important accomplishment for SLP.

Overview of SLP Functionality

SLP version 1 is described in RFC 2165. Drafts have already been submitted for version 2. This book refers to RFC 2165 and the current implementations of SLP. Where possible, this chapter gives hints on what the IETF (Internet Engineering Task Force) is working on. What SLP version 2 will look like cannot be determined at the time of writing. Not too many implementations of SLP version 1 exist yet. Novell NetWare 5 is an example of an operating system that uses SLP's functionality. IBM uses SLP with NetWare for SAA, and Hewlett-Packard says that JetAdmin 4.0 supports SLP.

SLP Processes

SLP communication includes several processes:

- **User agent (UA):** Initiates a discovery on behalf of an application. It understands the service and resource needs of the application and gets the information from a service or directory agent. A UA looks for a directory agent first. If it can't find a directory agent, it multicasts a general Service Request to the network segment. Any service agents that receive the Service Request and that are holding a matching Service Registration will respond to the Service Request.

▸ **Service agent (SA):** Works on behalf of a service. It responds directly to a UA's general multicast query for services. The SA can also register its service with one or more directory agents. SLP dynamically maintains Service Attributes so that the information provided to the UA is current.

▸ **Directory agent (DA):** Collects and maintains service information. When SAs discover the presence of a DA, they register their services with the DA. The SA is responsible for locating, contacting, and populating DAs with service information. The DA then replies to user agent Service Requests, if it maintains information about the requested service.

Scopes

Network resources can be collected together into administrative domains called *scopes*. Scopes are supported by UAs, SAs, and DAs. User agents are typically configured with the name of their administrative scope. This configuration can be done in one of three ways:

▸ Using DHCP (option 79)

▸ From the initial computer setup

▸ From directory agents

Each UA includes its configured scope in Service Requests, which enables access to services configured to operate within that scope. Scopes may be configured along the lines of administrative control, geographic locations, or network topology.

SLP Network Designs

Which of the preceding processes you use depends on the size and complexity of your network design. The following three scenarios are possible.

Small Network

If you have 50 servers or less, you can choose the small network design. This design has no DAs and no need for scopes. SAs reply directly to user agent multicasts. The number of 50 servers is an average random number. It is not a limitation of SLP. At what point you need to implement a DA is unique to every network and really depends on different factors, such as the capacity of the network segment, the traffic profile, the topology of your network, the average bandwidth utilization, and many more factors.

Figure 14.1 shows how SAs directly respond to a general SLP multicast request from a UA.

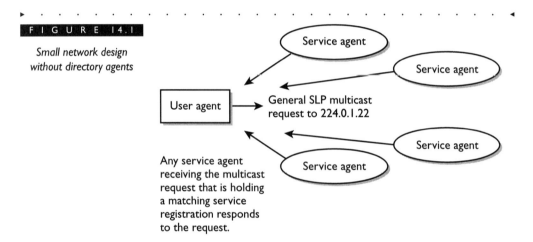

FIGURE 14.1

Small network design without directory agents

Medium-Sized Network

In a larger installation, you may not want hundreds of SAs to reply to queries from UAs. In this case, you implement DAs. When SAs come up and discover the presence of a DA, they register their service with it. Thereafter, the DA replies to requests from UAs on behalf of the SAs.

Figure 14.2 shows how SAs register their services with a DA and how the DA replies to the UA querying for a service.

FIGURE 14.2

A medium-sized network design with a directory agent

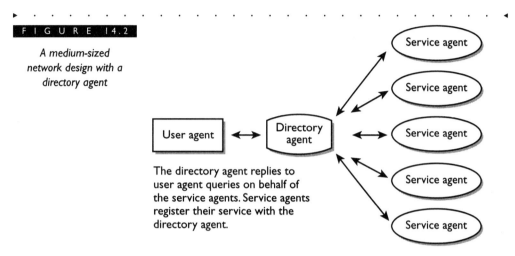

The directory agent replies to user agent queries on behalf of the service agents. Service agents register their service with the directory agent.

Large Network

For very large installations, and especially for networks that span WAN links, you can choose the large network design. In this design, the services are grouped together into scopes. For example, if your company has two sites, one in Zurich and one in Paris, you can configure a scope for each location. The UAs at each site are configured with the scope name of their location and the address of their local DA. This way, you will not have SLP queries crossing the WAN link. If users need access to remote services, you have to configure the UAs with both DAs' addresses. But, in this case, your SLP traffic crosses the WAN link.

You can also use this design to balance the load between multiple DAs. To do this, separate services into scopes and set up a DA for each scope. This way, one DA does not have to handle all SLP queries.

Figure 14.3 shows a design using directory agents and scopes.

FIGURE 14.3

Large network—logical grouping of services into scopes

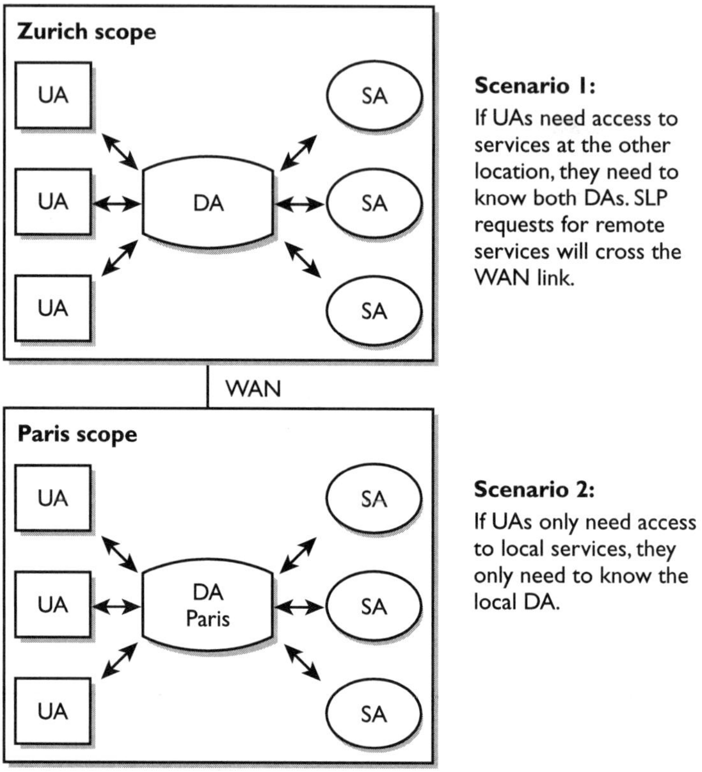
Zurich scope
UA
UA
UA
DA
SA
SA
SA
WAN
Paris scope
UA
UA
UA
DA
Paris
SA
SA
SA
Scenario 1:
If UAs need access to services at the other location, they need to know both DAs. SLP requests for remote services will cross the WAN link.
Scenario 2:
If UAs only need access to local services, they only need to know the local DA.

To allow for service access across the WAN link in this scenario, you could define an additional *unscoped directory agent*. By doing so, all services would register not only with their scoped DA, but also with the unscoped DA. The drawback in this scenario is that SLPv2 will no longer support the *unscoped* option. So you should not use this design.

The problem is that the current standard does not define a protocol for DA-DA communication. If that were available, the DAs could exchange service information, and UAs could find services at the remote location by talking to their local DA. Using SLP with Novell's NDS provides a wonderful replacement for this missing DA-DA communication (see Figure 14.4).

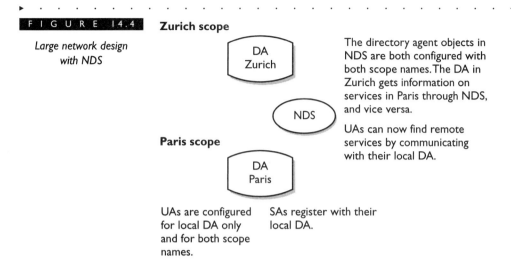

FIGURE 14.4

Large network design with NDS

Zurich scope

DA Zurich

NDS

The directory agent objects in NDS are both configured with both scope names. The DA in Zurich gets information on services in Paris through NDS, and vice versa.

Paris scope

DA Paris

UAs can now find remote services by communicating with their local DA.

UAs are configured for local DA only and for both scope names.

SAs register with their local DA.

When you use SLP with NDS, the two DAs, if configured for both scope names, exchange SLP information for remote services through NDS. SLP queries for remote services do not cross the WAN link, but are answered by the local DA.

This large network design can be quite complex. You can assign several scopes to a particular directory agent, and several directory agents to one scope.

According to RFC 2165, the terms "local" and "remote" should not be used to name your scopes. They are reserved for future use.

IMPORTANT

SLP Communications

UDP (User Datagram Protocol) or TCP (Transmission Control Protocol) can be used for transport of SLP communication. The registered port number for both transport protocols is 427. Most SLP communications use UDP. TCP can be used for bulk information transfer, which is traffic generated by a single request with multiple replies.

Several types of communications are possible with SLP:

▸ Service location general packets (to multicast address 224.0.1.22)

▸ Directory agent discovery packets (to multicast address 224.0.1.35)

▸ Internet Group Message Protocol (IGMP) multicast packets

▸ Unicast packets (to station address)

Locating a Directory Agent

A UA or SA can locate a DA in any of the following ways:

▸ **Configure the SLP device (a UA or SA) statically to use a specific DA.**
This option should be used only in networks in which the use of broadcast
or multicast discovery is impossible.

▸ **Use DHCP to configure hosts for a certain DA.** DHCP options 78 and
79 have been assigned for this purpose. Option 78 assigns the DA, and
option 79 assigns the scope name.

▸ **Locate a DA dynamically.** During the bootup process, an SLP device
sends a directory agent discovery multicast packet (multicast address
224.0.1.35), looking for a DA.

If no DA exists, the UA sends an SLP general multicast packet (multicast
address 224.0.1.22) to locate the requested service. Then service agents will reply
to the request.

Joining a Multicast Group

To join a multicast group, an SLP device uses IGMP, as described in Chapter 18.
The router decides whether or not to forward multicast packets to particular
subnetworks. IP routers forward multicast packets only to subnetworks in which
other devices have joined the multicast group. By using multicasting as opposed

to broadcasting, SLP reduces traffic on the network. In case your routers do not support IGMP, SLP can be configured to use broadcasting instead.

Refer to Chapter 4 to learn more about multicast and to Chapter 18 for information on IGMP (Internet Group Management Protocol).

X-REF

▶ . . . . ◀

SLP Header Structure

Figure 14.5 shows the fields in the SLP header, which are described next.

▶ . . . . ◀

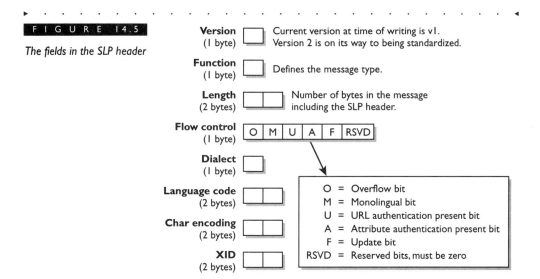

FIGURE 14.5

The fields in the SLP header

Version
(1 byte)
Current version at time of writing is v1.
Version 2 is on its way to being standardized.

Function
(1 byte)
Defines the message type.

Length
(2 bytes)
Number of bytes in the message including the SLP header.

Flow control
(1 byte)
O | M | U | A | F | RSVD

Dialect
(1 byte)

Language code
(2 bytes)

Char encoding
(2 bytes)

XID
(2 bytes)

O = Overflow bit
M = Monolingual bit
U = URL authentication present bit
A = Attribute authentication present bit
F = Update bit
RSVD = Reserved bits, must be zero

Version

This 1-byte field contains the version of SLP used. The current version is 1. Version 2 is on its way.

Function

This 1-byte field defines the type of the message. The currently defined operations are listed in Table 14.1.

TABLE 14.1 *SLP Message Types*	MESSAGE TYPE	ABBREVIATION	FUNCTION VALUE
	Service Request	SrvReq	1
	Service Reply	SrvRply	2
	Service Registration	SrvReg	3
	Service Deregister	SrvDereg	4
	Service Acknowledge	SrvAck	5
	Attribute Request	AttrRqst	6
	Attribute Reply	AttrRply	7
	DA Advertisement	DAAdvert	8
	Service Type Request	SrvTypeRqst	9
	Service Type Reply	SrvTypeRply	10

Length

This 2-byte field contains the length of the message in bytes including the SLP header.

Flow Control

Table 14.2 details the Flow Control bits.

Dialect

Dialect tags will be used by future versions of the Service Location Protocol to indicate a variant of vocabulary used. This field is reserved and *must* be set to 0 in the current version for compatibility with future versions of SLP.

T A B L E   1 4 . 2

The Flow Control Bits in the SLP Header

ABBREVIATION	NAME	DESCRIPTION
O	Overflow bit	If an SLP request results in a UDP reply that will overflow a datagram, the SA or DA sets the Overflow bit and sends as much data as it can fit into the UDP message. If the UA needs additional information, it initiates a TCP connection to the SA or DA and rerequests the information.
M	Monolingual bit	Requests with this bit set indicate the UA will accept responses only in the language that is indicated by the Service or Attribute Request. All Service Registrations declare the language in which the strings in the service attributes are written, by specifying the appropriate code in the message header. For each language the service advertises, a separate registration takes place. Each of these registrations uses the same URL to indicate that it refers to the same service. If a service is fully deregistered, then it needs to be deregistered only once. This effectively deregisters the service in all languages it has been registered in.
U	URL Authentication Present bit	If this bit is set, the URL is followed by a URL *authentication block*, which is used to authenticate Service Registrations and Deregistrations. Note: The current Novell implementation of SLP does not support this feature. The way authentication blocks work will be redesigned for SLPv2. Novell committed to support SLPv2 as soon as it is ready. This most likely will be the time at which it will support authentication of Service Registration and Deregistration.
A	Attribute Authentication Present bit	Authentication Present bit for attribute information. If this bit is set, the U bit must be set too.
F	Update bit	If this bit is set in a Service Acknowledgment, it means the DA has registered the service as a new entry, as opposed to an update.
RSVD	Reserved	These 3 bits are reserved and must be 0.

Language Code

This 2-byte field defines the language code to be applied to strings in the remainder of the message. This field will probably be phased out with version 2 of SLP.

Character Encoding

The characters making up strings within the remainder of the message may be encoded in any standardized encoding. Values for character encoding can be found in IANA's database: `http://www.isi.edu/in-notes/iana/assignments/character-sets`. The encoding will determine the interpretation of all character data that follows the SLP header. No way exists to mix ASCII and UNICODE, for example. All responses must be in the character set of the request or use US-ASCII. If a request is sent to a DA or SA, or a registration is sent to a DA that is unable to manipulate or store the character set of the incoming message, the request will fail. The SA or DA returns a CHARSET_NOT_UNDERSTOOD error in a SrvAck message in this case.

Transaction Identifier (XID)

This 2-byte field contains the transaction identifier. It is used to match requests with replies. The requestor creates an initial random number for the first request and increments it by one for each consecutive request. If the requestor has to retransmit the request because no answer is received, the XID should not increment.

Error Code

Some of the SLP frames have an Error Code field that comes directly after the XID. The values possible are shown in Table 14.3.

ERROR	VALUE
No Error	0
LANGUAGE_NOT_SUPPORTED	1
PROTOCOL_PARSE_ERROR	2
INVALID_REGISTRATION	3
SCOPE_NOT_SUPPORTED	4
CHARSET_NOT_UNDERSTOOD	5
AUTHENTICATION_ABSENT	6
AUTHENTICATION_FAILED	7

T A B L E   14.3

SLP Error Codes

The Use of URLs

The location of network services is represented as a URL (Uniform Resource Locator). You probably have used URLs before in your Web browser. The syntax and use of URLs is described in RFC 1738. SLP uses the *service:* URL scheme to specify the location of a service. Well-known service types are registered with the IANA, and templates are available as RFCs. Private service types may be supported.

Service types are used by SAs to register and deregister services with DAs. They are also used by DAs and SAs to return Service Replies to UAs. When URLs are registered, they have lifetimes and lengths. These values are associated with the URL for the duration of the registration. The association is known as the URL-entry and has the format shown in Figure 14.6.

F I G U R E   14.6

Format of the URL-entry

Lifetime (2 bytes) — The length of time (in seconds) that the registration is valid.

Length (2 bytes) — The length of the URL in bytes.

URL (Variable)

Authentication block — Only if U bit set in header.

Normally, a Service Request (SrvReq, value 1) returns a Service Reply (SrvRply, value 2). The exception to this rule is when a Service Request for the service type *directory-agent* is made. This Service Request is answered with a DA Advertisement (DAAdvert, value 8).

Without preconfiguration of a DA (by DHCP or manual configuration), a UA or SA sends a Service Request to discover a DA. It sends the Service Request to the directory agent discovery multicast address (224.0.1.35). No scope is included in this Service Request, so all DAs will respond.

Analyzing an SLP Session

So that you can become familiar with SLP, the following sections show some SLP-related communications.

SLP Device Registers Multicast Address

When an SLP device comes up, it first has to advertise its multicast address membership. It uses IGMP to do this. Figure 14.7 shows the frames pertaining to that process. Note the two frames. Frame 4 is a type 2 registration, which provides backward-compatibility with version 1 of IGMP.

F I G U R E 14.7

SLP device advertises multicast group membership

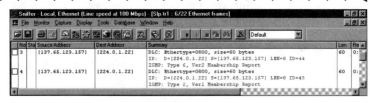

DA Discovery

In Figure 14.8, you see an SLP device looking for a DA. This can be a UA booting or an SA trying to locate a DA. Note the destination multicast IP address of 224.0.1.35 in the summary window. The message is addressed to UDP port 427 (shown in the summary window).

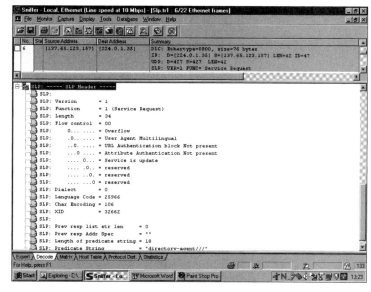

FIGURE 14.8

Directory agent discovery message

The Function field contains the message type 1, decoded as a Service Request (refer to Table 14.1). The Length field states the length, in bytes, which includes the SLP header. As mentioned earlier, the Dialect field currently isn't used and must be 0. At the end of the header, you can see a URL entry, as previously described in Figure 14.6. In this case, no specific service is mentioned, because the device looks for any DA. The first 2 bytes are both 0 in this message. They are followed by 2 bytes for the Length field and the URL for the service name.

Service Request/Reply

Figure 14.9 shows the SLP Service and Attribute Request and Reply communications of a booting NT Workstation that logs in to a NetWare 5 NDS tree. A filter was set on SLP to display the trace. For easier interpretation, the XID numbers were manually inserted on the summary window lines.

FIGURE 14.9

SLP Service and Attribute Request/Reply

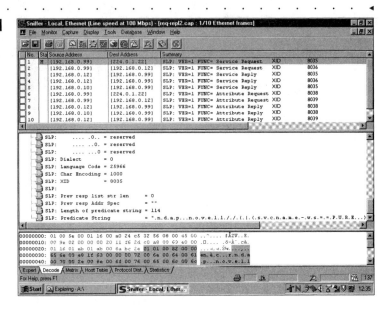

The NT client boots and issues a Service Request for the tree name. Note the Predicate String field in the detail window. The client looks for a service type ndap.novell, which means that it looks for an NDS server. The name of the tree that it tries to find is "Pure." The client issues two requests: one to the general multicast address (frame 1, XID 8035), and one to the DA (frame 2, XID 8036). Frame 3 is the DA's Service Reply to the Service Request in frame 1, and frame 4 is the DA's Service Reply to the unicast Service Request in frame 2 (compare XID). Another NetWare 5 server is in the tree, with an IP address of 192.168.0.10. Its services are registered with the DA, but it answers to the general Service Request issued in frame 1.

The same process happens with the Attribute Requests in frames 6 and 7. Frame 6 is the Attribute request to the general multicast address, and frame 7 goes out to the DA. Frame 8 is the DA's Attribute Reply to the general Attribute Request in frame 6, and frame 10 is the DA's Attribute Reply to the Attribute Request in frame 7. Frame 9 is the answer of the other server to the general Attribute Request.

DA Advertisement and Service Registration

Figure 14.10 shows the DA Advertisement and Service Registration frames. This trace was taken while loading SLPDA.NLM on a NetWare 5 server.

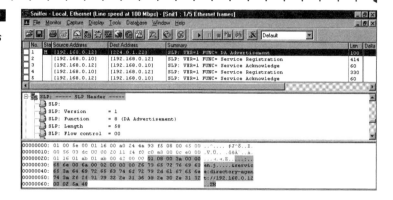

FIGURE 14.10

A DA comes up, advertises its presence, and SAs register with the DA

The DA Advertisement in frame 1 is addressed to the general multicast address of 224.0.1.22 and to UDP port 427. It is an SLP message of type 8, as you can see in the detail window. The Advertisement provides the IP address of the DA (shown in the hex window at the bottom).

Now, the other server with the IP address of 192.168.0.10 registers its services with the DA. These frames are not addressed to the multicast address. They use unicast. The SA takes the IP address for the DA from the DA Advertisement frame. The two Service Registration frames are frame 2 and frame 4. Both Service Registration frames are acknowledged by the DA. The service type advertised in frame 2 is `service:ndap.novell:///PURE`. This is the registration of the NDS tree name. In frame 4, the server registers the bindery name for the server. The entry is `service:bindery.novell:///GWPURE`. For a list of Novell service types, refer to Chapter 15. When registering with the DA, the SA does send a lot of additional SLP attribute information. It can currently be seen in the hex window of Sniffer Pro.

TIP

If the DA has been configured for specific scopes, the DA Advertisement message will contain the names of the supported scopes. The UA will add these names to its list of scopes that it is aware of. Many network administrators have chosen this method to control indirectly the scopes used by UAs, instead of configuring this through DHCP or local configuration. They configure the DAs with scope names and then control what DAs the UAs have access to.

Troubleshooting SLP

Your best friend in troubleshooting is always your analyzer. If you work with NetWare 5, the following utilities are available:

► On a Novell NetWare 5 server, use **DISPLAY SLP SERVICES** on the server console to view the registered services.

► Use **SLPINFO** on the command prompt of a Windows 95/98 or NT Workstation with Novell NetWare 5 Client software to view the local SLP configuration.

X-REF

For a detailed description of NetWare 5's implementation of SLP and related commands and utilities, refer to Chapter 15.

Case Study — What Can Go Wrong

The following case study presents a trace file that was taken because a user working on an NT Workstation could not log in to the network.

The Problem

Every time the user tries to log in, he gets the message `The tree or server cannot be found`. All other users have no problems connecting to the tree. We took the following trace file while the user logged in, and set a display filter on the NT Workstation's MAC address.

The Analysis

Figure 14.11 shows the trace file, which includes the following information:

FIGURE 14.11

Trace file summary

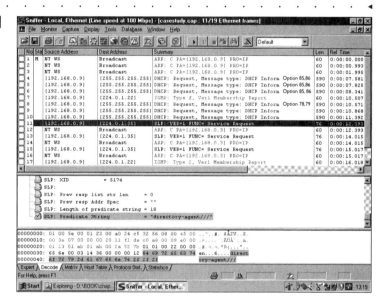

▸ **Frames 1 to 3:** The workstation is checking on its IP address (duplicate IP address test).

▸ **Frames 4 to 6:** DHCP Requests for options 85 (NDS server) and 86 (tree name). Because no DHCP server exists on this segment, no reply is made to these frames.

▸ **Frame 7:** The IGMP Membership Report for the SLP multicast address.

▸ **Frames 8 to 10:** These DHCP Requests ask for DHCP options 78 (DA) and 79 (scope name). Again, there is no reply, because no DHCP server is present.

▸ **Frames 11, 13, and 15:** Frame 11 is a Service Request for a DA, which is repeated in frames 13 and 15. But, no reply is made to this request.

▸ **Frames 12, 14, and 16:** Three ARP Requests for the IP address of 192.168.0.3. No reply.

At this point, the error message is displayed at the workstation. What's missing here? We know that the servers are up and running. Other users are logging in without problems. The unusual thing in this trace file is that it ARPs for an IP address and gets no reply, and no reply is made by a DA.

The Solution

The first thing we do is check the NetWare NT Client properties, by right-clicking the Network Neighborhood icon and checking the properties for the Novell Client for Windows NT, as shown in Figure 14.12.

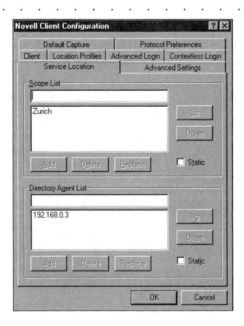

F I G U R E 14.12

The Service Location tab of the Novell Client Configuration dialog box

The Service Location tab indicates the reason that the workstation ARPed for the IP address of 192.168.0.3: the entry in the Directory Agent List. But no DA with this IP address is running, which is the reason that no reply is received. A further search through the Advanced Settings in the Novell Client Configuration dialog box, shown in Figure 14.13, indicates that the SLP Active Discovery parameter of a DA has been turned off. This means that the client doesn't multicast a Service or Attribute Request if no DA is running.

FIGURE 14.13

The Advanced Settings tab of the Novell Client Configuration dialog box

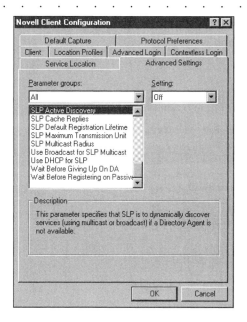

This user couldn't log in because no DA was there to be reached, and the user couldn't multicast for a service to be answered by an SA. The DA configured on its list was not up, and no backup DA was available to service the request.

Why could other users log in? Checking their SLP client properties, we found that they had been configured with a different DA in the Directory Agent List, and that DA was available. The IP address in the troubled client's Directory Agent List was a typo.

Summary

This chapter has explained how SLP communicates and how it eases service administration. It provides a dynamic and scaleable service location and reduces the number of broadcasts present in networks.

The next chapter introduces Novell's Implementation of TCP/IP. The advent of NetWare 5 and Pure IP communication presents many great new things to learn. You also meet SLP again, because NetWare 5 uses it.

## PART V

Vendor Implementation of TCP/IP

Novell TCP/IP Implementation

This chapter gives you an overview of new TCP/IP-related features with Novell NetWare 5. NetWare 5 includes DHCP and DNS services that are tied into NDS (Novell Directory Services). This chapter also looks at the NetWare 5 implementation of SLP (Service Location Protocol), which is the most important implementation of this new protocol at the time of writing.

This chapter gives you information that you can use to troubleshoot your TCP/IP NetWare environment, including as much real-world experience as currently available. This chapter does not explain how to install and configure NetWare 5 and TCP/IP with NetWare 5. A great Novell Press book is available that answers all of those questions in great detail: *Novell's Guide to NetWare 5 and TCP/IP,* by Drew Heywood. This chapter focuses on protocol-related issues only.

▶ · ◀

SNMP Support and Management

As Chapter 13 explains, SNMP (Simple Network Management Protocol) gives you all kinds of information regarding the health of your network. It needs two components: management agents on the hosts, and a management console that receives the messages and presents the information to you.

All NetWare platforms that support TCP/IP have built-in SNMP agent support. NetWare also includes tools for easy configuration and monitoring of SNMP. TCPCON is a server-based utility for monitoring and managing TCP/IP nodes on your network and is discussed in Chapter 13. I will show you certain useful screens for troubleshooting TCP/IP later in this chapter.

TCPCON can also be used to monitor and manage any SNMP device on your network. If you do not follow security rules by properly configuring your SNMP community names, people with access to TCPCON can access your routers or other devices and change configurations.

IMPORTANT

SNMP can also be used with protocols other than TCP/IP. On a NetWare server, you have IPXCON to manage SNMP over IPX (Internetwork Packet Exchange), and ATCON for SNMP over AppleTalk. These management consoles provide very basic SNMP management capabilities. If you need a more powerful network management tool, ManageWise may be your choice. It includes a complete SNMP management console.

To enable SNMP agent support on a NetWare server, you do not need to do anything specific. The SNMP.NLM includes SNMP agent support for all server-based protocols. Configuration of the agent is done through INETCFG, as described in Chapter 13. You can configure three different community names: a monitor community with read access to the MIB (Management Information Base, default set to "public"), a control community with read/write access to the MIB (disabled by default), and a trap community name that is sent with every trap message (set to "public" by default).

NOTE

If you are using third-party agents, remember that they usually have standard community names defined. They should always be changed according to your standards.

An SNMP agent is included with Novell Client for DOS, Windows 3.1x, and Windows 95/98. Choose the options for SNMP Agent and Host Resource MIB during the client installation program. The current NetWare 5 client for Windows NT does not include an SNMP agent. ManageWise includes enhanced SNMP agents for a variety of platforms, including Windows NT.

X-REF

For more information about SNMP and an explanation of all related terms, refer to Chapter 13.

TCPCON

TCPCON (TCP/IP Console) can, among other things, be used to monitor and manage the SNMP agents configured on your network. Many of the features of TCPCON are self-explanatory or described in the context-sensitive help. (As usual, press F1 for a description of the current field in any window.) This section highlights some specific features of TCPCON that are helpful for troubleshooting TCP/IP and routing problems.

Figure 15.1 shows the TCPCON main menu. On the first line in the upper part, you can check which host you are looking at. In this case, it is the local system. If you want to monitor another host, go to the SNMP Access Configuration selection in the Available Options menu. Two screens that you want to check when you troubleshoot your network are the IP Routing Table (to be seen on the Available Options Menu) and the ICMP Statistics, which you will find when you choose Statistics from the Available Options.

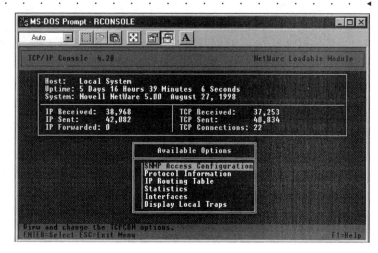

FIGURE 15.1

TCPCON main menu

After you choose IP Routing Table, you get the screen shown in Figure 15.2. It presents Route Selection Options, with which you can configure what you want to see. Note that I have chosen the Interfaces Option, which displays the list of my Interfaces. This shows two interfaces, one for each frame type loaded. You also see CMD (Compatibility Mode Driver), because SCMD.NLM is loaded on this server. (CMD is discussed later in this chapter.) You can choose whether you want to see all interfaces or just a selection.

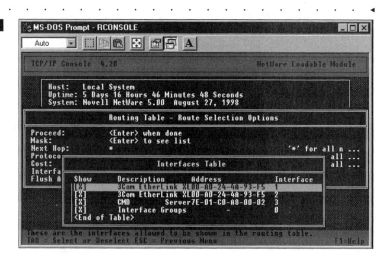

FIGURE 15.2

*The IP Routing Table —
Route Selection Options*

Now choose `Proceed:<Enter> when done` to view the routing table, which produces a list of all the routes in the table. Only one route is shown here, but it's enough to show you where to look at your routing table. And I hope yours looks a little more exciting. You can choose any of the routes in your routing table to look at the detailed information displayed about that route, as shown in Figure 15.3.

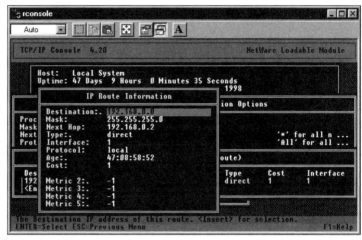

FIGURE 15.3

Detailed information about a routing entry

The IP Route Information displays the destination address, the mask associated with it, and the next hop to the destination. The Type field states whether the route is direct or remote. The Interface field tells you which interface is used to get to the destination. The Protocol field displays the routing mechanism through which this route was learned. So if this were a routed network that used different routing protocols, this field would indicate how this route got into the Routing Table. The Age field shows the age of the route entry. If you use a routing protocol that supports costs and metrics, they would be displayed in the Cost and Metric fields. Two types of fields appear in any TCPCON window:

▶ **Editable fields:** They are identified by an extra dot to the right of the colon following the field label. You can edit these fields and save the changes to the MIB of the node being managed. Destination, Type, and Age are examples of editable fields.

▸ **Noneditable fields:** They do not have the extra dot to the right of the colon. These fields are for display purposes only and can't be changed. The Mask and Next Hop fields are examples of noneditable fields.

Chapter 6 describes why the ICMP protocol is one of the best troubleshooting helpers in your network. With TCPCON, you can view ICMP statistics. Choose Statistics from the Available Options in the main menu, which presents you with a choice of all the TCP/IP protocols. Take some time to explore all the available statistics. ICMP was chosen for the screen shown in Figure 15.4.

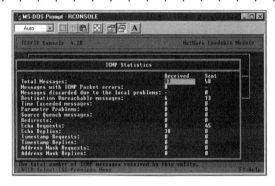

FIGURE 15.4

ICMP Statistics table in TCPCON

When I looked at this screen I wondered why there was a relatively high number of Echo Requests and Echo Replies. A check of the server showed that PING.NLM was running in the background, constantly pinging around. Make sure that you turn off such tools when you don't need them for troubleshooting purposes. Obviously, analyzing a trace file reveals the same things to you. You can set a filter on ICMP to get a quick overview of the health of your network (described in detail in Chapter 6).

NOTE

To log SNMP trap messages on your NetWare server, load the SNMPLOG.NLM after loading TCPIP. SNMPLOG.NLM is a background process that collects trap messages and stores them in the file sys:etc\snmp$log.bin. TCPCON reads this file running on the local server. Because the file has no size restrictions, make sure that you monitor its size periodically if you are logging traps.

DHCP SNMP Events
The SNMP events listed in Table 15.1 are supported with NetWare 5.

TABLE 15.1	EVENT	DESCRIPTION
DHCP SNMP Events	Critical events	Log file can't be opened
		Main thread cannot process lease expiration
	Major events	DHCPSRVR loaded/unloaded
		NDS update to subnet failed
	Warnings	Internal fault recovered
		Address not available
	Minor events	Decline generated against offered IP address

Pure IP

NetWare 5 finally offers Pure IP communication (sometimes referred to as Native IP during the beta cycle of the product). With all earlier versions of NetWare, IPX was the communication protocol. If someone wanted IP on the wire, they had to use NetWare/IP, which would only encapsulate the IPX packets into IP. IPX was always inside the IP packet (as described in Chapter 19).

With NetWare 5, the operating system has been rewritten to use IP as a transport without requiring IPX at all. This section explores what changes were necessary to make that transition.

NCP over IP
Novell's NetWare Core Protocol (NCP) is used for all communication with the server operating system. Figure 15.5 shows the communication model when NCP uses IPX. You need to understand this model to understand the changes made with NCP over IP.

▶ · ◀

SAP	RIP NLSP	Application NDS NCP	Application (connection- oriented)
IPX	IPX	IPX	SPX
			IPX
Data link layer			

SAP:	Service Advertising Protocol
RIP:	Routing Information Protocol
NLSP:	NetWare Link Services Protocol
NDS:	Novell Directory Services
NCP:	NetWare Core Protocol
IPX:	Internetwork Packet eXchange
SPX:	Sequenced Packet eXchange

In pre-NetWare 5 environments, SAP (Service Advertising Protocol), Bindery, and NDS are used for service location. Applications have to be written to use one or a combination of them. Application developers took a while to start using NDS, but now a wide variety of applications on the market support NDS. The SAP frames on the wire are what you want to get rid of when migrating to NetWare 5. SAP and IPX-RIP (Routing Information Protocol) both need IPX.

Figure 15.6 shows the communication model with Pure IP. With NetWare 5, SLP (Service Location Protocol) can be used for IP-based service location. SLP is mainly used to locate a connection server. Bindery, NDS, DHCP, and DNS can all be used for service location. SLP is the protocol that replaces SAP. IPX-RIP is replaced by IP-RIP, and NLSP (NetWare Link Services Protocol) is replaced by OSPF (Open Shortest Path First). NCP (NetWare Core Protocol) has been changed so that it is able to use IP. It has a new header structure, which is described later in the chapter.

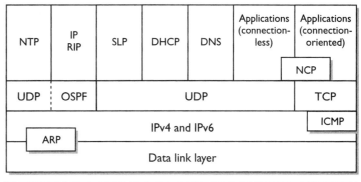

FIGURE 15.6

Pure IP

NTP	IP RIP	SLP	DHCP	DNS	Applications (connection-less)	Applications (connection-oriented)

NTP	: Network Time Protocol	UDP	: User Datagram Protocol
RIP	: Routing Information Protocol	OSPF	: Open Shortest Path First
SLP	: Service Location Protocol	TCP	: Transmission Control Protocol
DHCP	: Dynamic Host Configuration Protocol	IP	: Internet Protocol
DNS	: Domain Name System	ICMP	: Internet Control Message Protocol
NCP	: NetWare Core Protocol	ARP	: Address Resolution Protocol

Many applications on the market have been hard-coded to use IPX without using NCP. IPX-based applications also depend on SAP for service location. Other applications use SPX socket numbers. They do not work over Pure IP. You can still use them with CMD (Compatibility Mode). Refer to the section on CMD to learn more about this driver. Applications that work over Pure IP have to use NCP calls or IP. If they don't, you need Compatibility Mode (CMD).

TIP

Don't spend days trying to figure out whether your applications might work over Pure IP. Set up a test environment with Pure IP, install your applications, make sure IPX isn't in use, and find out whether they work.

Changes to Note with NetWare 5

Here are two important changes to be aware of in NetWare 5:

▶ IPX Watchdog is replaced by the *NCP TCP keepalive interval,* which is covered in more detail later in the chapter.

▶ Packet Burst isn't needed any more with Pure IP, because TCP has the streaming capability built in.

The New NCP Header

The NCP header structure has been modified for NetWare 5. Figure 15.7 shows the new NCP header.

F I G U R E   15.7

*New header fields in the
NCP header*

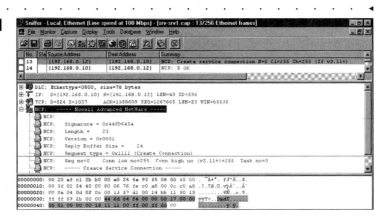

The first four fields, Signature, Length, Version, and Reply Buffer Size, are new in the NCP header. The Signature field uses 44 6d 64 54 for an NCP request. If you look at this in the hex window, you can see that it means DmdT, which stands for *Demand Transport.* In an NCP reply, this field is set to 74 4e 63 50, which means tNcP (transport is NCP).

Figure 15.8 is the decode of a server-to-server communication over Pure IP. Neat, eh? It shows two NetWare 5 servers communicating over IP. No IPX header is within the packet. Note the port number 524 in the TCP header. It is used for NCP over IP. The details for the new NCP header are shown in the detail window.

F I G U R E   15.8

*NCP communication over
Pure IP in a decode*

Protocols and Ports Used by NetWare 5 IP

Table 15.2 lists the ports used for NetWare 5 TCP/IP communication.

T A B L E 15.2	PORT	DESCRIPTION
Ports Used with NetWare 5 TCP/IP	UDP 524	NCP request over UDP. The source port will be a higher port, between 1024 and 65535.
	TCP 524	NCP request over TCP. The source port will be a higher port, between 1024 and 65535.
	UDP 427	SLP requests. The source port will be the same.
	TCP 427	SLP requests in the rare cases in which TCP is used for SLP. The source port will be the same.
	UDP 123	NTP for time synchronization. The source port will be the same.
	TCP 2302	CMD. The source port will be the same.
	UDP 2645	CMD. The source port will be the same.

You need to understand which port is used in which case, especially if you need to set up firewall exceptions.

NCP Requests—TCP and UDP 524

If you are running in Pure IP mode (not CMD) and are not dependent on SLP for locating your servers, all communication will go over this port. If you allow a destination TCP and UDP port 524 coming into the NetWare 5 server, and a source TCP and UDP port 524 going out from the NetWare 5 server, your communication will work. The source port used by the client making the connection will be a dynamic port between 1024 and 65535.

SLP Requests—TCP and UDP 427

If you want to locate your servers through SLP, you need to allow communication through TCP and UDP port 427. Both source and destination port are 427.

CMD Communication—TCP 2302 and UDP 2645

If you run CMD, you need to enable TCP 2302 and UDP 2645. Both the source port and destination port will use the same port number. All communication destined for an IPX device through a migration agent (MA) will use UDP packets. Also, the client connecting to the MA through CMD uses UDP. The only case in which TCP is used for CMD communication is when a NetWare 5 server running SCMD talks to an MA. Don't worry if you are not familiar with these terms yet — CMD is covered a little later in this chapter.

Novell Server Utilities for Configuration and Troubleshooting

The NetWare 5 server has many new utilities. A lot of documentation is already available, so this section simply lists the most important ones for NCP and IP.

Console Utilities

Table 15.3 shows useful and new utilities available on the server console.

T A B L E I 5.3	UTILITY	DESCRIPTION
Console Utilities	ncp addresses	Shows all registered NCP addresses for all protocols.
	config	Shows all loaded card drivers and binding information, including the CMD.
	protocols	Shows currently registered protocols, including frame type and protocol ID.
	ncp trace on <filename>/off	Displays NCP decodes to server screen or to file, if specified.
	ncp stats	Number of NCP requests processed.

Figure 15.9 shows a screenshot of my server after executing the `ncp stats`, `ncp addresses`, and `protocols` commands.

F I G U R E   I5.9

The output of the new console commands

Set Commands
Table 15.4 lists the set commands relating to IP communication on NetWare 5.

TABLE 15.4

Important TCP/IP and NCP Set Commands for NetWare 5

SET COMMAND	DESCRIPTION
tcp defend land attacks	Default is ON. You can keep the default setting of ON. It doesn't have much overhead. A *land attack* refers to a situation in which packets sent to a node have identical source and destination IP addresses and identical source and destination port numbers. Some IP stacks crash when they receive such a packet.
tcp defend syn attacks	Default is OFF. You should keep the default setting on a fileserver. Setting this parameter to ON would make sense on a firewall. If you install BorderManager on a NetWare 5 server, this parameter is set to ON by the installation program. A *syn attack* is when a node is flooded with syn packets (TCP handshake) to random and usually high port numbers until the processor is overloaded.
allow ip address duplicates	Default is OFF. By default, NetWare 5 does a duplicate IP address test before binding an IP address. Turning this parameter to ON would tell the server to bind the address even if it detects a duplicate IP address. Beware! Keep the default of OFF.
ncp tcp keepalive interval	Default is 9 minutes, 53.2 seconds; Range 0 to 15 hours. Set the delay before TCP keepalive closes idle NCP connections (0 never times out idle connections). This is the equivalent of the Watchdog packets in the IPX world. Tuning this parameter on dialup links may make sense. If you set it higher, you will have less keepalive packets. The price you pay is that idle connections stay open that much longer. You have to balance these requirements to find a proper value. Keep the default on regular LAN and WAN connections.
minimum ncp tcp receive window to advertise	Default is 4,096 bytes; Range 256 to 16,384. Set the minimum receive window size to advertise in the TCP header for NCP connections. Keep the default setting.
ncp tcp receive window	Default is 23,360 bytes; Range 1400 to 65,535. Set the advertised receive window on NCP connections. Changing this to the maximum can increase your performance. The default setting is a compromise. You can use 64K in the LAN and on a WAN with high

SET COMMAND	DESCRIPTION
	bandwidth. On slower WAN connections, you might have to go below the default. Tune this carefully and test it in your environment before implementing. To find the right setting, go to TCPCON, choose TCP Statistics. and watch for retransmits. If you have many retransmits, your setting is too high.
enable udp checksums on ncp packets	Default is 1 = checksum if client does; 0 = no checksums; 2 = require checksumming. Keep the default. UDP checksums can be important, as discussed in Chapter 9. This setting allows the server to checksum whenever the application does.
ncp protocol preferences	Default is empty. Set the preferred protocol order of the loaded transport protocols (TCP, IPX, UDP).

The New Environment in NetWare 5

Major changes have been made in the way that NetWare 5 handles Set Parameters. Although they are not protocol-related, they are mentioned here because many Set Parameters are discussed. And when you change Set Parameters on your NetWare 5 server, you need to understand how the server deals with them.

You probably already noticed that when you boot a NetWare 5 server, you see a message on the screen saying Refreshing the Environment from the NetWare Configuration File. NetWare 5 has a new feature called the *Registry* (also called the *environment*). Set Commands can be either permanent or temporary. Set Commands that are permanent are entered into the Registry. The Registry is a binary file that is stored in the c:\nwserver directory (or whatever your server boot directory is called). The filename is servcfg.000. It contains all the permanent settings and is read every time that you reboot the server (that's what the server is doing when it displays the Refreshing the Environment message). Most Set Commands, regardless of whether you configure them in Monitor.NLM or on the console prompt, are permanent. Set Parameters that are temporary are for such things as debug screens. Several new commands enable you to view the Registry, the most important of which are listed in Table 15.5.

	T A B L E 15.5	

Environment Commands for NetWare 5

COMMAND	DESCRIPTION
display environment	Displays all the entries in the environment.
display modified environment	Displays only the settings that have been changed from the default. Very cool. It even lists the default parameter with the current setting, making it easy to track what you have changed.
save modified environment <*filename*>	Saves to a file the modifications that you have made to your environment. It is a good idea to do that in regular intervals and keep a copy of this file on your backup. Use this command before you install a support pack, because your environment can be reset after the support pack installation. You can then use this backup file to restore your configuration.
reset environment	Resets your environment to all the default settings. This is the same as when you delete servcfg.000. In that case, the server comes up with all the default settings for NetWare 5.

TIP

For more information, refer to TID (Technical Information Document) 2946850. It is the best resource for an explanation about the environment and about the difference between persistent and nonpersistent set parameters and how to view and configure them.

Some Undocumented Parameters

Now that you know how the environment works, I am sure you are ready to find out about all the undocumented parameters. These parameters are *not* supported by Novell, which means that you use them at your own risk. So play with them on your test servers, and keep your production servers clean! Table 15.6 lists some of the undocumented parameters.

T A B L E   15.6

Undocumented Parameters

COMMAND	DESCRIPTION
set dhcp dump	Agent memory dump for debugging. Default 0; Range 0 to 2
set dhcp global poll	Change the DHCP poll interval. Do not change this on a production server, unless you know exactly what you are doing. Can also be set with the command load `DHCPSRVR.NLM -p <minutes>`. Default 30; Range 0 to 2415919103
set dhcp debug	Sets the DHCP debug level. Default 3; Range 0 to 3
set rip track log	Turns on the RIP track screen to be logged to a file. (You've been asking for this one a long time, right?) Default OFF; Range ON/OFF
set sap track log	Turns on the SAP track screen to be logged to a file. Default OFF; Range ON/OFF
set ipxrtr debug	Turning this option ON unhides hidden `IPXRTR` set commands. Default OFF. Be careful if you play with this option.
set tcp ip debug	Start or stop IP debug. Default 0; Range 0 to 4
set udp debug	Start or stop UDP debug. Default 0; Range 0 to 4
set tcp rip debug	Start or stop RIP debug. Default 0; Range 0 to 4
set tcp arp debug	Start or stop ARP debug. Default OFF; Range ON/OFF
set nds bootstrap interval	If this server does not hold a replica, this value specifies the address of a remote server with which it can perform tree connectivity operations (every 360 seconds).
set slp reset	Forces an SA to send a new Service Registration. Forces a DA to send a DA Advertisement. Flag will be reset to OFF.

Again, it cannot be repeated often enough: Turn OFF those debug screens when you don't need them—they use a lot of resources on your server.

IPX Compatibility Mode (CMD)

While pure IP is great, many applications on the market currently only support IPX. Novell, however, isn't going to abandon IPX support and built IPX Compatibility Mode into NetWare 5. Compatibility Mode enables running IPX-based applications and provides for a smooth transition from an IPX-only environment to a mixed-protocol or Pure IP world.

The Compatibility Mode Driver on a NetWare 5 server has two different operating modes:

▸ **CMD Server:** Enables IPX-dependent applications to work in a Pure IP network.

▸ **Migration Agent:** Enables communication between IPX and IP network segments. If you enable the Migration Agent, by default, the Backbone Support Gateway is enabled. The Backbone Support Gateway is responsible for tunneling IPX traffic through IP network segments.

If you configure a NetWare 5 server to support Pure IP (IPX not enabled), the Compatibility Mode Drivers are automatically enabled. These are the parameters:

▸ **LOAD SCMD:** Loads the CMD server.

▸ **LOAD SCMD /G:** Loads the Migration Agent, including the Backbone Support Gateway.

▸ **LOAD SCMD /BS:** In the first release of NetWare 5 (without Support Pack 1), this enabled the Backbone Support Gateway only. With the versions of SCMD.NLM included in Support Pack 1 or higher, the Migration Agent (MA) and Backbone Support (BS) functionalities have been merged into the single /G parameter, which automatically enables both MA and BS functionality. The /BS switch is still available for backward-compatibility, but does nothing more than /G alone does.

▸ **LOAD SCMD /SYNC:** Forces the CMD server to discover the MAs in the network and connect to one of them to get SAP/RIP information, to update its Routing Table.

▸ **LOAD SCMD /STAT:** Opens a separate SCMD information screen with useful information.

▸ **LOAD SCMD /SEARCH:** Lists the names of the services the CMD server or MA has located. Additional search parameters are available. To get a list of a specific service, enter **load scmd /search name=<service name>** or **load scmd /search net=<network number>**. The third option is to enter **load scmd /search /dump**. This creates a dump file in sys:etc\cmdstat.dat. The file can be viewed with any text editor. In this case, no information will be written to the CMD information screen.

If you install a NetWare 5 server with IP only, it will automatically enable CMD mode (load SCMD without options in autoexec.ncf). You cannot load SCMD if you have IPX bound on that server. If you remove IPX on a NetWare 5 server, you might want to check whether SCMD is loaded through the configuration files. On the other hand, when you need an MA and load SCMD.NLM /G, you need IPX and IP bound. The MA needs to see both worlds.

To view whether CMD is loaded, enter **config** at the console prompt. An additional board name will be listed. If you just loaded the CMD server, the board name will be CMD Server. If you loaded the MA, the board name will be Migration Agent. The board receives a system-generated fake node address, which always starts with 7E. The last 4 bytes represent the IP address and the driver is bound to the IPX network FFFFFFFD. This network number can be changed. (Table 15.7, later in the chapter, explains how to change the network number.)

Figure 15.10 shows the screen on my NetWare 5 server with the Migration Agent loaded.

► · ◄

FIGURE 15.10

The configuration screen of a NetWare 5 server with SCMD.NLM loaded

```
rconsole                                                      _ □ ✕
 Auto      ▾  ▢ ▤ ▤ ▣ ▣ ▣  A
              LAN protocol: ARP
              LAN protocol: IP Address 192.168.0.2 Mask FF.FF.FF.0(255.255.255.0)
                            Interfaces 1

3Com EtherLink XL and Fast EtherLink XL
     Version 3.10    May 26, 1998
     Hardware setting: Slot 3, I/O ports 6400h to 643Fh, Interrupt 9h
     Node address: 00A0244A93F5
     Frame type: ETHERNET_802.2
     Board name: 3C90X_1_E82
     LAN protocol: IPX network 0000AFFE

Compatibility Mode Driver
     Version 1.04c    August 13, 1998
     Hardware setting: I/O Port A55h
     Node address: 7E01C0A80002
     Frame type: CMD
     Board name: Migration Agent
     LAN protocol: IPX network FFFFFFFD

Tree Name: SILVIA
Bindery Context(s):
          .Zurich.Sunny

MARS:_
```

The Migration Agent must register itself with an SLP directory agent (DA), so that clients know where to find the service.

WARNING

The Migration Agent does not work without the presence of an SLP Directory Agent. So make sure that any node, workstation, or server that needs to use the MA is able to contact a DA on the network.

The Compatibility Mode on the server has many functions. This book is about troubleshooting TCP/IP, so CMD isn't covered in too much detail. (Novell's Web site has many white papers and Application Notes.) But with regard to TCP/IP and related protocols, you need to know that the CMD redirects outgoing SAPs to SLP and translates incoming SLP traffic to SAP and RIP. This way, pre-NetWare 5 clients are also supported. Outgoing IPX packets are encapsulated in UDP or TCP, and incoming encapsulated packets are decapsulated and delivered to the IPX stack.

This is very different from what NetWare/IP does. With NetWare/IP, NCP communication has always been based on IPX, which is encapsulated in IP. With NetWare 5, the NCP communication takes place over IP directly. (Refer to Figure 15.6 for an explanation of how this works.)

Figure 15.11 describes how the Migration Agent works.

▶ · ◀

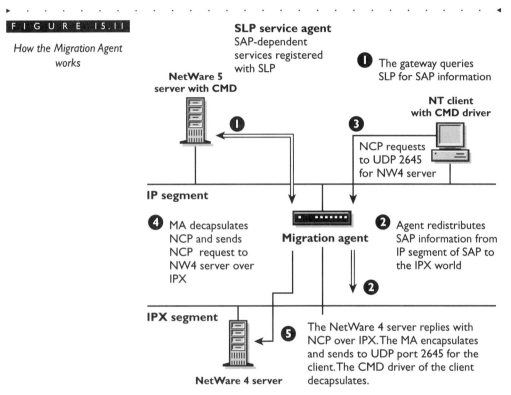

FIGURE 15.11

How the Migration Agent works

SLP service agent
SAP-dependent services registered with SLP

NetWare 5 server with CMD

① The gateway queries SLP for SAP information

NT client with CMD driver

③ NCP requests to UDP 2645 for NW4 server

IP segment

④ MA decapsulates NCP and sends NCP request to NW4 server over IPX

Migration agent

② Agent redistributes SAP information from IP segment of SAP to the IPX world

②

IPX segment

⑤ The NetWare 4 server replies with NCP over IPX. The MA encapsulates and sends to UDP port 2645 for the client. The CMD driver of the client decapsulates.

NetWare 4 server

The communication shown in the figure between the NT client on the IP segment and the NetWare 4 server in the IPX segment is further analyzed in a trace file later in this chapter. Now let us have a closer look at how the Migration Agent handles routing information. There are two cases:

1. An IP node connecting to an IPX node sends an encapsulated RIP query to the Migration Agent. The Migration Agent decapsulates the packet and sends it to the IPX segment.

2. When an IPX node connects to an IP node, the Migration Agent generates the RIP and advertises the IPX network.

CMD clients can be configured using DHCP. (Table 15.13, later in this chapter, lists the DHCP suboptions that are available for CMD configuration.) Figure 15.12 shows CMD mode in the trace file.

FIGURE 15.12

CMD mode in a decode

The NT workstation with the IP address `192.168.0.9` is a Pure IP client. The NetWare client was installed with the option IP with IPX Compatibility. These frames are part of the login sequence wherein the client executes the login script. The login script contains a map command to server Venus. The highlighted characters in the hex window show the client asking for the bindery service `Venus`. Venus is a NetWare 4.11 server that can only talk IPX. Frame 3 shows the Pure IP server Mars contacting Venus. The source address is the virtual IPX network number and the fake node address that the server assigns when SCMD.NLM is loaded. The frame goes from IPX socket 1105 to socket 16416 (dynamic sockets), and Mars requests a service connection to Venus, which is acknowledged in frame 4.

If you want LANalyzer for Windows to decode CMD mode properly, add the following line to the lzfw.ini file, at the end of the [Protocols] section: ipx(CMD)=NetWare,udp,TCP/IP,0x0A55,0,0xA55,0,0.

TIP

Some set commands relating to CMD settings on your NetWare 5 server are listed in Table 15.7.

T A B L E   15.7

Set Commands for NetWare 5 CMD

SET COMMAND	DESCRIPTION
ipx cmd mode routing	Configures whether IPX cmd mode routing is ON or OFF. If you load SCMD.NLM without options, ipx cmd mode routing is turned ON. If you load SCMD.NLM /G, ipx cmd mode routing is turned OFF. You should not change the value of this parameter. It will be removed in a future release of SCMD.NLM.
cmd network number	Default FF.FF.FF.FD This is the network number bound to the SCMD driver, which can be changed with this parameter, if desired. It can also be changed on the load command line when loading SCMD.NLM, by typing **load SCMD /net=xxxxxxxx**. On a NetWare 4 server, you would have to enter this network number on the load command in the autoexec.ncf to have it permanently changed. On a NetWare 5 server, the change is permanent (written to the environment). It is important to know that the cmd network number must not conflict with the ipx internal network number of any server or the ipx network number of any segment. Unload and reload SCMD.NLM after you have changed the network number. Also note that if you change the network number on the server, you have to adjust the settings on all servers and clients that use CMD, too.
preferred migration agent list	Default: all zeros, maximum of five addresses. List of the preferred MAs, separated by semicolons and ending with /. You configure this setting if you don't have multicast supported on your routers. This way, SCMD can find MAs on remote networks. Unload and reload SCMD after changing this setting. The limitation of five addresses is only for the setting of MAs in this list. It is not the maximum number of MAs this node can communicate with.

Continued

T A B L E   15.7

Set Commands for NetWare 5 CMD (continued)

SET COMMAND	DESCRIPTION
	In a future release of SCMD, it will be possible to disable SLP for MA discovery and get the MA list from a DHCP server.
cmd preferred ip address	Default: 00.00.00.00. The IP address that CMD uses for its functionality. On a server with multiple IP addresses, CMD or MA will bind to the lowest IP address by default. With this setting, you can specify which IP address to use. It can also be configured on the command line by typing **load SCMD /prefip=<ip address>**. Again, on a NetWare 4 server, you have to enter this load line into autoexec.ncf to make the change permanent. On NetWare 5, the change will be permanent and not reset to the default after rebooting. Unload and reload SCMD after changing this setting.

TIP

Check Novell's Web site for TID 2944065. This document is a central location summarizing TIDs and FAQs relating to SCMD, and it is updated regularly. The April 1999 AppNote contains an excellent article on CMD, including a lot of configuration information.

DNS

The new DNS services with NetWare 5 use NDS (Novell Directory Services) as their database. All DNS information is stored as objects in NDS (earlier versions of NetWare DNS services used Btrieve as their database). The NetWare 5 DNS server is BIND 4.9.6-compliant and supports most specifications of BIND 8.1.1. The DNS services are configured through a Java-based management console running on an NT Workstation with Novell NetWare 5 client software loaded. It is called *DHCP/DNS Management Console* (currently not integrated into ConsoleOne). Novell is actively developing DNS enhancements that will, among other things, fully support BIND 8.1. For users of previous Novell DNS versions, you need to know that NetWare 5's DNS supports multiple zones.

DNS — NDS Design

In a NetWare environment, there is no need for primary and secondary DNS servers for redundancy reasons, because the DNS data is stored as objects in NDS and replicated through NDS synchronization. Obviously, this is true only if you have properly partitioned and replicated your NDS database. If you have multiple NetWare 5 DNS servers running in your tree, they do not need to be configured as primary and secondary name servers. They are peers to each other and obtain their configuration information out of NDS.

Figure 15.13 shows the difference between a standard DNS world and the NetWare 5 DNS world.

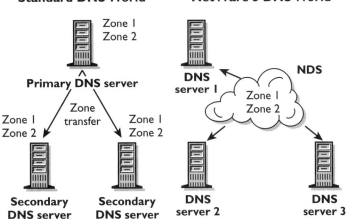

FIGURE 15.13

Comparison between standard DNS design and NetWare 5 DNS design

Standard DNS World

Zone 1
Zone 2
Primary DNS server

Zone transfer

Zone 1
Zone 2

Zone 1
Zone 2

Secondary DNS server

Secondary DNS server

The primary DNS server updates all secondaries with zone transfers.

NetWare 5 DNS World

DNS server 1

NDS

Zone 1
Zone 2

DNS server 2

DNS server 3

All the DNS servers are peers to each other. They receive their DNS data from NDS. Redundancy of DNS data is given by NDS replication.

Configuring NetWare's DNS to work with third-party, standard DNS servers is no problem. The NetWare DNS server can be either a primary DNS server and do zone transfers to third-party secondary servers, or a secondary server, receiving updates from a third-party master DNS server. The NetWare 5 DNS server populates its DNS database in NDS, and all other peer DNS servers get the data from NDS. The NetWare 5 DNS server can also be configured as a caching-only or forwarding DNS server. You can import any BIND-compliant host file to configure your DNS server.

X-REF

Refer to Chapter 12 to learn about DNS.

Figure 15.14 shows the interaction between a third-party primary DNS server and a NetWare 5 server configured as a secondary DNS server.

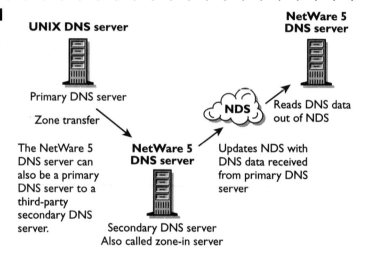

FIGURE 15.14

NetWare 5 DNS uploads data received through zone transfer into NDS

UNIX DNS server

NetWare 5 DNS server

Primary DNS server

Zone transfer

NDS

Reads DNS data out of NDS

The NetWare 5 DNS server can also be a primary DNS server to a third-party secondary DNS server.

NetWare 5 DNS server

Updates NDS with DNS data received from primary DNS server

Secondary DNS server
Also called zone-in server

NOTE

For DNS to work with NDS, several schema extensions have to be made. If you chose the installation of DHCP/DNS during NetWare 5 server installation, those schema extensions should have been added automatically. If this failed, or if you choose to install these services later, you can run DNIPINST.NLM on the server console to extend the schema.

Troubleshooting DNS on NetWare 5

Because DNS and DHCP services on NetWare 5 are such new products, we include a little more configuration information in this chapter. This will also help you to figure out how to troubleshoot these services.

NAMED.NLM Command-Line Options

To start a name server on NetWare 5, you have to load NAMED.NLM on the command line (you will probably add that command to your autoexec.ncf file). You have several options from which to choose when you load NAMED.NLM, as Table 15.8 overviews.

TABLE 15.8

NAMED.NLM Command-Line Options

OPTION	DESCRIPTION
-a	Activates auto-detect of new zones and is the default setting.
-b	Used to turn off auto-detect of new zones.
-f *file* [*context*]	Reads the file specified by *file*. The file must be a text file in BIND boot file format. The boot file specifies zones to be created in an NDS context specified by the *context* parameter.
-h	Displays the command syntax and options.
-l	Enables a DNS server to log in as an administrator, giving it the rights needed to create and delete zones from the command line.
-m *file* [*context*]	Creates a new primary zone as specified in the *file* parameter file. The data file is a BIND-format zone database file. Zone objects are placed in the context specified by *context*. Use this option to import a zone from a BIND server when moving support for the zone to a NetWare 5 DNS server.
-q	Disables verbose messages on the debug display. This is the default setting.
-r *zone*	Deletes the zone specified by *zone*.
-rp *characters*	If hostnames are generated dynamically by dynamic DNS, this specifies characters to be replaced by a dash (-) character.
-s [*zone*]	Displays status information. A *zone* name can be defined, if desired.
-u *file*	Updates an existing primary zone as specified in the *file* parameter file. The file is a BIND-format zone database file.
-v	Enables verbose messages on the debug screen, which is very helpful for troubleshooting, because you can view all the details occurring on the DNS server. Can be loaded after DNS server is up (re-entrantly).
-zi *zone*	Forces a zone-in transfer for a specified zone.

NAMED.NLM can be loaded re-entrantly to activate multiple options. When it loads, it reads the information from the RootServerInfo object in NDS. If it cannot find this object, it looks for the file sys:etc\dns\rootsrvr.dat.

Log Files

To enable event logging on your DNS server, you have to go to the DHCP/DNS Management Console. On the Options tab, configure the event log behavior. Then load CSATPXY.NLM on the server to retrieve logs from the DNS server in the Management Console. Consider adding the command LOAD CSATPXY to your autoexec.ncf file. Two types of log files are created: the *event log* shows you events, such as server startups, shutdowns, and alert messages, and the *audit trail log* gives you a history of DNS configuration events.

DHCP

The DHCP configuration is kept in NDS and is managed through the same Management Console as DNS services. A DHCP locator object is created in NDS which provides for fast lookups. DHCP configuration is very nice and flexible. You can have global configurations, subnet configurations, or specific client configurations. An Import/Export option is also offered, which is useful for customers with Novell DHCP services version 2. They can import their configuration into DHCP version 3 without needing to re-create all the information in NDS manually. NetWare 5's DHCP server also supports BOOTP clients. Addresses given out to BOOTP clients are always permanent.

TIP

Novell DHCP v2 uses a text file, sys:etc\dhcp.tab, to store the database. If you can save your third-party DHCP database in a text file with the same format, you can actually import any DHCP database into the NetWare 5 DHCP server. After you have configured your NetWare 5 DHCP server, use the Export option in the Management Console to create an additional backup of your configuration. It can be used to reimport the data in case of loss.

You can specify DHCP options for multiple subnets. The information is stored in NDS. Options can be assigned at three levels:

- **Global:** Options that apply to all subnets. They can be overridden by subnet or IP address options.

- **Subnet:** Options that apply to all clients on a subnet. They can be overridden by options assigned to a specific IP address.

- **IP address:** Options that apply only to the client described by a particular IP address object.

This approach is very versatile. It enables you to manage options easily for large groups of users, but you can still make exceptions for subnets or individual computers. According to Novell, NetWare 5 DHCP scales up to 10,000 nodes.

A hardware exclusion list is available in which you can deny services to unwanted devices, based on MAC address. DHCP can be configured to update DNS dynamically. The section "Dynamic DNS (DDNS)," later in the chapter, provides more details. You can also configure the DHCP server to do a ping test before giving out an IP address, thereby reducing the possibility of duplicate IP addresses on your network. Don't worry about a performance disadvantage here. Immediately after DHCPSRVR loads, it pings the first available IP address. When a client requests an address, it is immediately assigned. Then the DHCP server pings the next available address. The DHCP server also has extensive auditing capabilities and supports SNMP events. Refer to "SNMP Support and Management," earlier in this chapter, for more details.

The DHCP Management Console allows you to easily use DHCP options to configure your clients. You can choose them from a screen. You also can configure specific options not contained in the general list. However, certain IP addresses are invalid (as explained in Chapter 4). One example is the use of all ones or all zeros for the host ID. Novell's DHCP server automatically excludes invalid IP addresses from subnet and subnet address ranges by defining appropriate IP address objects.

Troubleshooting DHCP on NetWare 5
This section gives you a little starting help configuring and troubleshooting your NetWare 5 DHCP server.

DHCPSRVR.NLM Command-Line Options
To enable DHCP console logging, you can load DHCPSRVR.NLM with any of the options described in Table 15.9.

OPTION	DESCRIPTION

TABLE 15.9

DHCPSRVR.NLM Command-Line Options

OPTION	DESCRIPTION
-d1	Enables the background screen log of DHCP packets.
-d2	Enables the background screen log of DHCP packets and debug statements.
-d3	Combines -d1 and -d2 and writes the information to a log file at sys:etc\dhcp\dhcpsrvr.log. The information provided is very detailed and helpful when troubleshooting.
-s	Forces the DHCP server to read and write to the master NDS replica. Be careful when using this option. The Master Replica might be on the other side of a WAN link. We have not tested what happens if you change the configuration and the Master Replica Server is not available.
-p <minutes>	Configures the polling interval that DHCPSRVR.NLM uses to read its configuration from NDS. On a production server, you should leave the default, 30 minutes. During testing, this parameter can be reduced, to force DHCPSRVR.NLM to read its configuration more often.

Use these logging options when you need to troubleshoot. After everything is running fine, you should turn them off, to free up the resources for other server tasks.

Log Files

If you enable the log file, several events will be logged. This includes address deletion, address addition, address rejection, major SNMP events (refer to Table 15.1 for a list), renewal requests, and released addresses. You must load CSATPXY.NLM on the server to enable DNS/DHCP Management Console to retrieve logs from the DHCP server. Consider adding the command LOAD CSATPXY to your autoexec.ncf file, to make sure that the log file retrieval is enabled every time you restart the server

More Troubleshooting Files

When DHCPSRVR.NLM loads, it must read the DHCP locator object from NDS. Then it creates a file, sys:etc\dhcp\dhcploc.tab. This file keeps track of the synchronization with NDS and contains the global options and the excluded MAC addresses. If DHCPSRVR.NLM cannot find the locator object, it looks for this file. You can also copy this file from another server. When you unload DHCPSRVR.NLM, this file is a copy of the cache at unload time. When you reload DHCPSRVR.NLM and it can't connect to NDS for some reason, it reads this file.

Novell Server as DHCP Relay Agent

You can use a Novell server as a relay agent by loading BOOTPFWD.NLM. As Chapter 11 explains, you must configure the DHCP server's IP address on the relay agent.

The LOAD BOOTPFWD command has four options, described in Table 15.10. They should follow the IP address. If you don't specify options, you get a Help screen that displays all available options.

T A B L E 15.10	OPTION	PURPOSE
BOOTPFWD Options	SERVER=ipaddress	Specifies the address of a remote DHCP server to which BOOTPFWD is to forward BOOTP and DHCP requests.
	LOG=(YES | NO)	Specifies whether forwarding activity should be logged to the screen or a file.
	FILE=filename	Specifies the name of the log file. If no filename is specified, the log file is sys:etc\bootp.log.
	INFO	Displays current operational statistics.

The relay agent, also referred to as *bootp-forwarder*, can be configured through INETCFG. Go to Protocols ⇨ TCP/IP ⇨ Expert Configuration Options, and choose BootP Forwarding Configuration. Refer to TID 2920394 for more information.

NetWare-Related DHCP Options

Table 15.11 lists the new NDS- and SLP-related DHCP Options.

T A B L E 15.11	OPTION	DESCRIPTION
New DHCP Options for NDS and SLP	78	SLP directory agent
	79	SLP scope name
	85	NDS server
	86	NDS tree name
	87	NDS context

DHCP option 63 is particularly significant in the Novell world, because it is used to configure a variety of suboptions related to NetWare/IP and IPX compatibility support in NetWare 5. Suboptions 1 through 11 are associated with NetWare/IP and are documented in RFC 2242. Table 15.12 explains these options.

TABLE 15.12

Suboptions for DHCP Option 63 (NetWare/IP)

SUBOPTION	DESCRIPTION
1 NWIP_DOES_NOT_EXIST	The responding DHCP server does not have any NetWare/IP information configured.
2 NWIP_EXIST_IN_OPTIONS_AREA	All NetWare/IP information is present in the Options area of the DHCP Response packet.
3 NWIP_EXIST_IN_SNAME_FILE	All NetWare/IP information is present in the Sname and, if necessary, File fields of the DHCP Response packet. If used, the following DHCP server behavior is required: within the Options area, option 63 is present with its Length field set to 2. The first byte of the Value field is set to NWIP_EXIST_IN_SNAME_FILE tag, and the second byte is set to 0. Both option 62 and option 63 will be placed in the area covered by the Sname and File fields. Option 62 is encoded normally. Option 63 is encoded with its tag, length, and value. The Value field does not contain any of the first four suboptions described herein.
4 NWIP_EXIST_BUT_TOO_BIG	Neither the Options area nor the Sname field can accommodate the NetWare/IP information. If either suboption 2 or 3 is set, one or more of the following suboptions may be present.
5 NSQ_BROADCAST	Length is 1; value is 1 or 0. If the value is 1, the client should perform a NetWare Nearest Server query to find out its nearest NetWare/IP server.
6 PREFERRED_DSS	Length is ($n * 4$); value is an array of n IP addresses, each 4 bytes in length. The maximum number of addresses is five, so the maximum length value is 20. The list contains the addresses of n NetWare Domain SAP/RIP Servers (DSSs).
7 NEAREST_NWIP_SERVER	Length is ($n * 4$); value is an array of n IP addresses, each 4 bytes in length. The maximum number of addresses is five, so the maximum length value is 20. The list contains the addresses of n nearest NetWare/IP servers.

SUBOPTION	DESCRIPTION
8 `AUTORETRIES`	Length is 1; value is a 1-byte integer value indicating the number of times that a NetWare/IP client should attempt to communicate with a given DSS server at startup.
9 `AUTORETRY_SECS`	Length is 1; value is a 1-byte integer value indicating the amount of delay, in seconds, in between each NetWare/IP client attempt to communicate with a given DSS server at startup.
10 `NWIP_1_1`	Length is 1; value is 1 or 0. If the value is 1, the NetWare/IP client should support NetWare/IP version 1.1 compatibility. A NetWare/IP client needs this compatibility only if it will contact a NetWare/IP version 1.1 server.
11 `PRIMARY_DSS`	Length is 4; value is a single IP address. This field identifies the primary Domain SAP/RIP Server (DSS) for this NetWare/IP domain. NetWare/IP's administration utility uses this value as primary DSS server when configuring a secondary DSS server.

Three new suboptions, described in Table 15.13, are used to support IPX compatibility on NetWare 5.

T A B L E   15.13

Suboptions for DHCP Option 63 (IPX CMD)

SUBOPTION	NAME	DESCRIPTION
12	IPX network number	Specifies the virtual IPX network number used by the IPX Compatibility mode.
13	IPX stale time	Specifies the minimum interval, in minutes, that must expire before clients attempt to refresh their migration agent addressing information.
14	Migration Agents	Specifies a list of addresses for MA servers used by IP nodes to communicate with IPX nodes.

NOTE

As already mentioned in the section "DNS," for DNS/DHCP to work with NDS, several schema extensions have to be made. If you chose the installation of DHCP/DNS during NetWare 5 server installation, those schema extensions should have been added automatically. In case this failed or if you choose to install these services later, you can run DNIPINST.NLM on the server console and the schema will be extended.

Client Identifier with NetWare 5

DHCP has been updated with RFC 2131 (obsoletes RFC 1541). The new RFC adds several new features to DHCP. Two of them are that you can use a Client Identifier field as a substitute for using the MAC identifier and the Inform message. The Novell client software has a built-in mini-DHCP client that supports these new options. Note, though, that the Novell client for NT specifies the MAC address of the interface the request is being sent on in the client identifier field. For Windows 95/98, the Novell client is able to access the client identifier that the Microsoft DHCP client uses and, therefore, uses that value for the Client Identifier option in the DHCP Requests that are sent.

The Microsoft DHCP client is not configurable. To determine its level of support for DHCP, refer to the Microsoft documentation. Other, more-advanced DHCP clients that can be configured in a much more flexible way are available on the market, and they can be used with your Windows 95/98 or Windows NT clients.

TIP

For freaks only and at your own risk: As you know, almost anything in NT can be configured through the Registry Editor. If you want to manipulate the options that the DHCP client will request, go to the following path:
HKEY_LOCAL_MACHINE\SYSTEM\CurrentControlSet\Services\ DHCP\Parameters\Options. You will find a subset of keys with numbers. The numbers are the options that the DHCP client requests. You might be able to figure out how to add options manually.

Dynamic DNS (DDNS)

What is dynamic DNS? That is when DNS and DHCP learn to talk to each other. The DHCP server included with NetWare 5 can be configured to update the DNS database dynamically. When clients receive an IP address, DHCP updates DNS with the client's name and IP address. For example, if a client moves to a different subnet, DHCP removes the client's old resource record in DNS and adds a new one with the client's new IP address.

To have DDNS available, one of the zone's DNS name servers has to be configured as a DDNS server. The designated DDNS server communicates with DHCP and adds the DNS records to the NDS database. Other peer NetWare 5 DNS servers update their database records from NDS. When DHCP updates DNS resource records, it automatically increments the DNS SOA serial number so that the changes in DNS are propagated without administrative intervention.

To track DDNS activity on a NetWare 5 DNS server, check the sys:etc\ dhcp\dhcpdns.log. It keeps track of dynamic updates of DNS that can't be done because DNS isn't available.

▶ . . . . ◀

SLP

This chapter covers Novell's implementation of SLPv1 (Service Location Protocol version 1). Make sure that you understand the SLP concepts, as described in Chapter 14, before you read this section.

Novell has committed to support SLPv2 as soon as the standard is ready. The IETF working group is paying a lot of attention to making SLPv2 compatible with SLPv1. Novell is working on this, too, and its developers participate in the development of SLPv2. One fundamental change in SLPv2 will be that the *unscoped* scope will be removed. Every SA that registers a service with SLP will need to provide scope information. In the absence of an administrator-chosen scope, a default scope is assumed and registered. If you are implementing SLP now, it is a good idea to keep that in mind and work with a scope from the beginning. In NetWare 5 out of the box, a server can register with only a single scope. This limitation has been removed with Support pack 1 or higher.

Using SLP to locate an NDS server in your NetWare 5 environment is optional. If you use Pure IP, you can decide to go with DNS or DHCP for service location. The only case in which you really need SLP is if you need to emulate SAP/RIP. Then you need SLP with Compatibility Mode (CMD). But, you can't turn off SLP. As you will see in "Client Connection Sequence with Pure IP," later in the chapter, you can configure your clients so that you have no SLP frames on the wire. You have to play with the many client configuration options until you find what works best for you.

How to Configure a Directory Agent (DA)

A directory agent (DA) on a NetWare 5 server acts as a repository of all the services that service agents (SAs) have registered with. When a NetWare 5 client boots up using IP, it looks for a DA that can point it to the desired resources on the network. There are two ways to configure a DA:

▸ **Load SLPDA on the server and accept the default configuration.** This automatically creates an SLP scope unit and an SLP DA in your tree, and you are ready to go.

▸ **In NWAdmin32, create an SLP scope unit and an SLP DA.** Under the Configuration tab for the DA, select Host Server. Under the SLP Scope Units tab, add the scope to the Serviced Scope Units. Then load SLPDA on the server.

When the DA is initialized (when SLPDA is loaded), it looks for the NCP server object and checks for the attribute that states whether it is configured as a DA. SLPDA then finds the DA object in NDS and determines what scopes this DA supports. Next, it reads into memory all the objects within the supported scopes and sends out a DAAdvert message to advertise its presence. SAs register with the DA and refresh their information with the DA according to the *service lifetime* configured. For a NetWare 5 server SA, the default lifetime is 3,600 seconds (1 hour; see Table 15.15, later in the chapter), and for a NetWare 5 client SA, the default registration lifetime is 10,800 seconds (3 hours, see Table 15.16). Also refer to TID 2943614 for an overview of the SLP protocol.

As discussed in Chapter 14, the current SLP standard does not implement a protocol for communication between DAs. You should not use the unscoped option, because it will not be supported with the next version of SLP. If you point two DAs to the same scopes (in NWADMIN), they will know about each other's services through NDS. (Refer to Figure 14.4 in Chapter 14 on SLP.)

Common SLP Service Types

For a description of what service types are, refer to Chapter 14 or RFC 2165. The following list shows the most common SLP service types that you will find when analyzing your trace files taken in a NetWare 5 environment:

- **MGW.NOVELL:** Compatibility mode gateway/migration agents.

- **NDAP.NOVELL (NDS):** Comparable to SAP type 0x0278, with the difference that 0x0278 refers to an NDS tree and `ndap.novell` refers to an NDS partition in order to find the closest replica.

- **BINDERY.NOVELL (NetWare servers):** Compares to SAP type 0x0004.

- **SAPSRV.NOVELL:** NetWare 5 servers with IPX CMD loaded.

- **RMS.NOVELL:** Resource Management Service of NDPS.

- **SRS.NOVELL:** NDPS Broker.

- **RCONSOLE.NOVELL:** Java rconsole.

- **DIRECTORY.AGENT**

Figure 15.15 shows the service type in the decode. The service type isn't shown in the detail window; it is shown in the hex window, in which you can see that this client is looking for a service type `ndap.novell//` and for the tree named `SILVIA` (highlighted).

F I G U R E   15.15

The SLP service type in the decode

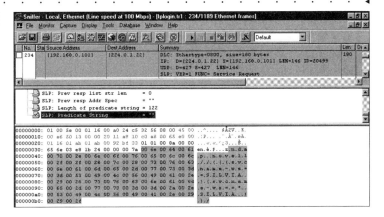

SLP Console and Set Commands for the NetWare 5 Server

Table 15.14 lists SLP-related commands that can be helpful in configuring and troubleshooting SLP.

T A B L E   15.14

SLP Console Commands

COMMAND	DESCRIPTION
slp open/close <*filename*>	The SLP trace file is created/closed in the root of Volume SYS.
display slp services	Displays all services registered with SLP. The server sends a Service Request frame (function 1), which is answered with a Service Reply (function 2).
display slp attributes	Displays all attributes of a given service. The server sends out an Attribute Request (function 6) and is answered with an Attribute Reply (function 7). In the current version of Sniffer Pro (2.1), the attribute information is not decoded in the detail window but can be seen in the hex window.
display slpda	Displays the list of SLP DAs and their current status. Includes IP address of DA and scope name.

Numerous SLP-related Set Commands also exist, as listed in Table 15.15.

T A B L E   15.15

SLP Set Commands

COMMAND	DESCRIPTION
set slp da discovery options	Values: 0 to 15 (default is 3) 0x01 = Use multicast DA advertisements 0x02 = Use DHCP discovery 0x04 = Use static file sys:etc\slp.cfg 0x08 = Scopes required If you work with the default setting of 3, multicast and DHCP are used. If you select option 0x04 to use the slp.cfg file and then modify slp.cfg, you must disable bit 0x04 and then re-enable bit 0x04 to force SLP to read the slp.cfg file. Good to know, eh?

COMMAND	DESCRIPTION
set slp tcp	Values: ON or OFF (default is OFF) Sets SLP to use TCP instead of UDP for transport. Do not turn on this option. TCP makes no sense with SLP, because SLP uses small packets and Request/Reply types of traffic. TCP would have great overhead but no advantage.
set slp debug	Values: 0 to 65535 (default is 0) 0x01 = COMM 0x02 = TRAN (TCP connection info) 0x04 = API (API calls and parameters) 0x08 = DA (DA errors) 0x010 = ERR (Misc. errors) 0x020 = SA (SA errors) These bits can be OR'd together for multiple values. All bits set would be 63 decimal, and the combination of COMM and API would be 5.
set slp multicast radius	Values: 0 to 32 (default is 32) Specifies the multicast radius; i.e., the number of routers the multicast packets will traverse. You could reduce this setting to avoid multicast packets to cross your WAN links. We recommend not changing this option. This is a configuration that should be handled by routers.
set slp broadcast	Values: ON or OFF (default is OFF) If set to ON, broadcast packets are used instead of multicast packets. Unless your routers do not support multicast, you should use multicast and leave this option at its default value.
set slp mtu size	Values: 0 to 24682 (default is 1450) This parameter sets the MTU size. This default is actually higher than what the RFC states. If you check the client settings, you'll find the RFC-conform setting of 1400.
set slp rediscover inactive directory agents	Values: 0 to 86400 (default is 60) The time period, in seconds, that SLP will wait to issue Service Requests to rediscover inactive DAs.
set slp retry count	Values: 0 to 128 (default is 3) The number of times SLP will retry to find a service, either by contacting a DA or by multicasting to the general service multicast address.

Continued

TABLE 15.15

SLP Set Commands (continued)

COMMAND	DESCRIPTION
slp scope list	Specifies a comma-delimited list of scope names. The TID says the maximum is 1,023 characters, whereas my server says the maximum is 184 characters. SAs and UAs operating on this server will use the scopes specified by this parameter. DAs are configured by the scopes specified in the NDS SLP DA object.
set slp sa default lifetime	Values: 0 to 65535 (default is 3600) Specifies the lifetime that an SLP service registration remains registered. The lifetime is sent with every Service Reply to a Service Request.
set slp event timeout	Values: 0 to 120 (default is 3) The number of seconds SLP will wait before timing out multicast packet requests.
set slp da heart beat time	Values: 0 to 65535 (default is 10800) Each DA multicasts a periodic *Heartbeat* packet to inform UAs and SAs that it is alive. This setting describes the interval, in seconds, between DA Heartbeat packets.
set slp close idle tcp connections time	Values: 0 to 86400 (default is 300) The number of seconds SLP waits before closing idle TCP connections.
set slp da event timeout	Values: 0 to 120 (default is 15) The number of seconds to wait before DA packet requests are timed out after it has tried for the number of times stated in the slp retry count.

SLP Settings on the Client

On the Windows 95/98 and Windows NT client, SLP is configured at two different places: the Service Location tab and the Advanced Settings tab of the client configuration dialog box. Table 15.16 shows the available parameters.

T A B L E   15.16

Client Set Parameters for SLP

ADVANCED SETTINGS PARAMETERS	DESCRIPTION
give up on requests to sas	Range: 1 to 60000 (seconds); default is 15 Specifies how long the client waits for a response to an SA multicast query. slp active discovery
on Windows NT client only	Range: ON or OFF If set to ON, the client uses active discovery (multicast or broadcast) for Service or Attribute Requests if there is no DA. Windows 95/98 clients are configured for this by using the Active Discovery check box on the Service Location tab.
static discovery check box	If you check the Static Discovery check box on the DA list page in the client properties, it changes the way the client discovers a DA. If not checked, the client will multicast to discover a DA. If checked, the client will only try the DAs in its configured DA list or those DAs received from a DHCP option 78 request.
slp cache replies	Range: 1 to 60 (minutes); default is 1 Specifies how long SLP will cache received replies for a given service or attribute. Increasing this value reduces the number of SLP queries that the client generates for a given service or attribute, thereby increasing the risk that the client is trying to use an obsolete service address.
slp default registration lifetime	Range: 60 to 60000 (seconds); default is 10800 Specifies how long a service is registered with SLP.
slp maximum transmission unit	Range: 576 to 4096; default is 1400 Specifies the MTU size for the link layer. The default value is suitable for Ethernet networks.
slp multicast radius	Range: 1 to 32; default is 32 Specifies the maximum number of subnets (number of routers plus 1) that SLP's multicast packets should traverse. A value of 1 confines multicasting to the local segment.
use broadcast for slp multicast	Range: OFF or ON If the network does not support multicast messages, change this setting to ON. This confines SLP to the local network. If possible, use multicast.

Continued

TABLE 15.16

Client Set Parameters for SLP (continued)

ADVANCED SETTINGS PARAMETERS	DESCRIPTION
use dhcp for slp	Range: ON or OFF If set to ON, the client uses DHCP to obtain SLP scope and DA configurations (options 78 and 79).
wait before giving up on da	Range: 1 to 60000 (seconds); default is 5 Specifies how long the client waits for a response to a DA query before giving up and reverting to active discovery.
wait before registering on passive da	Range: 1 to 60000 (seconds); default is 2 Specifies how long the client waits to register services following a *passive DA discovery*. A passive DA discovery is when the SA receives an unsolicited DA Advertisement because a DA just started.

Troubleshooting SLP

There are two troubleshooting tools available on the client. They are installed when you install the NetWare client that comes with NetWare 5.

Client Utilities and Configuration Options

Do you need to troubleshoot an SLP configuration? On a Windows 95/98 and Windows NT client with the client software for NetWare 5 installed, you can execute c:\novell\client32\slpinfo.bat on the command prompt to get configuration information for SLP. With the NT version of slp info, several switches can be used, which are explained on the help screen. The following is the output with the /all switch used.

```
****************************************************

***          Novell Client for Windows NT          ***

***          Service Location Diagnostics          ***

****************************************************
```

```
SLP Version:            1.0

SLP Start Time:         11:49:02am   1/19/1999

Last I/O:               1:51:50pm    1/19/1999

Total Packets:          Out: 80          In: 32

Total Bytes:            Out: 12002       In: 1040
```

```
SLP Operational Parameters                    Values
_____-         _____

Static Scopes                                 NO
Static Directory Agents                       NO
Active Discovery                              YES
Use Broadcast for SLP Multicast               NO
Use DHCP for SLP                              NO
SLP Maximum Transmission Unit                 1400 bytes
SLP Multicast Radius                          32 hops
```

```
SLP Timers                                    Values
_____-     _____

Give Up on Requests to SAs                    15 seconds
Close Idle TCP Connections                    5 minutes
Cache SLP Replies                             1 minute
SLP Default Registration Lifetime             10800 seconds
```

```
Wait Before Giving Up on DA                    5 seconds
Wait Before Registering on Passive DA          1-2 seconds



Scope Name                                     Source(s)
_____    _____

ZH                                             DA



DA IP Address    Source(s)    State    Local Interface
Scope(s)
_____-   ____-   __-   _____-   _____-

192.168.0.12     MCST         UP       192.168.0.99      ZH
192.168.0.12     MCST         UP       192.168.0.99      ZH



Local Interface    192.168.0.99
_____-

Operational State:       UP
Operating Mode(s):       MCAST
Last I/O:                1:51:50pm    1/19/1999
Total Packets:           Out: 80           In: 32
Total Bytes:             Out: 12002        In: 1040
Last Addr Out:           224.0.1.22
Last Addr In:            192.168.0.12
```

Play around with the other options to get more specific information on just what you need to know.

If you need to troubleshoot CMD mode, another nice utility can be executed on the client. The file is c:\novell\client32\cmdinfo.bat (this file is present only if you installed your clients with the IP with IPX Compatibility option). Execute the command **cmdinfo** on your command prompt, and it will produce the screen shown in Figure 15.16. This figure shows that the client knows the MA's IP address, but the MA is inactive.

You can execute the command with two options:

▸ -c — to display the active configuration

▸ -v — to load with verbose messaging

▸ · ◂

FIGURE 15.16

The output of cmdinfo.bat

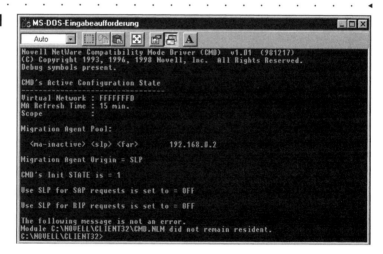

Further References on SLP

The following references contain valuable additional information on SLP:

▸ The Application Notes for September 98 and November 98 contain articles on SLP (`http://developer.novell.com/research`).

▸ TIDs (do a search on Novell's Knowledge Base, http://support.novell.com for SLP; many excellent documents are available).

▸ RFC 2165.

Multicast Forwarding Support

Currently, multicast routing is not mandatory for IP routing on the Internet. Therefore, not all the nodes constituting the Internet are multicast-routing-enabled. The result is that we have groups of nodes capable of multicast routing, separated by groups of nodes that are not capable of routing multicast packets. If we need multicast routing to work in such a scenario, we can configure tunnels between the groups of nodes that are able to route multicast packets.

As explained in Chapter 19, tunnels have two end nodes, which are associated with each other's IP address. The two end nodes of the tunnel can encapsulate the multicast packets they receive on one interface and send them as an IPv4 unicast packet through the tunnel to the other end node, thereby connecting the two multicast islands. The receiving end node decapsulates the unicast and forwards the multicast packets to other interfaces.

On a NetWare 5 server, you can enable this support by loading PIM.NLM. PIM stands for *Protocol Independent Multicasting*. PIM.NLM needs very little configuration. When you load it on the command line, it figures out the current IP bindings on the server and makes all the interfaces capable of routing multicast packets.

PIM.NLM is an implementation of a new experimental protocol that is described in RFC 2362. It uses a multicast address of 224.0.0.13, which is used by *all PIM routers*.

If you need to configure a tunnel, you have to specify the source and destination addresses of the tunnels in the sys:etc\pimtun.cfg file. The source and destination addresses should be bound addresses at either end of the tunnel for the tunnel to function properly. Obviously, the configuration at the other end of the tunnel has to match. The following is an example of a tunnel configuration:

You have two hosts and you want to enable a PIM tunnel. One host has the IP address of 10.0.1.1 and the other end node has the address 192.168.0.2.

▸ Host 10.0.1.1 has the following entry in its pimtun.cfg file:

```
10.0.1.1 192.168.0.2
```

▸ Host 192.168.0.2 has the following entry:

```
192.168.0.2 10.0.1.1
```

When PIM.NLM loads, it reads the configuration, and the tunnel comes up as a virtual interface. The two hosts will be recognized as neighbors.

If you load PIM.NLM with the debug option (**load pim debug**), you receive two lovely additional screens, described next.

A Debug Screen

This screen is blank, unless you enable the following parameters:

▸ set pim join prune debug = 1

▸ set pim hello debug = 1

▸ set pim graft debug = 1

▸ set pim assert debug = 1

▸ set pim all debug (turns on all the preceding options)

If you want to know what all of these terms are, refer to RFC 2362.

Remember that debug screens should be enabled only for troubleshooting purposes and should be turned off when not being used. They use a lot of your server's resources and there are so many of them, you can't keep them all running.

A Configuration and Monitoring Utility

Figure 15.17 shows the main menu of the PIM utility. It is shown here, because it can be used to view interesting protocol-related information that can't easily be found any other place.

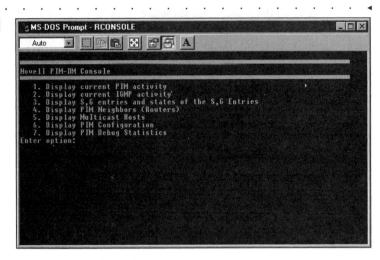

The main menu of the PIM utility

It is worth experimenting with this utility to see what statistics and information you can find. You can view the multicast host groups that have joined per interface. As Chapter 18 describes, IGMP registers multicast group membership. If you choose menu option 5, Display Multicast Hosts, you can see what multicast groups are registered per interface. Figure 15.18 is the output of that list.

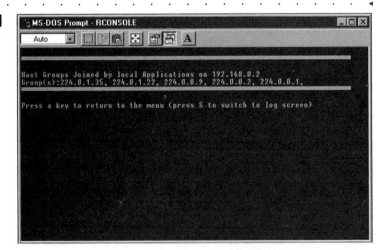

View the registered multicast groups

You see the list of multicast groups that have registered on my interface 192.168.0.2. The first two groups are the SLP multicast addresses. The RIP2 routers are 224.0.0.9, all routers on this subnet are 224.0.0.2, and all hosts on this subnet are 224.0.0.1. These are the multicast groups that my server is currently listening to.

Client Connection Sequences with Pure IP

To log in to a Pure IP network, a client needs to know the IP address of the server. A client can locate a server by using one of the following four methods:

▶ **Static configuration:** This option has two choices, depending on whether you want to use SLP. The client can use a hosts file that translates a server name to an IP address, which means that you don't use SLP for server location. If you want to use SLP, you can have a static configuration for a DA. In this case, you have to specify a DA in the client's Directory Agent List. You can enter into the Directory Agent List either the IP address or, to be flexible, the DNS name of the DA. If you enter the DNS name of the DA, the client uses DNS to resolve the server IP address. Obviously, the DNS server needs to be configured in the DNS tab of the TCP/IP properties.

▶ **DNS** can be used to resolve a server name to an IP address.

▶ **DHCP** can be used to provide the locations of NDS servers to the client.

▶ **SLP** can be used dynamically, and it will multicast for a DA when it comes up. If no DA responds, it multicasts to the general SLP multicast address, and SAs will respond to the UA via unicast. This actually limits the radius to the multicast domain the client can reach. If the routers do not support multicast, then the client (UA) will be able to discover only those DAs or SAs that reside on the same segment. In effect, if no DA or SA is in the same segment as the client, and if the routers do not support multicast, the client will not be able to locate any service through SLP. In that case, you need to use DHCP to provide the address of a DA, or configure a DA statically on the client.

Many ways and combinations exist for client connection sequences. Because this chapter can't cover them all, I decided that a good starting point would be to show how a client connection sequence looks with all the defaults. So what I have done is a new NT 4 Workstation installation with Service Pack 3. All protocols were removed except TCP/IP. The workstation and server services were also removed. The NetWare NT client was installed with the IP Only option. Version 4.60.128 of the NetWare 5 client is used, which was the most current version at the time of writing. This client is configured for a static IP address of 192.168.0.9. The trace file in Figure 15.19 shows how it looks with all the defaults. The following list describes the trace file:

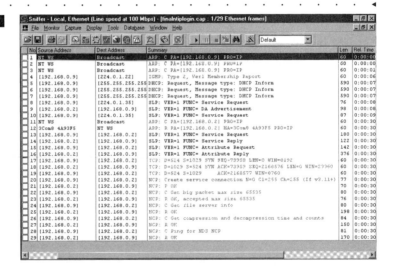

▸ **Frames 1 to 3:** Show how the client ARPs for its IP address to make sure that nobody else is using it.

▸ **Frame 4:** The client registers its IGMP membership for SLP.

▸ **Frames 5 to 7:** The client tries to get information from a DHCP server. It asks for options 78 (DAs) and 79 (Scope Name). Because no DHCP server is on this segment, there is no answer to these requests.

▸ **Frame 8:** An SLP request for a DA.

▸ **Frame 9:** The DA replies with a DA Advertisement. Note that the Service Request goes out to the multicast address, and the DA responds with a unicast.

▸ **Frame 10:** The client asks for a DA again, to check whether someone else might be answering.

▸ **Frames 11 and 12:** The client ARPs for the DA's IP address in frame 11, and the reply comes in frame 12.

▸ **Frames 13 and 14:** The client issues an SLP request for a service type ndap, including the tree name in frame 13. The server replies in frame 14, telling the client that it is an NDS server for the requested tree.

▸ **Frame 15:** The client requests attribute information about the address of the service.

▸ **Frame 16:** The DA sends all the attribute information. Now the client knows the server's address.

▸ **Frames 17 to 19:** The TCP handshake between the client and the NDS server.

In this example, the DA was loaded on the same server, and thus the client makes the TCP connection to the same server. The remaining frames show how the client and the server negotiate their NCP connection and how the client pings for NDS. All the following frames, which are not shown here, are the requests to NDS resolving the name and reading all attribute information from NDS, authenticating to the server, and executing the login script.

Playing around is fun. So look at the trace shown in Figure 15.20. It is a Pure IP login sequence, shown to the same point where the client pings for NDS. Note that this login only uses 14 frames to ping for NDS. What's the difference? It shows that you do not need SLP nor DHCP to log in to a tree. The configuration for this login sequence was as follows. The DNS server was running, with an A record for server mars.moon.universe.com. The client configuration was changed. The client was configured to use the DNS server with the address 192.168.0.2, and when prompted for the login in the dialog box, instead of entering the tree name, the DNS name of the login server was entered.

▶ • ◀

*NT client connection
sequence using DNS*

In frame 1, the client asks DNS for the IP address of its login server. The reply to this request is in frame 2, and frames 3 to 5 are the TCP handshake between the client and the login server. Then they create their NCP connection, and the client pings for NDS. Instead of 29 frames, as in the previous example, this has 14 frames. This login sequence could be two packets faster if you provide the IP address of the login server in place of the DNS name. But then you lose the flexibility that DNS offers.

WARNING

You can enter either an **IP** address or a **DNS** server name into the Tree Name field or into the Preferred Server field of the Login dialog box. Using the Preferred Server field is the better way. If you enter an IP address or a DNS name in the Tree Name field and that server happens to be in a different tree, the login and execution of the login script might cause problems. The server will not find the context specified in its database.

These two examples show the range of possibilities for designing your client connections. We have not even touched upon using DHCP yet. So carefully plan how you configure your clients, to get a flexible configuration and a fast login performance. And use your analyzers after you have made your design. The trace files will tell you how you can optimize the connection sequence.

NOTE

It is important to know that static client parameters override options received from DHCP. Options that you want to be configured through DHCP have to be cleared in the Network applet of Control Panel.

• • • • •

Before this book hits the shelves, newer, 32-bit clients will be out. Their login sequence might be a little different from what you find today. Once more, this is the reason for you to take your analyzers out of the dark and use them to design and troubleshoot your network. Novell is constantly working on the optimization of its communications and thus periodically makes changes in the client software and the server OS. So don't take the traces shown here for granted.

TIP

If you love these trace files without NetBIOS frames, then configure your NT Workstations like I configured mine. Disable Server Service, Workstation Service, and the NetBIOS Interface in the Control Panel. You have to live with the fact that every time you click properties of Network Neighborhood, Microsoft will ask whether you want to install Microsoft Networking. I'm sure a Registry key exists somewhere to disable that, but I haven't found it yet. Send me an e-mail if you find it.

► · ◄

Time Sync Processes

In the NetWare 4 world, SAP 0x026B is used by Time Providers to find each other and to advertise their presence to Secondary Time Servers. No SLP service type exists for Time Synchronization. In a Pure IP environment, you have to use configured lists. In the configured list, you can specify the name of the server (which implies that you use IPX and SAP 0x0004) or the NDS distinguished name, such as `server.resources.sunny.ch`. Your third option is to enter the IP address (which implies that you use TCP/IP).

The NetWare 5 Time Synchronization does not support DNS names. Otherwise, Time Synchronization works exactly as it does in NetWare 4. You have to apply the same rules and guidelines as with NetWare 4. If you state the IP address in the configured list, you are using NCP over UDP with port 524. You do not have to use NTP (Network Time Protocol, discussed in Chapter 18).

Novell is working on a new version of the TIMESYNC.NLM. It will be version 5.09 or higher. By the time you read this, this TIMESYNC.NLM will be released. The current version of NTP.NLM only implements an NTP client and can't be used as an NTP server to provide time to other servers. The new TIMESYNC.NLM will include NTP.NLM and can act as both NTP client (to receive time from an NTP time source) and NTP server (provide time via NTP to NTP clients). Thus, you'll be able to configure your Single Reference or Primary Servers to obtain their time from reference time sources on the Internet and distribute it to your secondary servers, all through NTP.

When you load NTP.NLM on your server, it reads the configuration in the sys:etc\ntp.cfg file. Check this file on your NetWare 5 server, and it will give you an explanation of how to configure it.

WARNING

Be careful when you load NTP.NLM on your production server. It will make changes to your timesync.cfg file without asking you. If you load it on a secondary or primary time server, the timesync server type will be changed to Single Reference Server.

► · ◄

BorderManager

Because BorderManager provides services that are closely related to TCP/IP and Internet issues, this section provides an overview of the product's functionality. Version 3 was just released and has many improvements over version 2. It is a well-established product that is known for being very flexible and that has great performance.

BorderManager has many different modules, and you can choose the ones that are important for your environment. Figure 15.21 gives an overview of the modules.

BorderManager is a great product. Learn about it and use it. Novell Press has a book available that covers BorderManager: *Novell's Guide to BorderManager*, by J. D. Marymee and Sandy Stevens.

FIGURE 15.21

The components of BorderManager

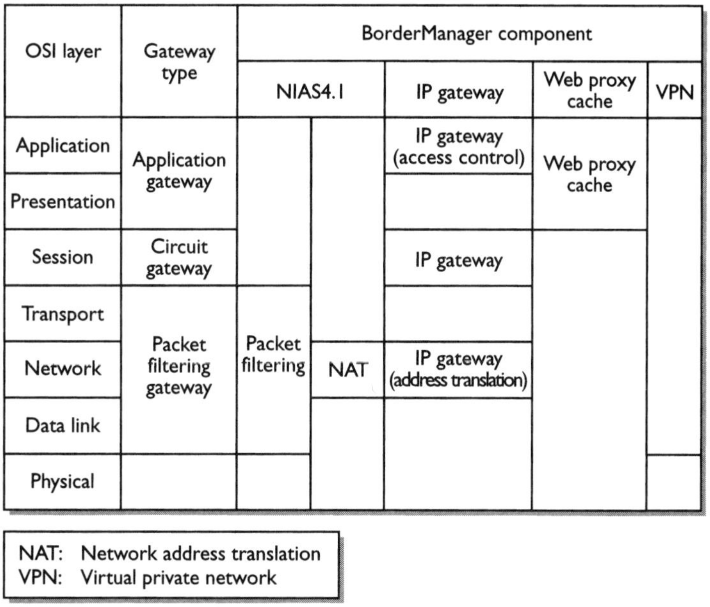

OSI layer	Gateway type	BorderManager component			
		NIAS4.1	IP gateway	Web proxy cache	VPN
Application	Application gateway		IP gateway (access control)	Web proxy cache	
Presentation					
Session	Circuit gateway		IP gateway		
Transport	Packet filtering gateway	Packet filtering			
Network		Packet filtering · NAT	IP gateway (address translation)		
Data link					
Physical					

NAT: Network address translation
VPN: Virtual private network

IPv6

Novell has already done a lot of work on a TCP/IP stack that supports IPv6. It is not contained in the current release of NetWare 5. Fact is, that since the common use of private IP addresses in combination with NAT (Network Address Translation) in many enterprises, the need for IPv6 to solve the address space problem is not so urgent any more. Novell is closely watching the market, and as soon as the demand for IPv6 becomes obvious, it will be ready to quickly release an IPv6 TCP/IP stack.

Protocol-Related Application Notes

The following Application Notes cover topics discussed in this chapter in more detail (available at `http://developer.novell.com/research`):

▸ April 99, Understanding the Advanced Settings in the Novell Client for Windows 95/98

▸ April 99, Configuration Parameters for the Compatibility Mode Driver

▸ March 99, Dynamically Discovering Services on an IP Network with SLP

▸ February 99, Migrating from NetWare/IP to NetWare 5 and Pure IP

▸ November 98, Novell DNS/DHCP Services, Design Issues and Troubleshooting

▸ September 98, Migrating to Pure IP with NetWare 5

▸ September 98, Compatibility Mode Installation and Configuration

▸ April 98, Easing TCP/IP Network Management with Novell's DNS/DHCP Services

▸ March 98, Maintaining IPX Compatibility During a Migration to TCP/IP

▸ March 98, Network Address Translator (NAT), Theory and Troubleshooting

Case Study — What Can Go Wrong

The following case study explains how a mixed-protocol environment works. This example was chosen because it illustrates the concepts well. Most of you will have a mixed NetWare 4/NetWare 5 environment, at least during a transition period. You might want to set up new clients with Pure IP and still be able to access NetWare 4 servers.

The Problem

We have a Microsoft NT 4 client with the latest Novell client software installed. It is a Pure IP client. During the install, the TCP/IP only option was chosen. The user's login script includes a map command to a NetWare 4 server. The user can log in to the NetWare 5 server, but the map to the NetWare 4 server cannot be done. The error message is `Drive map operation could not be completed, error code 8884`. The NetWare 5 server has the migration agent loaded and bindings for IPX and IP.

The Analysis

By examining the trace file taken during login, we find that the client issues a series of SLP requests for service type `bindery.novell:///VENUS`, with Venus being the name of the NetWare 4 server. But Mars, the NetWare 5 server, does not know about a bindery service `Venus`. Figure 15.22 shows the client's request for `VENUS` (highlighted in the hex window, following the entry for the service type `bindery.novell`).

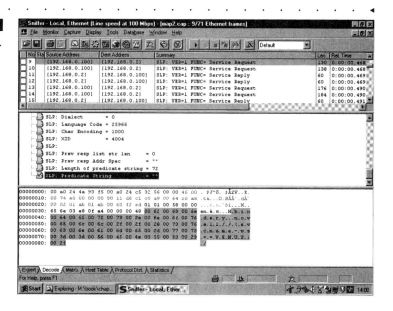

F I G U R E   1 5 . 2 2

The client's SLP Request for a bindery service

Next, we check what the NetWare 5 server knows about services. At the console, we use `display slp services` and `display servers`. The first command shows the entries in the SLP table, and the second command shows the server's SAP table. Figure 15.23 is the server's output to the two commands.

F I G U R E   15.23

The server's SLP and SAP tables

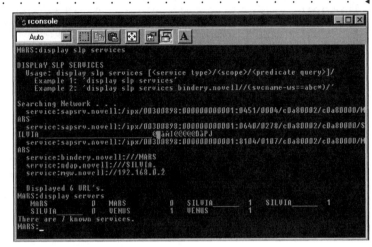

Mars can see three `sapsrv` services. This is the service type when CMD is loaded. The three entries present all refer to Mars. The first entry is for SAP type 0x0004 (bindery server), the second entry is for SAP type 0x0278 (NDS server), and the third entry is for SAP type 0x0107, which is there because RCONSOLE is loaded. Then Mars advertises itself as bindery service for Mars, as NDS server for tree name SILVIA (`ndap.novell`), and as a Migration Agent with the IP address of `192.168.0.2`. No entry for `bindery.novell:///VENUS`, right? So the server cannot give an answer to the client's SLP request for Venus.

By looking at the SAP table after issuing display servers, we can see that Mars is very well aware of Venus and can see it in its SAP table. But that's not enough. So how do we get this client to map to Venus?

The Solution

The solution is kind of simple. What the client needs is the CMD driver. Without Compatibility Mode, it will never be able to reach an IPX-based service of any kind.

So we reinstalled the Novell client software and chose the IP with IPX Compatibility option. Again, we took a trace file to see what the communication looks like. The client was now able to map a drive to the NetWare 4 server. Figure 15.24 displays the trace file.

Look at frame 1, which is highlighted. This is a UDP request going out from the client to UDP port 2645. That's the port number used for CMD. The data within the UDP packet (highlighted in the detail window and in the hex window) shows the client's request for volume data. Now the next frame is interesting. Server Mars, respectively the MA with the address FFFFFFFD.7E01C0A80064, makes an NCP request to server Venus. The internal IPX number for Venus is 290797. It is a request for the volume data mount number. By going inside this packet and looking at the hex decode of the NCP request, we find that it is exactly the same as the highlighted data portion in the first frame coming from the client. Venus replies to Mars in frame 3 with the volume data mount number. Frame 4 shows Mars replying to the client. To summarize, the client issues an NCP request for the map command. This request is encapsulated in a UDP packet by the CMD driver at the client. The NetWare 5 server with the MA loaded decapsulates the UDP request from the client and forwards the NCP request to the IPX service on behalf of the IP client. And for the NCP reply from the IPX service, the same process goes on in reverse order.

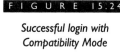

FIGURE 15.24

Successful login with Compatibility Mode

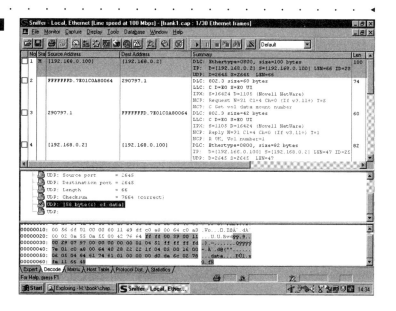

When the client was installed without a CMD driver, it would never issue this UDP request to port 2645 and, therefore, the MA could not forward the request to Venus.

Summary

This chapter has explained how Novell implements the Pure IP stack with NetWare 5. This is the first time NCP can communicate directly over IP without encapsulating IPX. This chapter has also touched on a lot of other TCP/IP-related issues in NetWare, such as SNMP, BorderManager, DHCP, and DNS services. The next chapter discusses Microsoft's implementation of TCP/IP.

Microsoft TCP/IP
Implementation

This chapter examines how Microsoft Windows products implement and use the TCP/IP protocol. TCP/IP is often used as the only protocol when installing a Microsoft NT Server, NT Workstation, or Windows 95/98 computer. Other protocols, such as NetBEUI and IPX/SPX, may also be installed on Windows products. This chapter focuses on the TCP/IP protocol only.

▶ . . . . ◀

Microsoft Networking Domain Overview

To begin networking within the Microsoft NT environment, at least one domain must be established. A *domain* is a logical grouping of computers that share a common domain database and security policies. Each domain within the NT network carries a unique name. For example, a Microsoft network with two domains may have domain names such as Accounting and Sales.

When a Microsoft network is first installed, the first NT Server is known as the *primary domain controller (PDC)*. The PDC controls the domain and maintains the domain-wide account database, called the *Security Accounts Manager (SAM)*. The PDC is then used to authenticate users and provide security access when users want to access the NT network. But what if the PDC fails? Could you lose the entire domain account database? The answer is yes, unless you have a backup, either in the form of an offline solution, such as a tape, or another computer that holds a copy of the SAM database. Most NT network implementations use both of these methods to back up the domain account database.

The computer that holds a secondary copy of the SAM database is called the *backup domain controller (BDC)*. The BDC simply receives copies of any account changes made to the PDC, ultimately keeping an exact duplicate copy of the SAM for use at any time. Though a BDC is not required, it is strongly recommended. The purpose of the BDC is twofold:

▶ Synchronize with the PDC to provide user account database backup

▶ Perform login authentication

You may place as many BDCs within the network as needed for backup purposes. As the network grows, a new domain may make its way into the NT network, as shown in Figure 16.1.

FIGURE 16.1

NT network with two domains

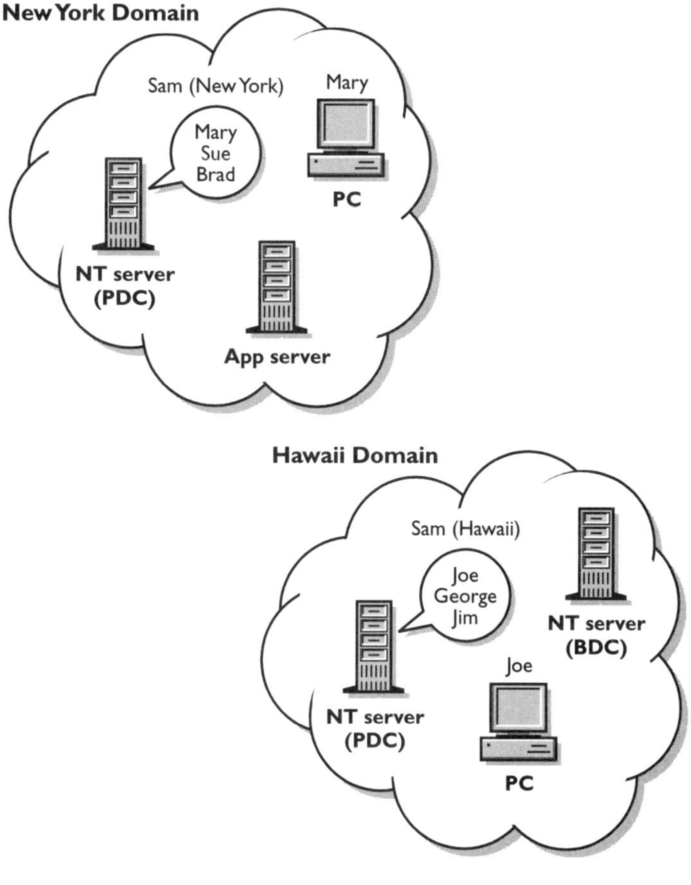

New York Domain

Sam (New York)   Mary

Mary
Sue
Brad

PC

NT server
(PDC)

App server

Hawaii Domain

Sam (Hawaii)

Joe
George
Jim

NT server
(BDC)

Joe

NT server
(PDC)

PC

In Figure 16.1, a second domain is added to the NT network. Notice that each domain has its own PDC—this is mandatory. In addition, each PDC has a database that contains only the user accounts for its own domain. New York has accounts for Mary, Sue, and Brad. Hawaii's PDC contains accounts for Joe, George, and Jim. Everybody is happy until one of the users needs to use resources in another domain. Suppose, for example, that Joe in Hawaii wishes to use the App

Server in New York for some very important business. To make this happen, the NT network administrator must establish a *trust relationship* between the domains, discussed next.

Communicating between Domains Using Trust Relationships

Figure 16.1 demonstrates two domains that are completely autonomous. This is fine until one user needs resources in another domain. The user, Joe, has a problem — because his name is not in the New York PDC's account database, the New York domain will not allow Joe access to the resources contained within the domain. Another problem exists, however. Although a *physical* link exists between New York and Hawaii, such as a point-to-point network link, no *logical* link exists between the domains. Once again, complete autonomy prevents Joe from accessing the App Server in New York.

To solve this problem, a *trust relationship* is established between the domains. A trust relationship allows one (local) domain to accept user accounts from another (remote) domain as valid accounts, and subsequently allows the user account access to local resources. This process takes place without the user account actually existing in the local domain.

A trust relationship can be set up either as a *one-way trust* or as *two one-way trusts* (sometimes referred to as a *two-way trust*). A one-way trust allows one domain to use resources in another, but it doesn't work the other way around. Two-way trusts, on the other hand, allow users from each domain to access resources in the other domain. In Figure 16.2, a one-way trust is established so that Joe can use the App Server.

In Figure 16.2, a one-way trust has been established between New York and Hawaii, so that Joe can use the App Server. The arrow in the diagram points to Hawaii, indicating that Hawaii is a *trusted domain*. It points away from the New York domain, which is considered to be the *trusting domain*. Seems like the arrow is pointing to the wrong domain, doesn't it?

F I G U R E   1 6 . 2

*A one-way trust relationship
is established.*

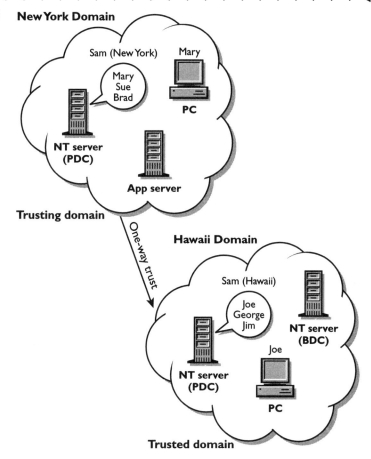

To understand the NT domain trust relationship, a few more details are necessary. First, in every trust relationship, one domain must be the trusting domain and one domain must be the trusted domain. The trusted domain is allowed to use the resources in the trusting domain. It's kind of like getting your hair cut. Consider this example: You are going to get your hair cut. You walk into the salon and sit down in the chair. The hairdresser (or stylist or barber) comes over to you with a pair of scissors in hand. Now, the question arises — *who trusts whom*? Of course, you trust the hairdresser to cut your hair. This is the same as New York trusting Hawaii to use its resources, which is why New York points to Hawaii — New York trusts Hawaii. When the haircut is complete, do you and the hairdresser switch places? Not usually, unless the hairdresser trusts you to cut his or her hair. This is a one-way trust in action.

Now, what if someone in New York needs to access the server in Hawaii? In this scenario, another trust relationship must be established, as shown in Figure 16.3.

FIGURE 16.3

A two-way trust relationship is established.

FIGURE 16.3

A two-way trust relationship is established.

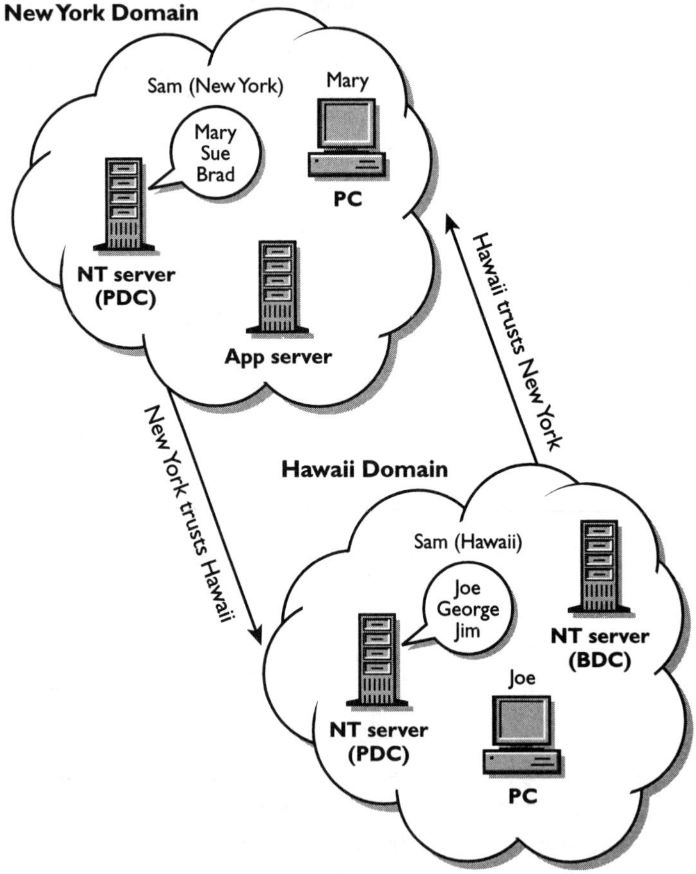

Configuring the Trust Relationship

When establishing a trust relationship, you must configure that trust relationship on both ends of the trust. The trust is set up on the PDC for each domain involved. One domain PDC will be the trusted domain and the other PDC will be the trusting PDC. To set up a trust, an NT network administrator uses an NT utility called User

Manager for Domains. This utility sets up user accounts, passwords, and other events, as well as trust relationships. The Trust Relationships dialog box is shown in Figure 16.4.

FIGURE 16.4

NT Trust Relationships setup screen

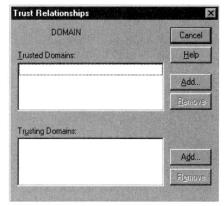

To use this screen, the administrator follows these general steps:

1. From the trusted domain, add the name of the trusting domain in he Trusting Domains box.

2. From the trusting domain, add the name of the trusted domain in the Trusted Domains box.

You can add a password when implementing the trust relationship. This is used for security in setting up the trust so that unauthorized users may not set up trusts.

As NT networks grow, many more domains may be established. As new domains are established, users may need to use resources within other domains. Very often, two-way trust relationships are established between domains to allow users the access they need. This may cause the trusts to become complicated. Consider the example shown in Figure 16.5.

▶ . . . . ◀

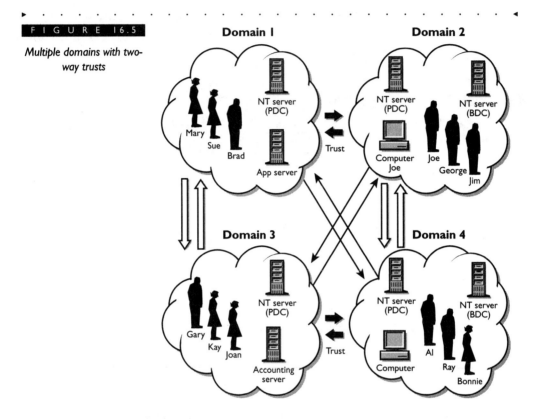

A company has four domains in which all users need access to resources in the other domains. The network administrator has set up individual trust relationships so that all users receive whatever resource they need. Unfortunately, the administrator has lost track of how many trust relationships are established! A count of the trust relationships indicates that the administrator must keep track of 12 trust relationships. The following is a formula that is used to calculate how many trust relationships you need for this fully trusting/trusted environment:

```
N*(N-1)
```

```
(N = Number of Domains)
```

Figure 16.5 has four domains. Plugging this into the formula, $4*(4 - 1) = 12$ trust relationships. What might happen if a new domain is installed? Where do the user accounts reside? How do you keep track of all the users? You can see that this is not an efficient management method. To make this network management more efficient, the setup of domains shown in Figure 16.6 is used.

▶ • ◀

FIGURE 16.6

Organized domains need fewer trust relationships.

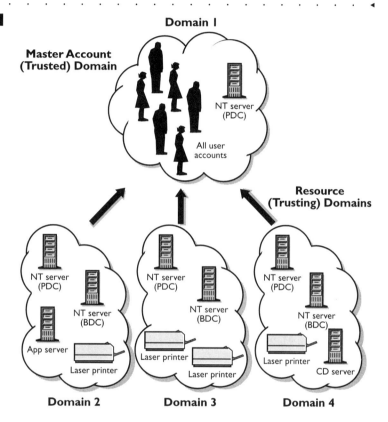

In Figure 16.6, the domains are reorganized into what Microsoft calls the *master domain model*. Using this model, a single (or master) domain contains the user accounts. The other domains simply contain resources. It does not matter where the physical users are — what matters is where their accounts reside. Notice also that the need for trust relationships is greatly reduced. When a user logs in to the network through the Domain 1 domain, the user is granted access to resources in other domains (if security rights allow), because of the trust relationship with Domain 1.

The network depicted in Figure 16.6 is a LAN divided into multiple domains. Multiple domains are not required, however. It is entirely possible to have a WAN with a single domain. To allow users to authenticate locally, BDCs are placed at the remote sites, and authentication traffic does not cross the WAN. BDCs are updated by the PDC from the master domain on a periodic basis.

 The Novell NDS for NT product allows NT users to authenticate through NDS, eliminating the need for trust relationships.

NOTE

Now that you have seen the basics of the Microsoft NT network domain structure, the following section takes a closer look at how TCP/IP is used in the Microsoft environment.

Dynamic Host Configuration Protocol (DHCP)

Chapter 11 explains how a client without a statically configured IP address could obtain one from a DHCP server by using the DHCP or BOOTP protocol. Within the Microsoft environment, a computer can either be a DHCP server (NT Server) or a DHCP client (NT Workstation, NT Server, or Windows 95/98). This section looks at how the server and client DHCP Services function.

Implementing the DHCP Server

The DHCP Server Service is included within the NT Server operating system. The Windows NT Server provides services to BOOTP clients in a limited capacity, assuming the current Service Pack is installed on the NT Server. To set up an NT-based DHCP server, a network administrator must perform the following steps:

1. Install the DHCP Server Service.

2. Configure a DHCP scope.

3. Configure DHCP scope options.

Install the DHCP Server Service

To install the DHCP Server Service, simply choose the Network option from the Control Panel on the Windows NT Server. Use the Services tab to display a list of currently installed services. Click the Add button to add the DHCP Server Service. The result is shown in Figure 16.7.

FIGURE 16.7

Installing the DHCP Server Service in an NT Server

With NT 4, this service and many others described in this chapter must be installed as a separate procedure after the operating system is functional. With Windows 2000 (initially called NT Server 5), the DHCP Server Service and other TCP/IP services, such as WINS and DNS, are automatically installed, but are not configured during the installation

The DHCP Service *must* be installed on an NT Server and not on an NT Workstation or Windows 95/98 computer. Additionally, the DHCP Service must be running before DHCP can be configured. The DHCP Service should run automatically when the server boots. If, for some reason, the DHCP Service is not running, you can manually start the DHCP Service in one of two ways:

1. Select Control Panel ➪ Services and find Microsoft DHCP Service in the list. Click Start to initialize the service.

2. At a command prompt, type **NET START DHCPSERVER**.

After the service is installed and running, you must configure an IP address scope.

Configure a DHCP Scope

After the service is installed, the DHCP server must be configured to give out appropriate addresses on the network. This is accomplished by using the DHCP Manager tool, shown in Figure 16.8.

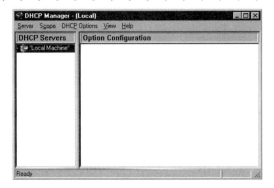

DHCP Manager tool main screen

You create the scope from within the DHCP Manager tool. Remember that a scope is used to give out IP addresses to clients that request them. Therefore, if you have more than one DHCP server on the network, you must make sure that they do not overlap IP addresses. DHCP servers do not talk to each other about the addresses they give out — they only maintain an internal database of used addresses. To create the scope, choose Scope ⇨ Create from the DHCP Manager main window. The Create Scope screen appears, as shown in Figure 16.9.

Figure 16.9 shows the options for creating the scope. You begin with the starting IP address in the range. In this case, the range begins with 192.168.1.50, which leaves all IP addresses below 50 for other devices that may need a static address, such as servers, printers, or routers. Next, you type in the ending address, which is 192.168.1.250 in this example. This means that the DHCP server will deliver addresses to clients with the range of 192.168.1.50 — 192.168.1.250.

You then fill in a subnet mask, exclusion range, and lease duration, in their respective fields. An *exclusion range* is a single IP address or multiple IP addresses that should not be given out. For example, suppose that a server has been configured to use IP address 192.168.1.100. DHCP could potentially give that address to a client, not knowing that the address was already in use by the server. So to prevent potential conflict, you simply exclude that address.

F I G U R E   16.9

DHCP Create Scope screen

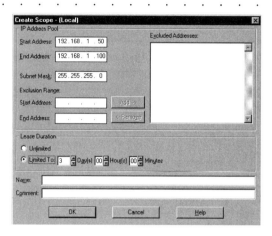

A *lease* is the length of time that a client may use an IP address. The default lease duration for a Microsoft DHCP server is three days, although the lease may be set for any number of days, up to 999 days, 23 hours, and 59 minutes.

You may give the scope a name, to define its purpose further, along with a user-defined comment. If another DHCP scope is needed in the future, you may add it to this or another server. However, you must realize that only one DHCP scope may be assigned to a specific subnet.

Through DHCP, you also can reserve IP addresses for specific clients. This is accomplished by clicking Scope ➪ Add Reservations within DHCP Manager. The Add Reserved Clients dialog box appears, as shown in Figure 16.10, in which an IP address of 192.168.1.150 is being reserved for Sue. To do this, DHCP requests the MAC address of the network interface card (NIC). DHCP will use the MAC information during the DHCP Request process to determine that this is a reserved lease.

For more information on DHCP Requests, refer to Chapter 11.

X-REF

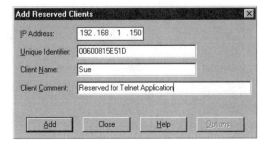

FIGURE 16.10

DHCP Add Reserved Clients dialog box

Configure DHCP Scope Options

After you configure a DHCP scope, you can give IP address and subnet mask information to each client automatically. But what if you want to give clients other information, such as DNS server names, default gateway addresses, or some other set of information? You can do this through the scope options setup within DHCP Manager. The following are the four levels of scope options:

▸ **Global:** Available to all DHCP clients; a global option is used to configure all clients with the exact same types of information, such as a DNS server.

▸ **Scope:** Available to all clients who lease an address from a particular scope. For example, you may have a different scope for each subnet, and each subnet may use a different default gateway. Therefore, you would configure the different gateway addresses using the scope option.

▸ **Default:** Modifies the default values for any one of the DHCP options.

▸ **Client:** Created for a specific client and uses a reserved DHCP address lease to give other DHCP options.

If more than one DHCP scope configuration method is used to set the same option, precedence occurs in the following order:

1. Client options

2. Scope options

3. Global options

4. Defaults

DHCP options are set using DHCP Manager. To choose an option, simply highlight the scope, and click Scope and the option type that you want to change. Figure 16.11 shows the dialog box for changing options for the scope.

▶ · ◀

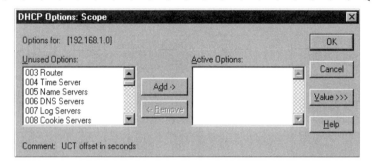

DHCP Options: Scope dialog box

RFC 2132 defines a long list of DHCP options that may be configured. Though many or all may be configured within DHCP Manager, only some of those options are used by Microsoft DHCP clients. Two types of options are used by the DHCP client:

▸ **DHCP protocol options:** Define specifics for the protocol, such as the type of message or lease time.

▸ **Information options:** Define variables, such as a default router or DNS server.

The options and their types for Microsoft DHCP clients are shown in Table 16.1.

TABLE 16.1

Frequently Used DHCP Server Options

OPTION TYPE	CODE	OPTION NAME	DESCRIPTION
Protocol	53	DHCP Message Type	Determines the type of DHCP message. Values for this option are the following: 1 – DHCPDISCOVER 2 – DHCPOFFER 3 – DHCPREQUEST 4 – DHCPDECLINE 5 – DHCPACK 6 – DHCPNAK 7 – DHCPRELEASE
Protocol	51	Lease Time	Allows the client to request a lease time, in seconds. Also used by the DHCP server to specify the lease time it is willing to offer.
Protocol	58	Renewal Time	The time interval from IP address assignment until the client requests an address renewal. The value is specified in seconds.
Protocol	59	Rebind Time	The time interval from IP address assignment until the client requests an IP address rebind. The value is specified in seconds.
Information	1	Subnet Mask	Specifies the client's subnet mask.
Information	3	Default Router	Specifies a list of IP addresses for routers on a particular subnet. Multiple routers should be listed in order of preference.
Information	6	DNS Server	Specifies a list of DNS servers available on the network, which should be listed in order of preference.
Information	15	Domain Name	Assigns a DNS domain name.
Information	44	NetBIOS Name Server (WINS)	Specifies a list of NetBIOS name servers, such as WINS, in order of preference.
Information	46	NetBIOS Node Type	Allows configuration of the client NetBIOS node type. Available values are the following: 0x1 – B-Node 0x2 – P-Node 0x3 – M-Node 0x4 – H-Node

OPTION TYPE	CODE	OPTION NAME	DESCRIPTION
Information	47	NetBIOS Scope ID	Similar to a domain name, the NetBIOS scope option specifies the NetBIOS scope ID for the client. Example: *clientname.netbios.com*

After you set the scope or global options within the DHCP server, clients will receive information as requested, such as a default router address or a DNS server address.

Configuring DHCP Clients

Just as a DHCP server must be configured to give out IP addresses, the client must be configured to receive IP addresses. Additionally, the client may be configured to receive other information from the DHCP server. Though the configuration process is similar in Windows NT Workstation, Windows 95, and Windows 98, the screens are not all exactly the same.

Before you can configure clients to request IP addresses from a DHCP server, you must install TCP/IP first. The DHCP configuration options for Windows 95/98 and NT clients are provided next.

Windows 95/98 DHCP Client Configuration

To configure a Windows 95/98 client for automatic IP address configuration, perform the following steps:

1. Go to Control Panel.

2. Choose Network (or right-click the Network Neighborhood icon and choose Properties).

3. Scroll down to the TCP/IP option and click Properties. (If more than one TCP/IP protocol is listed, choose the TCP/IP that corresponds with your NIC.)

4. From the TCP/IP Properties dialog box, choose the IP Address tab. Choose the Obtain an IP Address Automatically radio button, as shown in Figure 16.12.

FIGURE 16.12

Setting IP address automatic configuration for Windows 95/98

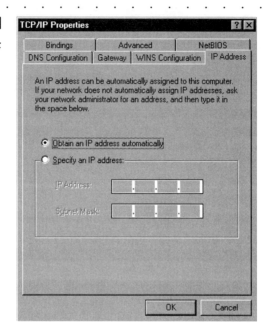

After the IP address is automatically configured, Windows 95 expects all other options to come from DHCP, including the DNS configuration, WINS setup, and default gateway information. To verify the configuration, use the **WINIPCFG** command, which displays the IP Configuration dialog box, shown in Figure 16.13.

Figure 16.13 displays quite a bit of information about the TCP/IP configuration for this workstation. Notice the adapter (MAC) address and other relevant information, including the IP address, subnet mask, DNS server, DHCP server, and default gateway. All of this information was pushed to the client through the DHCP options set in the server scope.

For an NT Workstation, the process is similar.

▶ · ◀

WINIPCFG from a Windows 95/98 client shows the IP Configuration dialog box

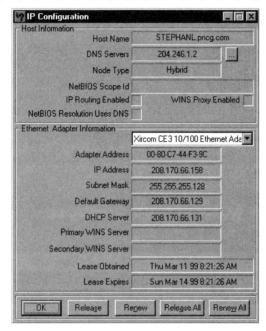

Windows NT Workstation DHCP Client Configuration

To configure a Windows NT Workstation client for automatic IP address configuration, perform the following steps:

1. Go to Control Panel.

2. Choose Network (or right-click the Network Neighborhood icon and choose Properties).

3. Click the Protocols tab

4. Scroll down to the TCP/IP option and click Properties.

5. From the TCP/IP Properties screen, choose the IP Address tab. Choose the Obtain an IP Address from a DHCP Server radio button, as shown in Figure 16.14.

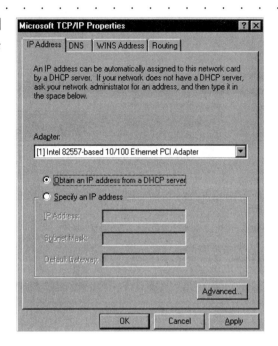

After the NT Workstation client is configured to use DHCP, other options may
be sent to the client from the DHCP server. To view the configuration, as shown
in Figure 16.15, use the **IPCONFIG /ALL** command.

Figure 16.15 displays the NT Workstation IP configuration screen from a
command prompt. Notice that the information includes the IP address, default
gateway, DNS server information, DHCP server use, and subnet mask, to name a
few. Other available options are discussed later in this chapter.

DHCP Relay Option and Multiple DHCP Servers

The discussion thus far has been the DHCP Service as it relates to a single
DHCP server on a single segment. DHCP looks for a server on a local segment to
supply IP addressing information. If a server is unavailable or not configured on a
local segment, how can a DHCP request be made to another server? The answer
is that a DHCP relay agent is used.

IPCONFIG /ALL shows the IP configuration on an NT Workstation.

```
Windows NT IP Configuration

Host Name  . . . . . . . . . . . . . . : ntws.pncg.com
    DNS Servers  . . . . . . . . . . . : 204.246.1.20
                                         204.70.128.1
    Node Type . . . . . . . . . . . . : Broadcast
    NetBIOS Scope ID . . . . . . . . . :
    IP Routing Enabled   . . . . . . . . : No
    WINS Proxy Enabled . . . . . . . . : No
    NetBIOS Resolution Uses DNS   . : No

Ethernet adapter E100B1:

    Description  . . . . . . . . . . . . : Intel EtherExpress PRO/100B PCI LAN Adapter
    Physical Address   . . . . . . . . . : 00-A0-C9-49-83-6E
    DHCP Enabled  . . . . . . . . . . . : Yes
    IP Address . . . . . . . . . . . . . : 208.170.66.157
    Subnet Mask . . . . . . . . . . . . : 255.255.255.128
    Default Gateway   . . . . . . . . . : 208.170.66.129
    DHCP Server . . . . . . . . . . . . : 208.170.66.131
    Lease Obtained . . . . . . . . . . : Saturday, March 13, 1999 9:15:43 AM
    Lease Expires . . . . . . . . . . . : Tuesday, March 16, 1999 9:15:43 AM
```

For details on DHCP Relay functionality, refer to Chapter 11.

X-REF

Microsoft NT Server implements the DHCP relay agent as an option on the DHCP server. When the DHCP relay agent is installed, requests from DHCP clients will be forwarded to another DHCP server, as shown in Figure 16.16.

In Figure 16.16, the DHCP client requests an IP address. The request is picked up by the relay agent (in this case, the NT Server) and passed on to the DHCP server on a different segment. The DHCP server, configured with scope information for both segments, returns IP addressing and other configured options to the relay agent, which in turn fulfills the client request.

▶ · ◀

FIGURE   16.16

DHCP relay agent forwards client DHCP requests

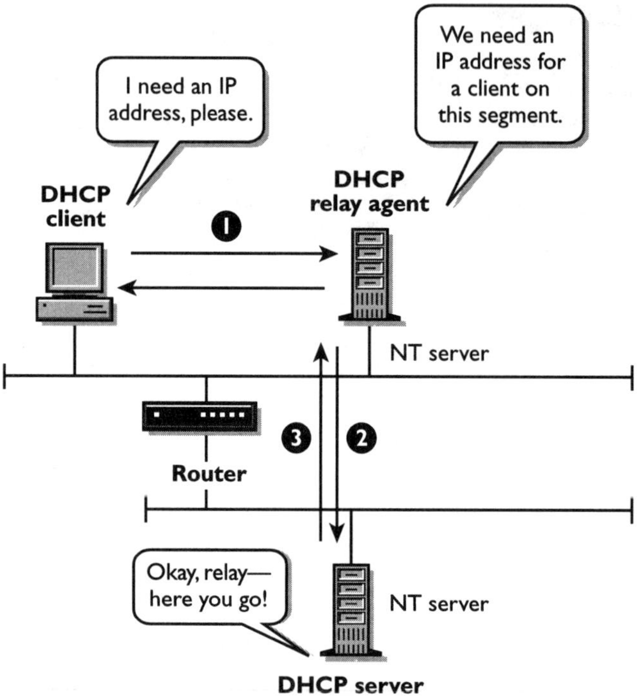

To configure the DHCP relay option in an NT Server, perform the following steps:

1. Go to Control Panel.

2. Choose Network (or right-click the Network Neighborhood icon, and choose Properties).

3. Click the Protocols tab.

4. Click the TCP/IP Protocol and click Properties.

5. Click the DHCP Relay tab.

6. Under the DHCP Servers box, click Add, and type the IP address of the server that will provide the IP addresses to the clients.

7. Click Add and then click OK.

The DHCP Relay tab of the TCP/IP Properties dialog box is shown in Figure 16.17.

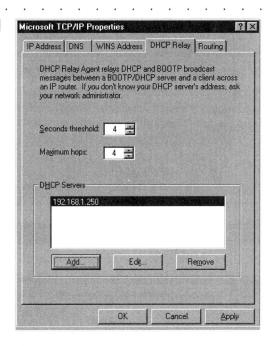

F I G U R E   16.17

DHCP Relay installation on an NT Server

NOTE

You cannot install DHCP Relay without installing DHCP Services on the NT Server.

Maintaining the DHCP Database

The DHCP database files are stored on the NT Server in the *systemroot*\ system32\dhcp directory. (The *systemroot* directory is generally the winnt directory, which is the default installation directory for NT Server.)

The DHCP Service consist of the following files:

▸ **Dhcp.mdb:** Main DHCP database file

▸ **Dhcp.tmp:** Holds temporary database information while the DHCP Service is running

▸ ***.log:** Transaction log files used to recover in the event of a failure or system crash

Generally, three maintenance items may take place with the DHCP database:

▸ Backing up

▸ Restoring a corrupt database

▸ Compacting the database

Backing Up the DHCP Database

By default, the DHCP database is backed up every 60 minutes. Backup copies of the DHCP database are stored in the *systemroot*\system32\dhcp\backup\jet\new directory.

The default backup interval may be changed by making a simple Registry edit using the REGEDIT or REGEDT32 command from the NT Server prompt. Use the utility to locate the following Registry key:

```
HKEY_LOCAL_MACHINE\SYSTEM\CurrentControlSet\Services\
DHCPServer\Parameters\BackupInterval
```

Change the interval as you wish. Figure 16.18 illustrates the Registry Editor and the BackupInterval key.

Restoring a Corrupt DHCP Database

As previously stated, a copy of the DHCP database is kept in the *systemroot*\ system32\dhcp\backup\jet\new directory. If a database file is corrupt or damaged, the easiest thing to do is simply to copy from the backup directory to the DHCP directory. This procedure may also be done from another media source, such as a tape backup.

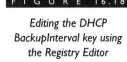

F I G U R E   16.18

Editing the DHCP BackupInterval key using the Registry Editor

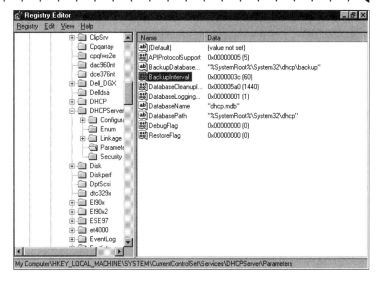

Compacting the DHCP Database

Occasionally, the DHCP database may need to be compacted. This procedure eliminates unnecessary entries from the database and refreshes the file for future use. The utility provided to compact the database is called JETPACK.EXE.

JetPack is a command-line utility that is run from the NT Server command window. It is located in the *systemroot*\system32 directory. To compact a DHCP database, use the following steps:

1. Stop the DHCP Server Service. This may be done from the Control Panel, Services applet, or from the command-line prompt. From the command line, type **NET STOP DHCPSERVER**.

2. From a command prompt, change to the *systemroot*\system32\dhcp directory. Run JetPack by using the following syntax:

```
jetpack dhcp.mdb filename.mdb
```

The *filename* may be anything you want. The DHCP.MDB file is compacted into the *filename.mdb*. Then the *filename.mdb* is copied to DHCP.MDB and the *filename.mdb* is deleted.

3. Restart the DHCP Server Service. This may be done from the Control
Panel, Services applet, or from the command-line prompt. From the
command line, type **NET START DHCPSERVER**.

A code of 0 will be returned when the JetPack operation is successful.
Occasionally, the JetPack utility will return an error code indicating some problem
with the compacting process. Table 16.2 lists some of the common JetPack errors.

TABLE 16.2	JETPACK CODE	DESCRIPTION
Common JetPack Error Codes	0	Successful Operation
	103	Could Not Start Thread
	105	System Busy Due to Too Many IOs
	319	Duplicated Item
	321	Some Versions Could Not Be Cleaned
	501	Log File Is Corrupt
	502	Last Log Record Read
	503	No Backup Directory Given
	504	The Backup Directory Is Not Empty
	505	Backup Is Active Already
	510	Fail When Writing to Log File
	514	Version of Log File Is Not Compatible with Jet Version
	516	Log Is Not Active
	519	Exceed Maximum Log File Number
	524	Could Not Delete Backup File
	525	Could Not Make Backup Temp Directory
	528	Current Log File Missing
	529	Log Disk Full
	1002	Invalid Name
	1011	Out of Memory
	1012	Maximum Database Size Reached

JETPACK CODE	DESCRIPTION
1014	Out of Database Page Buffers
1018	Read Verification Error
1020	Out of File Handles
1022	Disk IO Error
1023	Invalid File Path
1044	Filename Is Invalid
1051	Index Is in Use
1201	Database Already Exists
1202	Database in Use
1203	No Such Database
1204	Invalid Database Name
1207	Database Exclusively Locked
1803	Temp File Could Not Be Opened
1808	No Space Left on Disk
1809	Permission Denied
1811	File Not Found
1813	Database File Is Read Only

For a complete list of JetPack Error codes, go to support.microsoft.com **and request document Q172570.**

The JetPack utility can be used on other database files, such as the Windows Internet Naming Service (WINS) database, discussed later in this chapter.

NetBIOS over TCP/IP

NetBIOS was originally developed for IBM in the early 1980s to allow basic network communication on a single broadcast LAN segment. In other words, no routing was available for this protocol. To provide a routable transport for NetBIOS,

Novell developed NetBIOS over IPX in the early 1990s. Later, NetBIOS over TCP/IP was defined in RFCs 1001 and 1002. NetBIOS over TCP/IP is present in Microsoft products to allow coexistence with LAN Manager and MS-Net installations, as well as IBM LAN Server installations. Microsoft also supports NetBIOS on DOS, Windows 95/98, and NT Server and Workstation.

NetBIOS provides several services to the computer. Both connection-oriented session services and connectionless datagram services are provided, along with name services to identify each device on the network. Specifically, each of these services performs the following functions:

▶ **Name registration and verification:** Every resource in a NetBIOS framework is referenced by name. No lower-level information, such as MAC address, is available. NetBIOS registers each device on the network with a unique computer name. The name-registration portion of NetBIOS is responsible for adding new names and deleting names that are no longer in use.

▶ **Reliable session establishment and teardown:** The NetBIOS Session Service is a reliable exchange of information between two NetBIOS-enabled devices using the TCP transport. The Session Service is responsible for calling a remote device, listening for incoming calls, terminating connections, and communicating session status information.

▶ **Unreliable connectionless datagram data transfer:** The Datagram Service is used to transmit data using the UDP transport. Datagrams may be sent to a specific name, or broadcast over the network. The Datagram Service is responsible for sending and receiving application data and for sending and receiving broadcast datagrams.

▶ **General hardware control:** NetBIOS also has limited hardware control. NetBIOS is able to reset or initialize the local network interface, cancel a session, and obtain network interface adapter statistics.

NetBIOS actually acts as a session layer interface to the transport layer protocols, such as TCP. Figure 16.19 shows an analyzer view of the Request and Response packets when making a session connection to an NT Server. Packet 4 indicates that a user is making a session request. Packet 5 shows the session confirmation. The data portion of packet 4 shows the TCP header making the request to port 139 (NetBIOS) on the NT Server. Additionally, you can see the NetBIOS protocol on top of TCP.

F I G U R E   16.19

NetBIOS session request
and confirmation

Using NetBIOS Names

By using the NetBIOS protocol, you may find services and computers on the NT network by their NetBIOS names rather than just their IP or MAC addresses. A NetBIOS name is a unique, 16-byte address used to identify a NetBIOS resource on the network. A NetBIOS resource may be a computer name or a service running on a particular computer. For example, when a computer first boots up onto the network, it registers its unique NetBIOS name based on the computer name, as shown in Figure 16.20.

In Figure 16.20, all users on the network have unique names. If another device boots up with an identical name, such as Mary, and Mary already exists on the network, the new computer will not be allowed to register its NetBIOS name. In Figure 16.21, the NBTSTAT -r command has been used to view the registered NetBIOS names known to the NT Server.

FIGURE 16.20

*NetBIOS name registration
occurs during bootup.*

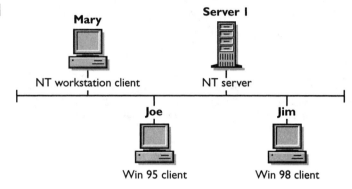

FIGURE 16.21

*NBTSTAT output from the
NT Server*

```
                                      temp
          Node IpAddress: [208.170.66.148]  Scope Id: [ ]
                       NetBIOS Local Name Table

             Name              Type        Status
          ----------------------------------------------------------------
          Registered Registered Registered Registered Registered Registered Regi
          stered Registered Registered Registered Registered Registered Register
          ed

          NTSERVER            <00>        UNIQUE
          NTSERVER            <20>        UNIQUE
          DOMAIN              <00>        GROUP
          DOMAIN              <1C>        GROUP
          DOMAIN              <1B>        UNIQUE
          NTSERVER            <03>        UNIQUE
          DOMAIN              <1E>        GROUP
          INet~Services       <1C>        GROUP
          DOMAIN              <1D>        UNIQUE
          IS~NTSERVER............ <00>    UNIQUE
          .._MSBROWSE__ ........<01>      GROUP
          NTSERVER            <6A>        UNIQUE
          NTSERVER            <87>        UNIQUE
```

For a full list of NBTSTAT command-line options, refer to Chapter 2.

X-REF

Notice in Figure 16.21 that the name NTSERVER and DOMAIN is listed more than once. To be able to register multiple services using the NetBIOS name, the name itself is limited to 15 characters. The sixteenth character is a hexadecimal value used to describe the specific service registered by that computer. For example, in Figure 16.21, after each NTSERVER entry, a different value is listed. These values indicate the type of service registered for that particular name. You can expect a server to register multiple values, such as a server computer name <20h>, workstation service <00h>, and messenger (message delivery) service <03h>.

The name DOMAIN is used to tell the NetBIOS devices that this computer is a domain master browser <1Bh>, a workstation service <00h>, and a domain controller <1Ch>, to name a few.

An NT Server may register itself many times, depending on the services installed. Using both the unique NetBIOS name and the sixteenth character describing the type of service request, devices may connect to each other over the NetBIOS protocol.

Additionally, a device may register itself as one of the following types:

▸ **Unique (U):** Only one IP address may be assigned to this name.

▸ **Group (G):** The single name may exist with many IP addresses. Designed to be used within a single subnet.

▸ **Multihomed (M):** Used to register a unique name when a computer has multiple network interfaces. The maximum number of addresses is 25.

▸ **Internet Group (I):** Special group used to manage Windows NT domain names.

▸ **Domain Name (D):** Specific to Windows NT 4 and used with domain registration.

Table 16.3 lists the common NetBIOS sixteenth-character types and their descriptions.

TABLE 16.3

NetBIOS Registration Types

NAME TYPE	HEX VALUE	REGISTRATION TYPE	DESCRIPTION
<computername>	00	Unique	Workstation Service
<computername>	01	Unique	Messenger Service
<\\—__MSBROWSE__>	01	Group	Master Browser
<computername>	03	Unique	Messenger Service
<computername>	06	Unique	RAS Server Service
<computername>	1F	Unique	NetDDE Service
<computername>	20	Unique	File Server Service
<computername>	21	Unique	RAS Client Service
<computername>	22	Unique	MS Exchange Interchange (MSMAIL)
<computername>	23	Unique	MS Exchange Store
<computername>	24	Unique	MS Exchange Directory
<computername>	30	Unique	Modem Sharing Server Service
<computername>	31	Unique	Modem Sharing Client Service
<computername>	43	Unique	SMS Clients Remote Control
<computername>	44	Unique	SMS Administrators Remote Control
<computername>	45	Unique	SMS Clients Remote Chat
<computername>	46	Unique	SMS Clients Remote Transfer
<computername>	4C	Unique	DEC Pathworks TCP/IP service on Windows NT
<computername>	52	Unique	DEC Pathworks TCP/IP service on Windows NT
<computername>	87	Unique	MS Exchange Message Transfer Agent
<computername>	6A	Unique	MS Exchange Internet Mail Connector
<computername>	BE	Unique	Network Monitor Agent
<computername>	BF	Unique	Network Monitor Application

NAME TYPE	HEX VALUE	REGISTRATION TYPE	DESCRIPTION
<username>	03	Unique	Messenger Service
<domain>	00	Group	Domain Name
<domain>	1B	Unique	Domain Master Browser
<domain>	1C	Group	Domain Controllers
<domain>	1D	Unique	Master Browser
<domain>	1E	Group	Browser Service Elections
<Inet~Services>	1C	Group	Internet Information Server
<IS~computername>	00	Unique	Internet Information Server
<computername>	2B	Unique	Lotus Notes Server Service
IRISMULTICAST	2F	Group	Lotus Notes
IRISNAMESERVER	33	Group	Lotus Notes
Forte_$ND800ZA	20	Unique	DCA IrmaLAN Gateway Service

Using a NetBIOS Scope

A NetBIOS scope is very similar to a DNS domain name. The syntax is the same, though it is *not* DNS. The *scope* is used to identify a group of computers that can use a registered name. The scope is simply an identifier that meets the domain name system requirements and is appended to the end of the NetBIOS name. For example, the computer named MARY might have a fully defined scope name of mary.company.com.

Multiple scopes may be defined to allow multiple computers with the same name to exist within different scopes in the network. Typically, in a NetBIOS network, only a single scope is used. NetBIOS scopes are configured from the WINS Address tab of the TCP/IP Properties dialog box, as shown in Figure 16.22.

RFC 1001 requires that each implementation of NetBIOS over TCP provide some way of managing the scope identifier, even though the scope ID is not required.

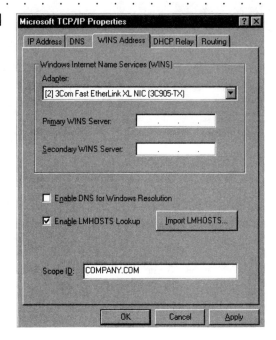

The NetBIOS Name Cache

NetBIOS names may either be loaded into a device's memory cache during normal use, or preloaded with a special file called the LMHOSTS file, which is discussed later in this chapter. Using the name cache reduces the amount of broadcasts required to locate a NetBIOS name within the network. By default, an entry remains in the NetBIOS name cache for 10 minutes, or 600,000 milliseconds. This can be changed by editing HKEY_LOCAL_MACHINE\ SYSTEM\CurrentControlSet\Services\NetBT\Parameters with the Registry Editor, shown in Figure 16.23.

Notice also in Figure 16.23 another Registry entry called Size/Small/Medium/Large. This value controls the size of the NetBIOS name cache on the computer. The default value is 1, which corresponds to a Small value of 16 name entries. A Medium value is equal to 2, which results in a name size cache of 64 names. A Large name cache value of 3 configures a name cache size of 128 entries.

FIGURE 16.23

Modifying the NetBIOS name CacheTimeout value with Registry Editor

Registry Editor

Registry   Edit   View   Help

Name	Data
[Default]	(value not set)
BcastNameQuery...	0x00000003 (3)
BcastQueryTimeout	0x000002ee (750)
CacheTimeout	0x000927c0 (600000)
EnableDNS	0x00000000 (0)
EnableLMHOSTS	0x00000001 (1)
EnableProxy	0x00000000 (0)
NameServerPort	0x00000089 (137)
NameSrvQueryCo...	0x00000003 (3)
NameSrvQueryTim...	0x000005dc (1500)
NbProvider	"_tcp"
ScopeID	""
SessionKeepAlive	0x0036ee80 (3600000)
Size/Small/Mediu...	0x00000001 (1)
TransportBindName	"\Device\"

Tree (left panel): MSExchange, MSExchange, MSExchange, MSExchange, Msfs, MSFTPSVC, Mup, Nbf, Ncr53c9x, ncr77c22, Ncrc700, Ncrc710, NDIS, NetBIOS, NetBIOSInfo, NetBT (Adapters, Enum, Linkage, Parameters, Security), NetDDE, NetDDEdsdm

My Computer\HKEY_LOCAL_MACHINE\SYSTEM\CurrentControlSet\Services\NetBT\Parameters

Address Resolution Protocol and the ARP Cache

Like all TCP/IP networks, Microsoft TCP/IP uses ARP to map IP addresses to MAC addresses. Ultimately, the MAC address is used to transmit data across routers to a final destination. Previously discovered IP-to-MAC address mappings are contained in the computer's ARP cache.

IMPORTANT

The ARP cache is not the same as the NetBIOS name cache. The NetBIOS name cache contains NetBIOS names, whereas the ARP cache contains IP and MAC addresses.

An ARP cache table is maintained for the network interface on the computer. To view the contents of a computer's ARP cache, simply use the ARP command, as shown in Figure 16.24.

X-REF

For a full list of ARP command-line parameters, refer to Chapter 2.

*ARP command shows local
ARP cache*

Each ARP cache entry has a potential lifetime of ten minutes. When an entry first goes into the ARP cache, a timestamp is created. If an entry is not used again within two minutes, the entry is deleted. If the entry is reused within the first two minutes, it remains in the ARP cache for ten minutes.

NetBIOS Name Resolution

Now that you have learned all about NetBIOS names, you are going to see how *name resolution* actually takes place within the network. What really happens when you type PING MARY, using the name instead of the IP address? Somehow, that name needs to be turned into an IP address. Name resolution is the process of mapping IP addresses to common names, such as NetBIOS names. By using name resolution, you can refer to computers by names that you can remember rather than by their IP addresses. This does not mean that you can eliminate the IP address, however. After the name resolution process takes place, ARP ultimately is still used behind the scenes to map the IP address to a MAC address, so that datagrams can be processed properly.

Within the Windows environment, standard TCP/IP services, such as DHCP, DNS, and ARP, are used extensively. One big difference with this environment is that it also allows you to name your computers by using NetBIOS names, such as Joe or Mary. However, an NT or Windows 95/98 computer may also have hostnames (such as mary.company.com) associated with them. Therefore, Windows computers must perform several types of resolution: they must get an IP address from DHCP, resolve IP addresses to MAC addresses by using ARP, resolve NetBIOS names by using a special process, and also resolve DNS hostnames by using a separate process. We will discuss these processes in this section.

IMPORTANT

Remember that a NetBIOS name is *not* a DNS hostname, although they may look the same. In reality, both types of name resolution take place through different processes.

Understand that the NetBIOS name resolution is completely independent from the DNS hostname resolution. A computer within a Microsoft network may have both of these names, as shown in Figure 16.25.

F I G U R E   16.25

Each device has both a NetBIOS name and a hostname.

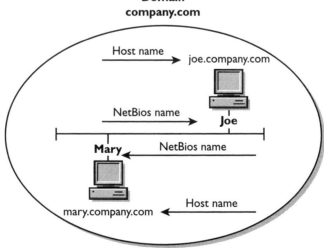

Having both a NetBIOS name and a hostname is kind of like having a key to the front door and a separate key to the back door in your home. The NetBIOS name is configured within the Identification tab of the Network dialog box, accessed via the Control Panel. In other words, it is the name of your computer. The hostname is configured through the TCP/IP Properties dialog box. Using the same name for both the NetBIOS and hostname is a very common practice.

To resolve NetBIOS names to IP addresses, a process called the Windows Internet Naming Service (WINS) must be invoked. Alternatively, a static text file called LMHOSTS may be used for NetBIOS name resolution. DNS hostname resolution, like that used on the Internet, is performed through the DNS Service or a static text file called HOSTS (this is not the same as the LMHOSTS file). This section looks at how you can find a device on an NT network, and how NetBIOS names are resolved.

Altogether, three methods are used by TCP/IP-enabled computers to find another computer on the NT network by using the NetBIOS name:

- ▶ Broadcast

- ▶ LMHOSTS file

- ▶ WINS

Before any type of NetBIOS resolution method is selected, the client always looks first in its own NetBIOS name cache. If the name is not found in the local cache, the client may use one or more methods to locate the NetBIOS name-to-IP address mapping. The next few sections examine how each of these methods is used in the Microsoft 95/98/NT environment.

Broadcast Name Resolution

Using the broadcast name resolution process, a computer that wants to resolve a NetBIOS name simply spits the broadcast resolution request onto the local segment and waits for a response. All computers on the local network receive the broadcast, and each computer checks its own local NetBIOS name information to see whether it owns the requested name. The computer that owns the NetBIOS name responds. Of course, any time that you use a broadcast on the network, it generates quite a bit of traffic. Additionally, most routers do not forward broadcasts. Therefore, this method is used in a small, single-segment network.

LMHOSTS File

The LMHOSTS (LAN Manager Hosts) file is a static text file used to resolve NetBIOS names to IP addresses of other NetBIOS-based hosts. When using the LMHOSTS file, each computer must have its own copy to be able to resolve the NetBIOS name.

If a computer is configured with an LMHOSTS file for NetBIOS name resolution, the file will be used only after an attempt is made to contact a WINS server. If no WINS server responds, the client will then use the broadcast resolution method. If still no response is forthcoming, the LMHOSTS file is used for resolution.

The LMHOSTS file is located in the \systemroot\system32\drivers\etc directory on the NT computer, or in the \windows directory of a Windows 95/98 computer. Each host defined on the network must be placed in the LMHOSTS file in order for name resolution to work properly. Each entry consists of one IP address and one NetBIOS name. Comments may be added by using the # sign. A sample LMHOSTS file is shown in Figure 16.26.

FIGURE 16.26

LMHOSTS file used for NetBIOS name resolution

```
                                        Lmhosts

208.107.66.128   ntserver1   #PRE   #DOM:networking    #net group's domain control l
er
208.107.66.152   servermain  #PRE              #source server
208.107.69.192   ntserver    #PRE              #needed for the include
208.107.70.156   ntbdc       #PRE              #needed for the include
145.30.56.109    sales                         #Outside Sales Server
145.30.92.76     molly                         #Molly's computer

#BEGIN ALTERNATE
#INCLUDE \\ntserver\public\lmhosts
#INCLUDE \\ntbdc\public\lmhosts
#END_ALTERNATE
```

In Figure 16.26, the LMHOSTS file contains entries for several main computers within the network. Notice that the IP address is followed by the computer name. In some cases, a special prefix is shown. The special prefix is indicated by an entry beginning with a # sign and shown in all caps. Two examples of the special prefixes shown in Figure 16.26 are the #PRE and #DOM entries. These are specific LMHOSTS file commands that designate a preloaded entry and a domain server. A list of common LMHOSTS special prefixes is shown in Table 16.4.

TABLE 16.4

LMHOSTS Predefined Special Prefix Keywords

PREDEFINED PREFIX	DESCRIPTION
#PRE	Preloads an entry permanently into the NetBIOS name cache. Generally used for servers and other heavily used devices.
#DOM:domain	Identifies a domain controller and reduces traffic for those devices wanting to log on and browse the network.
#BEGIN_ALTERNATE	Defines an alternate list for LMHOSTS files. The next command should be the #INCLUDE statement.
#INCLUDE	Specifies location of remote LMHOSTS files. Specified by the appropriate UNC path; i.e., \\ntserver\public\lmhosts.
#END_ALTERNATE	Stops processing alternate list of LMHOSTS files.
#MH	User for multiple entries with a multihomed computer (computer with multiple Network Interface Cards).

As the network gets larger, keeping track of the LMHOSTS file tends to become tedious. Additionally, problems associated with this manual configuration are numerous, including misspelled NetBIOS names, wrong IP addresses, multiple entries, and so on. Therefore, an automatic database to keep track of registered names and services is preferred. The automatic database is kept by a *NetBIOS name server*. Microsoft's NetBIOS name server (NBNS) is called the Windows Internet Naming Service (WINS).

Windows Internet Naming Service (WINS)

WINS is designed to resolve NetBIOS names to IP addresses while reducing the need for broadcast traffic. The WINS server is used to register, renew, release, and resolve NetBIOS names. DHCP can be configured to include a WINS server in its configuration, and DHCP clients can request WINS server information at bootup.

When a client wants to resolve a NetBIOS name, it first looks in its local NetBIOS name cache. If the name is not found in the local cache, the WINS server is contacted for resolution. After the WINS server answers the request and resolves the NetBIOS name, the client can use ARP to locate the MAC address of the destination.

The WINS architecture is a client/server architecture that consists of a WINS server and WINS clients. Windows NT, 95, and 98 can all be configured to use WINS. The WINS server establishes and maintains a dynamic database of NetBIOS names and IP address mappings. When a client needs to resolve a NetBIOS name, it simply queries the WINS server, as shown in Figure 16.27.

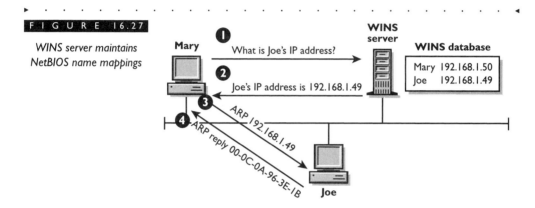

F I G U R E 16.27

WINS server maintains NetBIOS name mappings

In Figure 16.27, Mary wants to communicate with Joe, but does not know his IP address. Mary simply queries the WINS server and receives the IP address associated with Joe's computer. Mary's computer now performs an ARP request to find Joe's MAC address. When Joe's computer replies, communication begins between the two computers.

IMPORTANT

Remember, after a name resolution (either NetBIOS or WINS), IP-to-MAC address resolution must still be performed using ARP, unless the MAC address of the destination is already in the ARP cache.

All WINS communications are performed using UDP port 137. This is the port reserved for NetBIOS name service.

In addition to name queries, the WINS server performs three very important functions:

► Name registration

► Name release

▸ Name renewal

Next, take a look at how each of these three functions is implemented.

WINS Name Registration

When a computer is configured to use WINS, it sends a name registration request to the WINS server on bootup. The WINS server then looks at the registration request to see whether the name already exists in the database. If the name does not exist, the WINS server registers the NetBIOS name and IP address of the client.

If the name request contains a name already registered with the WINS database, the WINS server first *challenges* the registered owner of the name. The challenge is sent to the IP address of the registered computer three times. If the currently registered owner responds, the WINS server will not allow the new computer to claim the name. If the current owner does not respond, the WINS server allows the new computer to take the name. The WINS database then is updated with the IP address of the new client.

WINS Name Release

When a computer is shut down properly, it releases its computer name and IP address mapping through the use of a WINS Name Release message. This message is sent directly to the WINS server, informing it that the name is no longer needed. The WINS server then marks the name as released. The WINS server keeps the name until the *extinction interval* is reached, a variable time configured within the WINS server that defines how long WINS keeps an entry before marking it extinct and deleting it from the database.

If a computer is shut down improperly or abruptly, WINS does not receive a Name Release message, which causes one of two things to happen. If the computer reboots and attempts to reregister its name by using the same IP address as before the crash, the WINS server simply allows the name registration. However, if a client attempts to reregister its name by using a different IP address (as in the case of a DHCP server), the WINS server first attempts to contact what it thinks is the old client's IP address. If the client does not respond, the name reregistration takes place.

WINS Name Renewal

When the WINS client registers a computer name with the WINS server, the client receives a renewal time, called the *renewal interval,* for the computer name. The client is then required to renew its lease; if it doesn't, the WINS server releases the name. The client first attempts to renew its name registration after one-eighth of the renewal time has expired. Upon receipt of a successful name renewal, it then refreshes its registration when half the renewal interval has expired.

If a client attempts to renew its name and is unsuccessful, it keeps attempting to renew its registration every two minutes, until half the renewal interval has expired. The client then attempts to renew its name with a secondary WINS server, using the same procedure just described. If the registration renewal is unsuccessful, the WINS server will eventually release the name.

Implementing the WINS Server

WINS must be installed on at least one NT Server within the network. The installation and configuration of the WINS server can be performed in three steps:

1. Install the WINS Service.

2. Configure WINS.

3. Determine replication needs.

Install the WINS Service

To install the WINS Server Service, simply choose the Network option from the Control Panel. Use the Services tab to display a list of currently installed services. Click the Add button to add WINS. The result is shown in Figure 16.28.

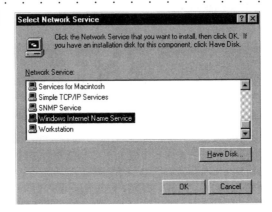

WINS installation screen

A single WINS server can typically handle the name resolution for an entire network, because a WINS request is a directed datagram, which does not eat up network bandwidth like a broadcast does. For fault tolerance, however, two WINS servers are recommended.

A single WINS server and backup server should be installed for every 10,000 WINS clients.

TIP

After WINS is installed, the computer must be rebooted. After the reboot, WINS is ready for configuration. The WINS Service should run automatically when the server boots, to configure the service. If the WINS Service is not running for some reason, you can manually start the WINS Service in one of two ways:

▶ From the Control Panel, select Services and then find the Microsoft WINS Server in the list. Click Start to initialize the service.

▶ At a command prompt, type **NET START WINS**.

Now that the service is installed and running, it can be configured.

Configure WINS

After you install WINS, the WINS Manager option appears on the menu. To use the WINS Manager, click Start ➪ Programs ➪ Administrative Tools ➪ WINS Manager. The opening WINS Manager screen will appear, as shown in Figure 16.29.

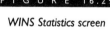

FIGURE 16.29

WINS Statistics screen

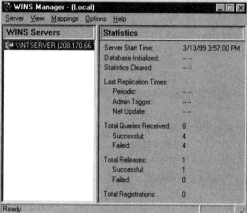

The WINS Statistics screen is a dynamic overview of the WINS server. The Statistics screen shows several variables, including:

- **Server Start Time:** The date and time the WINS Server Service was started.

- **Database Initialized:** The time when this WINS database was first initialized.

- **Statistics Cleared:** The time the statistics were last cleared.

- **Last Replication Times:** Times when the WINS server database was last replicated to a secondary WINS server, which can be performed in one of three ways:

  - **Periodic:** A normal replication that takes place based on the preferences set in the WINS Manager.

- **Admin Trigger:** A forced replication chosen by a network administrator.

- **Net Update:** An update that is performed as the result of a request from a secondary WINS server.

▸ **Total Queries Received:** The total number of resolution query requests received by the WINS server, along with the number of successful and failed resolutions.

▸ **Total Releases:** The total number of Name Release requests received by the WINS server, showing both successful and failed (or unreleased) names.

▸ **Total Registrations:** The total number of name registration requests received by the WINS server.

Remember that the WINS database is a dynamic database. Therefore, after the WINS Server Service starts, WINS begins populating the database immediately. To view the database, choose Mappings ⇨ View Database from the main screen, which displays the Show Database dialog box, shown in Figure 16.30.

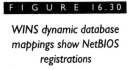

FIGURE 16.30

WINS dynamic database mappings show NetBIOS registrations

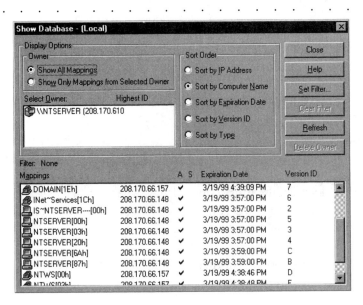

Figure 16.30 shows that the WINS database has several entries. Note that the NetBIOS name, plus the sixteenth character, is shown in each of the entries. This helps identify the registration type for each entry. Also notice that the IP address is shown for each entry, along with its status. The A type is an active (or dynamic) entry, while the S type shows any statically or manually entered entries, if they exist. You can view the expiration date of the NetBIOS name registration, as well as a unique Version ID, which is a field assigned by WINS to each entry to assist with replication to a secondary WINS server.

Determine Replication Needs

WINS servers can be configured so that database replication can take place between two or more servers, providing fault tolerance for the WINS Service. This is referred to as a *replication partnership*. The network administrator must explicitly set up a replication partnership between servers. In each partnership, a server is configured as either a pull partner or a push partner.

A *pull partner* is a server that pulls, or retrieves, the database entries from the other partner at specified intervals. This method is often used over slower WAN links that may be less busy at night. Figure 16.31 shows how a pull-partner relationship might work.

FIGURE 16.31

WINS pull partner pulls WINS database entries at specified intervals

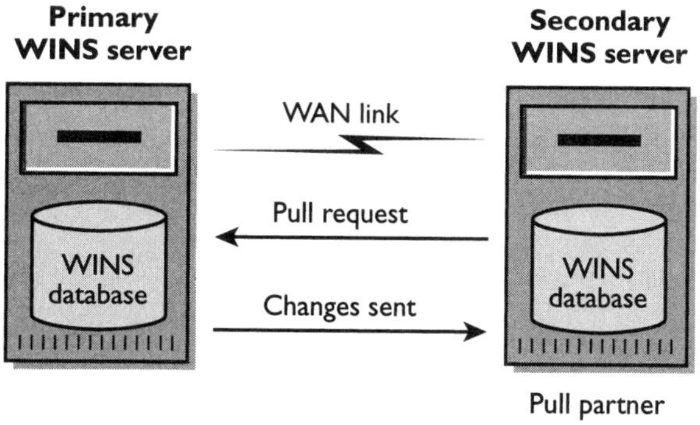

A *push partner* is a server that sends update notifications to the pull-partner server when the database has changed. The pull-partner server then requests the

updates, as shown in Figure 16.32. Replication partnerships are managed through the WINS Manager.

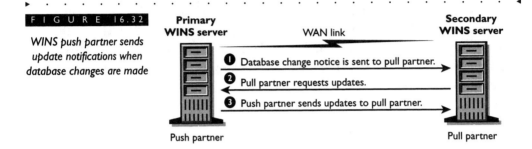

FIGURE 16.32

WINS push partner sends update notifications when database changes are made

Primary WINS server — WAN link — Secondary WINS server

❶ Database change notice is sent to pull partner.
❷ Pull partner requests updates.
❸ Push partner sends updates to pull partner.

Push partner   Pull partner

Automatic WINS Replication Partnerships

When you first bring up a WINS server, it will automatically send IGMP packets to multicast address 224.0.1.24. These multicast packets are sent by the WINS Service looking for possible replication partners. By default, this multicast occurs every 40 minutes. If other WINS servers are found on the network using the multicast, they are automatically configured as push and pull replication partners. Pull replication occurs every two hours, but occurs only if the network supports multicasting. If the network routers do not support multicasting, WINS servers will be able to find other WINS servers only on their local subnet, and not on other segments.

If you don't want these multicast packets to be sent, or want to change the multicast interval from 40 minutes, the following two Registry entries may be set, both of which are located in the HKEY_LOCAL_MACHINE\SYSTEM\ CurrentControlSet\Services\Wins\Parameters Registry key:

▸ **UseSelfFndPnrs key:** Only two values are possible: 0 and 1. The default is 0. If the parameter is set to 1 and the network supports multicasting, the WINS server automatically finds other WINS servers on the network and configures them as push and pull partners.

▸ **McastIntvl key:** Specifies the interval, in seconds, at which multicast packets are sent by WINS servers to announce their presence. The default is 2,400 seconds, or 40 minutes.

Configuring the WINS Client

Just as a WINS server must be configured to maintain the WINS database, the client must be configured to use WINS to resolve NetBIOS names. Though the configuration process is similar in Windows NT Workstation, Windows 95, and Windows 98, the screens are not all exactly the same.

Before you may configure clients to resolve NetBIOS names through WINS, you must first install TCP/IP. The following sections examine the WINS configuration options for Windows 95/98 and NT clients.

Windows 95/98 WINS Client Configuration

To configure a Windows 95/98 client to use WINS, you perform the following steps:

1. Go to Control Panel.

2. Choose Network (or right-click the Network Neighborhood icon and choose Properties).

3. Scroll down to the TCP/IP option and click Properties. (If more than one TCP/IP protocol is listed, choose the TCP/IP that corresponds with your network card.)

4. From the TCP/IP Properties screen, choose the WINS Configuration tab. Choose Enable WINS Resolution, and enter the Primary and Secondary WINS Server IP addresses, as shown in Figure 16.33.

In Figure 16.33, the IP address of the primary and secondary WINS servers have been entered. Because this client is also a DHCP client, a cleaner and more efficient method of distributing this information would be through the DHCP server. By selecting the Use DHCP for WINS Resolution radio button at the bottom of the screen, you can receive WINS parameters from DHCP and eliminate the need to configure each workstation separately.

For an NT Workstation, the process is similar.

▶ · ◀

FIGURE 16.33

WINS NetBIOS name resolution configuration for Windows 95/98

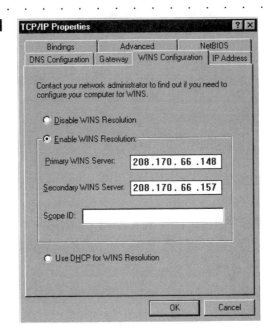

Windows NT Workstation Client Configuration

To configure a Windows NT Workstation client to use WINS for NetBIOS name resolution, perform the following steps:

1. Go to Control Panel.

2. Choose Network (or right-click the Network Neighborhood icon and choose Properties).

3. Click the Protocols tab.

4. Scroll down to the TCP/IP option and click Properties.

5. From the TCP/IP Properties screen, choose the WINS Address. Enter the IP addresses of the Primary and Secondary WINS Servers, as shown in Figure 16.34.

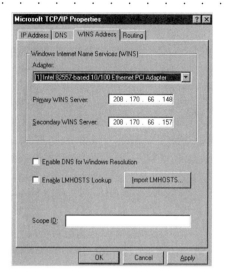

FIGURE 16.34

WINS client configuration for Windows NT Workstation

The NT Workstation will also use DHCP parameters for WINS if they are configured on the DHCP server. To verify that WINS parameters are working at the client, use the IPCONFIG /ALL command at the NT Workstation command prompt, or the WINIPCFG command at the Windows 95/98 Run command line. The WINS server addresses appear on the configuration screen.

Using NetBIOS Node Types to Control Name Resolution

A NetBIOS name may be resolved in a variety of methods, depending on the defined node type. A *node type* determines how a computer makes its way through the resolution process — should it broadcast or just use WINS? How does it know whether WINS is available? What about the LMHOSTS file?

Five types of methods are used to resolve NetBIOS names to IP addresses. Four of them are defined in RFCs 1001 and 1002, and the fifth, an enhanced broadcast, has been placed in use by Microsoft. The following are the four standard node types:

- ▸ B-node (Broadcast node)

- ▸ P-node (Peer-to-Peer node)

- ▸ M-node (Mixed node)

- ▸ H-node (Hybrid node)

The fifth node type is called the Microsoft Enhanced B-node. All five node types are discussed in this section.

B-Node (Broadcast) Resolution

The B-node method is the simplest to deploy and is generally the default in a small network. Using B-node resolution, a computer broadcasts the request onto the local network segment and waits for a response. When it receives a response, the computer places the newly acquired mapping into the NetBIOS name cache. This method has disadvantages, however. The biggest disadvantage is that broadcast traffic is sent everywhere on the network, which increases network traffic. Additionally, routers may not forward broadcasts, which makes name resolution impossible across multiple segments.

P-Node (Peer-to-Peer) Resolution

Using P-node resolution requires that a NetBIOS name server, such as WINS, is configured on the network. A P-node client that wants to resolve a NetBIOS name communicates directly with the WINS server. The advantage to this method is that it eliminates the broadcast traffic associated with the B-node. The disadvantage is the possible single point of failure if the WINS server goes down.

M-Node (Mixed) Resolution

The M-node resolution uses a combination of the B-node and P-node methods. When attempting to resolve a name, an M-node first broadcasts (B-node) and then contacts a NetBIOS name server as a P-node.

H-Node (Hybrid) Resolution

Like an M-node, the H-node uses a combination of the B-node and P-node resolution methods. The H-node firsts attempt to contact a NetBIOS name server (P-node) and then uses a B-node if resolution is unsuccessful.

Microsoft Enhanced B-Node

This node type is used by Microsoft to allow a broadcast method (B-node) to be used in conjunction with the LMHOSTS file. When resolving a NetBIOS name, an Enhanced B-node first broadcasts for the name. If unsuccessful, the client then checks the LMHOSTS file.

Because NetBIOS names can be entered in a HOSTS file, and WINS and DNS integration may be implemented, a host may also look to these options for resolution before returning an error message, which is why resolution sometimes takes so long.

Managing the WINS Database

The WINS database files are stored on the NT Server in the *systemroot*\system32\ wins directory. (The *systemroot* directory is generally the WINNT directory — this is the default installation directory for NT Server.)

The WINS installation consists of the following files:

- **Wins.mdb:** Main WINS database file

- **Winstmp.mdb:** Holds temporary database information while the WINS Service is running

- ***.Log and *.chk:** Transaction log files and checkpoint files used to recover in the event of a failure or system crash

Generally, you may perform the following maintenance items with the WINS database:

- Back up the WINS database

- Restore a corrupt WINS database

- Compact the WINS database

- Scavenge the WINS database

Backing Up the WINS Database

By default, the WINS database is *not* backed up. A backup directory must be specified from within the WINS Manager. To configure the backup from the WINS Manager, choose Mappings ➪ Back Up Database, specify a location for the backup files, and then click OK.

After you define the backup directory, the WINS database will back itself up every 24 hours.

Restoring a Corrupt WINS Database

If a WINS database becomes damaged, you may use one of two methods to restore the corrupt file:

- Start and stop the WINS Server Service. If the WINS server notices the corrupt file, it automatically restores a backup copy. You can do this from the command prompt by typing **NET STOP WINS**, or from the Services applet in the Control Panel. To restart the WINS Service, use the Services applet in Control Panel, or type **NET START WINS** from the command prompt.

- From within the WINS Manager program, choose Mappings ➪ Restore Database. This will also force a database restoration.

Compacting the WINS Database

Occasionally, the WINS database may need to be compacted, just like the DHCP database. The compacting procedure improves WINS performance and eliminates unnecessary entries. The same JetPack utility provided to compact the DHCP database is used with the WINS database.

To compact a WINS database, use the following steps:

1. Stop the WINS Server Service.

2. Open a command prompt and go to the *systemroot*\\system32\\wins directory.

3. Run the JetPack utility by using the following command-line syntax:

```
JETPACK wins.mdb filename.mdb
```

The *filename* may be anything that you wish. The wins.mdb file is compacted into the *filename.mdb*. Then the *filename.mdb* is copied to wins.mdb, and the *filename.mdb* is deleted.

4. Restart the WINS Server Service. This may be done from the Control Panel's Services applet or from the command-line prompt. From the command line, type **NET START WINS**.

Scavenging the Database

Occasionally, the WINS database should be manually cleared of old entries. This process is usually performed automatically by the WINS server, depending on the Extinction Timeout value set in the WINS server configuration. The process of cleaning out old entries, whether it is performed manually or automatically, is called *scavenging*.

To manually scavenge the WINS database, choose Mappings ⇨ Initiate Scavenging from the WINS Manager. The scavenging process then is queued and the database is verified and refreshed. Extinct entries are deleted, nonrenewed names still active are marked as released, and active names are revalidated.

Resolving Hostnames

Thus far, you have learned how NetBIOS names are resolved within the Microsoft network. Remember that each computer also has a *hostname* that is completely separate from the NetBIOS name configured for the computer.

Hostnames are very common to all TCP/IP environments. In fact, you probably use them every day on the Internet. A common use for a hostname is in a Web browser, such as when you type **www.novell.com** to reach a server that performs Web page services. When a non-NetBIOS application, such as a Web browser, requests name resolution, it does so by using the computer's hostname. Only NetBIOS applications use the NetBIOS name.

As previously mentioned, the hostname is separate from the NetBIOS name. One of the biggest differences between hostnames and NetBIOS names is that a NetBIOS name is only 15 characters (plus the sixteenth-character service identifier), and a hostname can be up to 256 characters. Some of the major differences between hostnames and NetBIOS names are listed in Table 16.5.

T A B L E   16.5

Differences between Hostnames and NetBIOS Names

FUNCTION	HOSTNAMES	NETBIOS NAMES
Overall length:	256-character string	15 characters
Configured in:	DNS Settings	Computer Identification tab
Names to IP addresses resolved by:	HOSTS file or DNS server (may be configured to use a NetBIOS name server)	LMHOSTS, broadcast, or NetBIOS name server, such as WINS

Two methods are used by TCP/IP-enabled computers to find another computer on the NT network by using the hostname:

► HOSTS file

► DNS

Before any resolution request is made, a host always checks its own hostname to see whether it is the destination host. Then it uses one of several methods to resolve the hostname. Microsoft allows a client to use standard hostname resolution, through either the HOSTS file or DNS. If neither method works, then the client attempts resolution through a NetBIOS name server (WINS), broadcast, and LMHOSTS file. This section looks at the HOSTS file and DNS to see how they are used in the Microsoft 95/98/NT environment.

HOSTS File

The HOSTS file is a static text file that is used to resolve hostnames to IP addresses. It provides cross-platform compatibility with other systems running TCP/IP-based services, such as UNIX or an AS/400.

When using the HOSTS file for resolution, each computer must have its own copy to be able to resolve the hostname. The HOSTS file may also resolve NetBIOS names. The HOSTS file is located in the \systemroot\system32\drivers\etc directory on the NT computer, and in the \windows directory of a Windows 95/98 computer. Each host requiring name resolution must be placed in the HOSTS file. Each entry consists of one IP address and one hostname. Comments are preceded with a # sign. A sample HOSTS file is shown in Figure 16.35.

FIGURE 16.35

Sample HOSTS file

```
# This is a comment line

208.170.66.159      server.company.com      # main server
208.170.66.148      client.company.com      # hostname for client

127.0.0.1           localhost
```

Figure 16.35 shows a comment line preceded by a # character. Next, the IP addresses and hostnames of a server and a client are shown, followed by another comment for each. With the HOSTS file, an IP address may be given several names. These additional names are called *aliases* and may be placed on the same line as the first hostname. Simply separate each alias with a space. Aliases commonly are used for servers, to hide the real name. Each entry in the HOSTS file is limited to 255 characters.

Unlike the LMHOSTS file, the HOSTS file does not allow the special characters, such as #PRE and #DOM, to preload names or set up domains. This is Microsoft-specific and only available in the LMHOSTS file. However, a NetBIOS name, such as Mary, can be placed in the HOSTS file with the appropriate IP address, and resolution will occur.

As the network grows, the maintenance of the HOSTS file becomes cumbersome. Each entry must be made using a text editor, and the entire HOSTS file must be distributed to each client on the network. To centralize the hostname-to-IP address mappings, a domain name server (DNS) may be placed in the network. The use of the DNS eliminates the need for the HOSTS file.

Domain Name Server (DNS)

Microsoft uses the hierarchical DNS system to map IP addresses to hostnames. The DNS Service included with NT Server complies with Internet standards and RFCs 1034 and 1035. Through the use of these standards, the Microsoft DNS system can be used just like a DNS-based database on another platform, such as UNIX.

For full details on how DNS works, refer to Chapter 12.

X-REF

Within the Microsoft network, as with any network, both DNS servers and DNS clients must be configured. This section examines this process. Additionally, it describes a Microsoft-specific method to integrate WINS and DNS name resolution.

▶ · ◀

Implementing the DNS Server

The DNS Server Service must be installed on a Windows NT Server. When the DNS Server Service is installed, clients may use the DNS database to resolve hostnames to IP addresses. To set up DNS on a server, an administrator must perform the following steps:

1. Install the DNS Service on a Windows NT Server.

2. Create a primary forward lookup zone.

3. Create a primary reverse lookup zone (optional).

4. Add records to the zone.

Each of these steps is described next in more detail.

Install the DNS Service on a Windows NT Server

To install the DNS Service, simply choose the Network option from the Control Panel on the NT Server. Use the Services tab to display a list of currently installed services. Click the Add button to add the DNS Service. The result is shown in Figure 16.36.

▶ · ◀

F I G U R E   16.36

DNS Server Service installation screen

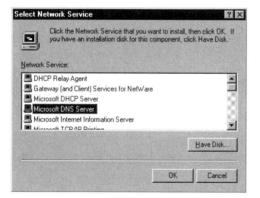

After you install the DNS Service, you must reboot the computer. After the reboot, the DNS Service is ready for configuration. The DNS Service should run automatically when the server boots, to configure the service. If the DNS Service is not running for some reason, you can manually start the DNS Service in either of two ways:

▸ Choose Control Panel ⇨ Services and find the Microsoft DNS Server in the list. Click Start to initialize the service.

▸ At a command prompt, type **NET START DNS**.

By default, the DNS server is a caching server only. During the DNS installation, a utility called DNS Manager was added to the Administrative Tools menu. Using that utility to view the initial DNS installation, we can see that a cache file has been included with our DNS server. The cache file includes the names of several top-level domain servers (called *root servers*), as shown in Figure 16.37.

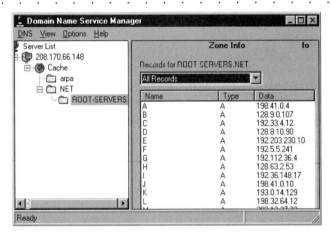

Though having the cache file is handy, it will not help you resolve DNS host-names within your organization or connect to the Internet properly, unless you configure your own zone files. You must first configure a primary forward lookup zone.

Create a Primary Forward Lookup Zone

As Chapter 12 explains, a zone may contain one or more domains, as well as one or more subdomains. The zone simply contains the DNS database files, and is considered to be authoritative for all the DNS information within the domains and subdomains contained in that file. The following is a description of the two types of zones:

▶ **Primary zone:** Contains its own Start of Authority resource record and depends entirely on the information contained within its own database files.

▶ **Secondary zone:** A read-only copy of an existing zone file; although not required, it is highly recommended. Basically, a secondary zone exists to serve as a backup for the primary zone. Additionally, the secondary zone can be used for name resolution and load balancing, and clients can be configured to use the secondary server instead of the primary when performing a name-resolution request. A secondary zone is created on a different server than the primary zone.

Additionally, a zone can be either a *forward lookup zone* or a *reverse lookup zone*. With a forward lookup zone, a client attempts to resolve an IP address by using a name, such as www.novell.com. (Chapter 12 calls these resolution queries either *iterative* or *recursive* queries.) Reverse lookups are addressed in the next section. All DNS servers must have a primary forward lookup zone, and this must be manually created by the network administrator.

To create a primary forward lookup zone, you use the following steps:

1. From the DNS Manager, click the server that represents the DNS name server.

2. Right-click and select New Zone.

3. A wizard appears. Choose Primary.

4. Enter the Zone Name and press the Tab key.

5. Enter a Zone Filename (the zone name plus a .dns extension; the extension is prefilled automatically after you press the Tab key).

6. Click Next and then click Finish.

After the new primary forward lookup zone has been created, it appears in the DNS Manager. A sample is shown in Figure 16.38, in which a primary zone, pncg.com, has been created. Notice that several records have already been added to the zone file. The SOA (Start of Authority) record identifies this server as the primary DNS server for this zone, while the NS (Name Server) and A (Address) records identify the server's name and IP address.

▶ . . . . ◀

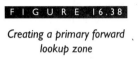

F I G U R E 16.38

Creating a primary forward lookup zone

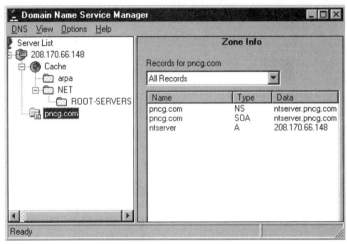

After creating the primary forward lookup zone, you must establish a primary reverse lookup zone.

Create a Primary Reverse Lookup Zone

With a reverse lookup, the client has the IP address and needs to resolve the hostname. Reverse lookups, also called *inverse queries,* are set up in a special domain called the in.addr.arpa domain. Using this special domain allows a name query to be resolved by using the IP address rather than the hostname.

Another reason this zone is important is that it allows users outside of your network to verify that you have a registered address. Usually, your Internet service provider (ISP) performs this registration process when you apply for a domain name on the Internet. Inside of your own network, the reverse lookup zone is created and synchronized with the forward lookup zone, to provide reverse name resolution. To set up a primary reverse lookup zone, take the following steps:

1. From the DNS Manager, click the server that represents the DNS name server.

2. Right-click and select New Zone.

3. A wizard appears. Choose Primary.

4. Enter the Zone Name and press the Tab key.

IMPORTANT

The zone name for the reverse lookup zone is the network portion of your IP address *in reverse*, followed by in-addr.arpa. (For example, if your network is 208.170.66, then the zone name is 66.170.208.in-addr.arpa.)

5. Enter a Zone Filename (the zone name plus a .dns extension; the extension is prefilled automatically after you press Tab).

6. Click Next and then click Finish.

After the new primary reverse lookup zone has been created, it appears in the DNS Manager. A sample is shown in Figure 16.39, which now has two primary zones — a forward lookup zone called pncg.com, and a reverse lookup zone called 66.170.208.in-addr.arpa. After you create both the forward and reverse lookup zones, you can begin adding records to the DNS database.

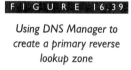

F I G U R E   16.39

Using DNS Manager to create a primary reverse lookup zone

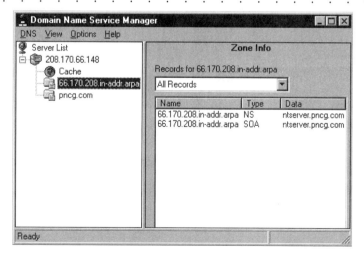

Add Records to the Zone

To add records to the zone file, you must first determine the type of record that you are going to use. Chapter 12 defines a broad variety of resource records (RRs) used by DNS, but a few essential records should be reviewed here. Some of the most common types of resource records are described in Table 16.6.

T A B L E   16.6

Common DNS Resource Records

RESOURCE RECORD TYPE	RESOURCE RECORD DESCRIPTION
Name Server (NS)	Identifies an authoritative DNS server to the domain.
Address (A)	In a *forward* lookup zone, maps a hostname to an IP address.
Start of Authority (SOA)	Identifies the primary source of information for the data contained in this DNS domain zone file.
Canonical Name (CNAME)	Creates an alias for a hostname.
Pointer (PTR)	In a *reverse* lookup zone, maps the IP address to a hostname. A PTR record can be created automatically while creating an Address record in a forward lookup zone.
Mail Exchange (MX)	Identifies the hostname of a server that will process or forward mail for a domain.

NOTE **Microsoft uses two special records, the WINS and WINS-R records, when integrating WINS and DNS Services. Integration of WINS and DNS is discussed later in this chapter.**

Now that you have reviewed the common record types, you can begin to populate the DNS database. Assume that you want to add the name of another server to the DNS database, so that users can resolve its name. To add the Address record for the server, follow these steps:

1. From the DNS Manager, right-click the primary forward lookup zone name.

2. Choose New Record. (The New Host option can also be chosen, to add an A Record quickly.)

3. Choose the record type and fill in the information. The properties may change according to the record type. Figure 16.40 shows that an A Record was chosen, thus requiring a Host Name and Host IP Address to be entered.

▶ • ◀

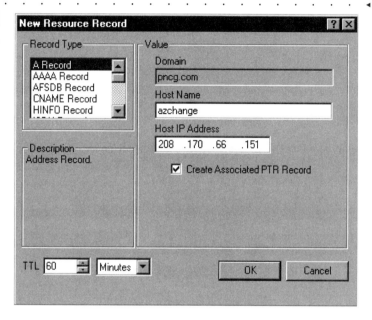

Notice in Figure 16.40 the option to create a PTR record in the reverse lookup zone. This is a time-saving feature, allowing you to make only one entry into the database instead of two. When the new A Record is created in the forward lookup zone, it immediately appears in the DNS database, as shown in Figure 16.41.

A record has been created for the second NT Server, called azexchange. Additionally, the automatically created inverse record for the azexchange server appears in the primary reverse lookup zone, as shown in Figure 16.42.

After the records have been added to the DNS database, a secondary DNS server should be installed for backup and redundancy.

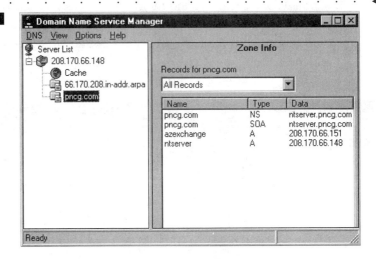

FIGURE 16.41

DNS database updated with new record

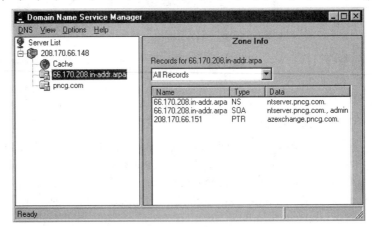

FIGURE 16.42

Reverse lookup records are automatically created

Managing the DNS Database

The DNS database files are stored on the NT Server in the *systemroot*\system32\dns directory. (The *systemroot* directory is generally the winnt directory—this is the default installation directory for NT Server.)

DNS database files are created as text files and follow the popular BIND (Berkeley InterNet Domain) implementation. These files may be modified by hand, if the administrator is aware of the proper syntax. Usually, the DNS Manager is used, given its graphical interface. The DNS installation consists of the following files:

- **Cache.dns:** Holds the DNS cache file included with the DNS server.

- **Boot.dns:** Special boot file that can be used by Microsoft DNS. If DNS uses the boot file, files must not be modified using the DNS Manager.

- ***Zonename*.dns:** Contains information for a particular zone. Several *zonename* files may be included within the DNS directory.

- ***Reverse zonename*.in-addr.arpa:** Contains the information relating to the reverse lookup for each zone. A reverse zone file will be present for each subnet ID.

Because the DNS database is essentially a text file, no packing or refreshing needs to be done. However, you should do a backup of this file, using an offline method, such as a tape drive.

▶ • ◀

Configuring the DNS Client

Just as the DNS server must be configured to maintain the DNS database, the client must be configured to use DNS to resolve hostnames. Though the configuration process is similar in Windows NT Workstation, Windows 95, and Windows 98, the screens are not all exactly the same.

Before you may configure clients to resolve hostnames through DNS, you first must install TCP/IP. This section looks at the DNS configuration options for Windows 95/98 and NT clients.

Windows 95/98 DNS Client Configuration

To configure a Windows 95/98 client to use DNS for hostname resolution, perform the following steps:

I. Go to Control Panel.

2. Choose Network (or right-click the Network Neighborhood icon and choose Properties).

3. Scroll down to the TCP/IP option and click Properties. (If more than one TCP/IP protocol is listed, choose the TCP/IP that corresponds with your network card.)

4. From the TCP/IP Properties screen, choose the DNS Configuration tab. Choose Enable DNS, and enter the hostname and domain name for the client. You must also configure the primary and secondary DNS server IP addresses, as shown in Figure 16.43.

FIGURE 16.43

DNS hostname resolution configuration for Windows 95/98

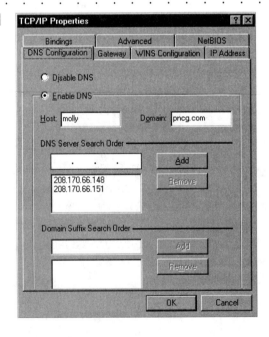

Because the client in Figure 16.43 is also a DHCP client, a cleaner and more efficient method of distributing this information would be through the DHCP server. When DNS information is configured at the DHCP server, the Windows 95/98 client automatically receives DNS server information on bootup. This is a preferred method, because you don't need to configure each workstation separately.

For an NT Workstation, the process is similar.

Windows NT Workstation Client Configuration

To configure a Windows NT Workstation client to use DNS for hostname resolution, perform the following steps:

1. Go to Control Panel.

2. Choose Network (or right-click the Network Neighborhood icon and choose Properties).

3. Click the Protocols tab.

4. Scroll down to the TCP/IP option and click Properties.

5. From the TCP/IP Properties screen, choose the DNS tab. Enter the hostname and domain name of the client. Enter the IP addresses of the primary and secondary DNS servers, as shown in Figure 16.44.

The NT Workstation will also use DHCP parameters for DNS if they are configured on the DHCP server. Like the Windows 95/98 clients, using DHCP to give client DNS configuration parameters is a very easy way to distribute the IP addresses of the DNS servers.

To verify that DNS parameters have been sent to the client, use the IPCONFIG /ALL command at the NT Workstation command prompt, or the WINIPCFG command at the Windows 95/98 Run command line. The DNS server addresses appear on the configuration screen.

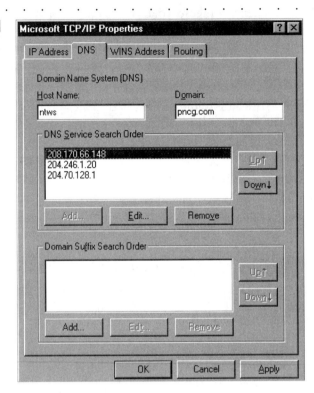

DNS client configuration for Windows NT Workstation

Integrating WINS and DNS

Microsoft allows the WINS and DNS technologies to be integrated within the same network. Using the WINS/DNS integration, a client may request a hostname that can be converted by DNS into a 15-character NetBIOS name, as shown in Figure 16.45.

▶ · ◀

WINS and DNS integration

The DNS server is able to communicate with the WINS server due to a special configuration option from within the DNS server. In each of the zones (both forward and reverse lookup), an option exists to allow WINS integration. To set up WINS integration, follow these steps:

1. From the DNS Manager, right-click the forward (or reverse) lookup zone.

2. Click Properties.

3. Choose the WINS Lookup tab.

4. Click the Enable WINS Integration checkbox, and add the IP address of the WINS server.

Repeat the process for the reverse lookup zone. When the integration is complete, two new records will be added to the DNS databases:

▶ WINS

▶ WINS-R

The WINS record enables the DNS server to convert the first portion of a full hostname to a single NetBIOS name. For example, using WINS integration, when a DNS server receives a request for mary.company.com and no DNS record exists for that host, the DNS server sends the NetBIOS name mary to the WINS server for resolution.

After the integration has been performed, the new record immediately exists in the DNS database, as shown in Figure 16.46.

FIGURE 16.46

WINS record exists in the DNS database after integration.

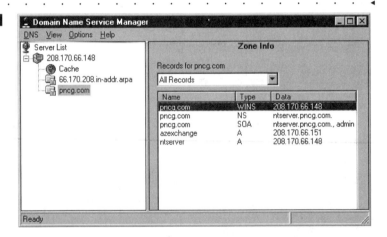

You must also perform the WINS integration steps in the reverse lookup domain to allow IP-to-hostname resolution.

IMPORTANT

The DNS server may reside on the same server as the WINS server, or it may point to another server for integration purposes.

Sample Network Configuration

Now that you have seen the components of the NT network, you are prepared to examine what a network configuration might look like in a real-life situation. In this case, we have a customer who has two locations connected via a WAN link. The bulk of the user load is at the main site, with approximately 300 users connected to the network. The remote site is home to about 50 occasional users. They want to install a domain structure, DHCP, WINS, and DNS to connect to the Internet. They have a permanent Internet connection at the main site and have registered their domain with their ISP. They have an existing DNS server on another platform that is BIND-compliant.

Given this situation, we have several items to look at. We will concentrate on the following areas:

- Domain structure: PDC/BDC placement

- DHCP server placement

- WINS server placement

- DNS server placement

- Client setup

Starting with the domain structure, we decide to create a single domain and have two servers — a PDC and BDC. We place the PDC at the main site, and install the BDC at the remote site. There, the BDC will perform login authentication for the remote users, eliminating logons across the WAN.

Next, we look at the DHCP server setup. Because this is across a WAN, we decide to install DHCP Services on each of the DCs, again, to eliminate that WAN traffic. Each DC is configured with two scopes: one scope gives 75 percent of the addresses on the local segment, and the other scope contains 25 percent of the addresses on the remote segment. (The terms *local* and *remote* change, depending on which location we are discussing.) DHCP relay agents are installed on the routers or the servers. This gives us fault tolerance in the event that one of our

DHCP servers goes down. A DHCP client can simply connect to the other DHCP server while repairs are made using the DHCP relay agent.

Next, we install a second set of computers, one at each location. We call these servers the name servers, and install both WINS and DNS on each server. The WINS servers are configured as replication partners, and the DNS servers are configured as primary and secondary servers, for fault tolerance.

When installing the clients, we request that all clients use DHCP to obtain their default gateway, WINS server, DNS server, subnet mask, node type, and lease duration. Multiple WINS and DNS servers are configured, for fault tolerance. When we put it all together, it looks the network shown in Figure 16.47.

F I G U R E   16.47

Sample Microsoft network configuration

Single Domain

Of course, several ways exist to set up any network. Things like cost and time, bandwidth speed, and so on are always factors in how many servers you decide to have. This is simply one way that this network may be set up.

Case Study — What Can Go Wrong

Misconfiguration, misconfiguration, misconfiguration! This is the biggest problem with any network, but when you add IP address-to-NetBIOS-to-DNS name mapping, DNS and WINS integration, and DHCP setup, things can go sour fast. This case study is an example of something we see quite a bit, and it should help you to understand the need for identical NetBIOS and WINS names. People often do not understand that the NetBIOS name on their computer is not the same as their DNS hostname. In fact, users rarely even know what these things are!

The Problem

A user on an NT network complains that a computer that she used to be able to use is no longer available to her. (Sound familiar?) All she knows is that she used to be able to PING APPSERVER, but now she can't. She proves it by showing us. She uses the PING command and gets the response shown in Figure 16.48.

FIGURE 16.48

PING APPSERVER results in bad IP address

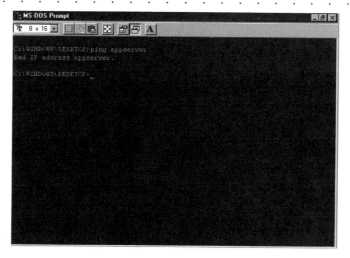

The Analysis

The first thing we suspect is name resolution. At this point, we are not quite sure whether we are trying to resolve a hostname or a NetBIOS name. Whenever we troubleshoot name resolution, we start by making sure IP connectivity is working. We get the IP address of the APPSERVER (208.170.66.157) from the network administrator and use the address to PING the host. We get a response.

We do not assume that we have the right IP address at this point, but continue anyway. Next, we look in a place where the IP-to-name address mapping might be kept—the DNS database. We find an entry in the DNS database for the APPSERVER at the correct address—208.170.66.157, as shown in Figure 16.49.

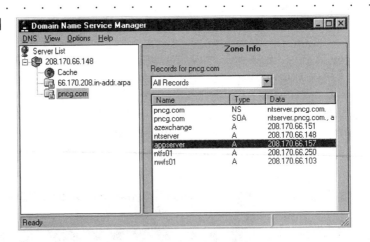

FIGURE 16.49

*DNS entry confirms
APPSERVER mapping*

So far so good. Next, we view the server's WINS configuration, as illustrated in Figure 16.50. The WINS database shows no APPSERVER entry. However, something very interesting catches our attention. The IP address 208.170.66.157 is registered to the name NTWS, which is why we cannot PING APPSERVER—WINS thinks that NTWS is at that address. A quick look at the NetBIOS name on the physical destination computer confirms that someone has changed the NetBIOS name. We change the NetBIOS name back to the APPSERVER and retry the PING command. Problem solved.

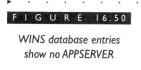

FIGURE 16.50

WINS database entries show no APPSERVER

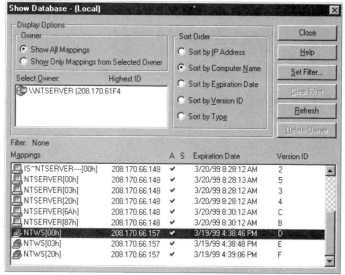

The Solution

Just by going through this short case study, you can see how important it is for NetBIOS names to be the same as hostnames, especially when WINS and DNS integration is configured. When a DNS client requests a name, and DNS sends it to WINS for resolution, DNS assumes that the NetBIOS name is the same as the hostname. When a user names his or her computer a different name to make their computer seem more personal, resolution will no longer work.

Summary

In this chapter, you learned how Microsoft implements TCP/IP in its Windows NT Server, Workstation, and Windows 95 and 98 products. You learned how the network structure is set up using domains, and how specific computers called domain controllers are called upon to manage those domains.

You also learned how a Windows network uses DHCP from the server and client side, and how a Windows computer resolves its own NetBIOS name using the WINS broadcast methods and static text files called LMHOSTS. Additionally, this chapter looked at hostname resolution using the Domain Name Server Service, and the different node types and procedures used in the NetBIOS resolution process.

## CHAPTER 17

UNIX TCP/IP
Implementation/
Configuration

The connection between UNIX and TCP/IP goes back to 1969. TCP/IP was developed on the UNIX platform. Today, everybody is using TCP/IP, and many of the UNIX-style utilities and methods have been ported to NetWare and Windows 95/NT systems. This chapter gives an overview of the main UNIX flavors available these days. One of the key things that you will notice is that, although each vendor has its own way of dealing with startup configurations, the utilities and tools are pretty much the same. Another key distinction is that UNIX development has grown into two separate streams—the Berkeley Software Distribution (BSD) stream and the System V stream.

This chapter intends to give credit to whom it is due. The TCP/IP protocol suite has its roots at the University of California, Berkeley. It has been developed in a project that started in 1969.

This chapter assumes that you are familiar with UNIX. If you are new to UNIX and want to start learning how to use it, many books and courses are available that can help you. This chapter does not intend to help you troubleshoot mixed UNIX-TCP/IP environments. This is beyond the scope of this book. Every TCP/IP stack, although written conforming to a standard, has its own personality. And as you know, that can create misunderstandings. So even if you have different versions of one operating system installed, you might run into trouble when they try to talk to each other. The goal of this chapter is to give you an overview of the main UNIXs that you can find on the market. Many flavors are available, so this chapter focuses on the mainstream UNIXs. This chapter also shows you the most common utilities available that relate to TCP/IP and to troubleshooting communications on a UNIX system.

► · ◄

History

UNIX was born at AT&T Bell Labs, developed and refined by Ken Thompson, Dennis Ritchie, and others. This early effort culminated in the seventh edition.

 The early efforts at AT&T Bell Labs are documented; if you are interested in more details, go to `http://cm.belllabs.com/ cm/cs/who/dmr/hist.html`. **Even the manuals of the seventh edition are still available at** `http://plan9.belllabs.com/ 7thEdMan/index.html`.

UNIX became very popular in the academic computer science community. AT&T made it available to universities at low cost. A second flavor of UNIX, Berkeley Software Distribution (BSD), came out of the University of California, Berkeley. It added virtual memory support, TCP/IP networking, and more. Figure 17.1 shows the UNIX tree.

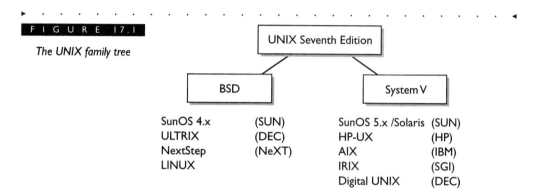

FIGURE 17.1

The UNIX family tree

The most popular UNIX version these days is probably Linux. This was developed independently from AT&T and Berkeley by a student at the University of Helsinki. More on Linux a little later in this chapter.

So TCP/IP was born in Berkeley and developed based on the ARPA Internet protocols. To dive into TCP/IP history, read RFC 1 (April 7, 1969) on host software, written by Steve Crocker at UCLA. It talks about the *interface message processor (IMP)*, later known as a *router*. RFC 114 (April 10, 1971) is the first RFC on FTP (File Transfer Protocol). John Postel wrote RFC 791 on IP in September 1981. In the years 1977 and 1978, TCP was split into TCP and IP. In 1983, UC Berkeley integrated TCP/IP into UNIX 4.2 BSD.

RFC 2555, an informational RFC, was released on April 7, 1999. It is called "30 Years of RFCs." It contains a recollection of the RFC editor, Joyce K. Reynolds, and of the three pioneers, Vint Cerf, Steve Crocker, and Jake Feinler. This 30th anniversary tribute was assembled in grateful admiration for John Postel's massive contribution to the RFC series.

NOTE

On October 16, 1998, John Postel died. Many tributes have been written to honor what he has done. His death leaves a huge hole in the Internet community. Visit his home page at `http://www.isi.edu/~postel/`. Two RFCs have been released as tributes to him. RFC 2468 was written by Vint Cerf on October 17, 1998. It is a very personal description of who John Postel was. RFC 2441, titled "Working with John," was written by Danny Cohen.

UNIX Flavors

This section lists the most important flavors of UNIX, starting with Linux.

Linux

Linux was developed by Linus Torvalds, a university student from Helsinki, Finland. Linus has reached legendary proportions for bringing to the industry one of the best gifts ever: a stable version of UNIX that is entirely free and includes a comprehensive set of tools that make it a useful business tool. Linux has also enjoyed the support of countless other developers who have enhanced it with their own utilities and programs. Today, versions of Linux are available for the x86, PowerPC, SPARC, Motorola, and other processor architectures. Linux is primarily a BSD UNIX, though some System V utilities and tools have been developed for it. Further to the BSD heritage, Linux is also plagued by a number of distributions (a *distribution* being a selection of tools and utilities that a company has decided to sell Linux with). Tools and configuration options vary slightly between distributions.

The Linux penguin, shown in Figure 17.2, was created by and is the property of Larry Ewing, at `http://www.isc.tamu.edu/~lewing/linux/`. If you want to know why Linus chose the penguin, visit `http://www.linux.org/info/penguin.html`. The site `http://www.linux.org` is a good starting point for Linux information in general. On January 25, 1999, the long-awaited Linux Kernel 2.2 was released.

▶ · ◀
FIGURE 17.2

The Linux penguin

Sun Solaris

Solaris, developed by Sun Microsystems, is currently in its second incarnation
with version 2.6. Solaris has been developed to run primarily on the SPARC
processor architecture, but ports have also been developed for the x86 architecture.
Solaris is one of the big players in current enterprise-wide UNIX deployments, and
much of this success has to do with the stability and scalability of the SPARC
architecture. Solaris 2.6 is compliant with AT&T's System V Release 4 version of
UNIX.

For references on SUN and Solaris, visit `http://www.sun.com.`

**For excellent information on how to tune your Solaris TCP/IP
stack, go to** `http://www.rvs.unihannover.de/people/
voeckler/tune/EN/tune.html`. **It is updated regularly and, yes, it is
written in English.**

IBM AIX

IBM AIX has been developed by IBM for use in its RISC- and PowerPC-based
systems. This version is also System V Release 4-compliant.

For general information on AIX, go to
http://www.rs6000.ibm.com/software.

For AIX TCP/IP configuration and troubleshooting information, refer to
http://www.rs6000.ibm.com/doc_link/en_US/a_doc_lib/aixbman/
commadmn/toc.htm.

Here's a site with tuning information for TCP/IP on RS6000 systems:
http://www.developer.ibm.com/library/aixpert/feb94/
aixpert_feb94_tcpip.html.

HP/UX

Developed by Hewlett-Packard, HP/UX is currently in release 11 and is also
System V Release 4-compliant. HP/UX currently runs on proprietary HP processors.
Rumors suggest that HP will be releasing an x86-based version of HP/UX some time
in the future.

For general information on HP/UX, go to the following site:
http://www.datacentersolutions.hp.com/2_2_index.html.

TCP/IP Utilities

This section lists the most common utilities that relate to TCP/IP and communications. Slight differences exist for the different flavors of UNIX, but
coverage of those differences is beyond the scope of this book.

Some of these UNIX utilities have been discussed previously in this book,
because they have been ported to the NetWare and Windows NT platforms. The
rest are unique to the UNIX operating system environment. This section is intended
to give you an overview of the available utilities. They are listed in Table 17.1.

TABLE 17.1

UNIX TCP/IP Utilities

UTILITY	DESCRIPTION
ifconfig	The main utility for setting up and checking the configuration of the TCP/IP interface. This utility is available on both systems V and BSD implementations of UNIX, with some slight variations in its use. When booting up your system, this utility is used to assign an IP address to each network interface, either through a static or dynamic setup. You can use it to detect bad IP addresses, incorrect subnet masks, and improper broadcast addresses.
ping	Use to verify communications and check routing tables. It also displays statistics on packet loss and delivery time. It has many options useful for troubleshooting and is available on most OSs. It is discussed in Chapter 4 (IP) and Chapter 6 (ICMP).
netstat	Use to view the TCP/IP services running, the ports they are using, and the number of users connected to each port. This command also displays routing and interface information. It has multiple options that can be used to view specific information.
route	Use to view, add, and remove static routes from the routing table.
traceroute	Similar to its Windows 95/98 and NT counterparts, this command lists all intermediate hops between the current system and the destination host. Refer to Chapter 6 for a detailed explanation of how this is done.
snoop	Found primarily on System V UNIX versions, such as Solaris, this command allows you to view the Internet traffic crossing the cable in real time. Essentially a built-in analyzer.
tcpdump	Like `snoop`, this command allows you to view IP traffic. Found primarily in BSD systems, such as Linux.
arp	Like its NT counterpart, allows you to view and change the local ARP cache.
nslookup	Use to troubleshoot DNS.
dig	Use to troubleshoot DNS. Similar to `nslookup`, but does not provide an interactive prompt.
ripquery	Can be used on systems running RIP. Provided as part of the `gated` software. Provides information on content of RIP update packets being sent or received. Depending on your UNIX flavor, this software is installed as a default or has to be installed separately. Check your UNIX documentation.
man <utility>	On all UNIX system, you should be able to get online help for all utilities by entering man followed by the utility name. This gives you a detailed description, with all possible options and examples of how to use the utility. Some UNIX flavors install the manuals by default, whereas others let you choose whether to install those files.

The /etc/inetd.conf File and Daemons

When a UNIX system boots, some of the automatically loaded drivers and services start via the use of *rc scripts*. The rc scripts usually start the network interfaces, the NFS server, and the Internet daemon. The latter is what controls the UNIX Internet services, including FTP, TELNET, HTTP, FINGER, SENDMAIL, and others. Upon startup, the Internet daemon (inetd) looks for its configuration file /etc/inetd.conf.

The /etc/services File

The /etc/services file is used as a list of variables for the /etc/inetd.conf file. It maps the port names to a number. This file is used frequently to determine which daemons run on which ports.

 A very good book to read to become familiar with TCP/IP network administration on the UNIX platform is *TCP/IP Network Administration*, by Craig Hunt (O'Reilly & Associates).

NOTE

Routing

On most UNIX systems, minimal routes are created with the ifconfig command. On Linux systems, you have to use the route command.

The route command builds a static routing table. Static routing is not really appropriate in larger networks. Routing protocols are used to update our routing tables dynamically. On most UNIX systems, RIPv1 (Routing Information Protocol) is supported. RIP is run by routed, which builds the routing table. If you want to use other routing protocols, such as OSPF (Open Shortest Path First) or BGP (Border Gateway Protocol), you have to use the software package called gated. The way different vendors implement OSPF varies a lot. Before you use a UNIX box as an OSPF router, make sure the implementation of OSPF is according to the standards.

In a network where you want OSPF as a routing protocol, you will probably choose to use dedicated hardware routers rather than a UNIX box.

TIP

DNS

UNIX implementations of DNS are based on BIND software, which includes both the DNS server and the DNS client software.

DNS in general is discussed in Chapter 12.

X-REF

This section summarizes the most important UNIX-specific things to remember regarding DNS.

Resolver Configuration

DNS configuration is split between the DNS client and the DNS server. At the client side, in the /etc directory, you can create a text file with the name resolv.conf. This file contains the domain name and IP addresses of the primary and secondary DNS servers, and is needed on both the DNS client and DNS server systems. A DNS server needs this file, too, because a DNS server can behave like a client and make requests to another DNS server if it cannot resolve a request locally (refer to Chapter 12 for more details).

Named Configuration

Named is used to configure the DNS name server. Several files are used to configure named, which are listed in Table 17.2. You can name these files as you wish, although descriptive filenames are advised. In most instances, the names given in Table 17.2 are used. One exception is named.ca, which is commonly known as root.cache.

TABLE 17.2	CONFIGURATION FILE	DESCRIPTION
Named Configuration Files	named.boot	Sets general parameters and points to sources of DNS information used by this name server
	named.ca	Contains the root DNS server list
	named.local	Used to locally resolve the loopback address
	named.hosts	The zone file that maps hostnames to IP addresses
	named.rev	The zone file for the in-addr.arpa domain for reverse lookups

DNS Troubleshooting Utilities

The two main utilities to troubleshoot DNS on UNIX are nslookup and dig. Nslookup is described in Chapter 12 on DNS. Dig is similar to nslookup, but it does not present the user with an interactive prompt.

NOTE

> **A good reference for help with troubleshooting DNS is *DNS & BIND*, by Paul Albitz and Cricket Liu (O'Reilly & Associates).**

▶ · ◀

BOOTP/DHCP

The bootpd daemon is the program that provides BOOTP functionality on a UNIX system. Some operating systems include this daemon, others don't. In any case, it will not run by default, so you have to enable it explicitly. If your operating system does not include bootpd, you can download it from the Internet.

To configure a UNIX system as a relay agent, use the bootpgw daemon. As Chapter 11 describes, BOOTP and DHCP requests don't cross routers because they are limited broadcasts. If your BOOTP/DHCP server is on a segment other than the one your clients are on, you need a relay agent.

Several implementations of DHCP are available for UNIX systems. Many commercial packages are offered by vendors that run on specific UNIX flavors.

BOOTP and DHCP are discussed in detail in Chapter 11.

X-REF

Summary

This chapter provides a summarized view of the history of UNIX, which is the mother of TCP/IP. It has shown the different mainstream UNIX flavors currently available on the market and has given an overview of the most common utilities related to TCP/IP communications.

## PART VI

Other TCP/IP
Communications and Issues

## CHAPTER 18

Miscellaneous TCP/IP Communications

This chapter covers miscellaneous protocols in an overview, so you should consider it as a starting guide only. This chapter first looks at the Network Time Protocol (NTP) and then examines the Internet Group Management Protocol (IGMP), which was briefly discussed in Chapter 4 on IP. IGMP is used for multicasting.

When it comes to routing, protocols can be categorized as either interior or exterior routing protocols. This chapter introduces two proprietary interior routing protocols. The Interior Gateway Routing Protocol (IGRP) and the Enhanced Interior Gateway Routing Protocol (EIGRP) are Cisco proprietary routing protocols. This chapter gives an overview of these two protocols and compares them to the other routing protocols covered in this book, RIP and OSPF. Exterior gateway protocols are not covered in this book.

Network Time Protocol (NTP)

NTP provides a mechanism to synchronize time on computers across an internet. The specification for NTP version 3 is defined in RFC 1305, which updates RFC 1119.

NTP is used to synchronize the time of a client or server with the time of another server or a reference time source. That reference time source can be a radio, satellite receiver, or modem. Typical NTP designs configure multiple redundant servers and diverse network paths to achieve high accuracy and reliability.

NTP is a complex, distributed network application and can be configured and used for different timekeeping scenarios, depending on the needs and the size of the network.

NTP is configured with configuration files on each participating host. The most important factor in providing accurate, reliable time is the selection of modes and servers to be used, which are stated in the configuration file. The existing NTP subnet consists of a multiply redundant hierarchy of servers and clients. Each level in the hierarchy is identified by a *stratum number*. For example, *primary servers* operate at stratum one and provide synchronization to *secondary servers* operating at stratum two, and so on. In this hierarchy, *clients* are servers that have no dependents.

The NTP subnet in early 1999 includes 78 public primary (stratum 1) servers that are synchronized directly to UTC by radio, satellite, or modem and are located in every continent of the globe. Usually, clients and time servers with few clients do not synchronize to primary servers. Additionally, 108 public secondary (stratum 2) servers are synchronized to the primary servers. They provide synchronization to a total of over 100,000 clients and servers on the Internet. Numerous other private primary and secondary servers exist that are not normally available to the public.

 To get an up-to-date list of public primary and secondary NTP time servers, go to `http://www.eecis.udel.edu/~mills/ntp/servers.htm`.

NTP is built on UDP, using port 123 as its source and destination port. The same number has been reserved as a TCP port number. The protocol definition deals a lot with areas of accuracy and synchronization. Discussion of NTP in detail is beyond the scope of this book. It is mentioned here because it is a standards-track protocol.

IGMP (Internet Group Management Protocol)

The Internet Group Management Protocol (IGMP) is used by IP hosts to report their multicast group memberships to routers. IGMP is at version 2 and is described in RFC 2236, which updates RFC 1112. Every host that wants to receive multicasts must have IGMP implemented. It is an integral part of IP, as is ICMP.

Overview of IGMP Functionality

Chapter 4 touches upon multicasting in its discussion of IP addressing rules and multicast addresses. Multicasting is a way of sending a message to multiple recipients. If you use broadcasting to send messages to multiple hosts, every host in the segment must process the frame, sometimes only to find out that it isn't interested in the information. With multicasting, only the hosts that listen to that multicast address have to process the frame. So, using multicasting conserves bandwidth in the network and processing power on the host.

Hosts can join and leave multicast groups dynamically. IGMP is the building block for multicasting.

Host Groups

A *multicast address* is recognized by its 4 high-order bits being 1110. This gives a decimal range of 224.0.0.0 to 239.255.255.255 for multicast addresses. A set of hosts that listen to the same address is called a *host group*. RFC 1700 lists permanently assigned multicast addresses. The Base Address of 224.0.0.0 is reserved and thus can't be used. The address of 224.0.0.1 is a special address called *All-Systems Group*. It refers to all the multicast-capable hosts and routers on a physical network. Every host automatically joins this group on all multicast-capable interfaces. The membership in this group is never reported with membership messages. Another common address is 224.0.0.2, which refers to *All Routers* on the physical network.

 For the most current list of multicast addresses, go to the following site: ftp://ftp.isi.edu/in-notes/iana/assignments/multicast-addresses.

IGMP Communications

When a multicast-capable host boots, it reports all the multicast groups for all interfaces by sending a *Membership Report* per group. The Membership Report is sent to every host group that the host is a member of. The only group to which it won't send a Membership Report is the All-Systems Group (224.0.0.1).

A multicast router sends a *General Membership Query* at regular intervals. It wants to know whether hosts belonging to the different groups are still active. The router sends out a query per interface. The Group Address field in the IGMP header is set to 0. A host will respond to such a query by sending a Membership Report for each group that is active.

The multicast router keeps a table that shows which of its interfaces has hosts in a certain host group. When the router receives a multicast packet to forward, it sends it out through all the interfaces that are listed to have members of that host group.

Figure 18.1 is a diagram of these communications. You may remember the analogy in Chapter 4 in which the multicast address is compared to the transmission frequency of a radio station. The radio station sends its program over a certain frequency. If you are interested in receiving the program, you tune your radio to listen to that frequency. Your neighbor, who is not interested in the same program, can tune his radio to a different frequency. Both of you get only what you want. With multicasting, you "tune" your interface to listen to certain host groups, and you get only the messages addressed to those groups.

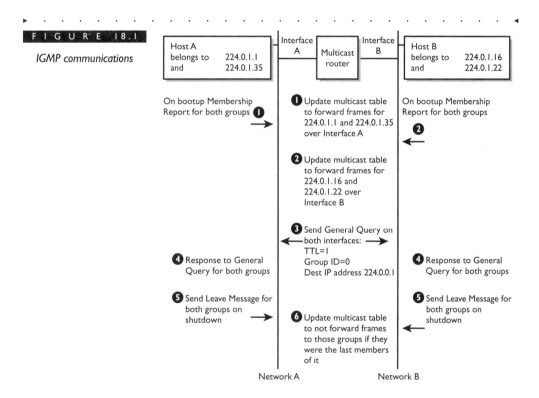

FIGURE 18.1

IGMP communications

IGMP Header Structure

The header of an IGMP message is shown in Figure 18.2. It has a fixed size and no room for options. It is an 8-byte message encapsulated in an IP datagram, with the following fields:

► . . . . ◄

FIGURE 18.2

IGMP header structure

Type
(1 byte)
With version 1 used to be
Version   4 bits
Type   4 bits

Max response time
(1 byte)
Unused field in version 1
Only used in membership query messages
In all other messages it is set to zero

Checksum
(2 bytes)
Calculated on entire IP payload

Group address
(4 bytes)

Total size: 8 bytes

► **Type:** One-byte field that states the type of the IGMP message. (Message types are listed in Table 18.1, later in the chapter.) In the previous version of IGMP, this used to be 4 bits for the version and 4 bits for the type, as shown in the decode of Figure 18.3.

► **Maximum Response Time:** One-byte field that was unused with version 1 of IGMP. It is meaningful only in Membership Query messages. This field specifies the maximum allowed time before a host sends a responding report. The unit is one tenth of a second. It is used for tuning purposes for IGMPv2 routers.

► **Checksum:** Two-byte field that is calculated on the whole IGMP message (entire IP payload). The checksum must be verified by a host before processing a packet.

► **Group Address:** Contains the 4-byte group address. In a General Membership Query, this address is set to 0. In a Group-Specific Query, it contains the group address being queried. In a Membership Report or Leave Group message, the Group Address field holds the IP multicast group address of the group being reported or left.

X-REF

Remember from Chapter 4 that multicast group addresses are recognized by their four high-order bits of 1110 **followed by the multicast group ID. The decimal address range is** 224.0.0.0 **through** 239.255.255.255**.**

Figure 18.3 shows the IGMP header in the decode.

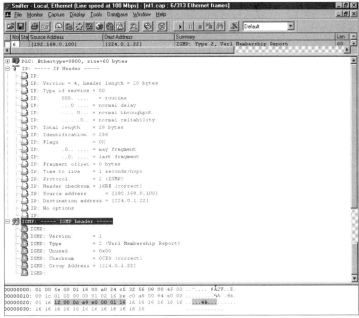

FIGURE 18.3

The IGMP header in the decode

This is a Membership Report message. The IP header in Figure 18.3 contains a few fields to note:

- **Total Length:** Set to 28 bytes, which includes the 20 bytes of the IP header plus the 8 bytes of the IGMP header

- **Time To Live (TTL):** Set to 1, because IGMP packets should not cross routers

- **Protocol:** Set to 2, for IGMP

- **Destination Address:** Set to the multicast group ID `224.0.1.22`, the general SLP (Service Location Protocol) multicast address

- **Maximum Response Time:** Decoded as unused

- **Group Address:** Set to 224.0.1.22

The IGMP header indicates that this is a Membership Report. The value 2 is according to RFC 1112, the version 1 definition. It is also used by version 2 for backward-compatibility.

NOTE

Chapter 6 on ICMP explains that when a router receives a datagram with a TTL of 1, it discards the datagram and sends back an ICMP *Time Exceeded* message. Multicast routers never issue Time Exceeded messages in response to a datagram destined to a multicast address.

Table 18.1 shows three types of IGMP messages. The fourth type is for backward-compatibility with IGMPv1.

TABLE 18.1

IGMP Message Types

TYPE NUMBER	NAME/SENT TO	DESCRIPTION
0x11	Membership Query General Query sent to All Systems Group (224.0.0.1) Group-Specific Query sent to the group being queried	Two types of Membership Queries exist: A *General Query* is used to learn which groups have members on an attached network. The Group Address field in the IGMP header is set to 0 in this case. A *Group-Specific Query* is used to learn whether a certain group has members on an attached network. The Group Address field is set to the group address of the group being queried.
0x16	Version 2 Membership Report Sent to the group being reported	Used to register with a multicast group
0x17	Leave Group sent to the All Routers Group (224.0.0.2)	Used to deregister for a certain multicast group
0x12	Version 1 Membership Report	Membership Report for backward-compatibility with IGMP version 1

Multicast routers use IGMP to learn which groups have members on each of their interfaces. A multicast router keeps a list of multicast group memberships for each attached network, and a timer for each membership. *Multicast group membership* means the presence of at least one member of a multicast group on a given attached network. It does not contain a list of all the members.

NOTE

RFC 2236 contains information about the requirements and configuration to have interoperability between IGMPv1 and IGMPv2 routers. Many timers are available for IGMP. They have default values and some of them can be used to optimize IGMP communications in your network. Again, refer to RFC 2236. It lists all the timers, with a detailed description and comments on how to use them for tuning.

Routing Issues

For multicast datagrams to be routed efficiently through an internetwork, routers need to know where multicast host groups exist. Unfortunately, no real standard currently exists for multicast routing. Routers need to support multicasting and be configured for it. Two protocols can propagate multicast routes:

▸ **Distance Vector Multicast Routing Protocol (DVMRP):** Derived from RIPv1 and described in RFC 1075 as an experimental protocol (back in 1988). DVMRP supports tunneling, which can be used to traverse networks that do not support multicasting.

▸ **Multicast OSPF (MOSPF):** Described in RFC 1584, this is a standards track protocol that was defined in 1994. It is based on OSPF version 2.

Cisco has a proprietary protocol called CGMP (*Cisco Group Management Protocol*). Refer to the Cisco site at `http://www.cisco.com/univercd/home/home.htm` for more information.

Nortel routers support IGMPv2 and use DVMRP or MOSPF. Nortel has a guide on its Web site called *Configuring IP Multicasting and Multimedia Services*. You will find a lot of information on IGMP, DVMRP, and MOSPF in that document. Its site is at `http://www.nortelnetworks.com`. Use the search engine to find the document.

In 1998, another experimental protocol was described, called *Protocol Independent Multicasting (PIM)*. The RFC number is 2362.

X-REF

Refer to Chapter 15 and the section "Multicast Forwarding Support" to learn how Novell implements PIM with PIM.NLM. Another good resource is RFC 1812. It is a standards track document that describes the requirements for IP version 4 routers. You will find a lot of useful information in there. It also covers multicast forwarding.

Interior and Exterior Gateway Protocols — An Overview

This section reviews some basic routing concepts and terms before diving into more details. These topics have been covered in other chapters already (Chapter 7 on RIP and Chapter 8 on OSPF). The concepts are summarized again as an introduction to the protocols discussed here.

A term that you find again and again is *autonomous system*. An autonomous system (AS) is a network under the same administration. It may consist of one segment or multiple segments connected through routers that belong to this system. All routers within an autonomous system must run the same routing protocol.

Interior Gateway Protocols

Interior gateway protocols are used *within* an autonomous system. Their task is to keep current their routing tables for the system. The following protocols are common IGPs:

- RIP (Routing Information Protocol)

- OSPF (Open Shortest Path First)

- IGRP (Interior Gateway Routing Protocol, Cisco)

- EIGRP (Enhanced IGRP, Cisco)

- IS-IS (Intermediate System-to-Intermediate System)

X-REF
To learn more about general routing concepts, refer to Chapter 4 on IP. To find more information about RIP, refer to Chapter 7. OSPF is covered in Chapter 8.

Exterior Gateway Protocols

Exterior gateway protocols are used to exchange routing information between networks that do not share common administration. They must isolate the autonomous systems that they connect. The following protocols are common exterior gateway protocols:

- ▶ BGP (Border Gateway Protocol)

- ▶ EGP (Exterior Gateway Protocol)

The interior and exterior gateway protocols can be used simultaneously by an internetwork. Exterior gateway protocols are not covered in this book.

IGRP (Cisco)

Interior Gateway Routing Protocol (IGRP) is an advanced Distance Vector Routing Protocol. Chapter 4 explains that routers using distance vector protocols know only about their next hops and learn their information from their neighbors. IGRP, which was developed by Cisco in the mid-1980s, is "advanced" because several features differentiate it from standard distance vector protocols, such as RIP:

- ▶ It is much more scalable because it overcomes RIP's 15-hop limit.

- ▶ Unlike standard distance vector protocols, it sends triggered updates when routes change; therefore, the response to network topology changes is much faster.

▸ IGRP has a much more sophisticated metric and provides a significant route selection flexibility. Factors like internetwork delay, bandwidth, reliability, and load are considered in the routing decision.

▸ IGRP can maintain up to four nonequal paths between a source and destination. Multiple paths can be used to increase bandwidth and to provide redundancy.

NOTE **RFC 2092 (informational RFC) defines extensions for RIP to trigger updates over WAN links. Any RIP stack implementation that uses these extensions is also capable of reducing traffic on a WAN, similar to IGRP.**

IGRP does not support variable-length subnet masking (VLSM). Refer to Chapter 4 to learn about subnet masking

Routers using IGRP broadcast routing table updates at 90-second intervals (configurable) to their neighbor routers. Periodically, the router broadcasts its entire routing table to its neighbors. The receiving router compares this table with its own. New destinations and paths are added to the routing table. The paths in the broadcast are compared with the existing paths, and the existing path is changed if a new path is better.

IGRP's composite metric is used to identify preferred routes. It takes into account the following components:

▸ Bandwidth (Kb per second) — default

▸ Delay (in 10th of microseconds) — default

▸ Reliability (based on keepalives) — configurable

▸ Loading (bits per second) — configurable

▸ MTU (smallest maximum transfer unit value in path) — configurable

The path with the smallest metric value is the best route. By default, IGRP only considers bandwidth and delay. But the other components are configurable by the administrator.

X-REF

If you are interested in how the metric is calculated, refer to the following document:
`http://www.cisco.com/univercd/cc/td/doc/product/software/`
`ios120/12cgcr/np1_r/1rprt1/1rigrp.htm#35451`.

The commands in Table 18.2 can be used to display IGRP routing information.

TABLE 18.2

Displaying IGRP Routing Information

COMMAND	DESCRIPTION
show ip route	Displays the routing table, which contains the list of all known networks and subnets and the metrics associated with each entry.
show ip protocols	Displays parameters, filters, and network information about the router.
show ip interfaces	Displays the status and global parameters associated with an interface.
debug ip igrp transaction	Displays transaction information on IGRP routing transactions. Disabled with **no debug ip igrp transaction**. Only enable this for troubleshooting.
debug ip igrp events	Displays a summary of the routing information. Disabled **with no debug ip igrp events**. Only enable this for troubleshooting.

EIGRP (Cisco)

Enhanced Interior Gateway Protocol (EIGRP), developed by Cisco, is a routing protocol that combines the advantages of distance-vector and link-state routing protocols. A router using a link-state routing protocol not only knows about its neighbors, it also has a map of the complete network.

IMPORTANT

EIGRP was significantly enhanced in IOS releases 10.3, 11.0, 11.1, and later. The implementation was changed to improve the performance on low-speed networks (including frame relay) and in configurations with many neighbors.

EIGRP has the following features:

- **Rapid convergence:** EIGRP achieves rapid convergence and avoids loops by using the *diffusing update algorithm (DUAL)*. It can quickly adapt to alternative routes by storing backup routes when available. If no appropriate route exists in the routing table, it queries its neighbors to discover an alternative route.

- **Reduced bandwidth usage:** EIGRP sends partial updates when a path changes or when the metric for a route changes. It does not send periodic updates. The information is only sent to routers that need it, unlike link-state protocols, which send change updates to all routers within their area.

- **Multiple network-layer support:** EIGRP has protocol-dependent modules that support AppleTalk, IP, and Novell's IPX.

- **Variable-length subnet masks (VLSMs):** Supported with EIGRP.

- **Novell IPX RIP/SAP Support:** Novell IPX RIP routers send out RIP and SAP updates every 60 seconds, regardless of whether a topology change has occurred. When EIGRP does incremental RIP and SAP updates, it sends out updates only when changes occur and sends only the information that has changed. EIGRP IPX networks also go beyond IPX RIP's 15-hop limit. EIGRP IPX networks have a diameter of 224 hops. Novell's IPX uses ticks and hop counts for path selection. EIGRP includes bandwidth and delay information to determine the best route.

- **Support for NLSP:** NetWare Link Services Protocol is Novell's Link State Routing Protocol. It is similar to OSPF. EIGRP routers support NLSP.

- **Support for AppleTalk:** AppleTalk updates routing tables periodically with the AppleTalk Routing Table Maintenance Protocol (RTMP), which uses hop counts to determine the best route. EIGRP for AppleTalk uses event-driven updates, which saves bandwidth, is more efficient, and calculates the metrics with a configurable combination metric. EIGRP routes are preferred to RTMP routes. EIGRP for AppleTalk can be used only in a environment without clients, because an AppleTalk client needs RTMP information locally.

Each EIGRP router maintains a *neighbor table* that lists all adjacent routers. EIGRP maintains a neighbor table for each protocol it supports. You can compare this table to the adjacencies database in OSPF. This table ensures bidirectional communication between directly connected neighbors. To build this table, an EIGRP router sends out multicast *Hello packets* to discover its neighbors and to exchange route updates. This is very much like OSPF's Hello packets. Hello packets are sent out periodically (60 second is the default) to verify the availability of the neighbors. The neighbor table contains information about the neighbor's address, the number of packets waiting in the queue to be sent, the average round-trip time to that neighbor, and the hold time, which is the interval to wait without receiving anything from the neighbor before considering the link as unavailable.

Each EIGRP router also maintains a *topology table* for each configured routing protocol. This table includes all the routes for all destinations that the router has learned. Each destination is listed along with all neighbors that can reach that destination, including the metrics for that path.

The router maintains one *routing table* for each protocol supported. It chooses the route to a destination from the topology table and places it in the routing table. If a destination has multiple routes, a *successor* route is selected as the primary route and is the one entered in the routing table. Backup routes to the successor route are kept in the topology table. They are called *feasible successors*. Up to five backup routes may exist per destination. EIGRP uses the same criteria as IGRP for calculating the metrics: bandwidth, delay, reliability, load, and MTU. EIGRP also uses the DUAL (diffusing update) algorithm, like IGRP.

EIGRP knows three different types of routes:

- **Internal:** Routes learned by EIGRP.

- **External:** Routes that are learned through another routing protocol and redistributed into EIGRP.

- **Summary:** Routes that EIGRP may dynamically create due to autosummarization or explicit summary route configuration.

Route selection is based on administrative distance. The default administrative distance for EIGRP is 90 (internal), 170 (external), or 5 (summary). For IGRP, the default administrative distance is 100, because internal EIGRP routes take precedence over IGRP routes, and IGRP routes are preferred to external EIGRP routes.

The router that learns about a topology change sends a multicast update packet to its neighbors. If it has to recalculate a route, it queries its neighbors to find an alternative route.

Table 18.3 lists some useful commands to view EIGRP routing information.

T A B L E 18.3

Displaying EIGRP Routing Information

COMMAND	DESCRIPTION
show ip eigrp neighbors	Displays the neighbor table.
show ip eigrp topology	Displays the topology table.
show ip route eigrp	Displays the entries in the EIGRP routing table.
show ip protocols	Displays the parameters and current state of the active routing protocol process, including the neighbors and distance information.
show ip eigrp traffic	Displays the number of EIGRP packets sent and received. Gives you statistics on Hello, Updates, Queries, Replies, and Acknowledgments.
show ipx route	Displays the content of the IPX routing table.
show ipx eigrp neighbors	Displays the IPX neighbors discovered by EIGRP.
show ipx eigrp topology	Displays the topology table for IPX.

To learn more about Cisco-specific protocols and products, go to its home page at `http://www.cisco.com/univercd/home/home.htm` **to find great technical documents, configuration information, case studies, troubleshooting guides, and design guidelines.**

Summary

This chapter has given an overview of some TCP/IP-related protocols. It covered NTP, the Network Time Protocol, which has been used for a long time and currently is at version 3. It also discussed IGMP, the Internet Group Management Protocol, which is the building block for multicasting. Applications that use broadcasting should, in the future, use multicasting instead. Finally, this chapter gave an overview of Cisco's two proprietary routing protocols, IGRP and EIGRP.

Tunneling can be used in many ways. The next chapter introduces the technique to you and shows the various implementations.

## CHAPTER 19

IP Tunneling

In a perfect world, all network systems are connected via the same protocols, and all protocols natively speak to each other. But in an imperfect world, disparate systems speak differently through protocol interpretation, and not all systems "understand" the TCP/IP protocols. Yes, we live in the imperfect world. To allow natively different systems to communicate over the TCP/IP suite of protocols, packets must be wrapped inside a User Datagram Protocol (UDP) or Transmission Control Protocol (TCP) transport header on the sending end and decoded or "unwrapped" at the receiving end. This process, known as *IP Tunneling,* or *encapsulation,* is quite widely used. This chapter explores the process of tunneling and some of the vendor implementations used today.

Overview of IP Tunneling

The following are three of the most frequently asked questions regarding the IP Tunneling process:

▶ What is IP Tunneling?

▶ What is the difference between IP Tunneling and encapsulation?

▶ Why tunnel?

What Is IP Tunneling?

IP Tunneling is the process of encapsulating (or "wrapping") data packets within an IP header to send data between systems. Tunneling assumes that a *tunnel server* (sometimes referred to as a *tunnel partner,* or *peer*) exists at each end of the wide area network (WAN) link, as shown in Figure 19.1.

FIGURE 19.1

Typical IP Tunnel Server scenario

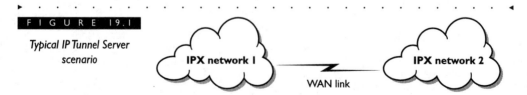

IPX network 1   WAN link   IPX network 2

In Figure 19.1, two sites are connected via a TCP/IP-only WAN. This WAN could be the Internet, or some other point-to-point link, such as an ISDN or T1 line. That part doesn't matter. What is important is that *only* TCP/IP is allowed on this link. Figure 19.1 also shows that the two remote sites only have IPX-based Novell networks on each side. Because the IPX networks communicate only by using this transport, and the network requires TCP/IP to get across the link, the data packets must be tunneled to reach their destination.

What Is the Difference between Tunneling and Encapsulation?

Some confusion occasionally arises over the words *tunneling* and *encapsulation*. To clarify the difference, the terms are specifically identified here:

▶ **Encapsulation:** Wrapping a packet inside an IP header. This may be done on a LAN or WAN. Encapsulation must be done before tunneling a packet, although a packet may be encapsulated and not tunneled. Figure 19.2 shows the structure of an encapsulated packet.

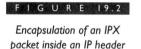

FIGURE 19.2

Encapsulation of an IPX packet inside an IP header

| MAC | IP | UDP | IPX/SPX packet | CRC |

▶ **Tunneling:** Assumes that tunnel servers are accepting and directing packets across a WAN or point-to-point link, such as that shown in Figure 19.1. Packets are encapsulated before being directed through the tunnel. The receiving tunnel server strips the header and sends the packet to the remote destination host.

These differences are explored further in this chapter.

Why Tunnel or Encapsulate?

Figure 19.1 shows a common situation in which a packet may be sent using an IP tunnel. When two networks using a protocol such as IPX require data transmission over a TCP/IP-only network, tunneling is required. However, many reasons exist why tunneling or encapsulation may take place. One of the most common emerging technologies that uses tunneling is the use of *Virtual Private Networks (VPNs)*. The VPN technology encapsulates IP within IP and tunnels it between servers, to provide data security over the Internet. Another popular encapsulation is Novell's NetWare/IP, which encapsulates IPX packets inside IP packets to provide TCP/IP services.

Do not confuse NetWare/IP with NetWare 5 Native IP. NetWare 5 Native IP uses true (nonencapsulated) TCP/IP communication.

X-REF

Microsoft uses both encapsulation and tunneling in its products. Another reason for encapsulation may be the transmission of IPv6 (version 6) packets over a standard IPv4 (version 4) internetwork. Each of these implementation methods is discussed in the next section.

Various Methods of Implementing Tunneling or Encapsulation

Vendors use tunneling and encapsulation in different ways.

Novell

To implement TCP/IP connectivity options, Novell offers several solutions, including IP Tunneling, IP Relay, and NetWare/IP. NetWare 5 offers true TCP/IP support without encapsulation. The following sections show how these solutions work.

IP Tunneling

Novell introduced the IP Tunneling feature in NetWare 3.11, and IP Tunneling has been available on every version of NetWare since that time. IP Tunneling is very popular when two IPX-based networks require communication over a dedicated TCP/IP-only link (as shown earlier, in Figure 19.1). Given the scenario just described, the complete tunneling process works like this:

1. Client sends IPX/SPX transmission from local network to the router (the destination is a computer on another network).

2. Router encapsulates data in a UDP and IP header and sends the packet to the remote peer.

3. The remote peer receives the tunneled packet and discards the IP and UDP headers.

4. Router delivers packet to the private LAN by using the IPX/SPX protocol.

This process is illustrated in Figure 19.3.

F I G U R E   19.3

The tunneling process

IP Tunneling is best used in an environment with few servers. Novell recommends a maximum of 10 peers in the tunnel network, for two reasons:

▶ Each server participating in the tunnel must be assigned a unique IP address along with the address of the other participating IP Tunnel servers in the partnership. The potential exists that all servers must somehow be connected to each other to perform tunnel operations, as illustrated in Figure 19.4.

▶ · ◀

FIGURE 19.4

IP tunnel partnerships must be defined at each server.

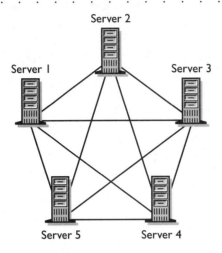

▶ IP Tunneling passes all IPX traffic, including SAP and RIP traffic, across the link. If you have many broadcasting devices and a slow link, broadcast packets can consume too much of the available bandwidth, which does not leave much room for application data.

IP Relay

IP Relay is similar to IP Tunneling insofar as it encapsulates IPX packets within UDP and then IP headers, to tunnel between servers. IP Relay, however, was designed for point-to-point WAN designs that use a star-type configuration, using a single server as a communication middle point. Figure 19.5 illustrates the star-type topology of IP Relay services.

In Figure 19.5, all servers have IP Relay loaded. The main (or hub) server contains a table of IP addresses for each remote server. The remote servers, however, do *not* contain the IP addresses for the hub server or for other remote servers. The hub server is the only server that knows how to contact each of the remote servers — therefore, the hub is responsible for initiating communications with any or all of the remote servers, using IP Relay. When an end node begins to communicate and wants to transmit from one LAN to another, the packet first passes through the hub and then to the remote router. This process is shown in Figure 19.6.

FIGURE 19.5

IP Relay is configured in a star topology.

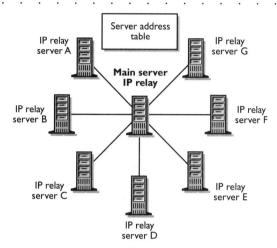

FIGURE 19.6

Packet communication process using IP Relay

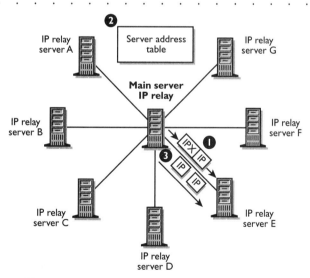

1 Hub server initiates IPX connection through IP relay services

2 Hub server maps IP address and establishes connection

3 Hub server sends IPX data through IP relay to remote server

IP Relay gives administrators a simpler way to manage IP communications between networks.

NetWare/IP

NetWare/IP is a product that is designed to allow NetWare servers to communicate using only TCP/IP. Though not a native (or "pure" IP) version of NetWare, NetWare/IP is a great way to begin moving from IPX-based versions of NetWare to a TCP/IP environment. NetWare/IP encapsulates all IPX packets inside a UDP packet, using ports 43981 and 43982, as shown in the trace in Figure 19.7.

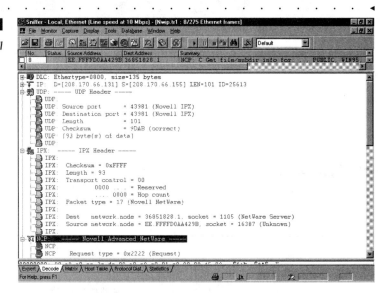

F I G U R E   19.7

NetWare/IP encapsulates all IPX/SPX communications inside a UDP header.

Notice the IPX header inside the UDP header in Figure 19.7. Because all traffic on a NetWare/IP network is encapsulated, the network communicates much like a normal TCP/IP network does. Clients must use proper IP addressing methods, network masks, and so on. Because NetWare/IP was designed to communicate with either IP- or IPX-based clients, IPX components still exist in this environment. The Domain SAP Server (DSS) is a series of NLMs that can be loaded on any NetWare version 3.1x, 4, or 5 server, or on a NetWare/IP 1.1 server. The DSS service provides Service Advertising Protocol (SAP) and Routing Information Protocol (RIP) information on request. This reduces the RIP and SAP broadcast traffic formerly seen on IPX networks, which was sent every 60 seconds, whether servers (or clients) requested that information or not.

Contrasting the encapsulation in NetWare/IP is NetWare 5. This operating system is capable of using straight, true TCP/IP to communicate with higher-level protocols, such as the NetWare Core Protocol (NCP), as shown in Figure 19.8.

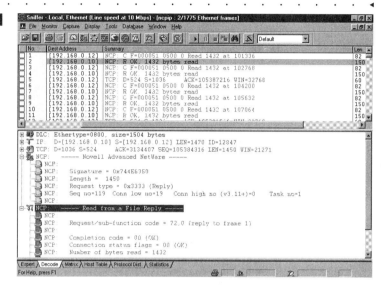

FIGURE 19.8

NetWare 5 pure IP has no encapsulation.

The TCP/IP services in NetWare 5 take advantage of both UDP and TCP. UDP is a *connectionless datagram transport,* which means that communication can be set up without a handshake. The TCP transport, on the other hand, is a *connection-oriented* transport protocol, which does require a handshake before communication can take place.

Refer to Chapters 9 and 10 for more information on the UDP and TCP transport protocols, respectively.

X-REF

Examples of UDP for NetWare 5 include SLP requests and CMD (compatibility mode) communication. Compatibility mode is used in NetWare 5 to allow an IP device to communicate with an IPX device, and when an application requires a direct IPX interface. NCP requests use TCP to communicate with the NetWare servers on TCP port 524.

Microsoft

Microsoft uses a form of TCP/IP encapsulation implementation to give TCP/IP services to the Windows environment. To communicate over a Windows network using "friendly" or NetBIOS names, the NetBIOS Frame Protocol (NBF) must be used. This protocol is used extensively in Windows networks.

NBF provides both unreliable and reliable services in the Windows environment. An example of an unreliable (or connectionless) service is a broadcast name advertisement, as shown in Figure 19.9.

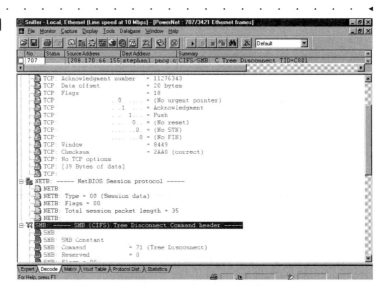

The NetBIOS protocol is implemented as the NetBIOS Session Protocol in the Sniffer screen shown in Figure 19.9. Notice the structure of the packet and how the NetBIOS protocol is sandwiched between TCP and the upper-layer communication protocol, Server Message Block (SMB). NetBIOS is required to identify the computer name, and is required in the Windows environment, which means that TCP does not directly communicate with the higher-layer protocol unless NetBIOS is present. However, NetBIOS was originally designed to run on a single physical network segment. As such, NetBIOS is nonrouteable. This can be a big problem in larger

Windows installations, because many network segments often are involved in a single LAN. Thus, using NetBIOS *over* TCP/IP allows the naming services of NetBIOS to be routed in the TCP/IP environment, much like a true TCP/IP packet would be routed.

For more information on the NetBIOS services and Windows TCP/IP implementation, refer to Chapter 16.

X-REF

NetBIOS has been implemented in networks such as LAN Manager, LAN Server, and many DOS-based networks. Hewlett-Packard, IBM, and Microsoft all use NetBIOS implementations for computer naming services. Implementations of NetBIOS also exist that run over IPX/SPX networks, such as a Windows NT Server running the NWLink protocol.

The Microsoft Windows environment also allows users to tunnel between networks using Virtual Private Network protocols. The VPN process is discussed later in this chapter.

IPv6 to IPv4

IPv6 is on the way. It is being implemented in today's corporate networks, right along with IPv4. IPv4 is today's most widely used standard for TCP/IP communication. But what happens when two IPv6 TCP/IP networks are connected over an IPv4 internetwork? Or how do you make the transition from IPv4 to IPv6 while making sure that everything is compatible? The answer is tunneling.

As just stated, the key to a successful transition to IPv6 is maintaining compatibility with the large, installed base of IPv4 hosts and routers. After all, simultaneously switching every device to IPv6 is impossible, and some devices may not be changed to IPv6 for years to come. Though that may not affect you in your IPv6 corporate network, what about communication on the Internet? You never know when you'll run into an IPv4 host, so it's best to be ready.

The IPv6 Tunneling Process

This type of tunneling is not unlike any other tunneling process described in this chapter. It is purely IP-within-IP encapsulation, through two different versions of IP. Consider the example network shown in Figure 19.10.

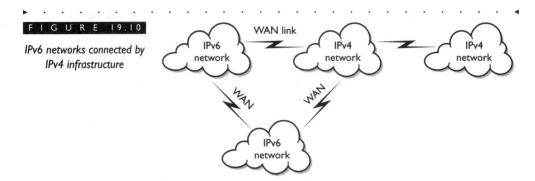

FIGURE 19.10

IPv6 networks connected by IPv4 infrastructure

In Figure 19.10, two sites at this company have been configured for IPv6. However, they are connected to other sites that contain IPv4 nodes, and by an IPv4 infrastructure. To communicate with each other, they must somehow have a common method between sites. Encapsulation and tunneling takes place using these steps:

1. The entry node of the tunnel (usually a router or server) takes the IPv6 packet and creates an encapsulating IPv4 header.

2. At the exit end of the tunnel, the exit node (again a router or server) receives the encapsulated packet.

3. The exit node strips and discards the IPv4 header.

4. The exit node sends the received IPv6 packet to the destination node.

This overview is illustrated further in Figure 19.11.

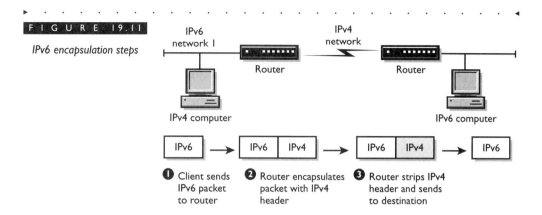

FIGURE 19.11

IPv6 encapsulation steps

IPv6
network 1

IPv4
network

Router

Router

IPv4 computer

IPv6 computer

IPv6 → IPv6 | IPv4 → IPv6 | IPv4 → IPv6

❶ Client sends
IPv6 packet
to router

❷ Router encapsulates
packet with IPv4
header

❸ Router strips IPv4
header and sends
to destination

Next, look a bit further into this process to see what the encapsulation process looks like from a packet view. When an IPv6 datagram is encapsulated, it is surrounded by an IPv4 header, as shown in Figure 19.12.

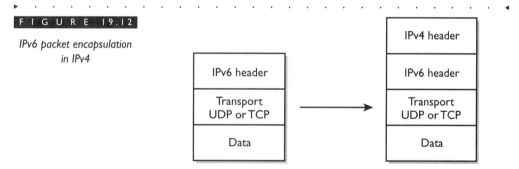

FIGURE 19.12

IPv6 packet encapsulation in IPv4

IPv6 header

Transport
UDP or TCP

Data

IPv4 header

IPv6 header

Transport
UDP or TCP

Data

Packet begins as an IPv6 packet...   and is encapsulated with an IPv4 header

This is quite a simple process from the sender's point of view. Wrap an IPv4 header around the IPv6 packet and send it on. But how does the exit (or *decapsulation*) node know when to strip the IPv4 header and process the packet as an IPv6 packet? The answer lies in the Protocol field of the IP header. Normally, this field contains the value assigned to the upper-layer protocol, such as 6 for TCP or 17 for UDP. In an encapsulated IPv6 packet, this field value is 41, as shown in Figure 19.13.

F I G U R E   19.13

Protocol field value is 41 in an encapsulated IPv6 packet

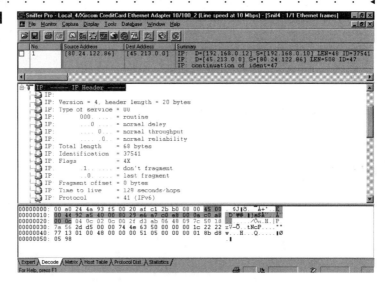

When an exit node receives a packet addressed to one of its own IPv4 addresses *and* the Protocol field value is 41, it then knows to strip the IPv4 header and submit the remaining IPv6 datagram for processing.

IPv6 Tunnel Types

Two types of tunneling are used with IPv6:

▶ Configured tunneling

▶ Automatic tunneling

Configured IPv6 Tunneling When configured tunneling is used, the tunnel endpoint address is determined by using the address information in the encapsulating node. For example, when an IPv6 packet is transmitted over a tunnel, the tunnel end node, such as a router or server, is used as the destination address for the IPv4 header, as shown in Figure 19.14.

FIGURE 19.14

Configured tunneling uses the tunnel end node address to send data

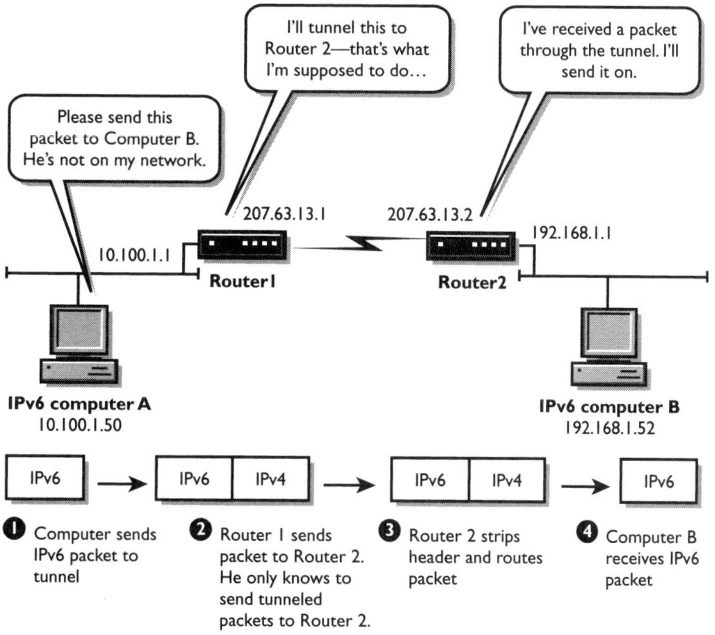

This is a good approach, but what if that tunnel endpoint node fails? How will encapsulated packets reach their destination? The answer is a twist on configured tunneling, using an IPv6 *anycast* method. An anycast is similar to an IPv4 multicast, but is used in a slightly different way, as shown in Figure 19.15.

► · ◄

FIGURE 19.15

Anycast vs. multicast

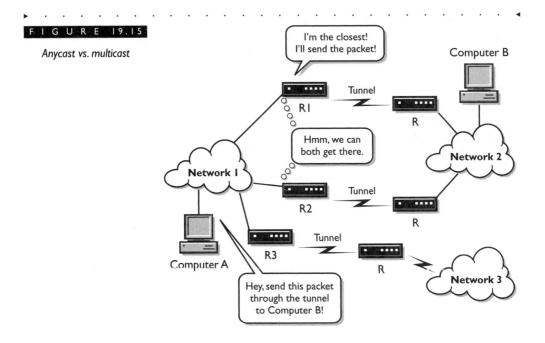

Figure 19.15 shows how an anycast communication is sent between a single sender and the nearest of several receivers in a group. A multicast, on the other hand, provides communication between a single sender and multiple receivers, not necessarily in a group. A common use for a multicast communication is for streaming video or audio, such as a live concert. A common use for anycast is to determine which gateway is closest when several possibilities exist for sending data. In a tunneling situation, anycast is used to allow all boundary routers in a group to accept tunneled IPv6 packets. This way, the nearest router will respond and decapsulate the packet. If a router fails, another router can accept the tunneled traffic.

Automatic IPv6 Tunneling   When using automatic tunneling, the tunnel endpoint is not necessarily the tunnel exit node. The endpoint address is determined from the packet being tunneled. Using this method, the destination IPv6 address must be an IPv4-compatible address, which is a 128-bit address that uses only the low-order 32 bits to determine destination addresses. The high-order 96 bits are identified by all zeroes, as shown in Figure 19.16.

▶ . . . . ◀

IPv4-compatible IP address

96-bits	32-bits
All zeroes	IPv4 address

IPv6 128-bit packet with IPv4 compatibility

Using the automatic method, the receiving (decapsulating) node takes the packet and extracts the IPv4-compatible component of the IPv6 address (the low-order 32 bits) and sends it to the destination. If the IPv6 address is not IPv4-compatible, automatic tunneling cannot be accomplished.

Virtual Private Networks

Virtual Private Networks (VPNs) are fast becoming a popular method for connecting two remote computers in different locations to a private network. These computers (or even remote offices) create a virtual link, or *tunnel,* between each other that provides a secure and private method for data transmission. This type of tunneling can take place over a public network, such as the Internet, or a private network, using the Point-to-Point Tunneling Protocol (PPTP). It is also sometimes referred to as *IP Tunneling.*

PPTP is implemented in a variety of ways. For example, Microsoft provides the PPTP protocol as part of its TCP/IP installation. Clients install the PPTP protocol and then are configured into VPNs. Many other vendors provide a hardware-based solution that allows VPN technology to be installed as a device on the network. Consider the following example, in which VPN technology might be used.

Suppose an office has several individual users that travel. To date, the users have been dialing in to the corporate network from their hotel rooms, which costs the company quite a bit in long-distance telephone charges. The company decides on a VPN solution, as shown in Figure 19.17.

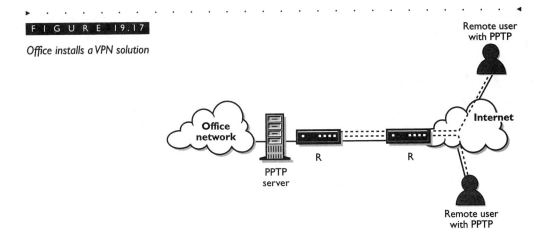

Office installs a VPN solution

Now, instead of dialing into the corporate network and accumulating long-distance expenses (and hotel surcharges), the remote user simply dials in to a local Internet service provider. From there, the user invokes the configured VPN, thus transferring data via a secure and private link between the remote user and the corporate office by using a local connection.

Understanding the PPTP Protocol

Although the PPTP protocol is becoming more widely used, it still is considered a "work in progress" by the Internet community. Guidelines have been defined for the overall operation and structure of the protocol, but have not yet been adopted as Internet standards.

The PPTP protocol is a tunneling protocol used specifically to tunnel the Point-to-Point Protocol (PPP) through an IP network. The PPP protocol has long been used by dial-up users and is responsible for encapsulating IP packets for use with a serial link, such as a dial-on-demand link. How perfect, then, that the PPP packet can be wrapped inside a PPTP packet, for a secure and private data communication method using a tunnel.

The PPTP protocol uses a client/server architecture to allow two systems to communicate over the tunnel. In a PPTP environment, one system (the server side) is usually configured to run on a device that uses the TCP/IP protocol and has some combination of hardware that uses IP, possibly LAN- or WAN-based hardware. This system is also directly connected to the LAN or WAN and is always available to the client. The client is usually a device that has dial-up capability and access to either a plain telephone line or ISDN line that is capable of using the PPP general operations and is configured to use the PPTP protocol.

PPTP Protocol Components

Two basic components are used for the PPTP protocol. These components must be established between each client/server pair using PPTP. For each pair, these processes must take place:

1. Establish a control connection

2. Create an IP tunnel

Step 1: Establish a Control Connection Before any PPP tunneling can occur between a client and a server, a control connection must be established. The *control connection* is a TCP session that is used to pass PPTP messages between both systems. It is responsible for establishing the connection, managing and releasing sessions, and exchanging information about the operating capability of the client/server pair. When a control connection is established, a session key is exchanged between the client and the server. This key is used by the client and server to identify uniquely the responsible session, because multiple sessions may be established with a particular device. A control connection can be initiated by either a client or server computer. The control-connection process is shown in Figure 19.18.

The control connection is established using destination TCP Port 5678. The source port is assigned to any unused port number.

After the control connection is established, the two systems may begin to communicate session information in the form of messages. Only certain message types may travel over a control connection. Remember, the control connection simply manages the connection, not the exchange of data, which is left up to the IP tunnel.

▶ · ◀

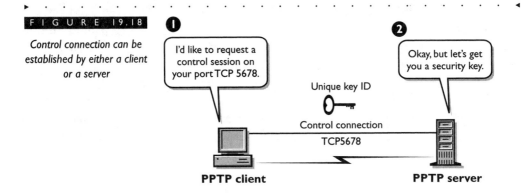

FIGURE 19.18

Control connection can be established by either a client or a server

Step 2: Create an IP Tunnel   After the control connection is established between a client/server pair, the IP tunnel must be created. This IP tunnel is used to carry all the user data for a particular session between a tunneled pair. Multiple sessions may occur between a server and clients, so a key is used to differentiate the sessions.

For each client/server pair, both a control connection and an IP tunnel *must* exist, as shown in Figure 19.19.

▶ · ◀

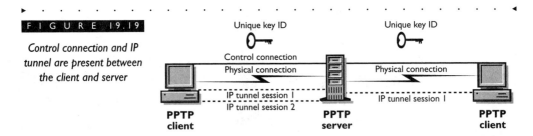

FIGURE 19.19

Control connection and IP tunnel are present between the client and server

While the user data is traveling through the IP tunnel, PPTP messages are traveling through the control connection to regulate the session. Messages may be passed to establish or clear user sessions, maintain the connection, or report errors. The following are the two types of PPTP messages:

▶ Management messages

▶ Control messages

Management messages are currently undefined, but several *control messages* exist that may be passed over the control connection. The currently defined messages can be grouped into four major categories:

- **Control Connection Management:** Manages initiation, continuity, and termination of the control connection.

- **Call Management:** Initiation, handshake, and termination of the phone call.

- **Error Reporting:** Error-reporting messages.

- **PPP Session Control:** Changes PPP parameters during a PPTP session.

The control messages and their meanings are shown in Table 19.1.

The Future for PPTP

The PPTP protocol has been an Internet draft standard for several years. It was last updated in December 1998. Though it currently has a growing popularity, another Internet draft is in the works. This Internet draft standard discusses the use of the *Layer 2 Tunneling Protocol (L2TP)* as a possible replacement for PPTP.

Today, the traditional dial-up network service on the Internet is for registered IP addresses only. These addresses are often given to dial-up users through a pool of registered addresses at the ISP. This sometimes makes communication difficult through corporate firewalls, because the user IP address changes each time a dial-up connection is established. The L2TP protocol will attempt to correct this situation by allowing corporations to assign IP addresses to VPN users, instead of requiring an ISP to assign an address. Security, authentication, and accounting issues are all addressed by this draft protocol.

Remaining competitive in today's business world requires the transmission of sensitive data quickly and securely. Yesterday's couriers and air mail are no longer quick enough. With Virtual Private Networking technology, businesses can support telecommuters, branch offices, and business partners with ease. Users on a VPN can transmit and receive documents around the globe knowing the data is secure, whether they are using today's or tomorrow's tunneling protocols.

TABLE 19.1
PPTP Control Messages

MESSAGE CATEGORY	MESSAGE NAME	CODE	DESCRIPTION
Control Connection Management	Start-Control-Connection-Request	1	Request to establish control connection.
	Start-Control-Connection-Reply	2	Reply to establish a control connection.
	Stop-Control-Connection-Request	3	Request to stop a control connection.
	Stop-Control-Connection-Reply	4	Reply to stop a control connection.
	Echo-Request	5	Similar to a "keep alive." Makes a request to the peer to announce its presence. May be initiated by either the client or server.
	Echo-Reply	6	Reply to the Echo Request.
Call Management	Outgoing-Call-Request	7	Request to establish an outbound call sent by the server to the client. Gives the client the information it needs to place a call to the server.
	Outgoing-Call-Reply	8	Reply in response to the Outgoing-Call-Request message.
	Incoming-Call-Request	9	Request by the client to the server to initiate a call. Gives the server parameter information for the incoming call, such as phone numbers.
	Incoming-Call-Reply	10	Reply in response to an Incoming-Call-Request message.
	Incoming-Call-Connected	11	Sent in response to a Incoming-Call-Reply message. This is the third step in the three-way handshake required to initiate a session.
	Call-Clear-Request	12	Request to disconnect a call sent by the server to the client.
	Call-Disconnect-Notify	13	Sent by the client to the server whenever a call is disconnected, either by a Call-Clear-Request or any other reason.
Error Reporting	WAN-Error-Notify	14	Sent by the client to the server to indicate WAN error conditions. The packet contains counters for various errors, including CRC, framing, hardware and buffer overruns, timeouts, and alignment errors.
PPP Session Control	Set-Link-Info	15	Sent from the server to the client to set options. Options can change during the life of the call.

Summary

This chapter looked at how tunneling and encapsulation work on TCP/IP-based networks. Different vendor implementations were discussed, as were possibilities for Virtual Private Networking (VPN) and expanding to IPv6. Trace files showed what encapsulation looks like against a pure TCP/IP-only environment.

## CHAPTER 20

IP Version 6

You have learned a lot about IPv4 throughout this book. This chapter now talks about IPv6. Does that mean you have to start from scratch? No, it does not. IPv4 has proven to be a very well-designed protocol. Otherwise, it would not have been so successful. IPv6 keeps many of the characteristics of IPv4. But, many lessons have been learned through all the years of working with version 4, and that knowledge has been built into IPv6. So, prepare to dive into the new version and find out what it offers.

The advent of IPv6 in your networks will not happen as fast as many expected only a short time ago. Everybody was running out of IP addresses. It is difficult to even get a Class C address. The additional address space offered by IPv6 was, for a long time, the main reason that everybody was looking for it to arrive. However, in today's networks, the widespread use of firewalls and NAT (Network Address Translation) has diminished the need for official IP addresses. Many companies internally use the reserved IP addresses (discussed in Chapter 4) and need only a few official IP addresses to be represented to the outside world.

Parts of the Internet backbone are currently running IPv6; so it is used, but you won't need IPv6 in your corporate network for a while.

► · ◄

Overview of IPv6 Functionality

IPv6, described in RFC 2460 (December 1998), obsoletes RFC 1883. With IPv6, a lot of work is in progress, so you should always make sure to work with the latest information. To understand the basics, RFC 2460 is a good starting point.

NOTE

At the end of this chapter, you'll find a table that lists the most important RFCs that relate to IPv6, as well as references to Internet sites from which you can get updated information.

IPv6 has the following new capabilities, which were partially integrated in IPv4 but will be mandatory for IPv6:

► Expanded addressing capabilities

► Header format simplification

▸ Improved support for extensions and options

▸ Flow labeling capability for support of real-time communication

▸ Auto-configuration

▸ Security

IPv6 Header Structure

The IPv6 header has a total fixed length of 40 bytes. It has an 8-byte header followed by two 16-byte fields for Source and Destination IP Address. Figure 20.1 shows the header format.

Version
(4 bits)

Traffic class
(1 byte)

Flow label
(20 bits)

Payload length
(2 bytes)

Next header
(1 byte)

Hop limit
(1 byte)

Source address
(16 bytes)

Destination address
(16 bytes)

Total length: 40 bytes fixed length

If you compare this header to the IPv4 header, you find that it looks much simpler. Six fields were removed:

- ▸ Header Length

- ▸ Type of Service

- ▸ Identification

- ▸ Flags

- ▸ Fragment Offset

- ▸ Header Checksum

Three fields have been renamed and slightly modified: Length, Protocol Type, and Time To Live (TTL). The Class and the Flow Label fields have been added. Remember from the IPv4 header that it has a variable length. The minimum is 20 bytes, but options can be added up to a maximum of 60 bytes.

IPv6 has a fixed-length header of 40 bytes. This doesn't mean that IPv6 cannot express options for special cases, but they are added by using *extension headers*, which are appended after the main header. That is the reason why the Header Length field was removed. You may wonder why the Header Checksum was removed. The advantage of this is that the header processing is done faster, and no need exists to check and update checksums at every router. Actually, many routers do not do the checksum test when routing packets, even with IPv4. The risk for undetected errors and misrouted packets is minimal, because checksumming is done at the media access level, too.

What about fragmentation and the missing Identification, Flags, and Fragment Offset fields? Remember fragmentation from IPv4? If a large packet has to be sent over a network supporting a small packet size, the IPv4 layer splits the packet into slices and sends multiple packets that have to be collected and reassembled at the destination host. If only one packet was missing, the whole transmission had to be redone. Very inefficient. In IPv6, the host should learn the MTU (maximum transfer unit) size through the procedure called *Path MTU Discovery*. IPv6 includes an end-to-end segmentation procedure. If the sending host wants to fragment a packet, it does so by using an extension header (discussed in more detail later in this chapter).

The TOS (Type of Service) field has been removed, too. It was not used by many applications, and IPv6 provides a different mechanism to handle preferences.

The following list describes the new fields in more detail:

▸ **Traffic Class (1 byte):** Replaces the 4 bits of the TOS field in IPv4, and is designed to facilitate the handling of real-time data.

▸ **Flow Label (20 bits):** Used to distinguish packets that require the same treatment. Packets sent by a given source to a given destination with a given set of options will have the same Flow Label. This field is intended to facilitate the handling of real-time traffic.

▸ **Payload Length (2 bytes):** The length of data carried after the header. This is handled differently than in the IPv4 world. Figure 20.2 explains the difference.

▸ **Next Header (1 byte):** Used to be the Protocol Type field in IPv4. It has been renamed to reflect the new organization of IP packets. If the next header is UDP or TCP, you will find the same protocol codes as in IPv4. It would be 6 for TCP or 17 for UDP. But, if *extension headers* are used with IPv6, this field will contain the type of the first extension header. That header will be located between the IP header and the TCP or UDP header. (Table 20.1, later in the chapter, lists possible values in the Next Header field.)

▸ **Hop Limit (1 byte):** In IPv4, the TTL field contains a number of seconds, indicating how long a packet can remain in the network before being destroyed. Most routers simply decrement this value by 1 at each hop. This field is called Hop Limit in IPv6, and the name reflects the change: the value in this field now expresses a number of hops instead of a number of seconds.

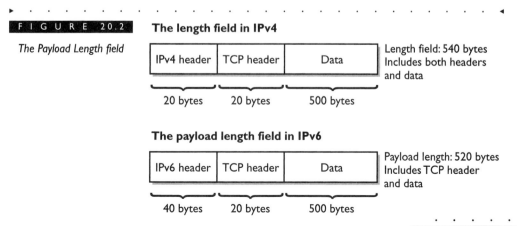

FIGURE 20.2

The Payload Length field

The length field in IPv4

IPv4 header	TCP header	Data
20 bytes	20 bytes	500 bytes

Length field: 540 bytes
Includes both headers and data

The payload length field in IPv6

IPv6 header	TCP header	Data
40 bytes	20 bytes	500 bytes

Payload length: 520 bytes
Includes TCP header and data

The Length Field in IPv4 includes the length of the IPv4 header, whereas the Payload Length field in IPv6 contains only the header and the data following the IPv6 header. The fact that the Payload Length field has 2 bytes limits the maximum packet size to 64 kilobytes. IPv6 has a *Jumbogram Option*, which supports bigger packet sizes, if needed.

Extension Headers

The IPv4 header has 40 bytes that can be used to specify options such as Security Options, Source Routing, or Timestamping. As you know, they are rarely used, because using them is a performance hit. The simpler a packet header, the faster the processing. IPv6 handles these options in additional headers, called *extension headers*.

In IPv6, you can have one or more extension headers between the IP header and the payload. The current IPv6 specification defines six extension headers:

- **Hop-by-Hop Options Header:** Extension headers are only processed by the final destination of a packet. This header is the exception to this rule. It contains information that has to be processed by every intermediate host (router).

- **Routing Header:** Contains a list of intermediate addresses through which the packet should be routed. It is a source route and can be strict or loose.

- **Fragment Header:** IPv6 routers do not fragment packets. IPv6 works much like IPv4 when the IPv4 Don't Fragment bit is set. But, in IPv6, a sending host can fragment a packet before it sends it out to the network. This will be done by inserting the Fragment Header after the IPv6 header, and will work very much like fragmentation in IPv4, with an Identification field and an Offset field. IPv6 also has a More Fragment bit, which is set in all packets except the last.

- **Destination Options Header:** This header type makes it possible to add functionality to IPv6 without having to define a new extension header type. The Destination Options header uses a single header type (60) that contains one or more options, identified by option types. It is used to carry optional information that only needs to be examined by a packet's destination node.

▸ **Authentication Header:** Used to provide connectionless integrity and data origin authentication for IP datagrams. It is described in RFC 2402.

▸ **Encrypted Security Payload:** Provides a mix of security services in IPv4 and IPv6. It is described in RFC 2406.

NOTE **The first four extension headers are described in RFC 2460. The Authentication Header is described in RFC 2402, and the Encrypted Security Payload is described in RFC 2406.**

Figure 20.3 explains how these headers can be piled onto each other.

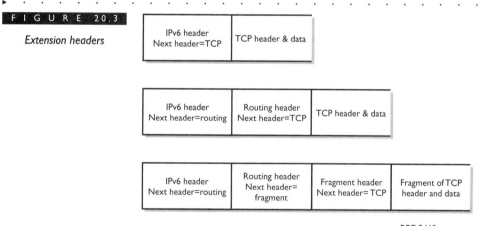

F I G U R E 20.3

Extension headers

RFC 2460

Note in this example that the Next Header field can either contain a protocol type for the next layer (UDP or TCP) or specify an extension header. Header type numbers are taken out of the same range of numbers and therefore shouldn't conflict with protocol type numbers.

Some numbers that you will find in the Next Header field are shown in Table 20.1.

	VALUE	DESCRIPTION
TABLE 20.1	0	Reserved and not used with IPv4 IPv6: Hop-by-Hop Option Header
Values in the Next Header Field	4	IPv6: IP (IPv4 encapsulation)
	6	TCP
	17	UDP
	43	Routing Header
	44	Fragmentation Header
	45	IDRP (Interdomain Routing Protocol)
	46	RSVP (Resource Reservation Protocol)
	51	Authentication Header
	52	Encrypted Security Payload Header
	58	ICMPv6
	59	No next header
	60	Destination Options Header

The processing order is determined by the order of the headers and, therefore, by the sending host. It will be demultiplexed in reverse order at the receiving host. The extension headers are all optional.

IPv6 Addressing

The address architecture with IPv6 has many similarities with the one used with IPv4. As in IPv4, an IPv6 address uniquely identifies an interface connected to a subnetwork. A multihomed station has as many IP addresses as interfaces. One difference is that, with IPv6, each interface can be identified by several addresses. The IPv6 Addressing Architecture is described in RFC 2373.

IPv6 addresses can be in one of three categories:

- **Unicast:** Uniquely identifies one interface.

- **Multicast:** Identifies a group of hosts. A packet sent to a multicast address will be processed by all members of the group.

- **Anycast:** Also identifies a group of hosts. A packet addressed to an anycast address will be delivered to only one of the group, usually the nearest member.

An IPv6 address has 128 bits, which are divided into eight 16-bit integers, separated by a colon. Each integer has 4 hexadecimal bits. A complete IPv6 address could look like this:

```
0123:0000:0000:0011:2233:4455:0000:7799
```

To make an administrator's life easier, some abbreviations are possible. A first rule is that *leading zeros can be skipped.* The preceding address then looks like this:

```
123:0000:0000:11:2233:4455:0000:7799
```

The next rule is that *consecutive fields of 0 can be replaced by a double colon.* This can be done once within an address. Now the example address looks like this:

```
123::11:2233:4455:0000:7799
```

Some IPv6 addresses are built by prepending zero bits to an IPv4 address. IPv6 introduces a specific format for these addresses. All the zeros can be expressed by a double colon, as you just read. The IPv4 address can be added in the common dotted decimal notation. So, the address would look like this:

```
::192.168.0.2
```

Initial Assignment

The addressing architecture for IPv6 defines several *Prefixes* that are used to identify special addresses, such as loopback or multicast addresses. The initial definition defined *Provider-Based Addresses.* With recent developments, this name has been changed to *Aggregatable Global Unicast Addresses.* Prefixes are also reserved for NSAP-compatible addresses and IPX-compatible addresses. The initial Prefix assigned for *Geographic Addresses* has been removed. Table 20.2 lists the reserved Prefixes, according to RFC 2373.

TABLE 20.2

Reserved IPv6 Prefixes

DESCRIPTION	PREFIX (BINARY)	FRACTION OF ADDRESS SPACE ASSIGNED
Reserved	0000 0000	1/256
Reserved for NSAP allocation	0000 001	1/128
Reserved for IPX allocation	0000 010	1/128
Aggregatable Global Unicast Addresses	001	1/8
Link-Local Unicast Addresses	1111 1110 10	1/1024
Site-Local Unicast Addresses	1111 1110 11	1/1024
Multicast Addresses	1111 1111	1/256

Aggregatable Global Unicast Addresses

Aggregatable Global Unicast Addresses are identified by the Prefix 001, as shown in Table 20.2. The Prefix is followed by five components. In the initial specifications, they were of variable length. This has been changed to fixed-length in the most current specification, to make renumbering easier. Figure 20.4 shows the address format and the five components.

FIGURE 20.4

Format of the Aggregatable Global Unicast Address

P 001	TLA	Res	NLA	SLA	Interface ID
3	13	8	24	16	64

Bits = Total 128

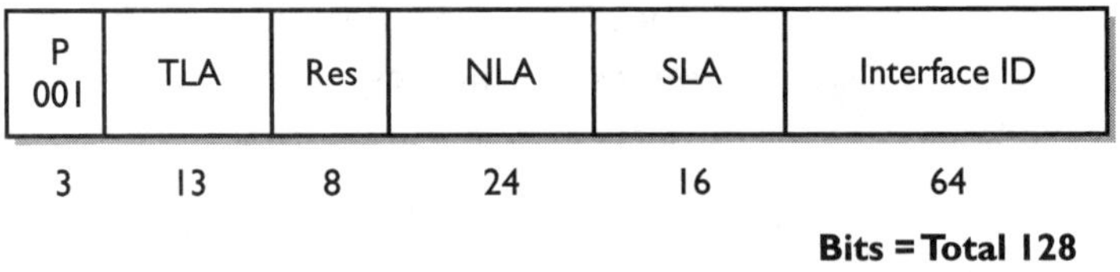

P : 001 Prefix for aggregatable global unicast addresses
TLA : Top level aggregator
Res : Reserved for future use
NLA : Next level aggregator
SLA : Site level aggregator

The *TLA (Top Level Aggregator)* is what used to be the Provider-Based ID. A TLA does not have to be an actual provider. At the core of the Internet, in the backbone, routing tables will need to have one entry per TLA for the routing inside the TLA. The *NLA (Next Level Aggregator)* replaces what used to be the Subscriber Identifier in earlier specifications. The last level in the hierarchy designates the *SLA (Site Level Aggregator)*. Changes in the most current specification basically keep the hierarchical structure defined earlier, but release it from the commercial relations to specific providers expressed in the old addressing structure.

Other Special Addresses

The *Loopback Address* is assigned out of the 0000 0000 address space. It has the value 0:0:0:0:0:0:0:1 and may be used by a node to send an IPv6 packet to itself.

A special IPv6 address is the *Unspecified Address,* which has a value of 0:0:0:0:0:0:0:0. It indicates the absence of an address and is used as a source address by a host that initializes its stack before it knows its IP address. It should never be assigned and should never appear as a destination address.

Unicast addresses can be distinguished from *multicast* addresses by the value of the high-order byte. An IPv6 address with a high-order byte of 1111 1111 is always a multicast address. Anything else is a unicast address. *Anycast* addresses are taken from the unicast address space. They cannot be distinguished from unicast addresses by their high-order byte value.

To get a list of the currently assigned IPv6 multicast addresses, refer to RFC 2375.

NOTE

The following are two special addresses that are defined for backward-compatibility with IPv4:

▸ **IPv6 Addresses with Embedded IPv4 Addresses:** Used to tunnel IPv6 packets dynamically over an IPv4 routing infrastructure. IPv6 nodes that utilize this technique are assigned special IPv6 unicast addresses that carry an IPv4 address in the low-order 32 bits. This type of address is called an *IPv4-compatible IPv6 address.*

▸ **IPv4-Mapped IPv6 Address:** Used to represent the addresses of IPv4-only nodes.

Both address formats are shown in Figure 20.5.

FIGURE 20.5

Special IPv6 address types for IPv4-compatibility

IPv4-compatible IPv6 address

0000 0000	0000	IPv4 address
80 bits	16 bits	32 bits

IPv4-mapped IPv6 address

0000 0000	FFFF	IPv4 address
80 bits	16 bits	32 bits

Refer to Chapter 19 on IP tunneling for detailed coverage of tunneling of IPv6 in IPv4.

X-REF

Chapter 4 (on IPv4) discusses how companies who are not connected to the Internet or using NAT (Network Address Translation) can use private addresses specified in RFC 1597. With IPv6, the same is provided by the *Site Local Addressing Prefix*. The Prefix 1111 1110 11 has been reserved for these organizations. A site local address will have this prefix followed by a set of zeros, the subnet ID, and the Interface Identifier. These addresses cannot be routed on the Internet and are only unique within a site.

The *Link Local Address Range* has been defined for hosts that do not have a provider-based or a site-local address yet. These addresses can be used only within a network segment and should never be routed. They are identified by the Prefix 1111 1110 10.

Autoconfiguration of IPv6 Hosts

IPv6 has an autoconfiguration mechanism that can be stateful or stateless.

With *stateless autoconfiguration* (RFC 2462), no manual configuration of hosts has to be done. A host can generate its own addresses by using a combination of locally available information and information advertised by routers. Routers advertise prefixes that identify the subnet(s) associated with a link, while hosts generate an Interface Identifier that uniquely identifies an interface on a subnet. An address is formed by combining the two. In the absence of a router, only Link-Local Addresses (described earlier in "IPv6 Addressing") can be generated. With a Link-Local Address, a host can only communicate with hosts on the same segment.

A node that starts initializing its IPv6 stack joins the *All Nodes* multicast group. Next, it sends a Solicitation message (ICMP message type 133) to the routers on the link, using the All Routers multicast address. The routers on the link are supposed to answer with a Router Advertisement message (ICMP message type 134).

With *stateful autoconfiguration*, hosts obtain interface addresses and/or configuration information and parameters from a server. This is the equivalent of DHCP for IPv6. Both autoconfiguration models can be combined. A host can generate its addresses by stateless autoconfiguration and obtain additional configuration information from a server.

To make sure that all configured addresses are unique, nodes run a *Duplicate Address Test* before assigning the address to an interface. The Duplicate Address Detection algorithm is performed on all addresses, independent of whether they are obtained through stateless or stateful autoconfiguration.

Duplicate Address Detection uses the *Neighbor Discovery* procedure, which is the IPv6 procedure that replaces the IPv4 protocols for address resolution and neighbor discovery. After configuring its IP address, the IPv6 host sends a Solicitation message toward that address. If a reply is made, it knows that the address is already being used by another host. It will then try another address, if possible, or display an error message.

Address Lifetime

IPv6 addresses have an associated, limited lifetime. With stateful autoconfiguration, the lifetime is configured on the server providing the address information. With stateless autoconfiguration, the lifetime is taken from the Prefix in the router's Router Advertisement.

When the lifetime expires, the address becomes invalid. When a TCP process on a host starts a connection, it can choose any of the local addresses as a source address for the communication. It should choose the one with the longest lifetime.

Routers send out Router Advertisements in regular intervals. Every host receives them and examines the Prefix in the Advertisement. If the Prefix is known, the host knows that it is still on the same link, and updates the lifetime of its address with the new one in the Router Advertisement. If the Prefix has changed, the host will autoconfigure a new address, reflecting the change in the network layout. Does it sound like better times are ahead for administrators?

Dynamic Host Configuration

The *Stateful Configuration Protocol* is known as DHCP in the IPv4 world. An IPv6 host will locate a DHCP server by sending out a DHCP Solicitation message to the multicast address of All DHCP Servers and Relay Agents. The messages will be sent using UDP port 546 for the server, and port 547 for the client. The server will reply with a *DHCP Advertisement* message. Now, the host requests configuration information by sending a *DHCP Request* message, which will be answered with a *DHCP Reply* message. Sounds quite familiar. A *DHCP Release message* can be issued by the client if it wants to release some configuration parameters. *DHCP Reconfigure* messages are sent by a server that wants to update a client's configuration with new parameters. The server will include the parameters in the message body, and then the client has to request these parameters by using a DHCP Request message.

The following multicast addresses are used:

► All DHCP Agents (servers and relays) must join the link-local *All-DHCP-Agents multicast group* at the address FF02:0:0:0:0:0:1:2.

► All DHCP servers must join the site-local *All-DHCP-Servers multicast group* at the address FF05:0:0:0:0:0:1:3.

► All DHCP relays must join the site-local *All-DHCP-Relays multicast group* at the address FF05:0:0:0:0:0:1:4.

IMPORTANT

Currently, no RFC for DHCPv6 exists. This is a work in progress and it might have many changes before it is standardized. We have summarized the information from the draft available at the `http://www.ietf.org` **site. The version of the draft was** `draft-ietf-dhc-dhcpv6-14.txt`, **dated February 1999. In that draft, you can also find a detailed description of the DHCPv6 communication processes, as well as packet descriptions and header formats.**

Packet Size Issues

IPv6 requires every link in the Internet to have an MTU of 1,280 bytes or greater. If a link cannot support that packet size in one piece, link-specific fragmentation and reassembly must be provided at a layer below IPv6. Links that have a configurable MTU (for example, PPP links) must be configured to have an MTU of at least 1,280 bytes. It is even recommended that they be configured with an MTU of 1,500 bytes or greater, to accommodate possible encapsulations.

It is strongly recommended that IPv6 nodes implement Path MTU Discovery (RFC 1981), with which they can discover and take advantage of path MTUs greater than 1,280 bytes.

ICMPv6

ICMP for IPv6 has been streamlined and extended. Some unused options from ICMPv4 were removed. Multicast functions that were governed by IGMP (Internet Group Management Protocol; refer to Chapter 19) have been incorporated into ICMP. The format of the ICMP header had to be extended to accommodate for IPv6 addressing. ICMPv6 is not compatible with ICMPv4. You may have noticed in Table 20.1 that it has been assigned a different value for the Next Header field. ICMP with IPv4 has the value 1. ICMPv6 has the Next Header value 58 in the IPv6 header.

The current specification (RFC 2463) defines 14 different types of ICMP messages, listed in Table 20.3.

TABLE 20.3

ICMPv6 Types

TYPE	DESCRIPTION	CODE
1	Destination Unreachable	0 – No Route to Destination 1 – Communication Administratively Prohibited 2 – not assigned 3 – Address Unreachable 4 – Port Unreachable
2	Packet Too Big	The Code field is not used. This message is used as part of the Path MTU Discovery process. It has a 4-byte field that contains the MTU for the next-hop link.
3	Time Exceeded	0 – Hop Limit Exceeded in Transit 1 – Fragment Reassembly Time Exceeded
4	Parameter Problem	0 – Erroneous Header Field 1 – Unrecognized Next Header Type 2 – Unrecognized IPv6 Option
128	Echo Request	
129	Echo Reply	
130	Group Membership Query	
131	Group Membership Report	
132	Group Membership Reduction	
133	Router Solicitation	
134	Router Advertisement	
135	Neighbor Solicitation	
136	Neighbor Advertisement	
137	Redirect	

All ICMP messages have a common format. They have an 8-byte header that contains the message Type (1 byte), Code (1 byte), and Checksum (2 bytes) fields. The following fields are of variable length and vary depending on what message type it is.

For a detailed explanation of all the different ICMPv6 message formats, refer to RFC 2463.

NOTE

. . . . . .

Other Protocol Changes for IPv6

Many protocols have to adapt to the changes with IPv6, as described next.

Checksums

Upper-layer protocols have to adapt to changes in IPv6. Transport protocols, such as TCP and UDP, create pseudoheaders when computing checksums. In that checksum computation, source and destination addresses are an important part of detecting misdelivery of a packet. These checksum calculations will have to be changed to use the 16-byte IPv6 address. Because IPv6 does not have a header checksum any more, checksumming at the upper layer becomes mandatory. With IPv4, checksumming with UDP was optional.

Routing Protocols

The size of routing tables is a big concern with IPv4. CIDR (Classless Interdomain Routing) was the short-term solution to these problems.

Exterior Gateway Protocols

The building blocks of the IPv4 Internet are autonomous systems (ASs). An AS is managed by a single administration and can be the network of an ISP (Internet service provider) or a large company. ASs use exterior gateway protocols to exchange routing information. The most commonly used protocol is BGP (Border Gateway Protocol). It uses the same route aggregation procedures required by CIDR. BGP is optimized to handle 32-bit IPv4 addresses. Because upgrading BGP to handle 128-bit IPv6 addresses was too difficult, the IPv6 world uses IDRP (Interdomain Routing Protocol) as an exterior gateway protocol. IDRP is defined in the ISO standard 10747. The discussion of IDRP is beyond the scope of this book.

Interior Gateway Protocols

Within ASs, interior gateway protocols are used to exchange intradomain routing information. The IETF working group is preparing updated versions of OSPF and RIP. Updates for other protocols, such as IS-IS and EIGRP, will probably follow. Currently, a draft exists for IGRPv6.

OSPF for IPv6 OSPF is the recommended protocol for intradomain routing. The changes that have to be made to update it to IPv6 are minimal. It will run on top of IPv6 and accommodate the new IPv6 address format. The OSPF database for IPv6 will not be shared with the IPv4 database. Currently, a draft exists for OSPF for IPv6.

RIPng for IPv6 RIPng (next generation) for IPv6 is described in RFC 2080.

DNS Changes

DNS has to adapt for the new IPv6 addresses. A new resource record (RR) has been defined for IPv6 and contains a 16-byte IP address. Its type has been set to *AAAA* and it is the equivalent for the A type used with IPv4. The value for this new record type is 28 (refer to Table 12.3 in Chapter 12). For reverse name resolution, the IPv4 specification uses the `in-addr.arpa` domain. This domain is used to retrieve the domain name associated with a given IP address. A similar service has been defined for IPv6. It is not as simple as with IPv4, however, because IPv6 addresses do not have a fixed boundary, as explained earlier in "IPv6 Addressing." The domain suffix used for IPv6 reverse name mapping is `.IP6.INT`.

The DNS extensions to support IPv6 are described in RFC 1886. They are designed to be compatible with existing software, and the support for IPv4 addresses is retained.

▶ · ◀

Transition Mechanisms

The key to a successful IPv6 transition is maintaining compatibility with IPv4 hosts and routers, while deploying IPv6. Most hosts in the Internet and in corporate networks will need to be compatible with IPv4 for a long time to come. Different techniques can be used to establish compatibility. RFC 1933 covers transition mechanisms in great detail. This section provides a summary for you.

Dual IP Layer

The easiest way for an IPv6 node to be compatible with IPv4 is to be a *Dual IP Layer* node. This is called an *IPv6/IPv4 node* in RFC 1933. Being a Dual IP Layer node means that the node can send and receive both IPv4 packets and IPv6 packets. It will be configured with one or more IPv4 addresses and one or more IPv6 addresses. The Dual IP Layer technique can be used in conjunction with the tunneling mechanisms. IPv6/IPv4 nodes can use the *stateless autoconfiguration* mechanisms (described earlier) or other techniques, such as DHCP for IPv6 to receive their IPv6 address. This can be an IPv6-only address or an IPv4-compatible address. This node can even receive its IPv4 address by known configuration mechanisms, such as DHCP for IPv4, and then map that address into a IPv4-compatible IPv6 address by prepending it with the 96-bit prefix 0:0:0:0:0:0.

NOTE **An IPv6/IPv4 host will have multiple DNS entries: an A Record for each IPv4 address and an AAAA Record for each IPv6 address. DNS and DNS Resolvers will need to support these multiple entries. More details are available in RFC 1933.**

IPv6-Over-IPv4 Tunneling

This is the technique of encapsulating IPv6 packets within IPv4 so that they can be routed across IPv4 infrastructures. It is described in Chapter 19 on IP Tunneling. The following are the two ways of tunneling:

▸ **Configured tunneling:** The IPv4 tunnel endpoint address is configured on the encapsulating node.

▸ **Automatic tunneling:** The IPv4 tunnel endpoint address is determined from the IPv4 address embedded in the IPv4-compatible destination address of the IPv6 packet. If the destination address is not an IPv4-compatible address, the packet cannot be tunneled using automatic tunneling. Therefore, IPv4-compatible addresses are assigned to IPv6/IPv4 nodes that support automatic tunneling. This special case of IPv6 addresses has been described in the section on IPv6 Addressing (refer to Figure 20.5). Nodes that are configured with IPv4-compatible addresses may use the complete address as their IPv6 address, and use the embedded IPv4 address as their IPv4 address.

IPv6 Trace Files

I am sure you would love to see some trace files with IPv6, right? You would not have bought this book if you weren't a packet freak.

The IPv6 Header

Figure 20.6 shows the details of an IPv6 header in a decode. Here, you can see all the fields that have been discussed in the section on the IPv6 header. The Traffic Class field in the latest RFC is decoded as the Priority field in SnifferPro. The Next Header field value in this case is the known protocol code for UDP, which is 17. The Destination IP Address field is ff02::9. This is the multicast address for RIP Routers, according to RFC 2375. In the UDP header, you can see Source and Destination Port 521. This is the port number for RIPng.

FIGURE 20.6

The IPv6 header

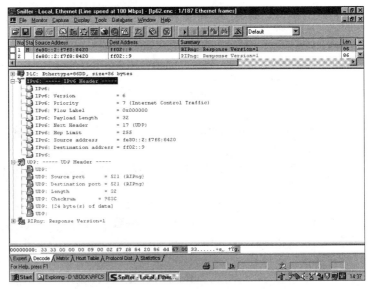

Neighbor Discovery

Figure 20.7 is a trace file that shows ICMPv6 communication; in this case, Neighbor Solicitation and Neighbor Advertisement frames. In the IPv6 header, you can see the Next Header value of 58 for ICMPv6. The details of the ICMP header show that this is a type 135 message: a Neighbor Solicitation message. Refer to Table 20.3 for the list of ICMP message types. The code for Neighbor Solicitation is 0. The Options section defines the address as a type 1 address, which is a Source Link Layer address. To interpret the last field in the ICMP header, you have to go down to the hexadecimal window, which shows the last 6 bytes of the source IP address. This can be seen in Figure 20.8.

FIGURE 20.7

ICMP Neighbor Solicitation frame

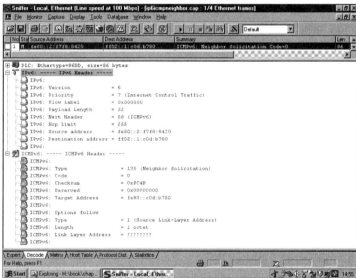

Figure 20.8 is the neighbor's answer to the Neighbor Solicitation message — a Neighbor Advertisement frame.

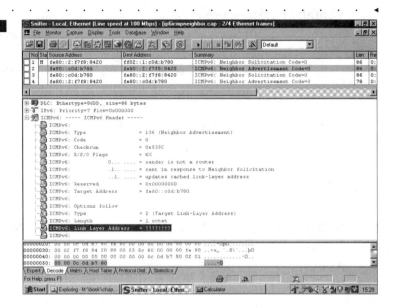

FIGURE 20.8

ICMP Neighbor Advertisement frame

The IPv6 header looks the same as in the Solicitation message. Only the IP source and destination addresses have changed. The ICMP message type is 136 for the Neighbor Advertisement. Flags can be set that indicate whether the neighbor is a router, whether the message was sent in response to a Solicitation, and whether the Advertisement should override an existing cache entry. This figure highlights the last field, showing the Link Layer Address. The highlighted fields in the hexadecimal window show the last 6 bytes of the source address.

If you want to learn all the details about neighbor discovery for IPv6, refer to RFC 2461.

NOTE

Extension Headers

Figure 20.9 shows the details of a frame that contains two extension headers between the IPv6 and the ICMPv6 headers.

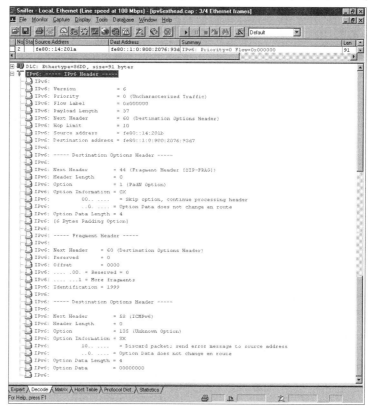

FIGURE 20.9

Extension headers

Remember from Figure 20.3 that extension headers can be piled onto each other. This detail window of an IPv6 packet shows multiple extension headers, which are differentiated by the *Next Header values* (described in Table 20.1). The IPv6 header indicates a Next Header value of 60 for the Destination Options. The Destination Options Header shows the Next Header value 44 for a Fragment Header. The Fragment Header contains the value 60 for another Destination Options Header. And, finally, the last Destination Options Header contains the value 58 for ICMP.

▶ · ◀

Further References on IPv6

This book is intended to be a TCP/IP troubleshooting book. This chapter on IPv6 does not intend to explain all there is to know about IPv6, but instead tries to give you a general understanding of the major changes and the most important things to know about migration issues. If you want to know it all, you will find many good books on the market that cover IPv6 in great detail.

NOTE

One book that I can recommend for further reading is *IPv6*, by Christian Huitema (Prentice Hall). The second edition was released in fall 1998. It covers all aspects of IPv6 in great detail. The author is the former head of the Internet Architecture Board (IAB) and has written numerous RFCs — Information from the source.

Read RFCs

The RFCs are the most important source of information on IPv6. Many Web sites are available on which you can search the RFCs by search terms. To find all related RFCs, do a search on **IPv6**. Table 20.4 lists the most important RFCs for IPv6.

T A B L E   20.4

Main RFCs on IPv6

DESCRIPTION	RFC NUMBER	DATE
Internet Protocol, Version 6 (IPv6) Specification	RFC 2460 Obsoletes RFC 1883	December 98
IPv6 Addressing Architecture	RFC 2373 Obsoletes RFC 1884	July 98
IPv6 Stateless Address Autoconfiguration	RFC 2462	December 98
Transition Mechanisms for IPv6 Hosts and Routers	RFC 1933	April 96
Internet Control Message Protocol (ICMPv6) for the Internet Protocol Version 6 (IPv6) Specification	RFC 2463 Obsoletes RFC 1885	December 98
Neighbor Discovery for IPv6	RFC 2461 Obsoletes RFC 1970	December 98

DESCRIPTION	RFC NUMBER	DATE
IPv6 Multicast Address Assignments	RFC 2375 Memo	July 98
Various RFCs that cover the implementation of IPv6 on different topologies	RFC 2464 on Ethernet RFC 2467 on FDDI RFC 2470 on Token Ring RFC 2491 on NBMA RFC 2492 on ATM RFC 2497 on ARCnet RIPng for IPv6 RFC 2080	January 97
Generic Packet Tunneling in IPv6	RFC 2473	December 98
DNS Extensions to Support IPv6	RFC 1886	December 95
Several SNMP MIBs have been defined	RFC 2452 for TCP RFC 2454 for UDP RFC 2465 for IPv6 RFC 2466 ICMPv6	

Internet References

After digesting all RFCs, you should definitely go on the Internet, especially for new technologies, because you can find the most up-to-date information there. Here's a short list of some cool sites with IPv6 information:

- ▶ For the latest developments in the IETF working groups, go to `http://www.ietf.org`.

- ▶ Sun Microsystems maintains a nice site with a good overview and many links to working groups, at `http://playground.sun.com/pub/ipng/html/ipng-main.html`.

- ▶ `http://www.ipv6.com` and `http://www.ipv6.org` are two sites with a lot of resources and further links.

The *6bone* is an IPv6 test network that has been built to assist in evolution and deployment of IPv6. Check out its site at `http://www.6bone.net`. Here's a list of some interesting links, to show what sort of information you can find at 6bone:

- 6bone Statistics, at `http://www.6bone.net/6bone_stats.html`

- 6bone Tools, at `http://www.6bone.net/6bone_tools.html`

- 6bone Routing Reports, at
  `http://www.merit.net/mail.archives/html/6bone-routing-report/`

- 6bone Odd Routing Reports, at
  `http://carmen.cselt.it/ipv6/bgp/odd-routes.html`

Wanna Play?

Would you like to play with and test IPv6? Here's some information about implementations of IPv6 that are available today:

- IBM AIX 4.3 ships with an IPv6 implementation

- BSDI's BSD/OS v4.0 ships with an IPv6 implementation

- Sun Solaris has a prototype implementation; for more information, go to
  `http://www.sun.com/solaris/ipv6/`

- Linux kernels version 2.2 and above ship with an IPv6 implementation

- Trumpet has an IPv6 Winsock implementation for testing; find more
  information at `http://www.trumpet.com.au/ipv6.htm`

- Microsoft Windows currently doesn't ship with an IPv6 implementation,
  but Microsoft Research has an alpha IPv6 stack; for more information, go
  to `http://www.research.microsoft.com/msripv6/`

- IBM OS/390 — more information is available at
  `http://www.software.ibm.com/network/commserver/downloads/demos/demo_csos390.html`

- Compaq Open VMS — find information at
  `http://www.digital.com/info/ipv6/host-implementation.html`

- Cisco has an IOS beta software program that supports IPv6; for more information, go to
  `http://www.cisco.com/warp/public/732/ipv6/index.html`

- Nortel Networks supports IPv6 in all routers with Version BayRS 12.0 and higher; a lot of IPv6 information can be found on its site at
  `http://www.nortelnetworks.com/`

This list might not be complete and I apologize to anyone not mentioned here. Regardless, this list will change a bit by the time you read this book. But, it is a starting point if you want to research.

Summary

This last chapter covered the main things to learn about IPv6. It looked at the header format and examined the new extension headers. You learned the IPv6 addressing rules and found out about autoconfiguration of IPv6 hosts, whether it be stateful or stateless. This chapter also gave some information about changes that have to be made to other protocols in order to adapt to IPv6. This chapter provides an outlook on a new protocol—one whose final arrival time in corporate networks is still uncertain. Time will tell.

Hex-Decimal-Binary Conversion Chart

HEX-DECIMAL-BINARY CONVERSION CHART

TABLE A.I

Hex-Decimal-Binary Conversion Chart

DECIMAL VALUE	HEXADECIMAL VALUE	BINARY VALUE	DECIMAL VALUE	HEXADECIMAL VALUE	BINARY VALUE
0	0	00000000	26	1a	00011010
1	1	00000001	27	1b	00011011
2	2	00000010	28	1c	00011100
3	3	00000011	29	1d	00011101
4	4	00000100	30	1e	00011110
5	5	00000101	31	1f	00011111
6	6	00000110	32	20	00100000
7	7	00000111	33	21	00100001
8	8	00001000	34	22	00100010
9	9	00001001	35	23	00100011
10	a	00001010	36	24	00100100
11	b	00001011	37	25	00100101
12	c	00001100	38	26	00100110
13	d	00001101	39	27	00100111
14	e	00001110	40	28	00101000
15	f	00001111	41	29	00101001
16	10	00010000	42	2a	00101010
17	11	00010001	43	2b	00101011
18	12	00010010	44	2c	00101100
19	13	00010011	45	2d	00101101
20	14	00010100	46	2e	00101110
21	15	00010101	47	2f	00101111
22	16	00010110	48	30	00110000
23	17	00010111	49	31	00110001
24	18	00011000	50	32	00110010
25	19	00011001	51	33	00110011

DECIMAL VALUE	HEXADECIMAL VALUE	BINARY VALUE	DECIMAL VALUE	HEXADECIMAL VALUE	BINARY VALUE
52	34	00110100	78	4e	01001110
53	35	00110101	79	4f	01001111
54	36	00110110	80	50	01010000
55	37	00110111	81	51	01010001
56	38	00111000	82	52	01010010
57	39	00111001	83	53	01010011
58	3a	00111010	84	54	01010100
59	3b	00111011	85	55	01010101
60	3c	00111100	86	56	01010110
61	3d	00111101	87	57	01010111
62	3e	00111110	88	58	01011000
63	3f	00111111	89	59	01011001
64	40	01000000	90	5a	01011010
65	41	01000001	91	5b	01011011
66	42	01000010	92	5c	01011100
67	43	01000011	93	5d	01011101
68	44	01000100	94	5e	01011110
69	45	01000101	95	5f	01011111
70	46	01000110	96	60	01100000
71	47	01000111	97	61	01100001
72	48	01001000	98	62	01100010
73	49	01001001	99	63	01100011
74	4a	01001010	100	64	01100100
75	4b	01001011	101	65	01100101
76	4c	01001100	102	66	01100110
77	4d	01001101	103	67	01100111

Continued

HEX-DECIMAL-BINARY CONVERSION CHART

T A B L E A.1

Hex-Decimal-Binary Conversion Chart (continued)

DECIMAL VALUE	HEXADECIMAL VALUE	BINARY VALUE	DECIMAL VALUE	HEXADECIMAL VALUE	BINARY VALUE
104	68	01101000	130	82	10000010
105	69	01101001	131	83	10000011
106	6a	01101010	132	84	10000100
107	6b	01101011	133	85	10000101
108	6c	01101100	134	86	10000110
109	6d	01101101	135	87	10000111
110	6e	01101110	136	88	10001000
111	6f	01101111	137	89	10001001
112	70	01110000	138	8a	10001010
113	71	01110001	139	8b	10001011
114	72	01110010	140	8c	10001100
115	73	01110011	141	8d	10001101
116	74	01110100	142	8e	10001110
117	75	01110101	143	8f	10001111
118	76	01110110	144	90	10010000
119	77	01110111	145	91	10010001
120	78	01111000	146	92	10010010
121	79	01111001	147	93	10010011
122	7a	01111010	148	94	10010100
123	7b	01111011	149	95	10010101
124	7c	01111100	150	96	10010110
125	7d	01111101	151	97	10010111
126	7e	01111110	152	98	10011000
127	7f	01111111	153	99	10011001
128	80	10000000	154	9a	10011010
129	81	10000001	155	9b	10011011

DECIMAL VALUE	HEXADECIMAL VALUE	BINARY VALUE	DECIMAL VALUE	HEXADECIMAL VALUE	BINARY VALUE
156	9c	10011100	182	b6	10110110
157	9d	10011101	183	b7	10110111
158	9e	10011110	184	b8	10111000
159	9f	10011111	185	b9	10111001
160	a0	10100000	186	ba	10111010
161	a1	10100001	187	bb	10111011
162	a2	10100010	188	bc	10111100
163	a3	10100011	189	bd	10111101
164	a4	10100100	190	be	10111110
165	a5	10100101	191	bf	10111111
166	a6	10100110	192	c0	11000000
167	a7	10100111	193	c1	11000001
168	a8	10101000	194	c2	11000010
169	a9	10101001	195	c3	11000011
170	aa	10101010	196	c4	11000100
171	ab	10101011	197	c5	11000101
172	ac	10101100	198	c6	11000110
173	ad	10101101	199	c7	11000111
174	ae	10101110	200	c8	11001000
175	af	10101111	201	c9	11001001
176	b0	10110000	202	ca	11001010
177	b1	10110001	203	cb	11001011
178	b2	10110010	204	cc	11001100
179	b3	10110011	205	cd	11001101
180	b4	10110100	206	ce	11001110
181	b5	10110101	207	cf	11001111

Continued

TABLE A.1

Hex-Decimal-Binary Conversion Chart (continued)

DECIMAL VALUE	HEXADECIMAL VALUE	BINARY VALUE	DECIMAL VALUE	HEXADECIMAL VALUE	BINARY VALUE
208	d0	11010000	232	e8	11101000
209	d1	11010001	233	e9	11101001
210	d2	11010010	234	ea	11101010
211	d3	11010011	235	eb	11101011
212	d4	11010100	236	ec	11101100
213	d5	11010101	237	ed	11101101
214	d6	11010110	238	ee	11101110
215	d7	11010111	239	ef	11101111
216	d8	11011000	240	f0	11110000
217	d9	11011001	241	f1	11110001
218	da	11011010	242	f2	11110010
219	db	11011011	243	f3	11110011
220	dc	11011100	244	f4	11110100
221	dd	11011101	245	f5	11110101
222	de	11011110	246	f6	11110110
223	df	11011111	247	f7	11110111
224	e0	11100000	248	f8	11111000
225	e1	11100001	249	f9	11111001
226	e2	11100010	250	fa	11111010
227	e3	11100011	251	fb	11111011
228	e4	11100100	252	fc	11111100
229	e5	11100101	253	fd	11111101
230	e6	11100110	254	fe	11111110
231	e7	11100111	255	ff	11111111

IP Addressing
Rules/RFC 1878

Table B.1 lists the variable length subnets from 1 to 32, the CIDR representation form (/x), and the decimal equivalents (M = Million, K = Thousand, and A, B, and C = traditional class values). The first three columns list the mask values in hex, CIDR, and decimal form.

TABLE B.I

Variable Length Subnets for IPv4

HEX	CIDR	DECIMAL	NUMBER OF ADDRESSES	CLASS
80.00.00.00	/1	128.0.0.0	2048M	128 A
C0.00.00.00	/2	192.0.0.0	1024M	64 A
E0.00.00.00	/3	224.0.0.0	512M	32 A
F0.00.00.00	/4	240.0.0.0	256M	16 A
F8.00.00.00	/5	248.0.0.0	128M	8 A
FC.00.00.00	/6	252.0.0.0	64M	4 A
FE.00.00.00	/7	254.0.0.0	32M	2 A
FF.00.00.00	/8	255.0.0.0	16M	1 A
FF.80.00.00	/9	255.128.0.0	8M	128 B
FF.C0.00.00	/10	255.192.0.0	4M	64 B
FF.E0.00.00	/11	255.224.0.0	2M	32 B
FF.F0.00.00	/12	255.240.0.	1024K	16 B
FF.F8.00.00	/13	255.248.0.0	512K	8 B
FF.FC.00.00	/14	255.252.0.0	256K	4 B
FF.FE.00.00	/15	255.254.0.0	128K	2 B
FF.FF.00.00	/16	255.255.0.0	64K	1 B
FF.FF.80.00	/17	255.255.128.0	32K	128 C
FF.FF.C0.00	/18	255.255.192.0	16K	64 C
FF.FF.E0.00	/19	255.255.224.0	8K	32 C
FF.FF.F0.00	/20	255.255.240.0	4K	16 C
FF.FF.F8.00	/21	255.255.248.0	2K	8 C
FF.FF.FC.00	/22	255.255.252.0	1K	4 C

HEX	CIDR	DECIMAL	NUMBER OF ADDRESSES	CLASS
FF.FF.FE.00	/23	255.255.254.0	512	2 C
FF.FF.FF.00	/24	255.255.255.0	256	1 C
FF.FF.FF.80	/25	255.255.255.128	128	1/2 C
FF.FF.FF.C0	/26	255.255.255.192	64	1/4 C
FF.FF.FF.E0	/27	255.255.255.224	32	1/8 C
FF.FF.FF.F0	/28	255.255.255.240	16	1/16 C
FF.FF.FF.F8	/29	255.255.255.248	8	1/32 C
FF.FF.FF.FC	/30	255.255.255.252	4	1/64 C
FF.FF.FF.FE	/31	255.255.255.254	2	1/128 C
FF.FF.FF.FF	/32	255.255.255.255	Single host route	

The number of available network and host addresses is derived from the number of bits used for subnet masking. The tables that follow depict the number of subnetting bits and the resulting network, broadcast address, and host addresses. Note that all-zero and all-one subnets are included in Tables B.2 and B.3 per the current standards-based practice for using all definable subnets.

Table B.2 represents traditional subnetting of a Class B network address.

Table B.3 represents traditional subnetting of a Class C network address (which is identical to extended Class B subnets).

TABLE B.2

Subnetting of a Class B Network Address

SUBNET MASK (BITS OF SUBNET HOSTS/SUBNET)	NUMBER OF NETS	NETWORK ADDRESS	HOST ADDRESS RANGE	BROADCAST ADDRESS
255.255.128.0	2 nets	N.N.0.0	N.N.0–127.N	N.N.127.255
1 bit subnet/32766		N.N.128.0	N.N.128–254.N	N.N.254.255
255.255.192.0	4 nets	N.N.0.0	N.N.0–63.N	N.N.63.255
2 bit subnet/16382		N.N.64.0	N.N.64–127.N	N.N.127.255
		N.N.128.0	N.N.128–191.N	N.N.191.255
		N.N.192.0	N.N.192–254.N	N.N.254.255
255.255.224.0	8 nets	N.N.0.0	N.N.0–31.N	N.N.31.255
3 bit subnet/8190		N.N.32.0	N.N.32–63.N	N.N.63.255
		N.N.64.0	N.N.64–95.N	N.N.95.255
		N.N.96.0	N.N.96–127.N	N.N.127.255
		N.N.128.0	N.N.128–159.N	N.N.159.255
		N.N.160.0	N.N.160–191.N	N.N.191.255
		N.N.192.0	N.N.192–223.N	N.N.223.255
		N.N.224.0	N.N.224–254.N	N.N.254.255
255.255.240.0	16 nets	N.N.0.0	N.N.0–15.N	N.N.15.255
4 bit subnet/4094		N.N.16.0	N.N.16–31.N	N.N.31.255
		N.N.32.0	N.N.32–47.N	N.N.47.255
		N.N.48.0	N.N.48–63.N	N.N.63.255

SUBNET MASK (BITS OF SUBNET HOSTS/SUBNET)	NUMBER OF NETS	NETWORK ADDRESS	HOST ADDRESS RANGE	BROADCAST ADDRESS
		N.N.64.0	N.N.64–79.N	N.N.79.255
		N.N.80.0	N.N.80–95.N	N.N.95.255
		N.N.96.0	N.N.96–111.N	N.N.111.255
		N.N.112.0	N.N.112–127.N	N.N.127.255
		N.N.128.0	N.N.128–143.N	N.N.143.255
		N.N.144.0	N.N.144–159.N	N.N.159.255
		N.N.160.0	N.N.160–175.N	N.N.175.255
		N.N.176.0	N.N.176–191.N	N.N.191.255
		N.N.192.0	N.N.192–207.N	N.N.207.255
		N.N.208.0	N.N.208–223.N	N.N.223.255
		N.N.224.0	N.N.224–239.N	N.N.239.255
		N.N.240.0	N.N.240–254.N	N.N.254.255
255.255.248.0	32 nets	N.N.0.0	N.N.0–7.N	N.N.7.255
5 bit subnet/2046		N.N.8.0	N.N.8–15.N	N.N.15.255
		N.N.16.0	N.N.16–23.N	N.N.23.255
		N.N.24.0	N.N.24–31.N	N.N.31.255
		N.N.32.0	N.N.32–39.N	N.N.39.255
		N.N.40.0	N.N.40–47.N	N.N.47.255

Continued

TABLE B.2

Subnetting of a Class B Network Address *(continued)*

SUBNET MASK (BITS OF SUBNET HOSTS/SUBNET)	NUMBER OF NETS	NETWORK ADDRESS	HOST ADDRESS RANGE	BROADCAST ADDRESS
		N.N.48.0	N.N.48–55.N	N.N.55.255
		N.N.56.0	N.N.56–63.N	N.N.63.255
		N.N.64.0	N.N.64–71.N	N.N.71.255
		N.N.72.0	N.N.72–79.N	N.N.79.255
		N.N.80.0	N.N.80–87.N	N.N.87.255
		N.N.88.0	N.N.88–95.N	N.N.95.255
		N.N.96.0	N.N.96–103.N	N.N.103.255
		N.N.104.0	N.N.104–111.N	N.N.111.255
		N.N.112.0	N.N.112–119.N	N.N.119.255
		N.N.120.0	N.N.120–127.N	N.N.127.255
		N.N.128.0	N.N.128–135.N	N.N.135.255
		N.N.136.0	N.N.136–143.N	N.N.143.255
		N.N.144.0	N.N.144–151.N	N.N.151.255
		N.N.152.0	N.N.152–159.N	N.N.159.255
		N.N.160.0	N.N.160–167.N	N.N.167.255
		N.N.168.0	N.N.168–175.N	N.N.175.255
		N.N.176.0	N.N.176–183.N	N.N.183.255
		N.N.184.0	N.N.184–191.N	N.N.191.255

SUBNET MASK (BITS OF SUBNET HOSTS/SUBNET)	NUMBER OF NETS	NETWORK ADDRESS	HOST ADDRESS RANGE	BROADCAST ADDRESS
		N.N.192.0	N.N.192–199.N	N.N.199.255
		N.N.200.0	N.N.200–207.N	N.N.207.255
		N.N.208.0	N.N.208–215.N	N.N.215.255
		N.N.216.0	N.N.216–223.N	N.N.223.255
		N.N.224.0	N.N.224–231.N	N.N.231.255
		N.N.232.0	N.N.232–239.N	N.N.239.255
		N.N.240.0	N.N.240–247.N	N.N.247.255
		N.N.248.0	N.N.248–254.N	N.N.254.255
255.255.252.0	64 nets	N.N.0.0	N.N.0–3.N	N.N.3.255
6 bit subnet/1022		N.N.4.0	N.N.4–7.N	N.N.7.255
		N.N.8.0	N.N.8–11.N	N.N.11.255
		N.N.12.0	N.N.12–15.N	N.N.15.255
		N.N.240.0	N.N.240–243.N	N.N.243.255
		N.N.244.0	N.N.244–247.N	N.N.247.255
		N.N.248.0	N.N.248–251.N	N.N.251.255
		N.N.252.0	N.N.252–254.N	N.N.254.255
255.255.254.0	128 nets	N.N.0.0	N.N.0–1.N	N.N.1.255
7 bit subnet/510		N.N.2.0	N.N.2–3.N	N.N.3.255

Continued

T A B L E B . 2

Subnetting of a Class B Network Address (continued)

SUBNET MASK (BITS OF SUBNET HOSTS/SUBNET)	NUMBER OF NETS	NETWORK ADDRESS	HOST ADDRESS RANGE	BROADCAST ADDRESS
		N.N.4.0	N.N.4–5.N	N.N.5.255
		N.N.250.0	N.N.250–251.N	N.N.251.255
		N.N.252.0	N.N.252–253.N	N.N.253.255
		N.N.254.0	N.N.254.N	N.N.254.255
255.255.255.0	255 nets	N.N.0.0	N.N.0.N	N.N.0.255
8 bit subnet/253		N.N.1.0	N.N.1.N	N.N.1.255
		N.N.252.0	N.N.252.N	N.N.252.255
		N.N.253.0	N.N.253.N	N.N.253.255
		N.N.254.0	N.N.254.N	N.N.254.255

T A B L E   B . 3

Subnetting of a Class C Network Address

SUBNET MASK (BITS OF SUBNET HOSTS/SUBNET)	NUMBER OF NETS	NETWORK ADDRESS	HOST ADDRESS RANGE	BROADCAST ADDRESS
255.255.255.128	2 nets	N.N.N.0	N.N.N.1–126	N.N.N.127
1 bit Class C/126		N.N.N.128	N.N.N.129–254	N.N.N.255
9 bit Class B				
255.255.255.192	4 nets	N.N.N.0	N.N.N.1–62	N.N.N.63
2 bit Class C/62		N.N.N.64	N.N.N.65–126	N.N.N.127
10 bit Class B		N.N.N.128	N.N.N.129–190	N.N.N.191
		N.N.N.192	N.N.N.193–254	N.N.N.255
255.255.255.224	8 nets	N.N.N.0	N.N.N.1–30	N.N.N.31
3 bit Class C/30		N.N.N.32	N.N.N.33–62	N.N.N.63
11 bit Class B		N.N.N.64	N.N.N.65–94	N.N.N.95
		N.N.N.96	N.N.N.97–126	N.N.N.127
		N.N.N.128	N.N.N.129–158	N.N.N.159
		N.N.N.160	N.N.N.161–190	N.N.N.191
		N.N.N.192	N.N.N.193–222	N.N.N.223
		N.N.N.224	N.N.N.225–254	N.N.N.255
255.255.255.240	16 nets	N.N.N.0	N.N.N.1–14	N.N.N.15
4 bit Class C/14		N.N.N.16	N.N.N.17–30	N.N.N.31
12 bit Class B		N.N.N.32	N.N.N.33–46	N.N.N.47
		N.N.N.48	N.N.N.49–62	N.N.N.63

Continued

T A B L E B.3

Subnetting of a Class C Network Address (continued)

SUBNET MASK (BITS OF SUBNET HOSTS/SUBNET)	NUMBER OF NETS	NETWORK ADDRESS	HOST ADDRESS RANGE	BROADCAST ADDRESS
		N.N.N.64	N.N.N.65–78	N.N.N.79
		N.N.N.80	N.N.N.81–94	N.N.N.95
		N.N.N.96	N.N.N.97–110	N.N.N.111
		N.N.N.112	N.N.N.113–126	N.N.N.127
		N.N.N.128	N.N.N.129–142	N.N.N.143
		N.N.N.144	N.N.N.145–158	N.N.N.159
		N.N.N.160	N.N.N.161–174	N.N.N.175
		N.N.N.176	N.N.N.177–190	N.N.N.191
		N.N.N.192	N.N.N.193–206	N.N.N.207
		N.N.N.208	N.N.N.209–222	N.N.N.223
		N.N.N.224	N.N.N.225–238	N.N.N.239
		N.N.N.240	N.N.N.241–254	N.N.N.255
255.255.255.248	32 nets	N.N.N.0	N.N.N.1–6	N.N.N.7
5 bit Class C/6		N.N.N.8	N.N.N.9–14	N.N.N.15
13 bit Class B		N.N.N.16	N.N.N.17–22	N.N.N.23
		N.N.N.24	N.N.N.25–30	N.N.N.31
		N.N.N.32	N.N.N.33–38	N.N.N.39
		N.N.N.40	N.N.N.41–46	N.N.N.47
		N.N.N.48	N.N.N.49–54	N.N.N.55

SUBNET MASK (BITS OF SUBNET HOSTS/SUBNET)	NUMBER OF NETS	NETWORK ADDRESS	HOST ADDRESS RANGE	BROADCAST ADDRESS
		N.N.N.56	N.N.N.57–62	N.N.N.63
		N.N.N.64	N.N.N.65–70	N.N.N.71
		N.N.N.72	N.N.N.73–78	N.N.N.79
		N.N.N.80	N.N.N.81–86	N.N.N.87
		N.N.N.88	N.N.N.89–94	N.N.N.95
		N.N.N.96	N.N.N.97–102	N.N.N.103
		N.N.N.104	N.N.N.105–110	N.N.N.111
		N.N.N.112	N.N.N.113–118	N.N.N.119
		N.N.N.120	N.N.N.121–126	N.N.N.127
		N.N.N.128	N.N.N.129–134	N.N.N.135
		N.N.N.136	N.N.N.137–142	N.N.N.143
		N.N.N.144	N.N.N.145–150	N.N.N.151
		N.N.N.152	N.N.N.153–158	N.N.N.159
		N.N.N.160	N.N.N.161–166	N.N.N.167
		N.N.N.168	N.N.N.169–174	N.N.N.175
		N.N.N.176	N.N.N.177–182	N.N.N.183
		N.N.N.184	N.N.N.185–190	N.N.N.191
		N.N.N.192	N.N.N.193–198	N.N.N.199
		N.N.N.200	N.N.N.201–206	N.N.N.207

Continued

TABLE B.3

Subnetting of a Class C Network Address (continued)

SUBNET MASK (BITS OF SUBNET HOSTS/SUBNET)	NUMBER OF NETS	NETWORK ADDRESS	HOST ADDRESS RANGE	BROADCAST ADDRESS
		N.N.N.208	N.N.N.209–214	N.N.N.215
		N.N.N.216	N.N.N.217–222	N.N.N.223
		N.N.N.224	N.N.N.225–230	N.N.N.231
		N.N.N.232	N.N.N.233–238	N.N.N.239
		N.N.N.240	N.N.N.241–246	N.N.N.247
		N.N.N.248	N.N.N.249–254	N.N.N.255
255.255.255.252	64 nets	N.N.N.0	N.N.N.1–2	N.N.N.3
6 bit Class C/2		N.N.N.4	N.N.N.5–6	N.N.N.7
14 bit Class B		N.N.N.8	N.N.N.9–10	N.N.N.11
		N.N.N.244	N.N.N.245–246	N.N.N.247
		N.N.N.248	N.N.N.249–250	N.N.N.251
		N.N.N.252	N.N.N.253–254	N.N.N.255

UDP/TCP Well-Known Port List

The Well-Known Ports are those from 0 through 1023. The Registered Ports are those from 1024 through 49151. The Dynamic and/or Private Ports are those from 49152 through 65535. Table C.1 lists only the Well-Known Ports due to space limitations.

TABLE C.1
UDP/TCP Well-Known Port List

KEYWORD	DECIMAL	DESCRIPTION	REFERENCES
	0/tcp	Reserved	
	0/udp	Reserved	
tcpmux	1/tcp	TCP Port Service Multiplexer	
tcpmux	1/udp	TCP Port Service Multiplexer	
compressnet	2/tcp	Management Utility	
compressnet	2/udp	Management Utility	
compressnet	3/tcp	Compression Process	
compressnet	3/udp	Compression Process	
#	4/tcp	Unassigned	
#	4/udp	Unassigned	
rje	5/tcp	Remote Job Entry	
rje	5/udp	Remote Job Entry	
#	6/tcp	Unassigned	
#	6/udp	Unassigned	
echo	7/tcp	Echo	
echo	7/udp	Echo	
#	8/tcp	Unassigned	
#	8/udp	Unassigned	
discard	9/tcp	Discard	
discard	9/udp	Discard	
#	10/tcp	Unassigned	
#	10/udp	Unassigned	

KEYWORD	DECIMAL	DESCRIPTION	REFERENCES
systat	11/tcp	Active Users	
systat	11/udp	Active Users	
#	12/tcp	Unassigned	
#	12/udp	Unassigned	
daytime	13/tcp	Daytime	[RFC 867]
daytime	13/udp	Daytime	[RFC 867]
#	14/tcp	Unassigned	
#	14/udp	Unassigned	
#	15/tcp	Unassigned (was netstat)	
#	15/udp	Unassigned	
#	16/tcp	Unassigned	
#	16/udp	Unassigned	
qotd	17/tcp	Quote of the Day	
qotd	17/udp	Quote of the Day	
msp	18/tcp	Message Send Protocol	
msp	18/udp	Message Send Protocol	
chargen	19/tcp	Character Generator	
chargen	19/udp	Character Generator	
ftp-data	20/tcp	File Transfer (Default Data)	
ftp-data	20/udp	File Transfer (Default Data)	
ftp	21/tcp	File Transfer (Control)	
ftp	21/udp	File Transfer (Control)	
ssh	22/tcp	SSH Remote Login Protocol	
ssh	22/udp	SSH Remote Login Protocol	
telnet	23/tcp	Telnet	
telnet	23/udp	Telnet	
	24/tcp	any private mail system	
	24/udp	any private mail system	

Continued

UDP/TCP WELL-KNOWN PORT LIST

T A B L E C . I

UDP/TCP Well-Known Port List (continued)

KEYWORD	DECIMAL	DESCRIPTION	REFERENCES
smtp	25/tcp	Simple Mail Transfer	
smtp	25/udp	Simple Mail Transfer	
#	26/tcp	Unassigned	
#	26/udp	Unassigned	
nsw-fe	27/tcp	NSW User System FE	
nsw-fe	27/udp	NSW User System FE	
#	28/tcp	Unassigned	
#	28/udp	Unassigned	
msg-icp	29/tcp	MSG ICP	
msg-icp	29/udp	MSG ICP	
#	30/tcp	Unassigned	
#	30/udp	Unassigned	
msg-auth	31/tcp	MSG Authentication	
msg-auth	31/udp	MSG Authentication	
#	32/tcp	Unassigned	
#	32/udp	Unassigned	
dsp	33/tcp	Display Support Protocol	
dsp	33/udp	Display Support Protocol	
#	34/tcp	Unassigned	
#	34/udp	Unassigned	
	35/tcp	any private printer server	
	35/udp	any private printer server	
#	36/tcp	Unassigned	
#	36/udp	Unassigned	
time	37/tcp	Time	
time	37/udp	Time	
rap	38/tcp	Route Access Protocol	

KEYWORD	DECIMAL	DESCRIPTION	REFERENCES
rap	38/udp	Route Access Protocol	
rlp	39/tcp	Resource Location Protocol	
rlp	39/udp	Resource Location Protocol	
#	40/tcp	Unassigned	
#	40/udp	Unassigned	
graphics	41/tcp	Graphics	
graphics	41/udp	Graphics	
name	42/tcp	Host Name Server	
name	42/udp	Host Name Server	
nameserver	42/tcp	Host Name Server	
nameserver	42/udp	Host Name Server	
nicname	43/tcp	Who Is	
nicname	43/udp	Who Is	
mpm-flags	44/tcp	MPM FLAGS Protocol	
mpm-flags	44/udp	MPM FLAGS Protocol	
mpm	45/tcp	Message Processing Module (recv)	
mpm	45/udp	Message Processing Module (recv)	
mpm-snd	46/tcp	MPM (default send)	
mpm-snd	46/udp	MPM (default send)	
ni-ftp	47/tcp	NI FTP	
ni-ftp	47/udp	NI FTP	
auditd	48/tcp	Digital Audit Daemon	
auditd	48/udp	Digital Audit Daemon	
tacacs	49/tcp	Login Host Protocol (TACACS)	
tacacs	49/udp	Login Host Protocol (TACACS)	
re-mail-ck	50/tcp	Remote Mail Checking Protocol	
re-mail-ck	50/udp	Remote Mail Checking Protocol	
la-maint	51/tcp	IMP Logical Address Maintenance	

Continued

TABLE C.1

UDP/TCP Well-Known Port List (continued)

KEYWORD	DECIMAL	DESCRIPTION	REFERENCES
la-maint	51/udp	IMP Logical Address Maintenance	
xns-time	52/tcp	XNS Time Protocol	
xns-time	52/udp	XNS Time Protocol	
domain	53/tcp	Domain Name Server	
domain	53/udp	Domain Name Server	
xns-ch	54/tcp	XNS Clearinghouse	
xns-ch	54/udp	XNS Clearinghouse	
isi-gl	55/tcp	ISI Graphics Language	
isi-gl	55/udp	ISI Graphics Language	
xns-auth	56/tcp	XNS Authentication	
xns-auth	56/udp	XNS Authentication	
	57/tcp	any private terminal access	
	57/udp	any private terminal access	
xns-mail	58/tcp	XNS Mail	
xns-mail	58/udp	XNS Mail	
	59/tcp	any private file service	
	59/udp	any private file service	
	60/tcp	Unassigned	
	60/udp	Unassigned	
ni-mail	61/tcp	NI MAIL	
ni-mail	61/udp	NI MAIL	
acas	62/tcp	ACA Services	
acas	62/udp	ACA Services	
whois++	63/tcp	whois++	
whois++	63/udp	whois++	
covia	64/tcp	Communications Integrator (CI)	
covia	64/udp	Communications Integrator (CI)	

KEYWORD	DECIMAL	DESCRIPTION	REFERENCES
tacacs-ds	65/tcp	TACACS-Database Service	
tacacs-ds	65/udp	TACACS-Database Service	
sql*net	66/tcp	Oracle SQL*NET	
sql*net	66/udp	Oracle SQL*NET	
bootps	67/tcp	Bootstrap Protocol Server	
bootps	67/udp	Bootstrap Protocol Server	
bootpc	68/tcp	Bootstrap Protocol Client	
bootpc	68/udp	Bootstrap Protocol Client	
tftp	69/tcp	Trivial File Transfer	
tftp	69/udp	Trivial File Transfer	
gopher	70/tcp	Gopher	
gopher	70/udp	Gopher	
netrjs-1	71/tcp	Remote Job Service	
netrjs-1	71/udp	Remote Job Service	
netrjs-2	72/tcp	Remote Job Service	
netrjs-2	72/udp	Remote Job Service	
netrjs-3	73/tcp	Remote Job Service	
netrjs-3	73/udp	Remote Job Service	
netrjs-4	74/tcp	Remote Job Service	
netrjs-4	74/udp	Remote Job Service	
	75/tcp	any private dial out service	
	75/udp	any private dial out service	
deos	76/tcp	Distributed External Object Store	
deos	76/udp	Distributed External Object Store	
	77/tcp	any private RJE service	
	77/udp	any private RJE service	
vettcp	78/tcp	vettcp	
vettcp	78/udp	vettcp	

Continued

UDP/TCP Well-Known Port List (continued)

KEYWORD	DECIMAL	DESCRIPTION	REFERENCES
finger	79/tcp	Finger	
finger	79/udp	Finger	
http	80/tcp	World Wide Web HTTP	
http	80/udp	World Wide Web HTTP	
www	80/tcp	World Wide Web HTTP	
www	80/udp	World Wide Web HTTP	
www-http	80/tcp	World Wide Web HTTP	
www-http	80/udp	World Wide Web HTTP	
hosts2-ns	81/tcp	HOSTS2 Name Server	
hosts2-ns	81/udp	HOSTS2 Name Server	
xfer	82/tcp	XFER Utility	
xfer	82/udp	XFER Utility	
mit-ml-dev	83/tcp	MIT ML Device	
mit-ml-dev	83/udp	MIT ML Device	
ctf	84/tcp	Common Trace Facility	
ctf	84/udp	Common Trace Facility	
mit-ml-dev	85/tcp	MIT ML Device	
mit-ml-dev	85/udp	MIT ML Device	
mfcobol	86/tcp	Micro Focus Cobol	
mfcobol	86/udp	Micro Focus Cobol	
	87/tcp	any private terminal link	
	87/udp	any private terminal link	
kerberos	88/tcp	Kerberos	
kerberos	88/udp	Kerberos	
su-mit-tg	89/tcp	SU/MIT Telnet Gateway	
su-mit-tg	89/udp	SU/MIT Telnet Gateway	

Port 90 also being used unofficially by Pointcast

· · · · ·

KEYWORD	DECIMAL	DESCRIPTION	REFERENCES
dnsix	90/tcp	DNSIX Securit Attribute Token Map	
dnsix	90/udp	DNSIX Securit Attribute Token Map	
mit-dov	91/tcp	MIT Dover Spooler	
mit-dov	91/udp	MIT Dover Spooler	
npp	92/tcp	Network Printing Protocol	
npp	92/udp	Network Printing Protocol	
dcp	93/tcp	Device Control Protocol	
dcp	93/udp	Device Control Protocol	
objcall	94/tcp	Tivoli Object Dispatcher	
objcall	94/udp	Tivoli Object Dispatcher	
supdup	95/tcp	SUPDUP	
supdup	95/udp	SUPDUP	
dixie	96/tcp	DIXIE Protocol Specification	
dixie	96/udp	DIXIE Protocol Specification	
swift-rvf	97/tcp	Swift Remote Virtural File Protocol	
swift-rvf	97/udp	Swift Remote Virtural File Protocol	
tacnews	98/tcp	TAC News	
tacnews	98/udp	TAC News	
metagram	99/tcp	Metagram Relay	
metagram	99/udp	Metagram Relay	
newacct	100/tcp	(unauthorized use)	
hostname	101/tcp	NIC Host Name Server	
hostname	101/udp	NIC Host Name Server	
iso-tsap	102/tcp	ISO-TSAP Class 0	
iso-tsap	102/udp	ISO-TSAP Class 0	
gppitnp	103/tcp	Genesis Point-to-Point Trans Net	
gppitnp	103/udp	Genesis Point-to-Point Trans Net	

Continued

T A B L E C . I

UDP/TCP Well-Known Port List (continued)

KEYWORD	DECIMAL	DESCRIPTION	REFERENCES
acr-nema	104/tcp	ACR-NEMA Digital Imag. & Comm. 300	
acr-nema	104/udp	ACR-NEMA Digital Imag. & Comm. 300	
cso	105/tcp	CCSO name server protocol	
cso	105/udp	CCSO name server protocol	
csnet-ns	105/tcp	Mailbox Name Nameserver	
csnet-ns	105/udp	Mailbox Name Nameserver	
3com-tsmux	106/tcp	3COM-TSMUX	
3com-tsmux	106/udp	3COM-TSMUX	
rtelnet	107/tcp	Remote Telnet Service	
rtelnet	107/udp	Remote Telnet Service	
snagas	108/tcp	SNA Gateway Access Server	
snagas	108/udp	SNA Gateway Access Server	
pop2	109/tcp	Post Office Protocol — Version 2	
pop2	109/udp	Post Office Protocol — Version 2	
pop3	110/tcp	Post Office Protocol — Version 3	
pop3	110/udp	Post Office Protocol — Version 3	
sunrpc	111/tcp	SUN Remote Procedure Call	
sunrpc	111/udp	SUN Remote Procedure Call	
mcidas	112/tcp	McIDAS Data Transmission Protocol	
mcidas	112/udp	McIDAS Data Transmission Protocol	
ident	113/tcp		
auth	113/tcp	Authentication Service	
auth	113/udp	Authentication Service	
audionews	114/tcp	Audio News Multicast	
audionews	114/udp	Audio News Multicast	
sftp	115/tcp	Simple File Transfer Protocol	

KEYWORD	DECIMAL	DESCRIPTION	REFERENCES
sftp	115/udp	Simple File Transfer Protocol	
ansanotify	116/tcp	ANSA REX Notify	
ansanotify	116/udp	ANSA REX Notify	
uucp-path	117/tcp	UUCP Path Service	
uucp-path	117/udp	UUCP Path Service	
sqlserv	118/tcp	SQL Services	
sqlserv	118/udp	SQL Services	
nntp	119/tcp	Network News Transfer Protocol	
nntp	119/udp	Network News Transfer Protocol	
cfdptkt	120/tcp	CFDPTKT	
cfdptkt	120/udp	CFDPTKT	
erpc	121/tcp	Encore Expedited Remote Pro.Call	
erpc	121/udp	Encore Expedited Remote Pro.Call	
smakynet	122/tcp	SMAKYNET	
smakynet	122/udp	SMAKYNET	
ntp	123/tcp	Network Time Protocol	
ntp	123/udp	Network Time Protocol	
ansatrader	124/tcp	ANSA REX Trader	
ansatrader	124/udp	ANSA REX Trader	
locus-map	125/tcp	Locus PC-Interface Net Map Ser	
locus-map	125/udp	Locus PC-Interface Net Map Ser	
nxedit	126/tcp	NXEdit	
nxedit	126/udp	NXEdit	
#unitary	126/tcp	Unisys Unitary Login	
#unitary	126/udp	Unisys Unitary Login	
locus-con	127/tcp	Locus PC-Interface Conn Server	
locus-con	127/udp	Locus PC-Interface Conn Server	
gss-xlicen	128/tcp	GSS X License Verification	

Continued

TABLE C.I

UDP/TCP Well-Known Port List (continued)

KEYWORD	DECIMAL	DESCRIPTION	REFERENCES
gss-xlicen	128/udp	GSS X License Verification	
pwdgen	129/tcp	Password Generator Protocol	
pwdgen	129/udp	Password Generator Protocol	
cisco-fna	130/tcp	cisco FNATIVE	
cisco-fna	130/udp	cisco FNATIVE	
cisco-tna	131/tcp	cisco TNATIVE	
cisco-tna	131/udp	cisco TNATIVE	
cisco-sys	132/tcp	cisco SYSMAINT	
cisco-sys	132/udp	cisco SYSMAINT	
statsrv	133/tcp	Statistics Service	
statsrv	133/udp	Statistics Service	
ingres-net	134/tcp	INGRES-NET Service	
ingres-net	134/udp	INGRES-NET Service	
epmap	135/tcp	DCE endpoint resolution	
epmap	135/udp	DCE endpoint resolution	
profile	136/tcp	PROFILE Naming System	
profile	136/udp	PROFILE Naming System	
netbiosns	137/tcp	NETBIOS Name Service	
netbiosns	137/udp	NETBIOS Name Service	
netbiosdgm	138/tcp	NETBIOSDatagramService	
netbiosdgm	138/udp	NETBIOSDatagramService	
netbios-ssn	139/tcp	NETBIOSSessionService	
netbios-ssn	139/udp	NETBIOSSessionService	
emfisdata	140/tcp	EMFIS Data Service	
emfisdata	140/udp	EMFIS Data Service	
emfiscntl	141/tcp	EMFIS Control Service	
emfiscntl	141/udp	EMFIS Control Service	

KEYWORD	DECIMAL	DESCRIPTION	REFERENCES
bl-idm	142/tcp	Britton-Lee IDM	
bl-idm	142/udp	Britton-Lee IDM	
imap	143/tcp	Internet Message Access Protocol	
imap	143/udp	Internet Message Access Protocol	
uma	144/tcp	Universal Management Architecture	
uma	144/udp	Universal Management Architecture	
uaac	145/tcp	UAAC Protocol	
uaac	145/udp	UAAC Protocol	
iso-tp0	146/tcp	ISO-IP0	
iso-tp0	146/udp	ISO-IP0	
iso-ip	147/tcp	ISO-IP	
iso-ip	147/udp	ISO-IP	
jargon	148/tcp		
jargon	148/udp	Jargon	
aed-512	149/tcp	AED 512 Emulation Service	
aed-512	149/udp	AED 512 Emulation Service	
sql-net	150/tcp	SQL-NET	
sql-net	150/udp	SQL-NET	
hems	151/tcp	HEMS	
hems	151/udp	HEMS	
bftp	152/tcp	Background File Transfer Program	
bftp	152/udp	Background File Transfer Program	
sgmp	153/tcp	SGMP	
sgmp	153/udp	SGMP	
netsc-prod	154/tcp	NETSC	
netsc-prod	154/udp	NETSC	
netsc-dev	155/tcp	NETSC	
netsc-dev	155/udp	NETSC	

Continued

· · · · ·

UDP/TCP WELL-KNOWN PORT LIST

T A B L E C.I

UDP/TCP Well-Known Port List (continued)

KEYWORD	DECIMAL	DESCRIPTION	REFERENCES
sqlsrv	156/tcp	SQL Service	
sqlsrv	156/udp	SQL Service	
knet-cmp	157/tcp	KNET/VM Command/Message Protocol	
knet-cmp	157/udp	KNET/VM Command/Message Protocol	
pcmailsrv	158/tcp	PCMail Server	
pcmailsrv	158/udp	PCMail Server	
nssrouting	159/tcp	NSS-Routing	
nssrouting	159/udp	NSS-Routing	
sg-mptraps	160/tcp	SGMP-TRAPS	
sg-mptraps	160/udp	SGMP-TRAPS	
sn-mp	161/tcp	SNMP	
sn-mp	161/udp	SNMP	
sn-mptrap	162/tcp	SNMPTRAP	
sn-mptrap	162/udp	SNMPTRAP	
cmipman	163/tcp	CMIP/TCP Manager	
cmipman	163/udp	CMIP/TCP Manager	
cmipagent	164/tcp	CMIP/TCP Agent	
smipagent	164/udp	CMIP/TCP Agent	
xnscourier	165/tcp	Xerox	
xnscourier	165/udp	Xerox	
snet	166/tcp	Sirius Systems	
snet	166/udp	Sirius Systems	
namp	167/tcp	NAMP	
namp	167/udp	NAMP	
rsvd	168/tcp	RSVD	
rsvd	168/udp	RSVD	

KEYWORD	DECIMAL	DESCRIPTION	REFERENCES
send	169/tcp	SEND	
send	169/udp	SEND	
print-srv	170/tcp	Network PostScript	
print-srv	170/udp	Network PostScript	
multiplex	171/tcp	Network Innovations Multiplex	
multiplex	171/udp	Network Innovations Multiplex	
cl/1	172/tcp	Network Innovations CL/1	
cl/1	172/udp	Network Innovations CL/1	
xyplex-mux	173/tcp	Xyplex	
xyplex-mux	173/udp Xyplex		
mailq	174/tcp	MAILQ	
mailq	174/udp MAILQ		
vmnet	175/tcp	VMNET	
vmnet	175/udp VMNET		
genrad-mux	176/tcp	GENRAD-MUX	
genrad-mux	176/udp	GENRAD-MUX	
xdmcp	177/tcp	X Display Manager Control Protocol	
xdmcp	177/udp	X Display Manager Control Protocol	
nextstep	178/tcp	NextStep Window Server	
nextstep	178/udp	NextStep Window Server	
bgp	179/tcp	Border Gateway Protocol	
bgp	179/udp	Border Gateway Protocol	
ris	180/tcp	Intergraph	
ris	180/udp	Intergraph	

Continued

TABLE C.1

UDP/TCP Well-Known Port List (continued)

KEYWORD	DECIMAL	DESCRIPTION	REFERENCES
unify	181/tcp	Unify	
unify	181/udp	Unify	
audit	182/tcp	Unisys Audit SITP	
audit	182/udp	Unisys Audit SITP	
ocbinder	183/tcp	OCBinder	
ocbinder	183/udp	OCBinder	
ocserver	184/tcp	OCServer	
ocserver	184/udp	OCServer	
remote-kis	185/tcp	Remote-KIS	
remote-kis	185/udp	Remote-KIS	
kis	186/tcp	KIS Protocol	
kis	186/udp	KIS Protocol	
aci	187/tcp	Application Communication Interface	
aci	187/udp	Application Communication Interface	
mumps	188/tcp	Plus Five's MUMPS	
mumps	188/udp	Plus Five's MUMPS	
qft	189/tcp	QueuedFile Transport	
qft	189/udp	QueuedFile Transport	
gacp	190/tcp	Gateway Access Control Protocol	
gacp	190/udp	Gateway Access Control Protocol	
prospero	191/tcp	Prospero Directory Service	
prospero	191/udp	Prospero Directory Service	
osu-nms	192/tcp	OSU Network Monitoring System	
osu-nms	192/udp	OSU Network Monitoring System	
srmp	193/tcp	Spider Remote Monitoring Protocol	
srmp	193/udp	Spider Remote Monitoring Protocol	

KEYWORD	DECIMAL	DESCRIPTION	REFERENCES
irc	194/tcp	Internet Relay Chat Protocol	
irc	194/udp	Internet Relay Chat Protocol	
dn-6nlmaud	195/tcp	DNSIX Network Level Module Audit	
dn-6nlmaud	195/udp	DNSIX Network Level Module Audit	
dn-6smmred	196/tcp	DNSIX Session Mgt Module Audit Redir	
dn-6smmred	196/udp	DNSIX Session Mgt Module Audit Redir	
dls	197/tcp	Directory Location Service	
dls	197/udp	Directory Location Service	
dlsmon	198/tcp	DNSIX Network Level Module Audit	
dlsmon	198/udp	Directory Location Service Monitor	
smux	199/tcp	SMUX	
smux	199/udp	SMUX	
src	200/tcp	IBM System Resource Controller	
src	200/udp	IBM System Resource Controller	
at-rtmp	201/tcp	AppleTalk Routing Maintenance	
at-rtmp	201/udp	AppleTalk Routing Maintenance	
at-nbp	202/tcp	AppleTalk Name Binding	
at-nbp	202/udp	AppleTalk Name Binding	
at-3	203/tcp	AppleTalk Unused	
at-3	203/udp	AppleTalk Unused	
at-echo	204/tcp	AppleTalk Echo	
at-echo	204/udp	AppleTalk Echo	
at-5	205/tcp	AppleTalk Unused	
at-5	205/udp	AppleTalk Unused	

Continued

TABLE C.1

UDP/TCP Well-Known Port List (continued)

KEYWORD	DECIMAL	DESCRIPTION	REFERENCES
at-zis	206/tcp	AppleTalk Zone Information	
at-zis	206/udp	AppleTalk Zone Information	
at-7	207/tcp	AppleTalk Unused	
at-7	207/udp	AppleTalk Unused	
at-8	208/tcp	AppleTalk Unused	
at-8	208/udp	AppleTalk Unused	
qmtp	209/tcp	The Quick Mail Transfer Protocol	
qmtp	209/udp	The Quick Mail Transfer Protocol	
z39.50	210/tcp	ANSI Z39.50	
z39.50	210/udp	ANSI Z39.50	
914c/g	211/tcp	Texas Instruments 914C/G Terminal	
914c/g	211/udp	Texas Instruments 914C/G Terminal	
anet	212/tcp	ATEXSSTR	
anet	212/udp	ATEXSSTR	
ipx	213/tcp	IPX	
ipx	213/udp	IPX	
vmpwscs	214/tcp	VM PWSCS	
vmpwscs	214/udp	VM PWSCS	
softpc	215/tcp	Insignia Solutions	
softpc	215/udp	Insignia Solutions	
CAllic	216/tcp	Computer Associates Int'l License Server	
CAllic	216/udp	Computer Associates Int'l License Server	
Dbase	217/tcp	dBASE Unix	
Dbase	217/udp	dBASE Unix	
Mpp	218/tcp	Netix Message Posting Protocol	
Mpp	218/udp	Netix Message Posting Protocol	

· · · · ·

KEYWORD	DECIMAL	DESCRIPTION	REFERENCES
Uarps	219/tcp	Unisys ARPs	
Uarps	219/udp	Unisys ARPs	
imap3	220/tcp	Interactive Mail Access Protocol v3	
imap3	220/udp	Interactive Mail Access Protocol v3	
fln-spx	221/tcp	Berkeley rlogind with SPX auth	
fln-spx	221/udp	Berkeley rlogind with SPX auth	
rsh-spx	222/tcp	Berkeley rshd with SPX auth	
rshspx	222/udp	Berkeley rshd with SPX auth	
cdc	223/tcp	Certificate Distribution Center	
cdc	223/udp	Certificate Distribution Center	
masqdialer	224/tcp	masqdialer	
masqdialer	224/udp	masqdialer	
#	225-241	Reserved	
direct	242/tcp	Direct	
direct	242/udp	Direct	
sur-meas	243/tcp	Survey Measurement	
sur-meas	243/udp	Survey Measurement	
dayna	244/tcp	Dayna	
dayna	244/udp	Dayna	
link	45/tcp	LINK	
link	45/udp	LINK	
dsp3270	46/tcp	Display Systems Protocol	
dsp3270	246/udp	Display Systems Protocol	
subntbcst_tftp	247/tcp	SUBNTBCST_TFTP	
subntbcst_tftp	247/udp	SUBNTBCST_TFTP	
bhfhs	248/tcp	bhfhs	
bhfhs	248/udp	bhfhs	
#	249255	Reserved	

Continued

· · · ·

TABLE C.1

UDP/TCP Well-Known Port List (continued)

KEYWORD	DECIMAL	DESCRIPTION	REFERENCES
rap	256/tcp	RAP	
rap	256/udp	RAP	
set	257/tcp	Secure Electronic Transaction	
set	257/udp	Secure Electronic Transaction	
yak-chat	258/tcp	Yak Winsock Personal Chat	
yak-chat	258/udp	Yak Winsock Personal Chat	
esrogen	259/tcp	Efficient Short Remote Operations	
esrogen	259/udp	Efficient Short Remote Operations	
openport	260/tcp	Openport	
openport	260/udp	Openport	
nsiiops	261/tcp	IIOP Name Service over TLS/SSL	
nsiiops	261/udp	IIOP Name Service over TLS/SSL	
arcisdms	262/tcp	Arcisdms	
arcisdms	262/udp	Arcisdms	
hdap	263/tcp	HDAP	
hdap	263/udp	HDAP	
bgmp	264/tcp	BGMP	
bgmp	264/udp	BGMP	
#	265-279	Unassigned	
http-mgmt	280/tcp	httpmgmt	
http-mgmt	280/udp	http-mgmt	
personal-link	281/tcp	Personal Link	
personal-link	281/udp	Personal Link	
cable-portax	282/tcp	Cable Port A/X	
cable-portax	282/udp	Cable Port A/X	
#	283-307	Unassigned	
novastorbakcup	308/tcp	Novastor Backup	

KEYWORD	DECIMAL	DESCRIPTION	REFERENCES
novastorbakcup	308/udp	Novastor Backup	
entrusttime	309/tcp	EntrustTime	
entrusttime	309/udp	EntrustTime	
bhmds	310/tcp	bhmds	
bhmds	310/udp	bhmds	
asip-webadmin	311/tcp	AppleShare IP WebAdmin	
asip-webadmin	311/udp	AppleShare IP WebAdmin	
vslmp	312/tcp	VSLMP	
vslmp	312/udp	VSLMP	
magenta-logic	313/tcp	Magenta Logic	
magenta-logic	313/udp	Magenta Logic	
opalis-robot	314/tcp	Opalis Robot	
opalis-robot	314/udp	Opalis Robot	
dpsi	315/tcp	DPSI	
dpsi	315/udp	DPSI	
decauth	316/tcp	decAuth	
decauth	316/udp	decAuth	
zannet	317/tcp	Zannet	
zannet	317/udp	Zannet	
#	318-320	Unassigned	
pip	321/tcp	PIP	
pip	321/udp	PIP	
#	322-343	Unassigned	
pdap	344/tcp	Prospero Data Access Protocol	
pdap	344/udp	Prospero Data Access Protocol	
pawserv	345/tcp	Perf Analysis Workbench	
pawserv	345/udp	Perf Analysis Workbench	
zserv	346/tcp	Zebra server	

Continued

UDP/TCP Well-Known Port List (continued)

KEYWORD	DECIMAL	DESCRIPTION	REFERENCES
zserv	346/udp	Zebra server	
fatserv	347/tcp	Fatmen Server	
fatserv	347/udp	Fatmen Server	
csi-sgwp	348/tcp	Cabletron Management Protocol	
csi-sgwp	348/udp	Cabletron Management Protocol	
mftp	349/tcp	mftp	
mftp	349/udp	mftp	
matiptypea	350/tcp	MATIP Type A	
matiptypea	350/udp	MATIP Type A	
matiptypeb	351/tcp	MATIP Type B	
matiptypeb	351/udp	MATIP Type B	
bhoetty	351/tcp	bhoetty (added 5/21/97)	
bhoetty	351/udp	bhoetty	
dtagstesb	352/tcp	DTAG (assigned long ago)	
dtagstesb	352/udp	DTAG	
bhoedap4	352/tcp	bhoedap4 (added 5/21/97)	
bhoedap4	352/udp	bhoedap4	
ndsauth	353/tcp	NDSAUTH	
ndsauth	353/udp	NDSAUTH	
bh611	354/tcp	bh611	
bh611	354/udp	bh611	
datex-asn	355/tcp	DATEX-ASN	
datexasn	355/udp	DATEX-ASN	
cloantonet-1	356/tcp	Cloanto Net 1	
cloantonet-1	356/udp	Cloanto Net 1	
bhevent	357/tcp	bhevent	
bhevent	357/udp	bhevent	

KEYWORD	DECIMAL	DESCRIPTION	REFERENCES
shrinkwrap	358/tcp	Shrinkwrap	
shrinkwrap	358/udp	Shrinkwrap	
tenebris-nts	359/tcp	Tenebris Network Trace Service	
tenebris-nts	359/udp	Tenebris Network Trace Service	
scoi2odialog	360/tcp	scoi2odialog	
scoi2odialog	360/udp	scoi2odialog	
seman-tix	361/tcp	Semantix	
seman-tix	361/udp	Semantix	
srssend	362/tcp	SRS Send	
srssend	362/udp	SRS Send	
rsvp_tunnel	363/tcp	RSVP Tunnel	
rsvp_tunnel	363/udp	RSVP Tunnel	
auroracmgr	364/tcp	Aurora CMGR	
auroracmgr	364/udp	Aurora CMGR	
dtk	365/tcp	DTK	
dtk	365/udp	DTK	
odmr	366/tcp	ODMR	
odmr	366/udp	ODMR	
mortgageware	367/tcp	MortgageWare	
mortgageware	367/udp	MortgageWare	
qbikgdp	368/tcp	QbikGDP	
qbikgdp	368/udp	QbikGDP	
rpc2portmap	369/tcp	rpc2portmap	
rpc2portmap	369/udp	rpc2portmap	
codaauth2	370/tcp	codaauth2	
codaauth2	370/udp	codaauth2	
clearcase	371/tcp	Clearcase	
clearcase	371/udp	Clearcase	

Continued

TABLE C.1

UDP/TCP Well-Known Port List (continued)

KEYWORD	DECIMAL	DESCRIPTION	REFERENCES
ulistproc	372/tcp	ListProcessor	
ulistproc	372/udp	ListProcessor	
legent-1	373/tcp	Legent Corporation	
legent-1	373/udp	Legent Corporation	
legent-2	374/tcp	Legent Corporation	
legent-2	374/udp	Legent Corporation	
hassle	375/tcp	Hassle	
hassle	375/udp	Hassle	
nip	376/tcp	Amiga Envoy Network Inquiry Proto	
nip	376/udp	Amiga Envoy Network Inquiry Proto	
tnETOS	377/tcp	NEC Corporation	
tnETOS	377/udp	NEC Corporation	
dsETOS	378/tcp	NEC Corporation	
dsETOS	378/udp	NEC Corporation	
is99c	379/tcp	TIA/EIA/IS-99 modem client	
is99c	379/udp	TIA/EIA/IS-99 modem client	
is99s	380/tcp	TIA/EIA/IS-99 modem server	
is99s	380/udp	TIA/EIA/IS-99 modem server	
hp-collector	381/tcp	hp performance data collector	
hp-collector	381/udp	hp performance data collector	
hp-managed-node	382/tcp	hp performance data managed node	
hp-managed-node	382/udp	hp performance data managed node	
hp-alarm-mgr	383/tcp	hp performance data alarm manager	
hp-alarm-mgr	383/udp	hp performance data alarm manager	
arns	384/tcp	A Remote Network Server System	

KEYWORD	DECIMAL	DESCRIPTION	REFERENCES
arns	384/udp	A Remote Network Server System	
ibm-app	385/tcp	IBM Application	
ibm-app	385/udp	IBM Application	
asa	386/tcp	ASA Message Router Object Def.	
asa	386/udp	ASA Message Router Object Def.	
aurp	387/tcp	Appletalk Update-Based Routing Pro.	
aurp	387/udp	Appletalk Update-Based Routing Pro.	
unidata-ldm	388/tcp	Unidata LDM Version 4	
unidata-ldm	388/udp	Unidata LDM Version 4	
ldap	389/tcp	Lightweight Directory Access Protocol	
ldap	389/udp	Lightweight Directory Access Protocol	
uis	390/tcp	UIS	
uis	390/udp	UIS	
synotics-relay	391/tcp	SynOptics SNMP Relay Port	
synotics-relay	391/udp	SynOptics SNMP Relay Port	
synotics-broker	392/tcp	SynOptics Port Broker Port	
synotics-broker	392/udp	SynOptics Port Broker Port	
dis	393/tcp	Data Interpretation System	
dis	393/udp	Data Interpretation System	
embl-ndt	394/tcp	EMBL Nucleic Data Transfer	
embl-ndt	394/udp	EMBL Nucleic Data Transfer	
netcp	395/tcp	NETscout Control Protocol	
netcp	395/udp	NETscout Control Protocol	
netware-ip	396/tcp	Novell NetWare over IP	
netware-ip	396/udp	Novell NetWare over IP	

Continued

T A B L E C . 1

UDP/TCP Well-Known Port List (continued)

KEYWORD	DECIMAL	DESCRIPTION	REFERENCES
mptn	397/tcp	Multi Protocol Trans. Net.	
mptn	397/udp	Multi Protocol Trans. Net.	
kryptolan	398/tcp	Kryptolan	
kryptolan	398/udp	Kryptolan	
iso-tsap-c2	399/tcp	ISO Transport Class 2 Non-Control over TCP	
iso-tsap-c2	399/udp	ISO Transport Class 2 Non-Control over TCP	
work-sol	400/tcp	Workstation Solutions	
work-sol	400/udp	Workstation Solutions	
ups	401/tcp	Uninterruptible Power Supply	
ups	401/udp	Uninterruptible Power Supply	
genie	402/tcp	Genie Protocol	
genie	402/udp	Genie Protocol	
decap	403/tcp	decap	
decap	403/udp	decap	
nced	404/tcp	nced	
nced	404/udp	nced	
ncld	405/tcp	ncld	
ncld	405/udp	ncld	
imsp	406/tcp	Interactive Mail Support Protocol	
imsp	406/udp	Interactive Mail Support Protocol	
timbuktu	407/tcp	Timbuktu	
timbuktu	407/udp	Timbuktu	
prm-sm	408/tcp	Prospero Resource Manager Sys. Man.	
prm-sm	408/udp	Prospero Resource Manager Sys. Man.	

KEYWORD	DECIMAL	DESCRIPTION	REFERENCES
prm-nm	409/tcp	Prospero Resource Manager Node Man.	
prm-nm	409/udp	Prospero Resource Manager Node Man.	
decladebug	410/tcp	DECLadebug Remote Debug Protocol	
decladebug	410/udp	DECLadebug Remote Debug Protocol	
rmt	411/tcp	Remote MT Protocol	
rmt	411/udp	Remote MT Protocol	
synoptics-trap	412/tcp	Trap Convention Port	
synoptics-trap	412/udp	Trap Convention Port	
smsp	413/tcp	SMSP	
smsp	413/udp	SMSP	
infoseek	414/tcp	InfoSeek	
infoseek	414/udp	InfoSeek	
bnet	415/tcp	BNet	
bnet	415/udp	BNet	
silverplatter	416/tcp	Silverplatter	
silverplatter	416/udp	Silverplatter	
onmux	417/tcp	Onmux	
onmux	417/udp	Onmux	
hyper-g	418/tcp	Hyper-G	
hyper-g	418/udp	Hyper-G	
ariel1	419/tcp	Ariel	
ariel1	419/udp	Ariel	
smpte	420/tcp	SMPTE	
smpte	420/udp	SMPTE	
ariel2	421/tcp	Ariel	

Continued

UDP/TCP WELL-KNOWN PORT LIST

UDP/TCP Well-Known Port List (continued)

KEYWORD	DECIMAL	DESCRIPTION	REFERENCES
ariel2	421/udp	Ariel	
ariel3	422/tcp	Ariel	
ariel3	422/udp	Ariel	
opc-job-start	423/tcp	IBM Operations Planning and Control Start	
opc-job-start	423/udp	IBM Operations Planning and Control Start	
opc-job-track	424/tcp	IBM Operations Planning and Control Track	
opc-job-track	424/udp	IBM Operations Planning and Control Track	
icad-el	425/tcp	ICAD	
icad-el	425/udp	ICAD	
smartsdp	426/tcp	smartsdp	
smartsdp	426/udp	smartsdp	
svrloc	427/tcp	Server Location	
svrloc	427/udp	Server Location	
ocs_cmu	428/tcp	OCS_CMU	
ocs_cmu	428/udp	OCS_CMU	
ocs_amu	429/tcp	OCS_AMU	
ocs_amu	429/udp	OCS_AMU	
utmpsd	430/tcp	UTMPSD	
utmpsd	430/udp	UTMPSD	
utmpcd	431/tcp	UTMPCD	
utmpcd	431/udp	UTMPCD	
iasd	432/tcp	IASD	
iasd	432/udp	IASD	
nnsp	433/tcp	NNSP	
nnsp	433/udp	NNSP	

KEYWORD	DECIMAL	DESCRIPTION	REFERENCES
mobileip-agent	434/tcp	MobileIP-Agent	
mobileip-agent	434/udp	MobileIP-Agent	
mobilip-mn	435/tcp	MobilIP-MN	
mobilip-mn	435/udp	MobilIP-MN	
dna-cml	436/tcp	DNA-CML	
dna-cml	436/udp	DNA-CML	
comscm	437/tcp	comscm	
comscm	437/udp	comscm	
dsfgw	438/ tcp	dsfgw	
dsfgw	438/udp	dsfgw	
dasp	439/tcp	dasp	[Thomas Obermait]
dasp	439/udp	dasp	[tommy@ inlab.m.eunet.de]
sgcp	440/tcp		
sgcp	440/udp	sgcp	
decvms-sysmgt	441/tcp	decvms-sysmgt	
decvms-sysmgt	441/udp	decvms-sysmgt	
cvc_hostd	442/tcp	cvc_hostd	
cvc_hostd	442/udp	cvc_hostd	
https	443/tcp	http protocol over TLS/SSL	
https	443/udp	http protocol over TLS/SSL	
snpp	444/tcp	Simple Network Paging Protocol	
snpp	444/udp	Simple Network Paging Protocol	
microsoft-ds	445/tcp	Microsoft-DS	
microsoftds	445/udp	Microsoft-DS	
ddm-rdb	446/tcp	DDM-RDB	
ddm-rdb	446/udp	DDM-RDB	
ddm-dfm	447/tcp	DDM-RFM	

Continued

UDP/TCP WELL-KNOWN PORT LIST

T A B L E C . I

UDP/TCP Well-Known Port List (continued)

KEYWORD	DECIMAL	DESCRIPTION	REFERENCES
ddm-dfm	447/udp	DDM-RFM	
ddm-ssl	448/tcp	DDM-SSL	
ddm-ssl	448/udp	DDM-SSL	
a-sservermap	449/tcp	AS Server Mapper	
as-servermap	449/udp	AS Server Mapper	
tserver	450/tcp	TServer	
tserver	450/udp	TServer	
sfs-smp-net	451/tcp	Cray Network Semaphore server	
sfs-smp-net	451/udp	Cray Network Semaphore server	
sfs-config	452/tcp	Cray SFS config server	
sfs-config	452/udp	Cray SFS config server	
creativeserver	453/tcp	CreativeServer	
creativeserver	453/udp	CreativeServer	
contentserver	454/tcp	ContentServer	
contentserver	454/udp	ContentServer	
creativepartnr	455/tcp	CreativePartnr	
creativepartnr	455/udp	CreativePartnr	
macon-tcp	456/tcp	macon-tcp	
macon-udp	456/udp	macon-udp	
scohelp	457/tcp	scohelp	
scohelp	457/udp	scohelp	
appleqtc	458/tcp	apple quick time	
appleqtc	458/udp	apple quick time	
ampr-rcmd	459/tcp	ampr-rcmd	
ampr-rcmd	459/udp	ampr-rcmd	
skronk	460/tcp	skronk	
skronk	460/udp	skronk	

KEYWORD	DECIMAL	DESCRIPTION	REFERENCES
datasurfsrv	461/tcp	DataRampSrv	
datasurfsrv	461/udp	DataRampSrv	
datasurfsrvsec	462/tcp	DataRampSrvSec	
datasurfsrvsec	462/udp	DataRampSrvSec	
alpes	463/tcp	alpes	
alpes	463/udp	alpes	
kpasswd	464/tcp	kpasswd	
kpasswd	464/udp	kpasswd	
digital-vrc	466/tcp	digital-vrc	
digital-vrc	466/udp	digital-vrc	
mylex-mapd	467/tcp	mylex-mapd	
mylex-mapd	467/udp	mylex-mapd	
photuris	468/tcp	proturis	
photuris	468/udp	proturis	
rcp	469/tcp	Radio Control Protocol	
rcp	469/udp	Radio Control Protocol	
scx-proxy	470/tcp	scx-proxy	
scx-proxy	470/udp	scx-proxy	
mondex	471/tcp	Mondex	
mondex	471/udp	Mondex	
ljk-login	472/tcp	ljk-login	
ljk-login	472/udp	ljk-login	
hybrid-pop	473/tcp	hybrid-pop	
hybrid-pop	473/udp	hybrid-pop	
tn-tl-w1	474/tcp	tn-tl-w1	
tn-tl-w2	474/udp	tn-tl-w2	
tcpnethaspsrv	475/tcp	tcpnethaspsrv	
tcpnethaspsrv	475/udp	tcpnethaspsrv	

Continued

T A B L E   C.1

UDP/TCP Well-Known Port List (continued)

KEYWORD	DECIMAL	DESCRIPTION	REFERENCES
tn-tl-fd1	476/tcp	tn-tl-fd1	
tn-tl-fd1	476/udp	tn-tl-fd1	
ss7ns	477/tcp	ss7ns	
ss7ns	477/udp	ss7ns	
spsc	478/tcp	spsc	
spsc	478/udp	spsc	
iafserver	479/tcp	iafserver	
iafserver	479/udp	iafserver	
iafdbase	480/tcp	iafdbase	
iafdbase	480/udp	iafdbase	
ph	481/tcp	Ph service	
ph	481/udp	Ph service	
bgs-nsi	482/tcp	bgs-nsi	
bgs-nsi	482/udp	bgs-nsi	
ulpnet	483/tcp	ulpnet	
ulpnet	483/udp	ulpnet	
integra-sme	484/tcp	Integra Software Management Environment	
integra-sme	484/udp	Integra Software Management Environment	
powerburst	485/tcp	Air Soft Power Burst	
powerburst	485/udp	Air Soft Power Burst	
avian	486/tcp	avian	
avian	486/udp	avian	
saft	487/tcp	saft Simple Asynchronous File Transfer	
saft	487/udp	saft Simple Asynchronous File Transfer	
gss-http	488/tcp	gss-http	

KEYWORD	DECIMAL	DESCRIPTION	REFERENCES
gss-http	488/udp	gss-http	
nest-protocol	489/tcp	nest-protocol	
nest-protocol	489/udp	nest-protocol	
micom-pfs	490/tcp	micom-pfs	
micom-pfs	490/udp	micom-pfs	
go-login	491/tcp	go-login	
go-login	491/udp	go-login	
ticf-1	492/tcp	Transport Independent Convergence for FNA	
ticf-1	492/udp	Transport Independent Convergence for FNA	
ticf-2	493/tcp	Transport Independent Convergence for FNA	
ticf-2	493/udp	Transport Independent Convergence for FNA	
pov-ray	494/tcp	POV-Ray	
pov-ray	494/udp	POV-Ray	
intecourier	495/tcp	intecourier	
intecourier	495/udp	intecourier	
pim-rp-disc	496/tcp	PIM-RP-DISC	
pim-rp-disc	496/udp	PIM-RP-DISC	
dantz	497/tcp	dantz	
dantz	497/udp	dantz	
siam	498/tcp	siam	
siam	498/udp	siam	
iso-ill	499/tcp	ISO ILL Protocol	
iso-ill	499/udp	ISO ILL Protocol	
isakmp	500/tcp	isakmp	
isakmp	500/udp	isakmp	

Continued

TABLE C.1

UDP/TCP Well-Known Port List (continued)

KEYWORD	DECIMAL	DESCRIPTION	REFERENCES
stmf	501/tcp	STMF	
stmf	501/udp	STMF	
asa-appl-proto	502/tcp	asa-appl-proto	
asa-appl-proto	502/udp	asa-appl-proto	
intrinsa	503/tcp	Intrinsa	
intrinsa	503/udp	Intrinsa	
citadel	504/tcp	citadel	
citadel	504/udp	citadel	
mailbox-lm	505/tcp	mailbox-lm	
mailbox-lm	505/udp	mailbox-lm	
ohimsrv	506/tcp	ohimsrv	
ohimsrv	506/udp	ohimsrv	
crs	507/tcp	crs	
crs	507/udp	crs	
xvttp	508/tcp	xvttp	
xvttp	508/udp	xvttp	
snare	509/tcp	snare	
snare	509/udp	snare	
fcp	510/tcp	FirstClass Protocol	
fcp	510/udp	FirstClass Protocol	
passgo	511/tcp	PassGo	
passgo	511/udp	PassGo	
exec	512/tcp	remote process execution	
comsat	512/udp		
biff	512/udp	used by mail system to notify users	
login	513/tcp	remote login a la telnet	
who	513/udp	maintains databases	

KEYWORD	DECIMAL	DESCRIPTION	REFERENCES
shell	514/tcp	cmd	
syslog	514/udp		
printer	515/tcp	spooler	
printer	515/udp	spooler	
videotex	516/tcp	videotex	
videotex	516/udp	videotex	
talk	517/tcp	like tenex link, but across	
talk	517/udp	like tenex link, but across	
ntalk	518/tcp		
ntalk	518/udp		
utime	519/tcp	unixtime	
utime	519/udp	unixtime	
efs	520/tcp	extended file name server	
router	520/udp	local routing process (on site)	
ripng	521/tcp	ripng	
ripng	521/udp	ripng	
ulp	522/tcp	ULP	
ulp	522/udp	ULP	
ibm-db2	523/tcp	IBM-DB2	
ibm-db2	523/udp	IBM-DB2	
ncp	524/tcp	NCP	
ncp	524/udp	NCP	
timed	525/tcp	timeserver	
timed	525/udp	timeserver	
tempo	526/tcp	newdate	
tempo	526/udp	newdate	
stx	527/tcp	Stock IXChange	
stx	527/udp	Stock IXChange	

Continued

T A B L E C . I

UDP/TCP Well-Known Port List (continued)

KEYWORD	DECIMAL	DESCRIPTION	REFERENCES
custix	528/tcp	Customer IXChange	
custix	528/udp	Customer IXChange	
irc-serv	529/tcp	IRC-SERV	
irc-serv	529/udp	IRC-SERV	
courier	530/tcp	rpc	
courier	530/udp	rpc	
conference	531/tcp	chat	
conference	531/udp	chat	
netnews	532/tcp	readnews	
netnews	532/udp	readnews	
netwall	533/tcp	for emergency broadcasts	
netwall	533/udp	for emergency broadcasts	
mm-admin	534/tcp	MegaMedia Admin	
mm-admin	534/udp	MegaMedia Admin	
iiop	535/tcp	iiop	
iiop	535/udp	iiop	
opalis-rdv	536/tcp	opalis-rdv	
opalis-rdv	536/udp	opalis-rdv	
nmsp	537/tcp	Networked Media Streaming Protocol	
nmsp	537/udp	Networked Media Streaming Protocol	
gdomap	538/tcp	gdomap	
gdomap	538/udp	gdomap	
apertus-ldp	539/tcp	Apertus Technologies Load Determination	
apertus-ldp	539/udp	Apertus Technologies Load Determination	
uucp	540/tcp	uucpd	
uucp	540/udp	uucpd	

KEYWORD	DECIMAL	DESCRIPTION	REFERENCES
uucp-rlogin	541/tcp	uucp-rlogin	
uucp-rlogin	541/udp	uucp-rlogin	
commerce	542/tcp	commerce	
commerce	542/udp	commerce	
klogin	543/tcp		
klogin	543/udp		
kshell	544/tcp	krcmd	
kshell	544/udp	krcmd	
appleqtcsrvr	545/tcp	appleqtcsrvr	
appleqtcsrvr	545/udp	appleqtcsrvr	
dhcpv6-client	546/tcp	DHCPv6 Client	
dhcpv6-client	546/udp	DHCPv6 Client	
dhcpv6-server	547/tcp	DHCPv6 Server	
dhcpv6-server	547/udp	DHCPv6 Server	
afpovertcp	548/tcp	AFP over TCP	
afpovertcp	548/udp	AFP over TCP	
idfp	549/tcp	IDFP	
idfp	549/udp	IDFP	
new-rwho	550/tcp	new-who	
new-rwho	550/udp	new-who	
cybercash	551/tcp	cybercash	
cybercash	551/udp	cybercash	
deviceshare	552/tcp	deviceshare	
deviceshare	552/udp	deviceshare	
pirp	553/tcp	pirp	
pirp	553/udp	pirp	
rtsp	554/tcp	Real Time Stream Control Protocol	
rtsp	554/udp	Real Time Stream Control Protocol	

Continued

. . . . .

TABLE C.I

UDP/TCP Well-Known Port List (continued)

KEYWORD	DECIMAL	DESCRIPTION	REFERENCES
dsf	555/tcp		
dsf	555/udp		
remotefs	556/tcp	rfs server	
remotefs	556/udp	rfs server	
openvms-sysipc	557/tcp	openvms-sysipc	
openvms-sysipc	557/udp	openvms-sysipc	
sdnskmp	558/tcp	SDNSKMP	
sdnskmp	558/udp	SDNSKMP	
teedtap	559/tcp	TEEDTAP	
teedtap	559/udp	TEEDTAP	
rmonitor	560/tcp	rmonitord	
rmonitor	560/udp	rmonitord	
monitor	561/tcp		
monitor	561/udp		
chshell	562/tcp	chcmd	
chshell	562/udp	chcmd	
nntps	563/tcp	nntp protocol over TLS/SSL (was snntp)	
nntps	563/udp	nntp protocol over TLS/SSL (was snntp)	
9pfs	564/tcp	plan 9 file service	
9pfs	564/udp	plan 9 file	
whoami	565/tcp	whoami	
whoami	565/udp	whoami	
streettalk	566/tcp	streettalk	
streettalk	566/udp	streettalk	
banyan-rpc	567/tcp	banyan-rpc	
banyan-rpc	567/udp	banyan-rpc	

KEYWORD	DECIMAL	DESCRIPTION	REFERENCES
ms-shuttle	568/tcp	microsoft shuttle	
ms-shuttle	568/udp	microsoft shuttle	
ms-rome	569/tcp	microsoft rome	
ms-rome	569/udp	microsoft rome	
meter	570/tcp	demon	
meter	570/udp	demon	
meter	571/tcp	udemon	
meter	571/udp	udemon	
sonar	572/tcp	sonar	
sonar	572/udp	sonar	
banyan-vip	573/tcp	banyan-vip	
banyan-vip	573/udp	banyan-vip	
ftp-agent	574/tcp	FTP Software Agent System	
ftp-agent	574/udp	FTP Software Agent System	
vemmi	575/tcp	VEMMI	
vemmi	575/udp	VEMMI	
ipcd	576/tcp	ipcd	
ipcd	576/udp	ipcd	
vnas	577/tcp	vnas	
vnas	577/udp	vnas	
ipdd	578/tcp	ipdd	
ipdd	578/udp	ipdd	
decbsrv	579/tcp	decbsrv	
decbsrv	579/udp	decbsrv	
sntp-heartbeat	580/tcp	SNTP HEARTBEAT	
sntp-heartbeat	580/udp	SNTP HEARTBEAT	
bdp	581/tcp	Bundle Discovery Protocol	
bdp	581/udp	Bundle Discovery Protocol	

Continued

TABLE C.1

UDP/TCP Well-Known Port List (continued)

KEYWORD	DECIMAL	DESCRIPTION	REFERENCES
scc-security	582/tcp	SCC Security	
scc-security	582/udp	SCC Security	
philips-vc	583/tcp	Philips Video-Conferencing	
philips-vc	583/udp	Philips Video-Conferencing	
keyserver	584/tcp	Key Server	
keyserver	584/udp	Key Server	
imap4-ssl	585/tcp	IMAP4+SSL (use 993 instead)	
imap4-ssl	585/udp	IMAP4+SSL (use 993 instead)	
password-chg	586/tcp	Password Change	
password-chg	586/udp	Password Change	
submission	587/tcp	Submission	
submission	587/udp	Submission	
cal	588/tcp	CAL	
cal	588/udp	CAL	
eyelink	589/tcp	EyeLink	
eyelink	589/udp	EyeLink	
tns-cml	590/tcp	TNS CML	
tns-cml	590/udp	TNS CML	
http-alt	591/tcp	FileMaker, Inc. — HTTP Alternate (see Port 80)	
http-alt	591/udp	FileMaker, Inc. — HTTP Alternate (see Port 80)	
eudora-set	592/tcp	Eudora Set	
eudora-set	592/udp	Eudora Set	
http-rpc-epmap	593/tcp	HTTP RPC Ep Map	
http-rpc-epmap	593/udp	HTTP RPC Ep Map	
tpip	594/tcp	TPIP	
tpip	594/udp	TPIP	

KEYWORD	DECIMAL	DESCRIPTION	REFERENCES
cab-protocol	595/tcp	CAB Protocol	
cab-protocol	595/udp	CAB Protocol	
smsd	596/tcp	SMSD	
smsd	596/udp	SMSD	
ptcnameservice	597/tcp	PTC Name Service	
ptcnameservice	597/udp	PTC Name Service	
sco-websrvrmg3	598/tcp	SCO Web Server Manager 3	
sco-websrvrmg3	598/udp	SCO Web Server Manager 3	
acp	599/tcp	Aeolon Core Protocol	
acp	599/udp	Aeolon Core Protocol	
ipcserver	600/tcp	Sun IPC server	
ipcserver	600/udp	Sun IPC server	
urm	606/tcp	Cray Unified Resource Manager	
urm	606/udp	Cray Unified Resource Manager	
nqs	607/tcp	nqs	
nqs	607/udp	nqs	
sift-uft	608/tcp	Sender-Initiated/Unsolicited File Transfer	
sift-uft	608/udp	Sender-Initiated/Unsolicited File Transfer	
np-mptrap	609/tcp	npmp-trap	
np-mptrap	609/udp	npmp-trap	
np-mplocal	610/tcp	npmp-local	
np-mplocal	610/udp	npmp-local	
np-mpgui	611/tcp	npmp-gui	
np-mpgui	611/udp	npmp-gui	
hm-mpind	612/tcp	HMMP Indication	
hm-mpind	612/udp	HMMP Indication	

Continued

UDP/TCP Well-Known Port List (continued)

KEYWORD	DECIMAL	DESCRIPTION	REFERENCES
hm-mpop	613/tcp	HMMP Operation	
hm-mpop	613/udp	HMMP Operation	
sshell	614/tcp	SSLshell	
sshell	614/udp	SSLshell	
sco-inetmgr	615/tcp	Internet Configuration Manager	
sco-inetmgr	615/udp	Internet Configuration Manager	
sco-sysmgr	616/tcp	SCO System Administration Server	
sco-sysmgr	616/udp	SCO System Administration Server	
sco-dtmgr	617/tcp	SCO Desktop Administration Server	
sco-dtmgr	617/udp	SCO Desktop Administration Server	
deiic-da	618/tcp	DEI-ICDA	
deiic-da	618/udp	DEI-ICDA	
digitalevm	619/tcp	Digital EVM	
digitalevm	619/udp	Digital EVM	
sco-websrvrmgr	620/tcp	SCO WebServer Manager	
sco-websrvrmgr	620/udp	SCO WebServer Manager	
e-scpip	621/tcp	ESCP	
e-scpip	621/udp	ESCP	
collaborator	622/tcp	Collaborator	
collaborator	622/udp	Collaborator	
aux_bus_shunt	623/tcp	Aux Bus Shunt	
aux_bus_shunt	623/udp	Aux Bus Shunt	
crypto-admin	624/tcp	Crypto Admin	
crypto-admin	624/udp	Crypto Admin	
decdlm	625/tcp	DEC DLM	
decdlm	625/udp	DEC DLM	

KEYWORD	DECIMAL	DESCRIPTION	REFERENCES
asia	626/tcp	ASIA	
asia	626/udp	ASIA	
passgotivoli	627/tcp	PassGo Tivoli	
passgotivoli	627/udp	PassGo Tivoli	
qmqp	628/tcp	QMQP	
qmqp	628/udp	QMQP	
3com-amp3	629/tcp	3Com AMP3	
3com-amp3	629/udp	3Com AMP3	
rda	630/tcp	RDA	
rda	630/udp	RDA	
ipp	631/tcp	IPP (Internet Printing Protocol)	
ipp	631/udp	IPP (Internet Printing Protocol)	
bmpp	632/tcp	bmpp	
bmpp	632/udp	bmpp	
servstat	633/tcp	Service Status update (Sterling Software)	
servstat	633/udp	Service Status update (Sterling Software)	
ginad	634/tcp	ginad	
ginad	634/udp	ginad	
rlzdbase	635/tcp	RLZ DBase	
rlzdbase	635/udp	RLZ DBase	
ldaps	636/tcp	ldap protocol over TLS/SSL (was sldap)	
ldaps	636/udp	ldap protocol over TLS/SSL (was sldap)	
lanserver	637/tcp	lanserver	
lanserver	637/udp	lanserver	
mc-nssec	638/tcp	mcns-sec	

Continued

T A B L E C . I

UDP/TCP Well-Known Port List (continued)

KEYWORD	DECIMAL	DESCRIPTION	REFERENCES
mc-nssec	638/udp	mcns-sec	
ms-dp	639/tcp	MSDP	
ms-dp	639/udp	MSDP	
entrust-sps	640/tcp	entrust-sps	
entrust-sps	640/udp	entrustsps	
rep-cmd	641/tcp	repcmd	
rep-cmd	641/udp	repcmd	
esroe-msdp	642/tcp	ESRO-EMSDP V1.3	
esroe-msdp	642/udp	ESRO-EMSDP V1.3	
sanity	643/tcp	SANity	
sanity	643/udp	SANity	
dwr	644/tcp	dwr	
dwr	644/udp	dwr	
pssc	645/tcp	PSSC	
pssc	645/udp	PSSC	
ldp	646/tcp	LDP	
ldp	646/udp	LDP	
dhcp-failover	647/tcp	DHCP Failover	
dhcp-failover	647/udp	DHCP Failover	
rrp	648/tcp	Registry Registrar Protocol (RRP)	
rrp	648/udp	Registry Registrar Protocol (RRP)	
aminet	649/tcp	Aminet	
aminet	649/udp	Aminet	
obex	650/tcp	OBEX	
obex	650/udp	OBEX	
ieee-mms	651/tcp	IEEE MMS	
ieee-mms	651/udp	IEEE MMS	

KEYWORD	DECIMAL	DESCRIPTION	REFERENCES
udlr-dtcp	652/tcp	UDLR_DTCP	
udlr-dtcp	652/udp	UDLR_DTCP	
repscmd	653/tcp	RepCmd	
repscmd	653/udp	RepCmd	
#	654-665	Unassigned	
mdqs	666/tcp		
mdqs	666/udp		
doom	666/tcp	doom Id Software	
doom	666/udp	doom Id Software	
disclose	667/tcp	campaign contribution disclosures — SDR Technologies	
disclose	667/udp	campaign contribution disclosures — SDR Technologies	
mecomm	668/tcp	MeComm	
mecomm	668/udp	MeComm	
meregister	669/tcp	MeRegister	
meregister	669/udp	MeRegister	
vacdsm-sws	670/tcp	VACDSM-SWS	
vacdsm-sws	670/udp	VACDSM-SWS	
vacdsm-app	671/tcp	VACDSM-APP	
vacdsm-app	671/udp	VACDSM-APP	
vpps-qua	672/tcp	VPPS-QUA	
vpps-qua	672/udp	VPPS-QUA	
cimplex	673/tcp	CIMPLEX	
cimplex	673/udp	CIMPLEX	
acap	674/tcp	ACAP	
acap	674/udp	ACAP	
dctp	675/tcp	DCTP	

Continued

TABLE C.1

UDP/TCP Well-Known Port List (continued)

KEYWORD	DECIMAL	DESCRIPTION	REFERENCES
dctp	675/udp	DCTP	
vpps-via	676/tcp	VPPS Via	
vpps-via	676/udp	VPPS Via	
vpp	677/tcp	Virtual Presence Protocol	
vpp	677/udp	Virtual Presence Protocol	
ggf-ncp	678/tcp	GNU Generation Foundation NCP	
ggf-ncp	678/udp	GNU Generation Foundation NCP	
mrm	679/tcp	MRM	
mrm	679/udp	MRM	
entrust-aaas	680/tcp	entrust-aaas	
entrust-aaas	680/udp	entrust-aaas	
entrust-aams	681/tcp	entrust-aams	
entrust-aams	681/udp	entrust-aams	
xfr	682/tcp	XFR	
xfr	682/udp	XFR	
corba-iiop	683/tcp	CORBA IIOP	
corba-iiop	683/udp	CORBA IIOP	
corba-iiop-ssl	684/tcp	CORBA IIOP SSL	
corba-iiop-ssl	684/udp	CORBA IIOP SSL	
mdc-portmapper	685/tcp	MDC Port Mapper	
mdc-portmapper	685/udp	MDC Port Mapper	
hcp-wismar	686/tcp	Hardware Control Protocol Wismar	
hcp-wismar	686/udp	Hardware Control Protocol Wismar	
asipregistry	687/tcp	asipregistry	
asipregistry	687/udp	asipregistry	
realm-rusd	688/tcp	REALM-RUSD	
realm-rusd	688/udp	REALM-RUSD	

KEYWORD	DECIMAL	DESCRIPTION	REFERENCES
#	689-703	Unassigned	
elcsd	704/tcp	errlog copy/server daemon	
elcsd	704/udp	errlog copy/server daemon	
agentx	705/tcp	AgentX	
agentx	705/udp	AgentX	
#	706	Unassigned	
borland-dsj	707/tcp	Borland DSJ	
borland-dsj	707/udp	Borland DSJ	
#	708	Unassigned	
entrust-kmsh	709/tcp	Entrust Key Management Service Handler	
entrust-kmsh	709/udp	Entrust Key Management Service Handler	
entrust-ash	710/tcp	Entrust Administration Service Handler	
entrust-ash	710/udp	Entrust Administration Service Handler	
cisco-tdp	711/tcp	Cisco TDP	
cisco-tdp	711/udp	Cisco TDP	
#	712-728	Unassigned	
netviewdm1	729/tcp	IBM NetView DM/6000 Server/Client	
netviewdm1	729/udp	IBM NetView DM/6000 Server/Client	
netviewdm2	730/tcp	IBM NetView DM/6000 send/tcp	
netviewdm2	730/udp	IBM NetView DM/6000 send/tcp	
netviewdm3	731/tcp	IBM NetView DM/6000 receive/tcp	
netviewdm3	731/udp	IBM NetView DM/6000 receive/tcp	
netgw	741/tcp	netGW	
netgw	741/udp	netGW	

Continued

TABLE C.1

UDP/TCP Well-Known Port List (continued)

KEYWORD	DECIMAL	DESCRIPTION	REFERENCES
netrcs	742/tcp	Network based Rev. Cont. Sys.	
netrcs	742/udp	Network based Rev. Cont. Sys.	
flexlm	744/tcp	Flexible License Manager	
flexlm	744/udp	Flexible License Manager	
fujitsu-dev	747/tcp	Fujitsu Device Control	
fujitsu-dev	747/udp	Fujitsu Device Control	
ris-cm	748/tcp	Russell Info Sci Calendar Manager	
ris-cm	748/udp	Russell Info Sci Calendar Manager	
kerberos-adm	749/tcp	kerberos administration	
kerberos-adm	749/udp	kerberos administration	
rfile	750/tcp		
loadav	750/udp		
kerbero-siv	750/udp	kerberos version iv	
pump	751/tcp		
pump	751/udp		
qrh	752/tcp		
qrh	752/udp		
rrh	753/tcp		
rrh	753/udp		
tell	754/tcp	send	
tell	754/udp	send	
nlogin	758/tcp		
nlogin	758/udp		
con	759/tcp		
con	759/udp		
ns	760/tcp		
ns	760/udp		

KEYWORD	DECIMAL	DESCRIPTION	REFERENCES
rxe	761/tcp		
rxe	761/udp		
quotad	762/tcp		
quotad	762/udp		
cycleserv	763/tcp		
cycleserv	763/udp		
omserv	764/tcp		
omserv	764/udp		
webster	765/tcp		
webster	765/udp		
phonebook	767/tcp	phone	
phonebook	767/udp	phone	
vid	769/tcp		
vid	769/udp		
cadlock	770/tcp		
cadlock	770/udp		
rtip	771/tcp		
rtip	771/udp		
cycleserv2	772/tcp		
cycleserv2	772/udp		
submit	773/tcp		
notify	773/udp		
rpasswd	774/tcp		
acmaint_dbd	774/udp		
entomb	775/tcp		
acmaint_transd	775/udp		
wpages	776/tcp		
wpages	776/udp		

Continued

T A B L E   C . I

UDP/TCP Well-Known Port List (continued)

KEYWORD	DECIMAL	DESCRIPTION	REFERENCES
multiling-http	777/tcp	Multiling HTTP	
multiling-http	777/udp	Multiling HTTP	
#	778-779	Unassigned	
wpgs	780/tcp		
wpgs	780/udp		
concert	786/tcp	Concert	
concert	786/udp	Concert	
qsc	787/tcp	QSC	
qsc	787/udp	QSC	
#	788-799	Unassigned	
mdbs_daemon	800/tcp		
mdbs_daemon	800/udp		
device	801/tcp		
device	801/udp		
#	802-809	Unassigned	
fcp-udp	810/tcp	FCP	
fcp-udp	810/udp	FCP Datagram	
#	811-827	Unassigned	
itm-mcell-s	828/tcp	itm-mcell-s	
itm-mcell-s	828/udp	itm-mcell-s	
pkix-3-ca-ra	829/tcp	PKIX-3 CA/RA	
pkix-3-ca-ra	829/udp	PKIX-3 CA/RA	
#	830-872	Unassigned	
rsync	873/tcp	rsync	
rsync	873/udp	rsync	
#	875-885	Unassigned	
iclcnet-locate	886/tcp	ICL coNETion locate server	

. . . . . .

KEYWORD	DECIMAL	DESCRIPTION	REFERENCES
iclcnet-locate	886/udp	ICL coNETion locate server	
iclcnet_svinfo	887/tcp	ICL coNETion server info	
iclcnet_svinfo	887/udp	ICL coNETion server info	
accessbuilder	888/tcp	AccessBuilder	
accessbuilder	888/udp	AccessBuilder	
cddbp	888/tcp	CD Database Protocol	
#	889-899	Unassigned	
omginitialrefs	900/tcp	OMG Initial Refs	
omginitialrefs	900/udp	OMG Initial Refs	
#	901-910	Unassigned	
xact-backup	911/tcp	xact-backup	
xact-backup	911/udp	xact-backup	
#	912-988	Unassigned	
ftps-data	989/tcp	ftp protocol, data, over TLS/SSL	
ftps-data	989/udp	ftp protocol, data, over TLS/SSL	
ftps	990/tcp	ftp protocol, control, over TLS/SSL	
ftps	990/udp	ftp protocol, control, over TLS/SSL	
nas	991/tcp	Netnews Administration System	
nas	991/udp	Netnews Administration System	
telnets	992/tcp	telnet protocol over TLS/SSL	
telnets	992/udp	telnet protocol over TLS/SSL	
imaps	993/tcp	imap4 protocol over TLS/SSL	
imaps	993/udp	imap4 protocol over TLS/SSL	
ircs	994/tcp	irc protocol over TLS/SSL	
ircs	994/udp	irc protocol over TLS/SSL	
pop3s	995/tcp	pop3 protocol over TLS/SSL (was spop3)	

Continued

T A B L E C.I

UDP/TCP Well-Known Port List (continued)

KEYWORD	DECIMAL	DESCRIPTION	REFERENCES
pop3s	995/udp	pop3 protocol over TLS/SSL (was spop3)	
vsinet	996/tcp	vsinet	
vsinet	996/udp	vsinet	
maitrd	997/tcp		
maitrd	997/udp		
busboy	998/tcp		
puparp	998/udp		
garcon	999/tcp		
applix	999/udp	Applix ac	
puprouter	999/tcp		
puprouter	999/udp		
cadlock	1000/tcp		
ock	1000/udp		
#	1001-1009	Unassigned	
#	1008/udp	Possibly used by Sun Solaris?	
surf	1010/tcp	surf	
surf	1010/udp	surf	
#	1011-1022	Reserved	
	1023/tcp	Reserved	
	1023/udp	Reserved	

RFC Index

This appendix lists the most common RFC numbers per protocol mentioned throughout the book. For a more complete list of RFCs, go to `www.rfc-editor.org/rfc.html`. There are many RFC indexes on the Web; this site lists a lot of them. Every RFC index site has a different look and feel and many of them have search capabilities. You'll find a link to your favorite RFC index from there.

Some important, basic RFCs that you should know:

▸ **RFC 2400** — known as *Internet Official Protocol Standard*. It tells you which RFC contains the latest version of an official Internet protocol and which protocols are official and which are unofficial.

▸ **RFC 1700** — known as *Assigned Numbers* Document. We have referred to this one many times throughout the book. It contains the assignment of protocol parameters for all the protocols in the TCP/IP suite.

▸ **RFC 1122 and 1123** — known as *Host Requirements* Documents. RFC 1122 covers the communication protocol layers and RFC 1123 covers the application layers.

▸ **RFC 1812** — known as *Requirements for IPv4 Routers.*

NOTE There is also a file available on RFC websites called `rfc-index.txt`, which is a useful citation of all RFCs in numerical order, currently up to RFC 2583. This is your fastest way of finding the latest RFC for a specific topic and to find out which RFCs have been updated or obsoleted by newer versions.

Each of the following tables lists RFCs mentioned in the chapters of this book. Table D.1 describes RFCs in Chapter 4.

T A B L E   D.1

Chapter 4: IP

DESCRIPTION	RFC
IP	RFC 791
Path MTU Discovery	RFC 1191
Definition of the Differentiated Services Field (DS Field) in the IPv4 and IPv6 Headers	RFC 2474 (obsoletes RFC 1349)
IPv4 Address Behaviour today	RFC 2101
Address Allocation for Private Internets	RFC 1918 (obsoletes RFC 1597)
Variable Length Subnet Table For IPv4	RFC 1878
An Architecture for IP Address Allocation with CIDR	RFC 1518
Classless Inter-Domain Routing (CIDR)	RFC 1519

Table D.2 covers RFCs mentioned in Chapter 6.

T A B L E   D.2

Chapter 6: ICMP

DESCRIPTION	RFC
ICMP	RFC 792
Internet Standard Subnetting Procedure	RFC 950 (updates 792)
ICMP Router Discovery Messages	RFC 1256
Source Quench Introduced Delay (SQuID)	RFC 1016

Routing protocol RFCs from Chapters 7 and 8 are described in Table D.3.

T A B L E   D.3

Chapters 7 and 8: Routing Protocols

DESCRIPTION	RFC
RIP Version 2 Protocol Analysis	RFC 1721
RIP Version 2 Protocol Applicability Statement	RFC 1722
RIP Version 2	RFC 2453

Continued

Table D.4 covers UDP/TCP RFCs discussed in Chapters 9 and 10.

The BOOTP/DHCP RFCs from Chapter 11 are given in Table D.5.

DESCRIPTION	RFC
DHCP	RFC 2131
DHCP Options and BOOTP Vendor Extensions	RFC 2132
DHCP Options for Novell Directory Services	RFC 2241

Table D.6 lists the RFCs relevant to Chapter 12.

T A B L E D.6

Chapter 12: DNS

DESCRIPTION	RFC
Structure and Identification of Management Information for TCP/IP-based Internets	RFC 1155 (obsoletes RFC 1034)
Domain Names — Implementation and Specification	RFC 1035
DNS Encoding of Network Names and Other Types	RFC 1101
New DNS RR Definitions	RFC 1183
Tools for DNS debugging	RFC 1713
DNS Extensions to support IP version 6	RFC 1886
Common DNS Operational and Configuration Errors	RFC 1912
Incremental Zone Transfer in DNS	RFC 1995
A Mechanism for Prompt Notification of Zone Changes (DNS NOTIFY)	RFC 1996
Dynamic Updates in the Domain Name System (DNS Update)	RFC 2136
Secure Domain Name System Dynamic Update	RFC 2137
Clarifications to the DNS Specification	RFC 2181
Selection and Operation of Secondary DNS Servers	RFC 2182
Domain Name System Security Extension	RFC 2535 (updates RFCs 2181, 1034, and 1035; obsoletes RFC 2065)
Negative Caching of DNS Queries	RFC 2308

Table D.7 lists the SNMP RFCs covered in Chapter 13. Many different RFCs are available that describe specific SNMP extensions. For more information, go to an RFC search engine and search for SNMP.

TABLE D.7

Chapter 13: SNMP

DESCRIPTION	RFC
Management Information Base for Network Management of TCP/IP-based internets (MIB-I)	RFC 1156 (historic)
Management Information Base for Network Management of TCP/IP-based internets (MIB-II)	RFC 1213
Structure and Identification of Management Information for TCP/IP-based internets	RFC 1155
SNMP Administrative Model	RFC 1351

Table D.8 gives SLP RFCs for Chapter 14.

TABLE D.8

Chapter 14: SLP

DESCRIPTION	RFC
Service Location Protocol	RFC 2165
Uniform Resource Locators	RFC 1738

Vendor implementation RFCs from Chapters 15 and 16 are given in Tables D.9 and D.10.

TABLE D.9

Chapter 15: Novell's Implementation

DESCRIPTION	RFC
DHCP Options for Novell Directory Services	RFC 2241
NetWare/IP Domain Name and Information	RFC 2242
Protocol Independent Multicast-Sparse Mode (PIM-SM)	RFC 2362

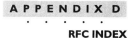

T A B L E   D.10

Chapter 16: Microsoft's Implementation

DESCRIPTION	RFC
Protocol standard for a NetBIOS service on a TCP/UDP transport: Concepts and methods	RFC 1001
Protocol standard for a NetBIOS service on a TCP/UDP transport: Detailed specifications	RFC 1002

Table D.11 describes miscellaneous RFCs covered in Chapter 17.

T A B L E   D.11

Chapter 17: Miscellaneous

DESCRIPTION	RFC
Network Time Protocol (Version 3) Specification, Implementation	RFC 1305
Internet Group Management Protocol, Version 2	RFC 2236

The IP Tunneling RFC from Chapter 19 is listed in Table D.12.

T A B L E   D.12

Chapter 19: IP Tunneling

DESCRIPTION	RFC
IP in IP Tunneling	RFC 1853

Finally, IPv6 RFCs given in Chapter 20 are listed in Table D.13.

T A B L E   D.13

Chapter 20: IPv6

DESCRIPTION	RFC NUMBER	DATE
Internet Protocol, Version 6 (IPv6) Specification	RFC 2460 (obsoletes RFC 1883)	December 98
IPv6 Addressing Architecture	RFC 2373 (obsoletes RFC 1884)	July 98

Continued

Analyzer Manufacturer List

TABLE E.1

Analyzer Manufacturer List

ANALYZER MANUFACTURER	WEB ADDRESS	PHONE	PRODUCT
AG Group, Inc.	www.aggroup.com	800-466-2447	EtherPeek
CompuWare	www.compuware.com	248 737-7300	EcoScope
Fluke Corporation	www.fluke.com	425-347-6100	LanMeter
Hewlett-Packard	www.hp.com	800-452-4844	Internet Advisor
Microsoft Corporation	www.microsoft.com	800-426-9400	SMS Server (NetMon)
Microtest	www.microtest.com	800-526-9675	Compas
Network Associates, Inc.	www.nai.com	408-988-3832	Sniffer (Pro, Basic)
Network Instruments, LLC	www.networkinstruments.com	800-526-7919	Observer
Novell	www.novell.com	800-453-1267	ManageWise
Precision Guesswork	www.guesswork.com	978-887-6570	LANWatch
Proteon	www.lantracer.com	888-757-2968	LanTracer
Shomiti Systems, Inc.	www.shomiti.com	888-746-6484	Surveyor
Technically Elite	www.tecelite.com or www.apptitude.com	800-474-7888	MeterWare
Triticom	www.triticom.com	612-937-0772	LanDecoder32
Vital Signs Software	www.vitalsigns.com	888-980-8844	NetMedic
Wandel & Golterman	www.wg.com	800-729-9441	LinkView/ Domino

Ethertype Assignments

Ethertype Assignments

ETHERNET (DECIMAL/HEX)	EXPERIMENTAL ETHERNET (DECIMAL/OCTAL)	DESCRIPTION	REFERENCES
0000/0000-05DC		IEEE802.3 Length Field	[XEROX]
0257/0101-01FF		Experimental	[XEROX]
0512/0200	512/1000	XEROX PUP (see 0A00)	[8,XEROX]
0513/0201		PUP Addr Trans (see 0A01)	[XEROX]
- /0400		Nixdorf	[XEROX]
1536/0600	1536/3000	XEROX NS IDP	[133,XEROX]
- /0660		DLOG	[XEROX]
- /0661		DLOG	[XEROX]
2048/0800	513/1001	Internet IP (IPv4)	[IANA]
2049/0801		X.75 Internet	[XEROX]
2050/0802		NBS Internet	[XEROX]
2051/0803		ECMA Internet	[XEROX]
2052/0804		Chaosnet	[XEROX]
2053/0805		X.25 Level 3	[XEROX]
2054/0806		ARP	[IANA]
2055/0807		XNS Compatability	[XEROX]
2056/0808		Frame Relay ARP	[RFC 1701]
2076/081C		Symbolics Private	[DCP1]
2184/0888-088A		Xyplex	[XEROX]
2304/0900		Ungermann-Bass net debugr	[XEROX]
2560/0A00		Xerox IEEE802.3 PUP	[XEROX]
2561/0A01		PUP Addr Trans	[XEROX]
2989/0BAD		Banyan VINES	[XEROX]
2990/0BAE		VINES Loopback	[RFC 1701]
2991/0BAF		VINES Echo	[RFC 1701]
4096/1000		Berkeley Trailer nego	[XEROX]

ETHERNET (DECIMAL/HEX)	EXPERIMENTAL ETHERNET (DECIMAL/OCTAL)	DESCRIPTION	REFERENCES
4097/1001-100F		Berkeley Trailer encap/IP	[XEROX]
5632/1600		Valid Systems	[XEROX]
16962/4242		PCS Basic Block Protocol	[XEROX]
21000/5208		BBN Simnet	[XEROX]
24576/6000		DEC Unassigned (Exp.)	[XEROX]
24577/6001		DEC MOP Dump/Load	[XEROX]
24578/6002		DEC MOP Remote Console	[XEROX]
24579/6003		DEC DECNET Phase IV Route	[XEROX]
24580/6004		DEC LAT	[XEROX]
24581/6005		DEC Diagnostic Protocol	[XEROX]
24582/6006		DEC Customer Protocol	[XEROX]
24583/6007		DEC LAVC, SCA	[XEROX]
24584/6008-6009		DEC Unassigned	[XEROX]
24586/6010-6014		3Com Corporation	[XEROX]
25944/6558		Trans Ether Bridging	[RFC 1701]
25945/6559		Raw Frame Relay	[RFC 1701]
28672/7000		Ungermann-Bass download	[XEROX]
28674/7002		Ungermann-Bass dia/loop	[XEROX]
28704/7020-7029		LRT	[XEROX]
28720/7030		Proteon	[XEROX]
28724/7034		Cabletron	[XEROX]
32771/8003		Cronus VLN	[131,DT15]
32772/8004		Cronus Direct	[131,DT15]
32773/8005		HP Probe	[XEROX]
32774/8006		Nestar	[XEROX]
32776/8008		AT&T	[XEROX]

Continued

Ethertype Assignments (continued)

ETHERNET (DECIMAL/HEX)	EXPERIMENTAL ETHERNET (DECIMAL/OCTAL)	DESCRIPTION	REFERENCES
32784/8010		Excelan	[XEROX]
32787/8013		SGI diagnostics	[AXC]
32788/8014		SGI network games	[AXC]
32789/8015		SGI reserved	[AXC]
32790/8016		SGI bounce server	[AXC]
32793/8019		Apollo Domain	[XEROX]
32815/802E		Tymshare	[XEROX]
32816/802F		Tigan, Inc.	[XEROX]
32821/8035		Reverse ARP	[48, JXM]
32822/8036		Aeonic Systems	[XEROX]
32824/8038		DEC LANBridge	[XEROX]
32825/8039-803C		DEC Unassigned	[XEROX]
32829/803D		DEC Ethernet Encryption	[XEROX]
32830/803E		DEC Unassigned	[XEROX]
32831/803F		DEC LAN Traffic Monitor	[XEROX]
32832/8040-8042		DEC Unassigned	[XEROX]
32836/8044		Planning Research Corp.	[XEROX]
32838/8046		AT&T	[XEROX]
32839/8047		AT&T	[XEROX]
32841/8049		ExperData	[XEROX]
32859/805B		Stanford V Kernel exp.	[XEROX]
32860/805C		Stanford V Kernel prod.	[XEROX]
32861/805D		Evans & Sutherland	[XEROX]
32864/8060		Little Machines	[XEROX]
32866/8062		Counterpoint Computers	[XEROX]
32869/8065		Univ. of Mass. at Amherst	[XEROX]

ETHERNET (DECIMAL/HEX)	EXPERIMENTAL ETHERNET (DECIMAL/OCTAL)	DESCRIPTION	REFERENCES
32870/8066		Univ. of Mass. at Amherst	[XEROX]
32871/8067		Veeco Integrated Auto.	[XEROX]
32872/8068		General Dynamics	[XEROX]
32873/8069		AT&T	[XEROX]
32874/806A		Autophon	[XEROX]
32876/806C		ComDesign	[XEROX]
32877/806D		Computgraphic Corp.	[XEROX]
32878/806E-8077		Landmark Graphics Corp.	[XEROX]
32890/807A		Matra	[XEROX]
32891/807B		Dansk Data Elektronik	[XEROX]
32892/807C		Merit Internodal	[HWB]
32893/807D-807F		Vitalink Communications	[XEROX]
32896/8080		Vitalink TransLAN III	[XEROX]
32897/8081-8083		Counterpoint Computers	[XEROX]
32923/809B		Appletalk	[XEROX]
32924/809C-809E		Datability	[XEROX]
32927/809F		Spider Systems Ltd.	[XEROX]
32931/80A3		Nixdorf Computers	[XEROX]
32932/80A4-80B3		Siemens Gammasonics Inc.	[XEROX]
32960/80C0-80C3		DCA Data Exchange Cluster	[XEROX]
32964/80C4		Banyan Systems	[XEROX]
32965/80C5		Banyan Systems	[XEROX]
32966/80C6		Pacer Software	[XEROX]
32967/80C7		Applitek Corporation	[XEROX]
32968/80C8-80CC		Intergraph Corporation	[XEROX]
32973/80CD-80CE		Harris Corporation	[XEROX]

Continued

Ethertype Assignments (continued)

ETHERNET (DECIMAL/HEX)	EXPERIMENTAL ETHERNET (DECIMAL/OCTAL)	DESCRIPTION	REFERENCES
32975/80CF-80D2		Taylor Instrument	[XEROX]
32979/80D3-80D4		Rosemount Corporation	[XEROX]
32981/80D5		IBM SNA Service on Ether	[XEROX]
32989/80DD		Varian Associates	[XEROX]
32990/80DE-80DF		Integrated Solutions TRFS	[XEROX]
32992/80E0-80E3		Allen-Bradley	[XEROX]
32996/80E4-80F0		Datability	[XEROX]
33010/80F2		Retix	[XEROX]
33011/80F3		AppleTalk AARP (Kinetics)	[XEROX]
33012/80F4-80F5		Kinetics	[XEROX]
33015/80F7		Apollo Computer	[XEROX]
33023/80FF-8103		Wellfleet Communications	[XEROX]
33031/8107-8109		Symbolics Private	[XEROX]
33072/8130		Hayes Microcomputers	[XEROX]
33073/8131		VG Laboratory Systems	[XEROX]
33074/8132-8136		Bridge Communications	[XEROX]
33079/8137-8138		Novell, Inc.	[XEROX]
33081/8139-813D		KTI	[XEROX]
- /8148		Logicraft	[XEROX]
- /8149		Network Computing Devices	[XEROX]
- /814A		Alpha Micro	[XEROX]
33100/814C		SNMP	[JKR1]
- /814D		BIIN	[XEROX]
- /814E		BIIN	[XEROX]
- /814F		Technically Elite Concept	[XEROX]
- /8150		Rational Corp	[XEROX]

· · · · · ·

ETHERNET (DECIMAL/HEX)	EXPERIMENTAL ETHERNET (DECIMAL/OCTAL)	DESCRIPTION	REFERENCES
- /8151-8153		Qualcomm	[XEROX]
- /815C-815E		Computer Protocol Pty Ltd	[XEROX]
- /8164-8166		Charles River Data System	[XEROX]
- /817D		XTP	[XEROX]
- /817E		SGI/Time Warner prop.	[XEROX]
- /8180		HIPPI-FP encapsulation	[XEROX]
- /8181		STP, HIPPI-ST	[XEROX]
- /8182		Reserved for HIPPI-6400	[XEROX]
- /8183		Reserved for HIPPI-6400	[XEROX]
- /8184-818C		Silicon Graphics prop.	[XEROX]
- /818D		Motorola Computer	[XEROX]
- /819A-81A3		Qualcomm	[XEROX]
- /81A4		ARAI Bunkichi	[XEROX]
- /81A5-81AE		RAD Network Devices	[XEROX]
- /81B7-81B9		Xyplex	[XEROX]
- /81CC-81D5		Apricot Computers	[XEROX]
- /81D6-81DD		Artisoft	[XEROX]
- /81E6-81EF		Polygon	[XEROX]
- /81F0-81F2		Comsat Labs	[XEROX]
- /81F3-81F5		SAIC	[XEROX]
- /81F6-81F8		VG Analytical	[XEROX]
- /8203-8205		Quantum Software	[XEROX]
- /8221-8222		Ascom Banking Systems	[XEROX]
- /823E-8240		Advanced Encryption Systems	[XEROX]
- /827F-8282		Athena Programming	[XEROX]
- /8263-826A		Charles River Data Systems	[XEROX]

Continued

T A B L E   F.1

Ethertype Assignments (continued)

ETHERNET (DECIMAL/HEX)	EXPERIMENTAL ETHERNET (DECIMAL/OCTAL)	DESCRIPTION	REFERENCES
- /829A-829B		Inst Ind Info Tech	[XEROX]
- /829C-82AB		Taurus Controls	[XEROX]
- /82AC-8693		Walker Richer & Quinn	[XEROX]
- /8694-869D		Idea Courier	[XEROX]
- /869E-86A1		Computer Network Tech	[XEROX]
- /86A3-86AC		Gateway Communications	[XEROX]
- /86DB		SECTRA	[XEROX]
- /86DE		Delta Controls	[XEROX]
- /86DD		IPv6	[IANA]
34543/86DF		ATOMIC	[Postel]
- /86E0-86EF		Landis & Gyr Powers	[XEROX]
- /8700-8710		Motorola	[XEROX]
34667/876B		TCP/IP Compression	[RFC 1144]
34668/876C		IP Autonomous Systems	[RFC 1701]
34669/876D		Secure Data	[RFC 1701]
- /880B		PPP	[IANA]
- /8A96-8A97		Invisible Software	[XEROX]
36864/9000		Loopback	[XEROX]
36865/9001		3Com(Bridge) XNS Sys Mgmt	[XEROX]
36866/9002		3Com(Bridge) TCP-IP Sys	[XEROX]
36867/9003		3Com(Bridge) loop detect	[XEROX]
65280/FF00		BBN VITAL-LanBridge cache	[XEROX]
- /FF00-FF0F		ISC Bunker Ramo	[XEROX]
65535/FFFF		Reserved	[RFC 1701]

Ethernet Vendor Addresses

TABLE G.1

Ethernet Vendor Addresses

ADDRESS	VENDOR (COMMENTS)
000001	SuperLAN-2U
000002	BBN (was internal usage only, no longer used)
000009	Powerpipes (?)
00000C	Cisco
00000E	Fujitsu
00000F	NeXT
000010	Hughes LAN Systems (formerly Sytek)
000011	Tektronix
000015	Datapoint Corporation
000018	Webster Computer Corporation (Appletalk/Ethernet Gateway)
00001A	AMD (?)
00001B	Novell (now Eagle Technology)
00001C	JDR Microdevices (generic, NE2000 drivers)
00001D	Cabletron
00001F	Cryptall Communications Corp.
000020	DIAB (Data Intdustrier AB)
000021	SC&C (PAM Soft&Hardware also reported)
000022	Visual Technology
000023	ABB Automation AB, Dept. Q
000024	Olicom
000029	IMC
00002A	TRW
00002C	NRC-Network Resources Corporation-MultiGate Hub1+, Hub2, etc.
000032	GPT Limited (reassigned from GEC Computers Ltd.)
000037	Oxford Metrics Ltd.
00003B	Hyundai/Axil (Sun clones)
00003C	Auspex

ADDRESS	VENDOR (COMMENTS)
00003D	AT&T
00003F	Syntrex Inc.
000044	Castelle
000046	ISC-Bunker Ramo, an Olivetti Company
000048	Epson
000049	Apricot Ltd.
00004B	APT (ICL also reported)
00004C	NEC Corporation
00004F	Logicraft 386-Ware P.C. Emulator
000051	Hob Electronic Gmbh & Co. KG
000052	Optical Data Systems
000055	AT&T
000058	Racore Computer Products Inc.
00005A	SK (Schneider & Koch in Europe and Syskonnect outside of Europe)
00005A	Xerox 806 (unregistered)
00005B	Eltec
00005D	RCE
00005E	U.S. Department of Defense (IANA)
00005F	Sumitomo
000061	Gateway Communications
000062	Honeywell
000063	Hewlett-Packard (LanProbe)
000064	Yokogawa Digital Computer Corp.
000065	Network General
000066	Talaris
000068	Rosemount Controls
000069	Concord Communications, Inc. (although someone said Silicon Graphics)
00006B	MIPS

Continued

TABLE G.1

Ethernet Vendor Addresses (continued)

ADDRESS	VENDOR (COMMENTS)
00006D	Case
00006E	Artisoft, Inc.
00006F	Madge Networks Ltd. (Token-ring adapters)
000073	DuPont
000075	Bell Northern Research (BNR)
000077	Interphase (used in other systems; e.g. MIPS, Motorola)
000078	Labtam Australia
000079	Networth Inc. (bought by Compaq, used in Netelligent series)
00007A	Ardent
00007B	Research Machines
00007D	Cray Research Superservers,Inc. [also Harris (3M) (old)]
00007E	NetFRAME multiprocessor network servers
00007F	Linotype-Hell AG (Linotronic typesetters)
000080	Cray Communications (formerly Dowty Network Services)
000081	Synoptics
000083	Tadpole Technology
000084	Aquila (?), ADI Systems Inc. (?)
000086	Gateway Communications Inc. (then Megahertz & now 3Com)
000087	Hitachi
000089	Cayman Systems (Gatorbox)
00008A	Datahouse Information Systems
00008E	Solbourne (?), Jupiter (?)
000092	Unisys, Cogent (both reported)
000093	Proteon
000094	Asante (MAC)
000095	Sony/Tektronix
000097	Epoch

ADDRESS	VENDOR (COMMENTS)
000098	Cross Com
000099	Memorex Telex Corporations
00009F	Ameristar Technology
0000A0	Sanyo Electronics
0000A2	Wellfleet
0000A3	Network Application Technology (NAT)
0000A4	Acorn
0000A5	Compatible Systems Corporation
0000A6	Network General (internal assignment, not for products)
0000A7	Network Computing Devices (NCD) (X-terminals)
0000A8	Stratus Computer, Inc.
0000A9	Network Systems
0000AA	Xerox
0000AC	Conware Netzpartner
0000AE	Dassault Automatismes et Telecommunications
0000AF	Nuclear Data [Acquisition Interface Modules (AIM)]
0000B0	RND (RAD Network Devices)
0000B1	Alpha Microsystems Inc.
0000B3	CIMLInc.
0000B4	Edimax
0000B5	Datability (Terminal Servers)
0000B6	Micro-matic Research
0000B7	Dove (Fastnet)
0000BB	TRI-DATA Systems Inc. (Netway products, 3274 emulators)
0000BC	Allen-Bradley
0000C0	Western Digital now SMC (Std. Microsystems Corp.)
0000C1	Olicom A/S
0000C5	Farallon Computing Inc.

Continued

. . . . .

917

Ethernet Vendor Addresses (continued)

ADDRESS	VENDOR (COMMENTS)
0000C6	HP Intelligent Networks Operation (formerly Eon Systems)
0000C8	Altos
0000C9	Emulex (Terminal Servers, Print Servers)
0000CA	LANcity Cable Modems (now owned by BayNetworks)
0000CC	Densan Co., Ltd.
0000CD	Industrial Research Limited
0000D0	Develcon Electronics, Ltd.
0000D1	Adaptec, Inc. ("Nodem" product)
0000D2	SBE Inc.
0000D3	Wang Labs
0000D4	PureData
0000D7	Dartmouth College (NED Router)
0000D8	old Novell NE1000's (before about 1987?) (also 3Com)
0000DD	Gould
0000DE	Unigraph
0000E1	Hitachi (laptop built-in)
0000E2	Acer Counterpoint
0000E3	Integrated Micro Products Ltd.
0000E4	mips?
0000E6	Aptor Produits De Comm Indust
0000E8	Accton Technology Corporation
0000E9	ISICAD, Inc.
0000ED	April
0000EE	Network Designers Limited (also KNX Ltd., a former division)
0000EF	Alantec (now owned by ForeSystems)
0000F0	Samsung
0000F2	Spider Communications (Montreal, not Spider Systems)

ADDRESS	VENDOR (COMMENTS)
0000F3	Gandalf Data Ltd. - Canada
0000F4	Allied Telesis, Inc.
0000F6	A.M.C. (Applied Microsystems Corp.)
0000F8	DEC
0000FB	Rechner zur Kommunikation
0000FD	High Level Hardware (Orion, UK)
0000FF	Camtec Electronics (UK) Ltd.
000102	BBN (Bolt Beranek and Newman, Inc.)
000143	IEEE 802
000150	Megahertz (now 3Com) modem
000163	NDC (National Datacomm Corporation)
000168	W&G (Wandel & Goltermann)
0001C8	Thomas Conrad Corp.
0001FA	Compaq (PageMarq printers)
000204	Novell NE3200
000205	Hamilton (Sparc Clones)
000216	ESI (Extended Systems, Inc.) (print server)
000288	Global Village (PCcard in Mac portable)
0003C6	Morning Star Technologies Inc.
000400	Lexmark (Print Server)
0004AC	IBM (PCMCIA Ethernet adapter)
000502	Apple (PCI bus Macs)
00059A	PowerComputing (Mac clone)
0005A8	PowerComputing
00060D	Hewlett-Packard (JetDirect token-ring interfaces)
000629	IBM RISC6000 system
00067C	Cisco
0006C1	Cisco

Continued

T A B L E   G.I

Ethernet Vendor Addresses (continued)

ADDRESS	VENDOR (COMMENTS)
000701	Racal-Datacom
00070D	Cisco (2511 Token Ring)
000852	Technically Elite Concepts
000855	Fermilab
0008C7	Compaq
001007	Cisco Systems (Catalyst 1900)
00100B	Cisco Systems
00100D	Cisco Systems (Catalyst 2924-XL)
001011	Cisco Systems (Cisco 75xx)
00101F	Cisco Systems (Catalyst 2901)
001029	Cisco Systems (Catalyst 5000)
00102F	Cisco Systems (Cisco 5000)
00104B	3Com (3C905-TX PCI)
00105A	3Com (Fast Etherlink XL in a Gateway 2000)
001060	Billington (Novell NE200 compatible)
001079	Cisco (5500 Router)
00107A	Ambicom (was Tandy?)
00107B	Cisco Systems
001083	HP-UX E 9000/889
0010A4	Xircom (RealPort 10/100 PC Card)
0010A6	Cisco
0010D7	Argosy (EN 220 Fast Ethernet PCMCIA)
0010F6	Cisco
001700	Kabel
002000	Lexmark (Print Server)
002005	simpletech
002008	Cable & Computer Technology

ADDRESS	VENDOR (COMMENTS)
00200C	Adastra Systems Corp.
002011	Canopus Co Ltd.
002017	Orbotech
002018	Realtek
00201A	Nbase
002025	Control Technology Inc. (Industrial Controls and Network Interfaces)
002028	Bloomberg
002029	TeleProcessing CSU/DSU (now owned by ADC/Kentrox)
00202B	ATML (Advanced Telecommunications Modules, Ltd.)
002035	IBM (mainframes, Etherjet printers)
002036	BMC Software
002042	Datametrics Corp.
002045	SolCom Systems Limited
002048	Fore Systems Inc.
00204B	Autocomputer Co Ltd.
00204C	Mitron Computer Pte Ltd.
002056	Neoproducts
002061	Dynatech Communications Inc.
002063	Wipro Infotech Ltd.
002066	General Magic Inc.
002067	Node Runner Inc.
00206B	Minolta Co., Ltd. (network printers)
002078	Runtop Inc.
002085	3COM SuperStack II UPS management module
00208A	Sonix Communications Ltd.
00208B	Focus Enhancements
00208C	Galaxy Networks Inc.
002094	Cubix Corporation

Continued

Ethernet Vendor Addresses (continued)

ADDRESS	VENDOR (COMMENTS)
0020A5	Newer Technology
0020A6	Proxim Inc.
0020A7	Pairgain Technologies, Inc.
0020AF	3COM Corporation
0020B2	CSP (Printline Multiconnectivity converter)
0020B6	Agile Networks Inc.
0020B9	Metricom, Inc.
0020C5	Eagle NE2000
0020C6	NECTEC
0020D0	Versalynx Corp. ("The One Port" terminal server)
0020D2	RAD Data Communications Ltd.
0020D3	OST (Ouet Standard Telematique)
0020D8	NetWave
0020DA	Xylan
0020DC	Densitron Taiwan Ltd.
0020E0	PreMax PE-200 (PCMCIA NE2000-clone card, sold by InfoExpress)
0020E5	Apex Data
0020EE	Gtech Corporation
0020F6	Net Tek & Karlnet Inc.
0020F8	Carrera Computers Inc.
0020FC	Matrox
004001	Zero One Technology Co Ltd. (ZyXEL?)
004005	TRENDware International Inc.; Linksys; Simple Net; all three reported
004009	Tachibana Tectron Co Ltd.
00400B	Crescendo (now owned by Cisco)
00400C	General Micro Systems, Inc.
00400D	LANNET Data Communications

ADDRESS	VENDOR (COMMENTS)
004010	Sonic (Mac Ethernet interfaces)
004011	Facilities Andover Environmental Controllers
004013	NTT Data Communication Systems Corp.
004014	Comsoft Gmbh
004015	Ascom
004017	XCd XJet - HP printer server card
00401C	AST Pentium/90 PC (emulating AMD EISA card)
00401F	Colorgraph Ltd.
004020	Pilkington Communication
004023	Logic Corporation
004025	Molecular Dynamics
004026	Melco Inc.
004027	SMC Massachusetts
004028	Netcomm
00402A	Canoga-Perkins
00402B	TriGem
00402F	Xlnt Designs Inc. (XDI)
004030	GK Computer
004032	Digital Communications
004033	Addtron Technology Co., Ltd.
004036	TribeStar
004039	Optec Daiichi Denko Co Ltd.
00403C	Forks, Inc.
004041	Fujikura Ltd.
004043	Nokia Data Communications
004048	SMD Informatica S.A.
00404C	Hypertec Pty Ltd.
00404D	Telecomm Techniques

Continued

Ethernet Vendor Addresses (continued)

ADDRESS	VENDOR (COMMENTS)
00404F	Space & Naval Warfare Systems
004050	Ironics, Incorporated
004052	Star Technologies Inc.
004053	Datum (Bancomm Division) (TymServe 2000)
004054	Thinking Machines Corporation
004057	Lockheed-Sanders
004059	Yoshida Kogyo K.K.
00405B	Funasset Limited
00405D	Star-Tek Inc.
004066	Hitachi Cable, Ltd.
004067	Omnibyte Corporation
004068	Extended Systems
004069	Lemcom Systems Inc.
00406A	Kentek Information Systems Inc.
00406E	Corollary, Inc.
00406F	Sync Research Inc.
004072	Applied Innovation
004074	Cable and Wireless
004076	AMP Incorporated
004078	Wearnes Automation Pte Ltd.
00407F	Agema Infrared Systems AB
004082	Laboratory Equipment Corp.
004085	SAAB Instruments AB
004086	Michels & Kleberhoff Computer
004087	Ubitrex Corporation
004088	Mobuis [NuBus (Mac) combination video/EtherTalk]
00408A	TPS Teleprocessing Sys. Gmbh

ADDRESS	VENDOR (COMMENTS)
00408C	Axis Communications AB
00408E	CXR/Digilog
00408F	WM-Data Minfo AB
004090	Ansel Communications (PC NE2000 compatible twisted-pair ethernet cards)
004091	Procomp Industria Eletronica
004092	ASP Computer Products, Inc.
004094	Shographics Inc.
004095	Eagle Technologies (UMC also reported)
004096	Telesystems SLW Inc.
00409A	Network Express Inc.
00409C	Transware
00409D	DigiBoard (Ethernet-ISDN bridges)
00409E	Concurrent Technologies Ltd.
00409F	Lancast/Casat Technology Inc.
0040A4	Rose Electronics
0040A6	Cray Research Inc.
0040AA	Valmet Automation Inc.
0040AD	SMA Regelsysteme Gmbh
0040AE	Delta Controls, Inc.
0040AF	Digital Products, Inc. (DPI)
0040B4	3COM K.K.
0040B5	Video Technology Computers Ltd.
0040B6	Computerm Corporation
0040B9	MACQ Electronique SA
0040BD	Starlight Networks Inc.
0040C1	Bizerba-Werke Wilheim Kraut
0040C2	Applied Computing Devices
0040C3	Fischer and Porter Co.

Continued

TABLE G.1

Ethernet Vendor Addresses (continued)

ADDRESS	VENDOR (COMMENTS)
0040C5	Micom Communications Corp.
0040C6	Fibernet Research, Inc.
0040C7	Danpex Corporation
0040C8	Milan Technology Corp.
0040CC	Silcom Manufacturing Technology Inc.
0040CF	Strawberry Tree Inc.
0040D0	DEC/Compaq
0040D2	Pagine Corporation
0040D4	Gage Talker Corp.
0040D7	Studio Gen Inc.
0040D8	Ocean Office Automation Ltd.
0040DC	Tritec Electronic Gmbh
0040DF	Digalog Systems, Inc.
0040E1	Marner International Inc.
0040E2	Mesa Ridge Technologies Inc.
0040E3	Quin Systems Ltd.
0040E5	Sybus Corporation
0040E7	Arnos Instruments & Computer
0040E9	Accord Systems, Inc.
0040EA	PlainTree Systems Inc.
0040ED	Network Controls International Inc.
0040F0	Micro Systems Inc.
0040F1	Chuo Electronics Co., Ltd.
0040F4	Cameo Communications, Inc.
0040F5	OEM Engines
0040F6	Katron Computers Inc.
0040F9	Combinet

ADDRESS	VENDOR (COMMENTS)
0040FA	Microboards Inc.
0040FB	Cascade Communications Corp.
0040FD	LXE
0040FF	Telebit Corporation (Personal NetBlazer)
004854	Digital SemiConductor (21143/2 based 10/100)
004F49	Realtek
004F4B	Pine Technology Ltd.
005004	3Com (3C90X)
00500F	Cisco
00504D	Repotec Group
00504E	UMC (UM9008 NE2000-compatible ISA Card for PC)
005050	Cisco
005069	PixStream Incorporated
0050BD	Cisco
0050E2	Cisco
005500	Xerox
006008	3Com (3Com PCI form factor 3C905 TX board)
006009	Cisco (Catalyst 5000 Ethernet switch)
006025	Active Imaging Inc.
00602F	Cisco
006030	VillageTronic (used on Amiga)
00603E	Cisco (100Mbps interface)
006047	Cisco
00604E	Cycle Computer (Sun MotherBoard Replacements)
006052	Realtek (RTL 8029 = PCI NE2000)
00605C	Cisco
006067	Acer Lan
006070	Cisco [routers (2524 and 4500)]

Continued

ETHERNET VENDOR ADDRESSES

Ethernet Vendor Addresses (continued)

ADDRESS	VENDOR (COMMENTS)
006083	Cisco (3620/3640 routers)
00608C	3Com (1990 onwards)
006094	AMD PCNET PCI
006097	3Com
0060B0	Hewlett-Packard
0060F5	Phobos FastEthernet for Unix WS
008000	Multitech Systems Inc.
008001	Periphonics Corporation
008004	Antlow Computers, Ltd.
008005	Cactus Computer Inc.
008006	Compuadd Corporation
008007	Dlog NC-Systeme
008009	Jupiter Systems (older MX-600 series machines)
00800D	Vosswinkel FU
00800F	SMC (Standard Microsystem Corp.)
008010	Commodore
008012	IMS Corp. (IMS failure analysis tester)
008013	Thomas Conrad Corp.
008015	Seiko Systems Inc.
008016	Wandel & Goltermann
008017	PFU
008019	Dayna Communications ("Etherprint" product)
00801A	Bell Atlantic
00801B	Kodiak Technology
00801C	Cisco
008021	Newbridge Networks Corporation
008023	Integrated Business Networks

ADDRESS	VENDOR (COMMENTS)
008024	Kalpana
008026	Network Products Corporation
008029	Microdyne Corporation
00802A	Test Systems & Simulations Inc.
00802C	The Sage Group PLC
00802D	Xylogics, Inc. (Annex terminal servers)
00802E	Plexcom, Inc.
008033	Formation (?)
008034	SMT-Goupil
008035	Technology Works
008037	Ericsson Business Comm.
008038	Data Research & Applications
00803B	APT Communications, Inc.
00803D	Surigiken Co Ltd.
00803E	Synernetics
00803F	Hyundai Electronics
008042	Force Computers
008043	Networld Inc.
008045	Matsushita Electric Ind Co
008046	University of Toronto
008048	Compex, used by Commodore and DEC at least
008049	Nissin Electric Co Ltd.
00804C	Contec Co., Ltd.
00804D	Cyclone Microsystems, Inc.
008051	ADC Fibermux
008052	Network Professor
008057	Adsoft Ltd.
00805A	Tulip Computers International BV

Continued

TABLE G.1

Ethernet Vendor Addresses (continued)

ADDRESS	VENDOR (COMMENTS)
00805B	Condor Systems, Inc.
00805C	Agilis (?)
00805F	Compaq Computer Corporation
008060	Network Interface Corporation
008062	Interface Co.
008063	Richard Hirschmann Gmbh & Co
008064	Wyse
008067	Square D Company
008069	Computone Systems
00806A	ERI (Empac Research Inc.)
00806B	Schmid Telecommunication
00806C	Cegelec Projects Ltd.
00806D	Century Systems Corp.
00806E	Nippon Steel Corporation
00806F	Onelan Ltd.
008071	SAI Technology
008072	Microplex Systems Ltd.
008074	Fisher Controls
008079	Microbus Designs Ltd.
00807B	Artel Communications Corp.
00807C	FiberCom
00807D	Equinox Systems Inc.
008082	PEP Modular Computers Gmbh
008086	Computer Generation Inc.
008087	Okidata
00808A	Summit (?)
00808B	Dacoll Limited

· · · · ·

ADDRESS	VENDOR (COMMENTS)
00808C	Netscout Systems (formerly Frontier Software Development)
00808D	Westcove Technology BV
00808E	Radstone Technology
008090	Microtek International Inc.
008092	Japan Computer Industry, Inc.
008093	Xyron Corporation
008094	Sattcontrol AB
008096	HDS (Human Designed Systems) (X terminals)
008098	TDK Corporation
00809A	Novus Networks Ltd.
00809B	Justsystem Corporation
00809D	Datacraft Manufactur'g Pty Ltd.
00809F	Alcatel Business Systems
0080A1	Microtest
0080A3	Lantronix (see also 0800A3)
0080A6	Republic Technology Inc.
0080A7	Measurex Corp.
0080AD	CNet Technology (used by Telebit, among others)
0080AE	Hughes Network Systems
0080AF	Allumer Co., Ltd.
0080B1	Softcom A/S
0080B2	NET (Network Equipment Technologies)
0080B6	Themis Corporation
0080BA	Specialix (Asia) Pte Ltd.
0080C0	Penril Datability Networks
0080C2	IEEE (802.1 Committee)
0080C6	Soho

Continued

Ethernet Vendor Addresses (continued)

ADDRESS	VENDOR (COMMENTS)
0080C7	Xircom, Inc.
0080C8	D-Link (also Solectek Pocket Adapters, and LinkSys PCMCIA)
0080C9	Alberta Microelectronic Centre
0080CE	Broadcast Television Systems
0080D0	Computer Products International
0080D3	Shiva (Appletalk-Ethernet interface)
0080D4	Chase Limited
0080D6	Apple Mac Portable (?)
0080D7	Fantum Electronics
0080D8	Network Peripherals
0080DA	Bruel & Kjaer
0080E0	XTP Systems Inc.
0080E3	Coral (?)
0080E7	Lynwood Scientific Dev Ltd.
0080EA	The Fiber Company
0080F0	Kyushu Matsushita Electric Co
0080F1	Opus
0080F3	Sun Electronics Corp.
0080F4	Telemechanique Electrique
0080F5	Quantel Ltd.
0080F7	Zenith Communications Products
0080FB	BVM Limited
0080FE	Azure Technologies Inc.
009004	3Com
009027	Intel
0090B1	Cisco
00902B	Cisco (Ethernet switches and light streams)

ADDRESS	VENDOR (COMMENTS)
009086	Cisco
009092	Cisco
0090AB	Cisco
0090B1	Cisco
0090F2	Cisco (Ethernet switches and light streams)
00A000	Bay Networks (Ethernet switch)
00A00C	Kingmax Technology Inc. (PCMCIA card)
00A024	3com
00A040	Apple (PCI Mac)
00A04B	Sonic Systems Inc. (EtherFE 10/100 PCI for Mac or PC)
00A073	Com21
00A083	Intel
00A092	Intermate International (LAN printer interfaces)
00A0AE	Network Peripherals, Inc.
00A0C8	Adtran, Inc.
00A0C9	Intel (PRO100B and PRO100+) (used on Cisco PIX firewall among others)
00A0CC	Lite-On (used by MacSense in Adapter for Mac, also seen in PCs)
00A0D1	National Semiconductor (COMPAQ Docking Station)
00A0D2	Allied Telesyn
00AA00	Intel
00B0D0	Computer Products International
00C000	Lanoptics Ltd.
00C001	Diatek Patient Managment
00C002	Sercomm Corporation
00C003	Globalnet Communications
00C004	Japan Business Computer Co. Ltd.
00C005	Livingston Enterprises Inc. [Portmaster (OEMed by Cayman)]
00C006	Nippon Avionics Co Ltd.

Continued

TABLE G.1

Ethernet Vendor Addresses (continued)

ADDRESS	VENDOR (COMMENTS)
00C007	Pinnacle Data Systems Inc.
00C008	Seco SRL
00C009	KT Technology(s) Pte Inc.
00C00A	Micro Craft
00C00B	Norcontrol A.S.
00C00C	ARK PC Technology, Inc.
00C00D	Advanced Logic Research Inc.
00C00E	Psitech Inc.
00C00F	QNX Software Systems Ltd. (also Quantum Software Systems Ltd.)
00C011	Interactive Computing Devices
00C012	Netspan Corp.
00C013	Netrix
00C014	Telematics Calabasas
00C015	New Media Corp.
00C016	Electronic Theatre Controls
00C017	Fluke
00C018	Lanart Corp.
00C01A	Corometrics Medical Systems
00C01B	Socket Communications
00C01C	Interlink Communications Ltd.
00C01D	Grand Junction Networks, Inc. (Cisco Catalyst also reported)
00C01F	S.E.R.C.E.L.
00C020	Arco Electronic, Control Ltd.
00C021	Netexpress
00C023	Tutankhamon Electronics
00C024	Eden Sistemas De Computacao SA
00C025	Dataproducts Corporation

ADDRESS	VENDOR (COMMENTS)
00C027	Cipher Systems, Inc.
00C028	Jasco Corporation
00C029	Kabel Rheydt AG
00C02A	Ohkura Electric Co
00C02B	Gerloff Gesellschaft Fur
00C02C	Centrum Communications, Inc.
00C02D	Fuji Photo Film Co., Ltd.
00C02E	Netwiz
00C02F	Okuma Corp.
00C030	Integrated Engineering B.V.
00C031	Design Research Systems, Inc.
00C032	I-Cubed Limited
00C033	Telebit Corporation
00C034	Dale Computer Corporation
00C035	Quintar Company
00C036	Raytech Electronic Corp.
00C039	Silicon Systems
00C03B	Multiaccess Computing Corp
00C03C	Tower Tech S.R.L.
00C03D	Wiesemann & Theis Gmbh
00C03E	Fa. Gebr. Heller Gmbh
00C03F	Stores Automated Systems Inc.
00C040	ECCI
00C041	Digital Transmission Systems
00C042	Datalux Corp.
00C043	Stratacom
00C044	Emcom Corporation
00C045	Isolation Systems Inc.

Continued

TABLE G.1

Ethernet Vendor Addresses (continued)

ADDRESS	VENDOR (COMMENTS)
00C046	Kemitron Ltd.
00C047	Unimicro Systems Inc.
00C048	Bay Technical Associates
00C049	US Robotics Total Control (tm) NETServer Card
00C04D	Mitec Ltd.
00C04E	Comtrol Corporation
00C04F	Dell
00C050	Toyo Denki Seizo K.K.
00C051	Advanced Integration Research
00C055	Modular Computing Technologies
00C056	Somelec
00C057	Myco Electronics
00C058	Dataexpert Corp.
00C059	Nippondenso Corp.
00C05B	Networks Northwest Inc.
00C05C	Elonex PLC
00C05D	L&N Technologies
00C05E	Vari-Lite Inc.
00C060	ID Scandinavia A/S
00C061	Solectek Corporation
00C063	Morning Star Technologies Inc. (may be miswrite of 0003C6)
00C064	General Datacomm Ind Inc.
00C065	Scope Communications Inc.
00C066	Docupoint, Inc.
00C067	United Barcode Industries
00C068	Philp Drake Electronics Ltd.
00C069	California Microwave Inc.

ADDRESS	VENDOR (COMMENTS)
00C06A	Zahner-Elektrik Gmbh & Co KG
00C06B	OSI Plus Corporation
00C06C	SVEC Computer Corp.
00C06D	Boca Research, Inc.
00C06F	Komatsu Ltd.
00C070	Sectra Secure-Transmission AB
00C071	Areanex Communications, Inc.
00C072	KNX Ltd.
00C073	Xedia Corporation
00C074	Toyoda Automatic Loom Works Ltd.
00C075	Xante Corporation
00C076	I-Data International A-S
00C077	Daewoo Telecom Ltd.
00C078	Computer Systems Engineering
00C079	Fonsys Co Ltd.
00C07A	Priva BV
00C07B	Ascend Communications (ISDN bridges/routers)
00C07D	RISC Developments Ltd.
00C07F	Nupon Computing Corp.
00C080	Netstar Inc.
00C081	Metrodata Ltd.
00C082	Moore Products Co
00C084	Data Link Corp. Ltd.
00C085	Canon
00C086	The Lynk Corporation
00C087	UUNET Technologies Inc.
00C089	Telindus Distribution
00C08A	Lauterbach Datentechnik Gmbh

Continued

Ethernet Vendor Addresses (continued)

ADDRESS	VENDOR (COMMENTS)
00C08B	RISQ Modular Systems Inc.
00C08C	Performance Technologies Inc.
00C08D	Tronix Product Development
00C08E	Network Information Technology
00C08F	Matsushita Electric Works, Ltd.
00C090	Praim S.R.L.
00C091	Jabil Circuit, Inc.
00C092	Mennen Medical Inc.
00C093	Alta Research Corp.
00C095	Znyx (Network Appliance); Jupiter Systems (MX-700); Apple (G3) all seen
00C096	Tamura Corporation
00C097	Archipel SA
00C098	Chuntex Electronic Co., Ltd.
00C09B	Reliance Comm/Tec, R-Tec Systems Inc.
00C09C	TOA Electronic Ltd.
00C09D	Distributed Systems Int'l, Inc.
00C09F	Quanta Computer Inc.
00C0A0	Advance Micro Research, Inc.
00C0A1	Tokyo Denshi Sekei Co
00C0A2	Intermedium A/S
00C0A3	Dual Enterprises Corporation
00C0A4	Unigraf OY
00C0A7	SEEL Ltd.
00C0A8	GVC Corporation
00C0A9	Barron McCann Ltd.
00C0AA	Silicon Valley Computer
00C0AB	Jupiter Technology Inc.

ADDRESS	VENDOR (COMMENTS)
00C0AC	Gambit Computer Communications
00C0AD	Computer Communication Systems
00C0AE	Towercom Co Inc. DBA PC House
00C0B0	GCC Technologies, Inc.
00C0B2	Norand Corporation
00C0B3	Comstat Datacomm Corporation
00C0B4	Myson Technology Inc.
00C0B5	Corporate Network Systems Inc.
00C0B6	Meridian Data Inc.
00C0B7	American Power Conversion Corp.
00C0B8	Fraser's Hill Ltd.
00C0B9	Funk Software Inc.
00C0BA	Netvantage
00C0BB	Forval Creative Inc.
00C0BD	Inex Technologies, Inc.
00C0BE	Alcatel - Sel
00C0BF	Technology Concepts Ltd.
00C0C0	Shore Microsystems Inc.
00C0C1	Quad/Graphics Inc.
00C0C2	Infinite Networks Ltd.
00C0C3	Acuson Computed Sonography
00C0C4	Computer Operational
00C0C5	SID Informatica
00C0C6	Personal Media Corp.
00C0C8	Micro Byte Pty Ltd.
00C0C9	Bailey Controls Co
00C0CA	Alfa, Inc.
00C0CB	Control Technology Corporation

Continued

Ethernet Vendor Addresses (continued)

ADDRESS	VENDOR (COMMENTS)
00C0CD	Comelta S.A.
00C0D0	Ratoc System Inc.
00C0D1	Comtree Technology Corporation (EFA also reported)
00C0D2	Syntellect Inc.
00C0D4	Axon Networks Inc.
00C0D5	Quancom Electronic Gmbh
00C0D6	JI Systems, Inc.
00C0D9	Quinte Network Confidentiality Equipment Inc.
00C0DB	IPC Corporation (Pte) Ltd.
00C0DC	EOS Technologies, Inc.
00C0DE	ZComm Inc.
00C0DF	Kye Systems Corp.
00C0E1	Sonic Solutions
00C0E2	Calcomp, Inc.
00C0E3	Ositech Communications Inc.
00C0E4	Landis & Gyr Powers Inc.
00C0E5	GESPAC S.A.
00C0E6	TXPORT
00C0E7	Fiberdata AB
00C0E8	Plexcom Inc.
00C0E9	Oak Solutions Ltd.
00C0EA	Array Technology Ltd.
00C0EC	Dauphin Technology
00C0ED	US Army Electronic Proving Ground
00C0EE	Kyocera Corporation
00C0EF	Abit Corporation
00C0F0	Kingston Technology Corporation

· · · · · ·

ADDRESS	VENDOR (COMMENTS)
00C0F1	Shinko Electric Co Ltd.
00C0F2	Transition Engineering Inc.
00C0F3	Network Communications Corp.
00C0F4	Interlink System Co., Ltd.
00C0F5	Metacomp Inc.
00C0F6	Celan Technology Inc.
00C0F7	Engage Communication, Inc.
00C0F8	About Computing Inc.
00C0FA	Canary Communications Inc.
00C0FB	Advanced Technology Labs
00C0FC	ASDG Incorporated
00C0FD	Prosum
00C0FF	Box Hill Systems Corporation
00DD00	Ungermann-Bass (IBM RT)
00DD01	Ungermann-Bass
00DD08	Ungermann-Bass
00E011	Uniden Corporation
00E014	Cisco
00E016	Rapid-City (now a part of Bay Networks)
00E018	Asustek (Intel 82558-based Integrated Fast Ethernet for WIM)
00E01E	Cisco
00E029	SMC EtherPower II 10/100
00E02C	AST built into 5166M PC motherboard (Win95 IDs as Intel)
00E034	Cisco
00E039	Paradyne 7112 T1 DSU/CSU
00E04F	Cisco
00E07D	Encore (Netronix?) (10/100 PCI Fast ethernet card)
00E081	Tyan Computer Corp. (Onboard Intel 82558 10/100)

Continued

Ethernet Vendor Addresses (continued)

ADDRESS	VENDOR (COMMENTS)
00E083	Jato Technologies, Inc.
00E08F	Cisco Systems (Catalyst 2900 series)
00E098	Linksys (PCMCIA card)
00E0A3	Cisco Systems (Catalyst 1924)
00E0B0	Cisco Systems (Various systems reported)
00E0B8	AMD PCNet (in a Gateway 2000)
00E0C5	BCOM Electronics Inc.
00E0ED	New Link
00E0F7	Cisco
00E0F9	Cisco
00E0FE	Cisco
020406	BBN (internal usage, not registered)
020701	Interlan (now Racal-InterLAN) [DEC (UNIBUS or QBUS), Apollo, Cisco]
020701	Racal-Datacom
026060	3Com
026086	Satelcom MegaPac (UK)
02608C	3Com (IBM PC, Imagen, Valid, Cisco, Macintosh)
02A0C9	Intel
02AA3C	Olivetti
02CF1F	CMC (Masscomp, Silicon Graphics, Prime EXL)
02E03B	Prominet Corporation (Gigabit Ethernet Switch)
02E6D3	BTI (Bus-Tech, Inc.) (IBM Mainframes)
048845	Bay Networks (token ring line card)
080001	Computer Vision
080002	3Com (formerly Bridge)
080003	ACC (Advanced Computer Communications)
080005	Symbolics (LISP machines)

ADDRESS	VENDOR (COMMENTS)
080006	Siemens Nixdorf (PC clone)
080007	Apple
080008	BBN (Bolt Beranek and Newman, Inc.)
080009	Hewlett-Packard
08000A	Nestar Systems
08000B	Unisys also Ascom-Timeplex (former Unisys subsidiary)
08000D	ICL (International Computers, Ltd.)
08000E	NCR/AT&T
08000F	SMC (Standard Microsystems Corp.)
080010	AT&T (misrepresentation of 800010?)
080011	Tektronix, Inc.
080014	Excelan (BBN Butterfly, Masscomp, Silicon Graphics)
080017	National Semiconductor Corp. (used to have Network System Corp., wrong NSC)
08001A	Tiara? (used to have Data General)
08001B	Data General
08001E	Apollo
08001F	Sharp
080020	Sun
080022	NBI (Nothing But Initials)
080023	Matsushita Denso
080025	CDC
080026	Norsk Data (Nord)
080027	PCS Computer Systems GmbH
080028	TI (Explorer)
08002B	DEC
08002E	Metaphor
08002F	Prime Computer (Prime 50-Series LHC300)
080030	CERN

Continued

Ethernet Vendor Addresses (continued)

ADDRESS	VENDOR (COMMENTS)
080032	Tigan
080036	Intergraph (CAE stations)
080037	Fuji Xerox
080038	Bull
080039	Spider Systems
08003B	Torus Systems
08003D	cadnetix
08003E	Motorola (VME bus processor modules)
080041	DCA (Digital Comm. Assoc.)
080044	DSI (DAVID Systems, Inc.)
080045	? (maybe Xylogics, but company claims not to know this number)
080046	Sony
080047	Sequent
080048	Eurotherm Gauging Systems
080049	Univation
08004C	Encore
08004E	BICC (3Com bought BICC, so may appear on 3Com equipment as well)
080051	Experdata
080056	Stanford University
080057	Evans & Sutherland (?)
080058	DECsystem-20
08005A	IBM
080066	AGFA (printers, phototypesetters, etc.)
080067	Comdesign
080068	Ridge
080069	Silicon Graphics
08006A	ATTst (?)

ADDRESS	VENDOR (COMMENTS)
08006E	Excelan
080070	Mitsubishi
080074	Casio
080075	DDE (Danish Data Elektronik A/S)
080077	TSL (now Retix)
080079	Silicon Graphics
08007C	Vitalink (TransLAN III)
080080	XIOS
080081	Crosfield Electronics
080083	Seiko Denshi
080086	Imagen/QMS
080087	Xyplex (terminal servers)
080088	McDATA Corporation
080089	Kinetics (AppleTalk-Ethernet interface)
08008B	Pyramid
08008D	XyVision
08008E	Tandem / Solbourne Computer (?)
08008F	Chipcom Corp.
080090	Retix, Inc. (bridges)
09006A	AT&T
10005A	IBM
100090	Hewlett-Packard (Advisor products)
1000D4	DEC
1000E0	Apple A/UX (modified addresses for licensing)
2E2E2E	LAA (Locally Administered Address) for Meditech Systems
3C0000	3Com [dual function (V.34 modem + Ethernet) card]
400003	NetWare (?)
444553	Microsoft (Windows 95 internal "adapters")

Continued

· · · · ·

APPENDIX G
. . . . .
ETHERNET VENDOR ADDRESSES

TABLE G.1

Ethernet Vendor Addresses (continued)

ADDRESS	VENDOR (COMMENTS)
444649	DFI (Diamond Flower Industries)
475443	GTC (not registered; this number is a multicast)
484453	HDS?
484C00	Network Solutions
4854E8	Winbond?
4C424C	Information Modes software modified addresses (not registered?)
525400	Realtek (UpTech? also reported)
52544C	Novell 2000
5254AB	REALTEK (a Realtek 8029 based PCI Card)
565857	Aculab plc (audio bridges)
800010	AT&T (misrepresented as 080010?)
80AD00	CNET Technology Inc. (probably an error, see instead 0080AD)
AA0000	DEC (obsolete)
AA0001	DEC (obsolete)
AA0002	DEC (obsolete)
AA0003	DEC (global physical address for some DEC machines)
AA0004	DEC (local logical address for DECNET systems)
C00000	Western Digital (may be reversed 00 00 C0?)
EC1000	Enance Source Co., Ltd. (PC clones?)
E20C0F	Kingston Technologies

Ethernet Multicast Addresses

ETHERNET MULTICAST ADDRESSES

Ethernet Multicast Addresses

ETHERNET ADDRESS	TYPE FIELD	USAGE
01-00-0C-CC-CC-CC	802	CDP (Cisco Discovery Protocol), VTP (Virtual Trunking Protocol)
01-00-0C-DD-DD-DD		CGMP (Cisco Group Management Protocol)
01-00-10-00-00-20	802	Hughes Lan Systems Terminal Server S/W download
01-00-10-FF-FF-20	802	Hughes Lan Systems Terminal Server S/W request
01-00-1D-00-00-00	802	Cabletron PC-OV PC discover (on demand)
01-00-1D-42-00-00	802	Cabletron PC-OV Bridge discover (on demand)
01-00-1D-52-00-00	802	Cabletron PC-OV MMAC discover (on demand)
01-00-3C-xx-xx-xx		Auspex Systems (Serverguard)
01-00-5E-00-00-00 through 01-00-5E-7F-FF-FF	0800	DoD Internet Multicast (RFC-1112)
01-00-5E-80-00-00 through 01-00-5E-FF-FF-FF		DoD Internet reserved by IANA
01-00-81-00-00-00		Synoptics Network Management
01-00-81-00-00-02		Synoptics Network Management
01-00-81-00-01-00	802	(snap type 01A2) Bay Networks (Synoptics) autodiscovery
01-00-81-00-01-01	802	(snap type 01A1) Bay Networks (Synoptics) autodiscovery
01-20-25-00-00-00 through 01-20-25-7F-FF-FF	873A	Control Technology Inc's Industrial Ctrl Proto.
01-80-24-00-00-00	8582	Kalpana Etherswitch every 60 seconds
01-80-C2-00-00-00	802	Spanning tree (for bridges)
01-80-C2-00-00-01 through 01-80-C2-00-00-0F	802	802.1 alternate Spanning multicast
01-80-C2-00-00-10	802	Bridge Management
01-80-C2-00-00-11	802	Load Server
01-80-C2-00-00-12	802	Loadable Device
01-80-C2-00-00-14	802	OSI Route level 1 (within area) IS hello?

ETHERNET ADDRESS	TYPE FIELD	USAGE
01-80-C2-00-00-15	802	OSI Route level 2 (between area) IS hello?
01-80-C2-00-01-00	802	FDDI RMT Directed Beacon
01-80-C2-00-01-10	802	FDDI status report frame
01-DD-00-FF-FF-FF	7002	Ungermann-Bass boot-me requests
01-DD-01-00-00-00	7005	Ungermann-Bass Spanning Tree
03-00-00-00-00-01	802	NETBIOS [TR?]
03-00-00-00-00-02	802	Locate — Directory Server [TR?]
03-00-00-00-00-04	802	Synchronous Bandwidth Manager [TR?]
03-00-00-00-00-08	802	Configuration Report Server [TR?]
03-00-00-00-00-10	802	Ring Error Monitor [TR?]
03-00-00-00-00-10	80D5	(OS/2 1.3 EE + Communications Manager)
03-00-00-00-00-20	802	Network Server Heartbeat [TR?]
03-00-00-00-00-40	802	Ring Parameter Monitor [TR?]
03-00-00-00-00-40	80D5	(OS/2 1.3 EE + Communications Manager)
03-00-00-00-00-80	802	Active Monitor [TR?]
03-00-00-00-01-00	802	OSI All-IS Multicast
03-00-00-00-02-00	802	OSI All-ES Multicast
03-00-00-00-04-00	802	LAN Manager [TR?]
03-00-00-00-08-00	802	Ring Wiring Concentrator [TR?]
03-00-00-00-10-00	802	LAN Gateway [TR?]
03-00-00-00-20-00	802	Ring Authorization Server [TR?]
03-00-00-00-40-00	802	IMPL Server [TR?]
03-00-00-00-80-00	802	Bridge [TR?]
03-00-00-01-00-00 through 03-00-40-00-00-00	802	user-defined (per 802 spec?)
03-00-00-20-00-00	802	IP Multicast Address (RFC 1469)
03-00-00-80-00-00	802	Discovery Client
03-00-FF-FF-FF-FF	802	All Stations Address

Continued

. . . . .

TABLE H.1

Ethernet Multicast Addresses (continued)

ETHERNET ADDRESS	TYPE FIELD	USAGE
09-00-02-04-00-01?	8080?	Vitalink printer messages
09-00-02-04-00-02?	8080?	Vitalink bridge management
09-00-07-00-00-00 through 09-00-07-00-00-FC	802	AppleTalk Zone multicast addresses
09-00-07-FF-FF-FF	802	AppleTalk broadcast address
09-00-09-00-00-01	8005	HP Probe
09-00-09-00-00-01	802	HP Probe
09-00-09-00-00-04	8005?	HP DTC
09-00-0D-XX-XX-XX	802	ICL Oslan Multicast
09-00-0D-02-00-00		ICL Oslan Service discover only on boot
09-00-0D-02-0A-38		ICL Oslan Service discover only on boot
09-00-0D-02-0A-39		ICL Oslan Service discover only on boot
09-00-0D-02-0A-3C		ICL Oslan Service discover only on boot
09-00-0D-02-FF-FF		ICL Oslan Service discover only on boot
09-00-0D-09-00-00		ICL Oslan Service discover as required
09-00-1E-00-00-00	8019?	Apollo DOMAIN
09-00-26-01-00-01?	8038	Vitalink TransLAN bridge management
09-00-2B-00-00-00	6009?	DEC MUMPS?
09-00-2B-00-00-01	8039	DEC DSM/DDP
09-00-2B-00-00-02	803B?	DEC VAXELN?
09-00-2B-00-00-03	8038	DEC Lanbridge Traffic Monitor (LTM)
09-00-2B-00-00-04		DEC MAP (or OSI?) End System Hello?
09-00-2B-00-00-05		DEC MAP (or OSI?) Intermediate System Hello?
09-00-2B-00-00-06	803D?	DEC CSMA/CD Encryption?
09-00-2B-00-00-07	8040?	DEC NetBios Emulator?
09-00-2B-00-00-0F	6004	DEC Local Area Transport (LAT)
09-00-2B-00-00-1x		DEC Experimental

ETHERNET ADDRESS	TYPE FIELD	USAGE
09-00-2B-01-00-00	8038	DEC LanBridge Copy packets (All bridges)
09-00-2B-01-00-01	8038	DEC LanBridge Hello packets (All local bridges) 1 packet per second, sent by the designated LANBridge
09-00-2B-02-00-00		DEC DNA Level 2 Routing Layer routers?
09-00-2B-02-01-00	803C?	DEC DNA Naming Service Advertisement?
09-00-2B-02-01-01	803C?	DEC DNA Naming Service Solicitation?
09-00-2B-02-01-09	8048	DEC Availability Manager for Distributed Systems DECamds
09-00-2B-02-01-02	803E?	DEC Distributed Time Service
09-00-2B-03-xx-xx		DEC default filtering by bridges?
09-00-2B-04-00-00	8041?	DEC Local Area System Transport (LAST)?
09-00-2B-23-00-00	803A?	DEC Argonaut Console?
09-00-39-00-70-00?		Spider Systems Bridge Hello packet?
09-00-4C-00-00-00	802	BICC 802.1 management
09-00-4C-00-00-02	802	BICC 802.1 management
09-00-4C-00-00-06	802	BICC Local bridge STA 802.1(D) Rev6
09-00-4C-00-00-0C	802	BICC Remote bridge STA 802.1(D) Rev8
09-00-4C-00-00-0F	802	BICC Remote bridge ADAPTIVE ROUTING (e.g. to Retix)
09-00-4E-00-00-02?	8137?	Novell IPX (BICC?)
09-00-56-00-00-00 through 09-00-56-FE-FF-FF		Stanford reserved
09-00-56-FF-00-00 through 09-00-56-FF-FF-FF	805C	Stanford V Kernel, version 6.0
09-00-6A-00-01-00		TOP NetBIOS.
09-00-77-00-00-00	802	Retix Bridge Local Management System
09-00-77-00-00-01	802	Retix spanning tree bridges
09-00-77-00-00-02	802	Retix Bridge Adaptive routing

Continued

TABLE H.1

Ethernet Multicast Addresses (continued)

ETHERNET ADDRESS	TYPE FIELD	USAGE
09-00-7C-01-00-01		Vitalink DLS Multicast
09-00-7C-01-00-03		Vitalink DLS Inlink
09-00-7C-01-00-04		Vitalink DLS and non DLS Multicast
09-00-7C-02-00-05	8080?	Vitalink diagnostics
09-00-7C-05-00-01	8080?	Vitalink gateway?
09-00-7C-05-00-02		Vitalink Network Validation Message
09-00-87-80-FF-FF	0889	Xyplex Terminal Servers
09-00-87-90-FF-FF	0889	Xyplex Terminal Servers
0D-1E-15-BA-DD-06		HP
33-33-00-00-00-00 through 33-33-FF-FF-FF-FF	86DD	IPv6 Neighbor Discovery
AB-00-00-01-00-00	6001	DEC Maintenance Operation Protocol (MOP) Dump/Load Assistance
AB-00-00-02-00-00	6002	DEC Maintenance Operation Protocol (MOP) Remote Console 1 System ID packet every 8-10 minutes, by every: DEC LanBridge DEC DEUNA interface DEC DELUA interface DEC DEQNA interface (in a certain mode)
AB-00-00-03-00-00	6003	DECNET Phase IV end node Hello packets 1 packet every 15 seconds, sent by each DECNET host
AB-00-00-04-00-00	6003	DECNET Phase IV Router Hello packets 1 packet every 15 seconds, sent by the DECNET router
AB-00-00-05-00-00 through AB-00-03-FF-FF-FF		Reserved DEC
AB-00-03-00-00-00	6004	DEC Local Area Transport (LAT) — old
AB-00-04-00-xx-xx		Reserved DEC customer private use
AB-00-04-01-xx-yy	6007	DEC Local Area VAX Cluster groups System Communication Architecture (SCA)

ETHERNET ADDRESS	TYPE FIELD	USAGE
CF-00-00-00-00-00	9000	Ethernet Configuration Test protocol (Loopback)
FF-FF-00-60-00-04	81D6	Lantastic
FF-FF-00-40-00-01	81D6	Lantastic
FF-FF-01-E0-00-04	81D6	Lantastic

Internet Multicast Addresses

T A B L E I.I

Internet Multicast Addresses

ADDRESS	DESCRIPTION	REFERENCE
224.0.0.0	Base Address (Reserved)	[RFC 1112, JBP]
224.0.0.1	All Systems on this Subnet	[RFC 1112, JBP]
224.0.0.2	All Routers on this Subnet	[JBP]
224.0.0.3	Unassigned	[JBP]
224.0.0.4	DVMRP Routers	[RFC 1075, JBP]
224.0.0.5	OSPFIGP All Routers	[RFC 2328, JXM1]
224.0.0.6	OSPFIGP Designated Routers	[RFC 2328, JXM1]
224.0.0.7	ST Routers	[RFC 1190, KS14]
224.0.0.8	ST Hosts	[RFC 1190, KS14]
224.0.0.9	RIP2 Routers	[RFC 1723, GSM11]
224.0.0.10	IGRP Routers	[Farinacci]
224.0.0.11	Mobile-Agents	[Bill Simpson]
224.0.0.12	DHCP Server/Relay Agent	[RFC1884]
224.0.0.13	All PIM Routers	[Farinacci]
224.0.0.14	RSVP-ENCAPSULATION	[Braden]
224.0.0.15	all-cbt-routers	[Ballardie]
224.0.0.16	designated-sbm	[Baker]
224.0.0.17	all-sbms	[Baker]
224.0.0.18	VRRP	[Hinden]
224.0.0.19–224.0.0.255	Unassigned	[JBP]
224.0.1.0	VMTP Managers Group	[RFC 1045, DRC3]
224.0.1.1	NTP Network Time Protocol	[RFC 1119, DLM1]
224.0.1.2	SGI-Dogfight	[AXC]
224.0.1.3	Rwhod	[SXD]
224.0.1.4	VNP	[DRC3]
224.0.1.5	Artificial Horizons-Aviator	[BXF]
224.0.1.6	NSS (Name Service Server)	[BXS2]

ADDRESS	DESCRIPTION	REFERENCE
224.0.1.7	AUDIONEWS-Audio News Multicast	[MXF2]
224.0.1.8	SUN NIS+ Information Service	[CXM3]
224.0.1.9	MTP Multicast Transport Protocol	[SXA]
224.0.1.10	IETF-1-LOW-AUDIO	[SC3]
224.0.1.11	IETF-1-AUDIO	[SC3]
224.0.1.12	IETF-1-VIDEO	[SC3]
224.0.1.13	IETF-2-LOW-AUDIO	[SC3]
224.0.1.14	IETF-2-AUDIO	[SC3]
224.0.1.15	IETF-2-VIDEO	[SC3]
224.0.1.16	MUSIC-SERVICE	[Guido van Rossum]
224.0.1.17	SEANET-TELEMETRY	[Andrew Maffei]
224.0.1.18	SEANET-IMAGE	[Andrew Maffei]
224.0.1.19	MLOADD	[Braden]
224.0.1.20	any private experiment	[JBP]
224.0.1.21	DVMRP on MOSPF	[John Moy]
224.0.1.22	SVRLOC	[Veizades]
224.0.1.23	XINGTV	[Gordon]
224.0.1.24	microsoft-ds	<arnoldm@ microsoft.com>
224.0.1.25	nbc-pro	<bloomer@ birch.crd.ge.com>
224.0.1.26	nbc-pfn	<bloomer@ birch.crd.ge.com>
224.0.1.27	lmsc-calren-1	[Uang]
224.0.1.28	lmsc-calren-2	[Uang]
224.0.1.29	lmsc-calren-3	[Uang]
224.0.1.30	lmsc-calren-4	[Uang]
224.0.1.31	ampr-info	[Janssen]

Continued

TABLE I.I

Internet Multicast Addresses (continued)

ADDRESS	DESCRIPTION	REFERENCE
224.0.1.32	mtrace	[Casner]
224.0.1.33	RSVP-encap-1	[Braden]
224.0.1.34	RSVP-encap-2	[Braden]
224.0.1.35	SVRLOC-DA	[Veizades]
224.0.1.36	rln-server	[Kean]
224.0.1.37	proshare-mc	[Lewis]
224.0.1.38	dantz	[Yackle]
224.0.1.39	cisco-rp-announce	[Farinacci]
224.0.1.40	cisco-rp-discovery	[Farinacci]
224.0.1.41	gatekeeper	[Toga]
224.0.1.42	iberiagames	[Marocho]
224.0.1.43	nwn-discovery	[Zwemmer]
224.0.1.44	nwn-adaptor	[Zwemmer]
224.0.1.45	isma-1	[Dunne]
224.0.1.46	isma-2	[Dunne]
224.0.1.47	telerate	[Peng]
224.0.1.48	ciena	[Rodbell]
224.0.1.49	dcap-servers	[RFC 2114]
224.0.1.50	dcap-clients	[RFC 2114]
224.0.1.51	mcntp-directory	[Rupp]
224.0.1.52	mbone-vcr-directory	[Holfelder]
224.0.1.53	heartbeat	[Mamakos]
224.0.1.54	sun-mc-grp	[DeMoney]
224.0.1.55	extended-sys	[Poole]
224.0.1.56	pdrncs	[Wissenbach]
224.0.1.57	tns-adv-multi	[Albin]
224.0.1.58	vcals-dmu	[Shindoh]

ADDRESS	DESCRIPTION	REFERENCE
224.0.1.59	zuba	[Jackson]
224.0.1.60	hp-device-disc	[Albright]
224.0.1.61	tms-production	[Gilani]
224.0.1.62	sunscalar	[Gibson]
224.0.1.63	mmtp-poll	[Costales]
224.0.1.64	compaq-peer	[Volpe]
224.0.1.65	iapp	[Meier]
224.0.1.66	multihasc-com	[Brockbank]
224.0.1.67	serv-discovery	[Honton]
224.0.1.68	mdhcpdisover	[Patel]
224.0.1.69	MMP-bundle-discovery1	[Malkin]
224.0.1.70	MMP-bundle-discovery2	[Malkin]
224.0.1.71	XYPOINT DGPS Data Feed	[Green]
224.0.1.72	GilatSkySurfer	[Gal]
224.0.1.73	SharesLive	[Rowatt]
224.0.1.74	NorthernData	[Sheers]
224.0.1.75	SIP	[Schulzrinne]
224.0.1.76	IAPP	[Moelard]
224.0.1.77	AGENTVIEW	[Iyer]
224.0.1.78	Tibco Multicast1	[Shum]
224.0.1.79	Tibco Multicast2	[Shum]
224.0.1.80	MSP	[Caves]
224.0.1.81	OTT (One-way Trip Time)	[Schwartz]
224.0.1.82	TRACKTICKER	[Novick]
224.0.1.83	dtn-mc	[Gaddie]
224.0.1.84	jini-announcement	[Scheifler]
224.0.1.85	jini-request	[Scheifler]
224.0.1.86	sde-discovery	[Aronson]

Continued

T A B L E   I.I

Internet Multicast Addresses (continued)

ADDRESS	DESCRIPTION	REFERENCE
224.0.1.87	DirecPC-SI	[Dillon]
224.0.1.88	BIRMonitor	[Purkiss]
224.0.1.89	3Com-AMP3 dRMON	[Banthia]
224.0.1.90	imFtmSvc	[Bhatti]
224.0.1.91	NQDS4	[Flynn]
224.0.1.92	NQDS5	[Flynn]
224.0.1.93	NQDS6	[Flynn]
224.0.1.94	NLVL12	[Flynn]
224.0.1.95	NTDS1	[Flynn]
224.0.1.96	NTDS2	[Flynn]
224.0.1.97	NODSA	[Flynn]
224.0.1.98	NODSB	[Flynn]
224.0.1.99	NODSC	[Flynn]
224.0.1.100	NODSD	[Flynn]
224.0.1.101	NQDS4R	[Flynn]
224.0.1.102	NQDS5R	[Flynn]
224.0.1.103	NQDS6R	[Flynn]
224.0.1.104	NLVL12R	[Flynn]
224.0.1.105	NTDS1R	[Flynn]
224.0.1.106	NTDS2R	[Flynn]
224.0.1.107	NODSAR	[Flynn]
224.0.1.108	NODSBR	[Flynn]
224.0.1.109	NODSCR	[Flynn]
224.0.1.110	NODSDR	[Flynn]
224.0.1.111	MRM	[Wei]
224.0.1.112	TVE-FILE	[Blackketter]
224.0.1.113	TVE-ANNOUNCE	[Blackketter]

ADDRESS	DESCRIPTION	REFERENCE
224.0.1.114	Mac Srv Loc	[Woodcock]
224.0.1.115	Simple Multicast	[Crowcroft]
224.0.1.116	SpectraLinkGW	[Hamilton]
224.0.1.117	dieboldmcast	[Marsh]
224.0.1.118	Tivoli Systems	[Gabriel]
224.0.1.119	pq-lic-mcast	[Sledge]
224.0.1.120	HYPERFEED	[Kreutzjans]
224.0.1.121	Pipesplatform	[Dissett]
224.0.1.122	LiebDevMgmg-DM	[Velten]
224.0.1.123	TRIBALVOICE	[Thompson]
224.0.1.124	UDLR-DTCP	[Cipiere]
224.0.1.125	PolyCom Relay1	[Coutiere]
224.0.1.126	Infront Multi1	[Lindeman]
224.0.1.127	XRX DEVICE DISC	[Wang]
224.0.1.128	CNN	[Lynch]
224.0.1.129–224.0.1.255	Unassigned	[JBP]
224.0.2.1	"rwho" Group (BSD) (unofficial)	[JBP]
224.0.2.2	SUN RPC PMAPPROC_CALLIT	[BXE1]
224.0.2.064–224.0.2.095	SIAC MDD Service	[Tse]
224.0.2.096–224.0.2.127	CoolCast	[Ballister]
224.0.2.128–224.0.2.191	WOZ-Garage	[Marquardt]
224.0.2.192–224.0.2.255	SIAC MDD Market Service	[Lamberg]
224.0.3.000–224.0.3.255	RFE Generic Service	[DXS3]
224.0.4.000–224.0.4.255	RFE Individual Conferences	[DXS3]
224.0.5.000–224.0.5.127	CDPD Groups	[Bob Brenner]
224.0.5.128–224.0.5.191	SIAC Market Service	[Cho]
224.0.5.192–224.0.5.255	Unassigned	[IANA]
224.0.6.000–224.0.6.127	Cornell ISIS Project	[Tim Clark]

Continued

INTERNET MULTICAST ADDRESSES

TABLE I.I

Internet Multicast Addresses (continued)

ADDRESS	DESCRIPTION	REFERENCE
224.0.6.128–224.0.6.255	Unassigned	[IANA]
224.0.7.000–224.0.7.255	Where-Are-You	[Simpson]
224.0.8.000–224.0.8.255	INTV	[Tynan]
224.0.9.000–224.0.9.255	Invisible Worlds	[Malamud]
224.0.10.000–224.0.10.255	DLSw Groups	[Lee]
224.0.11.000–224.0.11.255	NCC.NET Audio	[Rubin]
224.0.12.000–224.0.12.063	Microsoft and MSNBC	[Blank]
224.0.13.000–224.0.13.255	UUNET PIPEX Net News	[Barber]
224.0.14.000–224.0.14.255	NLANR	[Wessels]
224.0.15.000–224.0.15.255	Hewlett Packard	[van der Meulen]
224.0.16.000–224.0.16.255	XingNet	[Uusitalo]
224.0.17.000–224.0.17.031	Mercantile & Commodity Exchange	[Gilani]
224.0.17.032–224.0.17.063	NDQMDI	[Nelson]
224.0.17.064–224.0.17.127	ODN-DTV	[Hodges]
224.0.18.000–224.0.18.255	Dow Jones	[Peng]
224.0.19.000–224.0.19.063	Walt Disney Company	[Watson]
224.0.19.064–224.0.19.095	Cal Multicast	[Moran]
224.0.19.096–224.0.19.127	SIAC Market Service	[Roy]
224.0.19.128–224.0.19.191	IIG Multicast	[Carr]
224.0.19.192–224.0.19.207	Metropol	[Crawford]
224.0.19.208–224.0.19.239	Xenoscience, Inc.	[Timm]
224.0.20.000–224.0.20.063	MS-IP/TV	[Wong]
224.0.20.064–224.0.20.127	Reliable Network Solutions	[Vogels]
224.0.20.128–224.0.20.143	TRACKTICKER Group	[Novick]
224.0.21.000–224.0.21.127	Talarian MCAST	[Mendal]
224.0.252.000–224.0.252.255	Domain Scoped Group	[Fenner]
224.0.253.000–224.0.253.255	Report Group	[Fenner]

ADDRESS	DESCRIPTION	REFERENCE
224.0.254.000–224.0.254.255	Query Group	[Fenner]
224.0.255.000–224.0.255.255	Border Routers	[Fenner]
224.1.0.0–224.1.255.255	ST Multicast Groups	[RFC 1190,KS14]
224.2.0.0–224.2.127.253	Multimedia Conference Calls	[SC3]
224.2.127.254	SAPv1 Announcements	[SC3]
224.2.127.255	SAPv0 Announcements (deprecated)	[SC3]
224.2.128.0–224.2.255.255	SAP Dynamic Assignments	[SC3]
224.252.0.0–224.255.255.255	DIS transient groups	[Joel Snyder]
225.0.0.0–225.255.255.255	MALLOC (temp-renew 12/99)	[Handley]
232.0.0.0–232.255.255.255	VMTP transient groups (see single-source-multicast file)	[DRC3]
239.000.000.000–239.255.255.255	Administratively Scoped	[IANA,RFC 2365]
239.000.000.000–239.063.255.255	Reserved	[IANA]
239.064.000.000–239.127.255.255	Reserved	[IANA]
239.128.000.000–239.191.255.255	Reserved	[IANA]
239.192.000.000–239.251.255.255	Organization-Local Scope	[Meyer,RFC 2365]
239.252.000.000–239.252.255.255	Site-Local Scope (reserved)	[Meyer,RFC 2365]
239.253.000.000–239.253.255.255	Site-Local Scope (reserved)	[Meyer,RFC 2365]
239.254.000.000–239.254.255.255	Site-Local Scope (reserved)	[Meyer,RFC 2365]
239.255.000.000–239.255.255.255	Site-Local Scope	[Meyer,RFC 2365]

IP Option Numbers

TABLE J.1

IP Option Numbers

COPY	CLASS	NUMBER	VALUE	NAME	REFERENCE
0	0	0	0	EOOL End of Options List	[RFC 791, JBP]
0	0	1	1	NOP No Operation	[RFC 791, JBP]
1	0	2	130	SEC Security	[RFC 1108]
1	0	3	131	LSR Loose Source Route	[RFC 791, JBP]
0	2	4	68	TS Time Stamp	[RFC 791, JBP]
1	0	5	133	ESEC Extended Security	[RFC 1108]
1	0	6	134	CIPSO Commercial Security	[?]
0	0	7	7	RR Record Route	[RFC 791, JBP]
1	0	8	136	SID Stream ID	[RFC 791, JBP]
1	0	9	137	SSR Strict Source Route	[RFC 791, JBP]
0	0	10	10	ZSU Experimental Measurement	[ZSu]
0	0	11	11	MTUP MTU Probe	[RFC 1191]
0	0	12	12	MTUR MTU Reply	[RFC 1191]
1	2	13	205	FINN Experimental Flow Control	[Finn]
1	0	14	142	VISA Expermental Access Control	[Estrin]
0	0	15	15	ENCODE - ?	[VerSteeg]
1	0	16	144	IMITD - IMI Traffic Descriptor	[Lee]
1	0	17	145	EIP- ?	[RFC 1358]
0	2	18	82	TR - Traceroute	[RFC 1393]
1	0	19	147	ADDEXT - Address Extension	[Ullmann IPv7]
1	0	20	148	RTRALT - Router Alert	[RFC 2113]
1	0	21	149	SDB Selective Directed Broadcast	[Graff]
1	0	22	150	NSAPA NSAP Addresses	[Carpenter]
1	0	23	151	DPS Dynamic Packet State	[Malis]

ICMP Code Types
(v4 and v6)

The Internet Control Message Protocol, version 4 (ICMPv4) has many messages that are identified by a type field, as listed in Table K.1.

TABLE K.1

Internet Control Message Protocol v4 (ICMPv4) Type Numbers

TYPE	NAME	REFERENCE
0	Echo Reply	[RFC 792]
1	Unassigned	[JBP]
2	Unassigned	[JBP]
3	Destination Unreachable	[RFC 792]
4	Source Quench	[RFC 792]
5	Redirect	[RFC 792]
6	Alternate Host Address	[JBP]
7	Unassigned	[JBP]
8	Echo	[RFC 792]
9	Router Advertisement	[RFC 1256]
10	Router Selection	[RFC 1256]
11	Time Exceeded	[RFC 792]
12	Parameter Problem	[RFC 792]
13	Timestamp	[RFC 792]
14	Timestamp Reply	[RFC 792]
15	Information Request	[RFC 792]
16	Information Reply	[RFC 792]
17	Address Mask Request	[RFC 950]
18	Address Mask Reply	[RFC 950]
19	Reserved (for Security)	[Solo]
20–29	Reserved (for Robustness Experiment)	[ZSu]
30	Traceroute	[RFC 1393]
31	Datagram Conversion Error	[RFC 1475]

TYPE	NAME	REFERENCE
32	Mobile Host Redirect	[David Johnson]
33	IPv6 Where-Are-You	[Bill Simpson]
34	IPv6 I-Am-Here	[Bill Simpson]
35	Mobile Registration Request	[Bill Simpson]
36	Mobile Registration Reply	[Bill Simpson]
37	Domain Name Request	[Simpson]
38	Domain Name Reply	[Simpson]
39	SKIP	[Markson]
40	Photuris	[Simpson]
41–255	Reserved	[JBP]

Many of these ICMPv4 types also have a code field. Table K.2 lists the types again, this time with their assigned code fields.

T A B L E K.2

ICMPv4 Code Fields

TYPE	NAME/ASSIGNED CODE FIELDS	REFERENCE
0	Echo Reply Codes: 0 No Code	[RFC 792]
1	Unassigned	[JBP]
2	Unassigned	[JBP]
3	Destination Unreachable Codes: 0 Net Unreachable 1 Host Unreachable 2 Protocol Unreachable 3 Port Unreachable 4 Fragmentation Needed and Don't Fragment was Set 5 Source Route Failed 6 Destination Network Unknown 7 Destination Host Unknown 8 Source Host Isolated 9 Communication with Destination Network is Administratively Prohibited	[RFC 792]

Continued

TABLE K.2

ICMPv4 Code Fields (continued)

TYPE	NAME/ASSIGNED CODE FIELDS	REFERENCE
	10 Communication with Destination Host is Administratively Prohibited	
	11 Destination Network Unreachable for Type of Service	
	12 Destination Host Unreachable for Type of Service	
	13 Communication Administratively Prohibited	[RFC 1812]
	14 Host Precedence Violation	[RFC 1812]
	15 Precedence cutoff in effect	[RFC 1812]
4	Source Quench Codes: 0 No Code	[RFC 792]
5	Redirect Codes: 0 Redirect Datagram for the Network (or subnet) 1 Redirect Datagram for the Host 2 Redirect Datagram for the Type of Service and Network 3 Redirect Datagram for the Type of Service and Host	[RFC 792]
6	Alternate Host Address Codes: 0 Alternate Address for Host	[JBP]
7	Unassigned	[JBP]
8	Echo Codes: 0 No Code	[RFC 792]
9	Router Advertisement Codes: 0 No Code	[RFC 1256]
10	Router Selection Codes: 0 No Code	[RFC 1256]
11	Time Exceeded Codes: 0 Time to Live exceeded in Transit 1 Fragment Reassembly Time Exceeded	[RFC 792]
12	Parameter Problem Codes: 0 Pointer indicates the error 1 Missing a Required Option 2 Bad Length	[RFC 792] [RFC 1108]
13	Timestamp Codes: 0 No Code	[RFC 792]
14	Timestamp Reply Codes: 0 No Code	[RFC 792]

TYPE	NAME/ASSIGNED CODE FIELDS	REFERENCE
15	Information Request Codes: 0 No Code	[RFC 792]
16	Information Reply Codes: 0 No Code	[RFC 792]
17	Address Mask Request Codes: 0 No Code	[RFC 950]
18	Address Mask Reply Codes: 0 No Code	[RFC 950]
19	Reserved (for Security)	[Solo]
20–29	Reserved (for Robustness Experiment)	[ZSu]
30	Traceroute	[RFC 1393]
31	Datagram Conversion Error	[RFC 1475]
32	Mobile Host Redirect	[David Johnson]
33	IPv6 Where-Are-You	[Bill Simpson]
34	IPv6 I-Am-Here	[Bill Simpson]
35	Mobile Registration Request	[Bill Simpson]
36	Mobile Registration Reply	[Bill Simpson]

The Internet Control Message Protocol, version 6 (ICMPv6) has many messages that are identified by a type field [RFC 2463], as listed in Table K.3.

T A B L E   K . 3

Internet Control Message Protocol, version 6 (ICMPv6) Type Numbers

TYPE	NAME	REFERENCE
1	Destination Unreachable	[RFC 2463]
2	Packet Too Big	[RFC 2463]
3	Time Exceeded	[RFC 2463]
4	Parameter Problem	[RFC 2463]
128	Echo Request	[RFC 2463]

Continued

TABLE K.3

Internet Control Message Protocol, version 6 (ICMPv6) Type Numbers (continued)

TYPE	NAME	REFERENCE
129	Echo Reply	[RFC 2463]
130	Multicast Listener Query	[MC-LIST]
131	Multicast Listener Report	[MC-LIST]
132	Multicast Listener Done	[MC-LIST]
133	Router Solicitation	[RFC 2461]
134	Router Advertisement	[RFC 2461]
135	Neighbor Solicitation	[RFC 2461]
136	Neighbor Advertisement	[RFC 2461]
137	Redirect Message	[RFC 2461]
138	Router Renumbering	[Crawford]

Many of these ICMPv6 types also have a code field. Table K.4 lists the types again with their assigned code fields.

TABLE K.4

ICMPv6 Code Fields

TYPE	NAME/ASSIGNED CODE FIELDS	REFERENCE
1	Destination Unreachable Codes: 0 No route to destination 1 Communication with destination administratively prohibited 2 (Not assigned) 3 Address unreachable 4 Port unreachable	[RFC 2463]
2	Packet Too Big	[RFC 2463]
3	Time Exceeded Codes: 0 Hop limit exceeded in transit 1 Fragment reassembly time exceeded	[RFC 2463]
4	Parameter Problem Codes: 0 Erroneous header field encountered 1 Unrecognized Next Header type encountered 2 Unrecognized IPv6 option encountered	[RFC 2463]
128	Echo Request	[RFC 2463]

TYPE	NAME/ASSIGNED CODE FIELDS	REFERENCE
129	Echo Reply	[RFC 2463]
130	Multicast Listener Query	[MC-LIST]
131	Multicast Listener Report	[MC-LIST]
132	Multicast Listener Done	[MC-LIST]
133	Router Solicitation	[RFC 2461]
134	Router Advertisement	[RFC 2461]
135	Neighbor Solicitation	[RFC 2461]
136	Neighbor Advertisement	[RFC 2461]
137	Redirect Message	[RFC 2461]
138	Router Renumbering Codes: 0 Router Renumbering Command 1 Router Renumbering Result 255 Sequence Number Reset	[Crawford]

The IPv6 Neighbor Discovery has options that are identified by an Option Format Type field [RFC 2461], as listed in Table K.5.

TABLE K.5

IPv6 Neighbor Discovery Option Formats

TYPE	DESCRIPTION	REFERENCE
1	Source Link-layer Address	[RFC 2461]
2	Target Link-layer Address	[RFC 2461]
3	Prefix Information	[RFC 2461]
4	Redirected Header	[RFC 2461]
5	MTU	[RFC 2461]
6	NBMA Shortcut Limit Option	[IPV6-NBMA]
7	Advertisement Interval	[MOBILE-IPv6]
8	Home Agent Information	[MOBILE-IPv6]

TCP Options (Parameters)

Table L.1 lists TCP option numbers.

T A B L E L.1

TCP Option Numbers

KIND	LENGTH	MEANING	REFERENCE
0		End of Option List	[RFC 793]
1		No-Operation	[RFC 793]
2	4	Maximum Segment Size	[RFC 793]
3	3	WSOPT — Window Scale	[RFC 1323]
4	2	SACK Permitted	[RFC 1072]
5	N	SACK	[RFC 1072]
6	6	Echo (obsoleted by option 8)	[RFC 1072]
7	6	Echo Reply (obsoleted by option 8)	[RFC 1072]
8	10	TSOPT - Time Stamp Option	[RFC 1323]
9	2	Partial Order Connection Permitted	[RFC 1693]
10	3	Partial Order Service Profile	[RFC 1693]
11		CC	[RFC 1644]
12		CC.NEW	[RFC 1644]
13		CC.ECHO	[RFC 1644]
14	3	TCP Alternate Checksum Request	[RFC 1146]
15	N	TCP Alternate Checksum Data	[RFC 1146]
16		Skeeter	[Knowles]
17		Bubba	[Knowles]
18	3	Trailer Checksum Option	[Subbu & Monroe]
19	18	MD5 Signature Option	[RFC 2385]
20	SCPS	Capabilities	[Scott]
21		Selective Negative Acknowledgements	[Scott]
22		Record Boundaries	[Scott]
23		Corruption experienced	[Scott]
24		SNAP	[Sukonnik]

Table L.2 gives TCP alternate checksum numbers.

T A B L E   L.2

TCP Alternate Checksum Numbers

NUMBER	DESCRIPTION	REFERENCE
0	TCP Checksum	[RFC 1146]
1	8-bit Fletchers's algorithm	[RFC 1146]
2	16-bit Fletchers's algorithm	[RFC 1146]
3	Redundant Checksum Avoidance	[Kay]

APPENDIX M

DNS and DHCP/BOOTP Parameters

Table M.1 gives Domain Name System (DNS) parameters.

TABLE M.I

Domain Name System (DNS) Parameters

DECIMAL	NAME	REFERENCES
0	Reserved	[IANA]
1	Internet (IN)	[RFC 1035]
2	Unassigned	[IANA]
3	Chaos (CH	[RFC 1035]
4	Hesiod (HS)	[RFC 1035]
5–253	Unassigned	[IANA]
254	None	[Vixie]
255	Any [QCLASS Only]	[RFC 1035]
256–65534	Unassigned	[IANA]
65535	Reserved	[IANA]

In the Internet (IN) class, the following Resource Record (RR) types and QTYPEs are defined as listed in Table M.2.

TABLE M.2

*Resource Record (RR) Types
and QTYPEs*

TYPE	VALUE	MEANING	REFERENCES
A	1	A host address	[RFC 1035]
NS	2	An authoritative name server	[RFC 1035]
MD	3	A mail destination (Obsolete — use MX)	[RFC 1035]
MF	4	A mail forwarder (Obsolete — use MX)	[RFC 1035]
CNAME	5	The canonical name for an alias	[RFC 1035]
SOA	6	Marks the start of a zone of authority	[RFC 1035]
MB	7	A mailbox domain name (EXPERIMENTAL)	[RFC 1035]
MG	8	A mail group member (EXPERIMENTAL)	[RFC 1035]
MR	9	A mail rename domain name (EXPERIMENTAL)	[RFC 1035]

TYPE	VALUE	MEANING	REFERENCES
NULL	10	A null RR (EXPERIMENTAL)	[RFC 1035]
WKS	11	A well known service description	[RFC 1035]
PTR	12	A domain name pointer	[RFC 1035]
HINFO	13	Host information	[RFC 1035]
MINFO	14	Mailbox or mail list information	[RFC 1035]
MX	15	Mail exchange	[RFC 1035]
TXT	16	Text strings	[RFC 1035]
RP	17	For Responsible Person	[RFC 1183]
AFSDB	18	For AFS Data Base location	[RFC 1183]
X25	19	For X.25 PSDN address	[RFC 1183]
ISDN	20	For ISDN address	[RFC 1183]
RT	21	For Route Through	[RFC 1183]
NSAP	22	For NSAP address, NSAP style A record	[RFC 1706]
NSAP-PTR	23		
SIG	24	For security signature	[RFC 2065]
KEY	25	For security key	[RFC 2065]
PX	26	X.400 mail mapping information	[RFC 2163]
GPOS	27	Geographical Position	[RFC 1712]
AAAA	28	IP6 Address	[Thomson]
LOC	29	Location Information	[Vixie]
NXT	30	Next Domain	[RFC 2065]
EID	31	Endpoint Identifier	[Patton]
NIMLOC	32	Nimrod Locator	[Patton]
SRV	33	Server Selection	[RFC 2052]
ATMA	34	ATM Address	[Dobrowski]
NAPTR	35	Naming Authority Pointer	[RFC 2168]
KX	36	Key Exchanger	[RFC 2230]
CERT	37	CERT	[Eastlake]

Continued

T A B L E   M . 2

*Resource Record (RR) Types
and QTYPEs (continued)*

TYPE	VALUE	MEANING	REFERENCES
A6	38	A6	[Crawford]
DNAME	39	DNAME	[Crawford]
UINFO	100	[IANA-Reserved]	
UID	101	[IANA-Reserved]	
GID	102	[IANA-Reserved]	
UNSPEC	103	[IANA-Reserved]	
TKEY	249	TKEY	[Eastlake]
TSIG	250	Transaction Signature	[Vixie]
IXFR	251	Incremental transfer	[RFC 1995]
AXFR	252	Transfer of an entire zone	[RFC 1035]
MAILB	253	Mailbox-related RRs (MB, MG or MR)	[RFC 1035]
MAILA	254	Mail agent RRs (Obsolete — see MX)	[RFC 1035]
*	255	A request for all records	[RFC 1035]

Note that in RFC 1002, two additional types are defined:

| NB | 32 | NetBIOS general Name Service |
| NBSTAT | 33 | NetBIOS NODE STATUS |

It is not clear that these are in use; if so, their assignments conflict with those given in Table M.2.

Table M.3 gives domain system operation codes.

T A B L E   M . 3

Domain System Operation Codes

CODE	NAME	REFERENCES
0	Query	[RFC 1035]
1	Iquery	[RFC 1035]
2	Status	[RFC 1035]

CODE	NAME	REFERENCES
3	reserved	[IANA]
4	Notify	[RFC 1996]
5	Update	[Vixie]

Table M.4 gives domain system response codes.

T A B L E   M.4

Domain System Response Codes

OPCODE	NAME	MEANING	REFERENCES
0	NoError	No Error	[RFC 1035]
1	FormErr	Format Error	[RFC 1035]
2	ServFail	Server Failure	[RFC 1035]
3	NXDomain	Non-Existent Domain	[RFC 1035]
4	NotImp	Not Implemented	· [RFC 1035]
5	Refused	Query Refused	[RFC 1035]
6	YXDomain	Name Exists when it should not	[RFC 2136]
7	YXRRSet	RR Set Exists when it should not	[RFC 2136]
8	NXRRSet	RR Set that should exist does not	[RFC 2136]
9	NotAuth	Server Not Authoritative for zone	[RFC 2136]
10	NotZone	Name not contained in zone	[RFC 2136]

Table M.5 lists BOOTP vendor extensions and DHCP options.

T A B L E   M.5

BOOTP Vendor Extensions and DHCP Options

TAG	NAME	DATA LENGTH	MEANING
0	Pad	0	None
1	Subnet Mask	4	Subnet Mask Value
2	Time Offset	4	Time Offset in Seconds from UTC

Continued

TABLE M.5

BOOTP Vendor Extensions and DHCP Options (continued)

TAG	NAME	DATA LENGTH	MEANING
3	Router	N	N/4 Router addresses
4	Time Server	N	N/4 Timeserver addresses
5	Name Server	N	N/4 IEN-116 Server addresses
6	Domain Server	N	N/4 DNS Server addresses
7	Log Server	N	N/4 Logging Server addresses
8	Quotes Server	N	N/4 Quotes Server addresses
9	LPR Server	N	N/4 Printer Server addresses
10	Impress Server	N	N/4 Impress Server addresses
11	RLP Server	N	N/4 RLP Server addresses
12	Hostname	N	Hostname string
13	Boot File Size	2	Size of boot file in 512 byte chunks
14	Merit Dump File	N	Client to dump and name the file to dump it to
15	Domain Name	N	The DNS domain name of the client
16	Swap Server	N	Swap Server addeess
17	Root Path	N	Path name for root disk
18	Extension File	N	Path name for more BOOTP info
19	Forward On/Off	N	Enable/Disable IP Forwarding
20	SrcRte On/Off	1	Enable/Disable Source Routing
21	Policy Filter	N	Routing Policy Filters
22	Max DG Assembly	2	Max Datagram Reassembly Size
23	Default IP TTL	1	Default IP Time to Live
24	MTU Timeout	4	Path MTU Aging Timeout
25	MTU Plateau	N	Path MTU Plateau Table
26	MTU Interface	2	Interface MTU Size
27	MTU Subnet	1	All Subnets are Local
28	Broadcast Address	4	Broadcast Address

· · · · ·

TAG	NAME	DATA LENGTH	MEANING
29	Mask Discovery	I	Perform Mask Discovery
30	Mask Supplier	I	Provide Mask to Others
31	Router Discovery	I	Perform Router Discovery
32	Router Request	4	Router Solicitation Address
33	Static Route	N	Static Routing Table
34	Trailers	I	Trailer Encapsulation
35	ARP Timeout	4	ARP Cache Timeout
36	Ethernet	I	Ethernet Encapsulation
37	Default TCP TTL	I	Default TCP Time to Live
38	Keepalive Time	4	TCP Keepalive Interval
39	Keepalive Data	I	TCP Keepalive Garbage
40	NIS Domain	N	NIS Domain Name
41	NIS Servers	N	NIS Server Addresses
42	NTP Servers	N	NTP Server Addresses
43	Vendor Specific	N	Vendor Specific Information
44	NETBIOS Name Srv	N	NETBIOS Name Servers
45	NETBIOS Dist Srv	N	NETBIOS Datagram Distribution
46	NETBIOS Node Type	I	NETBIOS Node Type
47	NETBIOS Scope	N	NETBIOS Scope
48	X Window Font	N	X Window Font Server
49	X Window Manmager	N	X Window Display Manager
50	Address Request	4	Requested IP Address
51	Address Time	4	IP Address Lease Time
52	Overload	I	Overload "sname" or "file"
53	DHCP Msg Type	I	DHCP Message Type
54	DHCP Server Id	4	DHCP Server Identification
55	Parameter List	N	Parameter Request List
56	DHCP Message	N	DHCP Error Message

Continued

TABLE M.5

BOOTP Vendor Extensions and DHCP Options (continued)

TAG	NAME	DATA LENGTH	MEANING
57	DHCP Max Msg Size	2	DHCP Maximum Message Size
58	Renewal Time	4	DHCP Renewal (T1) Time
59	Rebinding Time	4	DHCP Rebinding (T2) Time
60	Class ID	N	Class Identifier
61	Client ID	N	Client Identifier
62	Netware/IP Domain	N	Netware/IP Domain Name
63	Netware/IP Option	N	Netware/IP sub Options
64	NIS-Domain-Name	N	NIS+ v3 Client Domain Name
65	NIS-Server-Addr	N	NIS+ v3 Server Addresses
66	Server-Name	N	TFTP Server Name
67	Bootfile-Name	N	Boot File Name
68	Home-Agent-Addrs	N	Home Agent Addresses
69	SMTP-Server	N	Simple Mail Server Addresses
70	POP3-Server	N	Post Office Server Addresses
71	NNTP-Server	N	Network News Server Addresses
72	WWW-Server	N	WWW Server Addresses
73	Finger-Server	N	Finger Server Addresses
74	IRC-Server	N	Chat Server Addresses
75	StreetTalk-Server	N	StreetTalk Server Addresses
76	STDA-Server	N	ST Directory Assistance Addresses
77	User-Class	N	User Class Information
78	Director Agent	N	Directory agent information
79	Service Scope	N	Service location agent scope
80	Naming Authority	N	Naming authority
81	Client FQDN	N	Fully Qualified Domain Name
82	Agent Circuit ID	N	Agent Circuit ID
83	Agent Remote ID	N	Agent Remote ID

TAG	NAME	DATA LENGTH	MEANING
84	Agent Subnet Mask	N	Agent Subnet Mask
85	NDS Servers	N	Novell Directory Services
86	NDS Tree Name	N	Novell Directory Services
87	NDS Context	N	Novell Directory Services
88	IEEE 1003.1 POSIX	N	IEEE 1003.1 POSIX Timezone
89	FQDN	N	Fully Qualified Domain Name
90	Authentication	N	Authentication
91	Vines TCP/IP	N	Vines TCP/IP Server Option
92	Server Selection	N	Server Selection Option
93	Client System	N	Client System Architecture
94	Client NDI	N	Client Network Device Interface
95	LDAP	N	Lightweight Directory Access Protocol
96	IPv6 Transitions	N	IPv6 Transitions
97	UUID/GUID	N	UUID/GUID-based Client Identifier
98	User-Auth	N	Open Group's User Authentication
99	Unassigned		
100	Printer Name	N	Printer Name
101	MDHCP	N	MDHCP multicast address
102–107	Removed/Unassigned		
108	Swap Path	N	Swap Path Option
109	Unassigned		
110	IPX Compatability	N	IPX Compatability
111	Unassigned		
112	Netinfo Address	N	NetInfo Parent Server Address
113	Netinfo Tag	N	NetInfo Parent Server Tag
114	URL	N	URL
115	Failover	N	DHCP Failover Protocol

Continued

. . . . .

TABLE M.5

BOOTP Vendor Extensions and DHCP Options (continued)

TAG	NAME	DATA LENGTH	MEANING
116–125	Unassigned		
126	Extension	N	Extension
127	Extension	N	Extension
128–254	Private Use		
255	End	0	None

ARP/RARP Parameters

ARP (Address Resolution Protocol)/RARP (Reverse Address Resolution Protocol) Parameters

NUMBER	OPERATION CODE(OP)	REFERENCES
1	REQUEST	[RFC 826]
2	REPLY	[RFC 826]
3	request Reverse	[RFC 903]
4	reply Reverse	[RFC 903]
5	DRARP-Request	[David Brownell]
6	DRARP-Reply	[David Brownell]
7	DRARP-Error	[David Brownell]
8	InARP-Request	[RFC 1293]
9	InARP-Reply	[RFC 1293]
10	ARP-NAK	[RFC 1577]
11	MARS-Request	[Armitage]
12	MARS-Multi	[Armitage]
13	MARS-Mserv	[Armitage]
14	MARS-Join	[Armitage]
15	MARS-Leave	[Armitage]
16	MARS-NAK	[Armitage]
17	MARS-Unserv	[Armitage]
18	MARS-Sjoin	[Armitage]
19	MARS-Sleave	[Armitage]
20	MARS-Grouplist-Request	[Armitage]
21	MARS-Grouplist-Reply	[Armitage]
22	MARS-Redirect-Map	[Armitage]
23	MAPOS-UNARP	[Maruyama]

Index

my2cents.idgbooks.com

Register This Book — And Win!

Visit **http://my2cents.idgbooks.com** to register this book and we'll automatically enter you in our fantastic monthly prize giveaway. It's also your opportunity to give us feedback: let us know what you thought of this book and how you would like to see other topics covered.

Discover IDG Books Online!

The IDG Books Online Web site is your online resource for tackling technology — at home and at the office. Frequently updated, the IDG Books Online Web site features exclusive software, insider information, online books, and live events!

10 Productive & Career-Enhancing Things You Can Do at www.idgbooks.com

- Nab source code for your own programming projects.

- Download software.

- Read Web exclusives: special articles and book excerpts by IDG Books Worldwide authors.

- Take advantage of resources to help you advance your career as a Novell or Microsoft professional.

- Buy IDG Books Worldwide titles or find a convenient bookstore that carries them.

- Register your book and win a prize.

- Chat live online with authors.

- Sign up for regular e-mail updates about our latest books.

- Suggest a book you'd like to read or write.

- Give us your 2¢ about our books and about our Web site.

You say you're not on the Web yet? It's easy to get started with IDG Books' *Discover the Internet,* available at local retailers everywhere.